TAX PLANNING FOR HIGHLY COMPENSATED INDIVIDUALS

ROBERT E. MADDEN

*Managing Partner, Mahn, Franklin & Goldenberg,
Washington, D.C.*

WARREN, GORHAM & LAMONT
Boston • New York

Copyright © 1983 by

WARREN, GORHAM & LAMONT, INC.
210 SOUTH STREET
BOSTON, MASSACHUSETTS 02111

ALL RIGHTS RESERVED

No part of this book may be reproduced in any form, by photostat, microfilm, xerography, or any other means, or incorporated into any information retrieval system, electronic or mechanical, without the written permission of the copyright owner.

ISBN 0-88262-896-8

Library of Congress Catalog Card No. 83-60090

This educational publication is designed to present information to professionals as an aid to independent research and preparation of materials. It is not to be regarded as providing opinion or advice for any individual case.

This publication is not intended to render legal or other professional services or advice. The appropriate professional should be consulted for any such services or advice.

PRINTED IN THE UNITED STATES OF AMERICA

Preface

THIS BOOK IS FOCUSED on tax planning devices most useful to "highly compensated individuals" — taxpayers who have a considerable amount of earned income as opposed to income received from business holdings or investments. The book's objective is to aid in the design of a plan that reduces the income tax impact on an individual's highly compensated status and that also provides for the preservation and transfer of the individual's estate at minimum tax cost.

Topical Organization. For convenience, planning for employment-related income, such as deferred compensation, stock options, and fringe benefits, is discussed separately from noncompensation income topics, such as tax shelters or the basic shifting of income or deductions from year to year. In other chapters, the book reviews the estate planning needs of highly compensated individuals. All too frequently, the client and his advisor fail to integrate lifetime income tax planning with the development of an overall estate plan. Unfortunately, this is often a serious oversight. A strategy that results in a minor income tax savings, and, at the same time, creates a potentially large estate tax liability, may prove to be very costly. Accordingly, this book emphasizes the compelling need to integrate lifetime income tax planning with a well-rounded estate plan.

Although many topics are discussed by necessity in separate income tax or estate planning sections, there is constant cross-referencing between these sections in an attempt to weave the various planning devices into an integrated tax plan.

Scope of Coverage. The basic thrust (indeed, the title) of this book is tax *planning* for the highly compensated individual. Accordingly, it focuses on the active use of certain devices and strategies to best advantage. For example, rather than reciting all details of the law governing compensation plans, the book describes those situations when it is best to use a given plan and outlines strategies for its most effective use.

The book assumes that the reader has a basic understanding of the essential provisions of the Internal Revenue Code. For instance, the chapter on tax shelters assumes an understanding of basic partnership

PREFACE

tax rules and discusses in detail only those aspects of partnership taxation that relate to problems and planning for investments in tax shelter syndications. The detailed discussions are all directly related to effective use of tax shelters for highly compensated individuals in order to lay a foundation for knowledgeable use of such devices rather than to outline everything the Code or the courts may say about them.

Certain tax planning situations may demand that the tax advisor go into more detailed research than is provided in this treatise. Since the book is not devoted solely to compensation planning, tax shelters, or estate planning, there are inevitably many details of these areas that could not fit into a single-volume discussion. My hope, however, is that the essentials are here — that the reader has a basis for undertaking a sophisticated overall tax plan for the highly compensated individual.

Acknowledgments. When I made the commitment to write this book in April 1980, I undertook it fully aware of the magnitude of the task. In the intervening period of time, however, there were two significant pieces of tax legislation that greatly impacted upon the subject matter and that necessitated numerous changes and updates. It was only because of the advice, help, and encouragement of my friends, business colleagues, and loved ones that I was able to persevere and finally publish this treatise.

To all those who have assisted me, I give my special thanks. These include: the fine people at Warren, Gorham & Lamont, especially Michael Coffey, whose suggestions, comments, and criticisms produced a far better product than I could have done alone; my colleagues at Mahn, Franklin & Goldenberg, who both tolerated and encouraged this project; Israel Grossman, for his tremendous assistance with Chapters 9 and 12; and Lynn, Maggie, and Michele, who typed more drafts and versions of this treatise than can be imagined and who will forever remember this project as "the damn book."

My biggest thanks, however, go to my wife, Mary Ann, and my daughter, Jennifer, for their support and understanding during the past two and one-half years. On far too many occasions I was an absent husband and father while I attempted to both write this book and cope with the demands of a busy legal practice. I could not have done it without their support.

ROBERT E. MADDEN

Washington, D.C.
January 1983

Summary of Contents

	Page
TABLE OF CONTENTS	vii

Part I — General Tax Planning Strategies

CHAPTER 1.	Profile of the Highly Compensated Individual	1-1
CHAPTER 2.	Income Tax Overview	2-1

Part II — Compensation Planning

CHAPTER 3.	Deferred Compensation	3-1
CHAPTER 4.	Property Transferred for the Performance of Services	4-1
CHAPTER 5.	Qualified Plans	5-1
CHAPTER 6.	Income Taxation of Life Insurance	6-1
CHAPTER 7.	Fringe Benefits.......................................	7-1

Part III — Noncompensation Planning

CHAPTER 8.	Tax Shelters	8-1
CHAPTER 9.	Grantor Trusts.......................................	9-1

Part IV — Estate Planning

CHAPTER 10.	Overview of Estate and Gift Taxation	10-1
CHAPTER 11.	Lifetime Gifts	11-1
CHAPTER 12.	Irrevocable Lifetime Trusts	12-1
CHAPTER 13.	Estate Taxation of Life Insurance	13-1

SUMMARY OF CONTENTS

Page

CHAPTER 14. Estate Planning for Compensation Plans........ 14-1

CHAPTER 15. Tax Planning With Wills............................ 15-1

CHAPTER 16. Private Annuities, Powers of Appointment 16-1

TABLE OF I.R.C. SECTIONS.. T-1

TABLE OF TREASURY REGULATIONS................................ T-9

TABLE OF REVENUE RULINGS, REVENUE PROCEDURES,
AND OTHER IRS RELEASES AND GUIDELINES................. T-13

TABLE OF CASES T-17

INDEX I-1

Table of Contents

Part I — General Tax Planning Strategies

Chapter 1
PROFILE OF THE HIGHLY COMPENSATED INDIVIDUAL

		Page
¶ 1.01	Inflation and the Highly Compensated	1-1
¶ 1.02	Types of Highly Compensated Individuals	1-2
	[1] Corporate Executives	1-2
	[2] Professionals	1-2
	[3] Professional Athletes	1-3
	[4] Entertainers or Artistic Performers	1-3
	[5] "Super Salesmen"	1-3
¶ 1.03	Tax Problems of the Highly Compensated	1-4

Chapter 2
INCOME TAX OVERVIEW

¶ 2.01	The Graduated Rate Structure	2-2
	[1] Rates of Taxation	2-2
	[2] Effect on Deductions	2-3
	[3] Effect on Credits	2-4
	[4] Indexing	2-4
¶ 2.02	Alternative Minimum Tax	2-5
	[1] Computation of Alternative Minimum Tax	2-5
	[2] Items of Tax Preference	2-7
	[a] Accelerated Depreciation on Real Property	2-7
	[b] Accelerated Depreciation on Leased Personal Property	2-8
	[c] Amortization of Certified Pollution Control Facilities	2-9
	[d] Incentive Stock Options	2-9

TABLE OF CONTENTS

		Page
	[e] Depletion	2-9
	[f] Intangible Drilling Costs	2-9
	[g] Accelerated Cost Recovery Deduction	2-10
	[h] Capital Gain	2-10
	[i] Miscellaneous Preference Items	2-10
	[3] Planning for the Alternative Minimum Tax	2-11
¶ 2.03	Taxation of Capital Gain	2-14
	[1] Basic Principles	2-14
	[2] Wash Sales	2-16
¶ 2.04	General Planning Strategies	2-18
	[1] Deferral of Income	2-19
	[2] Acceleration of Deductions	2-20
	[a] Accounting Method Must Clearly Reflect Income	2-21
	[b] Specific Deduction Limitations	2-21
	[3] Conversion of Ordinary Income Into Capital Gain	2-22
	[4] Avoiding Taxable Income	2-24
	[a] Tax-Exempt Bonds	2-24
	[i] Nontaxability of certain governmental obligations	2-24
	[ii] Indebtedness used to purchase tax-exempt securities	2-26
	[b] Tax-Free Exchanges	2-27
	[c] Avoidance of Tax on Sale of Residence	2-29
	[i] Replacement of residence	2-29
	[ii] Sale of residence by individuals who have attained age 55	2-30
	[d] Retention of Assets Until Death	2-32
	[5] Income Averaging	2-33

Part II — Compensation Planning

Chapter 3

DEFERRED COMPENSATION

¶ 3.01	Introduction	3-1
¶ 3.02	Pros and Cons of Deferred Compensation	3-2
	[1] Tax Planning Analysis	3-2
	[2] Economic Analysis	3-5

TABLE OF CONTENTS

		Page
	[a] Alternate Investment Opportunities	3-5
	[b] Risk of Deferral	3-6
	[c] Effect on Cash Flow	3-8
¶ 3.03	Tax Deferral — How to Achieve It	3-9
	[1] Avoiding Constructive Receipt	3-9
	[2] Economic Benefit Theory	3-11
	[3] Requirements for Deferral	3-13
	[a] Rev. Rul. 60-31	3-13
	[b] Requirements for Advance Rulings	3-16
¶ 3.04	Funding the Deferred Compensation Arrangement	3-17
¶ 3.05	Types of Deferred Compensation Arrangements	3-20
	[1] Investment-Type Arrangements	3-20
	[2] Investment in Employer Equities — The Phantom Stock Plan	3-21
	[3] Other Plans Involving Employer's Stock	3-23

Chapter 4

PROPERTY TRANSFERRED FOR THE PERFORMANCE OF SERVICES

¶ 4.01	Outline of Statutory Framework	4-1
¶ 4.02	Basic Concepts of Taxation Under Section 83	4-2
	[1] Determinants of Taxability	4-3
	[a] Transfer of Property	4-3
	[b] Substantial Risk of Forfeiture	4-5
	[c] Free Transferability of Property	4-7
	[2] Taxation of Nonqualified Options	4-8
	[3] Other Aspects of Section 83	4-11
	[a] Election to Include in Income	4-11
	[b] Holding Period and Basis	4-13
	[c] Employer Deduction	4-13
¶ 4.03	Types of Section 83 Plans	4-15
	[1] Nonqualified Stock Options	4-15
	[2] Stock Appreciation Rights	4-17
	[3] Restricted Stock Plans	4-19
¶ 4.04	Incentive Stock Options	4-20
	[1] Taxation to Employee	4-21
	[2] Qualification Requirements	4-22
	[3] Tax Planning	4-25

TABLE OF CONTENTS

Chapter 5

QUALIFIED PLANS

		Page
¶ 5.01	Income Tax Consequences	5-2
¶ 5.02	Types of Qualified Plans	5-4
	[1] Profit-Sharing Plans	5-4
	[2] Defined Benefit Pension Plans	5-6
	[3] Money Purchase Pension Plans	5-7
	[4] Target Benefit Plans	5-7
	[5] Stock Bonus Plans	5-8
	[6] Cash or Deferred Plans	5-9
	[7] Employee Stock Ownership Plans (ESOPs)	5-11
	[8] Payroll-Based Stock Ownership Plans (PAYSOPs)	5-13
	[9] Keogh Plans	5-14
¶ 5.03	Qualification Requirements Affecting the Highly Compensated	5-16
	[1] Antidiscrimination Requirements	5-17
	[2] Limitation on Contributions and Benefits	5-18
	[a] Defined Benefit Plans	5-18
	[b] Defined Contribution Plans	5-20
	[c] Multiple Plans	5-21
	[d] Keogh Plans	5-21
	[3] Voluntary Contributions	5-22
	[4] Top-Heavy Plans	5-25
¶ 5.04	Income Taxation of Distributions From Qualified Plans	5-27
	[1] Annuities or Periodic Payments	5-27
	[2] Lump-Sum Distributions	5-30
	[a] Definition of Lump-Sum Distributions	5-30
	[i] One taxable year of the recipient	5-31
	[ii] Balance to the credit of the employee	5-31
	[iii] Qualifying reasons for payment	5-32
	[iv] Five-year participation requirement	5-33
	[b] Capital Gains Taxation on Pre-1974 Benefits	5-34
	[c] Ten-Year Forward Averaging Rule	5-35
	[d] Unrealized Appreciation on Employer Securities	5-37
	[3] Choosing the Form of a Distribution	5-39
¶ 5.05	Rollovers	5-41
	[1] Section 402(a)(5) Rollovers	5-41
	[2] Rollovers by Spouse Upon Death of Plan Participant	5-43

TABLE OF CONTENTS

		Page
¶ 5.06	Individual Retirement Accounts (IRAs)	5-43
	[1] Qualification Requirements	5-44
	[a] Individual Retirement Accounts	5-44
	[b] Individual Retirement Annuities	5-45
	[c] Individual Retirement Bonds	5-46
	[2] Income Tax Consequences	5-46
	[a] Deductibility of Contributions	5-46
	[b] Distributions From IRAs	5-47
	[3] General Planning Comments	5-49

Chapter 6

INCOME TAXATION OF LIFE INSURANCE

¶ 6.01	Introduction	6-2
¶ 6.02	Income Tax Consequences of Life Insurance	6-2
	[1] Taxation of Life Insurance Proceeds	6-3
	[2] Deductibility of Premium Payments	6-5
	[3] Exchange of Policies	6-6
	[4] Systematic Borrowing of Cash Value	6-7
	[a] Denial of Interest Deduction	6-7
	[b] Exceptions to Denial of Interest Deduction	6-8
	[i] Four-out-of-seven exception	6-8
	[ii] The $100 exception	6-9
	[iii] Unforeseen events exception	6-9
	[iv] Trade or business exception	6-10
¶ 6.03	Group Term Life Insurance — Section 79	6-11
	[1] Taxability to the Employee	6-12
	[a] General Rule of Taxability	6-12
	[b] Exceptions to General Rule of Taxability	6-13
	[i] Terminated and retired employees	6-13
	[ii] Employer or charity as beneficiary	6-14
	[iii] Insurance in qualified plans	6-14
	[2] Requirements to Qualify Under Section 79	6-14
	[3] Groups of Fewer Than Ten Employees	6-17
	[4] Permanent Insurance Coverage Under a Group Term Plan	6-19
	[5] Coverage for Spouse or Children	6-20
¶ 6.04	Split-Dollar Insurance	6-20
	[1] Description	6-20

TABLE OF CONTENTS

		Page
	[2] Income Tax Consequences	6-21
	[3] Income Tax Planning	6-24
¶ 6.05	Life Insurance in Qualified Plans	6-26
	[1] Limitations on Coverage	6-27
	[2] Income Taxation of Value of Insurance in Qualified Plans	6-28
	[3] Income Taxation of Death Benefits	6-29
	[4] Planning Aspects	6-30
¶ 6.06	Retired Lives Reserve	6-31
	[1] Description	6-32
	[2] Income Taxation	6-32
	[3] Funding Vehicles	6-33
¶ 6.07	Key-Man Insurance	6-35

Chapter 7

FRINGE BENEFITS

¶ 7.01	Statutory vs. Nonstatutory Fringe Benefits	7-1
¶ 7.02	Health Plans — Insured	7-3
¶ 7.03	Health Plans — Noninsured Medical Reimbursement	7-4
	[1] Taxation in General	7-4
	[2] Antidiscrimination Requirements	7-5
	[3] Planning	7-7
¶ 7.04	Disability and Sickness Plans	7-9
	[1] Disability Plans	7-9
	[2] Workmen's Compensation	7-11
¶ 7.05	Educational Assistance Programs	7-12
¶ 7.06	Survivor's Death Benefits	7-16
¶ 7.07	Cafeteria Plans	7-18
¶ 7.08	Nonstatutory Fringe Benefits	7-20
	[1] Taxation of Fringe Benefits in General	7-21
	[2] Treasury Discussion Drafts	7-23
	[3] Planning for Specific Fringe Benefits	7-26
	[a] Basic Planning Factors	7-26
	[b] Financial Counseling	7-27
	[c] Conventions	7-28
	[d] Meals or Lodging	7-29

TABLE OF CONTENTS

Part III — Noncompensation Planning

Chapter 8

TAX SHELTERS

		Page
¶ 8.01	Introduction	8-2
	[1] Definition of a Tax Shelter	8-2
	[2] Goals of a Tax Shelter Program	8-4
	[a] Deferral of Taxes	8-4
	[b] Conversion of Ordinary Income to Capital Gain	8-5
	[c] Leverage	8-5
	[d] Investment With Limited Liability	8-6
¶ 8.02	Achieving Tax Classification as a Partnership	8-7
	[1] Tax Advantages of Partnership Status	8-7
	[2] Regulations Distinguishing Partnerships From Corporations	8-8
	[a] Continuity of Life	8-9
	[b] Centralization of Management	8-10
	[c] Limited Liability	8-11
	[d] Free Transferability of Interest	8-11
	[3] IRS Ruling Position on Limited Partnership Status	8-12
	[a] Net Worth Requirements	8-12
	[b] Limit on Aggregate Deductions	8-13
	[4] Court Challenges to Limited Partnership Status	8-14
	[5] Proposed Revision of Regulations	8-16
	[6] Planning to Achieve Partnership Status	8-17
¶ 8.03	Basis and At-Risk Rules	8-18
	[1] Determination of Basis	8-18
	[2] Effect of Partnership Borrowings	8-19
	[3] At-Risk Limitations	8-21
¶ 8.04	Hobby Loss Provisions	8-24
¶ 8.05	Retroactive Allocation of Losses	8-26
¶ 8.06	Deductibility of Fees and Expenses	8-27
	[1] Organizational Expenses	8-27
	[2] Construction Period Interest and Taxes	8-30
	[3] Intangible Drilling Expenses	8-31
¶ 8.07	Evaluating a Tax Shelter	8-31
	[1] Soundness of the Investment	8-32

			Page
	[2] Review of Tax Risks		8-33
	[3] Real Cost of the Investment		8-36
	[4] Promoter's "Track Record"		8-37
	[5] Ultimate Profit From the Transaction		8-39
¶ 8.08	Estate Planning for Tax Shelters		8-41

Chapter 9

GRANTOR TRUSTS

¶ 9.01	Objectives for Creation of Trusts	9-2
¶ 9.02	Basic Trust Provisions	9-3
¶ 9.03	Revocable Trusts Created for Purposes Other Than Tax Savings	9-6
	[1] Lifetime Use of Revocable Trusts	9-6
	[2] Post-Death Benefits	9-6
	[3] Income Tax Considerations	9-8
	[4] Gift and Estate Tax Consequences	9-11
¶ 9.04	Relinquishment of Ownership of Trust to Reduce Tax Liability	9-11
	[1] Grantor Owns Entire Trust	9-11
	[2] Grantor Owns Part of Trust	9-12
	[3] Grantor Retains Only Corpus Interest	9-13
¶ 9.05	"Clifford" Trusts	9-13
¶ 9.06	Taxation of "Clifford" Trusts	9-14
	[1] Income Tax Benefits	9-14
	[2] Grantor's Gift Tax Liability on Creation	9-15
¶ 9.07	Current Distribution or Accumulation of Trust Income	9-16
¶ 9.08	Restriction on Grantor's Powers to Transfer Trust Ownership for Income Tax Purposes	9-17
	[1] Reversionary Interest Must Be Relinquished for a Sufficient Period of Time	9-17
	[a] Earliest Permissible Time for Reacquisition	9-17
	[b] Postponement of Reacquisition Date	9-18
	[2] Power to Control Beneficial Enjoyment Must Be Curtailed	9-19
	[a] Grantor as Trustee	9-19
	[i] Retained powers subjecting grantor to tax	9-20
	[ii] Permissible retained powers	9-20

TABLE OF CONTENTS

		Page
[b] Person Other Than Grantor as Trustee		9-23
[c] Power to Remove Trustee		9-24
[d] Reciprocal Trusts		9-25
[3] Administrative Powers Exercisable by Grantor		9-25
[a] Grantor's Use of Administrative Powers to Directly Control Beneficial Enjoyment		9-25
[b] Offensive Administrative Powers Grantor Must Relinquish to Avoid Income Taxation		9-27
[c] Borrowing From Trust by Grantor		9-27
[4] Power to Revoke Subjecting Grantor to Tax		9-27
[5] Use of Trust Income for Benefit of Grantor		9-28
[6] Use of Trust Income for Support of Grantor's Dependents		9-29
¶ 9.09 Persons Other Than the Grantor as Owner of Trust		9-29
¶ 9.10 Grantor's Potential Estate Tax Liability		9-30
¶ 9.11 Alternative Methods of Achieving Income Tax Benefits From Transfer of Property		9-30
[1] Irrevocable Trusts		9-31
[2] Interest-Free Loans		9-31
[3] Comparison of Grantor Trusts and Alternative Methods of Transfer		9-32
[a] Outright Gifts		9-32
[b] Irrevocable Trusts		9-33
[c] Short-Term or "Clifford" Trusts		9-33
[d] Interest-Free Loans		9-34
[e] Interest-Free Loans to an Irrevocable Trust		9-35
¶ 9.12 Foreign Trusts		9-36

Part IV — *Estate Planning*

Chapter 10

OVERVIEW OF ESTATE AND GIFT TAXATION

¶ 10.01 Introduction		10-2
¶ 10.02 Basic Estate and Gift Tax Structure		10-5
[1] Computation of Estate Tax		10-5

TABLE OF CONTENTS xvi

	Page
[2] Unified Credit	10-7
[3] Credit for Tax on Prior Transfers	10-7
[a] Transfer of Property	10-8
[b] Computation of the Credit	10-9
[i] Value of the transferred property	10-9
[ii] Estate tax paid on transferred property	10-10
[iii] Decedent's estate tax attributable to transferred property	10-11
[4] Credit for State Death Taxes	10-11
¶ 10.03 Deductions From the Gross Estate	10-13
[1] Estate Administration Expenses	10-14
[a] General Limitations	10-14
[b] Allowable Deductions	10-15
[i] Funeral expenses	10-15
[ii] Probate and administration expenses	10-16
[iii] Executor's commissions	10-16
[iv] Other deductible expenses	10-17
[c] Planning for Section 2053 Deductions	10-17
[2] Claims Against the Estate	10-18
[a] General Conditions for Deduction	10-19
[b] Specific Types of Deductible Claims	10-20
[i] Taxes	10-20
[ii] Interest	10-21
[iii] Charitable pledges	10-22
[iv] Unpaid mortgages	10-22
[c] Planning for Claims	10-22
[i] Ascertaining potential claims	10-22
[ii] Ensuring proper documentation	10-23
[3] Losses During Administration	10-23
¶ 10.04 Tax on Generation Skipping Transfers	10-24
[1] Imposition of the Generation Skipping Tax	10-25
[2] Planning With Respect to the Tax on Generation Skipping Transfers	10-26
[a] Direct Bequests to Younger Generations	10-26
[b] The Income Exception	10-27
[c] The $250,000 Exclusion	10-29
¶ 10.05 Jointly Held Property	10-30
[1] General Rule of Taxation	10-30
[2] Joint Interests with Spouse	10-31

Chapter 11

LIFETIME GIFTS

		Page
¶ 11.01	Introduction	11-2
¶ 11.02	Outline of the Gift Tax Provisions	11-2
	[1] Unified System of Estate and Gift Taxation	11-2
	[2] Donee's Basis in Property	11-4
	[3] Annual Gift Tax Exclusion	11-4
	[4] Gift Tax Marital Deduction	11-7
	[5] Gifts in Contemplation of Death	11-8
¶ 11.03	What Is a Taxable Gift?	11-9
¶ 11.04	Estate and Income Tax Advantages of Making a Gift	11-14
	[1] Use of the Annual $10,000 Exclusion to Reduce the Estate	11-15
	[2] Removal of Subsequent Appreciation From Donor's Estate	11-17
	[3] Shifting the Incidence of Income Taxation	11-18
	[4] Removal of Gift Tax Paid From Decedent's Estate	11-19
	[5] Avoidance of Tax on Generation Skipping Transfers	11-19
¶ 11.05	Strategies for Gift Tax Reduction in General	11-20
¶ 11.06	Fractionalized Gifts	11-20
¶ 11.07	Net Gifts	11-23
¶ 11.08	Use of the Lifetime Credit	11-24
¶ 11.09	Interest-Free Loans	11-26
	[1] Gift Tax Consequences to the Lender	11-26
	[2] Income Tax Consequences to the Borrower	11-28
	[3] Tax Planning for Interest-Free Loans	11-30
¶ 11.10	Gifts to Minors	11-32
	[1] Section 2503(c) Trusts	11-33
	[a] Trustee's Discretion	11-33
	[b] Age of Distribution	11-35
	[c] Disposition on Death of Donee	11-38
	[2] Uniform Gifts to Minors Act — Custodial Transfer	11-40
	[3] Transfer to a Guardian	11-42
¶ 11.11	Gifts to Spouses	11-43

Chapter 12

IRREVOCABLE LIFETIME TRUSTS

		Page
¶ 12.01	Planning for the Use of Trusts	12-2
	[1] Definition of Irrevocable Trust	12-2
	[2] Transferor's Objectives	12-2
¶ 12.02	Grantor Trust as Alternative to Irrevocable Trust	12-3
	[1] Tax Consequences	12-3
	[2] Providing for Possibility of Grantor's Death During the Trust Term	12-4
	[3] Benefits of Grantor Trust vs. Irrevocable Trust	12-6
¶ 12.03	Estate Tax Considerations in Making Lifetime Irrevocable Gifts to Trusts	12-7
	[1] Current and Prior Law	12-7
	[2] Transfer of Non-Appreciating Property to Irrevocable Trust	12-8
	[3] Transfer of Potentially Appreciating Property	12-9
	[a] Examples of Tax Savings From Transfers to Irrevocable Trusts	12-9
	[i] Stock in closely held corporations	12-10
	[ii] Real estate	12-10
	[b] Exclusion of Transferred Property From Estate	12-11
¶ 12.04	Requirements for Removal of Transferred Property From Taxable Estate	12-11
¶ 12.05	Transfers for Consideration	12-12
¶ 12.06	Retention of Life Interest by Transferor	12-13
	[1] Includability in Transferor's Estate	12-13
	[2] Retention of Partial Interest	12-13
	[3] Retention of Implied Right	12-14
¶ 12.07	Use of Trust to Discharge Transferor's Obligations	12-15
	[1] Support Obligations	12-15
	[2] Obligations Other Than Support	12-16
¶ 12.08	Tax Consequences Affected by Identity of the Trustee	12-17
	[1] Transferor or Party Controlled by Transferor as Trustee	12-17
	[2] Power to Remove or Appoint Successor Trustees	12-19
	[3] Third Party as Trustee	12-21
	[4] Beneficiary as Trustee	12-21
¶ 12.09	Transferor's Retention of Administrative Powers	12-22

TABLE OF CONTENTS

		Page
¶ 12.10	Transferor's Retention of Power to Alter, Amend, Revoke, or Terminate Trusts	12-24
	[1] Includability in Transferor's Estate	12-24
	[2] Permissible Retained Powers	12-25
	[3] General Rules	12-27
¶ 12.11	Transfers Taking Effect at Transferor's Death	12-27
	[1] Includability in Transferor's Estate	12-27
	[2] Avoiding Application of Section 2037	12-28
¶ 12.12	Advantages and Disadvantages of Irrevocably Transferring Property Out of One's Estate	12-30

Chapter 13

ESTATE TAXATION OF LIFE INSURANCE

¶ 13.01	Significance of Life Insurance to the Estate	13-2
	[1] Liquidity	13-2
	[2] Building the Estate	13-3
	[3] Insurance for a Specific Purpose	13-3
¶ 13.02	General Principles of Estate Taxation of Life Insurance	13-4
	[1] Receivable by or for the Benefit of the Estate	13-4
	[2] Receivable by Other Beneficiaries	13-5
	[a] Incidents of Ownership in General	13-5
	[b] Incidents of Ownership Where Insured Is Trustee	13-6
	[c] Incidents of Ownership Where Policy Owned by Corporation	13-7
	[d] Controversy Regarding Incidents of Ownership	13-8
¶ 13.03	Removal of Life Insurance Proceeds from Decedent's Taxable Estate	13-11
	[1] In General	13-11
	[2] Gift Tax Consequences of Transfer of Life Insurance	13-11
	[3] Direct Transfer vs. Transfer in Trust	13-13
	[a] Direct Transfer to Other Individuals	13-13
	[b] Transfer in Trust	13-15
	[4] Gifts of Group Term Life Insurance	13-20
	[a] Requirements for an Effective Assignment	13-20
	[b] Incidents-of-Ownership Problems	13-20
	[c] Premium Payments as Gifts	13-21
¶ 13.04	Transfers of Life Insurance as Gifts in Contemplation of Death	13-22

TABLE OF CONTENTS

		Page
[1] Position of the Internal Revenue Service		13-23
[2] Planning to Avoid Gifts in Contemplation of Death		13-26
¶ 13.05 Gifts of Present Interests — The *Crummey* Trust		13-28
[1] Description of the Problem		13-28
[2] The *Crummey* Case		13-29
[3] Particular Problems With *Crummey* Provisions		13-30
[a] Increase in Annual Exclusion		13-30
[b] Notice of Demand Provisions		13-31
[c] Length of Withdrawal Period		13-32
[d] Multiple Beneficiaries		13-32
[4] Planning for Use of the *Crummey* Provision		13-34

Chapter 14

ESTATE PLANNING FOR COMPENSATION PLANS

¶ 14.01	Introduction	14-2
¶ 14.02	Income in Respect of a Decedent (IRD)	14-3
	[1] Purpose of IRD Rules	14-3
	[a] Definition of IRD	14-4
	[b] Timing and Character of IRD Income	14-5
	[c] Specific Examples of IRD Receivables	14-7
	[i] Noncompensation IRD items	14-7
	[ii] Compensation-related IRD items	14-8
	[2] Deductions in Respect of a Decedent	14-10
	[3] Income Tax Deduction for Estate Tax Attributable to IRD	14-12
	[a] General Method of Computation	14-12
	[b] Specific Computational Problems	14-13
	[i] Marital deduction	14-13
	[ii] Capital gain	14-15
	[iii] Lump-sum distributions from qualified plans	14-16
	[4] General Planning	14-16
¶ 14.03	Estate Planning for Deferred Compensation	14-17
	[1] Tax Consequences Under Section 2039(a)	14-18
	[2] Avoiding Estate Taxation — Death-Benefit-Only Plans	14-20
	[a] Early Cases Exclude Death-Benefit-Only Plans	14-20
	[b] The "Combination" Controversy	14-21
	[i] Early cases	14-21
	[ii] The *Schelberg* case	14-23

xxi TABLE OF CONTENTS

Page

        [iii] The *Siegel* case 14-24
    [c] The Problem of the Power to Amend 14-26
    [d] The Gift Tax Problem 14-28
    [e] Planning to Avoid Taxability 14-28
        [i] Separate plans 14-29
        [ii] Restriction on other post-retirement plans 14-29
        [iii] No power to amend 14-29
  [3] Review of Beneficiaries' Needs 14-29

¶ 14.04 Estate Planning for Stock Options and Section 83 Plans ... 14-31

¶ 14.05 Estate Planning for Qualified Retirement Plans 14-35
  [1] $100,000 Exclusion for Annuities 14-35
    [a] Requirements for Exclusion 14-35
        [i] Specifically enumerated type of plan 14-35
        [ii] Not payable to participant's executor 14-36
        [iii] Contributions must be made by employer 14-37
        [iv] Not applicable to lump-sum distributions 14-38
        [v] Benefits must be "receivable" under a plan 14-38
    [b] Additional Planning Considerations 14-40
        [i] Exclusion from spouse's estate 14-40
        [ii] Income tax status of beneficiary 14-42
  [2] Lump-Sum Distributions 14-43
  [3] Individual Retirement Accounts 14-45

Chapter 15

TAX PLANNING WITH WILLS

¶ 15.01 The Need for a Last Will and Testament 15-2
  [1] The Marital Deduction 15-3
  [2] Disposition of Decedent's Assets 15-3
  [3] Grant of Powers to Fiduciaries 15-4

¶ 15.02 Planning for the Use of the Marital Deduction 15-5
  [1] Tax Planning With Marital Deduction Provisions 15-5
    [a] General Principles 15-5
    [b] Economic Needs of the Spouse 15-9
    [c] Use of Unified Estate and Gift Tax Credit by Both
        Spouses 15-9
    [d] Effect of Progressive Rate Structure 15-11
    [e] Time Value of Money Saved by Use of Marital
        Deduction 15-11
    [f] Other Factors in Determining Size of Marital
        Bequest 15-14

TABLE OF CONTENTS

		Page
[2] Qualification for Marital Deduction		15-15
[a] Decedent Must Be Survived by Spouse		15-15
[i] Marital status		15-16
[ii] Survival		15-17
[b] Property Must Pass From Decedent to Spouse		15-18
[c] Property Must Be Included in Decedent's Gross Estate		15-19
[d] Citizenship or Residency		15-19
¶ 15.03 Terminable Interests and Transfers in Trust		15-20
[1] Definition of Terminable Interest		15-20
[2] Factors Making Terminable Interest Nondeductible		15-21
[a] Statutory Requirements		15-21
[b] Transfer of the Same "Property"		15-21
[c] Interpretation of State Law		15-22
[d] Contingent Interests		15-23
[3] Exceptions to Terminable Interest Rule		15-24
[a] Survival for a Limited Period of Time		15-24
[b] Life Estate With General Power of Appointment		15-26
[c] Life Insurance With Power of Appointment		15-32
[d] Qualified Terminable Interest Property		15-34
¶ 15.04 Drafting the Marital Deduction Provision		15-36
[1] Fractional Share Provisions		15-37
[2] Pecuniary Bequests		15-38
[3] Equalization Clauses		15-40
¶ 15.05 Other Tax Planning Devices Available by Will		15-43
[1] Disclaimers		15-43
[a] Requirements for Qualified Disclaimers		15-44
[b] Complete vs. Partial Disclaimers		15-47
[2] Charitable Bequests		15-48
[a] Estate Taxation of Charitable Bequests		15-48
[i] Eligible recipients		15-48
[ii] Allowable methods of charitable transfer		15-49
[iii] Additional requirements for charitable bequests		15-52
[b] Planning for the Charitable Deduction		15-53
[3] Income Tax Planning Considerations		15-54
[a] Heirs' Tax Situation		15-55
[b] Potential Sale of Bequeathed Property		15-55
[c] Estate and Spouse Filing Joint Return		15-56

Chapter 16

PRIVATE ANNUITIES, POWERS OF APPOINTMENT

		Page
¶ 16.01	Introduction	16-2
¶ 16.02	Private Annuities	16-2
	[1] Taxation of Private Annuities	16-3
	[2] Special Tax Problems for the Annuitant	16-5
	[a] Retention of Security	16-6
	[b] Retained Life Estate	16-7
	[c] Value of the Annuity Promise	16-8
	[d] Foreign Trusts	16-9
	[3] Tax Consequences to Transferee	16-10
	[4] Tax Planning With Private Annuities	16-12
	[a] Removal of Assets From the Estate	16-12
	[b] Liquidity	16-12
	[c] Disadvantages of the Private Annuity	16-13
	[d] Alternatives to the Private Annuity — Installment Sale of Property	16-14
¶ 16.03	Powers of Appointment	16-16
	[1] Definition of General Power of Appointment	16-16
	[2] Exclusions From Definition of General Power of Appointment	16-17
	[a] Ascertainable Standard Exclusion	16-17
	[b] Joint Power Exclusion	16-20
	[c] "5 + 5" Power	16-21
	[3] Factors Affecting Taxation of Powers of Appointment	16-22
	[a] Capacity to Exercise Power	16-23
	[b] Release of Power	16-23
	[c] Gift Tax Consequences	16-24
	[4] Planning Objectives for Powers of Appointment	16-24
	[a] Shifting of Assets	16-24
	[b] Access to Trust Corpus	16-25
	[c] Marital Deduction Qualification	16-25
¶ 16.04	Inflation Planning	16-25
Appendix	Present Worth of Annuity, Life Interest, Remainder Interest	16-29

TABLE OF CONTENTS

	Page
TABLE OF I.R.C. SECTIONS	T-1
TABLE OF TREASURY REGULATIONS	T-9
TABLE OF REVENUE RULINGS, REVENUE PROCEDURES, AND OTHER IRS RELEASES AND GUIDELINES	T-13
TABLE OF CASES	T-17
INDEX	I-1

PART I

General Tax Planning Strategies

CHAPTER 1

Profile of the Highly Compensated Individual

		Page
¶ 1.01	Inflation and the Highly Compensated	1-1
¶ 1.02	Types of Highly Compensated Individuals	1-2
	[1] Corporate Executives	1-2
	[2] Professionals	1-2
	[3] Professional Athletes	1-3
	[4] Entertainers or Artistic Performers	1-3
	[5] "Super Salesmen"	1-3
¶ 1.03	Tax Problems of the Highly Compensated	1-4

¶ 1.01 Inflation and the Highly Compensated

The dominant economic factor of our times has been inflation. The double-digit inflation of the late 1960s and the 1970s has had a profound effect upon our economic lives. First, it has drastically changed the way people invest, causing a substantial diversion of money into those assets that are perceived to react well to inflationary tendencies, such as real estate, gold and precious metals, antiques, art work, and petroleum products. As a result, the tendency to save has been discouraged. The fact that a particular article is likely to cost substantially more tomorrow has promoted a tendency either to consume rather than save or to invest in the types of assets mentioned above. Inflation has favored the borrower, the consumer, and the investor, as opposed to the saver or the lender.

Inflation has also had a profound impact upon our system of employee compensation. In order merely to keep pace with inflation, salaries have been pushed to higher plateaus. Incomes once thought to be extraordinary are now rather commonplace. Recently graduated professionals, such as engineers and lawyers, are commonly paid starting salaries of $30,000 or more. Bus drivers in large metropolitan areas earn salaries in excess of $20,000. On the other hand, increased costs of goods and services, plus the acceptance of women in the job marketplace, have increased the likelihood that both spouses will be regularly employed. A growing number of two-income families now have a relatively high amount of earned income. It is common to find that a young couple with both spouses working will have a combined income substantially in excess of $50,000.

These inflationary tendencies have created a situation in which a substantial portion of society is composed of highly compensated individuals. In addition to the escalation of two-income couples into the higher tax brackets, professionals, such as doctors, engineers, and corporate executives, of course, still command high compensation for their services throughout their careers. Other occupations, such as professional athletes or entertainers, may achieve a very highly compensated status for a more limited period of time. This book concerns those who have significant amounts of earned income *as employees* rather than the income as business *owners*. Consequently, the book concentrates on those tax planning techniques that are most relevant to high-income status rather than on income and estate planning related to ownership of a business. Although a substantial portion of this book is relevant to the owners of both public corporations and closely held businesses, this relevance evolves from their highly compensated status rather than from a discussion of tax issues relating to business ownership.

¶ 1.02 Types of Highly Compensated Individuals

[1] Corporate Executives

Corporate executives tend to remain in a high-income status throughout their careers, with steadily rising incomes during that period. Since they are employees rather than owners of a business, much of their lifetime tax planning centers around compensation-related benefits provided by their employers. Because of their consistent highly compensated status, corporate executives regularly build estates of significant size as their careers progress.

[2] Professionals

Professionals, such as doctors and lawyers, are similar to corporate executives in that they usually experience a consistently growing, high level of compensation throughout their careers. The one major difference between professionals and corporate executives is that their "employers" are often a group of other professionals organized either as a partnership or as a professional corporation.[1] Despite this difference, virtually all of the compensation planning devices, with the exception of stock plans and options,[2] are available to groups of professionals — although some are limited to those organized as corporations.

[3] Professional Athletes

The most distinguishing economic characteristic of the professional athlete is his relatively short span of extremely high earnings. Unlike the corporate executive, the athlete is not likely to maintain his highly compensated status until normal retirement age, but rather may suffer a severe drop in earnings in his mid- to late 30's as his athletic career ebbs. Consequently, tax planning for the professional athlete must be designed to take cognizance of this expected drop in earnings.

[4] Entertainers or Artistic Performers

The show business personality is likely to be subject to a wide fluctuation in earnings. Compensation may be extremely high in periods of popularity or when the performer has a successful venture, such as a long running television series or a popular film. On the other hand, the same individual may suffer periods of economic drought. As a consequence, tax planning for this individual must give preference to tax minimization during the peak periods.

[5] "Super Salesmen"

The "super" salesman is similar to the performer in that he may go through periods of wide variation in earnings. If he is consistently successful, his income patterns will be similar to the corporate executive's in that it will remain consistently high. It is much more common, however, even for successful salesmen, to see a wide variation in earnings.

---

[1] A discussion of the advantages and disadvantages of professional corporations is beyond the scope of this book. This issue includes many nontax issues and is covered adequately in other articles and treatises.

[2] This is discussed in Chapter 4. Ownership of professional corporations or partnerships is usually restricted to licensed professionals. In addition, such organizations usually distribute most of their earnings on an annual basis — thus limiting the value of any equity buildup.

¶ 1.03 Tax Problems of the Highly Compensated

From both an economic and tax planning standpoint, the highly compensated are a unique group. First, most members of this class have high amounts of earned income for varying periods of time. In addition, they are also likely to have or desire to have other compensatory benefits, such as a retirement plan, stock options, or deferred compensation. Moreover, those individuals who remain in a highly compensated status throughout their working careers or who, in the alternative, experience extremely high compensation for a more limited period of time usually accumulate substantial assets during the course of their lifetime. Typically, such individuals, as a group, possess large taxable estates, even though they may not have been born into a position of wealth.

Because highly compensated individuals have much in common from an economic standpoint, they are also faced with many similar tax planning problems. First, their highly compensated status usually results in a very high marginal income tax bracket. Until the enactment of the Economic Recovery Tax Act of 1981 (referred to throughout this book as the 1981 Act), tax brackets had not been regularly adjusted to counteract the effects of inflation, since Congress had frequently rejected various forms of tax indexing.[3] Thus, inflation has induced a bracket creep in our tax system with the result that many individuals or two-salaried couples are taxed at a marginal rate of 50 percent or more. As more and more individuals are taxed at high marginal rates, the need for income tax planning for these individuals becomes more acute. The natural consequence of high marginal rates has been the intensified search for any possible legal means of reducing one's income taxes. Inflation has also meant that the assets purchased by the highly compensated have appreciated greatly in value over the course of time. Accordingly, the possible sale of these assets inevitably creates the potential for a large capital gains tax.

Inflation has also had a significant impact upon estate planning. Since inflation has greatly increased the dollar value of virtually all assets, the highly compensated status of many such individuals or families has meant the accumulation of significant estates. The consequence has been to accentuate the need for tax planning for those estates

---

[3] Tax indexing is the automatic adjustment of tax brackets by the yearly changes in the consumer price index. The 1981 Act has adopted an indexing system but it does not begin until 1985. See discussion at ¶ 2.01[2].

that fall into the taxable category. Although both the Tax Reform Act of 1976 (the 1976 Act) and the 1981 Act increased the size of an estate that could be transferred on a tax-exempt basis,[4] inflation has quickly eroded the effect of many of these changes. To put it quite simply, with houses worth $100,000 and salaries of $50,000 per year quite commonplace, virtually all highly compensated individuals tend to possess an estate of the magnitude that creates substantial estate and tax planning needs.

---

[4] The uniform lifetime credit enacted in Section 2010 means that any estate with taxable assets of less than $600,000 will pass totally free of federal estate tax when the credit is fully phased in by 1987. Prior to that date the credit will exempt a substantially lesser amount. The use of the marital deduction and other available deductions and credits can substantially increase the amount that can be transferred tax-free.

CHAPTER 2

Income Tax Overview

		Page
¶ 2.01	The Graduated Rate Structure	2-2
	[1] Rates of Taxation	2-2
	[2] Effect on Deductions	2-3
	[3] Effect on Credits	2-4
	[4] Indexing	2-4
¶ 2.02	Alternative Minimum Tax	2-5
	[1] Computation of Alternative Minimum Tax	2-5
	[2] Items of Tax Preference	2-7
	[a] Accelerated Depreciation on Real Property	2-7
	[b] Accelerated Depreciation on Leased Personal Property	2-8
	[c] Amortization of Certified Pollution Control Facilities	2-9
	[d] Incentive Stock Options	2-9
	[e] Depletion	2-9
	[f] Intangible Drilling Costs	2-9
	[g] Accelerated Cost Recovery Deduction	2-10
	[h] Capital Gain	2-10
	[i] Miscellaneous Preference Items	2-10
	[3] Planning for the Alternative Minimum Tax	2-11
¶ 2.03	Taxation of Capital Gain	2-14
	[1] Basic Principles	2-14
	[2] Wash Sales	2-16
¶ 2.04	General Planning Strategies	2-18
	[1] Deferral of Income	2-19
	[2] Acceleration of Deductions	2-20
	[a] Accounting Method Must Clearly Reflect Income	2-21
	[b] Specific Deduction Limitations	2-21
	[3] Conversion of Ordinary Income Into Capital Gain	2-22
	[4] Avoiding Taxable Income	2-24
	[a] Tax-Exempt Bonds	2-24
	[i] Nontaxability of certain governmental obligations	2-24

	Page
[ii] Indebtedness used to purchase tax-exempt securities	2-26
[b] Tax-Free Exchanges	2-27
[c] Avoidance of Tax on Sale of Residence	2-29
[i] Replacement of residence	2-29
[ii] Sale of residence by individuals who have attained age 55	2-30
[d] Retention of Assets Until Death	2-32
[5] Income Averaging	2-33

¶ 2.01 The Graduated Rate Structure

This chapter reviews the basic provisions of the federal income tax system and their effect upon the highly compensated individual. This discussion sets the stage for the more detailed analysis of specific tax planning strategies that constitute the remainder of this book. No attempt is made to initiate a general discussion of what does or does not constitute taxable income or whether or not a specific payment by an individual is or is not a deductible expense. For example, discussions such as whether or not a payment constitutes a deductible medical expense under Section 213 of the Internal Revenue Code or whether a particular payment qualifies as interest deductible under Section 163 are more properly the topic of an overall treatise on income taxation and are not discussed herein. Rather, this chapter reviews those facets of income taxation that, by design or otherwise, tend to impact most heavily upon the highly compensated individual. The general tax planning strategies suggested by this statutory framework are then reviewed.

[1] Rates of Taxation

The graduated tax rate structure imposes a tax upon an individual's taxable income ranging from 11 percent to 50 percent.[1] Tax rates vary depending on whether the individual filing the income tax return is a married individual filing a joint return or a surviving spouse, a head of household, a single individual or a married individual filing a separate return. The Economic Recovery Tax Act of 1981 (the 1981 Act) introduced a series of rate reductions which, through 1984, have the effect of decreasing the rate of individual taxation by increasing the amount of taxable income that an individual is permitted to earn before a specific rate of taxation will apply. For example, for married individuals filing

---

[1] Prior to 1983, the lowest rate of taxation was 12 percent.

joint returns, all income in excess of $85,600 will be taxed at the 50 percent rate in 1982. The 50 percent bracket will not apply until taxable income exceeds $109,400 in 1983 and, in 1984, the 50 percent tax bracket will not become effective until the taxable income exceeds $162,400.

Despite this decrease in the rate of taxation implemented by the 1981 Act, the effect of the graduated rate structure remains the same. Once an individual or family unit filing a joint return crosses a particular bracket line, each incremental dollar of income will be taxed at a higher rate, and this will continue until the individual reaches the 50 percent bracket. At that time, all additional dollars of taxable income will be taxed at the 50 percent rate. In addition, the graduated rate structure is designed so as to move an individual into significant rates of taxation once he or she reaches middle income levels. For example, single individuals reach the 35 percent rate bracket in 1982 once taxable income exceeds $23,500. In 1983, the single individual will be in the 36 percent rate bracket when taxable income exceeds $28,800 and will be in the 38 percent bracket in 1984 when taxable income exceeds $34,100.

The effect of this graduated rate structure, which impacts most heavily upon middle income and highly compensated individuals, is to place a significant premium on sophisticated tax planning. For individuals who have moved into income brackets where additional income is taxed at rates of 40 percent and more, this tax planning becomes imperative.[2]

[2] Effect on Deductions

One effect of the graduated rate structure is that a deduction is generally worth more to the highly compensated than to other individuals. This is because as an individual's tax bracket increases, more tax dollars are saved by each deduction. For example, the individual in the 50 percent rate bracket will save fifty cents in taxation for each dollar of

---

[2] Prior to 1981, the tax rate schedule produced a so-called marriage penalty under which married taxpayers with relatively equal incomes would be taxed at higher marginal rates than if each particular taxpayer was single. In order to alleviate this inequity, married couples with two wage earners beginning in 1983 will get a deduction of 10 percent (5 percent for 1982) for the lesser of $30,000 or the qualified earned income of the spouse with the lower earned income. This translates into a maximum deduction of $3,000 in 1983 and thereafter. This deduction only applies to "qualified earned income" and does not apply to passive income or items that are not includable in gross income, received as a pension or annuity, payment or distributions from an IRA, received as deferred compensation, or received for services performed by an individual in the employ of his spouse. See generally I.R.C. § 221.

additional deductions, whereas the individual in the 20 percent rate bracket will only save twenty cents for each additional deductible dollar. Accordingly, the highly compensated individual has a strong incentive to search for additional deductible items.

Those items that can be paid for with pretax dollars will have a net out-of-pocket cost of fifty cents per dollar and will create a significant incentive for the making of such deductible payments. For example, one of the primary inducements to the real estate boom of the 1970s was the combination of rate bracket creep, which pushed many individuals into the 50 percent rate bracket, and the deduction for interest payments with respect to mortgages allowed by Section 163. This combination, together with spiraling house prices, led individuals to commit themselves to bigger and bigger mortgages. Most such individuals made a determination that they would rather pay the additional dollar of mortgage payment, since it would be deductible and probably have a net out-of-pocket cost of fifty cents on the dollar. Similar factors encourage year-end charitable giving or the payment of various fringe benefits through a corporate structure. In all of these cases, a motivating factor is the graduated rate structure, which creates a strong incentive for the highly compensated individual to search for deductions.

[3] Effect on Credits

An income tax credit reduces an individual's tax liability on a dollar-for-dollar basis and thus is a highly cherished item. It does not lower taxable income as a deduction does, but reduces the amount of tax dollars owed. For example, an investment tax credit of $25 will reduce the recipient's income tax liability by $25. Because the credit produces a direct dollar-for-dollar reduction in income tax liability, the effect of a credit is the same irrespective of the individual's income tax bracket. Accordingly, when Congress is in one of its reform moods, there is a tendency to legislate various income tax breaks in the form of a credit rather than a deduction, since this will provide the same dollar impact to lower-income groups as to the highly compensated.

[4] Indexing

Perhaps the most significant long-range change introduced into our income tax system by the 1981 Act was the enactment of the indexing provisions that become effective in 1985. Beginning in that year, the individual rate brackets, the personal exemption, and the zero-bracket amount will be adjusted for inflation each year.[3] The cost-of-living adjustment for any calendar year will be determined by the percentage by which the Consumer Price Index (CPI) for the preceding calendar year [4] exceeds the CPI for the calendar year 1983. The implementation of an indexing system means that the same dollar amount of income will be taxed at a lesser rate each year, and that the so-called bracket creep induced by increases in income designed merely to keep pace with inflation will presumably be halted.

Although the deferral of income has always been a basic tenet of income tax planning, the introduction of indexing into our income tax system will place an even greater emphasis on this particular planning strategy. Since a dollar of income will be taxed at a lesser rate in succeeding years, there is a substantial incentive to defer income until that succeeding year. This will be discussed more fully in reviewing general planning strategies for the highly compensated at ¶ 2.04[1].

¶ 2.02 Alternative Minimum Tax

Because of a congressional concern that high-income taxpayers were taking too great an advantage of so-called loopholes in the Internal Revenue Code, a special tax has been enacted with the stated purpose of imposing some tax on high-income individuals who take substantial advantage of various items of tax preference built into the Code. This tax, known as the alternative minimum tax,[5] was substantially strengthened by the Tax Equity and Fiscal Responsibility Act of 1982 (the 1982 Act), which at the same time repealed the former "add on" minimum tax imposed by Section 56.[6]

[1] Computation of Alternative Minimum Tax

Section 55 imposes an alternative minimum tax at a rate of 20 percent to the extent that the tentative tax computed under this Section produces an alternative minimum tax liability that exceeds the tax-

---

[3] I.R.C. § 1(f).

[4] The CPI for the preceding year is determined by the average of the CPI as of the close of the twelve-month period ending on September 30 of such calendar year. I.R.C. § 1(f)(4).

[5] I.R.C. § 55.

[6] These changes were effective for tax years beginning after December 31, 1982.

payer's regular tax liability for the taxable year. In order to assess potential liability under this section, the taxpayer must first compute his alternative minimum taxable income as defined in Section 55(b).

"Alternative minimum taxable income" is defined to mean the taxpayer's adjusted gross income for the year reduced by the alternative tax net operating loss deduction, the alternative tax itemized deductions, plus any amount included in income under Section 667, and increased by the items of tax preference.[7] The deductions that are allowed in determining the alternative tax itemized deductions are charitable contributions, medical expenses in excess of 10 percent of adjusted gross income, casualty losses in excess of 10 percent of adjusted gross income, the Section 691(c) deduction for estate taxes attributable to income in respect of a decedent, and a deduction for qualified interest.[8] "Qualified interest" basically means interest paid by a taxpayer with respect to his personal residence and a deduction for interest (other than housing interest) to the extent that such interest does not exceed the taxpayer's qualified net investment income for the year.[9]

After the alternative minimum taxable income is so computed, a tentative tax at the rate of 20 percent is imposed to the extent that this minimum taxable income exceeds the exemption amount. The exemption amount is $40,000 in the case of a joint return,[10] or $30,000 in the case of a single individual. The exemption amount in the case of a trust or estate is $20,000. The tax thus computed is compared to the taxpayer's regular liability for the year,[11] and the taxpayer is required to pay the higher of the two amounts.

---

[7] See discussion at ¶ 2.02[2].

[8] I.R.C. § 55(e).

[9] I.R.C. § 55(e)(3). Net income taken into account either directly or indirectly from a limited partnership interest or an interest in a Subchapter S corporation (in the case of a person who does not participate in the management of the corporation) will be investment income for the purpose of the net investment income limitation on the interest deduction. Interest on indebtedness incurred to acquire or carry such an interest will be "below the line interest" for purposes of the minimum tax, and therefore subject to the net investment income limitation on the interest deduction.

[10] The exemption amount in the case of a surviving spouse is also $40,000. This is reduced to $20,000 in the case of a married individual who files a separate return.

[11] The taxpayer's regular tax in essence means his income tax liability reduced by the various credits allowable under Subpart A of Part IV of Chapter 1 of the Code (other than Sections 31, 39, and 43). Consequently, the various income tax credits, such as the investment credit, reduce a taxpayer's regular tax

Consequently, the alternative minimum tax increases the taxpayer's liability only when it exceeds the tax liability that might otherwise be computed under normal means. The taxpayer computes his alternative minimum tax liability on Form 6251 to determine if he is liable for the tax. If the calculation on this form indicates that no alternative minimum tax is due, it need not be attached to the taxpayer's return. It is the position of the Service that the failure by a tax return preparer to report a Section 55 minimum tax liability resulting from a net capital gain deduction will give rise to the penalty under Section 6694(a) for a negligent or intentional disregard of rules and regulations.[12] In this ruling it was indicated that neither oversight nor basic lack of awareness of the minimum tax provisions will relieve the preparer of the negligence penalty. Consequently, despite the rather confusing nature of the alternative minimum tax, a failure to take cognizance of it in the preparation of an income tax return may lead to the imposition of the negligence penalty.

[2] Items of Tax Preference

The various items of tax preference that create a potential liability for the alternative minimum tax are set forth in Section 57(a). Most of these items of tax preference are deductions from the income tax, which tend to lower the regular tax paid and thus increase the likelihood for the imposition of the minimum tax. This is consistent with the theory that a minimum tax is imposed on those individuals who take what is presumably considered to be an excessive advantage of the various tax incentives built into the Code. The major items of tax preference for individuals are discussed below.

[a] Accelerated Depreciation on Real Property. For purposes of Section 57(a)(2), accelerated depreciation on real property is defined as the excess of any depreciation or amortization allowance over that which would have been allowed if the taxpayer had used the straight-line method of depreciation.[13] This particular item of preference is primarily applicable to property placed in service prior to 1981. (A

---

liability as defined in Section 55 and thus increase the potential for the application of the alternative minimum tax.

[12] Rev. Rul. 80-28, 1980-1 C.B. 304.

[13] This is determined without regard to Section 167(k).

separate item of preference is created with respect to post-1981 ACRS accelerated cost recovery.) Regulations under Section 57 indicate that the minimum tax paid with respect to such accelerated depreciation does not serve to increase the basis of the property.[14] Thus, the taxpayer encumbered by the alternative minimum tax is not able to recoup his payment by other means. It also should be noted that when accelerated depreciation is used, the depreciation in the later years will frequently fall below that which would have been allowed under the straight-line method. This negative difference between the accelerated and straight-line methods is not recognized for minimum tax purposes and cannot be netted out against other accelerated depreciation that benefits a taxpayer in the same year. Similarly, the regulations require the excess depreciation to be determined on each separate item of Section 1250 property with no netting.[15] Consequently, accelerated depreciation on a separate item of Section 1250 property will create a tax preference for a given year, irrespective of the fact that other properties use the straight-line method or that other properties that have used accelerated depreciation are now being depreciated at a rate that falls below the straight-line method.

[b] Accelerated Depreciation on Leased Personal Property. A tax preference is created to the extent that each item of Section 1245 property is subject to a lease and has depreciation that exceeds that which would be allowable had the taxpayer depreciated the property under the straight-line method for the taxable year. The concept behind this particular item of tax preference is very similar to that of accelerated depreciation with respect to real property and is aimed at the equipment leasing tax shelters that have been popular for many years. For purposes of calculating the amount that would have been allowable under the straight-line method, the taxpayer is not permitted to use the 20 percent variance associated with the asset depreciation range (ADR) in determining the estimated useful life as provided by Section 167(m)(1). Thus, any increase in depreciation using ADR created by electing a useful life shorter than the class life becomes a preference amount. This is true whether or not straight-line or accelerated depreciation is used. As is the case with Section 1250 property, the tax preference created by accelerated depreciation for personal property is determined on an item-by-item basis.

---

[14] Treas. Reg. § 1.57-1(b)(6).
[15] Treas. Reg. § 1.57-1(b)(1).

[c] Amortization of Certified Pollution Control Facilities. An item of preference is created with respect to certified pollution control facilities to the extent that the amortization allowable under the sixty-month write-off for the facilities allowed by Section 169 exceeds that otherwise allowable as depreciation under Section 167. The determination of the deduction otherwise allowable as depreciation under Section 167 is made by a reference to any permissible method, including accelerated methods that may be elected.[16] The calculation of this excess is again made on an item-by-item basis.

[d] Incentive Stock Options. With respect to a transfer of shares of stock pursuant to the exercise of a incentive stock option as defined in Section 422A, the amount by which the fair market value of the share at that time exceeds the option price is considered an item of tax preference.[17] As with other items of tax preference, the payment of the minimum tax has no effect on the basis of the optioned stock.[18]

[e] Depletion. The excess of the deduction for depletion allowable under Section 611 over the adjusted basis of the property at the end of the taxable year in question creates a further item of tax preference. Consequently, participants in most oil and gas tax shelters are likely to be faced with this particular preference item.

[f] Intangible Drilling Costs. A preference item is created if the taxpayer elects to deduct intangible drilling costs [19] to the extent that such excess intangible drilling costs exceed the net income of the taxpayer from oil, gas, and geothermal properties for the taxable year. Excess intangible drilling costs are defined in Section 57(a)(11)(B) as the excess of such intangible drilling costs over the amount that would have been allowable for the taxable year if such costs had been capitalized and the straight-line recovery of intangibles had been used with respect to such costs. Consequently, this preference does not apply to taxpayers who elect to capitalize their intangible drilling costs, nor does it apply to nonproductive wells. If a well is plugged and abandoned without having

---

[16] Treas. Reg. § 1.57-1(d)(4).

[17] This item of preference was added by the 1982 Act. The Conference Report indicates that this preference will not apply when there is an early disposition of the stock acquired through the exercise of the option.

[18] Treas. Reg. § 1.57-1(f)(7).

[19] I.R.C. § 263(c).

produced oil or gas in commercial quantities, it will be considered nonproductive and thus does not serve to create a preference item.

[g] Accelerated Cost Recovery Deduction. An item of tax preference added by the 1981 Act relates to the accelerated cost recovery deduction. This item of preference is created by comparing the amount, if any, by which a deduction allowable under Section 168(a) exceeds the deduction that would have been allowable for the taxable year had the property been depreciated using the straight-line method (with a half-year convention and without regard to salvage value) and a recovery period determined in accordance with the following table:

Type of Property	Recovery Period
3-year property	5 years
5-year property	8 years
10-year property	15 years
15-year public utility property	22 years

With respect to the recovery period for 15-year real property, the preference is created by the amount, if any, by which the deduction allowed under Section 168 exceeds the deduction that would have been allowable for the taxable year had the property been depreciated using a 15-year period and a straight-line method without regard to salvage value. Thus, if straight-line 15-year depreciation is used with respect to real property, no tax preference item will be created. If an accelerated method is used, a tax preference will be created to the extent that it exceeds the depreciation allowable under the straight-line method.

[h] Capital Gain. In a case of a taxpayer other than a corporation, an amount equal to the capital gain deduction for the taxable year determined under Section 1202 is a further item of tax preference. This deduction, which is equal to 60 percent of the net long-term capital gain, can produce a very significant preference item in a case of a taxpayer who realizes an exceedingly large capital gain in a particular taxable year.

[i] Miscellaneous Preference Items. Other items of preference include any amount of interest excluded from the taxpayer's gross income for the taxable year under Section 116 or 128.[20] Thus, interest

---

[20] I.R.C. § 57(a)(1).

under the $100 dividend and interest exclusion, the all-savers exclusion, and the 15 percent net income interest exclusion (which takes effect after 1984) will be added back into alternative minimum taxable income as a preference item.

Two other preferences were added by the 1982 Act. These are mining exploration and development costs to the extent of an amount equal to the amount allowable as a deduction under Sections 616(a) or 617.[21] In addition, circulation and research and experimental expenditures are now a preference item to the extent that the amount allowable as a deduction under Sections 173 or 174(a) for the taxable year exceeds the amount that would have been allowable for the taxable year if these expenditures had been capitalized and amortized ratably over the ten-year period beginning for the taxable year in which such expenditures were made.[22] Thus, to the extent that taxpayers elect ten-year amortization for either of these expenditures, no preference item will be created. A further item of preference created by Section 57(a)(7) is for reserves for losses and bad debts of financial institutions, to the extent that such reserves exceed the amount that would have been allowable had the institution maintained its bad debt reserve for all taxable years on the basis of actual experience.

[3] Planning for the Alternative Minimum Tax

The basic purpose behind the enactment of the alternative minimum tax was to ensure that high-income individuals who were paying low income taxes because of substantial use of tax preferences would pay at least some minimum rate of tax. A quick glance at the rules underlying the computation of the alternative minimum tax indicates that it does work toward this end. By adding back the capital gain deduction and the other commonly used preference items into a taxpayer's taxable income, the alternative minimum tax will ensure that a taxpayer who has substantial amounts of one or all of these preferences will pay some taxes, up to a maximum rate of 20 percent.

There are, however, situations where the alternative minimum tax will produce a surprising impact upon an individual's income tax liability even though he pays a substantial income tax in the year in question. One such situation where the alternative minimum tax will have a significant impact is where the taxpayer has a large ordinary loss in the same year that a substantial long-term capital gain has been

---

[21] I.R.C. § 57(a)(5).

[22] I.R.C. § 57(a)(6).

realized. In such a situation, the impact of the losses will be diluted by the alternative minimum tax. Another situation that may produce a significant alternative minimum tax liability is where a taxpayer has little or no ordinary income but has realized a substantial long-term capital gain or other preference items in a particular year.

Because the three basic factors that affect the imposition of the alternative minimum tax — regular tax liability, preference items, and the alternative minimum tax deductions — are clearly spelled out, planning for avoidance or minimization of the alternative minimum tax requires the tax planner to consider the interaction of these three factors. For example, it is obvious that the realization of substantial ordinary losses in the same year that there are many items of tax preference is likely to produce an alternative minimum tax liability, with the result that the impact of the losses will be minimized or wasted. Thus, it is usually prudent to determine if it is possible to postpone the realization of ordinary loss when the taxpayer has already realized a substantial capital gain in a particular year. Inasmuch as the tax bracket for both the alternative minimum tax and capital gains is equal (20 percent), the tax impact upon the capital gain is largely identical whether or not the alternative minimum tax is imposed. By realizing ordinary losses in the same year, the effect of these losses will be reduced because the alternative minimum tax will impose a tax liability on the gain irrespective of these losses. Thus, it is generally worthwhile to attempt to postpone these losses until the following taxable year. Another approach suggested is to recognize some additional amounts of ordinary income in order to offset these losses.[23] By paying this additional compensation in such a year, the taxpayer may be able to realize the income at a maximum rate of only 20 percent as opposed to other years in which he may be taxed at a 50 percent bracket. A similar means of controlling the alternative minimum tax would be to reduce, if possible, the amount of gain realized in a year by making an installment sale.

---

[23] This approach has been suggested by Streer, "The New Alternative Minimum Tax; Proper Planning Can Mitigate the Impact," 57 Taxes 97 (1979). The following formula has been suggested by the author to determine the approximate amount of additional compensation that can be received at an effective rate equal to the highest minimum tax bracket:

$$\text{Additional compensation} = \frac{\text{Alternative minimum tax} - \text{Normally computed tax liability}}{\text{Taxpayer's highest incremental tax rate} - 20\%}$$

When low income tax liability is produced by large ordinary losses, large capital gains and/or other preference items in a particular year are likely to create an alternative minimum tax liability. Careful planning requires a constant awareness of this fact and an attempt to ensure that this combination of factors is not present in a single taxable year. Of course, it is not always possible to avoid such a combination. For example, if a taxpayer has valuable tax shelter investments that throw off significant tax losses, and he is presented with a favorable opportunity to sell a capital asset for a significant long-term capital gain, the economic reality of the offer received may dictate accepting it, irrespective of the alternative minimum tax consequences. The alternative minimum tax at a maximum rate of 20 percent may not be significant enough to compel a taxpayer to turn his back on a substantial economic gain from the sale of an appreciated asset.

Another example may be a situation where a taxpayer whose business has produced substantial economic losses is offered an opportunity to sell an investment asset at a substantial gain. In such a case, the economic gain resulting from the sale of the asset may be required in order to help the taxpayer sustain himself because of business reversals. Again, although this may result in an alternative minimum tax liability, economic necessities may dictate a consummation of the sale. If, however, such economic necessities are not present, it may be possible to plan to avoid or minimize the alternative minimum tax by avoiding a combination of the previously described factors.

A tax advisor should generally be aware that an aggressive tax reduction program for a client based upon many of the items listed as preferences will create an alternative minimum tax liability. Accordingly, in evaluating a potential investment such as a real estate tax shelter, the advisor must attempt to make a determination as to whether or not a minimum tax liability will result, and if so, what its impact will be. Thus, one aspect of proper planning with respect to the minimum tax would be to attempt to direct the taxpayer so that the amount of preference items in any given year will be limited. If a taxpayer has substantial accelerated depreciation on real property in a particular year, that may not be the year to get involved in an oil drilling venture that will provide considerable intangible drilling expenses as an item of deduction. The taxpayer may be better off in waiting until the accelerated portion of his real estate deductions have receded somewhat before entering into another venture of this type.

Although the potential imposition of the alternative minimum tax is a negative factor that may influence a taxpayer's decision not to invest in a particular venture, the existence of this tax may not be such a negative influence as to completely eliminate the benefits of a particular transaction. In some instances, the alternative minimum tax will only reduce the benefits of the transaction but not make the transaction nonbeneficial. For example, the accelerated portion of real estate depreciation will save the 50 percent bracket taxpayer fifty cents for each dollar's worth of deduction. If the alternative minimum tax at a rate of 20 percent is imposed on the items of accelerated deduction, the effect will be to reduce the benefit of the accelerated portion of the depreciation deduction to thirty cents. In such a case, the benefit of the deduction will not be eliminated — only reduced. If the taxpayer is faced with an extremely high tax liability for that given year, it may be advantageous to proceed with a proposed transaction even though an item of tax preference will be created.

¶ 2.03 Taxation of Capital Gain

Gain from the sale of capital assets held for more than one year is accorded highly favorable tax treatment by the Code. As a result, a substantial incentive is created to structure a transaction so that gain will be subject to capital gain taxation.

[1] Basic Principles

An individual taxpayer is allowed a deduction from gross income in any taxable year in which the taxpayer has an excess of net long-term capital gain over a net short-term capital loss. The deduction is equal to 60 percent of the amount of such excess.[24] When this 60 percent deduction is multiplied by the 50 percent maximum rate bracket for individuals, it means that long-term capital gain for individuals is taxed at a maximum rate of 20 percent. Long-term capital gain is created by the sale of a capital asset held for more than one year. "Capital assets" are defined in Section 1221 of the Code as property held by a taxpayer but not including:

(1) stock in trade of the taxpayer or other property of a kind which would properly be included in the inventory of the taxpayer;

---

[24] I.R.C. § 1202(a). This deduction is an item of tax preference. See discussion at ¶ 2.02[2][h].

if on hand at the close of the taxable year, or property held by the taxpayer primarily for sale to customers in the ordinary course of his trade or business;

(2) property, used in his trade or business, of a character which is subject to the allowance for depreciation provided in section 167, or real property used in his trade or business;[25]

(3) a copyright, a literary, musical, or artistic composition, a letter or memorandum, or similar property, held by —

    (A) a taxpayer whose personal efforts created such property,

    (B) in the case of a letter, memorandum, or similar property, a taxpayer for whom such property was prepared or produced, or

    (C) a taxpayer in whose hands the basis of such property is determined, for purposes of determining gain from a sale or exchange, in whole or part by reference to the basis of such property in the hands of a taxpayer described in subparagraph (A) or (B);

(4) accounts or notes receivable acquired in the ordinary course of trade or business for services rendered or from the sale of property described in paragraph (1);

(5) a publication of the United States Government (including the Congressional Record) which is received from the United States Government or any agency thereof, other than by purchase at the price at which it is offered for sale to the public, and which is held by —

    (A) a taxpayer who so received such publication, or

    (B) a taxpayer in whose hands the basis of such publication is determined, for purposes of determining gain from a sale or exchange, in whole or in part by reference to the basis of such publication in the hands of a taxpayer described in subparagraph (A).[26]

In order to qualify for the net long-term capital gain deduction of 60 percent, the capital asset must be held for a period of one year. Thus, the sale of capital assets held for a period of less than a year will be considered short-term capital gain and will not qualify for the 60 percent deduction. This, in effect, means that a short-term capital gain will be taxed at ordinary income rates.

If an individual taxpayer has a loss from the sale or exchange of

---

[25] But see I.R.C. § 1231(b).

[26] I.R.C. § 1221.

capital assets, these losses shall only be allowed to the extent of the gains from such sales or exchanges plus, if such losses exceed such gains, the smallest of the following amounts:

(1) Taxable income for the taxable year reduced by the zero bracket amount;

(2) $3,000; or

(3) The sum of the excess of net short-term capital loss over net long-term capital gain and one half of the excess of the net long-term capital loss over the net short-term capital gain.[27]

Thus, as a practical matter, the deduction of excess capital losses is generally limited to $3,000 per year. Excess capital losses that are not allowable under the aforementioned rules may be carried over into succeeding taxable years.[28]

[2] Wash Sales

Section 1091(a) of the Code states that a loss from the sale of stock or securities will be disallowed if, within a period beginning thirty days before such sale and ending thirty days after such sale, the taxpayer has acquired or has entered into a contract or option to so acquire substantially identical stock or securities. Thus, if a taxpayer acquires Xerox stock within a sixty-one day period surrounding the sale of Xerox stock at a loss, his loss on the sale of such stock will be disallowed for tax purposes. This restriction, known as the wash sale provision of the Code, was designed to prevent a taxpayer from claiming a tax loss when, in reality, his economic position remains unchanged. In such a case, the taxpayer would, in effect, continue to hold the Xerox stock of equivalent amounts and remain in the same economic position as before.

If a loss is disallowed, the basis of the stock acquired within the prescribed period is adjusted as provided in Section 1091(d). The acquired stock assumes the basis of the stock sold and is adjusted upward or downward by the difference between the price at which the replacement stock was acquired and the price at which the original stock was sold. For example, if a taxpayer bought 100 shares of Xerox stock in 1965 for $100, sold the 100 shares on April 1, 1975 for $75, and

---

[27] I.R.C. § 1211(b)(1).

[28] I.R.C. § 1212(b).

purchased an additional 100 shares on April 15, 1975 for $80, his basis in the new stock would be $105 — the basis of the stock sold ($100) plus the amount by which the cost of the stock purchased exceeded the price at which the stock was sold ($5).[29] The loss would be disallowed because an identical security was purchased within 15 days of the sale of securities at loss. If the taxpayer had purchased the additional shares at $70, his basis in the new shares would be $95 — the $100 cost of the original shares less the difference between the purchase price of $70 and the sale price of $75.[30] Consequently, it is perhaps more accurate to state that Section 1091 merely postpones the disallowance of the capital loss rather than permanently denying it. An individual whose loss has been denied may merely wait thirty days from the later of the acquisition or the sale and again sell the stock at a loss in order to establish the loss for tax purposes.

The wash sale provisions often provide an unintended trap for taxpayers who are seeking to establish a capital loss to offset previously achieved gains. For example, a taxpayer who has already achieved a large taxable gain in a given year may realize that he can offset some of this taxable gain by recognizing a loss on certain stock that he owns whose present price is below his basis in the stock. Such a course of action frequently represents prudent tax planning as long as the taxpayer does not, within a period ending thirty days after the date of such sale, acquire substantially identical stock or securities. Any such acquisition will cause the loss on the sale of the stock to go unrecognized.

There has been frequent dispute as to when the stock or securities acquired are substantially identical to the ones that have been sold. The term "substantially identical" has been defined to mean approximation to identity, not mere similarity.[31] This definition allows a taxpayer a considerable amount of leeway in maintaining a relative economic position while still avoiding the wash sale rules. For example, a taxpayer could sell Mobil stock at a loss and purchase Exxon stock within the 30-day period and not be affected by Section 1091. Inasmuch as the issuers of the stock were different, the stock would not be considered substantially identical for wash sale purposes. Presumably, the taxpayer's economic position would remain relatively unchanged inas-

---

[29] See Treas. Reg. § 1.1091-2(a).

[30] Madden, "Restricted Stock, Wash Sales and a Declining Market; Traps for the Unwary," 75-8 Tax Mgmt.-Executive Compensation J. 4 (1975).

[31] Marie Hanlin, 38 B.T.A. 811 (1938), aff'd, 108 F.2d 429 (3d Cir. 1939).

much as these two securities are likely to move in the same direction in the stock market and both seem to offer the same relative degree of security. However, because it is theoretically possible for factors relating to one company to cause it to move in a different direction from the stock of the other, there is not substantial identity for Section 1091 purposes.

When common stock is sold and simultaneously warrants for stock of the same corporation are bought, they are held substantially identical for Section 1091 purposes.[32] Similarly, convertible preferred stock that has the same voting rights as common stock, is subject to the same dividend restriction, sells at prices that do not vary significantly from the conversion ratio, and is restricted as to convertibility, has been held to be substantially identical to common stock of the same company and was considered to be an option to acquire such stock.[33]

In determining whether bonds are substantially identical, both the Service and the courts tend to look at the maturity dates, interest rates and obligor to determine if there are material differences. For example, bonds of the same highway authority with different interest rates of 3.45 percent and 4.5 percent payable for forty years were held to be not substantially identical because of the difference in interest rates.[34] Treasury 6.8 percent bonds maturing in 1982 and not redeemable at par for payment of estate taxes, and Treasury 4.25 percent bonds maturing in 1992 redeemable for payment of estate taxes were not substantially identical.[35] The Service has ruled that bonds are substantially identical if not substantially different in material feature or because of differences in several material features considered together. Bonds must be compared as they existed when bought with bonds sold as they existed when sold. The same market value on a particular day and the same interest rates do not necessarily establish substantial identity.[36]

¶ 2.04 General Planning Strategies

The basic system of income taxation necessarily invites certain tax planning strategies. The remainder of this chapter discusses those general tax planning strategies that the tax system seems to suggest

---

[32] Rev. Rul. 56-406, 1956-2 C.B. 523.
[33] Rev. Rul. 77-201, 1977-1 C.B. 250.
[34] Rev. Rul. 60-195, 1960-1 C.B. 300.
[35] Rev. Rul. 76-346, 1976-2 C.B. 247.
[36] Rev. Rul. 58-211, 1958-1 C.B. 529.

strongly. Specific applications of these income tax planning strategies are discussed in Parts II and III of this book. In reviewing those specifics, however, it is well to bear in mind the general concepts of tax minimization. By keeping the general concepts constantly in view, the planning implications of the specific techniques will be more clearly understood.

[1] Deferral of Income

Perhaps the most obvious planning strategy suggested by the graduated rate structure is the deferral or postponement of the receipt of income. Because the graduated rate structure will typically impose a higher amount of taxation upon each additional dollar of income or will mean that each incremental dollar of income is taxed at a high marginal rate, it frequently is advantageous to defer the receipt of income until subsequent tax years. This particular concept is most viable in those situations where an individual is likely to be taxed at a lesser rate in a subsequent year. If, for example, an entertainer has an extremely lucrative year and does not expect to earn as much income in the year that follows, the postponement of income to that following year may mean that the income received in the subsequent year will be taxed at a lower rate. The same principal will hold true if a highly compensated individual is nearing retirement years in which his income will be significantly reduced.

In addition, the implementation of the indexing provisions of the Code that become effective in 1985 means that the same dollar amount of income will be taxed at a lesser rate in subsequent years. Accordingly, an individual whose income is holding relatively steady or level may find that there is some advantage to deferral. As this discussion implies, the concept of deferral will be most effective for those individuals whose income either widely fluctuates, is expected to diminish, or, at the very minimum, is holding steady. For those individuals such as corporate executives who are already in the 50 percent tax bracket with rising income, a deferral of income may produce little or no tax benefit, although the taxpayer will have the use of the money during the period of deferral. In those situations — particularly if the deferred income is not growing through investment, the executive may find it more advantageous to receive the income, pay the 50 percent tax, and invest the net amount.

It also should be briefly noted here that an individual cannot simply turn his back on income that he has a right to receive and thereby postpone the incidence of taxation to the following year. The principal of constructive receipt [37] is generally applicable when income is either credited to a taxpayer's account, set apart for him, otherwise made available so that he may draw upon it at any time, or made available so that he could have drawn upon it during a taxable year. This concept provides an overall limitation upon the ability of a taxpayer to defer income.[38]

[2] Acceleration of Deductions

A second principle of taxation suggested by our graduated income tax structure is the acceleration of deductions into a taxable year so as to reduce the taxpayer's income tax liability for that year. Because individuals are typically cash-basis taxpayers, this usually means that the payment of deductible expenses in a given year or the more aggressive use of certain types of deductions (such as the accelerated deduction for depreciation income) [39] is advantageous.

There are many specific examples to illustrate a taxpayer's ability to accelerate deductions. For example, he may make his fourth-quarter state estimated income tax payment (which is probably due on January 15 of the following year) on December 28 of a given year so as to accelerate that deduction into the current taxable year. Year-end charitable donations are also common. A taxpayer with extremely high income for a particular year may elect to use an accelerated form of depreciation on property purchased during that year rather than the straight-line method. Again, the impact of this election is to accelerate more deductions into the current taxable year.

Again, however, the wisdom of accelerating deductions depends upon the individual's particular tax situation. If an individual expects to receive significantly more income in the following year than the current year, it is foolish to accelerate deductions, since those deductions may be worth more to him in the year in which the higher taxable income will be received. On the other hand, an acceleration of deductions by a taxpayer who constantly remains in a high income tax bracket will postpone the payment of taxes and thus give the taxpayer the use of the money in the intervening period. Similarly, a taxpayer who has had

---

[37] See generally Treas. Reg. § 1.451-2.
[38] See Chapter 3 for a more extensive discussion of constructive receipt.
[39] I.R.C. § 168.

an exceedingly high income year will have an incentive to accelerate as many deductions as possible into that year. Although it is frequently prudent to attempt to accelerate deductions into a particular year, a taxpayer's ability to do this will be subject to two general limitations.

[a] Accounting Method Must Clearly Reflect Income. There is an overall limitation in the Code that the taxpayer's method of accounting must clearly reflect his income.[40] If this method of accounting does not clearly reflect income, the Commissioner has the power to make adjustments so that income will be clearly reflected. In other words, if the taxpayer's attempt to accelerate deductions is likely to create a material distortion of his income, this acceleration of deductions is subject to challenge by the Service. For example, when a cash-basis taxpayer prepaid five years' worth of interest on a loan, it was held to be a material distortion of his income and the deduction was denied.[41] A similar deduction was denied when a partnership's only transaction in a one-day taxable year was a prepayment of more than four years' worth of interest.[42] Although the prepayment of interest by cash-basis taxpayers has now partially been restricted by a statutory provision,[43] the principle that accelerating deductions cannot materially distort the taxpayer's income remains a viable overall concept that restricts taxpayers.

[b] Specific Deduction Limitations. In addition to the general limitation just discussed, the ability of a taxpayer to make a specific deduction can be reduced by statutory limitations upon a particular type of deduction. For example, Section 170(b) of the Code provides limitations that restrict a taxpayer's charitable deductions to certain specified percentages of adjusted gross income. As a general rule, most contributions are limited to 50 percent of the taxpayer's adjusted gross

---

[40] I.R.C. § 446(b).

[41] Sandor v. Comm'r, 62 T.C. 469 (1974), aff'd, 536 F.2d 874 (9th Cir. 1976).

[42] Resnik v. Comm'r, 66 T.C. 74 (1976), aff'd, 555 F.2d 634 (7th Cir. 1977).

[43] Section 461(g) of the Code limits a cash-basis taxpayer's deduction for interest allocable to a period beyond the close of a taxable year by requiring the deduction to be made in the year for which the interest is allocable. This section is not applicable to indebtedness incurred with respect to the taxpayer's principal residence if such payment of "points" is an established business practice in the area in which the indebtedness was occurred.

income [44] or 30 percent thereof if certain appreciated capital gain property is given to charity.[45]

Similarly, Section 163(d) provides a specific limitation on interest deductions directly connected with the production of investment income. This deduction for investment interest is limited to $10,000 [46] plus the taxpayer's net income from investment plus the amount, if any, by which certain deductions attributable to property subject to a net lease exceed the rental income from such property. Net investment income is defined to mean the excess of investment income over investment expenses. Investment income is statutorily defined to mean gross income from interest, dividends, rents, and royalties, plus net short-term capital gain attributable to the disposition of property held for investment and the amount treated under the recapture provisions of the Code as ordinary income, but only to the extent that such income, gain, and amounts are not derived from the conduct of a trade or business.[47] Consequently, excessive borrowing to carry investment properties that are not producing income may result in the limitation of a taxpayer's interest deduction for a particular year. Any deduction so disallowed, however, may be carried over into the succeeding taxable year.[48]

[3] Conversion of Ordinary Income Into Capital Gain

A further strategy suggested by the federal tax structure is to seek the realization of capital gain rather than ordinary income. Inasmuch as capital gains are taxed at a maximum rate of 20 percent as opposed to the ordinary income maximum rate of 50 percent, the realization of a capital gain is obviously beneficial. Consequently, the purchase of capital assets by high-income individuals, which do not produce significant income while being held [49] and which hopefully will appreciate while held, will create a considerable tax advantage, since the gain will

---

[44] See I.R.C. § 170(b)(1).

[45] See I.R.C. § 170(b)(1)(C). In addition, there is a 20 percent limitation on many contributions to private foundations.

[46] The limit on the deduction for investment interest is $5,000 in the case of married taxpayers filing separate returns.

[47] I.R.C. § 163(d)(3)(B).

[48] I.R.C. § 163(d)(2).

[49] The asset may also produce income that is sheltered by a depreciation deduction.

be taxed at capital gain rates. Thus, appreciating capital assets tend to be favored investments for the highly compensated individual.

Another method of turning ordinary income into capital gain is to acquire a depreciable asset and depreciate the basis of the asset against ordinary income. If the property can later be sold at a capital gain rate of taxation, the taxpayer may make up to a 30 percent profit (i.e., deduction against ordinary income at a 50 percent rate versus capital gain at a 20 percent rate) even if the asset is not sold for more than its original cost.

A taxpayer's ability to create such a gain by recovering the cost of depreciating assets against ordinary income and then selling at a capital gain is limited somewhat by the depreciation recapture rules contained in Sections 1245 and 1250 of the Code. Section 1245 provides that all gain arising on the disposition of tangible personal property that has been depreciated will be taxed at ordinary income rates to the extent of prior depreciation. The rule in regard to real property is not so restrictive.[50] Nonresidential real property that is depreciated on an accelerated method will be taxed similarly to personal property in that all gain to the extent of prior depreciation will be treated as ordinary income.[51] For residential real property, only the excess of the accelerated depreciation over that which would have been allowed if the taxpayer had used the straight-line method over a 15-year life will be recaptured as ordinary income.[52] On the other hand, if the straight-line method of cost recovery is used for residential or nonresidential property, all gain will be taxed at capital gain rates. Accordingly, by utilizing the straight-line method of cost recovery permitted under ACRS, a taxpayer will be able to depreciate the basis of such property against ordinary income and then to achieve capital gain if the property is later sold at an increment over its present basis.

A further means by which a corporate executive may convert ordinary income to capital gain is through the acquisition of incentive stock options that are now permitted by Section 422A.[53] By exercising

---

[50] I.R.C. § 1250.

[51] It should be remembered that even if this gain is recaptured at ordinary income rates, the taxpayer will have had the use of the money saved by the depreciation deduction in the intervening period.

[52] There are special recapture rules for various types of low-income property which generally phase out such recapture for accelerated depreciation over a 200-month period. See I.R.C. § 1250(a)(1)(B).

[53] See the discussion in Chapter 4.

this new type of qualified option, the executive will not realize taxable income, and any appreciation in the value of the stock subsequent to the option grant will be taxed at a capital gain rate (assuming certain holding period requirements are met). An executive may similarly set the stage for future capital gains by exercising a nonqualified stock option (and realizing income at that time if buying for less than fair market value) and holding the stock as an investment as it appreciates. Any subsequent gain will be taxed as a long-term capital gain if the holding period requirements are met.

Most opportunities to convert ordinary income into capital gain or to achieve capital gain are a result of holding long-term investment property. The highly compensated individual is often an appropriate individual to hold property for long-term gain since his highly compensated status provides sufficient day-to-day income to enable him still to live comfortably. The excess of such income over consumption needs and taxes provides the funds to enable this individual to make long-term investments which, in turn, provide a basis for favorable tax treatment.

[4] Avoiding Taxable Income

The previously mentioned tax planning devices involve either a means of deferring the taxation of income or reducing the rate of taxation by converting ordinary income into capital gain. In addition to these particular strategies, the Code contains certain statutory provisions for avoiding income taxation altogether. In the appropriate instance, one or more of these particular statutory devices may prove to be a useful means of avoiding taxation for the highly compensated individual.

[a] Tax-Exempt Bonds

[i] Nontaxability of certain governmental obligations. Section 103(a) of the Code creates a general rule that gross income does not include interest on the obligations of a state, a territory, a possession of the United States, or any political subdivision of the foregoing or of the District of Columbia. Thus, generally speaking, the interest income received from state or municipal bonds or obligations would be exempt from taxation. In addition, after creating a rule that so-called industrial development bonds are not tax-exempt, Section 103(b) creates exceptions to that rule that have the effect of making many such bonds tax-exempt. An industrial development bond is a bond issued by a normally tax-exempt municipal or state issuer, the proceeds of which are used directly or indirectly in a trade or business carried on by a person who is not an exempt person.[54] In the simplest terms, if the proceeds of municipal obligations are used to finance the business activities of a private concern, this obligation will be considered to be an industrial development bond. Those types of industrial development bonds that are tax-exempt relate to certain specifically exempt activities [55] or to certain small issues of industrial development bonds which, at the maximum, cannot exceed $10 million.[56]

Because the interest on tax-exempt and state obligations will be completely free of federal income tax,[57] the advantage of holding such obligations tends to increase as the taxpayer's tax bracket increases. For example, 10 percent interest on a municipal bond held by a 50 percent bracket taxpayer is the equivalent of earning 20 percent on a taxable basis, since this is an amount that would be required to be earned to produce the same yield. The equivalent yield for a 25 percent bracket taxpayer would only be 13.3 percent. Thus, the municipal bond typically has found most favor among the higher bracket taxpayers. Because such bonds are free of federal income tax, they usually bear a lower rate of interest than taxable securities of comparable quality. This interest differential is, generally speaking, not enough to eliminate the advantage of having received the income on such a bond on a tax-free basis. Thus, the high-income taxpayer who wishes to keep a portion of his

---

[54] I.R.C. § 103(b)(2)(A).

[55] Exempt activities described in Section 103(b)(4) of the Code are residential rental property if certain prescribed percentages of such property are used by individuals of low or moderate income, sports facilities, convention or trade show facilities, airports, docks, wharves, mass commuting facilities, parking facilities, or storage or training facilities directly related to any of the foregoing, sewage or solid waste disposal facilities or facilities for the local furnishing of electric energy or gas, air or water pollution control facilities, facilities for the furnishing of water and qualified hydroelectric generating facilities.

[56] Included in the $10 million limitation are capital expenditures with respect to such facilities, which are made within a six-year period beginning three years before the date of the issue and ending three years after the date of issue. I.R.C. § 103(b)(6)(D). In the case of facilities with respect to which an Urban Development Action Grant has been made under Section 119 of the Housing and Community Development Act of 1974, an additional $10 million of capital expenditures need not be taken into account. I.R.C. § 103(b)(6)(I).

[57] Such obligations will often be free of state income tax if the obligation was issued by a municipality in the state where the taxpayer resides.

investment in income-producing assets will often look to tax-exempt obligations issued under Section 103 of the Code to provide such exempt income.

[ii] Indebtedness to purchase tax-exempt securities. The existence of tax-exempt securities issued under Section 103 of the Code led astute taxpayers to consider borrowing money to purchase tax-exempt securities. Such a strategy would produce a double tax benefit in that the interest used to purchase the securities would be deductible from income, whereas the income produced by the obligation would not be taxable. This potential result, not surprisingly, led to the enactment of Section 265(2) of the Code, which denies a deduction for interest on indebtedness incurred or continued to purchase or carry obligations the interest on which is wholly exempt from federal income taxation. This section had the effect of denying an interest deduction in the hypothetical situation just described.

The Service guidelines for application of Section 265(2) are set forth in Rev. Proc. 72-18.[58] These guidelines determine that direct evidence of a purpose to carry tax-exempt obligations exists where tax-exempt obligations are used as collateral for indebtedness.[59] Direct evidence of a purpose to purchase tax-exempt obligations will exist where proceeds of indebtedness are used for and are directly traceable to the purchase of tax-exempt obligations. In the absence of such direct evidence, Rev. Proc. 72-18 sets forth certain guidelines to determine whether there is a direct relationship between the borrowing and the tax-exempt obligations. It is noted that a taxpayer may incur a variety of indebtedness of a personal nature ranging from short-term credit for purchases of goods and services for consumption or a mortgage incurred to purchase or improve a residence or other real property. Section 265(2) will not apply to indebtedness when an individual who holds municipal bonds incurs a mortgage to buy a residence instead of selling his municipal bonds to finance the purchase price. Presumably, Section 265(2) will not apply in similar circumstances when an individual incurred an interest expense on his bank credit card in a particular month.

Rev. Proc. 72-18 also states that a purpose to carry tax-exempt obligations will be inferred, unless rebutted by other evidence to the

---

[58] Rev. Proc. 72-18, 1972-1 C.B. 40, clarified by Rev. Proc. 74-8, 1974-1 C.B. 419.

[59] Wisconsin Cheeseman v. U.S., 388 F.2d 420 (7th Cir. 1968).

contrary, if the taxpayer has outstanding indebtedness not directly connected to personal expenditures nor incurred or continued in the active conduct of a trade or business while at the same time owning tax-exempt obligations. This inference will be made even though the indebtedness is ostensibly incurred or continued to purchase or to carry other portfolio investments.

Consequently, whenever a taxpayer who owns municipal obligations incurs investment indebtedness, there is a substantial possibility that Section 265(2) may deny the deduction for the interest payments. Although it is relatively clear that the borrowing of funds for personal needs while carrying tax-exempt obligations will not cause a deduction to be lost,[60] the incurring of indebtedness to purchase investment securities at the same time as municipal bonds are carried may result in a denial of the deduction.[61]

[b] Tax-Free Exchanges. A further means of avoiding taxation on the disposition of the property is to undertake a tax-free exchange as permitted by Section 1031 of the Code. This section provides that no gain or loss will be recognized if property held for a productive use in a trade or business or for investment [62] is exchanged solely for property of a like kind to be held either for productive use in trade or business or for investment. Thus, for example, if a taxpayer owns an office building as an investment and undertakes a like-kind exchange with another taxpayer who similarly owns an office building, no gain or loss will be recognized on the transaction assuming the various other technical requirements of Section 1031 have been met.

Critical to the determination of eligibility of tax-free status under Section 1031 is that the property both given and received must be investment property of a like kind and cannot consist of such property as stocks or securities. The term "like kind" as defined in the regulations [63] refers to the nature or character of the property and not to grade or quality. Under Section 1031, one kind or class of property may not be exchanged for property of a different kind or class. For example, the fact that real estate involved in an exchange is improved or unim-

---

[60] See Estate of Morris, ¶ 81,368 P-H Memo T.C.

[61] McDonough v. U.S., 577 F.2d 234 (4th Cir. 1978).

[62] Nonrecognition will not apply, however, to stock in trade or other property held primarily for sale, nor stocks, bonds, notes, choses in action, certificates in trust or beneficial interest, or other significant securities or evidences of the indebtedness or interest.

[63] Treas. Reg. § 1.1031(a)-1(b).

proved is not material because that fact only relates to the grade or quality of the property, not to its kind or class.

If money is received in connection with an exchange, it will be treated as boot and taxed accordingly. If the taxpayer's liabilities are assumed by the other party to the exchange, the amount of mortgages against the property transferred by that taxpayer which are assumed or taken subject to is considered to be money received in the exchange.[64] On the other hand, boot given by a taxpayer, such as the receipt of property subject to liabilities or mortgages, will reduce the amount of liabilities and mortgages that are treated as boot received by the taxpayer. Accordingly, mortgages both assumed and relieved in an exchange transaction are netted, and the taxpayer is taxed if he is relieved of more liabilities than he assumed.[65]

The principal areas of dispute under Section 1031 are whether or not the property exchanged is truly like-kind property and whether or not the mechanics of the transaction undertaken qualify as a like-kind exchange. Thus, for example, if there is either a three-corner exchange or an agreement upon the part of one party to acquire property in order to exchange it with the other taxpayer, there often is a question whether the mechanics of the transaction comport to Section 1031.[66] Similarly, if the property to be received in an exchange is not exactly similar to that which is given up, litigation may result.[67] Although the scope of both controversies is extensive and beyond the realm of this book, a taxpayer should be aware of these areas of concern and investigate the specifics of a proposed transaction if a like-kind exchange is contemplated.

A like-kind exchange may be a useful means for a taxpayer to avoid taxation when his basic purpose is to replace held property with more expensive property of the same kind. Thus, a taxpayer who owns a small office building and wishes, in effect, to sell and replace it with a larger

---

[64] Treas. Reg. § 1.1031(d)-2.

[65] If the liabilities assumed or taken subject to by the taxpayer exceed those assumed or taken subject to by the other party to the exchange, the excess does not reduce other boot such as cash received by the taxpayer. See Treas. Reg. § 1.1031(d)-2, Ex. 2.

[66] See, e.g., Starker v. U.S., 602 F.2d 1341 (9th Cir. 1979); Biggs v. Comm'r, 632 F.2d 1171 (5th Cir. 1980).

[67] See Century Elec. Co. v. Comm'r, 192 F.2d 155 (8th Cir. 1951) (exchange of a lease of thirty years or for a fee simple qualifies for a nonrecognition); Rev. Rul. 55-749, 1955-2 C.B. 295 (exchange of fee title for water rights qualified as like-kind exchange where under state law water rights were realty interests that were perpetual).

office building will be able to avoid taxation if he initiates a like-kind exchange for a larger building and allows the seller of the larger building to undertake the sale of his existing property. In such a case, the taxpayer will have been able to upgrade his holdings and yet avoid capital gain on the property that was disposed. The exchange provisions will generally not be useful for a taxpayer who is either selling out of a particular type of investment or downgrading his holdings, since the cash that will be received in such a transaction will be taxed as boot. For the highly compensated individual who is in the stage of acquiring or upgrading additional properties, the like-kind exchange provisions may be a useful means of avoiding taxation altogether at this time.

[c] Avoidance of Tax on Sale of Residence

[i] Replacement of residence. Further opportunities for the avoidance of income taxation are available on the sale of a taxpayer's residence. If the taxpayer sells his principal residence and, within a period beginning two years before the date of such sale and ending two years after, purchases and uses a new principal residence, the gain will be recognized only to the extent that the taxpayer's adjusted sales price of his old residence exceeds the cost of purchasing his new residence.[68] Accordingly, Section 1034 allows a taxpayer to sell his old residence and, if this property is replaced within a prescribed period with a residence costing at least as much, no gain will be taxed to the taxpayer from his original sale. This section is particularly useful to highly compensated individuals or upwardly mobile individuals who have a tendency to move into more expensive residences as their economic stature increases or, who, because of their upwardly mobile status, may undertake several moves.

The critical factors for qualification under Section 1034 are the two-year time frames surrounding the sale of the old residence and the fact that both the property sold and the property acquired must qualify as the taxpayer's principal residence. Thus, when the taxpayer purchases two residences with the proceeds from the sale of his principal residence, only the residence that qualifies as the principal residence at the end of the prescribed period would be considered for nonrecognition of gain.[69] This nonrecognition rule will apply separately to gains

---

[68] I.R.C. § 1034(a).
[69] Rev. Rul. 66-114, 1966-1 C.B. 181.

realized by a husband and wife from the sale of their residence where they have agreed to live apart and each has purchased and occupied a separate residence.[70] Questions as to whether or not the property sold was a taxpayer's principal residence frequently arise in the situation where the sold property had been rented to others prior to the time of sale. It has been held that actual occupancy of the old dwelling at the time of the sale is not required. Where a taxpayer has temporarily rented out property prior to the sale, nonrecognition may still be allowed.[71] If the period of rental becomes too long, the property will be considered to be abandoned by the taxpayer and thus not his principal residence.[72] On the other hand, the cases have uniformly held that the taxpayer must physically occupy his new home prior to the expiration of the replacement period.[73]

It must be stressed that Section 1034 is most useful to those upwardly mobile taxpayers who are at the stage of their career where they may be selling their residence and moving to larger property. If the cost of the replacement residence does not equal or exceed the cost of the residence that is sold, part of the gain will be recognized. It must be noted, however, that Section 1034 merely provides a deferral of taxation inasmuch as the basis of the new residence is reduced by an amount equal to the amount of gain that is not recognized from the sale of the old residence.[74] Thus, it is perhaps more accurate to describe Section 1034 as a deferral mechanism rather than a means of completely eliminating the taxation of the sale of one's residence.

[ii] Sale of residence by individuals who have attained age 55. In addition to Section 1034, which provides for an exclusion of gain from the sale of an individual's residence if he replaces it with another principal residence within a prescribed period, Section 121 of the Code creates a one-time exclusion of gain from the sale of a principal residence by an individual who has attained the age of 55. If a taxpayer has reached the age of 55 before the date of the sale or exchange, and during

---

[70] Rev. Rul. 74-250, 1974-1 C.B. 202.

[71] See Trisko v. Comm'r, 29 T.C. 515 (1957); Andrews v. Comm'r, ¶ 81,247 P-H Memo T.C.

[72] See Stolk v. Comm'r, 40 T.C. 345 (1963), aff'd, 326 F.2d 760 (2d Cir. 1964); Houlette v. Comm'r, 48 T.C. 350 (1967).

[73] Bayley v. Comm'r, 35 T.C. 288 (1960); Stanley v. Comm'r, 33 T.C. 614 (1959); Rev. Rul. 69-434, 1969-2 C.B. 163.

[74] I.R.C. § 1034(e).

the five-year period ending on the date of the sale or exchange he has owned and used the property as his principal residence for periods aggregating three years or more, he may exclude up to $125,000 of the gain on this sale. This particular exclusion will be inapplicable if either the taxpayer or his spouse has made a prior election to similarly exclude the gain from a sale or exchange.[75] In other words, the $125,000 exclusion is a one-time tax benefit. If property is held jointly by husband and wife as tenants in common or as tenants by the entirety, and if this couple files a joint return and if one spouse satisfies the age, holding, and use requirements, then both spouses will be treated as satisfying such requirement.[76]

If a taxpayer who has not made a previous election satisfies the age requirement, the principal conditions that must be met in order to qualify for the one-time exclusion are that the taxpayer must have owned and used the property as a principal residence in three of the five previous taxable years. Both the ownership and use tests must be met in order to qualify, but such tests need not be met simultaneously.[77] Thus, for example, if a taxpayer had used a property as his principal residence for the past five years but had rented it during three of the first five years of residence, he would not qualify for the exclusion under Section 121 because he had not owned the property for three years. Similarly, if the taxpayer had moved two and one-half years prior to the sale from one residence to another, he would not qualify under Section 121 because he did not satisfy either the ownership or use requirements for the property being sold. Although the Service has ruled that a short temporary absence, such as a vacation, will be counted as a period of use,[78] a longer absence, such as a one-year sabbatical by a college professor, will not be considered as a period of use.[79]

The requirement that only one exclusion may be elected by a taxpayer during his lifetime sometimes presents problems in the situation where one spouse has made an election prior to marriage. Thus, if a man married a woman who had previously joined in making an

---

[75] I.R.C. § 121(b)(2).

[76] I.R.C. § 121(d)(1). Where the taxpayer who met the age, holding, and use requirements entered into a binding contract to sell his principal residence but died before the sale was completed, his executor may elect to exclude the gain when he completes the sale after death. Rev. Rul. 82-1, 1982-1 I.R.B. 11.

[77] Rev. Rul. 80-172, 1980-2 C.B. 56.

[78] Treas. Reg. § 1.121-1(c).

[79] Treas. Reg. § 1.121-1(d), Ex. 4.

election while married to her first husband, he would be precluded from making an election under Section 121, even though he neither was married to her at the time she made an election nor received any tax benefit from it.

A Section 121 election presents a unique opportunity for a taxpayer who has attained the age of 55 to realize a gain on his principal residence without the imposition of tax on the first $125,000 of gain. If a taxpayer was selling a large residence and replacing it with a retirement condominium, Section 1034 might only defer a portion of the gain on that sale because the amount of proceeds reinvested did not equal the amount received from the sale of his residence. In such a case, he could use the provisions of Section 1034 to defer gain to the extent permitted by that section and, if he so qualified, use Section 121 to completely eliminate the taxation of the first $125,000 of gain that would otherwise be taxed. Consequently, this provision may be particularly useful to an individual who is downsizing a house or moving to retirement property of a lesser value than his current principal residence.

[d] Retention of Assets Until Death. Another often overlooked means of avoiding the taxable gain from the sale of an appreciating asset is to retain such asset until death. At that time, the basis of all assets held by a taxpayer will be stepped up to their date of death (or alternate valuation date) value [80] so that that particular asset may be sold by the taxpayer's heirs or estate at the date of death value without incurring a taxable gain. The step-up in basis at death rules frequently create an incentive for the retention of assets by elderly taxpayers who might otherwise have to pay a significant capital gain on assets that had appreciated in value. By merely retaining these assets until death, this large capital gains tax may be avoided.

In some instances, the retention of assets may prove to be impractical or counter-productive from an estate planning standpoint despite this tax benefit. For example, if a taxpayer is faced with liquidity problems in his estate, it may be advantageous to accept an attractive offer to sell a nonliquid asset despite the capital gains tax involved. In such a case, the advantages of achieving liquidity and disposing of an asset that might otherwise be difficult to sell, may far outweigh the disadvantage of having to pay capital gains tax. It also should be noted

---

[80] I.R.C. § 1014(a).

that forestalling the receipt of previously earned income until death will not necessarily avoid income taxation because Section 691 of the Code taxes income in respect of a decedent which is otherwise earned by a taxpayer prior to death.[81]

[5] Income Averaging

The income averaging provisions of the Code [82] are designed to offset some of the disadvantages that a graduated rate structure will impose upon an individual taxpayer whose income fluctuates widely from year to year. The general concept behind those provisions is that it is unfair to impose a steeply graduated tax upon an individual who has substantially increased his or her income after several lean years. The effect of the income averaging provisions in this situation is to moderate the graduated rate structure somewhat so that taxes will be imposed as if income had been earned at a more level rate over a several year period.

Generally speaking, an individual is eligible for income averaging if his taxable income for the current year exceeds, by at least $3,000, 120 percent of the average adjusted income for the four preceding base years. Thus, for example, if an individual had an average taxable income for four years of $10,000 and in the fifth year his income jumped to $25,000, he would be eligible for income averaging since this exceeded 120 percent of average base period income by at least $3,000. The tax on this income is five times the increase in the tax that would result from adding 20 percent of the amount subject to averaging to 120 percent of the average taxable income for the four preceding years. (The computations for income averaging are made and reported on Form 1040, Schedule G.)

Income averaging is available to individuals who are citizens or residents of the United States throughout the computation year.[83] The eligible individual must not have been a nonresident alien individual at any time during the five-year averaging period.[84] In addition to the

---

[81] I.R.C. § 691 will be discussed extensively in Chapter 14.

[82] I.R.C. §§ 1301–1305.

[83] I.R.C. § 1303(a). Accordingly, estates or trusts do not qualify for income averaging. See Treas. Reg. § 1.1303-1(a).

[84] I.R.C. § 1303(b).

residency and citizenship requirements, in order to qualify for income averaging an individual must meet the support test set forth in Section 1303(c). In general, the income averaging provisions will not apply if, for any base year (i.e., the previous four years), such individual and his spouse furnished less than one half of his support. The basic idea behind the support test is to exclude from income averaging those individuals who were not active members of the labor force during the previous four years. For example, because of the support test, an individual who was entirely supported by his parents for four years of college and who then entered the work force in the fifth year would not be eligible for income averaging.[85]

As might be expected, there has been a good deal of litigation concerning the question of whether or not an individual is providing his own support during the base period years. The Service has ruled that in determining whether an individual has furnished 50 percent or more of his support in base period years, a scholarship that is excluded from his gross income by Section 117 of the Code is considered to be support, but not support the individual furnished to himself.[86] This result seems consistent with the basic statutory purpose of the support test, which is to exclude from income averaging those individuals who were not truly members of the work force during the base period years. It should be noted, however, that the term "support" relates to payment of one's own expenses and is not necessarily synonymous with earned income. Thus, if an individual lived off his investments for four years and in the fifth year sought to income average, he would be eligible since he had provided his own support throughout the years he lived off his investments even though he had no earned income during that period.

Section 1303(c) provides three basic exceptions to the support requirement. These exceptions are:

(1) If the individual has attained the age of 25 during the tax year and during at least four of the taxable years beginning after he attained the age of 21 and ending with the computation year he was not a full-time student;

---

[85] However, see the exceptions to the support test discussed at ¶ 2.04[5] below.

[86] Rev. Rul. 75-40, 1975-1 C.B. 276. This position has generally been supported in litigation. See Heidel v. Comm'r, 56 T.C. 95 (1971); Frost v. Comm'r, 61 T.C. 488 (1974); Sharvy v. Comm'r, 67 T.C. 630 (1977), aff'd per curiam, 566 F.2d 1118 (9th Cir. 1977).

(2) More than one half of the individual's taxable income for the computation year is attributable to work performed by him in substantial part during two or more base period years; or

(3) The individual makes a joint return for the computation year and not more than 25 percent of the aggregate adjusted gross income for such individual and his spouse for the computation year is attributable to such individual.

The first exception will generally be beneficial to older individuals who spent some time in the work force and some time as a student after attaining the age of 21. The second exception is the so-called major accomplishment rule which would be applicable, for example, to individuals who spent two years writing a book [87] which produces substantial income in a third or fourth year. The third exception is designed to offset somewhat the harshness of the rule that if a joint return is to be filed for a computation year, both taxpayers must be eligible individuals in order to average income.[88] This exception means that if one spouse provided less than half of his or her support during the base period years, the couple will not be disqualified from income averaging on their joint return where less than 25 percent of the aggregate adjusted gross income for the computation year is attributable to that spouse.

As noted earlier, averageable income is computed by comparing taxable income for the current year and subtracting from that amount 120 percent of the average base period income. There must be more than a $3,000 difference between the two figures before income averaging may be elected.[89] The base period income for the previous four years is, generally speaking, the taxable income for such year increased by the excess of amounts excluded from gross income under Sections 911 and 931 over deductions allocable to such amounts.[90] The regulations take the position that the base period income for any taxable year may not be

---

[87] This is assuming that someone else furnished his support during such period.

[88] Treas. Reg. § 1.1303-1(a).

[89] Taxable income for the year is reduced for this purpose by any taxable income received under I.R.C. Section 72(m)(5) (amounts received from an H.R. 10 Plan subject to penalty tax) and any trust throwback income included under I.R.C. Section 667(a).

[90] Those adjustments generally relate to earned income from sources outside the United States and income from sources within the possessions of the United States.

¶ 2.04[5] GENERAL PLANNING 2-36

less than zero.[91] In addition, the tax court has held that the correct taxable income must be used for a base period year in computing the tax under the income averaging election for the computation year, even though an adjustment to such earlier year was barred by the statute of limitations. In *Unser v. Comm'r*,[92] income from the taxpayer's corporation was allocated to him under Section 482. An allocation was not made to the taxpayer for 1965 because of the statute of limitations. However, in computing the tax liability for the base years which included 1965, the Service was allowed to adjust the 1965 base as if an adjustment would have been made.

If a taxpayer's filing status changes from year to year, adjustments must be made in the taxpayer's base period income. For example, if a taxpayer changes from married to single or from married filing a joint return to married filing separate returns, there are numerous complexities involved. The Service sets forth the method for making computations in these situations in the regulations.[93] Although the detail and complexity of such computations are beyond the scope of this treatise, the taxpayer should generally be aware that a change in filing status will require adjustments to base period income and consult the regulations accordingly.

---

[91] Treas. Reg. § 1.1302-2(b)(1). This position has been sustained in litigation. See Beckman v. U.S., 396 F. Supp. 44 (D. Kan. 1975); Tebon v. Comm'r, 55 T.C. 410 (1970).

[92] Unser v. Comm'r, 59 T.C. 528 (1973); see also Coca v. Comm'r, 35 T.C.M. 1454 (1976); Rev. Rul. 74-61, 1974-1 C.B. 239.

[93] See Treas. Reg. § 1.1304-3(b); see also Mayer, "Income Averaging," 100-4th Tax Mgmt. Portfolio A15-A16, for a chart setting forth various computational methods related to change in filing status.

PART II
Compensation Planning

CHAPTER 3

Deferred Compensation

		Page
¶ 3.01	Introduction	3-1
¶ 3.02	Pros and Cons of Deferred Compensation	3-2
	[1] Tax Planning Analysis	3-2
	[2] Economic Analysis	3-5
	[a] Alternate Investment Opportunities	3-5
	[b] Risk of Deferral	3-6
	[c] Effect on Cash Flow	3-8
¶ 3.03	Tax Deferral — How to Achieve It	3-9
	[1] Avoiding Constructive Receipt	3-9
	[2] Economic Benefit Theory	3-11
	[3] Requirements for Deferral	3-13
	[a] Rev. Rul. 60-31	3-13
	[b] Requirements for Advance Rulings	3-16
¶ 3.04	Funding the Deferred Compensation Arrangement	3-17
¶ 3.05	Types of Deferred Compensation Arrangements	3-20
	[1] Investment-Type Arrangements	3-20
	[2] Investment in Employer Equities — The Phantom Stock Plan	3-21
	[3] Other Plans Involving Employer's Stock	3-23

¶ 3.01 Introduction

A substantial percentage of highly compensated individuals either enter into or actively consider entering into a deferred compensation arrangement with their employers. The basic thrust of such arrangements is to postpone the receipt of currently earned income until a later taxable year. If the deferral is successful for income tax purposes, a cash-basis taxpayer will not report the income until it is actually received in subsequent years.

The evaluation of a potential deferred compensation plan for a client or for a group of corporate employees involves several levels of analysis. First, the tax status of the employee must be evaluated to determine whether a deferral of compensation would be advantageous from an income tax standpoint. If a deferral is contemplated, the federal tax rulings and cases must be reviewed so as to ensure that the adopted plan meets the existing requirements for deferral. The employee's need for current income must be considered, as well as the ability of the employer to meet its commitments to pay the deferred income in the future. If these factors indicate that deferral would be advantageous, the various types of deferred compensation plans must be considered to determine their applicability to the specific situation. Finally, the tax advisor must take care to integrate the deferred compensation plan with his client's estate planning needs.[1] Only after an analysis of all of these factors has been made can a thoughtful and well-planned deferred compensation program be implemented.

¶ 3.02 Pros and Cons of Deferred Compensation

[1] Tax Planning Analysis

The basic tax planning concept that underlies deferred compensation arrangements is the postponement of the receipt of income for income tax purposes until a year in which the recipient's tax bracket is lower. That is, if an individual earns $10,000 in a year in which all additional income will be taxed at a marginal rate of 50 percent, his federal income tax on this incremental income will be $5,000. If receipt of this income is postponed until a year in which his additional income will be taxed at a marginal rate of 30 percent, his federal income tax on this deferred income will be $3,000. In such a case, the individual gains a $2,000 tax savings merely by postponing the receipt of income until the later year. Although this scenario clearly illustrates the benefit of deferred compensation, it is nonetheless necessary to undertake a careful analysis to determine if this savings will actually be achieved. It is frequently the case that the supposed tax benefits resulting from a deferral of receipt of income are often more illusory than real. Several recent factors have tended to smooth out the rate of taxation for highly compensated individuals (albeit at rather high rates), with the net

---

[1] Estate planning for deferred compensation plans is discussed at ¶ 14.03.

result that the deferral of income frequently produces little or no tax savings.

First, the Economic Recovery Tax Act of 1981 (the 1981 Act) reduced the maximum income tax rate on all income [2] from 70 percent to 50 percent as of January 1, 1982 and, at the same time, eliminated the need for the maximum tax on earned income.[3] Consequently, once an individual reaches a high level of compensation, his marginal income is taxed at relatively flat rates ranging from 45 to 50 percent. As a result, it often takes a very drastic drop in taxable income to reduce significantly an individual's tax bracket and, hence, his rate of taxation. For example, for taxable years beginning after 1983,[4] if an individual had taxable income of $165,000, his marginal income would be taxed at a rate of 50 percent if he was married and filed a joint return. If his taxable income dropped by $50,000, he would still be in the 49 percent tax bracket. Thus, at high income levels, the tax rates are relatively flat, with the effect that the benefit from deferral may be minimal.

Consequently, for deferral to achieve any significant tax savings for these individuals, there would have to be a drop in earnings well below present levels. Barring any extreme change in the rates of taxation or an unforeseen loss of employment, many highly compensated individuals are likely to remain in the 50 percent or greater tax bracket until retirement.[5] In addition, an individual receiving compensation of this magnitude is likely to accumulate enough rights under a qualified retirement plan so that his retirement annuity, or a combination of his retirement annuity and investment income, may keep him in the 50 percent tax bracket. Accordingly, a high-salaried corporate executive with a stable employment future may never have an effective rate of taxation significantly below 50 percent on marginal income. If this is the case, little or no tax savings can be expected from deferral.

On the other hand, the indexing provisions added by the 1981 Act [6] create a built-in incentive for tax deferral. For tax years beginning in

---

[2] The reduction applies to both personal service income and unearned income.

[3] Prior to the 1981 Act, I.R.C. § 1348 imposed a maximum tax rate of 50 percent on personal service income.

[4] This calculation does not take into account the effect of indexing.

[5] The alternative minimum tax on individuals under Section 55 must also be considered. This tax is discussed in depth at ¶ 2.02.

[6] I.R.C. § 1(f). See discussion at ¶ 2.01[2].

1985, this provision requires an adjustment to the tax rate brackets and the personal exemption for the previous year's increase in the Consumer Price Index (CPI). As a result, the same dollar amount of income will be taxed at a lesser rate in future years than it will be in the current taxable year. Consequently, indexing increases the possible tax benefits from deferral, especially if the deferral is combined with a significant reduction in income. Indexing of the personal income tax rates should serve to heighten the interest of compensation planners in deferred compensation plans.

The tax savings aspect of income deferral may be more significant for an individual whose income is subject to volatile swings or who is likely to have only a limited period of high earning potential. For example, a professional athlete may only be able to reasonably expect a ten- to fifteen-year period of high earnings given the general rules of longevity, or lack thereof, in his sport. A television performer or actor, unless an exception to the rule, may experience only a limited period of popularity and high earnings. In both cases, the likelihood of facing a substantial number of years of drastically reduced income means that the tax savings emanating from income deferral may be quite significant. It also may be that the deferral of income until the retirement years will produce a significant tax savings.

As the preceding discussion illustrates, it should not be taken for granted that a deferral of income will reduce income taxes. In many instances, if an individual is likely to remain at high income levels for a substantial period of time, it may be that no tax savings are achieved from the deferral of income. Although other factors may suggest the wisdom or necessity of deferral, even if the tax savings involved are likely to be minimal or nonexistent,[7] the establishment of a deferred compensation plan on an unverified assumption of tax savings will often produce a disappointing surprise to the recipient.

[2] Economic Analysis

Economic factors must also be evaluated in determining the wisdom of a deferred compensation arrangement. The three major questions to ask are:

---

[7] Factors that would make deferral attractive despite minimal tax savings may include the inability of an employer to increase the amount of current compensation or a concern that the funds may be squandered.

(1) Can the taxpayer do better by paying a current tax on the income and investing it — either himself or through investment advisors?

(2) How safe are the funds if deferral is elected?

(3) What effect does deferral have upon the taxpayer's current lifestyle and cash-flow position?

[a] **Alternative Investment Opportunities.** By entering into an arrangement that provides for the deferral of income, a taxpayer, by definition, elects not to have the funds made currently available to him. Inasmuch as deferral is only economically feasible for those individuals who are highly compensated and thus can elect to forego current income, deferral, in essence, means the nonreceipt of funds that might otherwise be available for investment purposes. Consequently, an alternative approach of paying a tax on current income and investing the remaining funds must be seriously considered.

If the taxpayer currently receives funds and pays a 50 percent tax on them, one half of these incremental funds would be available for investment purposes. If those remaining funds were invested and produced a return of 20 percent a year, the taxpayer would be economically far better off to have paid the tax and invested the funds than if he had deferred the amount in question and received it (and no more) ten years hence. Because of this factor, most long-term deferred compensation arrangements entered into today make some provision for earnings growth or investment of the deferred amount.[8] The deferred amounts may be invested in a specified manner, or the plan may provide for the employer to add interest annually to the deferred amount. If the plan being considered makes provision for investment experience, this factor must be weighed against the alternative uses of money available to the taxpayer. If the plan does not contemplate investment of deferred amounts, it is rare that a long-term deferral will be economically justified. If the taxpayer is simply going to receive the deferred amount several years hence, the plan is not likely to be worth the tax savings involved.

Other factors to weigh in considering these economic questions are the taxpayer's investment acumen and history, and his ability to handle large sums of money realistically. For instance, if there is a concern that

---

[8] Various types of deferred compensation arrangements and types of investment provisions acceptable to the Service are discussed in detail at ¶ 3.04.

the taxpayer will squander or consume the amount that is being considered for deferral, it may be advantageous in the long run to defer receipt, even if the tax advantages or other aspects of the program are not outstanding. Past investment experience on a taxpayer's part may also weigh heavily in the decision of whether or not to defer current income. If, for example, the taxpayer, despite his highly compensated position, has a history of bad investments or a considerable amount of debt arising from other experiences, it may be prudent to leave the deferred funds in his employer's hands so as to provide some protection from the taxpayer's creditors. In any event, the pros and cons of paying a current tax but making the funds presently available to the taxpayer for investment purposes must be closely analyzed.

[b] Risk of Deferral. A second economic factor to consider in choosing deferral is the risk of allowing the deferred amounts to remain with the taxpayer's employer. Because it is necessary that the deferred amount remain subject to the general creditors of the employer in order to achieve deferral for tax purposes,[9] the future economic viability of the employer must be weighed quite carefully. If the employer is financially unstable, in a volatile business, or in a highly cyclical industry, a plan in which the employee does not get paid until several years hence may mean that deferral creates severe economic risk. The risks of such deferral, even in large corporations, were vividly illustrated by the bankruptcy of the Penn Central Railroad. At the time that Penn Central went bankrupt, several of its salaried employees had accumulated approximately $10 million in deferred compensation benefits. Since the funds invested under this plan were subject to the claims of creditors of the company, substantial amounts of deferred benefits were lost. Under a court-approved settlement, the participants of the Penn Central plan were awarded approximately 25 percent of their deferred amounts.[10]

The Penn Central case, and other large bankruptcies in recent years, illustrate the dangers inherent in deferral. These dangers obviously increase the longer the deferral period. Accordingly, it is critical to

---

[9] See Rev. Rul. 60-31, 1960-1 C.B. 174. The requirements for deferral are discussed extensively at ¶ 3.03.

[10] In re Penn Cent. Transp. Co., 484 F.2d 1300 (3d Cir. 1973).

evaluate carefully the employer's financial health when making a decision whether or not to become a general creditor of that employer several years in the future.

Despite the Penn Central illustration, which indicates that deferred compensation creates economic risks even with a large-scale employer, the economic risk of deferral has always been considered greater if the employer is a small or closely held corporation. Such corporations are often dependent upon the particular business skills of one or two owners and tend not to have a perpetual existence such as that enjoyed by larger publicly held corporations. Consequently, in a closely held corporation whose principal owners are in their early 70s, it may be a poor choice for an executive to accept a deferred compensation arrangement. In such closely held situations, the wisdom of a deferred compensation arrangement will vary inversely to the dependency of the business on a single owner and the age and health of that owner.

A final factor that affects the economic risk of deferred compensation relates to the forfeiture conditions contained in the deferred compensation plan. The individual contemplating a deferred compensation plan must carefully evaluate the risks of forfeiture before agreeing to defer the receipt of significant amounts of income. For example, many deferred compensation plans include provisions that require the forfeiture of deferred compensation if a certain length of employment is not achieved. If the corporate executive has no real intention of leaving his present employer, such restrictions may be irrelevant. If, however, the executive is relatively young and upwardly mobile, the effect of such provisions upon his future job mobility must be carefully evaluated. Similarly, if the executive is working for a company where there is little job security or a history of employment instability, an agreement to defer compensation may be tantamount to an agreement never to receive such amounts. In such cases, the employee may be advised to use his bargaining power to seek expanded current compensation or a lengthy employment contract.[11]

---

[11] Forfeiture provisions are less common and rarely used in cases involving professional athletes or artistic performers. Because the employment arrangements in these cases are, by definition, relatively short-term, there is usually little concern on the employer's part about ensuring a long-term employment relationship. Conversely, there may be a greater concern about the long-range financial strength of the employer.

[c] **Effect on Cash Flow.** Another significant economic factor to weigh in determining the viability of deferral is the impact of the deferral on the cash flow of both the recipient and the employer. The deferral of income may provide the employee with a source of income in a future year when he may have a greater need for funds. This might be particularly true for an athlete who has a relatively short span of extremely high earnings or for a "super salesman" or a performer whose income is subject to a high degree of variation depending on the success of current projects. Such individuals typically have certain time frames in which extremely high income far exceeds their current cash requirements, and other years of restricted cash flow. In such a case, deferral can create a leveling of fluctuating income. On the other hand, if the recipient, such as a corporate executive, receives a relatively even but slowly rising source of cash flow and has a pressing need for funds, the deferral of income may deprive him of immediately needed cash-flow dollars. It is an axiomatic, but often overlooked, aspect of deferred compensation planning that the recipient employee must have a significantly high income base so as to enable him to maintain his desired standard of living without the deferred amounts. If deferral so severely restricts cash flow that it creates an economic hardship, it may be a case of tax planning overriding economic realities.

The employer similarly must weigh cash-flow considerations. Deferred compensation may enable an employer that is presently in a cash-flow bind to design a more attractive compensation package for its key employees by promising deferred compensation at a later date when better cash flow is anticipated. By utilizing this type of planning, the employer may be able to develop a greater overall compensation package for its key executives than current circumstances might otherwise permit and thus retain the services of important personnel. If the later receipt of deferred compensation is conditioned upon continuing employment through forfeiture devices or the like, effective long-term commitments from key personnel may be obtained. Deferred compensation may also be useful to the employer if reasonable compensation to the employee [12] is an issue. If there is a concern that this incremental amount of income might exceed the deduction allowed for reasonable compensation, postponing receipt (and corresponding postponement of the employer's deduction for it) could avoid this problem.

---

[12] I.R.C. § 162. See McLean & Martin, "Is 'Reasonable' Enough? The McCandless Doctrine," 54 Taxes 642 (1976).

¶ 3.03 Tax Deferral—How to Achieve It

If an analysis of all the relevant factors indicates that a deferred compensation arrangement is desirable, the next problem is to design a plan that will achieve the income tax goal of postponing current taxation. Unless the potential recipient can assure himself that current taxation will not result, he could be without the right to receive cash compensation and yet be liable for taxation on it despite income not yet received. Consequently, it is imperative to have a thorough understanding of the case law and rulings that address the question of whether a purported income tax deferral will be successful. In general, the principles of income tax deferral are governed by two general theories—the constructive receipt and economic benefit doctrines—as well as a body of Service rulings and cases interpreting these rulings.

[1] Avoiding Constructive Receipt

The doctrine of constructive receipt holds that an individual cannot defer the receipt of income for tax purposes by turning his back on income that he has an undisputed right to receive. If a taxpayer has an existing right to receive a specified amount of income, and subsequently refuses receipt of this income, current taxation will result. Unfortunately, the definition of constructive receipt is illusive and is often confused with other doctrines such as the economic benefit theory.[13] The regulations do not prove to be especially helpful in this regard, inasmuch as they define the term by using the word itself:

> Income although not actually reduced to a taxpayer's possession is constructively received by him in the taxable year during which it is credited to his account, set apart for him, or otherwise made available so that he may draw upon it any time, or so that he could have drawn upon it during the taxable year if notice of intention to withdraw had been given. However, income is not constructively received if the taxpayer's control of its receipt is subject to substantial limitations or restrictions.[14]

In *Corliss v. Bowers*,[15] Justice Holmes stated that "the income that is subject to a man's unfettered command and that he is free to enjoy at his

---
[13] See discussion at ¶ 3.03[2].
[14] Treas. Reg. § 1.451-2(a).
[15] 281 U.S. 376, 378 (1930).

¶ 3.03[1]

own option may be taxed to him as his income whether he sees fit to enjoy it or not." Thus, for example, if a plan were to provide that an individual has an election as to whether or not to receive income currently, and that election need not be made until the individual is to receive the payment, the doctrine of constructive receipt may apply.

Although the doctrine of constructive receipt is definitionally illusive, in practice there are certain principles that make it clear when the doctrine will be applied. For example, if an agreement to defer is consummated after earning compensation but prior to payment, there is greater likelihood that the Service will attempt to apply the constructive receipt doctrine.[16] However, an amendment to an existing deferred compensation arrangement to further defer a payment date will not constitute constructive receipt of the payment if the amendment is made prior to the time in which the taxpayer has a right to receive the deferred amounts.[17]

Although the doctrine of constructive receipt is theoretically applicable to elections made under qualified retirement plans, the Service has been relatively hesitant to apply the doctrine in this area. The 1981 Act amended Section 402(a) of the Code so as to eliminate the former requirement that benefits "made available" to employees under a qualified plan are taxable to them, even though such benefits are not actually distributed.[18] However, even prior to that amendment, in Rev. Rul. 55-423[19], the Service ruled that an employee is not in constructive receipt of income when, prior to the date that amounts are distributable to him under a qualified plan, he makes an irrevocable election to defer distribution to a fixed or determinable future. Similarly, in *Leavens v. Comm'r*,[20] the taxpayers were held not to be in constructive receipt of payments under qualified profit-sharing plans where, before the payment date, they elected to defer payments to a future date under a waiver agreement. The Third Circuit held that these benefits were not made available to the taxpayers until the deferred date. In other rulings the Service has found the constructive receipt doctrine inapplicable when an employee could only withdraw amounts from a qualified plan

---

[16] See, e.g., Willits v. Comm'r, 50 T.C. 602 (1968), acq., 1969-1 C.B. xxv; Laramy v. Comm'r, 25 T.C.M. 809 (1966).

[17] Goldsmith v. U.S., 586 F.2d 810 (Ct. Cl. 1978).

[18] I.R.C. § 402(a) as amended by the 1981 Act.

[19] 1955-1 C.B. 41.

[20] 467 F.2d 809 (3d Cir. 1972), rev'g 44 T.C. 623 (1965).

if an independent committee decided that financial hardship had been established, or if he could elect at any time prior to normal retirement to defer distribution until actual retirement.[21] In general, the Service's position has been that if a plan contains penalties for a withdrawal of funds, or if a prior irrevocable election to defer distribution to a fixed or determined time in the future is made, deferral for tax purposes will be permitted.[22] Despite the 1981 Act's amendment to Section 402(a), which should eliminate the constructive receipt problem for qualified plans, this authority that had developed in the qualified plan area may be useful in determining the application of the doctrine of constructive receipt to deferred compensation if the employee has too much control over the plan funds.[23]

[2] Economic Benefit Theory

The economic benefit theory holds that when the employee or independent contractor receives a transfer of property that confers an economic benefit, and this benefit has an equivalency of cash,[24] current taxation will result. Although Section 83 of the Code has preempted the field for determining when property received for the performance of services will be taxed, the theory of economic benefit still provides a background principle under which taxation of deferred compensation may result.[25] Generally speaking, the Service has attempted to apply this rule in situations where deferred amounts are funded via a trust arrangement or otherwise, or where property that does have a cash equivalency has been transferred to the employee.

---

[21] See Rev. Rul. 55-424, 1955-1 C.B. 42; Rev. Rul. 57-260, 1957-1 C.B. 164.

[22] Care should be taken in drafting a penalty provision, however, because of the limitations imposed on such penalties by ERISA. See generally Chapter 5.

[23] The doctrine of constructive receipt is also significant because of the recent popularity of cafeteria-type plans for compensating key executives as well as the so-called "cash or deferred" compensation plans. Cafeteria plans are discussed extensively at ¶ 7.07.

[24] A benefit may have the equivalency of cash if it is bankable. For example, a demand note payable by Exxon certainly would have the equivalency of cash.

[25] Regulations under Section 83 indicate that Section 83 is not applicable to an unsecured and unfunded promise of an employer to pay deferred compensation at a later date since the term "property" does not include an unsecured and unfunded promise to pay deferred compensation. Treas. Reg. § 1.83-3(e). Section 83 will be applicable to the transfer of notes or other evidences of indebtedness. See generally Chapter 4.

The case most frequently cited as an example of the economic benefit theory is *Cowden v. Comm'r.*[26] In *Cowden,* the taxpayer entered into an oil, gas, and mineral lease upon certain lands in Texas and became eligible to receive deferred payments of approximately $500,000 to be paid in the next two taxable years. The taxpayer then assigned a portion of the payments due from the oil company to a bank in which he was a director and received the face value of the amounts due, less a small discount. The Commissioner took the position that the taxpayer should be taxed on ordinary income on the fair market value of the contracts as of the date of execution. In reviewing this transaction the Fifth Circuit stated the following principle:

> We are convinced that if a promise to pay of a solvent obligator is unconditional and assignable, not subject to set-offs, and is of a kind that is frequently transferred to lenders or investors at a discount not substantially greater than the generally prevailing premium for the use of money, such promise is the equivalent of cash and taxable in like manner as cash would have been taxable had it been received by the taxpayer rather than the obligation.[27]

The court stressed that negotiability is not necessarily the equivalent of cash because an instrument may have been issued by a maker of doubtful solvency, or it may have been the type that is not readily bankable. It then reversed the case and sent it back to the Tax Court to reconsider the case consistent with its opinion because it felt that the Tax Court had given undue emphasis to the fact that deferral was entered into at the request of the taxpayers. On remand, the Tax Court held that the promise to pay was the equivalent of cash and thus should be taxed currently.[28]

In *Goldsmith v. U.S.,*[29] the Court of Claims upheld the basic nontaxability of a deferred compensation plan, but found that a portion of the amount deferred attributable to current life insurance benefits was taxable under the economic benefit doctrine. The deferred compensation plan in question provided certain death and disability benefits if the taxpayer died prior to the age of 65. These death benefits were far in excess of what would be received by the taxpayer if he were to terminate

---

[26] 289 F.2d 20 (5th Cir. 1961).
[27] Id. at 24.
[28] 20 T.C.M. 1134 (1961).
[29] 586 F.2d 810 (Ct. Cl. 1978).

his employment with a comparable amount of service.[30] Consequently, the court held that the value of this protection represented a current economic benefit, taxable to the extent of premiums on a comparable policy.

This "cash equivalency" rationale may not be applied where a negotiable right cannot be transferred to a lending institution without a substantial discount.[31] It also may be argued that because most unfunded obligations of an employer to pay future compensation cannot be transferred to a lender without a deep discount, this type of obligation is not of a nature that should be included in income under the economic benefit theory. However, because this theory exists and remains viable, it is advisable to include a nonassignability clause in deferred compensation contracts so as to preclude the possible applicability of the economic benefit doctrine.

[3] Requirements for Deferral

Although the constructive receipt and economic benefit theories provide an underlying rationale for the taxation of deferred compensation, the bulk of the guidance as to the achievement of deferral arises from the rulings and cases. To a large extent, the cases and rulings represent an effort to define the basic principles of economic benefit and constructive receipt. These cases and rulings have become so extensive and detailed, however, that they are often thought of as a separate body of law in and of themselves, and, in practical terms, they do define the parameters of taxation of deferred compensation.

[a] Rev. Rul. 60-31. The most comprehensive statement of the Service's position on deferred compensation is set forth in Rev. Rul. 60-31.[32] This ruling deserves thorough analysis because it still provides the basic principles for the taxation of deferred compensation today.[33]

---

[30] For example, if the taxpayer terminated employment after one year of service, he would receive ten annual payments of $633. If he were to die during the first year of employment, his beneficiaries would receive monthly benefits of $1,479.89 for ten years.

[31] See Warran Jones Co. v. Comm'r, 524 F.2d 788 (9th Cir. 1975).

[32] 1960-1 C.B. 174, Ex. 5, was modified by Rev. Rul. 70-435, 1970-2 C.B. 100.

[33] On February 3, 1978, the Service published Prop. Reg. § 1.61-16, which would have drastically changed the taxation of deferred compensation. In simplest terms, if the deferral was as a result of the employee's election, current

Generally speaking, in order to obtain deferral, the deferred compensation arrangement must remain an unsecured promise by the employer to pay a specified amount in the future. If the employee has a right to presently receive the amount set aside for his benefit, if the obligation has a cash equivalency, or if it is funded and separately set aside for the employee, current taxation will result.

Rev. Rul. 60-31 sets forth five different factual patterns and speaks to the taxability of each. In *situation 1*, the taxpayer and his employer entered into an arrangement whereby the taxpayer was entitled to receive certain amounts of additional compensation that would be credited to a bookkeeping reserve to be accumulated and paid in annual installments equal to one fifth of the reserve. The payments were to begin only after termination of the taxpayer's employment, the taxpayer becoming a part-time employee, or the taxpayer becoming partially or totally disabled. The reserve amounts were said to be only a contractual obligation and there was no intent that the amounts were to be held in trust by the corporation for the employee's benefit. This additional compensation was held to be taxable only when received by the taxpayer.

In *situation 2*, the corporation had established a plan whereby a percentage of the corporation's earnings was to be designated for division among the participants in a deferred compensation program. The amount was not currently paid to the participants but was set aside on the corporation's books as a separate account for each participant. Each account was also credited with the net earnings realized from investing any portion of the amount in an employee's account. Distributions were to be made when the employee reached the age of 60, was no longer employed by the company, or became totally disabled. Payments were said to be contingent on a noncompetition agreement and making the employee available to the corporation for consulting services after retirement. These amounts were similarly held to be nontaxable until actually received.

---

taxation would have resulted. As the result of considerable adverse comment, Congress added Section 132(a) to the Revenue Act of 1978, which stated that taxation of private deferred compensation plans is to be determined in accordance with the principles set forth in the regulations, rulings, and judicial decisions relating to deferred compensation that were in effect on February 1, 1978. As a result, the principles set forth in Rev. Rul. 60-31 and related cases and rulings retain continuing viability. For an extensive review of this legislative and regulatory dispute over deferred compensation see Fischer, "Deferred Compensation: Born Again — for Now" 37 N.Y.U. Inst. on Fed. Tax'n 28:00 (1979).

In *situation 3*, the taxpayer entered into a publishing agreement with a corporation containing relatively standard arrangements for the payment of royalties. In addition, on the same day a separate agreement was signed stating that, notwithstanding any provisions of the first contract, the publisher would not pay the taxpayer more than $100(x) in any one calendar year. Under this agreement, any sum in excess of this amount was to be carried over into succeeding accounting periods. As with the previously described arrangements, these amounts were not to be segregated from the publishing company's other resources. In this situation, the Service again held that the payments were taxable only upon receipt. In so holding, it was stressed that the arrangement was entered into before the royalties were earned and, indeed, prior to the time when the services were actually rendered. Because of this, the arrangement was held similar in effect to the first two situations in which deferral was permitted.

In *situation 4*, a football player entered into a contract under which he was to receive a bonus of $150(x). The contract provided that this sum was to be paid to an escrow agent designated by the football player, and the escrow agent agreed to pay this sum plus interest to the taxpayer in installments over a period of five years. The Service, citing the case of *E.T. Sproull v. Comm'r*,[34] held that the football player was taxable in the year in which the club unconditionally paid the amount over to the escrow agent.

In *situation 5*, the Service held that the profit-sharing arrangement between a boxer and a promoter constituted a joint venture, and the taxpayer's share of the receipts was currently taxable in his income under the general theory of partnership taxation set forth in Subchapter K of the Code. This example was later modified in Rev. Rul. 70-435.[35]

The examples set forth in Rev. Rul. 60-31 indicate that when, prior to performing any services, the taxpayer enters into an arrangement with his employer whereby he receives an unfunded promise to pay compensation in the future, deferral will result. If the deferred amounts are segregated into an account that is not subject to claim by the general creditors of the employer, the Service holds the deferred amount to be currently taxable. Thus, to achieve deferral, the employee must be willing to take the risk of becoming a general creditor of his employer. As noted earlier in this chapter (at ¶ 3.03[2]), this constitutes one of the

---

[34] 16 T.C. 244 (1951), aff'd, 194 F.2d 541 (6th Cir. 1952).

[35] 1970-2 C.B. 100. This new ruling substituted an example in which a true joint venture arrangement (which would be taxed as a partnership) existed.

basic economic questions that must be weighed by the employee in determining whether or not such an arrangement is advisable. To achieve the desired tax result from the deferral of income, the employee must also bear the economic risk of this deferral.

The Service further clarified its position on deferral in Rev. Rul. 69-650.[36] In this ruling, an employee could make a yearly election in the year prior to the rendering of services to defer receipt of either 5 percent or 10 percent of his salary for the following year. This election had to be made prior to December 31 for the following taxable year. The deferred amount was then credited to an account for the employee and was to be paid to the recipient over a ten-year period following the termination of his employment. This type of arrangement, providing for a regular election prior to the rendering of services, was similarly held to be effective in achieving deferral.

[b] Requirements for Advance Ruling. In Rev. Rul. 60-31, the Service stated that advance rulings would not be issued in specific cases involving deferred compensation. However, in 1964, the Service reevaluated this position and indicated that it would consider requests for advance rulings in regard to deferred compensation arrangements.[37] Seven years later, the Service set forth its ruling requirements for the issuance of an advance ruling. Rev. Proc. 71-19 [38] provides that to receive a ruling from the Service, the plan must meet the following requirements:

(1) The election to defer must be made before the beginning of the period of service for which the compensation is payable regardless of the existence of forfeiture provisions;

(2) If any elections are made subsequent to the beginning of the service period, the plan must set forth substantial forfeiture provisions that must remain in effect throughout the entire period of the deferral. Substantial forfeiture provisions will not be considered to exist unless its conditions impose a significant limitation or duty, which will require a meaningful effort on the part of the employee to fulfill, and there is a definite possibility that the event that will cause forfeiture could occur.[39]

---

[36] 1969-2 C.B. 106.

[37] See Rev. Rul. 64-279, 1964-2 C.B. 121.

[38] 1971-1 C.B. 698.

[39] One such forfeiture condition might be the necessity to remain an

However, in September 1977, the Service issued News Release IR-1881 suspending the issuance of advance rulings regarding nonqualified deferred compensation plans pending further review.[40] Rulings have now resumed.

¶ 3.04 Funding the Deferred Compensation Arrangement

Because of the concern that a deferred compensation arrangement that does not reflect investment experience is a plan of little utility, various types of deferred compensation arrangements have been suggested to credit the employee's account with a plan's investment experience. The concern relating to the security of the amounts deferred has similarly encouraged a wide variety of arrangements to provide greater economic safety for these plans. All of these arrangements must be considered in light of the basic principle that the amounts deferred must not be segregated in a trust fund and must remain subject to the general creditors of the employer.

The Service takes the position that if deferred amounts are placed in an irrevocable trust or escrow account and are not subject to forfeiture provisions of a substantial nature, the deferred amounts will be taxed to the employee. This position has been supported in litigation with the consequence that there appears to be little dispute on this point. In the case of *E.T. Sproull v. Comm'r*,[41] the employer placed the sum of $10,500 into a trust in 1945, with the trust instrument directing the trustee to pay half of the principal sum to the taxpayer in 1946 and the balance in 1947. The trust instrument contained no restrictions on the taxpayer's right to alienate his beneficial interest in the trust. The Tax Court held that the employee was taxable at the time of the transfer

---

employee for a given period of time. The Service also tends to impose other requirements for rulings, which are not published and which will vary from time to time. In general, these informal ruling requirements often relate to the time at which the employee designates the time and manner of payment and the degree of control the employee retains over the plan investments, if any. See, e.g., Field, "Deferred Compensation; Types and Use; How Far Can You Go To Provide Safety and Control; Executive Control Over Investments; Spendthrift Trusts; Inflation; Cost of Living Provisions." 35 N.Y.U. Inst. on Fed. Tax'n 1511, 1522 (1977).

[40] This suspension was a precursor to the issuance of Prop. Reg. § 1.61-16, which attempted to change the basic concept of taxation of deferred compensation. Section 132(a) of the Revenue Act of 1978 prevented these proposed regulations from becoming effective. See note 33, supra.

[41] Note 34, supra.

to trust. A similar result was reached in the case of *Jacuzzi v. Comm'r*.[42] Thus, it is evident that a funded trust or escrow arrangement will result in current taxation in the year of transfer to the trust.

Despite this relatively inflexible prohibition against a trust arrangement, there are methods available that have been approved by the Service to afford some degree of protection to the employee. First, it is clear that arrangements whereby the employer invests the deferred amounts will qualify for income tax deferral. If the employer invests, at its option, in property of its own choosing, deferral will be permitted, Although invested amounts must remain subject to the general creditors of the employer in order to meet the basic requirements for deferral, an investment arrangement offers the employee some protection in that, if the employer invests successfully, the plan will increase the amount of assets available to the employer to actually pay the deferred amounts.

The Service has ruled that an employer may, at its option, purchase a life insurance policy to fund a deferred compensation arrangement.[43] Under the example cited in the ruling, all rights to any benefits under the insurance contract are solely the property of the employer, and the proceeds of the contract are payable by the insurance company only to the employer.[44] It is the position of the Service that in such a case, the employee does not receive a present economic benefit from the policy, and consequently the basic concept of deferral is not defeated by the insurance funding.[45] If, however, the policy was transferred to the employee upon termination of employment, he would be taxable on the value of the policy received.[46] In Rev. Rul. 72-25,[47] the taxpayer and his employer entered into a deferred compensation agreement and the employer subsequently funded it with an annuity contract. The employer was the applicant, owner, and beneficiary of the annuity contract, and the contract remained subject to the general creditors of

---

[42] 61 T.C. 262 (1973).

[43] Rev. Rul. 68-99, 1968-1 C.B. 193.

[44] Such premium payments would not be deductible by the employer. I.R.C. § 264(a)(1).

[45] If the deferred compensation plan provides an insurance benefit in excess of deferred compensation itself, the employee is likely to be taxed on the economic benefit of that insurance. See Goldsmith v. U.S., 586 F.2d 810 (Ct. Cl. 1978).

[46] David Centre v. Comm'r, 55 T.C. 16 (1970).

[47] 1972-1 C.B. 127.

the employer. It was similarly held in this ruling that the income remained deferred until received or made available to the taxpayer.[48]

In its rulings the Service takes the position that the employer cannot be specifically required to hold any particular asset as a funding vehicle, and the employer must retain the right to veto any employee-directed investment. It is questionable whether this ruling position realistically defines the outer parameters of the law. The basic purpose of these investment vehicles is an attempt to create more assets for the employer so as to produce a greater likelihood that the funds will be available to pay the deferred compensation obligation. So long as the funds remain subject to the employer's creditors, they remain subject to the normal risks of investment and employer insolvency. Investment plans cannot, in and of themselves, ensure the availability of the funds when needed. Similarly, the mere fact that the investments are directed by the employee does not guarantee solvency.

Nevertheless, the compensation planner should be forewarned that an attempt to give the employee absolute control over the investment medium may generate Service resistance to the plan. Consequently, unless there is a compelling reason, which demands that the employee have absolute control over the investments, it would appear more prudent to allow the employer to retain an ultimate veto over the employee-chosen investment medium.

It also appears that the guarantee of the employer's obligations by a third party will not affect the basic deferred compensation scheme. In *Robinson v. Comm'r*,[49] deferred compensation for the prizefighter Sugar Ray Robinson was personally guaranteed by the president of the promotional corporation. The Tax Court held in this case that the taxpayer did not constructively receive funds payable in subsequent years under the deferral agreement. Consequently, the personal guarantee did not adversely affect the deferral.

The common thread of all these approved arrangements is that the employer invests the deferred amount in a funding vehicle designed to increase the assets available to the employer at the time the deferred compensation payments are scheduled to begin. Although none of these arrangements provides complete comfort to the employee, they do increase the likelihood of payment as agreed and also increase the size

---

[48] Under the deferred compensation arrangement in this ruling, the employee would also be credited with any gain or loss from the employer's investment, at its option, of all or any portion of the amount in his account.

[49] 44 T.C. 20 (1965), acq., 1970-2 C.B., xxiii, acq. corrected, 1976-2 C.B. 2.

of the ultimate payment to the employee. It must be emphasized, however, that if the employer is of questionable solvency, the ultimate assurance of payment does not exist. If the employer is of precarious financial condition, a deferred compensation arrangement would appear to be extremely unwise.[50]

¶ 3.05 Types of Deferred Compensation Arrangements

One of the great advantages of deferred compensation plans is their flexibility. Because these plans do not have to meet the coverage or funding requirements of qualified plans under Section 401(a) of the Code, they can be designed to accommodate widely varying individual circumstances. The Employee Retirement Income Security Act of 1976 (ERISA) basically exempts an unfunded arrangement maintained primarily for the purpose of providing deferred compensation for a select group of management or highly compensated employees.[51] Thus, such arrangements can be entered into with both a large group of upper management employees or a single individual, without having to wrestle with the discrimination requirements of qualified plans. Because of these factors, the flexibility of deferred compensation arrangements is almost limitless. As long as a plan meets the basic requirements to achieve deferral under the case law and rulings, the specific arrangements built into a plan can be almost as varied as the mind can conceive. There are, however, certain types of plans that tend to predominate or fall into certain defined groups.

[1] Investment-Type Arrangements

Probably the most frequently utilized plan is where the employer simply takes the deferred amount and invests it. As noted earlier,[52] the

---

[50] There are occasions where an executive will enter into a deferred compensation arrangement with his employer, even though there are grave concerns over ultimate payment. Often in such instances there are no other funds available to pay additional compensation to the executives. In such a case, the deferral concept is more of a myth unless the employer's economic fortune takes an upturn. If such an upturn does occur, the amounts payable under the deferred compensation arrangement will, in effect, be the executive's reward for remaining with the employer in economically difficult times. This type of arrangement, although similar on the surface to a normal deferred compensation plan, is in actuality quite different, inasmuch as it is entered into with the knowledge of strong likelihood of nonpayment.

[51] ERISA § 201(2).

[52] See discussion at ¶ 3.04.

Service has generally approved arrangements where the employer, at its option, invests in such articles as stocks and bonds, insurance contracts, annuity contracts, or the like. Another common arrangement is to credit the employee with interest annually on the amounts that have been deferred.[53] The deferred amounts may or may not be actually placed in an interest-bearing account, but the plan will often provide for crediting interest at an assumed rate.[54] The rates used in such types of plans are subject to a wide variation. For example, a plan may provide for a lesser rate of interest than the employee could achieve by his own investment because the employee will not be subject to current taxation on the interest so credited. Other plans credit interest at a higher rate or invest a deferred amount in interest-bearing accounts and credit the employee with actual experience. It must be remembered, however, that the employer will be subject to taxation on any interest actually received by it.

[2] Investment in Employer Equities — The Phantom Stock Plan

An alternative to investment of the deferred amounts is to tie the ultimate payment of the deferred compensation to the performance of the employer's stock. This alternative can provide for both equity appreciation and a continuing incentive to the employee to improve the performance of the company subsequent to deferral. Because this direct employment incentive remains even after the crediting of the deferred amounts, this type of plan has found a good deal of favor with corporate employers. One of the most common of such types of employer equity arrangements is the so-called phantom stock plan.

The phantom stock plan gains its name from the fact that there is no actual transfer of shares of the employer's stock. Under the typical phantom stock plan, the employee is credited with imaginary shares of the employer's stock under the terms set forth in the plan. Dividends paid with respect to the class of stock are then credited to the employee's account based on these imaginary or phantom shares.

The amount of the ultimate payment to the employee is then subject to a wide variety of arrangements. Some plans provide for

---

[53] Rev. Rul. 71-419, 1971-2 C.B. 220, approved a plan of this type.

[54] Many plans today use a variable rate of interest pegged to an easily recognizable source (such as the prime rate charged by a major bank) in order to adjust the return to market conditions.

payment to the employee of the excess of the fair market value of the stock on payment date over the fair market value of the stock when credited on the books, plus any dividends accrued in the interim. Other plans may provide for payment geared to the increase in the book value of the stock over the deferral period, or for some other criteria of measurement based on actual performance of the company, as opposed to market value of the stock.[55] The phantom stock plan terms for payment are often similar in scope or variety to straight deferred compensation plans. Payments may begin after a number of years or on the occurrence of a specified event such as death, disability, or retirement. Benefits may be paid in a lump sum or over a term of years and may or may not be subject to the election of the employee. Payments may actually be made in cash, employer stock, or a combination of the two.

Although the phantom stock plan has been more traditionally implemented by publicly traded companies, it may also be useful in a closely held corporation so long as there is an agreed-upon measuring device for value of the stock. In such a case, a phantom stock plan can provide the employer with the means of providing an equity incentive arrangement to key executive personnel without actually diluting the closely held ownership interests of the stockholders.[56] For the employee, the phantom stock plan (particularly if payments are made in cash) can provide a source of equity incentive for an individual without creating a concern over how to dispose of a minority interest in the stock of a closely held corporation.

For the executive, the phantom stock plan also provides the advan-

---

[55] This form of plan, which credits employees for an increase in book value, has become more popular in recent years because of the mediocre performance of the stock market during the last decade. Such plans usually adopt the theory that the stock market price of publicly traded stock does not always reflect the true value of such stock and is often affected by a wide variety of factors unrelated to the economic performance of the company.

[56] In adopting the phantom stock plan, the employer must be aware of the potential effect that the plan could have upon the estate planning arrangements of current stockholders. The measurement or valuation device used by the plan could be seized upon by the Internal Revenue Service for an estate tax or gift tax valuation controversy with the principal stockholders. In other words, a generous valuation formula used by an incentive compensation plan may provide a road map for the Internal Revenue Service to impose similar valuations upon the stock of the shareholders. Consequently, care should be taken in the design of the plan so as not to create any inconsistency with the estate plans of the owners of the closely held corporation.

tage of offering an opportunity for direct reward for superior corporate performance. If the executive is in a position to significantly affect the performance of the employer corporation, a phantom stock plan often will act as a valuable and lucrative means of rewarding an executive for his labors. This, however, assumes that the value of the employer's stock will positively reflect superior performance. If the stock is publicly traded on a national securities exchange and does not respond favorably to positive developments, a plan in which market performance is the measuring device may provide little incentive. Similarly, if factors unrelated to corporate performance were to seriously affect the measuring criteria, the incentive would also be lost or at least minimized. A further disadvantage of the phantom stock plan to the employee is that it ties payment solely to corporate performance. Thus, the phantom stock plan does little in the way of providing further security for payment to the employee and offers no assurances of payment of a specified amount.

As with any other deferred compensation plan, the employee will realize income when the payments are received. Because the crediting of the stock under a phantom stock plan is a mere bookkeeping entry and does not involve the actual transfer of property, this type of plan is similar to any other form of deferred compensation and is not subject to the rules of Section 83.[57] Unlike a plan where stock or other property is actually transferred, however, the executive will not receive property upon which future appreciation will be taxed as capital gain. The cash paid at the time specified in the plan, although based on performance of the employer's stock, will be taxable to the employee at ordinary income rates.

[3] Other Plans Involving Employer's Stock

There is a multiplicity of other types of plans involving stock of the corporate employer that traditionally have been thought of as forms of deferred compensation. These include stock purchase plans, which enable the employee to purchase stock of the employer (often at bargain rates or with employer-assisted financing). Another variation of this type of arrangement is a bargain transfer of stock to the employee, subject to certain forfeiture provisions so as to avoid taxability under Section 83 of the Code. Nonqualified stock options taxable under

---

[57] Treas. Reg. § 1.83-3(e).

Section 83 of the Code have also gained popularity.[58] Another type of popular plan involves the use of stock appreciation rights, either standing alone or granted in conjunction with a nonqualified stock option. Inasmuch as most of these types of plans involve a transfer of property to the employee, their taxability is governed under Section 83. These are discussed in depth in Chapter 4.

---

[58] Section 603(a) of the Tax Reform Act of 1976 eliminated qualified stock options granted after May 20, 1976. Section 422(c)(7) of the Code grandfathered certain options granted after that date under preexisting plans so long as they were exercised prior to May 21, 1981. The 1981 Act then reinstituted qualified options, now called incentive stock options. I.R.C. § 422A. Incentive stock options are discussed extensively in Chapter 4.

CHAPTER 4

Property Transferred for the Performance of Services

		Page
¶ 4.01	Outline of Statutory Framework	4-1
¶ 4.02	Basic Concepts of Taxation Under Section 83	4-2
	[1] Determinants of Taxability	4-3
	[a] Transfer of Property	4-3
	[b] Substantial Risk of Forfeiture	4-5
	[c] Free Transferability of Property	4-7
	[2] Taxation of Nonqualified Options	4-8
	[3] Other Aspects of Section 83	4-11
	[a] Election to Include in Income	4-11
	[b] Holding Period and Basis	4-13
	[c] Employer Deduction	4-13
¶ 4.03	Types of Section 83 Plans	4-15
	[1] Nonqualified Stock Options	4-15
	[2] Stock Appreciation Rights	4-17
	[3] Restricted Stock Plans	4-19
¶ 4.04	Incentive Stock Options	4-20
	[1] Taxation to Employee	4-21
	[2] Qualification Requirements	4-22
	[3] Tax Planning	4-25

¶ 4.01 Outline of Statutory Framework

One of the major provisions of the Tax Reform Act of 1969 was the addition of Section 83 to the Internal Revenue Code. This section and the regulations promulgated thereunder now provide the basic framework for the taxation of property [1] transferred in connection with the

---

[1] Treas. Reg. § 1.83-3(e). Property is defined to include real and personal property other than money or an unfunded and unsecured promise to pay

performance of services. Section 83 is applicable to many nonqualified plans involving transfer of the employer's stock to an employee, stock option plans, and many stock purchase plans. In addition, Section 422A was added to the Code by the Economic Recovery Tax Act of 1981 (the 1981 Act) to provide a new form of qualified stock option, known as an "incentive stock option." These sections, together with the statutory provisions for the taxation of qualified plans and the body of case law and rulings relating to deferred compensation,[2] form the basic guidelines for the taxation of executive compensation today.

¶ 4.02 Basic Concepts of Taxation Under Section 83

Because of the relatively recent enactment of Section 83 and the long delay in issuing final regulations thereunder,[3] most of the complexity in Section 83 relates to the statute itself and the regulations. As yet there is very little case law or ruling activity under that section.[4] Consequently, although the essential parameters of taxation under that section seem relatively well defined, many questions of interpretation still remain.

The basic rule of Section 83 is that if property is transferred to any person in connection with the performance of services, the excess of the fair market value of such property[5] over the amount, if any, paid for such property is includable in the gross income of the recipient in the

---

money in the future. In the case of a transfer of a life insurance contract, retirement income contract, or other contract providing life insurance protection, only the cash surrender value of the contract is considered to be property.

[2] Deferred compensation itself does not constitute a transfer of property, and it does not fall within the purview of Section 83. See generally Chapter 3.

[3] Regulations under Section 83 were first proposed in 1971 but were not finalized until July 24, 1978.

[4] The constitutionality of Section 83 has been upheld, Sakol v. Comm'r, 67 T.C. 986 (1977), aff'd, 574 F.2d 694 (2d Cir.), cert. denied, 439 U.S. 859 (1978).

[5] The determination of fair market value is made without regard to any restrictions on transfer other than a restriction that by its terms will never lapse. The courts have held that restrictions imposed by Section 16(b) of the Securities Exchange Act of 1934 are restrictions within the meaning of Section 83(a) of the Code, and thus the fair market value of property received is determined without regard to such restrictions. See Horwith v. Comm'r, 71 T.C. 932 (1979); Pledger v. Comm'r, 71 T.C. 618 (1979). As a result of these cases, the 1981 Act added a new Code Section 83(c)(3), which states that if a sale of property at a profit would subject a person to suit under Section 16(b), the person's rights in such property are subject to a substantial risk of forfeiture and are not transferable.

first year during which the rights of the person having the beneficial interest in such property are either transferable or not subject to a substantial risk of forfeiture. In simplest terms, if property is transferred to an employee or an independent contractor,[6] the recipient will be taxed on the difference between the fair market value of what he received and the amount that he paid for such property, whenever the property is no longer subject to a substantial risk of forfeiture or becomes freely transferable, whichever occurs first. Consequently, the three key determinants of taxability under Section 83 are:

(1) When does a transfer of property occur?
(2) What is a substantial risk of forfeiture?
(3) When is such property transferable?

Because taxability under Section 83 is determined by the occurrence of one of two specified events, the statute by its own terms allows the compensation planners to control the timing of taxation under this Section. By ensuring that transferred property has both restrictions on transferability and a substantial risk of forfeiture, current taxation can be prevented. Either or both of these restrictions can be dropped so as to create an incidence of taxability when it is most advantageous for the employee — from either an economic or a tax standpoint. Consequently, although Section 83 does, on occasion, create compensation income to the employee, it can, by careful control of the determinants of taxability, be utilized to control the timing of such income.

[1] Determinants of Taxability

[a] **Transfer of Property.** The concept of transfer is critical in determining the timing of taxation under Section 83. Unless there has been a transfer as set forth in the regulations, no taxation will occur. This may or may not be desirable depending on the facts and circumstances of each case. Since Section 83 provides for the taxation, at ordinary income rates, of the "spread" between the amount paid for property and its fair market value, designing an arrangement so that no transfer has occurred will avoid immediate taxation. The price paid for this tax deferral is that subsequent appreciation in the value of the

---

[6] Treas. Reg. § 1.83-1(a)(1) also provides that Section 83 is applicable to property transferred to an independent contractor.

property will also be taxed to the transferee at ordinary income rates at the time of deemed transfer. Section 83, in effect, provides a choice so that the person receiving the property rights may enjoy either a deferral of tax or capital gain on the appreciation of the property received, but not both. Unless the event triggering taxation under Section 83 occurs, the period for capital gain appreciation will not commence. Consequently, in those cases where it is thought likely that the property will appreciate substantially in value and be sold prior to death, it may be preferable to incur taxation under Section 83 so that this subsequent appreciation is realized as capital gain. An individual cannot both defer the tax and limit the amount to be taxed at ordinary income rates to the spread at the time at which the deferral began.

The regulations provide that for purposes of Section 83, a transfer of property occurs when a person acquires a beneficial ownership in such property.[7] The grant of an option to purchase property does not constitute a transfer.[8] The regulations also provide that if property is transferred and the amount paid consists solely of a nonrecourse liability,[9] the transaction will be considered in substance the same as the grant of an option. Finally, the regulations describe several factors to weigh in evaluating the facts and circumstances so as to determine whether a transfer has occured.[10] These factors are particularly applicable in a situation where property is transferred under conditions that require its return on the happening of an event that is *certain* to occur, such as the termination of employment. One such factor to evaluate is the similarity of the conditions relating to the transfer of an option. A second factor is the extent to which the consideration to be paid to the transferee upon surrendering the property does not approach the fair market value of the property at the time of surrender.[11] If the price to be paid on surrender is far below fair market value, the Service takes the

---

[7] Treas. Reg. § 1.83-3(a)(1).

[8] Treas. Reg. § 1.83-3(a)(2). See ¶ 4.02[2] for a discussion of the taxation of options.

[9] A nonrecourse liability is one that is secured only by the property in question and for which no individual is personally liable.

[10] Treas. Reg. §§ 1.83-3(a)(3)–1.83-3(a)(6).

[11] However, the existence of a nonlapse factor referred to in Treas. Reg. § 1.83-5(a) is not a factor indicating that no transfer has occured. See ¶ 4.03[3] for a discussion of restricted stock plans using nonlapse provisions, which require the employee to resell stock to the employer at a formula price upon termination of employment.

position that no transfer occurred in the first place. A final determinant of no transfer is the extent to which the transferee has not incurred the risk of a beneficial owner that the value of the property at the time of transfer might decline substantially. For example, if stock is transferred subject to the sole restriction that upon termination of employment the employee must sell the stock to the employer for the greater of its fair market value or the price paid for the stock, the employee has incurred no risk that the value of such stock will deline. Under these circumstances, no transfer will be deemed to have occurred.

[b] **Substantial Risk of Forfeiture.** The regulations under Section 83 adopt the terminology "substantially vested" and "substantially nonvested" property to describe the other triggering points for taxation under Section 83.[12] Property is said to be substantially vested for purposes of Section 83 (i.e., taxable) when it is either transferable or not subject to a substantial risk of forfeiture. Of these two factors, the one that is most critical in determining taxability under Section 83 is the existence of a substantial risk of forfeiture. When such a risk ceases to occur, taxability will result.

The regulations indicate that a substantial risk of forfeiture exists when rights of the property transferred are conditioned directly or indirectly upon the performance of substantial services by any person.[13] The regularity of the performance of such services and the time spent in performing such services tend to indicate whether the services required by a condition are substantial. It is the Service's position that if a person performing such services has the right to decline to perform them without forfeiture, this fact may tend to establish that the services are insubstantial. A forfeiture provision conditioned upon the employee committing a crime will not be considered substantial. The regulations further indicate that forfeiture conditioned upon a covenant not to compete with the taxpayer's employer will not ordinarily be considered a substantial risk of forfeiture unless the particular facts or circumstances indicate to the contrary. In determining whether a covenant not to compete constitutes a substantial risk of forfeiture, relevant factors to be considered are the age of the employee, the availability of alternative employment opportunities, the likelihood of the employee's

---

[12] Treas. Reg. § 1.83-3(b).
[13] Treas. Reg. § 1.83-3(c)(1).

¶ 4.02[1][b]

obtaining other employment, the degree of skill possessed by the employee, the employee's health, and the practice, if any, of the employer to enforce such covenants. Finally, there will be an inquiry into additional relevant factors in the case of property transferred to an employee of a corporation who owns a significant amount of the total combined voting power or value of all classes of stock of the employer corporation or of its parent corporation.[14]

Thus, the question of whether a substantial risk of forfeiture exists will be determined on a case-by-case facts and circumstances basis. The problem with this approach for the tax advisor is that it lessens the predictability of the tax consequences of any forfeiture provision. This is particularly critical if a plan, such as a restricted stock plan, is being designed so as to avoid immediate taxability to the employees. Certain parameters are quite clear, however. It is evident that a forfeiture provision conditioned upon completion of five additional years of employment with the same employer will be deemed a substantial risk of forfeiture under the regulations. At the other extreme, it is clear that a forfeiture provision conditioned upon a corporate executive not committing murder within the next five years will not be deemed to constitute substantial risk of forfeiture. The difficulty of prediction occurs with the many plans that fall into the middle of this spectrum. Even for these plans, however, the regulations provide a clear sense that those forfeiture provisions designed never to occur will be those that do not constitute a substantial risk.

For this reason, most Section 83 plans implemented today contain significant future employment obligations. Although this will undoubtedly ensure nontaxability under Section 83 until these provisions lapse, they do create a genuine risk that the executives will not enjoy the benefits of the property being transferred. For an executive or group of executives bargaining to establish an employment package, the benefits of tax deferral versus the possibility of forfeiture must be weighed. As is frequently the case, the price of tax deferral is an economic risk that

---

[14] Treas. Reg. § 1.83-3(c)(3). Those factors to be considered are (1) the employee's relationship to the other stockholders and extent of their potential control and possible loss of control of the corporation, (2) the position of the employee in the corporation and the extent to which he is subordinate to other employees, (3) the employee's relationship to its officers and directors, (4) the person or persons who must approve the employee's discharge and, (5) past actions of the employer in enforcing the provisions of these restrictions.

must be undertaken. In the case of a Section 83 plan, the risk may be that a forfeiture provision designed to ensure the deferral actually occurs so that the transferred property never becomes substantially vested in the employee.

[c] Free Transferability of Property. The other basic cornerstone of Section 83 is that property transferred to an individual in connection with the performance of services becomes taxable to him if such property becomes transferable. The regulations indicate that the rights in the property will become transferable if the transferee can assign his interest in the property to any person other than the transferor, but only if the rights in such property of the transferee are not subject to a substantial risk of forfeiture. Thus, if the person performing the services or receiving the property can sell, assign, or pledge his interest in the property to any person, and if the transferee is not required to give up the property or its value in the event the substantial risk of forfeiture materializes,[15] the property will be freely transferable. On the other hand, property is not considered to be transferable merely because the person performing the services or receiving the property may designate a beneficiary to receive the property in the event of death.

Although transferability in and of itself will make Section 83 property subject to immediate taxation, the transferability concept is not really an independent one. The term "transferability" is dependent upon whether or not the transferee will receive the property without becoming subject to a substantial risk of forfeiture. The fact that the recipient of the property can physically transfer it to another individual will be irrelevant if that individual is also subject to the same forfeitability conditions affecting the transferor. This definition emphasizes the fact that a restrictive legend should be placed upon the stock certificate itself in order to assure that potential transferees have knowledge of forfeitability conditions. Presumably, any person acquiring a stock certificate with knowledge of forfeitability conditions or restrictions on transferability would assume ownership subject to those restrictions. A bona fide purchaser with no knowledge of these conditions may possibly not be affected by them.[15a] Thus, if a Section 83 plan is being designed to defer taxation, care should be taken in restricting transfera-

---

[15] Treas. Reg. § 1.83-3(d).
[15a] U.C.C. § 8-301.

bility of the property and in noting any forfeitability conditions on the stock certificate itself in order to ensure that the stock will not be considered freely transferable.

[2] Taxation of Nonqualified Options

Section 83, together with incentive stock options issued under Section 422A, are the governing forces in determining the taxability of stock options. The basic parameters of taxability of nonqualified options, as set forth in Treas. Reg. § 1.83-7, are relatively simple. If an option has a readily ascertainable fair market value when granted, that option will be subject to immediate taxation under the rules set forth in Section 83(a).[16] In other words, upon the grant of an option with a readily ascertainable fair market value, the employee will be taxed immediately on the spread between the option price and fair market value of the underlying stock. If the option does not have a readily ascertainable fair market value at the time of the grant, the transferee will be taxed under the rules of Section 83(a) at the time of exercise or at the time of arm's-length disposition of the option, whichever occurs sooner. When an employee receives an option without a readily ascertainable fair market value and subsequently exercises it, the spread between the value of the stock and the exercise price (if any) will be taxed to that employee at the time of exercise.

Consequently, the concept of whether or not an option has readily ascertainable fair market value is critical in determining the timing of taxation of that option. Because of the restrictive position taken by the regulations, very few options will have a readily ascertainable fair market value at the time of grant. The regulations state that the value of an option is not readily ascertainable unless the option is actively traded on an established market.[17] If an option is not actively traded on an established market, it does not have a readily ascertainable fair market value unless the taxpayer can demonstrate that *all* of the following conditions exist:

(1) The option is transferable by the optionee;

(2) The option is exercisable immediately in full by the optionee;

---

[16] If the option were both nontransferable and subject to a substantial risk of forfeiture, taxation would be postponed until at least one of these restrictions was lifted.

[17] Treas. Reg. § 1.83-7(b)(1).

(3) The option or the property is not subject to any restriction or condition (other than a lien or a condition to secure payment of the purchase price) that has a significant effect on the fair market value of the option; and

(4) The fair market value of the option privilege is readily ascertainable according to Treas. Reg. § 1.83-7(b)(3).

The value of an option is not merely the difference that may exist at a particular time between the option exercise price and the value of the property subject to the option; it also includes the value of the option privilege for the remainder of the exercise period. For example, if an option exists for a period of ten years, it presumably would be necessary to consider the potential spread between fair market value and the option price ten years hence. Thus, the regulations take the position that, in order to determine if the option has a readily ascertainable fair market value, it is also necessary to consider whether the value of the option privilege for the life of the exercise period can be measured with reasonable accuracy.

These regulations make it virtually impossible to value an option at the time of grant, unless the option relates to the stock of a company that is publicly traded on one of the major exchanges, and unless the option itself is actively traded. In addition, most nonqualified options tend to contain restrictions such as a future employment obligation or limitations on transferability, which further complicate the problem of the valuation and also run counter to condition (3) above.

Because of this difficulty of valuing options, the Senate version of the Tax Reform Act of 1976 added a new subsection to Section 83 that would have allowed the recipient employee to elect to have his nonqualified option valued as a right. This subsection was stricken by the conferees who inserted language in the conference report indicating that it was the intention of the conferees that the Service should make every reasonable effort to value an employee's stock option at the time of issuance if the employee so elects.[18] As yet, the Service has done virtually nothing to carry out this intention expressed in the conference report.[19] The Service has requested the submission of public comments

---

[18] H.R. Rep. No. 94-1515, 94th Cong., 2d Sess. 438–439 (1976).

[19] Proposed regulations issued on September 20, 1977 contain a reporting provision under which an employee claiming that an option has a readily ascertainable fair market value can submit evidence to support immediate taxation. These proposed regulations do not, however, change the substance of

on the problem of how to value nonqualified options that are not actively traded on an established market.[20] No action has yet been taken on the comments received. It should be noted that this reticence of the Service to allow the immediate valuation of options may be somewhat shortsighted. Because the employer receives an offsetting deduction for the compensation income reported by the employee, very little revenue is produced by the taxable compensatory event.[21] In contrast, if the employee makes an early Section 83(b) election, the subsequent appreciation in the stock will be taxed as capital gain when the stock is sold and there will be no corresponding employer deduction. The Service undoubtedly could generate more revenue by encouraging an early valuation as of right and receiving a capital gains tax on the sale of the appreciated stock.[22]

If the underlying stock subject to a nonqualified option has a strong likelihood of increasing in value, an employee may want to have the option immediately taxed under Section 83. The fact that the regulations are restrictive in defining when an option has a readily ascertainable fair market value may mean that the employee will have to exercise the option in order to enable future appreciation of the underlying stock to be taxed at capital gain rates. It should also be noted that the regulations take the position that a grant of an option to purchase certain property does not constitute a transfer of such property.[23] Consequently, because there is no transfer, the election to include in

---

the requirement for establishing a readily ascertainable fair market value. Prop. Reg. §§ 1.83-6(s), 1.83-6(f). Subsections (e) and (f) remain in proposed form, although the Section 83 regulations have become largely finalized. Indeed, these regulations present an additional obstacle to immediate valuation by requiring the employer to submit a detailed explanation of the valuation method chosen, as well as a list of optionees and statements from them indicating their agreement with the employer's representations relating to value.

[20] 44 Fed. Reg. 20,538 (1979).

[21] Income is likely to be reported by a 50 percent individual taxpayer and a deduction taken by a 46 percent corporate taxpayer.

[22] Even if the Service were to become more lenient in allowing a valuation of nonqualified stock options as of right, there is a likelihood of frequent valuation controversies. These controversies will increase the cost of the process to the optionee — either by creating a higher value for the option or (even if the taxpayer prevails) by encumbering the valuation process with the costs of litigation.

[23] Treas. Reg. § 1.83-3(a)(2).

gross income as set forth in Section 83(b) of the Code [24] will not be available as of right unless the requirements of Treas. Reg. § 1.83-7 relating to the necessity for establishing a readily ascertainable fair market value have been met.

[3] Other Aspects of Section 83

[a] Election to Include in Income. Section 83(b) provides that the recipient of property may elect to include in his gross income, for the taxable year in which such property is transferred to him, the excess of the fair market value of such property at the time of transfer over the amount, if any, paid for such property. Thus, if property is both subject to a substantial risk of forfeiture and not freely transferable, an employee may elect to be taxed upon the receipt of property that would not otherwise be taxable *at that time*. If the Section 83(b) election is made, Section 83(a) will not apply with respect to the transfer of such property; and if the property is subsequently forfeited, no deduction will be allowed with respect to such forfeiture.

Section 83(b) thus provides a means for the recipient employee to elect immediate taxation on the property that is transferred to him. Although this will result in the receipt of ordinary income if the employee pays less than the fair market value for the property, any subsequent appreciation of the property will be taxed at capital gains rates if the holding period requirements are met. If the Section 83(b) election is made and the property is held until the date of death, the basis of the property will be stepped up to its date-of-death value. Consequently, the property may then be sold, if desired, without incurring a capital gains tax.

The Section 83(b) election provides a means of assuring that appreciation of the property subsequent to the election will not be taxed as compensation income at the price of subjecting that property to immediate taxation at the time of transfer. The tax value of making such an election must be weighed against the cost incurred if the property is subsequently forfeited under any forfeiture provisions accompanying the transferred property. If property that is the subject of a Section 83(b) election is forfeited, such forfeiture will be treated as a sale or exchange upon which there is a realized loss equal to the excess of the amount

---

[24] This is discussed at ¶ 4.03.

¶ 4.02[3][a] COMPENSATION PLANNING 4-12

paid for the property over the amount realized upon such forfeiture.[25] If the property is a capital asset in the hands of the taxpayer (as it almost always is), the loss will be a capital loss. For example, if an employee purchased stock of his employer that is worth $8 per share for a price of $2 per share and made a Section 83(b) election, he would be required to take into income $6 per share, representing the difference between the fair market value of the stock ($8) and the price that he paid ($2). If he subsequently left the employ of his employer and was required to forfeit the stock for a price of $1 per share, he would realize a loss on this forfeiture of $1 per share, representing the difference between the amount paid for the stock ($2 per share) over the amount realized on the forfeiture ($1 per share). If we assume that the stock was still worth $8 per share at the time of forfeiture, the remaining economic loss of $6 per share would be wasted for tax purposes. This clearly emphasizes that the main risk of a Section 83(b) election is that the amount taken into income may never be recouped for tax purposes if there is a subsequent forfeiture of the property. The significance of this risk, of course, will vary with the likelihood of forfeiture and the amount of income realized by making the Section 83(b) election. If there is little income realized, there is little tax risk in making the election.

The regulations set forth the procedure for making the Section 83(b) election [26] and also, not surprisingly, indicate that an election under Section 83(b) cannot be revoked except with the express consent of the Commissioner.[27] Consent will be given for revocation only in the case where a transferee is under a mistake of fact as to the underlying action and must be requested within sixty days of the date on which the mistake of fact first became known to the person who made the election.[28] Thus, the possibility of revoking a Section 83(b) election is quite narrowly restricted.

---

[25] Treas. Reg. § 1.83-2(a).

[26] Treas. Reg. § 1.83-2. The election must be made not later than 30 days after the date the property was transferred and may be filed prior to the date of the transfer. Treas. Reg. § 1.83-2(b). The election is made by filing a written statement containing the information specified in Treas. Reg. § 1.83-2(e). In addition, copies of this statement must be provided to the person for whom the services are performed and to the transferee if the transferee was not the person performing the services.

[27] Treas. Reg. § 1.83-2(f).

[28] The regulations specifically note that a mistake as to value, or a subsequent decline in value of the transferred property, or the failure to perform an act contemplated at the time of transfer does not constitute a mistake of fact.

[b] Holding Period and Basis. The holding period for property transferred under Section 83 will begin at the time the property becomes substantially vested.[29] However, if the person who has performed the services in connection with which property is transferred has made an election under Section 83(b), the holding period of the property will begin just after the date on which the property is transferred. In other words, the holding period for Section 83 property is equated with the timing of taxability under that Section. The deferral of taxation by the design of a plan containing a substantial forfeiture provision will also defer the date on which the holding period is deemed to begin for capital gain purposes. Conversely, the making of a Section 83(b) election will commence running of that holding period. The basis of the property received will reflect the amount paid for such property and any amount includable in the gross income of the person who performed the services.[30]

[c] Employer Deduction. The deduction allowed to the employer for the transfer of Section 83 property to an employee is equated quite closely to the incidence of taxation upon the employee. The regulations provide that the amount of deduction to the employer is equal to the amount includable as compensation in the gross income of the employee, but only to the extent that such amount meets the requirements of Section 162 or Section 212 and the regulations thereunder.[31] This deduction is allowable only for the taxable year of the employer in which the service provider has included such amount as compensation. For example, if the employer's fiscal year ends June 30, 1983 and a calendar-year employee realizes Section 83(a) income on September 30, 1983, the deduction to the employer will be allowed only for the taxable year ending on June 30, 1984.

There are two major exceptions under which an employer's deduction will not necessarily parallel the realization of income by an

---

[29] Treas. Reg. § 1.83-4(a).

[30] Treas. Reg. § 1.83-4(b)(1).

[31] The deduction must meet the requirements of Section 162 as an ordinary and necessary business expense or must meet one of the specified requirements for deductibility under Section 212. To be deductible under Section 212, the expense must be incurred (1) for the production or collection of income, (2) for the management, conservation, or maintenance of property held for the production of income, or (3) in connection with the determination, collection, or refund of any tax.

employee. First, the employer's deduction is subject to the normal requirements of Section 162 or Section 212 as to deductibility. Thus, the expenditure of compensation on behalf of the employee must either meet the requirements for an ordinary and necessary business expense set forth in Section 162 or must fall within the specific categories for deductability set forth in Section 212. The deduction will not be allowed if the transfer of property was a capital expenditure, an item of deferred expense, or an amount includable in the value of inventory items.

The other requirement, which first appeared in the final regulations,[32] is that the employer may deduct the includable amount only if the employer deducts and withholds upon such amount in accordance with Section 3402 of the Code. This withholding requirement is surprising inasmuch as it does not appear in the statute and did not appear in the proposed regulations. It suggests that the employer could be denied a deduction even when the employee actually correctly reports the income from the receipt of property and pays the appropriate tax on it. Since the basic legislative thrust of Section 83 was to coordinate the timing of income inclusion and the employer's deduction, this result seems somewhat ludicrous. In addition, the withholding requirement set forth in the regulations presents several practical problems. For example, what if an employee quit just after the taxable event but prior to the time where the employer had the opportunity to withhold? What if the holder of a nonqualified option was a former employee who was exercising his option subsequent to retirement? In such cases, withholding may prove to be impractical.

There also exists the problem of valuation of the property transferred. Inasmuch as the employer's withholding obligation is geared to the amount of income to the employee — a number that depends on the valuation of the property transferred — the employer may, in many cases, be faced with the difficult problem as to whether he has withheld the correct amount.

It has been suggested that the imposition of the Section 83 withholding requirement is yet another step in the Treasury's recent attacks on fringe benefits, deferred compensation, and the like. By increasing the practical problems surrounding the institution of Section 83 plans, the Service subtly discourages employers from instituting them. Precisely how these practical problems will be resolved remains to be seen. The employer corporation must, however, be aware that these problems

---

[32] Treas. Reg. § 1.83-6(a)(2).

exist when considering a Section 83 plan as part of its compensation package for executives.[33]

¶ 4.03 Types of Section 83 Plans

Section 83 is applicable to all transfers of property in connection with the performance of services. Inasmuch as the regulations define the term "property" to exclude only money and an unfunded and unsecured promise to pay money in the future, the scope of the plans that can fall within the auspices of Section 83 is almost limitless. In practice, however, the bulk of the plans in favor today that fall within the scope of this section may generally be classified into two categories: (1) nonqualified stock options and (2) restricted stock plans of various descriptions.

[1] Nonqualified Stock Options

A nonqualified stock option plan typically grants an employee the right to purchase a specified number of shares of his employer's stock at a stated price over a certain period of time. Because the nonqualified option need not conform to the restrictive statutory rules that encumber the incentive stock option,[34] there is a great deal of flexibility as to the design of these plans. Consequently, there need be no restrictions as to the timing of the exercise of the option, nor must the option price bear any specific relationship to the market value of the underlying stock. As noted earlier, virtually all nonqualified options will not have a readily ascertainable fair market value at the time of grant and, consequently, the taxable event under Section 83 will be postponed until the date of exercise. At that time, the employee will realize ordinary income in an amount equal to the spread between the price paid for the stock and its fair market value.

The exercise of the option may present a multiple cash-flow problem to the employee. First, the employee usually must pay cash to acquire the stock. The greater the option price, the higher the cash requirement. In addition, the employee will, at the same time, receive a

---

[33] There has been some indication that the Service is reconsidering its withholding requirement, but, as yet, no firm decision has been reached on this matter.

[34] This is discussed at ¶ 4.04.

substantial amount of noncash compensation in the form of Section 83 income, which will create additional cash requirements in order to pay the income tax. Fortunately for the employee, these two cash requirements work in diametrically opposed directions. The more closely the option price approximates the fair market value of the stock, the less will be the amount of income produced under Section 83. On the other hand, the greater the option spread (with its lesser cash requirement for purchase of stock), the higher will be the cash requirement in order to pay the income tax. Because of the cash bind that is frequently produced when the employee desires to exercise the option, many employers combine a nonqualified option plan with a program of making loans to the employee in order to finance the acquisition of the stock.[35] Because the corporate employer will receive a noncash deduction when the employee exercises the option and at the same time may be receiving cash for the purchase of the stock, there frequently is a ready source of cash flow to enable at least a partial financing of the stock acquisition.[36]

Another means of easing the financial burden upon an employee who is exercising a stock option is to allow payment for the stock with previously acquired stock of the corporate employer. For example, in Rev. Rul. 80-244,[37] an employee could exercise a nonqualified option by exchanging previously acquired shares having a fair market value equal to the option price. In that situation, the employee exercised his option to purchase 2,000 shares by exchanging 1,000 shares of stock he already owned. On this set of facts it was held that the transaction qualified for nonrecognition treatment under Section 1036(a) to the extent of 1,000 shares.[38] On the remaining shares the employee realized compensation income under Section 83. However, since the employee was allowed to use appreciated stock to exercise his option, the only cash demands were to pay the tax created by the income with respect to a portion of the shares. Consequently, the employee did not require cash for both the exercise of the option and the tax created by that exercise.

From the employee's standpoint, the nonqualified option offers

---

[35] If interest is charged on such a loan, it will be deductible by the employer when paid. Another possibility is to couple a nonqualified option with a stock appreciation right (SAR), the exercise of which provides cash to pay for exercised options. SARs are discussed at ¶ 4.03[2].

[36] The financing does not affect the question of taxability under Section 83.

[37] 1980-2 C.B. 234.

[38] The transaction was deemed to have created a carryover basis to the extent of the basis of the shares that were exchanged.

the advantage of extreme flexibility.[39] Assuming that the option extends for a reasonable period of time, the employee is provided with a good deal of latitude in deciding at what point, if any, to invest in his employer. Indeed, the investment can be withheld until there is the opportunity of reaping a substantial and immediate profit. Of course, the price paid for waiting will be taxation of the spread at ordinary income rates as opposed to an early exercise of the option, with the subsequent appreciation being taxed as capital gain. If the employee does not exercise the option and the employer subsequently encounters financial difficulty, the only loss will be one of lost expectations as opposed to an actual financial loss. Such a program, in effect, gives the employee a proprietary stake in his employer without undertaking any financial risk until the option is exercised.

Another way to defer taxation in connection with a nonqualified option plan is to impose a forfeiture requirement upon the shares acquired by exercising the option. For example, the employee could be required to forfeit the stock purchased (or resell it at the option price) if he ceased to be employed by his employer at any time within five years after the exercise of the option. Since this would constitute a substantial risk of forfeiture, if the forfeiture provisions lapsed over time (such as, for example, at a rate of 20 percent a year), the tax impact could similarly be spread out over that period of time. Again, however, the appreciation of the stock from the time of exercise until the taxable event when the forfeiture provisions lapsed would be taxed at ordinary income rates as opposed to capital gains. Such a plan is, however, fraught with danger for the employee. If he were to exercise the option, pay the exercise price, and pay the tax, he could be faced with the possibility of forfeiting stock on which he has already made a substantial investment. Thus, such a plan obliges the employee to evaluate the forfeiture risks for several years into the future.

[2] Stock Appreciation Rights

A recent development has been to combine the use of nonqualified options with stock appreciation rights (SARs) granted to the employee. Such a plan gives the employee the right to elect to surrender his right to

---

[39] The nonqualified option similarly provides flexibility to the corporate employer. For example, since there is no sequencing requirement as there is with incentive stock options, if the market price of the employer's stock fell, it could merely issue a new series of lower priced, nonqualified options, which could be immediately exercisable by its employees.

buy a share of stock, and the employer will then pay him the difference in value between the exercise price and the fair market value of the share of stock.[40] When the employee exercises the SAR, he relinquishes the right to exercise a nonqualified option on an equivalent number of shares.[41] The purpose of this type of plan is to permit the employee to obtain a sufficient amount of cash to pay the tax on the income realized from the exercise of both the nonqualified option and the stock appreciation right.

An additional advantage of the SAR to the corporate employer is that it (when not coupled with an option to purchase stock [42]) does not require the company to issue any stock to the employee. Consequently, there is no dilution of the current stockholders' equity interest with an SAR. This form of compensation thus enables the employer to provide an incentive to share in corporate growth without any corresponding transfer of ownership. An SAR may have an unfavorable impact upon the reported earnings of an accrual-basis employer, however. Sharp increases in the value of the employer's stock will result in a dramatic increase in accrued compensation and thus adversely affect reported earnings. SARs also require cash payments by the employer and thus do have a cash-flow impact.

In the case where an employee could exercise an SAR in lieu of a nonqualified option but the amount receivable under the SAR is limited to the option price, the Service ruled that the surrender of the related option upon exercise of the SAR is a loss of a valuable right and therefore a substantial limitation that precludes constructive receipt of income by virtue of the appreciation of the employer's stock.[43] Any cash payment received by exercise of the SAR would, of course, be includable in income in the year received.[44]

---

[40] The Service has ruled that payments received for the stock appreciation rights are includable in gross income in the year that the rights are exercised. Rev. Rul. 80-300, 1980-2 C.B. 165. That ruling further held that there was no constructive receipt on the part of the employee as the stock appreciates because the employee must surrender the right to future appreciation in the stock in order to receive the cash payment. This surrender of a valuable right precludes constructive receipt.

[41] SARs may also be issued by themselves so that they are not tied to the relinquishment of a nonqualified option.

[42] The conditions that must be imposed on SARs when coupled with an incentive stock option are discussed at ¶ 4.04.

[43] Rev. Rul. 82-121, 1982-25 I.R.B. 5.

[44] See note 40, supra.

[3] Restricted Stock Plans

The most frequently used form of restricted stock plan involves the sale of stock to an employee at a bargain price substantially below the fair market value of the stock. The purchased stock is then made subject to one of a number of conditions that constitute a substantial risk of forfeiture under the regulations. Frequently, the forfeiture provisions will lapse ratably over a period of time (such as at the rate of 10, 20, or 25 percent per year) so that the employee will recognize income in installments as the forfeiture provisions lapse. The amount of the bargain element varies a great deal from plan to plan, as does the degree of employer assistance in enabling the employee to purchase the stock. It is common for employers to provide financing to enable the stock purchase or, at the very least, to guarantee a third-party loan to the employee.

The tax and economic considerations for a restricted stock plan are very similar to those of the nonqualified stock option. The employer receives a noncash deduction for the bargain element of the purchase plus some cash for the payment of the purchase price. In addition, by the use of forfeiture provisions tied to length of employment, the employer tends to create a plan that induces long-term employment stability among key executives. The employee is able to acquire an equity interest in his employer at a bargain price but, just as with the nonqualified option, he is faced with a substantial cash requirement in order to purchase the stock and pay the income taxes involved. Employer financing plus a staggered phase-out of the forfeiture provisions in regard to the stock can substantially ease this burden.

The executive who participates in a restricted stock plan must weigh the fact that the acquisition of employer equities results in tying his economic future to that of his employer to a greater degree. If the employer is shaky financially or faces an uncertain economic future, the employee must weigh the question of whether he would be better off bargaining for increased current compensation and investing the funds elsewhere. On the other hand, a restricted stock plan or option plan might provide a means for a financially troubled employer to offer an inducement to key employees to remain with the corporation during financially troublesome times. If these employees do stay and assist in turning around the corporation's finances, they will be rewarded by their equity participation in the strengthened corporation.

There are other variations on restricted stock plans under Section 83 using nonlapse provisions. A nonlapse provision is one that will always remain with the equity involved, such as a requirement that an employee must resell his stock to this employer upon termination of employment at a formula price (i.e., book value or a predetermined multiple of earnings). Transfers under these arrangements may be made to the employee for a consideration equal to the formula price or may be made without consideration. If the transfer is made at the formula price, the employee would not have any immediate taxable income because he purchased the stock for its presumed fair market value.[45] When the employee resells the stock to his employer upon termination of employment or death, the taxable gain, if any, would be considered as capital gain. If the stock is transferred for bargain price to the employee, he, of course, will realize Section 83 income on the transfer, unless the nonlapse provision is also combined with a provision creating a substantial risk of forfeiture. If such is the case, the taxable event will occur when the forfeiture provision lapses.

One advantage of the nonlapse provision in such a situation is that it simplifies the problem of valuation in computing the taxable gain upon the lapse of the forfeiture provision. It also minimizes estate tax valuation problems if the employee should die while owning the restricted stock.[46] Settling these valuation questions may be particularly important if the employer is a closely held corporation where valuation of stock would ordinarily constitute a significant problem. Moreover, by utilizing a nonlapse provision requiring the employee to resell the stock to his employer at a formula price, the employer can assure itself that the stock will not be publicly traded and will always be returned to the corporation. By combining the forfeiture provisions with a nonlapse formula, the employer may also create the previously discussed inducements to continued long-term employment.

¶ 4.04 Incentive Stock Options

The 1981 Act added a new type of stock option to the Code [47] known as an "incentive stock option." This statutory form of stock option, which in many ways resembles the pre-1976 qualified options under

---

[45] Treas. Reg. § 1.83-5(a) indicates that in the case of property subject to a nonlapse provision, the price determined under the formula price will be considered to be the fair market value of the property unless established to the contrary by the Commissioner.

[46] See the discussion of estate planning for options and other Section 83 plans at ¶ 14.04.

[47] I.R.C. § 422A.

Section 422, will provide a major tool for compensation planners.[48] It is likely that many corporate employers will adopt the incentive stock option as a part of their compensation packages for highly compensated executives. Consequently, incentive stock options can be expected to form a major tax-planning tool for such executives.

[1] Taxation to Employee

No tax consequences result from the grant of an incentive stock option to an employee or the exercise of that option by the employee. Thus, when a corporate employer adopts an incentive stock option plan and, as a result, grants an executive the right to purchase a certain number of shares, no taxable income will accrue to that employee. Similarly, when the employee exercises his option, no income tax will be incurred. If the employee holds the stock for at least two years from the date of the option grant and for at least one year after the stock was transferred to him, the disposition of this stock will generally be taxed at capital gains rates. At the time of sale, the spread between the option price and the sales price will be subject to taxation at the maximum capital gains rate of 20 percent.[49]

Correspondingly, the grant of an incentive stock option creates no tax consequences for the corporate employer. The employer does not

---

[48] Qualified options granted under Section 422[b] of the Code were required to have an option price that was not less than the fair market value of the stock at the time the option was granted. In addition, the option could not have been exercised while any statutory stock option granted to the employee before that particular option was outstanding; the option must have been exercised during the employee's lifetime, only by him; and must have been transferable only by will or intestacy. Immediately after the grant of the qualified stock option, the optionee was not allowed to own stock or options representing more than 5 percent of the total voting power or value of all classes of stock in the corporation, and the option must have been exercisable while the optionee was employed by the corporation, its parent, or subsidiary, or within three months from termination of employment. The options were required to be granted within ten years from the earlier of the date of adoption of the qualified plan or approval of the stockholders of the company and must not have been exercisable more than five years after the date of the grant.

[49] Both the exercise of the incentive stock option and the sale of the stock at a capital gain create potential liability for the alternative minimum tax. See ¶ 2.02. If all the requirements for an incentive stock option are met other than the holding period requirements, the employee will receive ordinary income equal to the lesser of (1) the fair market value of the stock on the date of the exercise minus the option price or (2) the amount realized on the disposition minus the option price. The employer is allowed a corresponding deduction at that time. Temp. Reg. § 14a.422A-1, Q & A 2.

receive a deduction when the option is granted, nor does it receive a deduction upon the employee's exercise of the stock option rights. A disposition of the stock by the employee does not result in any tax consequences to the employer.

[2] Qualification Requirements

In order to receive the previously described tax treatment, an incentive stock option must conform to a rather stringent set of statutory requirements. The option grant must meet *all* of the following requirements:

(1) The option must be granted pursuant to a plan that specifies the aggregate number of shares to be issued and the employees eligible to receive such options. The plan must be approved by the stockholders of the corporation within twelve months before or after the date on which the plan is adopted;

(2) The option must be granted within ten years from the date the plan is adopted or from the date the plan is approved by the stockholders, whichever is earlier;

(3) The option must not be exercisable after the expiration of ten years from the date the option is granted;

(4) The option price must not be less than the fair market value of the stock at the time the option is granted;[50]

(5) The option must not be transferable by the individual other than by will or by the laws of descent and distribution and must be exercisable during his lifetime only by him;

(6) The grantee at the time the option is granted must not own stock possessing more than 10 percent of the total combined voting power of all classes of stock of the employer corporation or its parent or subsidiary corporation;[51]

---

[50] If the option fails to qualify under this subsection because there was a failure in an attempt made in good faith to meet the fair market value requirements, the fair market value requirement will be considered to have been met. I.R.C. § 422A(c)(1).

[51] The ten-percent shareholder rule is waived if, at the time the option is granted, the option price is at least 110 percent of the fair market value of the stock subject to the option, and the option by its terms is not exercisable after the expiration of five years from the date the option is granted. I.R.C. § 422A(c)(8).

(7) The option must not be exercisable while there is outstanding any previously granted incentive stock option to the same individual to purchase stock of his employer corporation;[52]

(8) In the case of an option granted after December 31, 1980, under the terms of the plan, the aggregate fair market value of the stock for which any employee may be granted options in any calendar year cannot exceed $100,000 plus any unused limit carryover to such year.[53]

The incentive stock option rules are applicable to options granted on or after January 1, 1976 and exercised on or after January 1, 1981, or outstanding on that date. In the case of an option granted prior to January 1, 1981, Section 422A applies only if the corporation granting the option elects to have those amendments made by that Section applied to the option. In order to qualify for the favorable tax treatment provided by an incentive stock option plan, the employee must hold the transferred shares for at least one year after the transfer and cannot dispose of the shares within two years of the date of the original option grant. In addition, in order to qualify for this treatment, the individual must be an employee of the granting corporation (or a related corporation) at all times beginning on the date of the grant of the option and ending on a date three months before the date of exercise.[54] In other words, any outstanding incentive stock options must be exercised within three months after leaving the employment of the granting employer. If an employee who has acquired a share of stock by the exercise of an incentive stock option makes a disposition of the stock within a two-year period from the grant of the option and sustains a loss on the disposition, the amount includable in the gross income of the

---

[52] This is the so-called sequencing rule, which can present serious problems to the plan if the price of the stock falls below an option price on previously issued options. The Service takes the position that the cancellation of an earlier option will not permit a subsequent option to be exercised any sooner. See Temp. Reg. § 14a.422A-1, Q & A 7. Because of the sequencing rule, an employer may want to consider faster vesting of options or a reduction in the option term. See Sollee, "Planning for the New Incentive Stock Options in Light of the Temporary Regs.," 56 J. Tax'n 194 (1982).

[53] To the extent $100,000 exceeds fair market value of the stock for which the employee was granted options in any calendar year after 1980, one half of the excess shall be unused limit carryover to each of the three succeeding calendar years. I.R.C. § 422A(c)(4)(a). The dollar limit applies to the fair market value of the stock granted. See Temp. Reg. § 14a.422A-1, Q & A 17.

[54] The employment relation requirement is waived in the case of the death of an employee. Temp. Reg. § 14a.422A-1, Q & A 2(b).

employee as compensation attributable to the exercise of the option will not exceed the excess, if any, of the amount realized on the sale or exchange over the adjusted basis of the shares.

The statute specifically permits an optionee to have the right to receive additional compensation in cash or other property at the time of exercise of the incentive stock option if the additional amount is includable in income under Section 83 of the Code.[55] This raises the possibility of combining an incentive stock option with other forms of nonqualified compensation into a single compensation package. In conjunction with this, the Service has taken the position that a tandem stock option [56] is not permitted, since a tandem arrangement may be used to evade the Section 422A qualification requirements.[57] An incentive stock option may be issued in tandem with a stock appreciation right, so long as the SAR by its terms meets the following requirements:

(1) The SAR will expire no later than the expiration of the underlying incentive stock option.

(2) The SAR may be for no more than 100 percent of the spread.

(3) The SAR is transferable only when the underlying incentive stock option is transferable and under the same conditions.

(4) The SAR may be exercised only when the underlying incentive stock option is eligible to be exercised.

(5) The SAR may be exercised only when there is a positive spread.[58]

If these requirements are met, a tandem incentive stock option–SAR will be considered exercised in full when either the underlying incentive stock option or SAR is exercised. Additionally, the SAR may be paid in either cash or property or a combination thereof, so long as the Section 83 inclusion rule applies to any property so transferred.

The Service has taken the position that both an incentive stock option and a nonqualified option may be granted pursuant to one plan, so long as the plan by its terms meets all of the incentive stock option

---

[55] I.R.C. § 422A(c)(5)(B).

[56] A tandem stock option is a stock option where two options are issued together and the exercise of one will eliminate the right to exercise the other.

[57] Temp. Reg. § 14a.422A-1, Q & A 39.

[58] Temp. Reg. § 14a.422A-1, Q & A 39. See ¶ 4.03[2] for a discussion of stock appreciation rights.

qualification requirements; and that each option granted pursuant to the plan must be clearly identified as to its status — i.e., qualified or nonqualified.[59] The plan need only specify the total number of shares issued rather than the aggregate number of incentive stock options and nonincentive stock options. Again, however, the incentive stock option and the nonqualified stock option must not be exercisable in a tandem arrangement.

The Code specifies that incentive stock option treatment will be available if an employee may exercise his incentive stock option with previously acquired employer stock.[60] As noted earlier,[61] the Service has ruled in the situation where an optionee exercises a nonqualified option by the exchange of previously acquired stock, to the extent that the fair market value of the shares received by the employee is equal to the fair market value of the shares surrendered, that no gain is recognized to the employee under the provisions of Section 1036. If this ruling is made applicable in the case of incentive and stock options, the employee may be able to effectively pyramid his holdings with no tax consequences. At this time, however, the Service has ruled that it will not issue advance rulings as to whether Rev. Rul. 80-244 is applicable to incentive stock options.[62]

[3] Tax Planning

The favorable tax treatment accorded to incentive stock options is likely to make them very popular as compensation planning devices. The employee who is the recipient of the option does not realize any income on the exercise of the option even if the value of the stock has appreciated substantially over the option price. Not until the stock is sold does the employee realize taxable income. At that time, the employee presumably has the cash available from the sale of the stock in order to pay the tax and then is taxed at a capital gains rate, which cannot exceed 20 percent.

The incentive stock option thus provides a very valuable form of incentive compensation to be included in executive compensation packages. At little or no out-of-pocket cost to the employer, it can

---

[59] Temp. Reg. § 14a.422A-1, Q & A 20.

[60] I.R.C. § 422A(c)(5)(A).

[61] See text accompanying note 37, supra.

[62] Rev. Proc. 82-18, 1982-11 I.R.B. 23.

provide a fringe benefit to its key executives who also receive favorable tax treatment, and it also creates an incentive to remain with the company as the value of its stock increases.[63] The compensation planner must not lose sight of the fact, however, that the value of the incentive stock options to employees is heavily dependent upon the growth in value of the corporate stock. Since the option grant must be made at a price equal to the fair market value of the stock, the option itself will have little value if there is not a corresponding growth in stock prices. During the 1970s, the qualified stock option then permitted by Section 422 lost favor with many compensation planners because the stock market remained flat. The incentive stock option will similarly lose popularity if the stock market does not favorably perform.

A comparison between the incentive stock option and a nonqualified option granted under Section 83 indicates that, at least on the surface, the incentive stock option provides much more favorable tax treatment to the recipient employee. The Section 83 option results in the realization of ordinary income upon the exercise of the option, whereas the incentive stock option creates no taxable event for the employee until the stock is sold (and then at capital gains rates). There will thus be a tendency among many compensation planners to automatically dismiss the nonqualified option as the viable planning alternative and to turn most of their attention to the incentive stock option. It is a mistake, however, to automatically reach such a conclusion. There are many instances where the nonqualified option granted under Section 83 may be more appropriate as a compensation planning device.

The biggest drawback to the incentive stock option is its restrictiveness. In order to receive the favorable tax treatment, the option plan must meet all of the requirements set forth in Section 422A(b). Perhaps the most troublesome of these requirements are the holding period limitations, the sequencing rule, the requirement that the option price must equal the fair market value at the time of the grant, and the restriction upon grants to substantial shareholders.

In order to qualify as an incentive stock option, the stock acquired by option cannot be disposed of before the expiration of two years from the date of the option grant or until the stock itself has been held for one year. If an option is granted just prior to an increase in the value of

---

[63] This incentive is enhanced if the incentive stock option rights are subject to a vesting arrangement.

corporate stock, the recipient employee, even if he immediately exercises the option, must hold the stock for a period of at least two years from the time of the option grant. This may somewhat limit his flexibility in realizing gain if there happens to be a very favorable moment in the stock market. In contrast, stock acquired under a Section 83 option that was exercised immediately could be sold after the one-year holding period had expired so as to achieve capital gain. Thus, the holding period requirements for incentive stock options do somewhat limit an employee's flexibility. An employer may, however, view this inflexibility as a positive aspect, inasmuch as it does create a more long-term incentive to retain the employer's stock rather than simply playing the stock market.

The second requirement of the incentive stock option, which may prove troublesome in some cases is that the option price must equal the fair market value at the time of grant. There is no such requirement for nonqualified options. Thus, the employer cannot, under an incentive stock option plan, grant an immediate bargain to its employees. Although the bargain granted under a nonqualified Section 83 option is taxable at ordinary income rates at the time of exercise, it does represent an economic gain to the employee. Thus, if an employer grants a nonqualified option to purchase stock worth $110 to an employee at $10 per share, the employee will recognize income of $100 if he immediately exercises the option. Assuming that the employee then pays $50 in tax on the option spread, he is still $50 ahead economically.

On the other hand, the option granted under an incentive stock plan must rely on future appreciation to reward the employee. Although this creates a long-term incentive for a stable employment relationship, it does limit the employer's ability to immediately reward key employees through the stock option device. It also must be remembered that the employer gets a deduction corresponding to the amount realized in compensation income by the employee under a Section 83 plan. This deduction is very popular with corporate employers since a significant deduction can be created by a noncash expenditure. The inability of an employer to realize a corresponding deduction under an incentive stock option plan may limit its popularity with corporate employers.

Finally, it should be noted that the grant of an incentive stock option to corporate employees who own more than 10 percent of the corporate stock is limited unless the option price equals 110 percent of the fair market value, and unless the exercise period is limited to five years. Consequently, in many closely held corporations and smaller entities, the incentive stock option may be either unavailable as a reward for key employees or, if available, the terms may be so unfavorable as not to provide a significant incentive. In addition, the dollar limitation on incentive stock options may be too small in some cases. In these entities, the nonqualified option granted under Section 83 or a combination of qualified and nonqualified options may prove to be more popular.

Consequently, although the incentive stock option does create very favorable tax treatment to the recipient employee, there are limitations upon its use. In order for such a plan to be implemented by the corporate employer, the various restrictions necessary for qualification must be consistent with the employer's desires regarding the stock option plan, and the employer must be willing to forgo the deductions that would otherwise result from a Section 83 plan. If, however, the requirements for an incentive stock option do seem reasonable in light of a particular set of circumstances, such a plan can provide a valuable long-term economic incentive to an employee when combined with favorable tax treatment. In many cases, however, a combination of an incentive stock option and another nonqualified plan, such as an SAR or a nonqualified option, may result in the most favorable compensation package.

CHAPTER 5

Qualified Plans

		Page
¶ 5.01	Income Tax Consequences	5-2
¶ 5.02	Types of Qualified Plans	5-4
	[1] Profit-Sharing Plans	5-4
	[2] Defined Benefit Pension Plans	5-6
	[3] Money Purchase Pension Plans	5-7
	[4] Target Benefit Plans	5-7
	[5] Stock Bonus Plans	5-8
	[6] Cash or Deferred Plans	5-9
	[7] Employee Stock Ownership Plans (ESOPs)	5-11
	[8] Payroll-Based Stock Ownership Plans (PAYSOPs)	5-13
	[9] Keogh Plans	5-14
¶ 5.03	Qualification Requirements Affecting the Highly Compensated	5-16
	[1] Antidiscrimination Requirements	5-17
	[2] Limitation on Contributions and Benefits	5-18
	[a] Defined Benefit Plans	5-18
	[b] Defined Contribution Plans	5-20
	[c] Multiple Plans	5-21
	[d] Keogh Plans	5-21
	[3] Voluntary Contributions	5-22
	[4] Top-Heavy Plans	5-25
¶ 5.04	Income Taxation of Distributions From Qualified Plans	5-27
	[1] Annuities or Periodic Payments	5-27
	[2] Lump-Sum Distributions	5-30
	[a] Definition of Lump-Sum Distributions	5-30
	[i] One taxable year of the recipient	5-31
	[ii] Balance to the credit of the employee	5-31
	[iii] Qualifying reasons for payment	5-32
	[iv] Five-year participation requirement	5-33
	[b] Capital Gains Taxation on Pre-1974 Benefits	5-34
	[c] Ten-Year Forward Averaging Rule	5-35
	[d] Unrealized Appreciation on Employer Securities	5-37
	[3] Choosing the Form of a Distribution	5-39

		Page
¶ 5.05	Rollovers	5-41
	[1] Section 402(a)(5) Rollovers	5-41
	[2] Rollovers by Spouse Upon Death of Plan Participant	5-43
¶ 5.06	Individual Retirement Accounts (IRAs)	5-43
	[1] Qualification Requirements	5-44
	[a] Individual Retirement Accounts	5-44
	[b] Individual Retirement Annuities	5-45
	[c] Individual Retirement Bonds	5-46
	[2] Income Tax Consequences	5-46
	[a] Deductibility of Contributions	5-46
	[b] Distributions From IRAs	5-47
	[3] General Planning Comments	5-49

¶ 5.01 Income Tax Consequences

If a highly compensated individual were to ask his tax advisor for an opinion as to the best available tax shelter, the reply would almost invariably be "a qualified plan." Although this answer might surprise the client, it is probably accurate. Generally speaking, no other tax planning vehicle can match the qualified plan as a means of providing for the tax-free accumulation of wealth.

A qualified plan allows an employer to make tax-deductible contributions to the plan on behalf of its participating employees. These contributions are not currently taxable to the employee nor are the earnings of the plan's trust taxable either to the trust or to the employee. Thus, the contributions to the plan are allowed to multiply and grow on a tax-free basis until distribution to the employee or his beneficiaries. For the highly compensated individual who has substantial contributions made on his behalf, this can allow a tremendous accumulation of funds, which become available to the employee or his beneficiaries at retirement, disability, death, or termination of employment.

Many qualified plans also permit, within prescribed limits, voluntary contributions by the employee. Although these contributions are not necessarily deductible by the employee,[1] the earnings on the voluntary contributions are not taxable to him. This can further accelerate the tax-free accumulation of funds in the plan. Additionally, beginning with

---

[1] See discussion at ¶ 5.03[3].

calendar year 1982, qualified plan participants who have earned income may also make contributions to an Individual Retirement Account (IRA), which are deductible up to a maximum of $2,000 per year.[2] Consequently, the highly compensated individual may have the opportunity to increase the amount of assets sheltered from tax in a qualified plan above and beyond the level of his employer's contributions.

Distributions from a qualified plan may receive favorable income tax treatment as well. Lump-sum distributions from a qualified plan may be taxed either at capital gains rates or under a special ten-year forward averaging provision that produces much more favorable tax consequences than normal methods of calculation.[3] Installment payments of benefits defer the tax on the unpaid distributions, thereby enabling a further tax-free buildup of funds inside the plan. Nondeductible voluntary contributions can be recovered from the plan tax-free. Even if the distributions are not subject to a favorable method of taxation, the fact that they are likely to be made after retirement may mean that the recipient is in a lower income tax bracket than at the time the contributions were made. If this is indeed the case, there will be this additional factor, which significantly reduces the tax burden upon distribution.

Because the basic assumption underlying this book is that the highly compensated individual does not control his corporate employer, the planning aspects to be discussed herein will not concentrate on plan design. A detailed discussion of this topic, and of the numerous requirements imposed for plan qualification by the Employee Retirement Income Security Act of 1974 (ERISA), is beyond the scope of this treatise. Consequently, the planning reviewed in this chapter starts with an assumption that the highly compensated individual's employer already has a plan in existence and that because of the antidiscrimination requirements imposed by ERISA, the plan cannot be individually tailored to benefit one or a particular group of highly compensated individuals. Consequently, most tax planning with respect to qualified plans revolves around methods to maximize employee participation in the plan or plans maintained by his employer and to minimize the tax on the distributions from the trust.

---

[2] The maximum is $2,250 in the case of a spousal IRA. IRAs are discussed extensively at ¶ 5.06.

[3] See discussion at ¶ 5.04[2].

¶ 5.02 Types of Qualified Plans

Within the scope of the ERISA requirements,[4] the variety of qualified plans is almost limitless. There are plans that promise specific retirement benefits, plans that set a goal towards the provision of certain retirement benefits but do not promise those benefits, and plans that promise no specific amount of benefits but rather distribute whatever happens to be in an employee's account to him or his beneficiary at the time selected for payment under the plan. Qualified plans may make distributions in cash or in employer stock or partly in cash and partly in stock. Employer contributions may be allocated to an employee based upon compensation, years of service, or a combination of these factors. These contributions may or may not be integrated with social security — that is, the plan might only take cognizance of compensation of the employee in excess of the social security wage base. The plan may be funded totally with employer contributions or may reflect contributions by both the employee and the employer. An employee's years of service under the plan are also likely to affect his rights to accrue benefits that have been allocated to his account.

Although the factors just discussed, and many others, create a wide variety of qualified plans, ERISA has mandated many similarities in plans because of its minimum participation rules, vesting requirements, and limitations upon benefits. The types of qualified plans tend to fall into generalized categories, with considerable variation among the plans in each of these categories. The basic types of qualified plans are discussed below.

[1] Profit-Sharing Plans

A profit-sharing plan is perhaps the most commonly used form of qualified plan. A profit-sharing plan is a defined contribution plan, in that the employer's contributions are either fixed by formula or determined at the discretion of the company's board of directors. The profit-sharing plan thus does not promise the employee a specific retirement benefit, but rather allocates contributions made on behalf of its employees to individual accounts maintained for each participant. The employee will then be entitled to these contributions, plus any earnings and less any losses with respect to his account, at the time specified for

---

[4] See discussion at ¶ 5.03.

payment under the plan — typically retirement, termination of employment, death, or disability.

Contributions to a profit-sharing plan must be made out of the employer's current or accumulated profits. Plans that allocate a stated percentage of the employer's profits for the current year do provide more certainty of contributions to the employee but represent a greater commitment on the part of the employer. Plans that leave the determination of the amount of annual contribution entirely to the discretion of a company's board of directors (but, of course, subject to the overall requirement that contributions must be made out of current or accumulated profits) have become increasingly popular in recent years. Such an arrangement gives a great deal of latitude to the corporate employer to adjust for profit fluctuations from year to year and to balance these fluctuations with other demands upon the corporation's cash or its overall income tax picture. Although this indefinite formula permits a corporation to omit contributions in lean years, the employer must make recurring and substantial contributions to the plan in order to maintain qualification.[5]

After contributions have been made to the profit-sharing plan, a critical factor with respect to each employee is the formula which allocates these contributions to that individual employee's account. Typically, contributions are allocated to an individual employee's account on the basis of either basic compensation or total compensation, with compensation perhaps integrated with social security. Forfeitures from employees who have left the employer prior to becoming fully vested will generally be allocated under the same formula or on the basis of account balances.

Employer contributions to a profit-sharing plan in any single year are limited to 15 percent of the compensation paid to all employees covered by the plan.[6] If the employer contributes less than this amount in any given year, it receives a contribution carryover, which may be

---

[5] Treas. Reg. § 1.401-1(b)(2). The regulations state as follows:
The term plan implies a permanent as distinguished from a temporary program....In the case of a profit-sharing plan..., it is not necessary that the employer contribute every year or that he contribute the same amount in accordance with the same ratio every year. However, merely by making a single or occasional contribution of the profits for employees does not establish a plan of profit sharing. To be a profit-sharing plan, there must be recurring and substantial contributions out of profits for the employees.

[6] I.R.C. § 404(a)(3)(A).

deducted in subsequent years subject to an overall limitation equal to 25 percent of covered compensation.[7]

Profit-sharing plans are generally popular with younger employees, inasmuch as they tend to provide greater benefits for them. Profit-sharing plans may favor younger employees because contributions will be made over a longer period of time and the total benefits payable under the plan are directly related to years of service. In addition, because the individual employee's account is credited with its proportionate share of earnings of the plan, these earnings will also accrue and compound over a substantial period of time. It should be noted, however, that a profit-sharing plan means that the individual employee's account bears the investment risks of the plan. If the plan contributions are poorly invested, or if the plan suffers significant losses, the employee's account will similarly suffer.

[2] Defined Benefit Pension Plans

A defined benefit pension plan differs from a profit-sharing plan in that it promises the participant a specific benefit based on a formula contained in the plan. The employer will make actuarially determined contributions to the plan in an amount necessary to provide the participants with the promised benefits. Benefits under a defined benefit pension plan are typically related to both compensation and years of service with the employer. Thus, a plan may promise to pay a participant a sum equal to 2 percent of compensation multiplied by the number of years of service. Alternatively, a plan may promise a specific fixed dollar benefit per year of service to the participants. Compensation would then be determined under the method set forth in the plan, such as, for example, average compensation for the five years preceding retirement or termination. In contrast to a profit-sharing plan, forfeitures by employees who leave the employer prior to vesting of benefits are used to reduce employer contributions rather than to increase the benefits payable to the plan participants.[8]

Pension plan formulae that do not take cognizance of years of service tend to favor older employees, in that the employer must make larger contributions with respect to these employees in order to fund the

---

[7] Id. Limitations on benefits with respect to individual plan participants are discussed at ¶ 5.03[2].

[8] I.R.C. § 401(a)(8).

benefits promised under the plan. Thus, an employer who is contemplating the implementation of a qualified plan may favor a defined benefit pension plan over other options that are available if that employer has older employees it particularly wishes to benefit.

In general, defined benefit pension plans are somewhat more costly and complex to administer than defined contribution plans because of the need for actuarial services for the determination of contributions. In addition, defined benefit plans are required to pay premiums to the Pension Benefit Guarantee Corporation (PBGC) in order to provide termination insurance for participants. If an employer terminates a defined benefit plan without sufficient assets to meet the obligations of the plan, it also faces a potential liability to PBGC of up to 30 percent of its net worth in order to meet this deficiency.[9] Accordingly, the employer contemplating the selection of plans will have to weigh the additional costs and risks of a defined benefit plan against the advantages of providing definitely determinable benefits to its employees and the ability to channel larger contributions to older employees it wishes to reward.

[3] Money Purchase Pension Plans

A money purchase pension plan, although denominated as a pension plan, is actually a defined contribution plan. The employer's contribution to the plan is fixed by a determinable formula, but no specific pension is guaranteed. The employee receives the amount contained in his individual account which benefits or suffers, as the case may be, from the plan's investment experience. In this respect, a money purchase pension plan is similar to a profit-sharing plan. A money purchase plan differs from a profit-sharing plan in that the employer's contributions are not dependent upon corporate profits and are based on a definite formula, such as a given percentage of compensation. Just as with a pension plan, forfeitures under the plan are used to reduce the employer's contributions rather than being reallocated among the plan participants.

[4] Target Benefit Plans

A target benefit plan is like a pension plan in that it is aimed toward providing an employee with a specific retirement benefit. The employer

---

[9] ERISA § 4062(b).

makes contributions that are determined so as to provide the targeted amount of benefits at retirement. The employee, however, actually receives the benefit that is provided by employer contributions plus plan earnings. Consequently, depending upon the investment experience of the plan, the actual benefit may be more or less than the amount that is planned or "targeted." A target benefit is thus a defined contribution plan and is subject to contribution limitations applied with respect to such plans. As a defined contribution plan, it is somewhat easier to administer than a defined benefit plan and also is not subject to Pension Benefit Guarantee Corporation insurance requirements.

[5] Stock Bonus Plans

The regulations [10] define a stock bonus plan as a plan to provide employees or their beneficiaries with benefits similar to those of profit-sharing plans, except that such benefits are distributable in stock of the employer and that contributions by the employer are not necessarily dependent upon the profits. If the employer's contributions are dependent upon profits, the plan may enable the employees or their beneficiaries to participate not only in the profits of the employer, but also in the profits of an affiliated employer who is entitled to deduct contributions to the plan under Section 404(a)(3)(B) of the Code. The regulations [11] further indicate that, for purposes of allocating or distributing the stock of the employer, such a plan is subject to the same requirements as a profit-sharing plan.

Stock bonus plans traditionally could make distributions only in stock of the corporate employer. However, for years beginning after 1980, a stock bonus plan will not be disqualified if it provides for distributions of cash rather than employer stock.[12] A plan that distributes cash must give employees the right to demand the distribution of benefits in the form of employer stock, and if the employer's securities are not readily tradable on an established market, the employees must have a right to require the employer to repurchase such securities under a fair valuation formula ("put option").[13] In the case of an employer whose charter or bylaws restrict the ownership of substantially all outstanding employer securities to employees or to a trust described in

---

[10] Treas. Reg. § 1.401-1(a)(2)(iii).
[11] Treas. Reg. § 1.401-1(b)(1)(iii).
[12] I.R.C. § 401(a)(23).
[13] I.R.C. § 409A(h).

Section 401(a) of the Code, it is not necessary for the plan to provide the participants a right to demand the distribution of their benefits in the form of employer stock.[14] A plan will be deemed to be in compliance with this put option requirement if it provides the put option for a period of at least sixty days following the date of distribution of stock of the employer and, if the put option is not exercised with a sixty-day period, for an additional period of at least sixty days in the following plan year.[15]

[6] Cash or Deferred Plans

A cash or deferred plan is a qualified profit-sharing or stock bonus plan that gives employees the option of making contributions to the plan in lieu of receiving cash payments as salary. A cash or deferred plan thus provides employees with the opportunity to make contributions to a qualified plan, which are excludable from income subject only to the overall ERISA limitations contained in Section 415 of the Code. The employer may or may not make contributions to the plan in addition to these elective employee contributions. Such a cash or deferred plan permits substantially higher deductible contributions than may be made to an Individual Retirement Account (IRA) or made as a voluntary contribution to a qualified plan under Section 219 of the Code.[16] In addition, employee contributions to a cash or deferred plan reduce the W-2 compensation and, for lower paid employees, may also reduce social security taxes as well as income taxes. Because a cash or deferred plan is a qualified plan, distributions from such a plan are subject to the lump-sum distribution rules of Section 402(e)(4) of the Code.[17] This is unlike an IRA, where all of the distributions are taxable as ordinary income.

Cash or deferred plans are finding increasing favor with corporate employers because of the flexibility they afford employees to either receive compensation in cash or have it contributed to a qualified plan. For the highly compensated individual with constant concerns about

---

[14] I.R.C. § 409A(h)(2). The Economic Recovery Tax Act of 1981 also added a provision to provide that banks prohibited by law from redeeming or purchasing their own securities need not meet the put option requirements if the plan provides that participants who are entitled to a distribution from the plan shall have a right to receive a distribution in cash. I.R.C. § 409A(h)(3).

[15] I.R.C. § 409A(h)(4).

[16] See discussion of these limitations at ¶ 5.03[2].

[17] See discussion at ¶ 5.04.

tax planning, this type of flexibility can be extremely useful and important. In addition, a cash or deferred plan may be an appropriate vehicle for an employer to establish a qualified plan without making a significant cash commitment to the plan. Such a plan can serve as an initial retirement vehicle and then be expanded at a later time.

In order to qualify for income tax deferral under Section 402(a)(8) of the Code, a cash or deferred plan must meet the qualification requirements set forth in Section 401(k). This section imposes three major qualification requirements in addition to those qualification requirements normally imposed upon a profit-sharing or stock bonus plan. The first of these major requirements is that the deferred amounts attributable to the employees' election to defer must not be distributable to participants or other beneficiaries earlier than upon retirement, death, disability, separation from service, hardship, or the attainment of age 59½ and will not be distributable merely by reason of the completion of a stated period of participation or the lapse of a fixed number of years.[18] Consequently, the cash or deferred plan requires a longer period of deferral than is normally mandated for the profit-sharing plan.[19] The second major requirement imposed upon cash or deferred plans is that the employee's right to his accrued benefit derived from employer contributions made to the trust pursuant to his election must be nonforfeitable.[20] This requirement is similar to that imposed upon employee voluntary contributions and seems to follow the general concept that any amounts contributed to a plan at the election of an employee must be nonforfeitable.

The third and perhaps most critical requirement imposed upon cash or deferred plans is the special participation and antidiscrimination requirement contained in Section 401(k)(3) of the Code. This section sets forth two mechanical tests which can be used to satisfy the nondiscrimination requirements of Section 401(a)(4). The first test is that the actual deferral percentage for the group of highly compensated employees must not be more than the actual deferral percentage of all other eligible employees multiplied by 1.5.[21] Thus, for example, if the lower paid group of employees was deferring on the average of 4 percent of their compensation, the highly compensated employees as a group

---

[18] I.R.C. § 401(k)(2)(B).

[19] There is no requirement that participants in a profit-sharing plan reach the age of 59½ before commencing distributions.

[20] I.R.C. § 401(k)(2)(C).

[21] I.R.C. § 401(k)(3)(A)(i).

could defer up to 6 percent of their compensation. For purposes of Section 401(k), a highly compensated employee is defined as any employee who is more highly compensated than two-thirds of all eligible employees.[22] The second alternative test is that the excess of the actual deferral percentage for the group of highly compensated employees over that of all other employees is not more than three percentage points and that the actual deferral percentage for the group of highly compensated employees must not be more than the actual deferral percentage of all other eligible employees multiplied by 2.5.[23] The Service has always expressed a concern about cash or deferred arrangements because there is a tendency on the part of highly compensated employees to make greater contributions to a plan than lower paid employees. If, however, the cash or deferred plan meets either of the two antidiscrimination tests outlined above, it will qualify under Section 401(a)(4).

Cash or deferred plans may become exceedingly popular in the future because of the flexibility afforded by such plans and because of their appeal to employers who may not have the economic ability to fund more costly types of plans. Section 401(k) is relatively new and untested, however, and has not yet become the subject of final regulations. Consequently, many technical problems remain to be ironed out with respect to such plans.[24]

[7] Employee Stock Ownership Plans (ESOPs)

Section 4975(e)(7) defines an employee stock ownership plan as a defined contribution plan that is a qualified stock bonus plan or a stock bonus plan and a money purchase plan, both of which are qualified under Section 401(a) and designed to invest primarily in qualifying employer securities. "Qualifying employer securities" refers to the common stock issued by the employer that is readily tradable on an established securities market. If there is no readily tradable common

---

[22] I.R.C. § 401(k)(4).

[23] I.R.C. § 401(k)(3)(A)(ii).

[24] For example, how does an employer insure that elective contributions which are at the discretion of the employee meet the antidiscrimination standards just discussed? One means of insuring this qualification is a so-called recharacterization formula whereby any amounts contributed by the upper one-third of employees in excess of the safe harbor rules would be recharacterized as voluntary employee contributions. The precise status of such clauses remains uncertain. See Lewis, "Cash or Deferred Profit Sharing Plans: Recent Developments and Issues," 1982-15 Tax Mgmt. Memo. 3.

stock, the term refers to common stock issued by the employer that carries a combination of voting power and dividend rights equal to, or in excess of, that class of the employer's common stock that has the greatest voting power and dividend right.[25] Noncallable preferred stock is treated as a qualifying employer security if this stock is convertible at any time, if it is stock that meets the aforementioned requirements, and if such conversion is at a reasonable price.[26]

Like a stock bonus plan, contributions to an ESOP are not necessarily dependent upon employer profits. Similarly, an ESOP no longer has to make distributions entirely in employer stock, but may distribute cash subject to the rules previously discussed with respect to stock bonus plans. ESOPs are exempted from the ERISA requirement that prohibits the lending of money or other extension of credit between the qualified plan and the employer or majority shareholder.[27] Accordingly, ESOPs are frequently leveraged in order to enable the purchase of employer stock. In order to be exempted from the prohibited transaction rules, the loan to a leveraged stock ownership plan must be primarily for the benefit of participants and beneficiaries of the plan, it must be at a reasonable rate of interest, and any collateral that is given to a disqualified person by the plan may consist only of the qualifying employer securities.[28] Because of this ability to leverage the ESOP stock, ESOPs are frequently promoted as a vehicle of corporate finance or as a means of solving estate planning problems of shareholders of a closely held corporation.[29]

The utility of an ESOP as an employee benefit plan has been improved somewhat, since the plan is now permitted to make distributions in cash. This alleviates the problem of making a distribution of employer securities to an employee in a situation where there is no market for the closely held stock being distributed.

---

[25] I.R.C. §§ 4975(e)(8), 409A(l).

[26] I.R.C. § 409A(l)(3).

[27] I.R.C. § 4975(c)(1)(B).

[28] I.R.C. § 4975(d)(3).

[29] The ESOP can be designed so that it borrows funds to purchase stock of the corporate employer which it uses as security for the loan. The employer then makes deductible contributions to the plan in an amount sufficient to allow the trust to amoritize the loan. It also should be noted that if the employer contributes stock directly to the ESOP, it may serve as a cash raising device for a profitable corporation, inasmuch as the employer will receive a deduction for a non-cash contribution. The tax savings involved may then be used for other business needs.

[8] Payroll-Based Stock Ownership Plans (PAYSOPs)

A tax credit employee stock ownership plan (PAYSOP) is a defined contribution plan that meets the qualification requirements of Section 401(a) of the Code, is designed to invest primarily in employer securities, and also meets the special qualification requirements set forth in Section 409A and also in Section 44G(c).[30] If a plan meets the PAYSOP requirements, the employer establishing the plan will receive a payroll credit based on a percentage of compensation paid or accrued to all employees who are participants in the plan.[31] This credit is available in calendar years 1983-1987. Contributions to this plan must be made in the form of employer securities or, if cash is contributed, it must be used within thirty days to purchase employer securities.[32]

In addition to the normal qualification requirements, the PAYSOP must meet the requirements of Section 409A. The primary requirements are that the plan provide that employer securities transferred to it shall be allocated to the accounts of participants who are employed at the end of the year and that the plan allocate the securities to the particpants in proportion to the ratio of each participant's compensation to the compensation of all of the participants.[33] Each participant must have a nonforfeitable right to any security allocated to his account.[34] A PAYSOP must meet the voting rights requirements set forth in Section 409A(e). Consequently, if the employer has a registration-type class of securities, each participant in the plan must be entitled to direct the plan as to the manner of voting of the securities that are allocated to his account. For closely held securities, the participant must be able to direct the voting for securities allocated to his

---

[30] I.R.C. §§ 409A(a), 44G(c). This latter section imposes certain additional antidiscrimination requirements and mandates that the securities be transferred to the plan no later than thirty days after the due date (including extensions) for the taxable year.

[31] I.R.C. §§ 44G(a)(1), 44G(a)(2). The amount of the credit is limited by Section 44G(b)(1) to the first $25,000 of tax liability, plus 90 percent of the excess over $25,000.

[32] I.R.C. § 44G(c)(4). An employer receiving this credit will not be allowed a deduction under Sections 162, 212, or 404. I.R.C. § 44G(c)(5).

[33] I.R.C. § 409A(b)(1). Only the first $100,000 of compensation may be considered. I.R.C. § 409A(b)(2).

[34] I.R.C. § 409A(c). Any security allocated to a participant's account under the Plan cannot be distributed to him prior to the end of eighty-four months after the allocation of the security except in the case of death, disability, separation from service, or certain corporate reorganizations. I.R.C. § 409A(d).

account only for those corporate matters which by law or charter must be decided by more than a majority vote of the outstanding common shares voted.[35]

Distributions from a PAYSOP may be in either employer securities or cash. However, for taxable years beginning after 1981, the participants may be able to demand that the benefits be distributed in the form of employer securities, except in the case of a corporation whose charter or bylaws restrict the ownership of substantially all outstanding employer securities to employees or to a trust [36] described in Section 401(a). If the corporate employer is of the type whose securities are not readily tradable on an established market, plan participants must have a put option to compel the employer to purchase securities distributed to them.[37]

The PAYSOP has gained popularity with employers because it provides a direct tax credit for a contribution that does not have to be made in cash. The employer contribution thus generates cash by a direct reduction in the company's federal income tax. In addition, the PAYSOP gives the employee-participants in the plan a direct stake in their company's future and is considered by many compensation specialists to be an effective incentive for corporate employees. Although the vesting requirements are more stringent than in the typical corporate plan and there is a requirement for pass-through of voting rights, many employers consider these detriments to be more than an even trade for the tax credit received for a stock contribution.

[9] Keogh Plans

A Keogh, or H.R. 10, plan is a qualified plan for self-employed individuals. The initial statutory framework for establishing such a plan is contained in Section 401(c) of the Code, which treats an unincorporated business as the employer of its owners who participate in a Keogh plan and which also defines self-employed participants as employees.[38]

---

[35] Typical causes for a vote requiring the approval of more than a majority of shares might be amendment of the corporate charter, liquidation, or merger. This particular requirement in many cases acts as an inhibiting factor for the establishment of a PAYSOP by a closely held corporation. Many such corporations do not wish to have their employees voting on extraordinary corporate matters.

[36] I.R.C. § 409A(h).

[37] I.R.C. § 409A(h)(1)(B). This requirement is described more extensively at ¶ 5.02[5].

[38] I.R.C. §§ 401(c)(1), 401(c)(4).

In order to qualify as an employee for Keogh plan purposes, an individual must derive earned income from the trade or business with respect to which the qualified plan is established. The term "earned income" is defined as net earnings from self-employment, but only with respect to a trade or business in which the personal services of the taxpayer are a material income-producing factor.[39] Although a Keogh plan must meet the general requirements for qualification that apply to corporate plans, it is also subject to certain additional qualification requirements. The most prominent of these requirements is the limitation upon benefits which, at least prior to 1984, is substantially less than the limitation allowed with respect to other qualified plans.[40] These additional requirements for qualification are particularly noteworthy if an owner-employee is a participant in the plan. An owner-employee is an employee who owns the entire interest in an unincorporated trade or business or, in the case of a partnership, a partner who owns more than 10 percent of either the capital interest or the profits interest in such a partnership.[41] The most significant of these requirements with respect to owner-employees are:

(1) If the plan is a profit-sharing plan, it is required to contain a definite formula for determining contributions on behalf of employees other than owner-employees;[42]

(2) The employees' rights to or derived from the contributions under the plan must be nonforfeitable at the time the contributions are paid to or under the plan;[43]

---

[39] A self-employed individual may establish a Keogh plan even if he is employed as an employee in another business, and, even in this capacity, he is covered by a qualified plan. Treas. Reg. § 1.401-10(b)(3)(ii). See Pulver v. Comm'r, T.C. Memo. 1982-437, where an employed chief engineer who was additionally paid a percentage of sales of his inventions marketed by the company was held to be a self-employed person eligible to establish a Keogh plan.

[40] See generally discussion at ¶ 5.03[2][c].

[41] I.R.C. § 401(c)(3).

[42] I.R.C. § 401(d)(2)(B). Thus, the plan cannot provide for discretionary contributions as is frequently the case with a profit-sharing plan. This requirement, along with the other special requirements for Keogh plans listed below, were generally repealed by the 1982 Act, which has as its general goal the equalization of qualification requirements between Keogh plans and other qualified plans. These changes are effective for years beginning after December 31, 1983. At that time a Keogh plan, like other qualified plans, will be subject to special qualification requirements if it is a so-called top-heavy plan. See generally ¶ 5.03[4].

[43] I.R.C. § 401(d)(2)(A).

(3) The plan must benefit each employee in the trade or business who has three or more years of service other than any owner-employee who does not consent to be covered under the plan;[44]

(4) Integration with social security benefits is not permitted for a defined benefit Keogh plan [45] or is severely restricted in the case of a defined contribution plan;[46] and

(5) No distributions must be made to an owner-employee (except in the case of disability) prior to reaching the age of 59½.[47]

The Keogh plan may be in the form of either a defined contribution plan or a defined benefit plan. It is also subject to the other normal ERISA requirements, such as the antidiscrimination rules of Section 401(a)(4) and the minimum age and service requirements of Section 410. Despite these additional limitations, the Keogh plan does serve as a means of providing retirement benefits to the highly compensated employee of an unincorporated business or an owner-employee of such business. The same tax benefits that generally apply to corporate plans, such as deductibility of contributions, deferral of tax on earnings, and favorable tax treatment of distributions, are generally applicable to Keogh plans.

¶ 5.03 Qualification Requirements Affecting the Highly Compensated

In order to achieve status as a qualified plan, a plan must meet the numerous and often confusing technical requirements mandated by ERISA. These requirements impose, for example, minimum age and service requirements for participation,[48] minimum vesting standards,[49] and requirements for the accrual of benefits.[50] The detailed requirements contained in these and other sections, together with the Service's interpretations of these requirements, have a tendency to

---

[44] I.R.C. § 401(d)(3).

[45] I.R.C. § 401(j)(4).

[46] I.R.C. § 401(d)(6).

[47] The plan must contain such restrictions on distributions to an owner-employee even if the plan is terminated. Rev. Rul. 65-21, 1965-1 C.B. 174.

[48] I.R.C. § 410(a)(1).

[49] I.R.C. § 411(a).

[50] I.R.C. § 411(b).

greatly limit the individuality of design of qualified plans. A detailed discussion of these qualification requirements could itself fill a book and is beyond the scope of this treatise. There are, however, certain qualification requirements that most significantly impact upon the highly compensated individual and that should be briefly noted here.

[1] Antidiscrimination Requirements

Perhaps the requirement for qualification that most significantly affects the highly compensated individual is contained in Section 401(a)(4), which states that the contributions or benefits provided under a qualified plan cannot discriminate in favor of employees who are officers, shareholders, or highly compensated individuals. In addition, the plan must be so designed as not to discriminate in favor of officers, shareholders, or the highly compensated in terms of eligibility to participate in the plan.[51] Consequently, qualified plans differ greatly from nonqualified arrangements that may be established for a select group of highly compensated employees. ERISA requires that the qualified plan be established to benefit the bulk of the corporation's employees.[52]

Consequently, although a qualified retirement plan may greatly benefit the highly compensated individuals who are employed by a particular company, the plan cannot be established solely to benefit that group. It is possible, however, to provide substantially greater benefits for the highly compensated employee than for other employees under the qualified plan. The antidiscrimination requirements do not mean that each employee who participates under a plan must receive precisely the same benefits. Section 401(a)(5) of the Code specifically provides that a classification will not be considered discriminatory

---

[51] I.R.C. § 410(b) requires that either (1) 70 percent or more of all employees must benefit under the plan, or (2) 80 percent or more of all employees who are eligible to benefit under the plan if 70 percent or more of all of the employees are eligible to benefit under the plan must benefit under the plan excluding in each case employees who have not satisfied the minimum age and service requirements, if any, prescribed by the plan as a condition of participation. Or, in the alternative, some other classification must be set up by the employer and found by the Secretary not to be discriminatory.

[52] Unionized employees may be excluded in determining whether or not the coverage test has been met if the employer can show that retirement benefits were the subject of good faith bargaining between employee representatives and the employer. I.R.C. § 410(b)(3)(A).

merely because it excludes employees whose wages fall below the social security wage base or because the plan is limited to salaried or clerical employees. Furthermore, a plan will not be considered discriminatory within the meaning of the Code merely because the contributions or benefits on behalf of the employees under the plan bear a uniform relationship to the total compensation or the basic or regular rate of compensation for such employees.[53] Although these requirements are far more complex than appears on the surface of the language of the Code, the basic message is that benefits under a qualified plan may be related to compensation. In this respect, and subject to the limitations on benefits (which are discussed at ¶ 5.03[2]), a plan may be weighted in favor of the highly compensated individual. It is this factor that permits the accumulation of very substantial benefits for the highly compensated individual under a qualified plan.

The antidiscrimination requirements do mean that a qualified plan is not an individually designed executive benefit but rather a benefit available to substantial percentages of a corporation's employees who are permissibly established as a unit of participation for the qualified plan. Within these parameters, the use of an allocation formula that is based upon compensation and/or that excludes compensation below the social security wage base can provide substantially more benefits to the highly compensated individual than to other corporate employees. The limitations upon these benefits will be discussed next.

[2] Limitation on Contributions and Benefits

After the antidiscrimination requirements, the aspect of qualified plans that most significantly affects the highly compensated individual is the limitation on benefits and contributions, which is largely contained in Section 415 of the Code. These limitations have the effect of placing a cap upon the contributions and benefits that an individual can receive under a qualified plan. Although these limitations do exist, they are of a nature that permits the payment of significant benefits under a qualified plan.

[a] Defined Benefit Plans. Section 415(b) states that, with respect to a participant in a defined benefit plan, the annual benefit cannot

---

[53] I.R.C. § 401(a)(5).

exceed the lesser of $90,000 (as adjusted annually for inflation) or 100 percent of the participant's average compensation for his high three years.[54] This limitation, which is applicable to all new plans and to existing plans for years beginning after 1982, was substantially reduced by the Tax Equity and Fiscal Responsibility Act of 1982 (the 1982 Act). Prior to the passage of that act, the annual adjustment for inflation had raised the dollar limitation to an amount equal to $136,425 in 1982. Limitations of this magnitude led to a certain amount of public outcry, with the result that the 1982 Act contained several significant pension reform provisions. The change that perhaps has the greatest impact on the highly compensated individual is the reduction in the benefit limitations.

The cost of living adjustment to the limitations for defined benefit plans and defined contribution plans (see ¶ 5.03[2][b]) was also changed by the 1982 Act so as to freeze the benefit limitations until January 1, 1986.[55] At that time, adjustments will be made for increases in the cost of living that will be similar to procedures used to adjust the primary insurance amounts under Section 215(i)(2)(A) of the Social Security Act.[56] The base for such adjustments will be the calendar quarter beginning October 1, 1984.

Section 415(b) of the Code also contains several adjustments that have the effect of reducing the limitations just discussed. That section defines the annual benefit as benefits payable annually in the form of a straight-life annuity.[57] If the benefit is payable in any other form, the benefit paid must be adjusted to the actuarial equivalent of the defined annual benefit. If the benefit is paid in the form of a qualified joint and survivor annuity, as defined in Section 401(a)(11)(G)(iii), no adjustment is required. If the retirement income benefit is scheduled to commence prior to age 62, in order to determine compliance with the dollar

---

[54] Average compensation for the high three years is defined in I.R.C. § 415(b)(3) to be the period of consecutive calendar years during which the participant both was an active participant in the plan and had the greatest aggregate compensation from the employer.

[55] I.R.C. § 415(d)(3).

[56] I.R.C. § 415(d)(1).

[57] The Service has ruled that a limitation year for purposes of determining benefit limitations is a calendar year unless a different twelve-month period is elected. Rev. Rul. 75-481, 1975-2 C.B. 188, as modified by Rev. Rul. 77-24, 1977-1 C.B. 122. Different limitation years may be chosen for different plans. Rev. Rul. 79-5, 1979-1 C.B. 165.

¶ 5.03[2][b]   COMPENSATION PLANNING   5-20

limitation (but not the compensation limitation) an actuarial adjustment is required so that the benefit is the equivalent of the benefit commencing at age 62.[58] Conversely, the benefit limitation is raised if benefits commence after age 65.[59] If the employee has less than ten years of service with the employer, the limitation is reduced based on the ratio of the number of years of service to ten.[60] Thus, if an employee retired with five years of service, the limitations for defined benefit plans would equal 50 percent of the general limitations described in Section 415(b)(1). Finally, there is a de minimis limitation contained in Section 415(b)(4) if the total annual benefits do not exceed $10,000. The only adjustment required for this de minimis limitation is if the employee has fewer than ten years of service.

[b] Defined Contribution Plans. Limitations with respect to defined contribution plans are expressed in the form of annual additions to a participant's account rather than to the annual benefit that is payable. These limitations, contained in Section 415(c)(1), restrict the annual additions to an individual's account to the lesser of $30,000 (adjusted annually commencing in 1986 for cost of living increases) or 25 percent of the participant's compensation for the year in question. The annual additions to an individual's account are defined to be the sum of employer contributions, the lesser of the amount of employee contributions in excess of 6 percent of his compensation or one half of the employee contributions, and forfeitures under the plan.[61] Forfeitures are considered an annual addition for a particular year if the forfeiture is allocated to an individual's account as of any day during that year.[62] Mandatory and voluntary employee contributions are

---

[58] I.R.C. § 415(b)(2)(C). If, however, the benefit commences on or after age 55, the limitation does not have to be reduced below $75,000. The adjustment must be based on an interest rate assumption of not less than the greater of 5 percent or the rate specified in the plan.

[59] In such a case, the interest rate assumption shall not be greater than the lesser of 5 percent or the rate specified in the plan. Rev. Rul. 79-90, 1979-1 C.B. 156, requires that a plan specify the actuarial assumptions used to determine benefit equivalence.

[60] I.R.C. § 415(b)(5).

[61] I.R.C. § 415(c)(2). Employee contributions for the second limitation described above are determined without regard to any rollover contributions and without regard to employee contributions to a simplified employee pension allowable as a deduction under Section 219(a) and without regard to deductible employee contributions within the meaning of I.R.C. § 72(o)(5).

[62] Treas. Reg. § 1.415-6(b)(5).

considered annual additions if the contributions are actually made within thirty days after the end of the plan year.[63]

[c] Multiple Plans. If an individual is a participant in both a defined benefit plan and a defined contribution plan maintained by the same employer, a limitation is imposed whereby the sum of the defined benefit plan fraction and the defined contribution plan fraction for any year may not exceed 1.0.[64] The defined benefit plan fraction is a fraction, the numerator of which is the projected annual benefit of the particular participant under the plan and the denominator of which is the lesser of 125 percent of the maximum dollar limitation for the year or 140 percent of average compensation for the three consecutive years.[65] The defined contribution plan fraction is a fraction, the numerator of which is the annual additions to the participant's account as of the close of the year and the denominator of which is the lesser of 125 percent of the maximum dollar limitation for the year or 140 percent of 25 percent of compensation for such year and for each prior year of service with the employer.[66]

[d] Keogh Plans. A Keogh plan maintained for self-employed individuals is subject to special limitations until years commencing after December 31, 1983. At that time, Keogh plans will become subject to the general limitations on corporate plans just discussed. In order for such amounts to be deductible in any taxable year prior to 1984, the contributions to a Keogh plan on behalf of any employee cannot exceed the lesser of $15,000 or 15 percent of the earned income derived by such employee from the trade or business with respect to which the plan is established.[67] The compensation base that may be taken into account under a plan may not exceed the first $200,000 of compensation.[68] If a defined contribution plan takes compensation in excess of $100,000 into account, contributions on behalf of each employee, other than an owner-employee to the plan, must be made at a rate of not less than 7.5

---

[63] Treas. Reg. § 1.415-6(b)(7)(iii).

[64] I.R.C. § 415(e)(1). Prior to the enactment of the 1982 Act, the limitation was 1.4.

[65] I.R.C. § 415(e)(2).

[66] I.R.C. § 415(e)(3).

[67] I.R.C. § 404(e)(1).

[68] I.R.C. § 401(a)(17).

percent.[69] Thus, until 1984, the limitations with respect to contributions to a Keogh plan are significantly lower than either the corporate defined benefit or defined contribution limitations.

The limitation on benefits for a defined benefit Keogh plan is specified in Section 401(j) to require that there will be reasonable comparability between the basic benefit accruing under the plan and the benefit that would be provided under a defined contribution Keogh plan.[70] The basic benefit is defined to mean a benefit in the form of a straight-life annuity commencing at the later of age 65 or the day five years after the day the participant's current period of participation began under a plan that provides no ancillary benefits and to which the employees do not contribute.[71] This basic benefit cannot exceed the sum of the products for each plan year of participation of the participant's annual compensation (not in excess of $100,000) for such year and the applicable percentage set forth in Section 401(j)(3).[72] If the defined benefit Keogh plan uses a compensation base in excess of $100,000, the annual benefit accrual for employees may not be a percentage of compensation that is less than one half of the applicable percentage set forth in the tables in Section 401(j)(3).[73]

[3] Voluntary Contributions

Voluntary contributions by an employee to a qualified plan serve as a means of increasing the tax-free buildup of assets in a plan. Prior to 1982, voluntary contributions to an employer plan were nondeductible. Beginning that year, however, a participant in a qualified plan may make contributions to an Individual Retirement Account up to a maximum of $2,000 [74] or 100 percent of compensation. If a plan participant does not make deductible contributions to an IRA, he may make a similar amount of voluntary deductible contributions to a qualified plan if permitted by the plan.

Even if such contributions are not deductible by the employee, they

---

[69] I.R.C. § 401(a)(17)(B)(i).

[70] I.R.C. § 401(j)(1).

[71] I.R.C. § 401(j)(5)(A).

[72] I.R.C. § 401(j)(2). The applicable percentage in I.R.C. § 401(j)(3)(A) is indicated in a table that sets forth specified percentages which decrease as the participant ages.

[73] I.R.C. § 401(a)(17)(B)(ii).

[74] The maximum is $2,250 in the case of a spousal IRA.

do serve a useful tax planning purpose in that the earnings on these contributions will not be currently taxed to the employee. Consequently, it is frequently prudent from a tax planning standpoint for the highly compensated employee to make voluntary contributions if permitted to do so by his employer's plan. It should be noted, however, that the lesser of the amount of employee contributions in excess of 6 percent of his compensation, or one half of the employee's contributions, will be counted as annual additions to the plan for purposes of computing the limitation on contributions to a defined contribution plan under Section 415(c)(1).[75]

The Service has long expressed the opinion that voluntary contributions to qualified plans must be subject to some sort of reasonable limitation. This position was recently affirmed in Rev. Rul. 80-350,[76] which indicates that employee contributions will be deemed reasonable if they do not exceed 10 percent of the employee's aggregate compensation for all years since he became a participant in the plan.[77] Such voluntary contributions must be used only for the purpose of providing benefits to the employee as an addition to the benefits provided by employer contributions. This 10 percent limitation is applied on a cumulative basis to all qualified plans covering a particular employee.[78] The plan may permit the withdrawal of employee contributions under certain specified circumstances.[79] Mandatory contributions or voluntary contributions that provide a base for employer contributions may only be withdrawn in accordance with the same standards that are applicable to the normal distribution of employer contributions under the plan.[80]

---

[75] I.R.C. § 415(c)(2)(B).

[76] 1980-2 C.B. 133.

[77] Voluntary contributions with respect to an owner-employee under a Keogh plan are limited to the lesser of $2,500 or 10 percent of earned income or the amount of the contribution that would be contributed if such contribution were made at the rate of contributions permitted to be made by employees other than owner-employees. I.R.C. § 4972(c). If there are no employees other than owner-employees, no voluntary contributions will be permitted.

[78] Rev. Rul. 69-627, 1969-2 C.B. 92.

[79] Rev. Rul. 60-323, 1960-2 C.B. 148. Prior to the enactment of the 1981 Act, an employee faced the problem of constructive receipt if the plan permitted the withdrawal of earnings on employee contributions. The removal of the "made available" language from I.R.C. § 401(a) should mean that such earnings will not be taxable unless actually withdrawn from the plan.

[80] Rev. Rul. 72-275, 1972-1 C.B. 109.

It also should be noted that if a plan provides for mandatory employee contributions, the Service requires that these contributions be limited to 6 percent or less of the employee's compensation for the year.[81] Even if this limitation applies, however, the employee can still make voluntary contributions up to the 10 percent limit if permitted by the plan.[82] In addition, the plan is still subject to the overall antidiscrimination requirements.

The basic advantage of voluntary contributions is the tax-free compounding of earnings within the ambit of the qualified plan. This can greatly increase the amount of funds that are available to the employee at retirement age, since the amount that would otherwise be taxed is available to serve as a base for further growth and earnings. In addition, if the employee removes these voluntary contributions in installments, that portion remaining in the plan will continue to grow on a tax-free basis until actually withdrawn from the plan.

The ability to make voluntary contributions may be especially valuable to the highly compensated individual whose employer has already contributed the maximum amount permissible under Section 415. Because of the definition of the term "annual addition" relating to the limitations on contributions to a defined contribution plan,[83] the employee is always able to contribute up to 6 percent of his compensation for the limitation year even if his annual additions otherwise equal the maximum amount that are permissible. If the employer has not contributed the maximum permissible amount, the employee may make additional voluntary contributions, subject to the 10 percent limitation, so long as these contributions do not create an annual addition in excess of the maximum limitations. In the case of pension plans, the Service has ruled that employee contributions to a defined benefit plan are to be measured under the defined contribution plan rules.[84] The employee contributions are thus considered a separate defined contribution plan subject to the fraction limitation of 1.0 discussed above with respect to a combination of plans. This often will enable a larger voluntary contribution in the situation where an

---

[81] Rev. Rul. 57-163, 1957-1 C.B. 128. Mandatory contributions to a Keogh plan are seemingly precluded if any owner-employee is covered under the plan. Treas. Reg. § 1.401-12(e)(1).

[82] Rev. Rul. 70-658, 1970-2 C.B. 86.

[83] Discussed at ¶ 5.03[2][b].

[84] Rev. Rul. 75-481, 1975-2 C.B. 188, as modified by Rev. Rul. 78-57, 1978-1 C.B. 128.

employer is already providing the maximum defined benefit permissible under Section 415(b).

If voluntary contributions are permitted by the plan in which a highly compensated individual participates, they should always be considered a potential means for tax deferral. Unlike municipal bonds, voluntary contributions placed in interest bearing accounts do not bear a market risk. The voluntary contribution thus provides a unique vehicle for the tax-free accumulation of funds without some of the fluctuations and attendant worries of the bond market.

[4] Top-Heavy Plans

The 1982 Act added a new concept to the qualified plan area known as top-heavy plans.[85] The top-heavy plan rules will be applicable to all qualified plans for years beginning after December 31, 1983. These requirements will apply to both corporate plans and Keogh plans and will essentially replace the special qualification requirements that have been applicable to Keogh plans. If a plan is classified as a top-heavy plan, it must meet certain specified vesting requirements, minimum benefit requirements, and limitations on compensation in order to retain its qualification.

A "top-heavy plan" is defined to mean any plan wherein the present value of cumulative accrued benefits for key employees under the plan exceeds 60 percent of the present value of the cumulative accrued benefits for all employees or, in the case of a defined contribution plan, if the aggregate amount of the accounts of key employees under the plan exceeds 60 percent of the aggregate of the accounts of all employees under the plan.[86] "Key employees" are defined to mean any participant in the plan who, during the plan year or during any of the four preceeding plan years, is an officer of the employer, one of the ten employees owning the largest interest in the employer, a 5-percent owner of the employer, or a one-percent owner of the employer having an annual compensation from the employer of more than $150,000.[87] Thus, a top-heavy plan in simplest terms is one that provides more than 60 percent of the present value of its benefits to officers or owner-employees. These requirements will generally have the most applicabil-

---

[85] See generally I.R.C. § 416.

[86] I.R.C. § 416(g)(1).

[87] I.R.C. § 416(i)(1)(A).

ity in the case of smaller employers, where the retirement plans are designed to primarily benefit owners or key officers.

If the plan is denominated as a top-heavy plan, several significant limitations become effective. First, such a plan is required to adopt either a vesting schedule, under which all employees with three years of service are 100 percent vested, or a six-year graded vesting plan, in which an employee with two years of service is 20 percent vested and vests an additional 20 percent per year so that he or she is 100 percent vested after six or more years of service.[88] In addition, a top-heavy plan must provide certain minimum benefits to all participants who are not key employees. In the case of a defined benefit plan, this means the lesser of 2 percent multiplied by the number of years of service with the employer or 20 percent of the employee's average compensation for the high five years.[89] In the case of a defined contribution plan, the employer is required to make minimum contributions of at least 3 percent of compensation for non-key employees.[90] Such plans cannot take social security contributions into account in meeting these minimum benefit requirements.[91] The other major limitation upon top-heavy plans is that the plan cannot take more than $200,000 of annual compensation into account.[92] This $200,000 limitation is adjusted for cost of living increases in the same manner as the benefit limitations under Section 415.[93]

The top-heavy plan requirements will impact most severely on highly compensated employees because of the additional requirements that such plans will impose upon the corporate employer. Because of these additional vesting and minimum contribution requirements for non-key employees, many corporate and noncorporate employers who

---

[88] I.R.C. § 416(b)(1).

[89] I.R.C. § 416(c)(1).

[90] I.R.C. § 416(c)(2).

[91] I.R.C. § 416(e).

[92] I.R.C. § 416(d)(1).

[93] In addition, if a top-heavy group maintains multiple plans, the 125 percent limitation contained in I.R.C. §§ 415(e)(2)(B) and 415(e)(3)(B) must be adjusted downward to 100 percent unless both the minimum benefits and contributions on behalf of non-key employees are increased by an additional percentage point and no more than 90 percent of the aggregate benefits and account balances are provided to key employees. I.R.C. § 416(h)(2). Thus, for example, the minimum contribution percentage on a defined contribution plan would be 4 percent rather than 3 percent and the minimum benefit on the defined benefit plans would be at least 3 percent per year rather than 2 percent.

fit into this category are likely to reconsider the question of whether it is appropriate to maintain a qualified plan or whether benefits under such a plan should be reduced. In other words, by imposing these additional requirements for non-key employees, the cost of maintaining such a plan will be greatly increased. In many cases, this is likely to lead the corporate employer to either terminate an existing qualified plan or to reduce overall benefits under it. In either case, there will be a negative impact upon the highly compensated executive currently covered under a qualified plan that now becomes subject to these rules.

Moreover, because of the elimination of the special Keogh plan qualification requirements and the application of the top-heavy plan rules to both Keogh and corporate plans, a major incentive to do business in the corporate form will have been eliminated. Consequently, it is likely that many highly compensated professionals will now choose not to incorporate.

¶ 5.04 Income Taxation of Distributions From Qualified Plans

Because of the extensive requirements of ERISA relating to the design and operation of qualified plans — most notably the antidiscrimination provisions — and because the highly compensated individual may not have significant input as to the plan design, tax planning with respect to qualified plans often is limited to an analysis of the income tax and estate tax [94] consequences of distributions from such plans. The factors that are generally most relevant to these planning considerations are the form of the distribution, its timing, and a choice of beneficiary for payments that do not directly go to the plan participant. The first component in making this analysis is an understanding of the income tax treatment of the various methods of distribution from a qualified plan.

[1] Annuities or Periodic Payments

Distributions from a qualified plan that do not constitute a lump-sum distribution [95] are, by virtue of Section 402(a)(1), taxable under Section 72 of the Code as annuities. This latter section provides that

---

[94] Discussed at ¶ 14.05.
[95] Discussed at ¶ 5.04[2].

annuities are generally taxed as if each payment constituted both a recovery of the annuitant's cost of the contract and taxable income. The ratio of the annuitant's investment in the contract to the total anticipated return under the contract provides the exclusion ratio that determines the nontaxable portion of each annuity payment.[96] Thus, under the typical annuity arrangement, each payment is considered partially a recovery of the annuitant's investment in the contract and partially a distribution of taxable income based upon gains provided by the annuity. An exception is made to this method of taxation where the employee's or annuitant's investment in the contract will be entirely recovered in the first three years of payment.[97] In this situation, the employee will recover his investment in the contract on a tax-free basis during this three-year period and all subsequent payments will be taxable to him.

Thus, in simplest terms, all annuity distributions from a qualified plan will be taxable to the recipient unless the employee has made an investment in the annuity contract.[98] Usually, but not always, such an investment will occur when there is a contributory type of plan. If the employee has made contributions to the plan, such contributions will be returned tax-free. If these contributions will be recovered within the first three years from the annuity starting date, there will be no taxable income received until all such payments have been recovered. If the amount of such payments will not be recovered within the three-year period, they will be considered as being received pro rata over the expected life of the annuity payments and, consequently, a portion of each year's payments will be considered a tax-free recovery of basis. Annuity payments under most qualified plans tend to fall within the three-year rule either because the employer has made all contributions

---

[96] I.R.C. § 72(b).

[97] I.R.C. § 72(d).

[98] I.R.C. § 72(p), which was added by the 1982 Act, treats loans from qualified plans as a taxable distribution under the Section 72 annuity rules. This requirement does not apply to the extent that a loan (when added to the outstanding balance of all other loans from the plan made on, before or after August 13, 1982) does not exceed the lesser of $50,000 or one-half of the present value of the employee's nonforfeitable accrued benefit (but not less than $10,000). This exception will not be applicable unless the loan by its terms is required to be repaid within five years. A five-year repayment requirement does not apply to any loan used to acquire, reconstruct, or substantially rehabilitate any dwelling unit that is to be used as a principal residence of the participant or a member of his family. This rule is applicable to loans made on or after August 13, 1982.

to the plan or because the ratio of employee to employer contributions is relatively small.

Although the employee's investment in the contract will basically consist of his own contributions to the retirement plan, certain employer contributions will be considered as part of this investment. In determining the amounts contributed by the employee, his investment will also consist of the amounts contributed by his employer that were includable in the gross income of the employee.[99] The major effect of this rule is to include such items as life insurance protection provided under a qualified plan (which is taxable to the employee) as a portion of his investment in the contract. The regulations [100] provide that the amount includable in gross income of the employee for life insurance protection is considered as premiums or other consideration paid or contributed by the employee only with respect to the benefits attributable to the contract providing life insurance protection.[101] Thus, to the extent that an employee is taxed on life insurance protection provided by a qualified plan, this will be considered as consideration paid by him as part of his investment in the contract.[102]

Also, it should be noted that in determining an employee's investment in the contract in order to offset income, this investment in the contract can only be used to offset payments made under the same contract. The regulations provide that each separate program of the employer consisting of interrelated contributions and benefits is considered a separate contract.[103] In a situation where an employee has previously included amounts in income representing insurance protection under an insurance policy and where the cash surrender value of the policy plus amounts from an investment account were used to purchase an annuity contract, the Service held that the employee's investment in the contract did not include those amounts previously taken into income.[104] The Service rationalized that the consideration

---

[99] I.R.C. § 72(f).

[100] Treas. Reg. § 1.72-16(b)(4).

[101] The income taxation of life insurance protection provided under a qualified plan is discussed extensively at ¶ 6.05.

[102] Treas. Reg. § 1.72-16(b)(4) also provides that life insurance protection included in the gross income of an owner-employee under a Keogh plan is not treated as part of that owner-employee's investment in the contract.

[103] Treas. Reg. § 1.72-2(a)(3). This rule is applicable to distributions commencing after October 20, 1960.

[104] Rev. Rul. 67-336, 1967-2 C.B. 66.

paid by the employee was for life insurance protection under the surrendered policy as opposed to the separate annuity contract that was purchased with the cash surrender value of the policy plus investment account funds. Consequently, although life insurance protection provided under a retirement income contract will be considered part of the employee's investment in that contract, it is important that the payments be considered to have been made under a single contract in order to increase the amount that may be recovered tax-free by the employee.[105]

[2] Lump-Sum Distributions

A lump-sum distribution, as defined in Section 402(e)(4)(A) of the Code, is subject to favorable income tax treatment in several respects. A portion of the lump-sum distribution may be subject to capital gain taxation with a maximum tax rate of 20 percent. The remainder can be subject to tax under a special ten-year forward averaging provision that has the effect of greatly reducing the impact of income taxes upon the distribution. In addition, there may be excluded from income at the time of the distribution the net unrealized appreciation attributable to any securities of the employer corporation that are being distributed. Consequently, in order to undertake a proper decision as to the form of distribution from a qualified plan, it is necessary to understand these special tax rules that are applicable to lump-sum distributions.

[a] Definition of Lump-Sum Distributions. The first step in determining the taxation of lump-sum distributions is to determine precisely which type of distribution qualifies for taxation under Section 402(e)(4)(A). This section defines a lump-sum distribution to be a distribution or payment within one taxable year of the recipient of the balance to the credit of an employee, which becomes payable to the recipient on account of the employee's death, after the employee attains age 59½, on account of the employee's separation from service, or after the employee has become disabled (within the meaning of Section

---

[105] See also Rev. Rul. 68-647, 1968-2 C.B. 47, which finds a single contract where the employee could transfer contributions made on his behalf between a variable annuity fund and a fixed income fund under the same program. In this Revenue Ruling, the Service considered the variable annuity fund and fixed annuity fund as part of a single interrelated program and thus a single contract for purposes of I.R.C. § 72.

72(m)(7)). The payment must be from a trust that forms part of a qualified retirement plan. The statute further specifies that for purposes of this section, the balance to the credit of the employee does not include the accumulated deductible employee contributions under the plan. Each of these major requirements is discussed below.

[i] **One taxable year of the recipient.** The first requirement for qualification as a lump-sum distribution is that the distribution be within one taxable year of the participant.[106] It should be noted at the outset that this does not require that the distribution be made in one payment — only that the payments be received in one taxable year. It also should be noted that there is no requirement that the payment be made in the same taxable year as the prescribed event that triggers the distribution. Thus, an employee could retire from service on December 31 of a given year and receive a lump-sum distribution the following January without loss of ability to be taxed under the lump-sum distribution provisions.

[ii] **Balance to the credit of the employee.** The second requirement for lump-sum distribution treatment as described in Section 402(e)(4)(A) is that the distribution constitute the balance to the credit of the employee, which becomes payable because of one of the specified events. This requirement is imposed at the time that distribution or payment commences.[107] The proposed regulations take the position that a distribution made before the death of the employee will not preclude an amount paid on account of the death of the employee from being treated as a lump-sum distribution by the recipient.[108] Thus, if an employee had received annuity payments prior to this death and, upon his death, a lump-sum distribution were paid to his widow, this distribution would be treated as a distribution of the balance to the credit of the employee. In addition, lump-sum distribution treatment is accorded a distribution if an additional amount is paid for the last year of service at a later date. The proposed regulations with respect to lump-sum distributions [109] took the position that lump-sum treatment was not available if payments were made to more than one person unless the

---

[106] I.R.C. § 402(e)(4)(A).

[107] Prop. Reg. § 1.402(e)-2(d)(1)(ii)(A).

[108] Prop. Reg. § 1.402(e)-2(d)(1)(ii)(B).

[109] Prop. Reg. § 1.402(e)-2(d)(1)(iii).

entire amount of the distribution was included in the income of the employee on whose account the distribution was made. The Service has announced, however, that final regulations under this section will allow lump-sum distributions in a situation where there are multiple distributees.[110]

[iii] **Qualifying reasons for payment.** Lump-sum distribution treatment is available only if the payment is made to the recipient for one of the reasons specified in Section 402(e)(4)(A). The acceptable reasons for payment are (1) death of the employee, (2) attainment of age 59½ (or later), (3) employee's separation from service, or (4) disability.[111] Separation from service as a triggering event is inapplicable in the case of self-employed individuals and owner-employees, and the disability requirement is only applicable in a case of such individuals.

Most of the controversy surrounding these requirements has related to the question of whether there has been a separation from service. This controversy usually arose in one of two situations: (1) if the employee continued to render some services to his employer or (2) in a corporate reorganization where an employee was performing the same job but technically for a different corporate employer. In considering whether or not an individual who is continuing to render services has separated from service, the critical factor usually is whether or not an employee-employer relationship has been maintained.[112]

In *Estate of Fry v. Commissioner,*[113] it was held that a lump-sum distribution was not on account of separation from service where the employee continued to work for his employer subsequent to reaching retirement age and after receiving the distribution. However, where an employee agreed to render part-time consulting service for an employer subsequent to retirement, lump-sum distribution treatment was accorded.[114] In this latter situation the consulting contract specified that the individual would not be subject to the direction and control of his former employer. This is the usual factor that is applied to determine

---

[110] See T.I.R. 1426 (Dec. 15, 1975).

[111] That is, within the meaning of I.R.C. § 72(m)(7).

[112] But see Rev. Rul. 81-26, 1981-1 C.B. 200, where a change in an individual's status from employee to partner was not considered a separation from service even though he would not technically be considered an employee for employment tax purposes.

[113] 19 T.C. 461 (1952), aff'd, 205 F.2d 517 (3d Cir. 1953).

[114] See Rev. Rul. 69-647, 1969-2 C.B. 100.

whether an employee-employer relationship exists and is critical in determining whether there is a separation from service.

The other major area of controversy as to whether there has been a separation from service occurs where there has been a corporate acquisition or reorganization. The Service's most recent position on this controversy is expressed in Rev. Rul. 79-336.[115] In this ruling, the former employer transferred all of its assets to a new employer, who continued the business that was previously conducted. The employees received their full account balances under the previous employer's profit-sharing plan but continued to work at their same jobs. On this set of facts, the Service held that there was not a separation from service and, therefore, lump-sum distribution treatment was unavailable.[116] This distribution could, however, qualify for a tax-free rollover if the requirements of Section 402(a)(5) and 402(a)(6)(B) were met. The Service has also held this principle applicable to the situation in which an employee performs the same services for a partnership that succeeded his corporate employer.[117] It must be noted, however, that if the employee whose separation from service is being questioned has reached the age of 59½, the distribution will qualify for lump-sum distribution treatment because of having satisfied the age requirement. Consequently, the question of whether or not there has been a separation from service is primarily critical for employees who are less than that age.

With respect to the lump-sum treatment because of death, a distribution will qualify under Section 402(e)(4)(A) regardless of the employee actually having received prior distributions. In addition, the five-year participation requirement [118] is waived with respect to distributions occurring by reason of death.

[iv] Five-year participation requirement. An employee must have been a plan participant for five or more taxable years preceding

---

[115] 1979-2 C.B. 187.

[116] See Gegax v. Comm'r, 73 T.C. 329 (1979). The Tax Court has adopted the Service's position that a separation from service does not occur when an employee continues in the same job after the employer has changed as a result of a corporate acquisition or reorganization.

[117] Rev. Rul. 80-129, 1980-1 C.B. 86. See also Rev. Rul. 81-141, 1981-1 C.B. 204, where there was not separation from service when an employee continued working for a subsidiary corporation after it was transferred to new owners.

[118] Discussed at ¶ 5.04[2][a][iv].

the taxable year of the distribution in order to be eligible for lump-sum distribution treatment.[119] Thus, if an amount that would otherwise be a lump-sum distribution is distributed to an employee who has completed only four taxable years of participation in the plan before the first day of the taxable year in which the amount was distributed, that employee is not entitled to use the provisions of Section 402(e) with respect to the amount distributed.[120] The five-year requirement is not applicable for purposes of determining capital gains treatment for the distribution with respect to pre-1974 participation. It only affects the employee's ability to use the ten-year forward averaging provision of Section 402(e)(1).

[b] Capital Gains Taxation on Pre-1974 Benefits. The portion of the lump-sum distribution attributable in whole or in part to pre-1974 participation in the employer's plan will be subject to taxation at capital gains rates.[121] The amount subject to capital gains taxation is determined by multiplying the total amount of the distribution by a fraction, the numerator of which is the number of calendar years of active plan participation prior to 1974 and the denominator of which is the total number of calendar years of active plan participation.[122] The amount that is potentially subject to capital gains taxation is not dependent on the actual amount of contributions made prior to 1974 but rather upon the ratio of the number of years of pre-1974 participation to the number of years of total participation. Consequently, for the participant in a qualified retirement plan whose coverage under the plan predates 1974, a significant amount of the lump-sum distribution may be subject to taxation at favorable capital gains rates. If, as is usually the case, the dollars contributed have increased steadily over time, it is likely that the

---

[119] I.R.C. § 402(e)(4)(H).

[120] Prop. Reg. § 1.402(e)-2(e)(3).

[121] I.R.C. § 402(a)(2).

[122] Prop. Reg. § 1.402(e)-2(d)(3)(ii) takes the position that the number of calendar years of active plan participation shall be the number of calendar months during the period beginning on the first month in which the employee became a participant under a plan and ending with the earliest of (1) the month in which the employee receives a lump-sum distribution under the plan, (2) in the case of an employee who is an employee within the meaning of I.R.C. § 402(c)(1), the month in which the employee separates from service, (3) the month in which the employee dies, or (4) in the case of an employee within the meaning of Section 401(c)(1), who receives a lump-sum distribution on account of disability, the first month in which he becomes disabled within the meaning of I.R.C. § 72(m)(7).

number of dollars subject to capital gains taxation will be far greater than the number actually contributed prior to 1974.

[c] Ten-Year Forward Averaging Rule. The portion of the lump-sum distribution attributable to post-1973 participation in a qualified plan will be taxed as ordinary income, subject to the taxpayer's option to elect the ten-year forward averaging provisions of Section 402(e). This provision treats that portion of the lump-sum distribution as if it were received evenly over a ten-year period and taxes it separately from other income. The tax is computed by multiplying 10 times the tax that would be due on $2,300,[123] plus one tenth of the total taxable amount over the minimum distribution allowance.[124] This tax is multiplied by a fraction which consists of the ordinary income portion of the distribution [125] over the total taxable amount. The effect of this calculation is to tax the lump-sum distribution at substantially lower rates than would be applied if the entire distribution was bunched into one year and taxed in the same manner as any other ordinary income.[126]

As was alluded to above, lump-sum distributions less than $70,000 are subject to a minimum distribution allowance.[127] This allowance is the lesser of $10,000 or one-half of the total taxable amount reduced by 20 percent of the amount by which the total taxable amount exceeds $20,000. The minimum distribution allowance further tends to reduce the tax on smaller distributions. However, by virtue of the formula just discussed, the allowance is completely phased out for distributions in excess of $70,000.[128]

In order to receive the benefits of the ten-year forward averaging for lump-sum distributions, the taxpayer must make an election. This

---

[123] This is the zero-bracket amount for single individuals.

[124] I.R.C. § 402(e)(1)(C). The total taxable amount is defined in I.R.C. § 402(e)(4)(D) to be the amount of the lump-sum distribution that exceeds the sum of the amounts considered to be contributed by the employee and the net unrealized appreciation attributable to the distribution which consists of securities of the employer corporation.

[125] That is, based on post-1973 years of active participation in the plan.

[126] This is particularly the case if the recipient has substantial amounts of other income.

[127] I.R.C. § 402(e)(1)(D).

[128] When the lump-sum distribution is paid as a death benefit, the amount subject to the ten-year averaging is reduced by the amount of the estate tax deduction attributable to the distribution under I.R.C. § 691(c). This is discussed in more detail at ¶ 14.02[3][b][iii].

¶ 5.04[2][c]

election is made by filing Form 4972 as part of the taxpayer's income tax return for the taxable year.[129] The proposed regulations also take the position that not more than one election may be made under this Section with respect to an employee after such employee has attained age 59½.[130]

In addition to the election to have the portion of the lump-sum distribution attributable to post-1973 participation taxed under the ten-year forward averaging provision, a taxpayer may also elect to have the entire distribution taxed pursuant to this provision in lieu of having the pre-1974 portion taxed as a capital gain.[131] This election, once made, is irrevocable and is applicable to all lump-sum distributions. The election to treat the lump-sum distribution as subject to the ten-year forward averaging provisions will not be made available if an employee had received a distribution after December 31, 1975, a portion of which was treated as long-term capital gain.[132]

An analysis of which method of taxation should be elected with respect to a lump-sum distribution generally requires a computation of the applicable tax under each of the aforementioned methods in order to determine which one will be most favorable to a particular taxpayer. Typically, it will be advantageous to elect the ten-year forward averaging provisions as opposed to merely being taxed under normal methods of computation. On the other hand, the choice between capital gains taxation for pre-1974 participation, as opposed to having the entire distribution taxed under Section 402(e), is not always so clear. A calculation should be made under both methods — particularly because of the irrevocability of an election to treat the whole distribution as subject to Section 402(e). The reduction in the maximum rate of capital gains taxation to 20 percent (as well as a similar cap upon the alternative minimum tax) has made capital gains taxation more favorable than had been the case prior to 1981. On the other hand, the 1981 Act also reduced tax rates significantly for all individuals and the alternate minimum tax will be applicable to the capital gains portion. Consequently, the only intelligent manner of making a choice between the two forms of taxation on pre-1974 distributions is to make both calculations with respect to the taxpayer for the year in question and to similarly

---

[129] Prop. Reg. § 1.402(e)-3(c)(2).
[130] Prop. Reg. § 1.402(e)-3(a).
[131] I.R.C. § 402(e)(4)(L).
[132] Prop. Reg. § 1.402(e)-14(b).

evaluate the estate tax consequences. The tax advisor should, however, be aware that this alternative exists and should explore its possibilities carefully prior to filing the return for the year in which the lump-sum distribution is received.

[d] Unrealized Appreciation on Employer Securities. The net unrealized appreciation attributable to any portion of a lump-sum distribution that consists of employer securities is excluded from income of the recipient.[133] This nontaxability holds true even if the recipient has not been a participant in the plan for five years as is normally required by Section 402(e)(4)(H).[134] It should be noted, however, that this complete exclusion for unrealized appreciation of employer securities is only applicable in the case of a lump-sum distribution. For a distribution that does not qualify for lump sum treatment, only the unrealized appreciation attributable to amounts contributed by the employee is so excluded.[135]

This exclusion has the effect of postponing taxation on those securities until they are sold or otherwise disposed of in a taxable transaction. The regulations [136] indicate that the gain on a subsequent transaction attributable to the unrealized appreciation will qualify for long-term capital gain treatment at the time of disposition irrespective of the holding period of the stock. Any gain in excess of the amount of net unrealized appreciation will be considered long-term or short-term capital gain, depending upon the holding period of the securities in the hands of the distributee.[137] The Service has ruled that this holding period begins on the date of distribution to the employee rather than on the date that the plan allocated stock to the employee's account.[138] The effect of these rules is to allow the gain attributable to net unrealized appreciation at the time of the lump-sum distribution to be always taxed at capital gains rates at a time and manner to be selected by the employee.

---

[133] I.R.C. § 402(e)(4)(D)(ii) excludes from the definition of the total taxable amount received on a lump-sum distribution the net unrealized appreciation attributable to that part of the distribution which consists of the securities of the employer corporation so distributed.

[134] I.R.C. § 402(e)(4)(J).

[135] I.R.C. § 402(a)(1).

[136] Treas. Reg. § 1.402(a)-1(b)(1)(i).

[137] Id.

[138] Rev. Rul. 81-122, 1981-1 C.B. 202.

If the employer securities received in the distribution have a fair market value that is less than the employee's contribution, the Service has ruled that no deductible loss is sustained upon a distribution of these securities from a qualified plan.[139] In this ruling, the Service took the position that the distribution of the securities does not constitute a closed and completed transaction within the meaning of Section 165 until the distributee subsequently disposes of the stock in a sale or exchange. The Service did indicate, however, that the employee may recognize this loss on a subsequent sale or exchange.[140] In the situation where the distribution consisted of the worthless stock of a bankrupt employer, the Service has considered the transaction to be closed and thus eligible for loss treatment.[141]

For purposes of the lump-sum distribution rules, the meanings of the terms "securities" and "securities of the employer corporation" are determined by reference to Section 402(a)(3).[142] That section defines the securities to mean only shares of stocks and bonds or debentures issued by a corporation with interest coupons in registered form and includes securities of both a parent and a subsidiary corporation of the employer corporation.[143]

Most problems concerning whether or not a participant has received shares of his employer corporation relate to the situation where there has been a corporate reorganization in one form or another. For example, Rev. Rul. 73-29 [144] considered the situation where employees, who worked in a portion of a business that was sold to an acquiring corporation, became employees of the purchasing corporation. In this situation, shares of stock of their former employer were held previously by a trust of a qualified plan while the participant was an employee of that company. On this set of facts, the Service ruled that a subsequent transfer of the assets in their accounts to the acquiring corporation's profit-sharing trust did not change the status of the shares as securities of the employer corporation. In another ruling, where a

---

[139] Rev. Rul. 71-251, 1971-1 C.B. 129.

[140] The Service has ruled that this same principle requiring the nonrecognition of a loss applies to a distribution from a qualified plan of nonemployer stock having fair market value less than the employee's contribution. Rev. Rul. 72-15, 1972-1 C.B. 114.

[141] Rev. Rul. 72-328, 1972-2 C.B. 224.

[142] I.R.C. § 402(e)(4)(K).

[143] I.R.C. §§ 402(a)(3)(A), 402(a)(3)(B). The term "subsidiary corporation" is defined in I.R.C. § 425(f).

[144] 1973-1 C.B. 198.

successor corporation had exchanged its stock for stock of the former corporate employer held by the employee's trust, the shares of this corporation were held to be securities of the employer corporation for purposes of Section 402(a)(1).[145] However, it should be noted that if, at the time of the merger, the participant employee elects to withdraw his securities from the qualified plan, it is possible that the distribution will not be considered a lump-sum distribution and only the net unrealized appreciation attributable to employee contributions would be excludable.[146]

[3] Choosing the Form of a Distribution

It should be evident from the preceding discussion that the different income tax consequences of a distribution in the form of an annuity and a distribution in the form of a lump sum (and, indeed, the difference in taxation that can be applicable to a lump-sum distribution) creates the opportunity for income tax planning with respect to the distribution. Consequently, it is incumbent upon the highly compensated individual and his advisor to weigh these tax consequences and, consistent with the individual's economic needs, make a determination of the most favorable form of payment. In many circumstances, the lump-sum distribution will produce the most favorable income tax consequences because the ten-year forward averaging method is computed as a separate tax and because the pre-1974 portion of the distribution may be taxed at the capital gains rate, which cannot exceed 20 percent. This will be particularly true if the recipient of the income has significant amounts of other income. On the other hand, if the recipient's income is likely to drop significantly within the next year or so, and if there are employee contributions that will be recovered tax-free within the ambit of the three-year rule relating to the payment of annuities, the effective rate of taxation on the annuity distribution may not be as onerous as initially appears on the surface. A further income tax consideration may be the employee's ability to receive a lump-sum distribution and roll it over into an individual retirement account.[147]

At the time the decisions are being made as to the most favorable

---

[145] Rev. Rul. 73-312, 1973-2 C.B. 142.

[146] See Rev. Rul. 72-440, 1972-2 C.B. 225. In this ruling, the Service rationalized that inasmuch as the distribution did not result from a separation from service, it did not qualify as a lump-sum distribution within the meaning of I.R.C. § 402(e)(4)(A).

[147] See generally ¶ 5.05.

income tax consequences of a distribution from a qualified plan, care must be taken not to overlook the estate tax consequences of the same decision.[148] Generally speaking, the payment of benefits in the form of an annuity will mean that the first $100,000 of benefits which remain to be paid to the survivor will not be subject to estate tax because of the provisions of Section 2039(c). On the other hand, immediate receipt of a lump-sum distribution will move the proceeds into the taxable estate of the recipient and potentially subject it to estate tax. In addition, if the employee's beneficiary will receive a lump-sum distribution at his death, an estate tax exclusion may be obtained, but only at the expense of forgoing favorable income tax treatment.[149] Consequently, these estate tax consequences should not be overlooked when reviewing the income tax consequences of the various distribution alternatives.

A final factor to be considered in determining the form of distribution is the potential investment opportunities and growth available to the qualified plan proceeds. If the plan participant received a lump-sum distribution, he or she may be able to invest the net proceeds available after taxes and achieve a significant rate of return. On the other hand, the annuity payable by the plan, or an election to receive benefits in installments, may or may not credit a comparable rate of return in determining the precise amount of the annuity payable to both the employee and the survivor.[150] Personal health factors may also enter into this analysis. For example, if a particular plan does not offer a term-certain option with respect to its annuities, and if both the employee-participant and his spouse are in poor health, it may make more economic sense to receive a lump-sum distribution because of limited life expectancies. Only after an analysis of all these factors — income tax consequences, estate tax consequences, and economic factors — have been weighed can a decision be made as to the preferable form of payment of the employee's benefit in the qualified plan. Because the size of these potential benefits in the case of a highly compensated individual is likely to be quite significant, considerable care should be used in making this determination.

---

[148] These tax consequences are extensively discussed at ¶ 14.05.

[149] See generally, I.R.C. § 2039(f) and the discussion at ¶ 14.05.

[150] Any such earnings on amounts that remain with the plan will, of course, accumulate tax-free until distributed.

¶ 5.05 Rollovers

As an alternative to the tax treatment of lump-sum distributions (discussed at ¶ 5.04[2]) the recipient of a lump-sum distribution may elect to postpone taxation on the amount received by rolling it over into an IRA or other eligible retirement plan as described in Section 402(a)(5)(D)(iv). The effect of such a rollover will be to postpone taxation on the amount so received until the funds are actually withdrawn from the IRA.[151] This can allow for the additional tax-free accumulation of funds.

[1] Section 402(a)(5) Rollovers

Section 402(a)(5) of the Code permits an employee to defer the receipt of taxable income if the balance to the credit of an employee in a qualified trust is paid to him in a qualifying rollover distribution, if the employee transfers any portion of that property he receives in such a distribution to an eligible retirement plan, and, in the case of a distribution of property other than money, if the amount so transferred consists of the property distributed.[152] In order to avoid taxation, the transfer to the eligible retirement plan must be made within sixty days following receipt of the property.[153] A qualifying rollover distribution is one or more distributions made within one taxable year of the employee on account of (1) termination of the plan in which the trust is a part,[154] (2) a lump-sum distribution, or (3) a distribution of accumulated deductible employee contributions within the meaning of Section 72(o)(5).[155] In the case of lump-sum distribution, the five-year active participation requirement that is normally applicable to such distributions is waived for rollover purposes.

The term "eligible retirement plan" is defined to mean an individual retirement account, an individual retirement annuity described in Section 408(b), a retirement bond described in Section 409, a qualified

---

[151] The taxation of IRAs is discussed generally at ¶ 5.06.

[152] The transferee may also sell the property distributed to him and transfer an amount equal to the proceeds of the sale into an eligible retirement plan. I.R.C. § 402(a)(6)(D).

[153] I.R.C. § 402(a)(5)(C).

[154] In the case of a profit-sharing or stock bonus plan, a rollover qualifies if there is a complete discontinuance of contributions under such plan.

[155] I.R.C. § 402(a)(5)(D).

trust, and an annuity plan described in Section 403(a).[156] Thus, the employee has a good deal of latitude as to the type of plan into which he can transfer the proceeds. It also should be noted that the statute specifically authorizes partial rollovers. Accordingly, it is possible for the employee to retain a portion of the lump-sum distribution that is distributed to him and transfer the remainder into another vehicle such as an IRA. This does give the employee the flexibility to defer taxation on a portion of the lump-sum distribution that is received.[157] If the employee does take advantage of a partial rollover, he will lose the ability to use the ten-year averaging provisions for the remaining portion that is taken into income.[158] It also should be noted that employee contributions cannot be rolled over, although the earnings on such contributions may be transferred to an eligible retirement plan.

The availability of the rollover provisions offers another unique tax planning opportunity to the highly compensated individual to defer income tax on the amounts that have been accrued for his benefit under a qualified plan. Under these provisions, an employee may receive a lump-sum distribution upon retirement — say, at age 65 — and transfer the amount received into an IRA. As will be more fully discussed at ¶ 5.06, distributions from this IRA need not commence until the individual reaches the age of 70½ — thereby offering the opportunity for tax-free accumulation of funds for several more years. This technique may be particularly useful if the individual employee has substantial amounts of income from other sources, such as a deferred compensation plan, and will have no actual need for the funds during that period. Although the ability of an individual to use this technique is largely dependent on his economic ability to forgo immediate receipt of the funds, in the appropriate case the rollover may be a valuable item of tax planning.

The rollover technique may also be especially valuable in the situation where an individual is in receipt of a lump-sum distribution because of the termination of a qualified plan in which he is a participant. In this case, the rollover will avoid the premature recognition of income and permit the participant to continue the tax-free accumulation of funds until a normal retirement age. In this respect it may also facilitate the sale of closely held businesses in the situation where major

---

[156] I.R.C. § 402(a)(5)(D)(iv).

[157] The 1982 Act permits partial rollovers on distributions from an IRA. I.R.C. § 408(d)(3)(D).

[158] I.R.C. § 402(a)(6)(C).

stockholders might otherwise be concerned about the tax consequences flowing from the termination of a qualified plan upon this sale. As such, the rollover provisions may encourage an otherwise prudent economic move by the owners of a closely held business by not creating a concern as to the income tax consequences of the discontinuance of their qualified plan.

[2] Rollovers by Spouse Upon Death of Plan Participant

Section 402(a)(7) permits a rollover in a situation where a spouse receives a lump-sum distribution from a qualified plan on the death of a participant. If the distribution is received in property other than money, the amount transferred must also consist of the property distributed. In the case of a 402(a)(7) rollover, the transfer must be made to an individual retirement plan.[159] Accordingly, in the case where the spouse of a deceased plan participant receives a substantial lump-sum distribution, Section 402(a)(7) presents an attractive tax planning option. The recipient may elect to have the distribution taxed under the favorable rules applicable to lump-sum distributions or, in the alternative, may elect to defer income taxation by rolling the amount so received into an IRA. The latter option may be especially valuable if the spouse has considerable other resources and thus is able to benefit from the further tax-free buildup of funds in the IRA.

¶ 5.06 Individual Retirement Accounts (IRAs)

An Individual Retirement Account, or IRA, has become the generic name for an individually directed and established savings program that permits individuals having earned income and their spouses to make tax-deductible contributions to a retirement savings program. This program is in many respects similar to a qualified plan. These retirement savings programs, as any casual reader of advertisements by financial institutions will note, can permit a significant tax-free accumulation of funds. Because of this opportunity, the IRA is a tax

---

[159] A spousal rollover under I.R.C. § 402(a)(7) may also contain estate tax advantages. I.R.C. § 2039(f)(2) provides an estate tax exclusion for lump-sum distributions if the recipient elects to treat the distribution "as taxable under Section 402(a) (without the application of paragraph (2) hereof)." Since the rollover rules are contained in I.R.C. § 402(a)(7), a spouse seemingly would not have to forgo the estate tax exclusion in order to take advantage of the rollover provisions. See generally ¶ 14.05.

planning and savings device that should be seriously considered by virtually every highly compensated individual.

[1] Qualification Requirements

There are several types of plans that can be described under the generic heading of IRA. These include individual retirement accounts described in Section 408(a), individual retirement annuities described in Section 408(b), and retirement bonds described in Section 409. Of these various types of accounts, the most popular by far is the individual retirement account, as most typically offered by financial institutions, insurance companies, and brokerage houses.

[a] Individual Retirement Accounts. An individual retirement account is described in Section 408(a) as a trust created or organized in the United States for the exclusive benefit of an individual or his beneficiaries that meets the following requirements:[160]

(1) Except in the case of rollover contributions, no contribution will be accepted unless it is in cash and is not in excess of $2,000 on behalf of any individual;

(2) The trustee is a bank or other person who demonstrates to the satisfaction of the Secretary of the Treasury that it will administer the trust consistent with the requirements of Section 408;

(3) No part of the trust funds will be invested in life insurance contracts;

(4) The interest of the individual in the balance of his account is nonforfeitable;

(5) The assets of the trust will not be commingled with other property except in a common trust fund or investment fund;

(6) The entire interest of an individual for whose benefit the trust is maintained will be distributed to him no later than the close of the taxable year in which he attains the age of 70½, or will be distributed over the life of such individual, or the life of such individual and his spouse, or over a period not extending beyond the life expectancy of such individual and his spouse; and

(7) If an individual for whose benefit the trust is established dies before the entire interest has been distributed to him or prior to the

---

[160] See generally I.R.C. § 408(a).

commencement of the distribution, the entire interest or the remainder will be distributed within five years after his death or after the death of his surviving spouse.[161]

Prior to the enactment of the 1981 Act, an individual could not make tax-deductible contributions to an IRA if he was also a participant in a qualified plan. The original concept behind the enactment of the IRA provisions was to allow a means of retirement savings for individuals who were not participants in other qualified plans. Indeed, the deduction limits on IRAs were purposefully set relatively low so as to not encourage organizations to avoid the establishment of qualified plans because their executives could contribute large sums of money to IRAs. Although the concept of relatively low limits on IRA contributions has not changed, the requirement prohibiting contributions to IRAs if an individual is also a participant in a qualified plan has been removed. Accordingly, a highly compensated individual or any other participant in a qualified plan may now make tax-deductible contributions to an IRA in addition to his participation in a qualified plan.

[b] Individual Retirement Annuities. An individual retirement annuity is an annuity contract or an endowment contract issued by an insurance company that meets the following requirements:[162]

(1) The contract is not transferable by the owner;

(2) Under the contract the premiums are not fixed, the annual premium on behalf of any individual will not exceed $2,000, and any refund of premiums will be applied before the close of the calendar year following the year of the refund toward the payment of future premiums or the purchase of additional benefits;

(3) The entire interest of the owner will be distributed to him no later than the close of the taxable year in which he attains the age of $70\frac{1}{2}$, or will be distributed over the life of the owner or the lives of the owner and his spouse over a period not extending beyond the life expectancy of the owner or the life expectancy of the owner and his spouse;

(4) If the owner dies before his entire interest is distributed to him or prior to the commencement of distributions, the entire interest or the

---

[161] I.R.C. § 408(a)(7). This requirement is inapplicable if distributions over a term certain commenced before the death of the individual for whose benefit the trust was maintained and the term certain was within the limitations of I.R.C. § 408(a)(6).

[162] See generally I.R.C. § 408(b).

remaining portion will be distributed within five years after his death or the death of his surviving spouse;[163] and

(5) The entire interest of the owner is nonforfeitable.

The individual retirement annuity is thus an IRA purchased in the form of an annuity contract that contains relatively similar requirements to those relating to individual retirement accounts. The individual retirement annuity provides an alternative vehicle for the accumulation of retirement benefits as opposed to the IRA, which is typically invested in an interest-bearing account, certificate of deposit, or more traditional investments, such as stocks or bonds.

[c] **Individual Retirement Bonds.** A third type of individual retirement arrangement is a retirement bond described in Section 409. This bond is an obligation issued by the U.S. Government under the Second Liberty Bond Act, which by its terms or by regulation provides (1) for the payment of interest or investment yield only upon redemption, (2) that no interest is payable if the bond is redeemed within twelve months after its issuance, (3) that it ceases to bear interest or will provide investment yield on the earlier of (a) the date on which the individual in whose name it is purchased attains age 70½ or (b) five years after the date on which the registered owner dies but not later than the date on which he would have attained age 70½ had he lived, and (4) that the registered owner may not contribute on behalf of any person for the purchase of such bonds in excess of $2,000 for any taxable year and is not transferable.[164]

Although individual retirement bonds do offer the additional advantage of being exempt from state taxation, they basically have found limited acceptance as an individual retirement vehicle because of the difference between the interest rates available on such bonds and that which is available from other commercial sources. Because of this factor, such retirement bond programs are now virtually extinct.

[2] Income Tax Consequences

[a] **Deductibility of Contributions.** The 1981 Act increased the allowable deduction for a contribution to an IRA to the lesser of $2,000

---

[163] I.R.C. § 408(b). Again, the five-year requirement is waived if distributions for a term certain commenced before the death of the owner and the term certain is within the ambit of I.R.C. § 408(b)(3).

[164] I.R.C. § 409(a).

or an amount equal to the compensation includable in an individual's gross income for the taxable year.[165] Thus, any individual with at least $2,000 of earned income in a calendar year may contribute up to that amount annually to an individual retirement account and receive a deduction for it. This ability to make a tax-deductible contribution to an IRA is available, irrespective of the fact that the individual is also a participant in a qualified plan. Alternatively, a participant in a qualified plan may claim a deduction for voluntary contributions to the qualified plan up to the IRA limitations if his plan permits him to do so. In order to be entitled to the deduction, the taxpayer's contribution must be made no later than the due date, including extensions, for his tax return for the year.[166] The IRA contribution is deductible from gross income and consequently is available to a taxpayer even if he does not itemize deductions.[167]

In lieu of the foregoing, an individual may establish a so-called spousal IRA, which allows an individual with a nonworking spouse to make a deductible contribution up to the lesser of $2,250 or 100 percent of compensation.[168] In order to establish a spousal IRA, the working spouse must establish either a single IRA in which he and his spouse have separate subaccounts or establish separate IRAs for each spouse. Prior to the 1981 Act, all contributions were required to be allocated 50 percent to the account of each spouse. Under current law, however, so long as $250 is allocated to the account of each spouse, the remainder of the contribution may be allocated in any proportion so desired.

An IRA operates similarly to a qualified plan in that the earnings of the IRA account are not taxable to the participant or the trust so long as they remain in the IRA account. This, of course, permits the individual's contribution to not only provide a tax deduction for the year when made but also to grow and compound on a tax-free basis so long as it remains within the retirement plan.

[b] Distributions from IRAs. Essentially, all distributions from an IRA account are taxable to the recipient. When an individual commences to withdraw funds that have been accumulated in the IRA account, he will be considered to have received ordinary income and will be taxed accordingly. Lump-sum distributions from an IRA are not

---

[165] I.R.C. § 219(b)(1).
[166] I.R.C. § 219(f)(3).
[167] I.R.C. § 62(10).
[168] I.R.C. § 219(c).

subject to the ten-year forward averaging provisions that are contained in Section 402(e)(4)(A). Thus, a lump-sum distribution from an IRA may produce unfavorable income tax consequences because of the bunching of income involved. Although income averaging may somewhat ameliorate the effect of this bunching, this is one factor to consider when weighing the consequences of whether or not to rollover a lump-sum distribution from a qualified plan into an IRA account.[169] If that rollover contribution is made, taxation of the distribution from an IRA will not be subject to the favorable income tax treatment provided by Section 402(e)(4)(A).[170]

As was noted earlier, distributions from an IRA must commence no later than the time at which the participant reaches the age of 70½. In addition, if a distribution is made from an IRA to an individual for whose benefit the account or annuity was established prior to the individual reaching the age of 59½, the proceeds will be taxable and the recipient will also be obligated to pay a penalty equal to 10 percent of the amount of distribution includable in his gross income.[171] This provision is designed to discourage the use of IRAs to accumulate tax-free funds that are then distributed at the participant's discretion. It also ensures that the IRA is used as a retirement savings vehicle. The 10-percent penalty tax is not applicable, however, in the case of disability.[172] The penalty tax is also not applicable to a distribution at death, inasmuch as the distribution in such a case could not be made to the individual who had established the account.

---

[169] One technique sometimes used by a highly compensated individual who continues to consult with his former employer is to establish a consulting company with a qualified plan. This enables this individual to roll his distribution into a qualified plan rather than an IRA and thus preserve his ability to make a future lump-sum distribution subject to the ten-year forward averaging rules.

[170] It should be noted that for property acquired by an IRA after December 31, 1981, the acquisition by an IRA or by an individually directed account under a plan described in I.R.C. § 401(a) of any "collectible" will be treated as a distribution from the account in an amount equal to the cost of such collectible. I.R.C. § 408(n)(1). Collectibles are defined to be any work of art, rug or antique, metal or gem, stamp or coin, alcoholic beverage, or other tangible personal property specified in regulations or rulings issued by the Secretary. I.R.C. § 408(m)(2). This provision has effectively eliminated the future investment by IRAs in such collectibles.

[171] I.R.C. § 408(f)(1).
[172] I.R.C. § 408(f)(3).

[3] General Planning Comments

The IRA offers a unique tax planning opportunity to the highly compensated individual in that it provides a vehicle to make tax-deductible contributions that will subsequently produce earnings that will not be taxed until distribution to the participant or his beneficiaries. The IRA also offers estate tax advantages that are discussed at ¶ 14.05[3]. Although the $2,000 (or $2,250, in the case of a spousal IRA) contribution limit is relatively low, a contribution of even this amount over the period of many years, when compounded at high rates of interest, will produce a very substantial accumulation of funds. Consequently, the highly compensated individual is likely to find a significant tax advantage in the establishment of an IRA even if he is also a participant in a qualified plan or other deferred compensation arrangement. In virtually all cases, unless the individual has an acute cash shortage, the establishment of an IRA will almost always be recommended.[173] If the highly compensated individual is not a participant in a qualified plan, the establishment of an IRA would appear to be almost mandatory — both as a means of tax savings and as a method of accumulating some funds for retirement years.

---

[173] There is no requirement for the regularity of contributions to an IRA account. Unlike the situation with a qualified plan, a highly compensated individual may make contributions to his IRA account in some years and none in others depending upon his cash requirements, or he may vary the amounts contributed each year for the same reason. The IRA thus offers considerable flexibility in the amount and timing of contributions.

CHAPTER 6

Income Taxation of Life Insurance

		Page
¶ 6.01	Introduction	6-2
¶ 6.02	Income Tax Consequences of Life Insurance	6-2
	[1] Taxation of Life Insurance Proceeds	6-3
	[2] Deductibility of Premium Payments	6-5
	[3] Exchange of Policies	6-6
	[4] Systematic Borrowing of Cash Value	6-7
	[a] Denial of Interest Deduction	6-7
	[b] Exceptions to Denial of Interest Deduction	6-8
	[i] Four-out-of-seven exception	6-8
	[ii] The $100 exception	6-9
	[iii] Unforeseen events exception	6-9
	[iv] Trade or business exception	6-10
¶ 6.03	Group Term Life Insurance — Section 79	6-11
	[1] Taxability to the Employee	6-12
	[a] General Rule of Taxability	6-12
	[b] Exceptions to General Rule of Taxability	6-13
	[i] Terminated and retired employees	6-13
	[ii] Employer or charity as beneficiary	6-14
	[iii] Insurance in qualified plans	6-14
	[2] Requirements to Qualify Under Section 79	6-14
	[3] Groups of Fewer Than Ten Employees	6-17
	[4] Permanent Insurance Coverage Under a Group Term Plan	6-19
	[5] Coverage for Spouse or Children	6-20
¶ 6.04	Split-Dollar Insurance	6-20
	[1] Description	6-20
	[2] Income Tax Consequences	6-21
	[3] Income Tax Planning	6-24
¶ 6.05	Life Insurance in Qualified Plans	6-26
	[1] Limitations on Coverage	6-27
	[2] Income Taxation of Value of Insurance in Qualified Plans	6-28

		Page
[3]	Income Taxation of Death Benefits	6-29
[4]	Planning Aspects	6-30
¶ 6.06	Retired Lives Reserve	6-31
[1]	Description	6-32
[2]	Income Taxation	6-32
[3]	Funding Vehicles	6-33
¶ 6.07	Key-Man Insurance	6-35

¶ 6.01 Introduction

It is rare that a corporate employer does not maintain some form of group term coverage for its employees. With perhaps the exception of health insurance plans, no type of fringe benefit is as common as employer-provided life insurance. Life insurance also has been frequently used to fund qualified pension or profit-sharing plans. In addition, other types of insurance programs have been developed that are more specifically aimed at providing coverage for the highly compensated employee. Included among these are split-dollar insurance plans, retired lives reserve plans, and key-man insurance.

Life insurance as a fringe benefit has become quite popular among highly compensated employees. Not only does this coverage provide the economic protection enabling an employee's beneficiaries to maintain an accustomed standard of living, but these various plans can also provide substantial income tax benefits to the employee.

This chapter reviews the income taxation of life insurance plans, with particular emphasis on those plans that are most commonly provided as a corporate fringe benefit. It first discusses the basic income tax consequences that flow from the purchase of life insurance policies and the receipt of the proceeds from such policies. Specific forms of employer-provided coverage are then reviewed. Included in this review are Section 79 plans, split-dollar insurance, insurance in qualified plans, retired lives reserve, and key-man insurance. Estate planning in regard to life insurance is not discussed in this chapter, but rather is reviewed extensively in Chapter 13.

¶ 6.02 Income Tax Consequences of Life Insurance

Before discussing the income tax planning for life insurance as a fringe benefit, it is proper to review the general income tax characteristics associated with buying and holding it.

[1] Taxation of Life Insurance Proceeds

Section 101(a)(1) of the Code provides a general rule that the proceeds of a life insurance contract payable upon death of the insured do not create taxable income. Consequently, even though the beneficiaries of a life insurance policy may realize a substantial economic gain by the receipt of the proceeds, this gain will not generally be taxable. Treasury regulations have extended this exclusion to death benefit payments having characteristics of life insurance — proceeds payable by reason of death under contracts such as workman's compensation insurance or accident and health insurance.[1]

The exclusion from income taxation of life insurance proceeds does not, however, apply in a case where a policy has been transferred for valuable consideration.[2] In such a case, the amount excluded from gross income is limited to the actual value of the consideration paid, plus the premiums or other amounts subsequently paid by the transferee. For example, if someone were to purchase a $100,000 life insurance policy from the insured for $5,000 and subsequently pay an additional $5,000 in premiums prior to the death of the insured, the transferee would receive taxable income of $90,000 ($100,000 proceeds less $5,000 consideration, less $5,000 premium payments).

To complicate matters further, the Code makes the transfer for valuable consideration rule inapplicable in two situations: (1) if the basis of the contract in the hands of the transferee is determined in whole or in part by reference to the basis in the hands of the transferor and (2) if such transfer is to the insured, a partner of the insured, a partnership in which the insured is a partner, or a corporation in which the insured is a shareholder or officer.[3] Thus, if a corporation receives a life insurance policy as a result of a tax-free reorganization, the transfer for valuable consideration rule will not be applicable. Similarly, if an insured individual sells his life insurance policy to his partnership or to a corporation in which he is a shareholder or officer, the proceeds will be allowed the full exclusion provided by Section 101(a)(1).

The regulations [4] provide that in a case of a gratuitous transfer of a life insurance contract, the amount of the proceeds excludable under

---

[1] Treas. Reg. § 1.101-1(a)(1).
[2] I.R.C. § 101(a)(2).
[3] I.R.C. §§ 101(a)(2)(A), 101(a)(2)(B).
[4] Treas. Reg. § 1.101-1(b)(2).

Section 101(a)(1) is limited to the amount that would have been excludable by the transferor if no such transfer had taken place, plus any premiums and other amounts subsequently paid by the transferee. The purpose of this regulation is to prevent an individual who owns an insurance policy, the proceeds of which will be taxable because it was purchased for valuable consideration, from circumventing this taxation by making a subsequent gift to a related transferee. For example, if an individual sold a $100,000 life insurance policy to an unrelated party for $5,000, and this buyer subsequently made a gift of this policy to his wife, the wife would be taxable on the proceeds received less the $5,000 paid and less any premiums subsequently paid by either the husband or the wife.[5]

If the beneficiary of a life insurance policy, the proceeds of which are excludable under Section 101(a)(1), chooses to receive the proceeds in a form other than a lump-sum payment, Sections 101(c) and 101(d) of the Code will affect the taxation of the proceeds, although they do not disturb the basic exclusion. Section 101(c) indicates that if the life insurance proceeds are left with an insurer under an agreement whereby interest payments will be paid thereon, the interest payments will be includable in gross income. This provision applies to payments of interest earned with respect to policy proceeds on any amount excluded from gross income held without substantial diminution of the principal amount during the period in which such interest payments are being made or credited to the beneficiaries of the policy.

Inasmuch as the interest payments on the policy proceeds held by the insurer will be fully taxable, the beneficiary should decide whether to leave the principal with the insurer, based upon the rate of interest paid and the security of the payor as compared to the return and safety of other available investment opportunities. Typically, the rate of interest paid by insurers is lower than can be obtained from comparable safe sources. If this is the case, the combination of higher rates available elsewhere and the fact that Section 101(c) makes the insurer's interest payments fully taxable would indicate that the most prudent course of action is to receive the entire proceeds in full (and tax-free) and invest them elsewhere.

If the beneficiary chooses to receive the principal amount in installments, Section 101(d) becomes applicable. This section states that the principal amount of the policy will be prorated and excluded from

---

[5] See Treas. Reg. § 1.101-1(b)(5), Ex. 6.

income, and any excess over this prorated amount will be taxable. Section 101(d)(1)(B) of the Code provides an additional exclusion, however, where the life insurance proceeds are being paid to the surviving spouse of the insured. In this situation, an additional $1,000 per year over the prorated principal amount will be excludable from income. This additional exclusion may prove to be beneficial to the spouse of a highly compensated individual who may herself be in a high tax bracket because of substantial inheritance or independent sources of income. This section will allow up to $1,000 of what is, in essence, interest to be excluded from the spouse's taxable income and can mean an additional tax savings of up to $500 per year. The additional exclusion, provided by Section 101(d)(1)(B), will not be available, however, if the entire principal amount is left with the insured so as to draw interest;[6] it is only applicable in a situation where there are prorated payments of principal. This additional exclusion should not, however, obscure a close analysis of the return actually being paid by the insurer. If the rate of return paid by the insurer is considerably below what can be obtained elsewhere, the additional tax savings generated by Section 101(d)(1)(B) may be more than counter-balanced by the income that is lost by not seeking investments with a greater rate of return.

[2] Deductibility of Premium Payments

Premium payments on personally owned life insurance policies are considered personal expenses and are not deductible by the insured. Thus, if an individual procures an insurance policy on his own life and makes the premium payments thereon, no tax benefit will ensue.[7] If, however, the premiums are paid by an employer for insurance on the life of an employee, these payments will be deductible by the employer as an ordinary and necessary business expense under Section 162 of the Code.[8] The major exceptions to this rule of deductibility in an employment context occur when the corporation itself is the beneficiary of the life insurance policy [9] or when amounts are paid or accrued as a result of

---

[6] I.R.C. § 101(c), as discussed above in this paragraph, governs this situation.

[7] If the insured designates a charity as the beneficiary of the policy, the premium payments will qualify as a charitable deduction.

[8] This assumes, of course, that the compensation paid by the employer is reasonable in amount.

[9] I.R.C. § 264(a)(1).

a plan that contemplates the systematic direct or indirect borrowing of all increases in cash value of the policy.[10] If the highly compensated individual also happens to be an owner or part owner of a business enterprise, the purchase of life insurance through the business enterprise will, under most circumstances, transform what is otherwise a nondeductible personal expense into a deductible item. This serves to explain one of the reasons for the popularity of life insurance as a fringe benefit.

Generally speaking, the purchase of a life insurance policy for the benefit of an employee will create taxable income to that employee. The major exception to this rule is in the case of the first $50,000 of group term insurance purchased under a plan that qualifies under Section 79 of the Code.[11] As later discussions in this chapter of the various types of insurance show, the amount of income taxable to the employee that is created by the insurance is frequently less than the actual cost of the insurance to the employer. In such a case, a very favorable tax situation is created — a full deduction for the cost of the insurance by the employer and a reduced amount of taxable income charged to the employee.

[3] Exchange of Policies

Section 1035 of the Code specifically provides that no gain or loss shall be recognized on (1) an exchange of a life insurance contract for another life insurance contract, (2) a contract of endowment insurance for another contract of endowment insurance that provides for regular payments beginning at a date not later than the date payments would have begun under the contract exchanged, (3) a contract of endowment insurance for an annuity contract, or (4) an annuity contract for another annuity contract. Section 1035 is only applicable to exchanges of the aforementioned policies on the same insured.[12] The regulations [13] similarly take the position that the exchange of an annuity contract for another annuity contract is limited to the case where the same person or persons are the obligee or obligees under the contract received in exchange as under the original contract. Section 1035 does not apply to transactions involving the exchange of an endowment contract or an

---

[10] I.R.C. § 264(a)(3). This is discussed extensively at ¶ 6.02[4].

[11] This is discussed extensively at ¶ 6.03.

[12] Treas. Reg. § 1.1035-1(c).

[13] Id.

annuity contract for a life insurance contract, nor does it apply to an annuity contract exchanged for an endowment contract. Accordingly, exchanges of the types of policies mentioned in Section 1035 for identical types of policies or for policies specifically mentioned as being permissible in an exchange that relates to the same insured individual may be made on a tax-free basis by the insured.

Section 1035 may be particularly valuable for those highly compensated individuals who are insured under older life insurance policies whose yield has become vastly outdated. In those instances, the insured individual can exchange the policy as outlined herein without any concern that the exchange will produce taxable income. If the insured had surrendered the policy for its cash surrender value, to the extent that the cash received exceeded total premiums paid (net of dividends), taxable income would have been created.

[4] Systematic Borrowing of Cash Value

[a] **Denial of Interest Deduction.** Section 264(a)(3) of the Code denies a deduction for any amount paid or accrued on indebtedness incurred or continued to purchase or carry a life insurance policy, endowment, or annuity contract [14] pursuant to a plan of purchase that contemplates a systematic, direct or indirect, borrowing of part or all of the increases in cash value of such contract either from the insurer or otherwise. After a whole life insurance policy has been in existence for two or three years, it is typical that the annual increments in the cash value of the policies are more than enough to make the annual premium payments for the policy. Thus, it is quite easy for the policy holder to finance the continued payment of premiums by borrowing against the policy an amount equal to the annual increment in the cash value. Section 264(a)(3) denies a deduction for the interest payments on such loans if they are found to be a part of a plan that contemplates systematic borrowing of this cash value increment. The amount of the deduction disallowed by this section is determined with reference to the entire amount of borrowing to purchase or carry the contract and is not limited to the borrowing of the increase in cash value.[15]

Unless a taxpayer can demonstrate otherwise, in a case of borrow-

---

[14] This is applicable to annuity contracts other than a single premium contract or contract treated as a single premium life insurance, endowment, or annuity contract that is covered by I.R.C. § 264(a)(2).

[15] Treas. Reg. § 1.264-4(b).

ing in connection with premiums for more than three years, the existence of a plan for systematic borrowing will be presumed.[16] In addition, such a plan may come into existence at any time during the seven-year period following the taxpayer's purchase of the insurance contract or following a substantial increase in premiums on the contract. The borrowing that constitutes such a plan may be by direct or indirect means.[17] For example, if an individual borrowed money from a bank to pay premiums on a life insurance contract and then borrowed an increase in cash value on the policy in order to repay the bank loans, this undoubtedly would be considered within the definition of an indirect plan under Section 264(a)(3) if done on a systematic basis.

[b] Exceptions to Denial of Interest Deduction. Section 264(c) of the Code sets forth four major exceptions to the denial of a deduction under Section 264(a)(3), which are discussed below.

[i] Four-out-of-seven exception. If four of the first annual premiums due during the initial seven-year period after the purchase of the policy are paid by a means other than indebtedness, Section 264(a)(3) will be inapplicable.[18] If there is a substantial increase in any annual premium on the contract, a new seven-year period begins to run.[19] If the taxpayer borrows an amount that is more than the annual premium on the policy, that borrowing will first be attributable to the current policy year, and then attributable to the premiums for prior policy years. Thus, the payment of the first four premiums will not necessarily provide a safe harbor to the taxpayer if, during the fifth year, the insured were to borrow the entire amount of the accrued cash value of the policy. This may be illustrated by the following example set forth in the Regulations:[20]

> Example 1. *A*, a calendar year taxpayer using the cash receipts and disbursements method of accounting, on January 1, 1964, purchases from a life insurance company a policy in the amount of $100,000 with an annual gross premium of $2,200. For the first four policy years, *A* initially pays the annual premium by means

---

[16] Treas. Reg. § 1.264-4(c)(1)(i).
[17] Treas. Reg. § 1.264-4(c)(2).
[18] I.R.C. § 264(c)(1).
[19] Treas. Reg. § 1.264-4(d)(1)(i).
[20] Treas. Reg. § 1.264-4(d)(1)(iv), Ex. 1.

other than borrowing. On January 1, 1968, pursuant to a plan referred to in paragraph (a) of this section, *A* borrows $10,000 with respect to the policy. Such borrowing is considered first attributable to paying the premium for the year 1968 and then attributable to paying the premiums for the years 1967, 1966, 1965 and 1964 (in part). No deduction is allowed for the interest paid by *A* on the $10,000 indebtedness during the year 1968.

Accordingly, by paying the premiums by means other than borrowing during four of the first seven years of the existence of an insurance contract, the taxpayer will fall within the safe harbor provisions of Section 264(c)(1) provided that in the remaining three years of the first seven, his borrowings with respect to the policy do not exceed the premium that is due in those years. If the borrowing in those three years does exceed the total amount of premiums due, the taxpayer may be surprised to find that the attribution of the indebtedness to an earlier policy year removes him from the Section 264(c)(1) exception.

[ii] **The $100 exception.** If the total amounts paid or accrued by an individual do not exceed $100, the deduction will not be disallowed.[21] This particular exception is of limited utility because of the extremely small amount involved. Because most highly compensated individuals have policies of such magnitude that the total amount of interest paid on the indebtedness would far exceed $100, this exception will rarely apply. Where the amount so paid or accrued during the taxable year exceeds $100, the entire amount is subject to the general rule of Section 264(a)(3).[22]

[iii] **Unforeseen events exception.** If the amount paid or accrued by the taxpayer on indebtedness was incurred because of an unforeseen substantial loss of a taxpayer's income or an unforeseen substantial increase in financial obligations, the deduction will not be denied.[23] The regulations [24] take a relatively stringent view as to what is or is not foreseeable. For example, it is indicated that college expenses are foreseeable. However, if college expenses substantially increase, then to the extent that such increases are unforeseen, this exception will apply. Other unforeseen expenses noted are unexpected medical

---

[21] I.R.C. § 264(c)(2).
[22] Treas. Reg. § 1.264-4(d)(2).
[23] I.R.C. § 264(c)(3).
[24] Treas. Reg. § 1.264-4(d)(3).

expenses or interest when the taxpayer is laid off from his job and, for that reason, systematically borrows against the cash value of a previously purchased contract.

Because this particular exception, by definition, relates to unforeseen events, it is difficult, if not impossible, to plan for its use. The existence of this exception may offer some assurance to a highly compensated taxpayer who has whole life policies in existence and is faced with unexpected expenditures or an unforeseen drop in income. In such a case, Section 264(c)(3) will offer some assurance that his interest deductions with respect to the borrowings will not be denied by virtue of a need to repeatedly take out policy loans to carry his life insurance policy.[25]

[iv] **Trade or business exception.** The final exception to the general denial of the deduction for systematic policy borrowing is the trade or business exception of Section 264(c)(4). In order to qualify under this exception, the indebtedness must be in connection with his trade or business and must be incurred to finance business obligations rather than to finance cash value life insurance. For example, if a taxpayer purchases life insurance as part of the collateral for a loan to finance the expansion of inventory or for capital improvements for his business, the deduction for interest on the loan will not be denied under Section 264(a)(3). Borrowing by a taxpayer to finance business life insurance such as key-man, split-dollar, or stock retirement plans is not considered to be incurred in conjunction with the taxpayer's trade or business within the meaning of this exception.[26]

This exception is perhaps the most difficult to interpret and is subject to the most controversy — particularly in the situation where ordinary business borrowings occur simultaneously with the purchase of life insurance policies. For example, the regulations discuss an instance where a corporation borrows substantial sums to carry on its business every year and also agrees to provide a retirement plan for the employees and purchases level premium life insurance to fund its obligation under the plan. The mere fact that the corporation purchases

---

[25] If the loss of income was caused by disability, the premiums may be automatically waived by a disability premium rider in the contract. In such a case, the borrowed proceeds would be available for other, and perhaps more pressing, purposes.

[26] Treas. Reg. § 1.264-4(d)(4).

cash-value life insurance will not cause its deduction for interest paid on its normal indebtedness to be denied, even though the policy is later used as part of the collateral for its normal indebtedness.[27] On the other hand, where a corporation maintained a retirement plan financed by the purchase of level premium whole life insurance and annually borrowed approximately 95 percent of the cash value of each policy in order to make premium payments under the plan, the borrowing was held not to be within the Section 264(c)(4) exception.[28] Thus, borrowing to fund an employee's retirement plan was not held to be an indebtedness incurred in connection with the employer's trade or business.

In one of the few cases decided under this section, a deduction was denied when an employer had purchased cash-value life insurance in order to secure payments under a corporate buy-out agreement and then systematically borrowed against the cash value of the policy.[29] The court stated that it was clearly the intent of Congress in creating the trade or business exception to Section 264(a)(3) not to allow a taxpayer to deduct interest on cash-value indebtedness incurred to finance the very insurance that created the cash value. The debt against the cash value must be incurred for a business purpose apart from the insurance plan itself before the interest paid becomes deductible under Section 264(c)(4).[30]

The trade or business exception will be available only in those instances where the utilization of the borrowing is clearly traced to business needs other than the carrying of the life insurance policies. Even if the policies themselves are used for a valid business purpose, such as the funding of a retirement plan or the funding of a buy-out agreement, the deduction will still be disallowed if the borrowing is undertaken merely as a means of carrying the policies themselves.

¶ 6.03 Group Term Life Insurance — Section 79

The most prevalent form of insurance provided by corporate employers is group term life. Term insurance has proven popular with corporate employers for many reasons. First, term insurance is the least

---

[27] Treas. Reg. § 1.264-4(d)(4), Ex. 1.

[28] Rev. Rul. 81-255, 1981-2 C.B. 79.

[29] American Body & Equip. Co. v. U.S., 511 F.2d 647 (5th Cir. 1975). The borrowings occurred during the first six years of the policy's existence.

[30] Id. at 649.

expensive form of insurance coverage, since it provides for no build-up of cash value. Consequently, the purchase of a group term policy by an employer enables it to provide the maximum amount of economic protection to its employees for the dollars that it is willing to spend on this particular fringe benefit. Second, unless there are problems of unreasonable compensation involved, the cost of this coverage is fully deductible by the employer for federal income tax purposes. Group term insurance is also relatively easy to administer, since it involves merely making beneficiary cards available to employees and the payment of premiums on a monthly basis. Finally, group term insurance does provide substantial income tax benefits to the covered employees. The precise form of these benefits and the requirements for qualification as group term insurance under Section 79 are discussed below.

[1] Taxability to the Employee

[a] General Rule of Taxability. If the particular form of insurance provided qualifies under Section 79 of the Code, the employee need only include the cost of this coverage in income to the extent that the insurance provided exceeds $50,000. In other words, the first $50,000 of group term insurance coverage may be provided tax-free to the employee. In addition to the exclusion of the first $50,000 of group term coverage, the cost of coverage in excess of this amount is "determined on the basis of uniform premiums (computed on the basis of five year age brackets) prescribed by Regulations by the Secretary."[31] These costs, as established in Table I of the regulations,[32] are often lower than the

---

[31] I.R.C. § 79(c).

[32] Treas. Reg. § 1.79-3(d)(2) sets forth these costs as follows:

Five-Year Age Bracket	Monthly Cost Per $1,000 of Insurance
Under 30	$ .08
30-34	.10
35-39	.14
40-44	.23
45-49	.40
50-54	.68
55-59	1.10
60-64	1.63

It should be noted that although these rates are low by historical standards, many newer term policies do charge rates that are considerably less than Table I rates.

actual cost of the insurance coverage. Accordingly, the amount of income that must be reported by the employee for this excess coverage may be less than the actual cost of the insurance. This means that it is possible for the employer, in many instances, to provide substantial insurance coverage to highly compensated individuals with very little out-of-pocket cost to that employee.[33]

[b] Exceptions to General Rule of Taxability. Section 79(b) provides three exceptions to this general rule of taxability for coverage in excess of $50,000.

[i] Terminated and retired employees. The first exception under Section 79(b) is for the cost of group term insurance on the life of an individual that is provided after the individual has terminated his employment with the employer and either has reached retirement age with respect to the employer or is disabled within the meaning of Section 72(m)(7).[34] An employee will be considered to have terminated employment when he no longer renders services to that employer as an employee.[35] If covered by a written pension or annuity plan, the employee will be considered to have reached retirement age when, under the plan, he can retire without the employer's consent and still receive immediate *full* retirement benefits, or when he has reached the age at which it is the practice of the employer to terminate members of his class of employees.[36]

If there is no retirement plan, the retirement age will be considered to be the age at which it has been the practice of the employer to terminate members of the class of employees to which the employee last

---

[33] The employee's out-of-pocket cost for the excess insurance coverage would only be his maximum tax bracket times the Table I cost of the excess insurance coverage provided.

[34] Section § 72(m)(7) of the Code provides that an individual will be considered to be disabled "if he is unable to engage in any substantial gainful activity by reason of any medically determinable, physical or mental impairment which can be expected to result in death or to be of long, continued, and indefinite duration. An individual shall not be considered to be disabled unless he furnishes proof of the existence thereof in such form and manner as the Secretary may require."

[35] Treas. Reg. § 1.79-2(b)(2). Thus, for example, an individual may be rendering services as a consultant or as an independent contractor to his former employer and yet be considered to have terminated employment.

[36] Treas. Reg. § 1.79-2(b)(3).

belonged, provided the age is reasonable in view of all the pertinent facts and circumstances. If neither of these factors is present, the retirement age will be considered to be 65. Consequently, post-retirement group term insurance coverage that satisfies these conditions as to termination of employment and retirement will be tax-free to the covered employee.

[ii] Employer or charity as beneficiary. The second exception under Section 79(b) is for the cost of any portion of group term life insurance on the life of the employee, provided that either the employer is directly or indirectly the beneficiary (which would make the cost of such policy nondeductible to the employer) or if a qualified charity described in Section 170(c) of the Code is the sole beneficiary. Thus, for example, if the insurance provided is key-man insurance and payable to the employer, the employee will not be required to take the cost of this excess coverage into income. This seems only fair and logical because the employee does not truly benefit by such a policy. The exception for policy proceeds payable to a qualified charity has a similar logical basis. Presumably, if the employee was required to take the cost of such insurance coverage into income, he could immediately deduct that cost as a charitable contribution. The net result of that would be the same as the noninclusionary language contained in Section 79(b)(2)(D).[37]

[iii] Insurance in qualified plans. The final exception under Section 79(b) is for the cost of any group life insurance provided under a contract to which Section 72(m)(3) applies. This refers to insurance protection provided under a qualified pension, profit-sharing, or stock bonus plan, or under a qualified annuity plan if the proceeds of such a contract are payable directly or indirectly to a participant in such trust or a beneficiary of such participant. In such a case, the taxability or nontaxability of this coverage will be determined under Section 72(m)(3) of the Code. This is discussed in detail at ¶ 6.05.

[2] Requirements to Qualify Under Section 79

In order to receive the favorable tax benefit provided by Section 79 of the Code, the life insurance provided must meet the definition of

---

[37] The regulations do clearly provide that the cost of insurance, which is not taken into income under this section, does not entitle the employee to a charitable deduction under Section 170. Treas. Reg. § 1.79-2(c)(3)(i).

group term life insurance set forth in the regulations [38] under Section 79. These requirements are:

(1) The insurance must provide a general death benefit that is excludable from gross income under Section 101(a) of the Code;

(2) The insurance is provided to a group of employees;

(3) The insurance is provided under a policy carried directly or indirectly by the employer;

(4) The amount of insurance provided to each employee must be computed under a formula that precludes individual selection.[39]

This formula must be based on factors such as age, years of service, compensation, or position. The condition that the formula must preclude individual selection is satisfied even if the amount of insurance provided is determined under a limited number of alternative schedules that are based on the amount each employee elects to contribute.

Accordingly, although a group term life insurance plan that qualifies under Section 79 must provide broadly based coverage, the uniform factors referred to above can allow an employer to design a plan that can provide considerably more coverage to the highly compensated individual than the bulk of other employees. For example, if coverage is based solely on compensation under a formula that provides insurance in an amount equal to five times salary, the individual who earns $10,000 must be provided with $50,000 worth of insurance coverage, whereas the executive earning $150,000 could be covered for $750,000. Other neutral factors, such as age, will also tend to favor the highly compensated employee in that such individuals tend to be long-service employees. Consequently, the Section 79 plan is frequently designed to provide substantial insurance benefits with favorable tax consequences to a highly compensated group of officer-employees.

---

[38] Treas. Reg. § 1.79-1(a).

[39] The requirement that the amount of insurance coverage must be computed pursuant to a formula that precludes individual selection was upheld by the Tax Court in Towne v. Comm'r, 78 T.C. 54 (1982). In *Towne,* a $500,000 policy on the life of the corporate president was superimposed upon a group term plan under which all other employees received coverage of one times salary with a maximum coverage of $25,000. The individual policy for the president was held not to be part of a plan of group term insurance. See Kunkle, "Tax Court in *Towne* Takes Tough Tack Toward Perceived Abuses in Group-Term Plans," 57 J. Tax'n 82 (1982).

Effective for taxable years beginning after December 31, 1983, the $50,000 exclusion for group term life insurance will not apply with respect to any key employee [40] if such a plan is found to be discriminatory [41] as to eligibility to participate or as to the type and amount of benefits available under the plan in favor of the key employees.

A plan will be found to be nondiscriminatory if such a plan benefits 70 percent or more of all employees of the employer, at least 85 percent of all employees who are participants under the plan are not key employees, or if such a plan benefits employees under a classification found by the Secretary not to be discriminatory in favor of key employees.[42] In the case of a group insurance plan that is part of a cafeteria plan, a plan may satisfy eligibility requirements by meeting the requirements of Section 125 of the Code. For purposes of determining compliance with these requirements, the employer may exclude employees who have not completed three years of service, who are part-time or seasonal employees, who are members of a collective bargaining unit,[43] and employees who are nonresident aliens and who received no earned income from the employer that constitutes income from sources within the United States.[44]

A plan will be nondiscriminatory as to benefits if the benefits available to all participants who are key employees are available to all other participants. Thus, a plan that provided the same benefits to both key employees and non-key employees clearly would be nondiscriminatory. Section 79(d)(5) does provide that a plan will not be discriminatory merely because the amount of life insurance of the employees under a plan bears a uniform relationship to the total or basic compensation of such employees. It can reasonably be expected that the Service will take the position that if a plan does not provide insurance in a uniform relationship to compensation, it will be considered discrimina-

---

[40] As defined in I.R.C. § 416(i)(1). A key employee is defined to mean any participant who at any time during the plan year or any of the four preceding plan years is an officer, one of the ten employees owning the largest interests in the employer, a five-percent owner of the employer, or a one-percent owner of the employer having compensation from the employer in excess of $150,000.

[41] I.R.C. § 79(d)(1).

[42] I.R.C. § 79(d)(3).

[43] If the benefits provided under the plan were the subject of good faith bargaining between the employee representatives and the employer.

[44] I.R.C. § 79(d)(3)(B).

tory. Consequently, the antidiscrimination rule will, in many instances, reduce the amount of group term life insurance that can be provided to a key employee and still preserve the $50,000 exclusion. Becuase of the relatively low rate of taxation on excess group term life insurance, the employer and the employee will have to weigh whether the $50,000 exclusion or the rate of taxation provided by the Section 79 plan is more valuable than the benefits of providing discriminatory amounts of insurance under a Section 79 plan to key employees. In most cases, it is likely that the conclusion will be to preserve the $50,000 exclusion, since the amount of insurance provided can bear a uniform relationship to compensation. In such cases, additional insurance can be provided outside of the ambit of the Section 79 group term plan.

[3] Groups of Fewer Than Ten Employees

Even if the aforementioned requirements for group term coverage are met, the policy cannot qualify as group term insurance unless, at some time during the calendar year, it is provided to at least ten full-time employees who are members of the group of employees.[45] This requirement will be waived if the following three conditions are met:

(1) The insurance is provided to all full-time employees of the employer, or if evidence of insurability affects eligibility, to all full-time employees who provide evidence of insurability satisfactory to the insurer;[46]

(2) The amount of insurance is computed either as a uniform percentage of compensation or on the basis of coverage brackets established by the insurer. In general, no bracket may exceed two and one-half times the next lower bracket, and the lowest bracket must be at least 10 percent of the highest bracket;[47] and

(3) Evidence of insurability affecting an employee's eligibility for insurance or the amount of insurance provided to that employee is limited to a medical questionnaire completed by the employee that does not require a physical examination.[48]

---

[45] Treas. Reg. § 1.79-1(c)(1).

[46] Id.

[47] The insurer may establish a separate schedule coverage for brackets for employees who are over age 65, but no bracket in the over age 65 schedule may exceed two and one-half times the next lower bracket, and the lowest bracket in the over age 65 schedule must be at least 10 percent of the highest bracket in the basic schedule.

[48] Treas. Reg. § 1.79-1(c)(2)(iii).

Employees need not be taken into account if they are denied insurance because they have not been employed for a waiting period specified in the policy (not to exceed six months), or if they are part-time employees whose customary employment is not for more than twenty hours in any week or five months in any calendar year, or because they have reached age 65.[49]

The basic thrust of these regulations is that group term insurance provided in a company that has ten or fewer full-time employees must meet somewhat more stringent requirements in order to qualify under Section 79. The Service has taken a more inflexible position with respect to qualification issues for a plan with ten or fewer employees. For example, where an insurer was bound, after insurability was established based solely on a medical questionnaire, to issue insurance for each employee in specified amounts at no more than a guaranteed premium and that premium could be reduced upon the employee's medical examination, the plan was held not to qualify as group term insurance under Section 79.[50] Similar restrictive rulings have been issued with respect to the limitations on the size of the insurance coverage provided. For example, a life insurance plan covering fewer than ten employees that would meet the requirements of the regulations only if all three of its coverage brackets were taken into account did not qualify as group term life insurance if no employee had ever been covered under the middle bracket provided under the plan.[51] Thus, proper brackets that prove to be illusory because they are never used by an employer will disqualify a plan with fewer than ten employees under Section 79.

Although the coverage that may be provided to a highly compensated employee is somewhat more restricted in the situation where there are ten or fewer employees, it is still possible to design a plan that provides generous coverage to corporate executives. For example, if the minimum amount of insurance provided under a plan were $30,000, it would be possible to provide up to $300,000 of coverage to highly paid corporate executives if the proper brackets were established throughout the plan.

---

[49] Treas. Reg. § 1.79-1(c)(4).
[50] Rev. Rul. 75-528, 1975-2 C.B. 35.
[51] Rev. Rul. 80-220, 1980-2 C.B. 35.

[4] Permanent Insurance Coverage Under a Group Term Plan

Considerable controversy has centered around whether an employer may provide permanent insurance in conjunction with a group term plan. This so-called group permanent insurance may only be provided under a plan that qualifies under Section 79 if the following requirements are met:

(1) It is designated in writing which part of the death benefit provided to each employee is group term life insurance;

(2) The part of the death benefit designated as group term life insurance is not less than the difference between the total death benefit provided under the policy and the employee's deemed death benefit at the end of the year;[52]

(3) The employee may elect to decline or drop the permanent benefits; and

(4) The death benefit designated as group term life insurance is not reduced because of an employee's election to decline or drop the permanent benefit.[53]

If Section 79 plans provide group permanent insurance, the permanent benefit is fully includable in the income of the employee under the formula set forth in the regulations. Inasmuch as this cost approximates the actual full cost of the permanent element of this insurance, it provides little or no tax benefit to that employee. Because of this, the provision of permanent insurance under a Section 79 plan does not find substantial favor among corporate employers who are seeking to provide special benefits for their highly compensated employees. It generally is much more favorable from an income tax standpoint to provide either additional term insurance under Section 79, which will only be taxed at the favorable Table I rates, or split-dollar life insurance [54] for the highly compensated executive.

---

[52] The deemed death benefit is computed under Treas. Reg. § 1.79-1(d).

[53] Treas. Reg. § 1.79-1(b)(1). The procedure to determine the cost of permanent benefits and deemed death benefits provided under the life insurance policies that include both group term life insurance and permanent benefits is set forth in Rev. Proc. 79-29, 1979-1 C.B. 571.

[54] See discussion at ¶ 6.04.

[5] Coverage for Spouse or Children

If a group plan does provide coverage to an employee's spouse and/or children, the employee may be taxable with respect to such coverage. If the coverage for a spouse or a child does not exceed $2,000, it will not be taxable to the employee.[55] If coverage is provided in excess of this amount, the cost of the entire amount of insurance coverage will be includable in the employee's gross income based on the Table I rates. Consequently, there is some benefit if dependent coverage is provided under a Section 79 plan in that a minimal amount may be excluded from income or, if coverage exceeds this minimal amount, the taxation of the entire proceeds will be at the Table I rates.[56] Although such coverage will not provide a substantial benefit to the highly compensated employee, it may be another small benefit to be added when developing a tax-favored package for corporate executives.

¶ 6.04 Split-Dollar Insurance

A popular fringe benefit for key executives in recent years has been the so-called split-dollar life insurance plan. This type of plan has gained popularity, not only for its income tax and estate planning benefits,[57] but also because it can be arranged for key employees on an individual basis and in a discriminatory fashion if desired.

[1] Description

Split-dollar insurance gains its name from the fact that both the benefits received from the insurance policy and the costs thereof are split between a corporate employer and the covered employee. Under the typical arrangement, the employer pays the portion of the premium equal to the annual increase in the policy's cash surrender value, and the employee pays the balance of the premium. Upon the death of the employee, the employer receives the portion of the insurance proceeds equal to the greater of the cash surrender value of the policy immediately prior to death or the total amount of premiums paid by that employer. The balance of the proceeds are paid to the designated beneficiary of the policy. Under this type of split-dollar plan, the only cost to the employer is the lost use of the money while it is tied up in the

---

[55] Treas. Reg. § 1.61-2(d)(2)(ii)(b).

[56] Treas. Reg. § 1.79-3(d)(2). These rates are set forth in note 32 supra.

[57] See generally discussion at ¶¶ 13.02–13.03.

policy. Pursuant to this basic split-dollar plan, the employee's required contributions are substantial in the early years of the policy before the cash value begins to accumulate. In later years, as the cash value builds, the employee's contributions drop—many times to nothing. Consequently, after the initial investment, the employee receives a considerable amount of insurance protection at little or no cost to him.

Because of the initial high outlay required of employees under the traditional split-dollar arrangement, other variations on the plan have been developed to relieve the employee's burden. One such arrangement is the level-contribution method whereby the employee contributes a level payment over the life of the policy rather than a variable amount. The level-premium variation results in the employee contributing less in the early years of the policy than he might under the basic split-dollar plan but more in the later years. Another common variation is for the employer to pay the entire cost of the policy premiums while still retaining a split-dollar interest (i.e., the cash value buildup) in the policy proceeds.

There are two basic structural patterns for implementing a split-dollar plan—the endorsement method and the collateral assignment method. Under the endorsement method, the employer becomes the owner of a policy on the employee's life and assumes responsibility for premium payments. The employer then enters into a split-dollar agreement with the employee whereby the employee agrees to reimburse his employer for the appropriate portion of the premiums. Typically, there is a special endorsement to the policy to protect the employee's rights under the plan.

The collateral assignment method involves the employee or a third party, such as the employee's spouse, becoming the owner of the policy. The employer then agrees to lend the employee an amount equal to the annual increment in the cash value of the policy. To secure this loan, the employee collaterally assigns the policy to the employer and agrees to repay the loan upon separation from service of the employee or upon death.

[2] Income Tax Consequences

The Service's position in regard to taxation of split-dollar arrangements is set forth in Rev. Rul. 64-328.[58] In essence, this ruling states that the employee must include in income the economic benefit of the

---

[58] 1964-2 C.B. 11, as amplified by Rev. Rul. 66-110, 1966-1 C.B. 12; Rev. Rul. 67-154, 1967-1 C.B. 11.

¶ 6.04[2]

insurance arrangement derived from employer contributions. The amount included in income is reduced to the extent that the employee contributes to the premium payments. This economic benefit is measured by the so-called P.S. 58 Tables, which have been published by the Service.[59] The P.S. 58 Tables contain the government's assumed rates for the purchase of term insurance at various ages. Consequently, if the rates on a particular policy are higher than those assumed in the P.S. 58 Tables, the employee is required to take into income only the amount set forth in the Table. This represents one of the potential tax benefits from a split-dollar arrangement and is discussed in more detail later.[60] If the insurance company's standard rates for initial issue individual one-year term policies are lower than the P.S. 58 rates, these lower rates may be used in the calculation of taxable income.[61]

In addition to the foregoing, the policy dividends on an insurance policy may present another potential source of taxable economic benefit to the employee. If the policy dividends are paid to the employee in cash, used to purchase paid-up additions in which the employee has a nonforfeitable interest, or used to purchase one-year term insurance under a so-called fifth dividend option, then the actual amount of any dividend used in any of these manners is taxable to the employee.[62] If the dividends are used to purchase paid-up additions to the policy and the employer is entitled to the cash value of these additions, only the cost of the insurance protection purchased for the employee with these dividends is a taxable economic benefit. If the dividends reduce the employer's contribution to the premium payments, then the dividend will not be taxable to the employee.

The Service has extended its position in regard to the taxation of a split-dollar plan to those situations in which the employee is an indirect beneficiary of the split-dollar arrangement. In Rev. Rul. 78-420,[63] the Service discussed two situations where an individual, other than the employee or former employee whose life was insured, was the owner of an insurance policy. In the first situation, a corporation entered into a split-dollar arrangement with a key employee. Upon his retirement, the taxpayer's son, who was also an employee of the corporation, became

---

[59] See Rev. Rul. 55-747, 1955-2 C.B. 228, as modified by Rev. Rul. 66-110, 1966-1 C.B. 12.

[60] See discussion at ¶ 6.04[3].

[61] Rev. Rul. 67-154, 1967-1 C.B. 11.

[62] Rev. Rul. 66-110, 1966-1 C.B. 12.

[63] 1978-2 C.B. 67.

the new owner of the life insurance policy on his father's life. In the second situation, the corporation had entered into a split-dollar arrangement with the wife of a taxpayer for the purchase of a life insurance policy that insured the life of her employee-husband. In both situations, it was held that the arrangements were of the type that was contemplated by Rev. Rul. 64-328. Consequently, in each case the taxpayer was required to include in income the value of the insurance protection in excess of the premiums paid by him.[64] In both cases the value of the insurance protection was deemed to be an economic benefit to the employee, although in one case he was not the insured and in the other he was not the policy owner.

Although a split-dollar arrangement may discriminate among employees, it is generally inadvisable to establish a split-dollar arrangement solely for the benefit of shareholders, and most particularly, if the shareholders are not employees. In Rev. Rul. 79-50,[65] the Service ruled that a split-dollar arrangement for a nonemployee shareholder required that the shareholder treat the value of the insurance protection as a distribution by the corporation to him. As a result, the split-dollar arrangement resulted in dividend treatment to the shareholder. The distinction between a dividend and additional compensation in this particular situation was undoubtedly more critical prior to the enactment of the Economic Recovery Tax Act of 1981 (the 1981 Act) when dividends were subject to taxation at a potentially higher rate of tax than was earned income. With the reduction of the maximum income-tax bracket to 50 percent, this distinction is no longer as critical as it was before. Nevertheless, Rev. Rul. 79-50 represents the Service's attempt to impute income in a split-dollar situation, irrespective of the technical arrangement that is devised. In other words, when a corporation enters into a split-dollar arrangement, the Service usually looks for an appropriate individual to charge with the income produced by the economic value of the insurance protection.

Finally, it should be noted that the employer is not allowed a deduction for any portion of the premium paid by it, since it is a beneficiary of the policy.[66] Consequently, although the employer may eventually recoup all dollars paid in a split-dollar arrangement once it

---

[64] In addition, the premiums deemed paid by the taxpayer were deemed to be transferred by the taxpayer to his wife for gift tax purposes and thus were subject to the gift tax.

[65] 1979-1 C.B. 138.

[66] See I.R.C. § 264(a)(1). See also Rev. Rul. 64-328, note 58 supra.

collects its allocable portion of the policy proceeds, the loss of the use of the money in the interim will not be mitigated by a deduction. This is true even though the employee may be required to take a certain portion of the premiums paid into income.

[3] Income Tax Planning

As was noted in the beginning of the discussion of split-dollar plans, these types of arrangements have become very popular in recent years. There are many reasons that underlie this increased popularity. From an employee's standpoint, a split-dollar arrangement offers the opportunity to obtain substantial insurance coverage at little or no cost — particularly in later years when the employer's contribution would cover all or virtually all of the premiums. In addition, since the trend is toward "employer pay all" variations on the split-dollar arrangement, this particular advantage is magnified.

Split-dollar plans hold two particularly salient advantages from the employer's standpoint. First, because there are no antidiscrimination requirements involved, a split-dollar plan can be individually tailored to reward key employees or a group of highly compensated executives. Thus, for example, a split-dollar plan can be instituted for upper-level corporate officers without the encumbrances that sometimes underlie a group insurance plan. Second, the employer will eventually recover the cost of its payments to the insurance company because of the cash buildup under the policy. Accordingly, its only cost is the lost use of the money paid for the policy prior to death or cancellation of the policy.[67] The significance of the loss of the use of the funds will vary depending upon the number of policies involved and the amount that the employer is required to invest in such policies. If, however, a restricted number of executives are covered by split-dollar plans, the employer will only have a limited amount of funds tied up in the policies.

The split-dollar arrangement may also provide certain income tax advantages to the employee, inasmuch as his taxable income in regard to the plan will be the P.S. 58 costs of the plan minus his contributions. If these P.S. 58 costs are less than the actual premium paid by the employer, the employee will receive a valuable benefit for a signifi-

---

[67] During periods of high interest rates or tight money, this factor obviously becomes more significant to many corporate employers. On the other hand, the detrimental aspects of loss of use of money can be alleviated somewhat if the employer is able to borrow against the policy.

cantly less tax cost than its actual value. This benefit will be particularly significant if the premiums charged for the policy are fairly high — for example, in the situation where the insured individual is rated in a high-risk category. Even if the P.S. 58 costs are not significantly lower than the actual premium paid, the employee will still obtain a valuable benefit in that his out-of-pocket costs for the insurance coverage will only be its tax cost — i.e., the amount he is required to take into income times his highest marginal rate bracket. For instance, if the monthly P.S. 58 costs on a particular insurance policy were $110 and if the insured were in a 50 percent rate bracket, his out-of-pocket costs for $110 worth of insurance per month would be only $55. If the actual monthly premiums on his policy were $200, the employee would be paying only approximately one fourth of the cost of the monthly premiums in order to obtain valuable insurance coverage. This gap between out-of-pocket cost and actual cost of the insurance policy illustrates one reason for the popularity of split-dollar plans. It should also be noted that it is possible for the employee to reduce his taxable income by paying part of the P.S. 58 costs himself.

One of the disadvantages of a split-dollar arrangement results from the annual increase in P.S. 58 costs as the insured grows older. The P.S. 58 costs move in the same direction as premiums on a term insurance policy and thus increase with age. This factor may or may not prove detrimental in a particular case. Inasmuch as the income of many highly compensated individuals increases with age, the employee presumably would have the increased economic ability to pay the taxes generated by the growing P.S. 58 costs. If these costs become burdensome, the split-dollar arrangement can be dropped or, in the alternative, the employer may give an annual bonus to the employee large enough to pay the taxes generated by the P.S. 58 costs. If a bonus arrangement is adopted, the employer should be careful not to tie it directly into the split-dollar arrangement, since the premium payments for such a plan are nondeductible. If the bonus is tied too closely to the split-dollar plan, the Service may take a position that it also is nondeductible as representing premium payments on the split-dollar insurance. If it is the employer's intention to present the employee with a bonus to cover the taxes generated by the P.S. 58 costs, it should merely pay annual bonuses in amounts not necessarily equal to the taxes generated by P.S. 58 premium costs, and should do so without any specific written agreement tying the bonuses into split-dollar arrangements.

In summary, a split-dollar plan can be an individually tailored arrangement, which provides both tax and economic benefits to the employee and allows the employer to eventually recover its payments under the plan upon disbursement of the policy proceeds. The wisdom of instituting a split-dollar arrangement in any particular case will of course depend on a tax and economic analysis of the facts relating to the particular employee's desirable coverage and the cost of the policy being proposed. A split-dollar plan should clearly be considered among the various alternative possibilities being weighed when designing an insurance package for key corporate executives.

¶ 6.05 Life Insurance in Qualified Plans

A further use of life insurance is to fund a death benefit under a qualified pension or profit-sharing plan.[68] Several factors have led to the inclusion of death benefits in the qualified plan. Perhaps the most significant of these was a desire to provide death benefit protection under the terms of the plan so as to protect the employee's family in the event of early death. In other words, the plan was looked at as not only a means of securing the retirement of a participant, but also as a means of providing protection to that participant's family if he did not live to reach retirement age. In addition, individual insurance policies were often used as a means of funding retirement benefits. As cash values accumulated under individual policies, this buildup in cash values could be used to pay a portion of the retirement benefits for those employees who lived to retirement age. Although this particular means of funding has receded because the rise in interest rates in recent years has made the return on many whole life policies obsolete, this particular reason for life insurance funding still remains viable in some cases. Funding a retirement plan with life insurance benefits was also used in many cases because of the ease of administration involved. An employer, in conjunction with its insurance carrier, could merely purchase the appropriate insurance policies necessary to fund a particular benefit and allow the insurance company to handle most of the administrative chores involved with the plan. Particularly in the case of

---

[68] This section will discuss the income tax consequences of and planning for life insurance used to fund a death benefit in a qualified pension or profit sharing plan. Tax planning related to qualified plans themselves is discussed in Chapter 5. A discussion of estate planning relative to qualified plans may be found at ¶ 14.05.

smaller employers, the ease of administration factor was quite sign)frcant in leading to a determination to utilize this form of funding.

In weighing the tax and fringe benefit value of the insurance coverage provided under a qualified plan, it is usually pertinent to make a comparison vis-à-vis the same type of coverage provided under a Section 79 plan.[69] Only by comparing the two types of coverage can an intelligent decision be made as to the most viable alternative in a particular case.

[1] Limitations on Coverage

A basic factor that affects the amount of life insurance protection that can be provided under a qualified plan is the requirement that the provision of such insurance must be incidental to the plan.[70] For a defined benefit or pension plan, the death benefits provided cannot exceed more than 100 times the projected monthly benefit under the plan.[71] Thus, if a participant is projected to receive a $2,000 a month pension benefit, the amount of life insurance protection provided under the plan cannot exceed $200,000. Under a defined contribution or profit-sharing plan, the whole life insurance premiums must be less than one-half the aggregate amount of employer contributions and forfeitures allocated to the employee's account.[72] In addition, at retirement, the ordinary life insurance policies held for the participant in a profit-sharing plan must be converted into cash, converted into an annuity, or distributed. This 50 percent limitation relates only to those contributions made during the last two years of the plan.[73] If term insurance is provided rather than whole life insurance, the limitation in

---

[69] This is discussed at ¶ 6.03. A good article comparing insurance coverage under a qualified plan with similar coverage under a Section 79 plan is found in Nasuti, "A Comparison of Life Insurance in Qualified Plans With Group Term and Group-Permanent Life Insurance in Section 79 Plans," 57 Taxes 602 (1979).

[70] Treas. Reg. § 1.401-1(b)(1)(i) (pension plan), Treas. Reg. § 1.401-1(b)(1)(ii) (profit sharing plans).

[71] Rev. Rul. 61-212, 1961-2 C.B. 20.

[72] Rev. Rul. 66-143, 1966-1 C.B. 79, as clarified by Rev. Rul. 68-31, 1968-1 C.B. 151.

[73] It should be noted, however, that the entire amount of voluntary contributions made by an employee may be used to purchase life insurance, Rev. Rul. 69-408, 1969-2 C.B. 59.

a case of a profit-sharing plan drops to 25 percent of the contributions and forfeitures allocated to a participant's account, rather than 50 percent. In contrast to the above-noted limitation, the amount of insurance provided under a Section 79 plan is only subject to the basic limitation that compensation paid to any employee must be a reasonable amount in order to be deducted.

[2] Income Taxation of Value of Insurance in Qualified Plans

If life insurance is provided under a qualified plan, the value of the pure life insurance protection must be included in the income of the participant for the taxable year in which the employer's contributions are applied for the purchase of such insurance.[74] The amount that is included in the income of the participant is calculated based on the P.S. 58 cost as published by the Service.[75] If the insurer's current premium rates for individual one-year term life insurance available to standard risks are lower than the P.S. 58 cost, these lower rates may be used provided they are the rates charged for initial insurance and are not dividend option rates such as those applicable to the fifth dividend option.[76]

If the insurance coverage is provided by a whole life policy, the amount of term insurance upon which the employee is taxed is based on the difference between the proceeds of life insurance payable to the participant and the cash value of the policy. For example, if the proceeds of the policy are $100,000 and the policy has a cash value of $32,000 at year end, the employee is considered to be covered by term insurance in the amount of $68,000. He would then be taxed on the value of $68,000 of insurance as calculated under the P.S. 58 Table.

Although an employer generally cannot make contributions to a qualified plan with respect to a retired employee, life insurance coverage may be continued on the life of a participant after retirement. It should be noted, however, that the P.S. 58 cost is relatively high after age 65 so that such continued coverage may produce unfavorable tax consequences to the retired employee. In contrast, under Section 79(b), the cost of group term life insurance is apparently not includable in the

---

[74] I.R.C. § 72(m)(3)(b).
[75] See Rev. Rul. 55-747, 1955-2 C.B. 228, Rev. Rul. 66-110, 1966-1 C.B. 12.
[76] See Rev. Rul. 67-154, note 61 supra.

income of the insured if he is no longer an employee and has either reached retirement age or has become permanently disabled.[77]

Looking solely at the question of current income taxation to the insured, group term insurance under Section 79 is obviously more beneficial than term insurance under a qualified plan. Section 79 coverage excludes the first $50,000 of coverage from taxation and coverage in excess of that amount is taxed under the Table I rates. In contrast, the P.S. 58 rates under which term coverage under a qualified plan are taxed create taxable income substantially in excess of the Table I rates. If permanent insurance is provided, however, a different result is obtained. No income is allocated to the employee in regard to the permanent portion of insurance coverage under a qualified plan. The cost of permanent insurance provided in conjunction with a Section 79 plan is fully taxable to the employee.

[3] Income Taxation of Death Benefits

A lump-sum distribution from a qualified plan attributable to life insurance will be excludable from income under Section 101(a)(1) of the Code to the extent that the insurance proceeds exceed the cash surrender value of the policy immediately prior to death.[78] The cash value portion of the policy will be taxed in accordance with the normal rules relative to the taxation of distributions from qualified plans.[79] Thus, in essence, the death benefits attributable to pure term insurance coverage under a qualified plan are excludable from income, whereas the cash benefit portion is potentially subject to taxation. The amount ineligible for the Section 101(a)(1) exclusion may be excluded from income, however, to the extent that the $5,000 death benefit exclusion of Section 101(b) is applicable or to the extent attributable to contributions by the employee. The P.S. 58 costs included in the income of the employee are deemed to have been a contribution by the employee for this purpose.[80]

If the distribution from a life insurance policy under a qualified plan is made other than in a form that qualifies as a lump sum under

---

[77] This exception to the normal rule of taxability to the employee is discussed at ¶ 6.03[1][b][i]. The concept of continuing group term coverage for retired employees under a retired lives reserve plan will be discussed in ¶ 6.06.

[78] Treas. Reg. § 1.72-16(c)(2)(ii).

[79] See generally ¶ 5.04.

[80] See Treas. Reg. §§ 1.72-16(b)(4) and 1.72-16(c)(3), Ex. 1.

Section 402(e)(4), all amounts distributed will be taxable when received to the extent that they exceed the beneficiary's basis in the policy. If a participant has included the cost of the pure insurance protection under the qualified plan in his gross income, this amount will be included as part of his basis that may be used to reduce the amount of income to the beneficiary that will be taxable.[81]

[4] Planning Aspects

In deciding whether or not to provide life insurance coverage as part of a qualified plan, there are three essential factors to be weighed, in addition to the value of the insurance protection provided. The first of these considerations is the potential use of the cash value of life insurance policies as a means of funding retirement payments and the use of such insurance to ease the administrative hassles of maintaining a qualified plan. These are considerations unrelated to the tax consequences of such coverage to the employee and mainly represent employer decisions related to the type and scope of the qualified retirement plan to be provided.

The second major consideration is the amount of insurance coverage that can be provided under a qualified plan relative to the needs of the employee. Because of the requirement that the insurance coverage provided by a qualified plan must be incidental to the other benefits provided, the limitations on coverage under such a plan may not allow the employer to provide the desired amount of coverage for key highly compensated employees.[82] This does not necessarily preclude the inclusion of life insurance coverage in a qualified plan, but may mean that additional coverage must be provided elsewhere.

The third factor is a comparison of the income tax costs and benefits of insurance under such a plan to alternate types of coverage, such as a Section 79 plan or a split-dollar arrangement. Generally speaking, Section 79 plans provide more favorable income tax treat-

---

[81] See Treas. Reg. § 1.72-8(a)(1). If this basis is recoverable within three years, all payments received are tax-free until the basis is recovered. I.R.C. § 72(d). If the contributions will not be recovered within three years, then the amount of such basis will be prorated over the period in which it is anticipated that the basis will be recovered.

[82] The antidiscrimination requirements of ERISA also preclude the design of such coverage solely to benefit highly compensated executives. See generally ¶ 5.03[1].

ment if pure term insurance is involved.[83] If, however, whole life insurance is involved, the qualified plan offers certain advantages in that the cost of the permanent element of the insurance is not included in the participant's income. In addition, a comparison with split-dollar insurance reveals that, although the employee will report taxable income under the P.S. 58 Tables under both types of plans, the contribution of an employer to a qualified plan will be deductible, whereas the payment under a split-dollar plan will not provide such a deduction to the employer. Accordingly, the provision of such whole life insurance under a qualified plan may produce more tax benefits to the corporate employer, although it will not be able to recoup a portion of the insurance proceeds as it will under the split-dollar plan.

Only after the employer has weighed all these factors can an intelligent decision relative to the best means of providing insurance coverage be reached. Because no one type of coverage provides a clear advantage in all instances, it is often the case that insurance coverage will be provided under several types of plans offered by the same employer.

¶ 6.06 Retired Lives Reserve

Because many employers drop their group term life insurance coverage for employees who retire, the retired employee may often find that he is faced with a substantial reduction in life insurance protection. Although other retirement benefits, such as payments under qualified pension and profit-sharing plans or deferred compensation plans, may be scheduled to commence upon retirement, the employee may often feel that the loss of life insurance protection will create an economic uncertainty for his dependents. Although the possibility exists that the employee can purchase insurance coverage, term insurance at the normal retirement age is prohibitively expensive or possibly unobtainable due to insurability problems. Accordingly, compensation planners frequently perceive a need to design a benefit package to retain some

---

[83] Insurance under a qualified plan may offer some estate tax benefits because of the exclusion of certain distributions from a qualified plan from the estate tax under Section 2039(c). Lump-sum distributions from a plan may be excluded from a decedent's gross estate if they are not payable to the decedent's estate and if the recipient elects to forgo the ten-year forward averaging income treatment. The estate taxation of distributions for qualified plans will be discussed more extensively in ¶ 14.05.

form of life insurance protection for retired employees. This has led to the development of the retired lives reserve concept.

[1] Description

A retired lives reserve is a fund established by an employer to provide a means of funding the cost of continued group term insurance benefits for retired employees. The fund allows the employer to allocate the cost of providing term insurance to retired employees over the working lifetimes of those employees on, presumably, a level-premium basis. Under this plan, the employer makes annual contributions to the fund during the employee's working years in an amount necessary to continue post-retirement insurance coverage. Upon retirement, the fund will make payments to the insurer in order to sustain coverage.

[2] Income Taxation

The employer's contributions to a retired lives reserve will be deductible in the year paid or accrued if the contributions meet the requirements established by the Service in various rulings. In order to be deductible, the following requirements must be met:

(1) The balance in the reserve fund must be held solely for the purpose of providing life insurance coverage for active or retired employees as long as any active or retired employee remains alive;

(2) The amount added to the fund is no greater than an amount that would otherwise be required to fairly allocate the cost of the life insurance coverage provided over the working lives of the employees insured under the fund; and

(3) The employer has no right to recapture any portion of the monies in the retired lives fund so long as any active or retired employee remains alive.[84]

In order to avoid distortions of the employer's taxable income, payments made to the reserve fund must be actuarially determined and made on a level basis.[85] Contributions to the retired lives reserve are, of course, subject to the normal requirements for reasonableness of compensation.

---

[84] Rev. Rul. 69-382, 1969-2 C.B. 28.

[85] Rev. Rul. 73-599, 1973-2 C.B. 40. Section 404(a) generally prohibits an employer deduction for many forms of deferred compensation unless various

Although there are no definitive rulings by the Service on this point, insurance coverage provided by a retired lives reserve apparently will not create taxable income to an employee either before or after retirement. During the employee's working career, he has no vested rights either to the money contributed to the retired lives reserve fund or to the post-retirement insurance coverage. Under most such plans, if the employee leaves the employment of the employer prior to retirement, no post-retirement insurance coverage will be provided. Accordingly, in such a situation, Section 83(a) of the Code would preclude taxability.[86] As noted earlier in the discussion of Section 79 insurance plans,[87] Section 79(b)(1) excludes from income the cost of group term insurance provided for employees who have terminated employment and reached the employer's normal retirement age. This section apparently mandates the conclusion that the post-retirement insurance coverage provided by the corporate employer does not create taxable income for the employee.[88] Although the Service has never officially confirmed this interpretation, it has issued several rulings with respect to the topic of retired lives reserve and has never taken the position in any of these rulings that post-retirement taxable income is created. Given the Service's proclivity to seize upon the potential taxability of employer-provided fringe benefits, one must assume that this interpretation of nontaxability is relatively secure.

[3] Funding Vehicles

There are three potential means of maintaining a retired lives reserve fund — a nonexempt trust, an exempt trust under Section

---

requirements contained in that section are met. It appears, however, that a retired lives reserve is an employee benefit plan rather than a deferred compensation plan and therefore is excluded from the application of Section 404(a). See Treas. Reg. § 1.404(a)-1(a)(2); Rev. Rul. 69-478, 1969-2 C.B. 29.

[86] See generally Chapter 4.

[87] See discussion at ¶ 6.03.

[88] The word "apparently" is used here because the conclusion of nontaxability in this situation is largely dependent upon an interpretation that Section 79(b)(1) overrides the general principles of taxation found in Section 83 in the case of post-retirement group term coverage. Such an interpretation is in accordance with the normal rules of statutory construction, which provide that the more specific section will override a statute of general applicability unless there is a clear indication to the contrary. An extended discussion of the statutory construction involved here may be found in Roberts & Martin, "Group Life Insurance," 387 Tax Mgm't at A-21 — A-24.

501(c)(9) of the Code, and a reserve maintained by a life insurance company. In most situations, however, the reserve maintained by the life insurance company is the only practical funding vehicle. Although contributions to a nonexempt trust will not create taxable income to that trust, any investment income earned by the trust will be taxable. Because this taxability reduces the amount of insurance that can be obtained per dollar of employer contribution, a nonexempt trust is often inappropriate. A Section 501(c)(9) trust alleviates the problem of taxability, but the requirements necessary in order to obtain tax-exempt status will often preclude the use of such a trust. The Service interprets Section 501(c)(9) as containing relatively broad eligibility requirements [89] and also requiring that no part of the net earnings of the trust will enure to the benefit of any private shareholder or individual.[90] As a result, the payment of disproportionate benefits to highly compensated executives may disqualify a plan under Section 501(c)(9) [91]. Consequently, if a corporate employer is desirous of limiting the benefits provided by a retired lives reserve to select groups of employees, the Section 501(c)(9) trust will be the wrong funding vehicle.

Because of the drawbacks of both the exempt and the nonexempt trust, the most commonly utilized funding mechanism is simply the maintenance of a reserve by a life insurance company. Not only does this reserve held by the life insurance company alleviate any potential tax problems to the corporate employer, it also provides a relatively simple means of administering the plan. The employer merely makes the appropriate contributions to the insurance company and is relieved of the subsequent administrative burdens involved.

A retired lives reserve may provide an additional valuable fringe benefit for the highly compensated individual. Because the insurance coverage provided will not be subject to taxation, such a plan enjoys a very favorable tax status. In addition, the assurance of post-retirement life insurance benefits provides a known source of liquid funds to the highly compensated individual for estate administration purposes, such as the payment of taxes or administration expenses. Accordingly, the retired lives reserve has gained in popularity in recent years — particularly in those situations where the reserve can be feasibly established for a limited number of employees.

---

[89] Treas. Reg. § 1.501(c)(9)-2.
[90] Treas. Reg. § 1.501(c)(9)-1.
[91] Treas. Reg. § 1.501(c)(9)-2(b)(1)(i).

¶ 6.07 Key-Man Insurance

A key-man insurance policy is one in which the proceeds are payable to the corporation in order to compensate for the loss caused by the death of key personnel. Because it is designed to benefit the employer corporation, it is not really per se a fringe benefit and consequently will not be discussed extensively here. The theory behind the purchase of such insurance is that often, particularly in a small corporation, the loss of a key officer is likely to have an immediate and detrimental effect on the corporation. By collecting insurance proceeds on the life of this individual, the corporation often will be provided with needed funds in order to ease the transition caused by the loss of this individual. As such, key-man insurance is more in the nature of protection for the remaining shareholders or corporate executives than a benefit to the decedent.

Key-man insurance is often confused with life insurance used to fund a corporate buy-out agreement in order to redeem the stock of a deceased shareholder. Although in both cases the insurance proceeds are payable to the corporation, in the case of the buy-out agreement the proceeds will actually be paid to the decedent's estate or a beneficiary thereof, whereas in the key-man insurance situation the proceeds will be retained by the corporation. The former type of insurance is used to protect the corporate officer by ensuring a market for the sale of his stock, whereas in the latter situation the insurance is designed to protect the corporation against loss.

Because the proceeds of key-man insurance are payable to the corporation, the premium payments will not be deductible.[92] On the other hand, the payment of the proceeds normally will not create taxable income to the corporation.[93] Consequently, one detrimental aspect of the purchase of such insurance is that it must be paid for with after-tax dollars that cannot be recouped on a tax-free basis until the death of the insured. Accordingly, the question of whether or not to purchase such insurance often becomes a balance between the lost use of these after-tax dollars versus the perceived impact of the death of the insured individual. The question of whether or not to purchase such insurance is not really one of tax planning.

Although, as stated previously, key-man insurance is not normally

---

[92] I.R.C. § 264(a)(1).
[93] I.R.C. § 101(a)(1).

considered a fringe benefit as such, there are at least two particular situations in which there will be some perception that the purchase of this insurance is a fringe benefit. First, if the insured individual has family members who will remain as stockholders or officers of the corporation, the purchase of key-man insurance on his life may be viewed as a means of providing for the continuity of the corporation for his survivors. Consequently, although this insurance may not directly benefit him, the benefit to his heirs may cause it to be viewed in a favorable light. Second, other corporate stockholders and officers may view the purchase of key-man insurance as a fringe benefit to them. By providing this insurance protection that will be payable to the corporation, their sense of security and confidence in the future continuity of the corporation will be enhanced. As such, the purchase of such insurance may help to retain valuable secondary personnel who might otherwise be concerned about the dominant status of a single individual.

CHAPTER 7

Fringe Benefits

		Page
¶ 7.01	Statutory vs. Nonstatutory Fringe Benefits	7-1
¶ 7.02	Health Plans — Insured	7-3
¶ 7.03	Health Plans — Noninsured Medical Reimbursement	7-4
	[1] Taxation in General	7-4
	[2] Antidiscrimination Requirements	7-5
	[3] Planning	7-7
¶ 7.04	Disability and Sickness Plans	7-9
	[1] Disability Plans	7-9
	[2] Workmen's Compensation	7-11
¶ 7.05	Educational Assistance Programs	7-12
¶ 7.06	Survivor's Death Benefits	7-16
¶ 7.07	Cafeteria Plans	7-18
¶ 7.08	Nonstatutory Fringe Benefits	7-20
	[1] Taxation of Fringe Benefits in General	7-21
	[2] Treasury Discussion Drafts	7-23
	[3] Planning for Specific Fringe Benefits	7-26
	[a] Basic Planning Factors	7-26
	[b] Financial Counseling	7-27
	[c] Conventions	7-28
	[d] Meals or Lodging	7-29

¶ 7.01 Statutory vs. Nonstatutory Fringe Benefits

Employer-provided fringe benefits granted to highly compensated employees have long proved to be popular, with both employers and employees. Fringe benefits, at the same time, have generated a good deal of tax controversy. Fringe benefits and "perks" have gained favor among the highly compensated because they generally provide a nontaxable benefit to the employee in an area where he would often have to spend after-tax dollars to obtain the same item or service. Such benefits also provide a deduction to the employer and a means of providing extra compensation to the highly compensated individual. Because such benefits frequently have been concentrated on the highly compensated, controversy has often ensued over the discriminatory nature of these benefits and the question of their taxability.

There are two basic types of fringe benefits that are provided to the highly compensated employee. The first group of benefits is that specifically permitted by statute. The second type has been developed over the years under a wide variety of plans that have no specific basis in the Code. These nonstatutory benefits usually involve the payment of a particular expense by the employer or the provision of goods and services to the employee. Through a long series of cases, rulings, and administrative customs, each of these plans has developed its own particular status as to taxability or nontaxability.

Statutorily authorized fringe benefits have usually found their way into the Code as a result of legislative pressure by particular groups that took the position that specific employee fringe benefits are socially desirable. In many instances, Congress has responded with legislation specifically permitting such fringe benefits and providing an exclusion from income for those benefits that fall within the definition of a particular Code section. Often, the statutory licensing of a specific fringe benefit was followed by a number of actions perceived as abuses requiring further legislative correction. One of the most frequently cited abuses for various benefits has been the restriction of such benefits to the highly compensated. Thus, there has been a legislative tendency, when Congress is in one of its "reform" moods, to modify the statutory exemption for a particular benefit with requirements that such benefits be provided to the bulk of a company's employees on a nondiscriminatory basis. This tendency has had the effect of limiting the utility of many statutorily authorized fringe benefits unless the employer was willing to provide such benefits to his entire work force.

The greatest portion of this chapter (¶¶ 7.02–7.07) reviews the statutorily authorized fringe benefits that are most frequently used by the highly compensated with the exception of stock ownership and qualified plans and life insurance, which are specifically covered in Chapters 4–6. The last section of this chapter (¶ 7.08) reviews many of the specifics and controversies surrounding nonstatutory fringe benefits.

¶ 7.02 Health Plans — Insured

Employer-paid health insurance plans are so commonplace for all employees, including the highly compensated, that little thought is given to their tax implications. Such plans provide a substantial economic and tax benefit to the employee and must not be overlooked when developing a fringe benefit package for the highly compensated. Although the Code no longer provides an individual deduction for health insurance premiums,[1] these premiums may be added together with other medical expenses and deducted under Section 213(a)(1) of the Code to the extent that they exceed 5 percent of the individual's adjusted gross income. Many highly compensated individuals cannot benefit from the Section 213(a)(1) deduction because medical expenses, except in the unusual situation, will not exceed 5 percent of their adjusted gross income. Consequently, the deduction provided by Section 213 is of only limited utility to the highly compensated individual.

In addition to economic comfort, a health insurance plan also provides substantial income tax benefits. First, the premiums paid by the employer are not taxable to the covered employee.[2] In addition, benefits provided by health insurance policies are not taxable to the employee unless they exceed the medical expenses incurred or unless they were with respect to expenses for which the employee had previously taken a deduction on his income tax return.[3] Consequently, a well-designed health insurance plan will provide economic protection for coverage of medical expenses on a tax-free basis.

The exclusion under Section 106 for health insurance premium payments has been, unlike many other exclusionary provisions of the Code, rather generously interpreted by the Service. For example, it has been ruled that the employer's reimbursement to employees for premiums paid on their individual policies is not taxable.[4] Similarly, retired

---

[1] I.R.C. § 213(a)(2) was eliminated by the 1982 Act beginning in 1983.

[2] I.R.C. § 106 provides that gross income does not include contributions by the employer to accident or health plans for compensation (through insurance or otherwise) to his employees for personal injuries or sickness.

[3] I.R.C. § 105(b). See also Rev. Rul. 69-154, 1969-1 C.B. 46, which indicates that the proportion of excess indemnification received under a medical insurance policy attributable to employer contributions is includable in the employee's taxable income.

[4] Rev. Rul. 75-241, 1975-1 C.B. 316.

employees have not been taxed on amounts that an employer pays on their behalf to health plans covering both active and retired employees.[5] However, where a plan provided that, upon retirement, an employee may receive a cash payment for accumulated sick leave or have the same amount applied to the cost of insurance, the employer's payment for such insurance has been held to be taxable.[6] If no option to receive cash is available, the amount paid for insurance is not includable in gross income under the exclusionary rule of Section 106 of the Code.

Because of the tax benefits provided by medical insurance coverage, as well as the protection against economic loss, the highly compensated individual must not overlook the value of a health insurance plan in evaluating the totality of his employment-related compensation package. It should be noted, however, that there is a wide variation among plans in terms of the specifics of the coverage provided. This is particularly true of those types of plans that provide dollar limitations on benefits. In those plans, unless there is coordination with a major medical policy, the dollar limitations may provide inadequate coverage due to the inflationary tendencies of medical costs. Consequently, in considering a new employment situation, it is advisable to specifically evaluate the coverage provided by a plan. In the situation where there is a continuing employment relationship, it is advisable for both the employer and the employee to review annually health insurance coverage to ascertain whether it continues to remain adequate.

¶ 7.03 Health Plans — Noninsured Medical Reimbursement

[1] Taxation In General

Although Section 105(a) of the Code provides that amounts received by an employee through accident or health insurance for personal injuries or sickness are to be included in the employee's gross income to the extent that they are paid by the employer, Section 105(b) immediately provides a major exception to that rule. Section 105(b) states that, in the case of amounts attributable to deductions allowed under Section 213, gross income does not include amounts referred to in Subsection 105(a) if such amounts are paid by an employer to reimburse a taxpayer for expenses incurred by him for medical care (as defined in

---

[5] Rev. Rul. 62-199, 1962-2 C.B. 38.
[6] Rev. Rul. 75-539, 1975-2 C.B. 45.

Section 213(e)) of the taxpayer, his spouse, or his dependents. This statutory exclusion of reimbursements for medical expenses induced many employers to create medical reimbursement plans to compensate their key employees for uninsured medical expenses. Such plans were often provided in conjunction with a basic health insurance plan and usually were limited to a select group of executives or stockholders.[7]

Medical reimbursement plans proved to be very popular with the highly compensated for several reasons. First, these plans provided favorable tax treatment in that the payments were not taxable income to the executive and yet were deductible by the employer. Second, the medical expense deduction provided by Section 213 of the Code frequently was of little value to the highly compensated employee because of the requirement that such expenses, in order to be deductible, must exceed 5 percent of the taxpayer's adjusted gross income.[8]

[2] Antidiscrimination Requirements

The tendency of most medical reimbursement plans to limit their benefits to the highly compensated led to significant public pressure for reform. As a result, Section 105(h) was added to the Code, effective for taxable years beginning after December 31, 1979, to require that such plans be nondiscriminatory. Consequently, unless a noninsured medical reimbursement plan meets the antidiscrimination requirements of Section 105(h), the income tax exclusion under Section 105(b) will either no longer be available or will be greatly reduced.

Section 105(h) basically provides that a self-insured medical reimbursement plan will qualify for income tax exclusion only if the plan does not discriminate in favor of highly compensated individuals as to eligibility to participate and if the benefits provided under the plan do not discriminate in favor of participants who are highly compensated individuals.[9] The regulations take the position that plan benefits will not satisfy the antidiscrimination requirements unless *all* the benefits provided for highly compensated individuals are provided for all other participants.[10] This test is applied to benefits subject to reimbursement

---

[7] Plans that were limited to stockholders created a danger that payments under the plans would be considered as dividends.

[8] Prior to 1983, such expenses were deductible if they exceeded 3 percent of adjusted gross income.

[9] I.R.C. § 105(h)(2).

[10] Treas. Reg. § 1.105-11(c)(3)(i).

under the plan rather than to actual benefit payments or claims made. Plans are allowed to establish limits for reimbursement, but the regulations indicate that any maximum limit attributable to employer contributions must be uniform for all participants and may not be modified by reason of a participant's age, years of service, or salary.[11]

A plan will not be discriminatory in terms of eligibility if 70 percent or more of all employees are eligible to participate, or if 80 percent or more of all employees who are eligible to benefit under the plan (if 70 percent or more of all employees are eligible to benefit under the plan) are eligible to participate.[12] For purposes of determining eligibility, the Code provides that it is permissible to exclude from consideration employees who have not completed three years of service, employees who have not attained age 25, part-time or seasonal employees, employees not included in the plan who are members of a bargaining unit for which accident and health benefits were the subject of good faith bargaining, and employees who are nonresident aliens who receive no earned income from U.S. sources.[13] The regulations indicate that employees whose customary weekly employment is less than thirty-five hours, if other employees in similar work with the same employer have substantially more hours, and seasonal employees whose customary annual employment is less than nine months, if other employees in similar jobs with the same employer work substantially more months, will be considered to be part-time. In addition, any employee whose customary weekly employment is less than twenty-five hours or any employee whose customary annual employment is less than seven months may be considered as part-time or seasonal.[14]

For purposes of Section 105(h), the term "highly compensated individual" is defined to mean an individual who is (1) one of the five highest paid officers, (2) a shareholder who owns[15] more than 10 percent in value of the stock of the employer, or (3) the highest paid 25 percent of all employees.[16] If a plan is found to provide a discriminatory benefit to a highly compensated individual, all of such benefits will be

---

[11] Id.

[12] I.R.C. § 105(h)(3)(A)(i).

[13] I.R.C. § 105(h)(3)(B).

[14] Treas. Reg. § 1.105-11(c)(2)(iii)(C). See also H.R. Rep. No. 1800, 95th Cong., 2d Sess. 254 (1978).

[15] The attribution rules of I.R.C. § 318 would apply.

[16] I.R.C. § 105(h)(5).

considered to be excess reimbursement and, hence, taxable to that individual. If a plan is found to be discriminatory as to coverage, a portion of that benefit will be held to be a taxable excess reimbursement. The amount of the excess reimbursement considered to be taxable is determined by multiplying the total amount reimbursed times a fraction, the numerator of which is the total amount reimbursed during the plan year to all highly compensated individuals and the denominator of which is the total amount reimbursed during that year to all participants. If, however, benefits are paid to participants who are not highly compensated individuals, they may still be excluded from gross income even if the plan is found to be discriminatory.[17]

The regulations take the position that reimbursements paid under a plan for medical diagnostic procedures for an employee (but not an employee's dependent) will not be considered to be part of a medical reimbursement plan subject to Section 105(h).[18] This exception is limited to diagnostic procedures such as routine medical examinations, blood tests, and X rays and does not include expenses incurred for the treatment, cure, or testing of a "known illness or disability." The Service also takes the position that these diagnostic procedures must be performed at a facility that provides no services other than medical and ancillary services and that does not include any incidental expenses for food or lodging.[19] Presumably, this means that the highly compensated employee cannot be sent to a luxurious health spa for his medical checkup. However, this section clearly allows a corporation to provide complete medical checkups on an annual basis to its highly compensated employees.

[3] Planning

Despite Section 105 (h), a medical reimbursement plan may still remain a very valuable fringe benefit to the highly compensated. For example, many corporate employers may not object to instituting a medical reimbursement plan that meets the nondiscrimination requirements of Section 105(h). This may be particularly true in smaller corporations, where limited numbers of lower paid employees might be eligible, or where, because of turnover and the age of lower paid

---

[17] Treas. Reg. § 1.105-11(a).
[18] Treas. Reg. § 1.105-11(g)(1).
[19] Id.

employees, the bulk of such employees may be legally excluded from coverage. Second, the requirements of Section 105(h) are applicable only to noninsured medical reimbursement plans. The section contains no prohibition against an employer instituting a discriminatory insured plan for its highly compensated employees. The regulations provide that an insured plan involves the shifting of risk of loss to an unrelated third party.[20] Thus, according to the regulations, a cost-plus policy or a policy that merely provides administrative or bookkeeping services is considered self-insured for purposes of Section 105. However, a plan is not considered self-insured merely because one factor that the insurer uses in determining the premium is the employer's prior claims experience.

The regulations in regard to shifting of the risk were issued partially in response to the offering of several cost-plus type insurance plans by insurers immediately after the enactment of Section 105(h). There are, however, policies being written and new types of plans being developed by insurers which will be designed to provide excess medical coverage to the highly compensated. Thus, the implementation of an insured plan can circumvent the requirements of Section 105(h) and provide favorable tax treatment to the corporate executive.

Even if a medical reimbursement plan is found to be discriminatory, it still may be economically beneficial to the highly compensated employee. For example, if a plan is found to be discriminatory as to coverage, only a fraction of the benefit paid will be taxable. If 50 percent of the benefits paid under a plan are distributed to highly compensated individuals and the plan is found to be discriminatory as to coverage, only one half of each dollar paid to the highly compensated under the medical reimbursement plan would be taxed. If this individual is in the 50 percent tax bracket, the net cost of each dollar of reimbursement to him will be twenty-five cents. Thus, in the proper set of circumstances, a considerable dollar savings can still be achieved. Moreover, even if the amount paid is fully taxable, the employee may still substantially benefit from reimbursement of cost if the payments would not have been deductible under Section 213 because they are below the dollar limitations.[21] In such a case, he will be paying, at most, fifty cents on the dollar in tax for each dollar expended for medical treatment. If medical

---

[20] Treas. Reg. § 1.105-11(b)(1)(ii).

[21] The expenses must be of the *type* that would be deductible under I.R.C. § 213.

expenses are of such a magnitude as to be in the deductible category, the employee will be no worse off economically and will have the comfort of knowing that the money is available to pay unexpected medical bills. In such a case, the benefit is economic rather than tax oriented.

Consequently, there are many situations where a medical reimbursement plan may be a desirable fringe benefit for both the highly compensated individual and the employer. Under some circumstances, an uninsured plan, even if it is found to be discriminatory, may be beneficial. In other cases, an insured plan for selected highly compensated employees may be the most desirable alternative. In any event, the antidiscrimination rules of Section 105(h) should not preclude the consideration of a medical reimbursement plan for the highly compensated individual, since, unless there are unreasonable compensation problems, the payments will be deductible by the employer in any event.

¶ 7.04 Disability and Sickness Plans

Many employers offer disability income plans to their employees which, in effect, provide income protection in the event that the employees' physical condition makes it impossible to work. In addition, all states have enacted workmen's compensation statutes which provide for certain payments in the event of job-related injuries. The tax status of such payments is discussed in this section.

[1] Disability Plans

The disability income provisions of the Code have been so emasculated that these sections can be expected to provide little or no benefit to the highly compensated. Section 105(d) of the Code provides for an exclusion of disability payments to a taxpayer who has not attained age 65 before the close of the taxable year and who has retired because of a permanent and total disability. This exclusion is limited to payments of $100 per week and is phased out on a dollar-for-dollar basis to the extent that the taxpayer's income for the year exceeds $15,000.[22] Thus, if an individual has retired with a permanent disability and has income in excess of $20,200, this exclusion will be totally inapplicable.

---

[22] I.R.C. § 105(d)(3). In the case of married individuals, the phaseout is applied with respect to their combined adjusted gross income. I.R.C. § 105(d)(5)(B)(ii). The $100 per week limitation is applied separately to each spouse. I.R.C. § 105(d)(5)(B)(i).

¶ 7.04[1]

In addition to the low dollar limitation, Section 105(d) is also limited by a narrow definition of total and permanent disability. An individual is said to be totally and permanently disabled if he is unable to engage in any substantial gainful activity by reason of any medically determinable physical or mental impairment that can be expected to result in death or that has lasted, or can be expected to last, for a continuous period of not less than twelve months.[23] Individuals claiming this exclusion must present medical evidence on an annual basis on Form 2440 in order to justify the exclusion.[24] This definition of disability is much narrower than that contained in many commercial disability income policies, which only require that an individual be unable to carry out the duties for which he is suited by reason of training, experience, or education. Finally, in order to claim the exclusion, a married taxpayer must file a joint return unless he has lived apart from his spouse at all times during the taxable year.[25] An individual who is also eligible for an annuity described in Section 72 of the Code may make an election, which must be irrevocable, to take the Section 72 election in lieu of the Section 105(d) exclusion.

Because of the very limited tax benefit provided by the Section 105(d) exclusion, this section will have very little applicability to the highly compensated. Most planning in regard to disability plans for the highly compensated will relate to the amount and extent of coverage under a disability insurance program rather than the limited tax benefits provided by the Code. For example, in reviewing a disability insurance policy on behalf of a highly compensated individual, the tax advisor should carefully review the limits of the policy so as to ascertain the level of benefits provided and to coordinate potential payments under such a policy with other benefits (such as deferred compensation or distributions from a qualified plan) that may also be provided in the event of disability. The definition of disability under the policy should be carefully reviewed to determine its relationship to the individual's present occupation rather than to his ability to perform any task at all. The critical questions in reviewing a disability plan are the amount and extent of coverage rather than tax planning per se. Although the Section

---

[23] I.R.C. § 105(d)(4).

[24] Prop. Reg. § 1.105-9(a)(2). The requirement for furnishing evidence annually is waived if the medical evidence furnished indicates there is no reasonable probability of the taxpayer's condition improving in the future.

[25] I.R.C. § 105(d)(5)(A).

105(d) exclusion should not be ignored, it is unlikely to be of much practical benefit to an individual who has been in a highly compensated status.

[2] Workmen's Compensation

Amounts received under workmen's compensation acts of the various states as compensation for personal injuries or sickness are excludable from gross income by virtue of Section 104(a)(1) of the Code. Both the regulations under this section and the interpretive rulings have given a broad interpretation to this exclusion. The regulations indicate that the exclusion is applicable to statutes in the nature of a workmen's compensation act which provide compensation to employees for personal injuries or sickness incurred in the course of employment.[26] The critical factors appear to be that the payments be mandated by statute and that they be compensation for occupational injury or illness. The exclusion is also applicable to compensation paid under a workmen's compensation act to a survivor or survivors of a deceased employee. It is inapplicable to any retirement pension or annuity to the extent it is determined by reference to the employee's age, length of service, or prior contributions.

The Service has issued numerous rulings interpreting this section, but most are of narrow applicability, inasmuch as they relate to specific municipal situations.[27] Other rulings demonstrate the broad definition given by the Service to laws considered to be in the nature of a workmen's compensation act. For example, the Service ruled that payments made to disabled coal miners under the Black Lung Benefits Act of 1972 are excludable under Section 104(a)(1).[28] The $50,000 payment made under federal law by the Law Enforcement Assistance Administration to dependents of an officer killed in the line of duty is similarly excludable.[29] Relatively informal, legally mandated payments also seem to qualify for exclusion. For example, a municipal ordinance providing a pension to surviving spouses of volunteer firefighters killed

---

[26] Treas. Reg. § 1.104-1(b).

[27] See, e.g., Rev. Rul. 72-45, 1972-1 C.B. 34 (New York City policemen and firemen); Rev. Rul. 72-44, 1972-1 C.B. 32 (New Orleans disabled firemen); Rev. Rul. 75-500, 1975-2 C.B. 44 (District of Columbia police and firemen, United States Park Police Force).

[28] Rev. Rul. 72-400, 1972-2 C.B. 75.

[29] Rev. Rul. 77-235, 1977-2 C.B. 45.

in the course of duty was held to be in the nature of workmen's compensation and excludable from the spouse's gross income.[30] The Service has also ruled that payments made to a county police officer injured in the line of duty pursuant to a collective bargaining agreement incorporated by reference into the county code were excludable from gross income.[31] Consequently, the tendency appears to be that payments are excludable under Section 104(a)(1) as long as they are made for job-related injury or illness, and are mandated by some form of state, federal, or municipal statute. If the payments reflect other characteristics, such as length of service or employee contributions, they will be evaluated under other sections of the Code, such as those relating to retirement benefits.

Quite obviously, there is no tax planning involved in regard to the Section 104(a)(1) exclusion, since one presumably does not plan to incur an occupational injury or disease. The tax planner must bear in mind, however, that that exclusion is available under the appropriate set of circumstances and is available irrespective of the income level of the recipient. Thus, for example, if a highly compensated person becomes disabled and receives numerous job-related benefits in addition to workmen's compensation, the Section 104(a)(1) exclusion is still available in spite of those other benefits received.

¶ 7.05 Educational Assistance Programs

The Revenue Act of 1978 added a new fringe benefit to the Code entitled Educational Assistance Programs. Under a plan that meets the statutory requirements,[33] an employee does not have to include the value of the educational benefits provided in his income. As was true of

---

[30] Rev. Rul. 72-291, 1972-1 C.B. 36. Duty disability payments paid under a municipal statute to disabled firefighters prior to reaching their normal retirement age were similarly held to be excludable. Rev. Rul. 80-14, 1980-1 C.B. 33.

[31] Rev. Rul. 81-47, 1981-1 C.B. 55. However, payments made by a municipality to a disabled police officer who has returned to work and is assigned to light duty because injury keeps the officer from performing regular police duties were held not excludable. Rev. Rul. 80-137, 1980-1 C.B. 36.

[32] This is assuming the continued availability of workmen's compensation.

[33] I.R.C. § 127. This section contains a "sunset provision" (I.R.C. § 127(d)) so that it will not be applicable to taxable years beginning after December 31, 1983. Whether or not this program will be extended remains to be seen, although there is generally a legislative tendency for extension of such exclusionary provisions.

many legislative enactments during the decade of the 1970s, this section contains broad antidiscrimination requirements so that the program cannot be specifically directed toward the highly compensated. If the employer does establish such a broadly based program, this particular fringe benefit can be very valuable to the highly compensated individual.

Although the concept of employer-financed educational benefits is not new, the enactment of Section 127 of the Code was an attempt to ameliorate long-standing confusion and controversy relating to such programs. Prior to the enactment of this section, an employee was required to report educational assistance payments as income and then, if possible, attempt to justify a deduction for such expenditures under Section 162 as a business expense. The result of this particular situation was a long-running controversy between the Service and taxpayers over what educational expenses were deductible under that section, and a confusing and uneven interpretation of the law.

The regulations under Section 162 take the position that, for an educational expense to be deductible, the education must maintain or improve a skill required by the individual in his employment or other trade or business, or meet the express requirements of the individual's employer or the requirements of applicable law or regulations, imposed as a condition to the retention by the individual of an established employment relationship, status, or rate of compensation.[34] Educational expenditures designed to meet the minimum educational requirements for qualification in an employment or other trade or business, or of the type that will lead to qualifying an individual for a new trade or business, were considered to be nondeductible personal expenses.[35] As might be expected, the cases and rulings interpreting these regulations are legion and often confusing. Typically, controversy centered on the issue of whether an individual was maintaining or improving skills required by his existing trade or business [36] or whether or not an individual was meeting minimum educational requirements

---

[34] Treas. Reg. § 1.162-5(a).

[35] Treas. Reg. §§ 1.162-5(b)(2) — 1.162-5(b)(3).

[36] See Welsh v. U.S., 210 F. Supp. 597 (N.D. Ohio 1962), aff'd, 329 F.2d 145 (6th Cir. 1964) (deduction allowed for law school courses taken to improve taxpayer's proficiency as revenue agent); Watson v. Comm'r, 31 T.C. 1014 (1959), nonacq. 1963-1 C.B. 5 (internist allowed deduction for costs of psychiatric training designed to improve his skill as internist); Crashley v. Comm'r, ¶ 79,513 P-H Memo. T.C. (deduction denied hockey player for leadership course since it

to qualify for a profession.[37] If an educational assistance plan does not qualify under Section 127, the educational assistance recipient may still try to satisfy the requirements for deductibility under Section 162.[38] Plans that qualify under Section 127, however, eliminate the need to undertake this risky and often confusing course of action.

If a plan meets the requirements of Section 127, the type of assistance that may be furnished is quite broad. The employer may pay expenses on behalf of the employee for books, tuition, and supplies and equipment. However, the educational assistance cannot include meals, lodging, or transportation, nor can it include any payment for any course or other education involving sports, games, or hobbies.[39] There are, however, no express requirements that the training be related to the particular job in question. Consequently, a professional sports team or league could establish an educational assistance program to train athletes for a profession to be entered after their retirement from professional sports. A corporate employer could render assistance to corporate executives who are studying for a law degree or a master's degree in business to enhance their promotion possibilities.

In order to qualify under Section 127, the employer is required to have a written plan for the exclusive benefit of his employees.[40] The employees cannot have an option to take cash in lieu of the educational benefits and there must be "reasonable notification" of the availability and terms of the program to all eligible employees. The plan itself need not be funded in advance. The major requirement of Section 127, however, is the antidiscrimination provision. In order to qualify under this section, the plan cannot be discriminatory in favor of employees who are officers, owners, or highly compensated employees or their dependents. In addition, not more than 5 percent of the amounts paid or incurred by the employer for educational assistance during the plan year may be provided for the class of individuals who are shareholders

---

did not improve skills required for his business); Lage v. Comm'r, 52 T.C. 130 (1969), acq., 1969-2 C.B. xxiv (deduction allowed company vice-president for tutoring by management expert designed to improve job skills).

[37] See Garwood v. Comm'r, 62 T.C. 699 (1974) (substitute teacher had not met minimum requirements for permanent teaching position); Rev. Rul. 71-58, 1971-1 C.B. 55 (employed teacher meeting minimum educational requirements for permanent teaching certificate in one state may deduct costs of educational courses to qualify as a teacher in a second state).

[38] I.R.C. § 127(c)(6).

[39] I.R.C. § 127(c)(1).

[40] See generally I.R.C. § 127(b).

or owners, each of whom owns more than 5 percent of the stock or capital or profits interest in the employer.[41] However, the program will not be considered discriminatory merely because the utilization rates for different types of educational assistance made available under the program are different or because successful completion or attaining a course grade is required or considered in determining reimbursement under a program.

There are, quite obviously, certain inherent limitations upon the utility of a Section 127 educational assistance program for the highly compensated individual. First, the program cannot be designed specifically for the highly compensated and must be offered by the employer to a broad class of employees. Second, many individuals reach highly compensated status because they are educated and are not really in need of educational assistance. This is not always the case, however. Professional athletes may require education for their later transition to nonathletic endeavors. Highly compensated entertainers may effectively use additional education in order to manage their financial empires. Business executives may desire further education in order to expand their promotion possibilities. Almost any highly compensated individual can benefit from refresher and updating courses in order to keep current in his area of expertise.

In each of these cases, an educational assistance program can provide a significant benefit to the highly compensated because of the nontaxable nature of the benefits. If the highly compensated individual had to pay for the program himself and could not sustain a Section 162 deduction, he would undoubtedly have to earn twice as much as the cost of the program in order to generate the after-tax dollars necessary to pay for it. Even if the cost of the program ultimately proved to be deductible, the individual might face a long and costly struggle with the Service to sustain the deduction. Consequently, a Section 127 program allows the highly compensated individual (and anyone else who is eligible) to participate in an educational program on a tax-free basis without a protracted tax struggle. Because of the antidiscrimination provisions in the statute, such a program may not be appropriate for many employers. If it is appropriate, it can be a valuable fringe benefit to the corporation's employees — including the highly compensated.[42]

---

[41] I.R.C. § 127(b)(3).

[42] It should be noted that I.R.C. § 127, unlike many provisions, specifically allows an unincorporated business or a partnership to be treated as an employer for purposes of this section. I.R.C. § 127(c)(3).

¶ 7.06 Survivor's Death Benefits

Section 101(b) of the Code excludes from gross income amounts received by the beneficiaries or the estate of an employee, if such amounts are paid by or on behalf of an employer by reason of that employee's death.[43] This benefit is limited to $5,000 and does not apply to amounts with respect to which the employee possessed, immediately before his death, a nonforfeitable right to receive while living.[44] This exclusion is also inapplicable to amounts received by a surviving annuitant under a joint and survivor's annuity contract after the first day of the first period for which an amount was received as an annuity by the employee (or would have been received by the employee if he had lived).[45]

This exception for benefits to which the employee had a nonforfeitable right while living is inapplicable to lump-sum distributions made by a qualified pension or profit-sharing plan, under an annuity contract or under a plan described in Section 403(a) or under an annuity contract purchased by an employer that is an organization referred to in Section 170(b)(1)(A)(ii) or that is a religious organization exempt from tax under Section 501(a).[46]

Most of the controversy relating to the Section 101(b) death benefit exclusion relates the question of whether or not the employee would have had a vested interest in the particular benefit if he had lived or

---

[43] For years beginning after 1983, the Tax Equity and Fiscal Responsibility Act of 1982 amended I.R.C. § 101(b)(3) so as to remove the exclusion of the self-employed from the definition of "employee" for purposes of I.R.C. § 101(b). Thus, after that date, the death benefit exclusion will apply to Keogh plan distributions.

[44] I.R.C. § 101(b)(2). See generally discussion at ¶ 14.03[2], which deals with the estate tax consequences of employee death-benefit-only plans.

[45] I.R.C. § 101(b)(2)(C). In Rev. Rul. 81-121, 1981-1 C.B. 43, the Service ruled that if a disabled federal employee had not made the election under I.R.C. § 105(d)(6) to treat disability retirement income as annuity income, the payments received by the spouse upon the death of the employee before age 65 qualify for the Section 101(b) exclusion. If an election had been made, the annuity starting date would have occurred in the year of election and thus the amounts receivable by the spouse would not be eligible for the exclusion because of I.R.C. § 101(b)(2)(C).

[46] I.R.C. § 101(b)(2)(B), "but only with respect to that portion of such total distribution payable which bears the same ratio to the amount of such total distribution payable which is includable in gross income, as the amounts contributed by the employer for such annuity contract which are excludable from gross income under Section 403(b) bear to the total amounts contributed by the employer for such annuity contract."

whether or not the payment constituted income payable to the employee during his life as compensation. The regulations take the position that the exclusion does not apply to amounts constituting income payable to the employee during his life as compensation for services, such as bonuses or payments for unused leave or uncollected salary.[47] If an individual dies while gainfully employed he typically will be owed that portion of his salary that accrued during the pay period immediately prior to his death, and accrued but unused vacation pay or sick leave. The payment of these amounts by the employer will not be eligible for the Section 101(b) exclusion. To be excluded, the death benefit must, in effect, be a separate and distinct payment from these previously accrued items.

In the rulings issued by the Service relating to the forfeitability question, the fact that the benefit accrues by reason of the death of the employee and thereafter could not be cancelled does not defeat the exclusion.[48] The critical factor is whether or not the employee was vested in such amounts prior to his death. For example, if bonuses subject to being "earned out" were awarded, but were payable after decedent's death, and bonuses awarded after a decedent's death would have been forfeitable immediately before his death, the aggregate amount of such bonuses not exceeding the statutory limitation was found to be excludable.[49]

Although the exclusion provided by Section 101(b) is small in terms of today's dollars, a death benefit that is excludable under this section is valuable to the highly compensated employee because his survivors typically remain in a relatively high income tax bracket — at least for the year of death. Consequently, by structuring a death benefit plan that meets the relatively simple requirements of Section 101(b), the employer can ensure that at least $5,000 will be sheltered from taxation in the event of the employee's death. It also should be noted that there are no antidiscrimination provisions in Section 101(b). Consequently, a plan can be maintained on a relatively informal basis for selected highly compensated employees.

In addition to the tax benefit provided, a death benefit payable under this section can also ensure that a surviving spouse has available immediately a significant amount of cash unencumbered by any pro-

---

[47] Treas. Reg. § 1.101-2(a)(2).
[48] Rev. Rul. 55-228, 1955-1 C.B. 231.
[49] Rev. Rul. 68-124, 1968-1 C.B. 44.

bate proceedings. This may be particularly important if the decedent had not undertaken sufficient tax planning so that the survivor had a certain amount of assets in his own name. Also, in some jurisdictions, state inheritance tax freezes are placed upon bank accounts immediately after the death of an individual. Consequently, by making a death benefit payment available to a surviving spouse shortly after the death of an employee, a company can provide funds for living expenses or funeral costs to meet the minimum needs of the surviving spouse until the estate can be opened or insurance proceeds collected. Thus, the employee death benefit can provide the double advantage of being tax-free and immediately available.[50]

¶ 7.07 Cafeteria Plans

A "cafeteria plan" is an employee benefit plan under which the employee can choose from among a group of benefits, some of which may be taxable and some nontaxable. The name evolved from the "pick and choose" aspect of the plan, not unlike a cafeteria line. Nontaxable benefits that may be chosen under such a plan can include, for example, group term life insurance up to the statutory maximum of $50,000, accident and health insurance, medical reimbursements under a qualified medical reimbursement plan, education benefits, and group legal services.[51] In the alternative, an employee may be able to elect to receive cash in lieu of these benefits.

Cafeteria plans have had a legislative history typical of many fringe benefits. After several companies had implemented such plans, legislative and regulatory concern arose over whether the ability to select cash under a plan created a taxable benefit. In response to this controversy, ERISA gave temporary approval to cafeteria plans in existence on June 27, 1974, but provided that plans enacted after that date would result in taxable income to participants to the extent that they could have elected taxable benefits. This legislation was originally scheduled to expire on January 1, 1977, but was extended by the Tax Reform Act of 1976 until

---

[50] Many companies that have such programs make it their practice to pay the death benefit to a surviving spouse immediately upon hearing of the employee's death. Much of the value of such a fringe benefit, particularly because of the dollar limitation on the exclusion, is dependent upon rapid payment by the employer.

[51] These benefits must also meet the requirements of I.R.C. § 120.

January 1, 1978. Finally, the Revenue Act of 1978 added a permanent section to the Code,[52] providing for the taxation of cafeteria plans. This statute, in essence, provides that if a plan meets the specific statutory requirements, the fact that an employee could elect among several benefits would not render the benefits taxable. As was typical with the legislation enacted during this period, in order to qualify under Section 125, a cafeteria plan must meet the restrictive antidiscrimination provisions of that section.

In order to qualify under Section 125, a plan cannot discriminate in favor of highly compensated participants.[53] Highly compensated participants are defined as officers, 5-percent shareholders, highly compensated individuals, or spouses of any of the above.[54] Employees with fewer than three years of service may be excluded provided they begin participation no later than the first day of the plan year after they have completed their eligibility requirements. If a plan provides health benefits, there are special antidiscrimination provisions requiring that the benefits for the highly compensated and non-highly compensated be relatively equal.[55] A plan that qualifies under this section cannot include a plan that provides for deferred compensation. However, it may include a profit-sharing or stock bonus plan that includes a qualifying cash or deferred arrangement as defined in Section 401(k)(2) to the extent of amounts that a covered employee may elect to have the employer pay as a contribution to a trust under such a plan on behalf of the employee.[56] If a plan does not qualify under this section, the right to receive cash under such a program will trigger taxation in the participant's tax year in which the tax plan year ends.

Because of the antidiscrimination provisions contained in this section, cafeteria plans cannot be a fringe benefit designed specifically for the highly compensated.[57] If any employer has instituted a plan on a company-wide basis, it may be of particular value to the highly compensated individual to the extent that he may choose nontaxable

---

[52] I.R.C. § 125.

[53] I.R.C. § 125(b). In determining whether or not a plan discriminates, certain controlled groups will be treated as a single employer. I.R.C. § 125(g)(4).

[54] I.R.C. § 125(e)(1).

[55] I.R.C. § 125(g)(2).

[56] I.R.C. § 125(d)(2).

[57] I.R.C. § 125(b).

benefits in lieu of the cash that may be an alternate selection under the plan. Consequently, the role of the tax advisor reviewing a cafeteria plan for a highly compensated individual will be to point out those benefits that are nontaxable among the selection provided. There will be a tendency on the part of the highly compensated to select those nontaxable benefits that are available — particularly if the benefits available have a value to that individual.

Certain employers feel that a cafeteria plan has particular utility to them in that it will allow them to make extra cash available to lower paid employees and to make nontaxable fringe benefits available to higher-paid employees under the same plan. From the employer's standpoint, it also emphasizes the dollar cost of fringe benefits and, as such, illustrates their value to the employee. Section 125 makes it imperative from both the employee's and employer's standpoints that the plan does qualify under that nondiscrimination section. If it does not, the highly compensated individual may be in a position of choosing a non-cash benefit and yet being taxed as if cash were received.

¶ 7.08 Nonstatutory Fringe Benefits

Despite the large number of fringe benefits whose tax status has been specifically dictated by statute, the ingenuity of corporate employers in providing a varied benefits package to its highly compensated employees has far outstripped the ability of Congress to respond legislatively to each particular benefit. Nonstatutory fringe benefits have taken a variety of forms whose diversity is almost endless. Employers have provided cars to corporate executives, secured country club memberships, arranged for the private use of the corporate plane, established executive dining rooms, and furnished exclusive hunting lodges. The list goes on and on.

Nonstatutory fringe benefits have long proved popular with both the employee and the employer. The employer has typically deducted the expense of making these benefits available to the employee while the employee has claimed that the benefits provided are nontaxable. In many cases, these claims have either been upheld or not challenged because they have slipped through upon audit. Consequently, as long as marginal income tax rates remain high, there will be a continuing attempt to devise a wide variety of fringe benefits whose taxation is not specifically covered by the Code.

[1] Taxation of Fringe Benefits in General

In theory, there should be no controversy surrounding the taxation of employer-provided fringe benefits. They should all be taxable. A perusal of the basic statutory and regulatory authorities unequivocally supports this contention. The regulations give an exceedingly broad interpretation to the definition of gross income. They state that "Gross income includes income realized in any form, whether in money, property or services. Income may be realized, therefore, in the form of services, meals, accommodations, stock, or other property, as well as cash."[58] The Supreme Court has also defined the concept of income in an expansive manner. In the case of *Comm'r v. Smith*[59] the Court, in holding the grant of a stock option to be a taxable event, stated what has come to be the most widely quoted definition of gross income: "Section 22(a) of the Revenue Act is broad enough to include in taxable income any economic or financial benefit conferred on the employee as compensation, whatever the form or mode by which it is affected."[60] Similarly, in *Comm'r v. LoBue*,[61] the Court broadly stated a definition of gross income as follows: "In defining 'gross income' as broadly as it did in Section 22(a), Congress intended to 'tax all gains except those specifically exempted.' [And that] When assets are transferred by an employer to an employee to secure better services they are plainly compensation."[62] Finally, in *Comm'r v. Duberstein*,[63] the Supreme Court was faced with the issue of whether a taxpayer who was not an employee received taxable income when a business associate presented him with a new Cadillac in appreciation for certain business referrals that had been made. In reviewing the *Duberstein* case, the Court refused to adopt the government's urgings that it formulate a new test for the definition of income and responded by saying:

> We think, to the extent they are correct, that these propositions are not principles of law but rather maxims of experience that the tribunals which have tried the facts of cases in this area have

---

[58] Treas. Reg. § 1.61-1(a).
[59] 324 U.S. 177 (1945).
[60] Id. at 181.
[61] 351 U.S. 243 (1956).
[62] Id. at 245-246.
[63] 363 U.S. 278 (1960).

enunciated in explaining their factual determinations. Some of them simply represent truisms. Others are overstatements of possible evidentiary inferences relevant to a factual determination on the totality of circumstances in the case...but these inferences cannot be stated in absolute terms.[64]

Duberstein thus recognized the practical situation that had developed over the years. Despite the broad language in the statute, regulations, and previously decided cases, many fringe benefits that had escaped taxation evolved over the years. There was no clear-cut rule or enunciated standard to guide either taxpayers or practitioners in determining which benefits were taxable and which were not.

Why then had this deviation developed from a relatively clear statutory and case law mandate? First, many benefits provided were of such a trivial nature that it did not pay the Service either in terms of absolute dollars or the ill will generated to tax these items. Items such as Christmas turkeys or the establishment of a first-aid station in an office proved to be too trivial to cause the Service to seek taxation. Second, the lack of uniform, easily understandable rules in the area had encouraged Service agents either to ignore various benefits or to develop tacit understandings with corporate employers as to the degree of benefits that would be permitted without its employees' incurring taxation. Additionally, administrative convenience often dictated the result. If a corporate employer was being audited, a separate matter involving a highly compensated executive would have to be initiated if the agent felt that, for example, use of the corporate car represented income to that executive. Since the agent was primarily concerned with the corporation's tax liability and since the dollar amounts regarding corporate car use may have been relatively minimal, it often was easier to ignore the latter issue and concentrate on the broader concerns of corporate tax liability. Although there are numerous cases where zealous Service agents pursued the taxation of corporate-provided fringe benefits,[65] the norm of behavior was otherwise. Finally, the so-called audit lottery contributed to many items being nontaxable. The particular entity providing the fringe benefit, or the recipient thereof, may simply not

---

[64] Id. at 287.

[65] A frequent means of raising these issues is in regard to FICA, FUTA, and income tax withholding. See Internal Revenue Manual Supplement 45G-30 (Jan. 14, 1981) for IRS instruction to agents for handling these issues.

have been audited for a period of years or, if audited, the issue may not have been picked up by the examining agent.

The Service itself contributed to this general lack of uniformity whereby certain benefits were not considered as taxable. For example, in the early days of the Code, the Service ruled that railroad passes provided for railroad employees were nontaxable gifts [66] and that supper money was excludable from gross income.[67] The rulings were, of course, pushed to the utmost limits by both employees and employers and led to such consequences as free airline tickets for airline employees not being taxed and executive dining suites not being compensatory.

As a result of this situation, the taxability of nonstatutory fringe benefits has developed over the years with very little logic. Although, in theory, all employer-provided fringe benefits were taxable as compensation to the employee, practices developed whereby some benefits were taxed and others were not. Administrative convenience, Service rulings, and pure oversight led to the exclusion of some items and the taxability of others. Predictability remained difficult and frequently subject to the vagaries of the audit lottery.

[2] Treasury Discussion Drafts

In an attempt to provide some uniformity for this topic, the Department of the Treasury on September 3, 1975 issued a discussion draft of proposed regulations that attempted to provide a set of uniform rules for the taxation of fringe benefits. This discussion draft set forth three basic rules for determining whether or not a fringe benefit should be taxable to an employee.

(1) Employees do not have taxable compensation where the employer makes available to employees facilities, goods, or services that exist incidentally to the employer's trade or business but only under the following circumstances:

  (a) The facilities, goods, or services are properly used by the employer in its trade or business and do not exist primarily for the benefit of the employees;

  (b) The facilities, goods, or services do not cause the employer to incur substantial additional costs in making them available; and

---

[66] O.D. 946, 4 C.B. 110 (1922).

[67] O.D. 514, 2 C.B. 90 (1918).

(c) The facilities, goods, and services are made available to employees generally or to reasonable classifications of employees determined on the basis of the nature of their work, seniority, duties, or other factors (but not including classifications primarily including only the most highly compensated employees).

(2) Benefits would not be taxable under a de minimis exception under which individual benefits will not be treated as compensation where they are so small that accounting for them is unreasonable or administratively impractical.

(3) Where benefits do not fall under these general rules, a facts-and-circumstances test would be considered with emphasis on nine factors set forth in the regulations.[68]

---

[68] The nine factors proposed were:

(1) The cost incurred by the employer in providing the benefit is not identifiable or is not significant in relation to the fair market value of the benefit received by the employee;

(2) The personal use occurs during, immediately before, or immediately after working hours at or near the business premises of the employer and has a proximate relation to work performed by the employee;

(3) The benefit is provided to employees generally or to reasonable classifications of employees determined, for example, on the basis of the nature of their work, seniority, or similar factors (but not including classification primarily including only the most highly compensated employees);

(4) The benefit is similar to a service or other benefit that is commonly provided by state or local governments in the United States, but is not readily available to employees because of the location of their employment;

(5) The benefit accommodates an important requirement of the employer or relieves the employer of significant expense or inconvenience;

(6) The benefit is reimbursement of a greater-than-usual item of expense that was incurred by the employee for a purpose normally thought primarily personal but which was incurred because a business requirement of the employer prevented the employee from obtaining the item in the ordinary manner;

(7) The benefit is provided primarily to insure the employee's safety by protecting against a significant risk arising from the employment relation;

(8) The benefit is not a substantial amount absolutely or in comparison to the employee's stated compensation; and

(9) The item generally is not thought of as constituting compensation includable in gross income.

Prop. Regs. § 1.61-16(b).

The first discussion draft generated both substantial criticism [69] and a good deal of controversy. Questions were raised as to whether the general rules proposed were workable, relating to the valuation of fringe benefits, and over the seeming emphasis of the proposed regulations on highly compensated corporate executives. Consequently, the proposed discussion draft did not generate any support and was withdrawn on September 28, 1976.

Subsequent to the withdrawal of the discussion draft, Congress enacted the Fringe Benefits Act,[70] which prohibited the issuance of fringe benefit regulations prior to January 1, 1980. This legislation was later extended to June 1, 1981 and, finally, the 1981 Act extended it further — until December 31, 1983. The purpose for this legislative moratorium was to allow Congress to study the situation and to consider remedial legislation. Although some congressional study has been undertaken at this point, no concrete legislation has yet been formulated.

With this background, a second discussion draft of proposed regulations was issued by the Carter administration on January 16, 1981.[71] This second discussion draft established a general rule of includability in gross income of any property, service, or facility furnished by an employer to or for the benefit of an employee in consideration of the employee's performance of services. There are three exceptions to this general rule. First, there is an exception, which is probably unnecessary, for any benefits subject to an explicit statutory provision. Second, there is an exception for what is termed to be "a working condition" — an exception that somewhat resembles the convenience-of-the-employer test developed under the case law. Finally, there is an exception on the grounds of administrative convenience. Because the second discussion draft was issued in the waning days of the Carter administration and was controversial in nature, the tax community immediately questioned the likelihood of these proposals becoming effective. The Reagan administration did initially indicate that it preferred a regulatory solution to the problem and responded by stating that it was working on its own draft proposals.[72] Approximately one month later, however, the

---

[69] See, e.g., Elwood, "Incidental Fringe Benefits — General Principals and an Allocation Approach to Valuation," Tax Mgmt. Memo. 76-16 (1976).

[70] Fringe Benefits Act, Pub. L. No. 95-427 (1978).

[71] Prop. Regs. § 1.61-17-22.

[72] See joint statement John E. Chapoton, assistant secretary for tax policy, and Internal Revenue Service Commissioner Roscoe L. Egger, Jr. at *Hearings of*

administration announced that it would issue no regulations or rulings altering the treatment of fringe benefits until July 1, 1982 so as to allow Congress to study the issue.

In summary, despite the issuance of two discussion drafts by the Treasury and congressional study of the issue for a substantial period of time, there appears to be no immediate likelihood of the issuance of a comprehensive set of rules relating to the taxation of fringe benefits.

Accordingly, the highly compensated individual and his advisor are faced with the task of determining the taxability of a particular fringe benefit on a case-by-case basis according to existing rulings, regulations, and cases. Although, as has been indicated earlier in this chapter, all such benefits provided in the nature of compensation are theoretically taxable, in practice many are not.

[3] Planning for Specific Fringe Benefits

The implementation of a specific nonstatutory fringe benefit for a corporate executive or other highly compensated employee typically has as its goal the providing of benefits of a nontaxable nature to the employee. Consequently, the cases and rulings relating to some of the more significant nonstatutory fringe benefits that are often provided to the highly compensated individual are reviewed below. Because of the unlimited variety of these benefits, it would be virtually impossible to review every type of fringe benefit in the context of this treatise.

[a] **Basic Planning Factors.** In considering the implementation of a specific fringe benefit there are certain basic planning factors which must be considered in every case. The more important considerations are the following:

(1) Generally speaking, the more lavish the benefit provided, the stronger the likelihood of taxation. Service agents have long focused their attention on some of the more obvious abuses in the fringe benefit area. Thus, such agents regularly review the flight logs of corporate aircraft to look for personal use of the plane and have focused on such other expensive items as corporate yachts or hunting lodges. Conse-

---

the House Ways and Means Select Revenue Measures Subcommittee on Taxation of Fringe Benefits, May 13, 1981, reprinted in BNA Daily Tax Report No. 92, May 13, 1981.

quently, the more opulent the benefit, the more likely that it will attract attention from a Service agent whose economic condition and expectations are likely to be far lower than the individual who received the benefit.

(2) If there is to be allocation between personal and business use, accurate records should be maintained. Areas such as travel and entertainment [73] or the allocation of automobile costs between personal and business use have always demanded detailed record keeping. This same rule holds true for any other situation in which allocations take place. As a general rule, if an individual has relatively accurate and extensive records, there is a more favorable chance of resolving the matter on a reasonable basis with the agent who is auditing the case.

(3) Consider making the benefit more widely available. The chances of a negative reaction from an agent are often lessened if a benefit is more widely available than if it is available to just a few top corporate executives. The antidiscrimination legislation contained in ERISA and in several of the statutorily provided fringe benefits has frequently led agents to focus upon those benefits that are only provided to a select few. Consequently, it may be useful in some cases to expand the eligibility list. For example, if the corporation decided to furnish a gym at its main office, it would be preferable to make this facility available to a broader class of employees, such as all office employees, rather than to just selected officers. In such a case, the same purpose may be accomplished but with less of a Service backlash.

(4) Remember that a benefit, even if taxable, will still benefit the highly compensated employee. If a benefit is held to constitute taxable income to an employee, his out-of-pocket cost for that benefit will be limited to the tax paid. Consequently, assuming that a highly compensated executive is in the 50-percent tax bracket, his net out-of-pocket cost for that benefit will be fifty cents on the dollar. In addition, he may be able to argue successfully for a lower valuation of the benefit on his own tax return in order to reduce this cost even further. Finally, in certain cases, he may be able to reduce part of the taxable income with an offsetting deduction.

[b] Financial Counseling. With the preceding discussion as a background, let us consider several fringe benefits that are often provided to upper level corporate employees. One particular benefit that has gained a good deal of popularity with corporate executives in recent

---

[73] Entertainment expenses are subject to the specific statutory dictates of I.R.C. § 274(a).

years has been the establishment of a financial counseling program for highly compensated employees.

This benefit has proven popular for several reasons. First, the affected employees, because of their income levels, are of the type who frequently can benefit from these services. In addition, highly compensated individuals such as corporate executives often tend to be so busy that they ignore their own financial planning or simply let it slip. When the employer institutes a program to provide this service, however, the employees who are eligible to participate will generally want to take advantage of this benefit and, in effect, are forced to undertake this planning. Consequently, employers have instituted programs providing the services of financial planners, estate planners, or tax attorneys to selected groups of executive employees. The Service has ruled that financial counseling fees paid by a corporation for the benefit of its executives are includable in taxable income.[74] However, if fees are incurred for tax or investment advice, they will be deductible by the executive under Section 212 of the Code. Consequently, such services can be provided to the executive employee at a relatively nominal cost to him.

[c] Conventions. On many occasions, the taxability or nontaxability of a particular employer-provided item will depend upon whether the use was primarily for personal or business purposes. This is particularly true of items such as convention trips or the use of automobiles, where both personal and business motives are inherently present. For example, where a business motive is a primary one, the value of an employer-paid trip to a convention is not taxable income to the employee.[75] Where the convention trip is intended more as a paid holiday or where business is not the primary motive, taxable income will result to the employee.[76] If an employee and spouse attend a

---

[74] Rev. Rul. 73-13, 1973-1 C.B. 42. See also Merians v. Comm'r, 60 T.C. 187 (1973), which held that the portion of an estate planning fee attributable to tax advice was deductible under I.R.C. § 212(3). In that case the deduction was limited to 20 percent of the fee paid because of the vagueness of the testimony presented.

[75] See U.S. v. Gotcher, 401 F.2d 118 (5th Cir. 1968); People's Life Ins. Co. v. U.S., 373 F.2d 924 (Ct. Cl. 1967); Acacia Mut. Life Ins. Co. v. U.S., 272 F. Supp. 188 (D.Md. 1967).

[76] See, e.g., Campbell Sash Works, Inc. v. U.S., 217 F. Supp. 74 (N.D. Ohio 1963). McCann v. U.S., 81-2 U.S.T.C. ¶ 9689 (Ct. Cl. Trial Div. 1981). Deductions for foreign conventions held outside of North America are specifically (and more stringently) covered by I.R.C. § 274(h).

convention, taxability of the spouse's employer-paid expenses depends on whether or not the spouse is actually involved in the convention proceedings [77] or the degree to which the employer insisted upon the spouse's attendance.[78] The taxability of employer-provided automobiles similarly depends upon the extent of personal use.[79]

In each of the above-noted cases, advance planning can help to make the employer's payment of the executive's expenses nontaxable. If a convention is to be undertaken, it should be planned so that there are sufficient business purposes to justify the employer payment of expenses. The program should be designed to include significant business meetings with preprinted programs and course materials to provide extrinsic evidence of the business purpose. Employees who attend may be required to submit a report on the convention to their employer. If spouses are to attend the convention, the nontaxable nature of their attendance may be sustained if the employer requires their attendance and designs the convention program so that they actively participate in the proceedings. If the use of an employer-provided car is contemplated, logs can be kept of business trips or business usage of the car. In such a case, accurate record-keeping may sustain an argument of predominate business use.

Advance planning and careful record-keeping can be useful in precluding taxability in those types of areas which are frequently questioned by Service agents. If the situation is clearly abusive, however, this type of cosmetic planning is still likely to fail. For example, the need for two business executives who live in New York to hold a winter meeting in Acapulco is somewhat dubious at best. Other meetings or conventions arranged for a limited number of executives at a distant locale or resort raise similar suspicions. The fact remains that if an employer-paid trip or expense is blatantly abusive, the cleverest papering will not be effective.

[d] Meals or Lodging. Another common battleground in the fringe benefit area relates to meals or lodging, either paid for or furnished by the employer. The Code specifically excludes from gross income of an employee the value of any meals or lodging furnished to him, his spouse, or any of his dependents by or on behalf of his

---

[77] See Peoples Life Ins. Co. v. U.S., note 75 supra.

[78] U.S. v. Disney, 413 F.2d 783 (9th Cir. 1969).

[79] Of course, records to support the extent of business use are also important.

¶ 7.08[3][d] COMPENSATION PLANNING 7-30

employer *for the convenience of the employer* but only if, in the case of meals, the meals are furnished on the business premises of the employer or, in the case of lodging, the employee is required to accept such loding on the business premises of his employer as a condition of his employment.[80] As might be expected, there are numerous cases and rulings under Section 119 relating to the issue of what is for the convenience of the employer or the employer's requirement to live on particular premises. Most of these cases, however, relate to such issues as meals furnished to waitresses [81] or cash allowances furnished to state troopers [82] and are not of particular relevance to the highly compensated.

The Tax Court has ruled that where top executives of a corporation meet on a daily basis for a staff luncheon whose purpose it is to conduct the company's business, the value of the meals will not be included in the employee's income.[83] The Service has also ruled that supper money paid to employees who voluntarily work overtime is not taxable to them where such payment is not considered additional compensation and is not charged to the salary account.[84] This presumably would cover the situation where the executive is reimbursed for supper when working late. The Tax Court has held, however, that an employer's reimbursement of amounts paid by employees for lunches when entertaining others are taxable income to the employees and a nondeductible personal expense. In this particular instance, the taxpayers normally expended similar amounts on themselves whether or not they conducted business at lunch.[85]

Section 274(e)(1) makes the general rules of Section 274(a) inapplicable to business meals and sets forth somewhat more liberal rules for deductibility. That subsection is applicable to:

Business Meals — Expenses for food and beverages furnished to any individual under circumstances which (taking into account the surroundings in which furnished, the taxpayer's trade, business, or income producing activity and the relationship to such trade,

---

[80] I.R.C. § 119(a).

[81] Treas. Reg. § 1.119-1(d), Ex. 1.

[82] Comm'r v. Kowalski, 434 U.S. 77 (1977).

[83] Comm'r v. Mabley, 24 T.C.M. 1974 (1965).

[84] O.D. 514, C.B. 90 (1920).

[85] Fenstermaker v. Comm'r, 37 T.C.M. 898 (1978).

business or activity of the persons to whom the food and beverages are furnished) are of a type generally considered to be conducive to a business discussion.[86]

The Service's position on dealing with this section on business meals is set forth in Rev. Rul. 63-144.[87] This ruling emphasizes that it is not actually necessary to discuss business at the meal as long as there is a business relationship and the atmosphere is conducive to a business discussion. It takes the position, for example, that floor shows or large cocktail parties have distracting influences and thus are not a business meal within the definition of Section 274(e)(1). Such expenses must be judged under the more stringent rules of Section 274(a)(1).

The area of nonstatutory fringe benefits is an area of both legal confusion and increasing interest on the part of both the Service and the highly compensated. As inflation pushes individuals into higher tax brackets, there is a natural tendency to attempt to avoid taxation by receiving benefits in kind. The failure of the Service and Congress to develop a uniform set of rules in this area has led to the situation wherein the taxability or nontaxability of such benefits is judged on a case-by-case basis. This, quite naturally, leads to an attitude on the part of many corporate employers to see how much they can get away with without detection. Certain lines that should not be crossed have been the subject of either litigation and/or rulings and are clearly defined. Below that line is a substantial gray area that undoubtedly represents a future battleground between the highly compensated and the Service.

---

[86] I.R.C. § 274(e)(1).
[87] 1963-2 C.B. 129.

PART III
Noncompensation Planning

CHAPTER 8

Tax Shelters

		Page
¶ 8.01	Introduction	8-2
	[1] Definition of a Tax Shelter	8-2
	[2] Goals of a Tax Shelter Program	8-4
	[a] Deferral of Taxes	8-4
	[b] Conversion of Ordinary Income to Capital Gain	8-5
	[c] Leverage	8-5
	[d] Investment With Limited Liability	8-6
¶ 8.02	Achieving Tax Classification as a Partnership	8-7
	[1] Tax Advantages of Partnership Status	8-7
	[2] Regulations Distinguishing Partnerships From Corporations	8-8
	[a] Continuity of Life	8-9
	[b] Centralization of Management	8-10
	[c] Limited Liability	8-11
	[d] Free Transferability of Interest	8-11
	[3] IRS Ruling Position on Limited Partnership Status	8-12
	[a] Net Worth Requirements	8-12
	[b] Limit on Aggregate Deductions	8-13
	[4] Court Challenges to Limited Partnership Status	8-14
	[5] Proposed Revision of Regulations	8-16
	[6] Planning to Achieve Partnership Status	8-17
¶ 8.03	Basis and At-Risk Rules	8-18
	[1] Determination of Basis	8-18
	[2] Effect of Partnership Borrowings	8-19
	[3] At-Risk Limitations	8-21
¶ 8.04	Hobby Loss Provisions	8-24
¶ 8.05	Retroactive Allocation of Losses	8-26
¶ 8.06	Deductibility of Fees and Expenses	8-27
	[1] Organizational Expenses	8-27
	[2] Construction Period Interest and Taxes	8-30
	[3] Intangible Drilling Expenses	8-31

		Page
¶ 8.07	Evaluating a Tax Shelter	8-31
	[1] Soundness of the Investment	8-32
	[2] Review of Tax Risks	8-33
	[3] Real Cost of the Investment	8-36
	[4] Promoter's "Track Record"	8-37
	[5] Ultimate Profit From the Transaction	8-39
¶ 8.08	Estate Planning for Tax Shelters	8-41

¶ 8.01 Introduction

No topic elicits more interest from highly compensated individuals than tax shelters. As soon as an individual reaches a highly compensated status and begins to pay a considerable amount of his income to the federal government, the first question usually asked is: How can I shelter my income? Consequently, the tax advisor is often faced with the question of investing in tax shelters and the potential need to evaluate such shelters at the earliest stages of tax and financial planning.

[1] Definition of a Tax Shelter

Although most highly compensated individuals have a general understanding of what constitutes a tax shelter, precise definitions are somewhat elusive. Proposed regulations issued by the Service relating to tax opinion letters given by practitioners in tax shelter transactions define a "tax shelter" as "a sale, offering, syndication, promotion, investment or other transaction in which the claimed tax benefits are likely to be perceived by the taxpayer as the principal reason for his or her participation."[1] The Joint Committee on Internal Revenue Taxation has defined a "real estate tax shelter" as "an investment in which a significant portion of the investor's return is derived from the realiza-

---

[1] Prop. Reg. to amend 31 C.F.R. pt. 10 (Treas. Dep't Circular 236); § 10.33(c)(2), 45 Fed. Reg. 58, 594 (1980). The Prop. Reg. in the introductory material attempts to define "abusive tax shelters" as those in which "it is contemplated that the aggregate deductions, credits and other allowances that a taxpayer may claim within 24 months of his or her initial cash outlay will equal or exceed the amount of such cash outlay (disregarding any cash to be obtained by borrowing, except full-recourse borrowings from financial institutions unrelated to the taxpayer, promoter, or other participants)."

tion of tax savings on other income as well as the receipt of tax-free cash flow from the investment itself."[2]

Perhaps a more realistic definition is that a tax shelter is an investment designed to produce tax losses to the investor which can be used to offset other income so as to reduce the investor's taxes. Viewed in this manner, a tax shelter can range in magnitude from an individually owned investment in a rental condominium to a participation with many other investors in a public offering. Examining the full range of shelter investments is important because all too often tax shelters are only thought of as the many prepackaged syndicated offerings that are readily available today. An individual investment in a medium such as rental real estate may be an effective shelter, as is an investment held jointly by a small, closely knit group of friends. In all of these investments, the critical notion for tax shelter purposes is the production of tax (but not economic) losses to offset other income.[3]

Anyone considering tax shelters must constantly keep in mind the ebb and flow of legislative and regulatory attitudes that affect the taxation of shelters. For example, public outcry concerning high-income individuals who pay little or no income tax instigated substantial congressional activity in the tax shelter area during the 1970s. The result of this activity was a wide variety of statutory provisions enacted by the Tax Reform Act of 1976 and by the Revenue Act of 1978. On the other hand, many provisions of the Economic Recovery Tax Act of 1981 (the 1981 Act), such as the reduced taxation of capital gains, faster depreciation writeoffs, and liberalization of tax credits for rehabilitation expenditures, have encouraged participation in many types of shelter programs. Thus, the shelter investor must be constantly alert to legislative changes. Last year's tax advice may rapidly become out of date.

Tax shelter investments must also be made with a constant reference to the Service's attitude relating to these programs. The Service, in

---

[2] Joint Comm. on Internal Revenue Taxation, 94th Cong., 2d Sess. *Handbook on Tax Shelters* (1976).

[3] The ratio of tax losses to cash invested is still frequently used as a means of evaluating a tax shelter investment. For example, a shelter that is said to produce losses of 3-to-1 means that the tax writeoff for the year in question will equal three times the cash invested in that year. If an individual is in a 50 percent tax bracket and invested $1,000 in a 3-to-1 shelter, the tax savings to that individual of $1,500 (produced by losses of $3,000) will exceed his cash investment for that year.

recent years, has greatly stepped up its activity in the tax shelter area. It has issued numerous rulings designed to curb some of the most abusive tax shelter programs and has also announced a policy of intensified audits for those tax shelters producing large tax losses.[4] In addition, the Service has shown an inclination to litigate various tax shelter issues that might be considered open areas under the law. The consequence of this activity is that the investor can expect that the tax shelter investment will be scrutinized closely by the Service.

[2] Goals of a Tax Shelter Program

[a] **Deferral of Taxes.** Essential to the concept of many tax shelters is the principle of deferral of taxes. In effect, such tax shelters utilize accelerated deductions in order to enable the participant to borrow money interest-free from the federal government. By utilizing accelerated deductions,[5] the participant in such transactions has funds currently available that he would otherwise use to pay taxes. These funds then can be invested to increase the taxpayer's net worth or for other personal purposes. Although the taxpayer may ultimately have to pay the same amount of taxes, the time of payment will be deferred to the taxpayer's advantage. For example, if a taxpayer in the 50 percent bracket can accelerate $10,000 of deductions into a given year, such as by making a $10,000 charitable contribution on December 31, he will save $5,000 in taxes. This money is then available for investment or consumption purposes until the taxes fall due.

Every taxpayer can benefit from the deferral of taxes since these funds will be available for personal use during the deferral period. A further advantage occurs if the taxpayer is in a lower bracket when the taxes fall due. Thus, a taxpayer whose income fluctuates downward will benefit even more from a tax-deferral type of shelter since the deductions will be received in high-income years and subsequent income will be taxed at a lower rate. Consequently, deferral types of shelters might be particularly appropriate for individuals experiencing very high income years, such as athletes or entertainers.

It also must be emphasized that the indexing provisions of the 1981

---

[4] See the I.R.S. Examination of Tax Shelters Handbook.

[5] An example of such accelerated deductions would be rapid depreciation of real property.

Act [6] substantially increase the value of tax deferral. Indexing means that the same dollar amount of income will be taxed at a lower rate in subsequent years as tax brackets are automatically adjusted for inflation. Conversely, a deduction of the same dollar amount is worth more today than tomorrow, since the income it offsets would be taxed in higher brackets today.

[b] Conversion of Ordinary Income to Capital Gain. A second goal of tax shelter operation is the conversion of ordinary income into capital gain. For example, a taxpayer must deduct depreciation against ordinary income. If the asset is later sold and the excess of the amount received over the adjusted basis is treated as capital gain, the taxpayer will have had the advantage of a deduction against ordinary income and the resultant income being taxed at capital gains rates. Although the depreciation recapture rules of Sections 1245 and 1250 have tended to mitigate against this principle, these recapture rules are not applicable in all situations. Consequently, in those situations, it is still possible to convert ordinary income into capital gain.

The 1978 and 1981 Acts, which have reduced the maximum capital gains rate to 20 percent, increase the advantage of realizing capital gain. A deduction against a 50 percent income tax rate, taxed at a 20 percent capital gains rate when property is sold, immediately achieves a 30 percent savings on the dollars involved. If, in the interim, indexing has also adjusted the tax brackets involved, the savings will be even greater. Accordingly, the tax savings from dollars deducted against ordinary income and later taxed at capital gains rates can be quite staggering.

[c] Leverage. Many tax shelters also use leverage to increase a taxpayer's deductions per dollar of investment. Leverage is generally the use of borrowed money by a taxpayer to invest in a particular shelter. This principle [7] enables the taxpayer to use borrowed money to create tax deductions and to invest his own funds elsewhere. Assuming that the taxpayer's investments are profitable, this principle maximizes the use of the taxpayer's own funds in order to achieve both gain and

---

[6] The indexing provisions become effective in 1985. These are discussed at ¶ 2.01[2].

[7] Leverage is subject to the basis limitations of partnership taxation and the at-risk rules of Section 465.

deductions. As the percentage of borrowing increases in a transaction, so does the rate of return and deduction to actual investment. In addition, the interest paid on the borrowed funds is deductible by the taxpayer.[8]

[d] Investment with Limited Liability. A further goal of most tax shelter investments is to structure the transaction so that the investor's liability is limited to a known amount. Most such investments are organized as limited partnerships with high-income investors admitted as limited partners. In the properly structured investment, the limited partner's liability will be limited to his agreed-upon contribution to the entity. Thus, just as with a corporation, the downside risk is known in advance. It must be emphasized, however, that limited liability is somewhat more difficult to achieve in a limited partnership than in a corporation because of the requirements of the Uniform Limited Partnership Act (U.L.P.A.). The partnership agreement must carefully and specifically set forth the parameters of the limited partner's capital contribution. In addition, the limited partner cannot participate in the management of the entity [9] if limited liability is to be achieved. The limited partner must remain a passive investor. If, however, these organizational requirements are complied with, the limited partner can limit the magnitude of his economic risk.

The types of investments offered in syndicated tax shelter transactions are as varied as the mind can conceive. The most common types of investment for tax shelter transactions are real estate, oil and gas, farming and cattle, timber, equipment leasing, coal, and motion pictures. Shelters have been offered in such other exotic areas as tropical plants, almond groves, art prints, and bibles. Because a detailed evaluation of the tax consequences of each of these types of investments would take several volumes, no attempt will be made in the chapter to present a complete analysis of the tax consequences of each type of tax shelter. Rather, the following section will discuss the general principles relating to the taxation of tax shelters and some specific problems relating to the more popular types of shelter programs. This will be followed by a

---

[8] Subject to the investment interest limitation of Section 163(d) and the prohibition against using borrowed funds to purchase or carry tax exempt obligations set forth in Section 265(2). This latter limitation is discussed at ¶ 2.04[4][a][ii].

[9] Nor should he have a right to participate in management under the partnership agreement.

discussion of rules for the evaluation of tax shelter investments and an analysis of the peculiar estate planning problems relating to shelters.

¶ 8.02 Achieving Tax Classification as a Partnership

[1] Tax Advantages of Partnership Status

The most critical early hurdle faced by a particular tax shelter operation is to be classified for tax purposes as a partnership. It is partnership classification that enables tax losses to be passed through to the investors [10] to shelter other income. The partnership itself is not taxed as an entity, as is a corporation, but rather all deductions, losses, credits, and income are passed through to its partners in allocable shares.[11] If a particular entity is not taxed as a partnership, the distributable shares of the partnership losses cannot be allocated to the various investor-partners and, hence, there is no shelter.[12]

Most tax shelter operations are organized as limited partnerships under U.L.P.A., which has been enacted by all the states. These entities generally have one or more general partners,[13] who usually are designees of or are related to the tax shelter promoter. The general partners manage the operation for the limited partners, whose role is that of passive investors. Under U.L.P.A.,[14] the liability of limited partners is statutorily limited to their agreed-upon capital contribution to the partnership so long as they maintain their passive role and do not assume active control over the investment. The limited partnership form is favored for use in tax shelter investments for three basic reasons. First, it enables the tax losses from the investment to be passed through to the limited partners to shelter their other income. Second, it

---

[10] An individually owned investment that produces a tax shelter (such as a rental condominium) does not, of course, require a separate entity in order to pass through tax losses since the property can be operated as a sole proprietorship.

[11] I.R.C. § 701.

[12] Most tax shelter investments, if they were classified as a corporation, would not qualify in the past as a Subchapter S corporation because a significant percentage of their income was derived from passive sources. See I.R.C. § 1372(e)(5). Even though the passive income limitations are largely eliminated for new S corporations, the investor in an S corporation may not have a sufficient tax basis to generate the desired amount of losses.

[13] Such entities may or may not be corporations.

[14] U.L.P.A. § 17.

provides a limitation upon their liability — the comfort that economic losses cannot exceed an agreed-upon amount in most instances. Third, because the limited partner by definition is a passive investor in the partnership, there is no necessity to assume an active managerial role over the investment. In a typical tax shelter operation, the investor depends on [15] someone else to manage the investment.

[2] Regulations Distinguishing Partnerships From Corporations

The tax classification of an entity as a partnership or as a limited partnership is a complex issue and does not necessarily parallel state law definitions. The term "partnership" is defined by the Code to be a "syndicate, group, pool, joint venture or other unincorporated organization, through or by means of which any business, financial operation, or venture is carried on, and which is not, within the meaning of this title, a trust or estate or a corporation."[16] The term "corporation" is defined to include "associations, joint stock companies, and insurance companies."[17] An organization that qualifies as a limited partnership under state law may be classified for tax purposes as a partnership or as an association taxable as a corporation, depending upon the various characteristics of that entity. The regulations [18] describe six characteristics that are found in a pure corporation:

(1) associates;
(2) an objective to carry on business and divide the gains therefrom;
(3) continuity of life;
(4) centralization of management;
(5) liability for corporate debts limited to corporate property (limited liability); and
(6) free transferability of interest.

The regulations then go on to state that an organization will be treated as an association taxable as a corporation if the corporate characteris-

---

[15] As discussed at ¶ 8.07, infra, such dependence can be costly.
[16] I.R.C. § 7701(a)(2).
[17] I.R.C. § 7701(a)(3).
[18] Treas. Reg. § 301.7701-2.

tics are such that the organization more nearly resembles a corporation than a partnership or trust.[19]

In distinguishing between a corporation and a partnership, those characteristics that are common to both (associates and an objective to carry on a business and divide the gains therefrom) are eliminated from consideration. Consequently, the remaining four characteristics — continuity of life, centralization of management, limited liability, and free transferability of interest — must be evaluated to determine how a particular organization will be classified. Present regulations state that an unincorporated organization will not be classified as an association taxable as a corporation unless the organization has more corporate than noncorporate characteristics.[20] If an unincorporated association has two corporate and two noncorporate characteristics, it will be classified as a partnership for tax purposes. Three corporate characteristics are required for an unincorporated organization to be taxable as a corporation.[21]

The Code itself does not mention the limited partnership as a distinct form of entity.[22] An organization that qualifies as a limited partnership under state law may be classified for tax purposes as a partnership or as an association taxable as a corporation. A limited partnership will be treated as an association taxable as a corporation if, applying the principles set forth in Reg. § 301.7701-2, the organization more nearly resembles a corporation than a partnership or other business entity.

[a] **Continuity of Life.** The regulations state that if the death, insanity, bankruptcy, retirement, resignation, or expulsion of any member results in a dissolution of the organization, continuity of life does not exist.[23] In addition, if the retirement, death, or insanity of the

---

[19] Treas. Reg. § 301.7701-2(a)(1); see also Morrissey v. Comm'r, 296 U.S. 344 (1935).

[20] Treas. Reg. § 301.7701-2(a)(3).

[21] These regulations, known as the Kintner Regulations (named after U.S. v. Kintner, 216 F.2d 418 (9th Cir. 1954)), evolved from a long-running battle between the I.R.S. and the earliest professional corporations. At that time, the I.R.S. took the position that professional corporations should be classified as partnerships for tax purposes. These Regulations, which thus preceded many of today's concerns relating to tax shelter investments, are somewhat more favorable to partnership classification than the I.R.S. would probably desire today.

[22] See I.R.C. §§ 7701(a)(2)-7701(a)(3).

[23] Treas. Reg. § 301.7701-2(b)(1).

general partner in a limited partnership causes the dissolution of the partnership unless the remaining members agree to continue the partnership, continuity of life simply does not exist.[24] If, despite any provisions in the partnership agreement, a member has the power under local law to dissolve the organization, the organization lacks continuity of life for tax purposes. A limited partnership organized under U.L.P.A. possesses the characteristics just discussed, which could result in a dissolution of the organization under local law in many circumstances. Consequently, the regulations specifically state that a limited partnership subject to a statute corresponding to U.L.P.A. lacks continuity of life.[25]

[b] Centralization of Management. The regulations indicate that centralized management means a concentration of continuing exclusive authority to make independent business decisions on behalf of the organization that do not require a ratification by members of the organization. Thus, there is not centralization of management when the centralized authority is merely to perform a ministerial act as an agent at the discretion of a principal.[26] The regulations also note that because of the mutual agency relationship between members of a general partnership subject to a statute corresponding to the Uniform Partnership Act, such a partnership cannot possess effective concentration of management powers and therefore cannot possess centralized management. In addition, the regulations note that limited partnerships subject to a statute corresponding to the U.L.P.A. do not generally have centralized management, but centralized management ordinarily does exist in such a limited partnership if substantially all the interests in the partnership are owned by the limited partners. The Service has not published a ruling that specifically defines when "substantially all" the interests in a partnership are owned by the limited partners. However, there is at least one example in the regulations [27] that finds centralized manage-

---

[24] See Glensder Textile Co. v. Comm'r, 46 B.T.A. 176 (1942).

[25] Section 20 of the Uniform Limited Partnership Act states that the retirement, death, or insanity of a general partner dissolves the partnership unless the business is continued by the remaining general partners either under a right to do so stated in the partnership certificate or with the consent of all members.

[26] Treas. Reg. § 301.7701-2(c)(3).

[27] Treas. Reg. § 301.7701-3(b)(2), Ex. 1.

ment to exist where the general partners owned in excess of 5 percent of the interest in the limited partnership.[28] Consequently, many limited partnerships that are owned predominantly by the limited partners possess this corporate characteristic. If the limited partners retain a high percentage of ownership, they often have to take extra care to ensure that they do not possess the other corporate characteristics discussed in ¶ 8.02[2].

[c] **Limited Liability.** The regulations state that "personal liability means that a creditor of an organization may seek personal satisfaction from a member of the organization to the extent that the assets of such organization are insufficient to satisfy the creditor's claim."[29] The regulations also take the position that in a case of an organization formed as a partnership, personal liability does not exist with respect to a general partner when he has no substantial assets and when he is merely a "dummy" acting as agent of the limited partners. Even if a general partner has no substantial assets, personal liability exists with respect to such general partner when he is not merely a dummy acting as agent of the limited partnership. If the organization is engaged in financial transactions that involve large sums of money and if the general partners have substantial assets (other than their interest in the partnership), there exists personal liability although the assets of the general partners would be insufficient to satisfy any substantial portion of the obligations of the organization.

[d] **Free Transferability of Interest.** The regulations state that an organization has the corporate characteristic of free transferability of interest only if each of its members or those members owning substantially all the interest in the organization have the power, without the consent of other members, to substitute for themselves a person who is not a member of the organization. Moreover, the regulations hold that no free transferability of interest exists if, under local law, a transfer of the member's interest results in a dissolution of the old organization and a formation of the new organization. In a situation where a transferee does not become a substitute limited partner except with the

---

[28] See also Treas. Reg. § 301.7701-(2)(g), Exs. 4, 5, 6, and the discussion of Rev. Proc. 74-17, 1974-1 C.B. 438, at ¶ 8.02[3][b].

[29] Treas. Reg. § 301.7701-2(d)(1).

unanimous consent of the general partners, the characteristic of the free transferability of interests does not exist.[30]

The regulations thus provide a relatively clear guideline on how to achieve limited partnership status. Continuity of life will almost always be avoided by proper organization under the U.L.P.A. Centralized management can be avoided, but only if the general partner has a substantial ownership position. Limited liability can be avoided through the creation of personal liability on a general partner who is not a "dummy." Finally, restrictions on transferability must be inserted.

[3] IRS Ruling Position on Limited Partnership Status

In addition to the aforementioned regulations, the Service has published two revenue procedures that set forth its ruling position as to when an entity will be classified as a limited partnership.

[a] Net Worth Requirements. In Rev. Proc. 72-13,[31] the Service announced that it will not issue a ruling that classifies an organization as a limited partnership where a corporation is the sole general partner if any one or more of the following conditions are present:

(1) The limited partners own, directly or indirectly, individually or in the aggregate, more than 20 percent of the stock of the sole corporate general partner, or any affiliates thereof;[32]

(2) The net worth of the sole corporate general partner (exclusive of its partnership interest) is not at least equal to the lesser of $250,000 or 15 percent of the total contributions to the partnership where contributions to the organization are less than $2,500,000;

(3) Where the contributions to the organization exceed $2,500,000, and the net worth of the sole corporate general partner (exclusive of its partnership interest) is less than 10 percent of such contributions;

(4) The sole corporate general partner has interests in more than one partnership, and the net worth requirement set forth in item (2) above is not satisfied as to each such partnership (excluding from sole general partner's net worth the interest in each such partnership); and

---

[30] Treas. Reg. §§ 301.7701-2(e)(1), 301.7701-3(b)(2), Ex. 1.
[31] 1972-2 C.B. 735.
[32] The concept of affiliates is defined in I.R.C. § 1504(a).

(5) The purchase of a limited partnership interest by the limited partner entails either mandatory or discretionary purchase or option to purchase any type of security of the sole corporate general partner or its affiliate.

This ruling is aimed at the situation whereby the limited partners would establish a dummy corporation to act as general partner of a newly formed partnership with a result that no person really had any personal liability. To date, this so-called net worth requirement has not been applied to the situation where there is an individual general partner, nor has it ever been tested in court. Most practitioners familiar with this area advise their clients to abide by these net worth requirements when there is a corporate general partner. In addition, if there is an individual general partner, this individual should be a person of substance rather than someone who was selected because he is judgment-proof.

[b] Limit on Aggregate Deductions. In Rev. Proc. 74-17,[33] the Service set forth additional restrictions on its ruling policy in regard to classification of limited partnerships. Ordinarily, to obtain a favorable ruling, the interests of all general partners taken together in each material item of the partnership — income, gain, loss, deduction, or credit — must be equal to at least one percent of each such item at all times during the existence of the partnership. In addition, the aggregate deductions to be claimed by the partners as their distributive shares of partnership losses for the first two years of operation of the limited partnership cannot be anticipated to exceed the amount of equity capital invested in the limited partnership. Finally, a creditor who makes a nonrecourse loan to the limited partnership must not have or acquire at any time as a result of making the loan any direct or indirect interest in the profits, capital, or property of the limited partnership other than as a secured creditor. Revenue Procedure 74-17 states that the above-mentioned rules are "to be applied only in determining whether ruling and determination letters will be issued and are not intended to be substantive rules for the determination of partnership status and are not to be applied as criteria for the audit of taxpayers' returns." That statement is somewhat gratuitous inasmuch as a ruling position such as this tends to become a substantive standard over time.

---

[33] 1974-1 C.B. 438.

Again, however, this particular revenue procedure has not been challenged or sustained in court.

Of the guidelines set forth in Rev. Proc. 74-17, the most critical is the indication that the losses for the first two years cannot exceed the amount of equity capital invested. Until the advent of the at-risk rules [34] set forth in Section 465 of the Code, this requirement was the most difficult to meet. The at-risk rules, which, in most cases other than real estate investments, limit deductions to the amount of equity capital invested, have in many instances made this particular requirement somewhat superfluous.

[4] Court Challenges to Limited Partnership Status

In recent years, the Service has also exhibited a tendency to challenge the partnership status claimed by limited partnerships, with the result of injecting some uncertainty to this area of the law. The first such case was *Zuckman v. U.S.*[35] In this case, the Court of Claims upheld the partnership status of a limited partnership organized under Missouri law. The general partner was a corporation having no substantial assets and that was a wholly owned subsidiary of a corporation wholly owned by one of the limited partners. Although the *Zuckman* holding favored the taxpayer, the case illustrated the point that the Service was willing to challenge the classification of a Uniform Limited Partnership Act type of organization as a partnership for tax purposes, despite the intimation in the regulations that such organizations will almost automatically qualify as a partnership. The case also illustrated that the Court of Claims has been a relatively favorable forum for taxpayers to litigate this issue.

In contrast to *Zuckman*, the Tax Court, in *Comm'r v. Larson*,[36] had considerable difficulty in classifying two California limited partnerships as partnerships for federal tax purposes. In *Larson*, the Service challenged the partnership status of two limited partnerships organized under the California Limited Partnership Statute. The Tax Court originally ruled on October 21, 1975 that the partnerships in *Larson* were taxable as corporations and, consequently, the partners were not entitled to deduct their allocable share of partnership losses. After many commentators had noted that the original *Larson* opinion largely

---

[34] The at-risk rules are discussed at ¶ 8.03[3], infra.
[35] 524 F.2d 729 (Ct. Cl. 1975).
[36] 66 T.C. 159 (1976).

ignored existing Service regulations,[37] that opinion was withdrawn. Subsequently, a divided Tax Court held that these partnerships were indeed taxable as partnerships. In so holding, the court ruled that the partnerships in question possessed two characteristics that are critical to classification as a corporation: centralized management and free transferability of interest. Since the partnerships were found not to possess corporate characteristics of limited liability and continuity of life, the Tax Court felt compelled under the existing regulations to hold the organizations taxable as partnerships. Since these organizations possessed two corporate characteristics and two noncorporate characteristics, and had no other significant corporate or noncorporate characteristics, they could not be classified under the regulations as corporations. The Service initiated, but later withdrew, an appeal of the final decision of the Tax Court.

The Service has announced[38] that it will follow the *Larson* decision and it has also announced that the absence or presence of the following factors will not be of critical importance in classifying an entity as a partnership:

(1) The division of limited partnership interests into units or shares and the promotion and marketing of such interests in a manner similar to corporate security;

(2) The managing partner's right or lack of the discretionary right to retain or distribute profits according to the needs of the business;

(3) The limited partner's right or lack of the right to vote on the removal and election of the general partners and the right or the lack of the right to vote on the sale of all or substantially all of the assets of the partnership;

(4) The limited partnership interest being represented or not being represented by certificates;

(5) The limited partnership's observance or lack of observance of corporate formalities and procedures;

(6) The limited partners being required or not being required to sign the partnership agreement; and

(7) The limited partnership providing a means of pooling investments while limiting the liability of some of the participants.

---

[37] Treas. Reg. § 301.7701-2.
[38] Rev. Rul. 79-106, 1979-1 C.B. 448.

[5] Proposed Revision of Regulations

In reaching its conclusion in *Larson*, the Tax Court seemingly suggested that if the regulations were phrased in a different manner it might rule otherwise. Thus, many tax practitioners felt that it was possible to interpret the *Larson* case as a suggestion that the Service should amend the regulations so as to be more restrictive in recognizing partnership status. Indeed, in January 1977, the Service did promulgate a proposed regulation under Section 7701, which would have significantly affected the method of classification of a business organization that possessed both corporate and noncorporate characteristics.[38a]

The proposed regulation adopted a "resemblance" test for the classification of business organizations. Under this test, the four primary characteristics by which a business organization is classified as either a partnership or an association taxable as a corporation were retained, but the degree to which the organization possessed each of these characteristics had to be tested in order to determine its proper classification. For example, if an organization possessed the characteristic of continuity of life under certain circumstances (if, for example, the death of a general partner would not cause a dissolution of the organization), the fact that continuity of life existed in this particular type of situation would have to be considered in determining the overall classification of the organization. More significantly, the proposed regulation limited the so-called preponderence test, under which an unincorporated business organization lacking two of the four corporate characteristics would automatically be considered as a partnership for tax purposes. In effect, a business organization would have to lack three of these characteristics to be assured of tax classification as a partnership. If the organization only lacked two of the corporate characteristics, the facts and circumstances underlying each characteristic would have to be weighed to determine the organization's classification. The proposed regulation also amended the test for each of the aforementioned characteristics, in general, to make partnership classification more difficult. This proposed regulation was immediately the subject of considerable adverse commentary. It was ordered withdrawn shortly after its release.[39]

[38a] Prop. Reg. §§ 301.7701-2, 301.7701-3, 42 Fed. Reg. 1038 (Jan. 5, 1977), withdrawn, 42 Fed. Reg. 1489 (Jan. 7, 1977).

[39] Subsequently, the Carter administration in its 1978 proposals for tax reform sought to limit the availability of tax advantages normally associated

[6] Planning to Achieve Partnership Status

The net result of *Larson* and other Service activity was to interject uncertainty into the critical area of partnership classification. In a relatively short period, the Service had announced a restrictive ruling position for the classification of an entity as a limited partnership, had shown a tendency to challenge in court the tax classification of a validly organized limited partnership, and had issued proposed regulations that would have drastically decreased the likelihood of partnership classification for many limited partnerships.

This degree of activity has slowed somewhat in recent years. The January 1977 proposed regulation has not been reissued and there has not been a major court challenge to the tax status of limited partnerships that would weaken the precedent set forth in *Larson* and *Zuckman*. With the precedent established in these cases, most practitioners feel relatively confident of achieving partnership classification if the guidelines set forth in the regulations and in the two revenue procedures issued by the Service are followed. The regulations and revenue procedures are discussed at ¶¶ 8.02[3][a] and 8.02[3][b].

It is particularly critical in establishing a limited partnership to insure that the general partner is not a "dummy" having no economic viability. This means that it is advisable either to follow the net worth requirements for corporate general partners set forth in Rev. Proc. 72-13 or to be sure that an individual general partner is a person of substance. Since most tax shelter limited partnerships do possess centralized management,[40] it is important that the limited liability criterion not be met. In addition, it is usually advisable to place relatively stringent restrictions on the transferability of a limited partner's interest so that free transferability of interest will not exist. Correct adherence to the standards of the Uniform Limited Partnership Act almost always means that there will be no continuity of life. Accordingly, if these guidelines are carefully followed, partnership status will usually be assured under current interpretations of the law.

Given the frequent concern expressed by the Service with tax

---

with widely held limited partnerships. Under their proposal, a limited partnership with more than 15 limited partners would be taxed as a corporation rather than a partnership. This proposal was defeated in committee and therefore not included in the Revenue Act of 1978. It is not likely to be resurrected in the near future.

[40] Management is generally centralized because substantially all the interests are typically owned by the limited partners.

shelter limited partnerships, it is reasonable to assume that the Service's attack on tax shelter limited partnerships has not permanently abated. The focus of concern has merely shifted in recent years from classification of an entity as a limited partnership to other areas.[41]

¶ 8.03 Basis and At-Risk Rules

The question of the tax basis for partners is extremely significant to the subject of tax shelters because the tax basis, together with the at-risk rules, places a limitation upon the amount of losses that each partner can deduct from a tax shelter operation. Each partner is generally permitted to offset his distributive share of partnership losses against income derived from other sources. However, a partner's distributive share of partnership deductions is not allowed as a deduction against other income to the extent it exceeds the adjusted basis for his partnership interest at the end of the year in which the deductions arise.[42] Thus, a partner, including a limited partner, cannot deduct partnership losses in excess of the basis of his partnership interest. Any deductions so disallowed, however, will be allowed as a deduction in subsequent years to the extent that the partner's adjusted basis for his partnership interest at the end of any such year exceeds zero before reduction by his loss for such year. The amount of deductible losses may be further limited by the at-risk rules set forth in Section 465 of the Code. This limitation, together with its interplay with the Section 704(d) rule on deductions not exceeding basis, is discussed at ¶ 8.03[3].

[1] Determination of Basis

A partner's basis for his partnership interest initially consists of the amount of money he contributes to the partnership plus the adjusted basis of any property he contributes, increased by the amount, if any, of the gain recognized by him at the time of contribution.[43] The adjusted basis of his partnership interest will be increased by the sum of his distributive share for the taxable year and the prior year's taxable income of the partnership, income of the partnership exempt from tax,

---

[41] See, e.g., ¶ 8.06, infra, discussing the legitimacy of deductions for partnership fees and expenses.

[42] I.R.C. § 704(d).

[43] I.R.C. § 722.

and the excess of deductions for depletion over the basis of the property subject to depletion. His basis will be decreased (but not below zero) by distributions by the partnership and by the sum of his distributive share for the taxable year and prior taxable years of losses of the partnership and expenditures of the partnership not deductible in computing its taxable income and not properly chargeable to its capital account and decreased (but not below zero) by the amount of the partner's deduction for depletion under Section 611 with respect to oil and gas wells.[44] Thus, in simplest terms, a partner's tax losses in any given year reduce the basis of his partnership interest. Consequently, to the extent that these losses reduce the basis of his partnership interest below zero, these losses will be disallowed.

[2] Effect of Partnership Borrowings

Borrowings by the partnership may also have a substantial effect on the tax basis of a partner's partnership interest. The effect of such borrowings will vary for the limited partners, depending on whether the indebtedness is recourse or nonrecourse.[45] Generally speaking, any increase in any partner's share of liabilities of the partnership or any increase in a partner's individual liabilities by reason of the assumption by such partner of partnership liabilities is considered a contribution of money by the partner and has the effect of increasing the basis of his partnership interest.[46] Conversely, any decrease in a partner's share of the liabilities of a partnership or any decrease in a partner's individual liabilities by reason of the partnership's assumption of such individual liabilities is considered a distribution of money to the partner by the partnership, with a resultant decrease in basis.[47] For purposes of Section 752, a liability to which the property is subject, to the extent of the fair market value of such property, will be considered as a liability of the owner of the property.[48] Because of the language in Section 752, the discharge of a partnership liability, be it recourse or nonrecourse, is treated as a receipt of money by the partner. Consequently, to the extent

---

[44] I.R.C. § 705.

[45] Nonrecourse liabilities are secured only by the property that is the subject of the borrowings; no individual is personally liable for the repayment of such debts.

[46] I.R.C. § 752(a).

[47] I.R.C. § 752(b).

[48] I.R.C. § 752(c).

that the liability being discharged exceeds the limited partner's basis in such property, taxable income will be produced.

In the landmark case of *Crane v. Comm'r*,[49] the court held that the tax basis of property subject to a mortgage includes the amount of the mortgage even though the owner of the property assumes no personal liability on the mortgage debt, and that when property subject to a liability is sold, the amount realized includes the amount of the unassumed mortgage. Because of a footnote in the *Crane* case, many commentators initially felt that the amount of income that could be realized on the discharge of a mortgage indebtedness was limited to the fair market value of the property.[50] Subsequent cases have, however, largely eliminated the argument that there is a fair market value limitation upon the amount realized from the discharge of a nonrecourse liability.[51]

If the partnership indebtedness is recourse, a partner's share of partnership liabilities will be determined in accordance with his ratio for sharing losses under the partnership agreement. In the case of a limited partnership, a limited partner's share of the partnership recourse liabilities will not exceed the difference between his actual contribution credited to him by the partnership and the total contribution that he is obligated to make under the limited partnership agreement.[52] Where neither of the partners nor the partnership has any personal liability with respect to a partnership liability (i.e., nonrecourse liability), then all of the partners, including limited partners, are considered as sharing the liability in the same proportion in which they share profits. Consequently, limited partners have generally been able to add the amount of partnership nonrecourse liabilities to the income tax basis of their partnership interest, whereas the basis increase permitted by recourse financing is limited to the limited partner's

---

[49] 331 U.S. 1 (1947).

[50] Footnote 37 in *Crane* (id. at 14) states as follows:

> Obviously, if the value of the property is less than the amount of the mortgage, a mortgagor who is not personally liable cannot realize the benefit equal to the mortgage. Consequently, a different problem might be encountered where a mortgagor abandoned the property or transferred it subject to the mortgage without receiving boot. This is not the case here.

[51] Millar v. Comm'r, 67 T.C. 656 (1977), aff'd, 577 F.2d 212 (3d Cir. 1978); Woodsam Assocs. v. Comm'r, 16 T.C. 649 (1951), aff'd, 198 F.2d 357 (2d Cir. 1952). But see Tufts v. Comm'r, 651 F.2d 1058 (5th Cir. 1981), rev'g 70 T.C. 756 (1978).

[52] Treas Reg. § 1.752-1(e).

agreed-upon capital contribution. For this reason, nonrecourse financing has been especially prevalent in the operation of tax shelters because it provided a means of increasing a limited partner's basis beyond his capital contribution and, hence, increased the amount of losses that he could deduct.

The use of nonrecourse financing has been significantly curbed in recent years by attacks on two fronts. First, the Service has issued rulings designed to limit the addition to basis created by nonrecourse financing far in excess of the value of the property securing the loan.[53] The Service has basically taken the position that the tax basis of property cannot be artificially inflated by nonrecourse financing in an amount that significantly exceeds the fair market value of the secured property. The Service also ruled that a nonrecourse loan made by a general partner of a limited partnership to the limited partners of a portion of their subscription in the partnership is a capital contribution by the general partner rather than a loan and will be added to the basis of the general partner's interest, rather than to the basis of the limited partners.[54] Second, the at-risk rules of Section 465 of the Code have also greatly restricted the utility of nonrecourse financing in most tax shelter areas with the exception of investment in real estate.[55]

[3] At-Risk Limitations

The at-risk limitations, which were first added to the Code in 1976 and expanded upon in 1978, provide a further limitation on the amount of losses a limited partner may deduct in any tax year. Basically, a limited partner may not deduct from his taxable income any amount attributable to his limited partnership losses in excess of the lesser of (1) the adjusted tax basis of his interest at the end of the partnership year or (2) the amount that the limited partner is considered to have at risk with respect to the activities of the limited partnership at the end of the limited partnership's tax year in which the loss occurs. The at-risk limitations, which are essentially applicable to all activities other than investment in real estate, limit the amount of losses that an individual may deduct to the amount he is considered to have at risk in a given period.[56] These limitations are also applicable to subchapter S corpora-

---

[53] See Rev. Rul. 77-110, 1977-1 C.B. 58; Rev. Rul. 78-29, 1978-1 C.B. 62; Rev. Rul. 80-42, 1980-1 C.B. 182.

[54] Rev. Rul. 72-135, 1972-1 C.B. 200.

[55] Other than mineral property.

[56] I.R.C. § 465(a)(1).

tions and corporations in which five or fewer individuals own (actually or constructively) more than 50 percent in value of the outstanding stock. The amounts considered at risk by a taxpayer include the amount of money and the adjusted basis of other property contributed by the taxpayer for the activity, amounts borrowed by the taxpayer with respect to the activity and amounts borrowed for which the taxpayer is either personally liable for repayment or for which he has pledged property (other than the property used in the activity) as security, to the extent of the net fair market value of the taxpayer's interest in such property.[57] The Code expressly states that a taxpayer should not be considered at risk with respect to amounts protected against loss through nonrecourse financing, guarantees, stop-loss agreements, or other similar arrangements.[58]

The major effect of Section 465 has been to place limitations upon the use of nonrecourse financing to increase the losses of taxpayers beyond their capital contributions in most tax shelter transactions. The only significant exception to this rule is in the case of real property, which is specifically excluded from the at-risk limitations.[59] Accordingly, the use of nonrecourse financing in real estate syndications is still quite prevalent. In such cases, the rulings relating to fair market value, nonrecourse financing by general partners, and other such limitations on artificially inflated loans must be carefully scrutinized.[59a]

The 1978 Act provided that if a limited partner's amount at risk is reduced below zero, the limited partner must recognize income to the extent that his at-risk basis is reduced below zero.[60] The limited partner is allowed a deduction for recaptured amounts included in taxable income if in a subsequent taxable year he increases his amount at risk. This situation could occur if loans that were previously made on a recourse basis became nonrecourse after a period of time, or if the partnership made certain distributions to a partner.

---

[57] I.R.C. § 465(b).

[58] I.R.C. § 465(b)(4).

[59] Section 465(c)(3)(D) of the Code excludes the holding of real property (other than mineral property) from the at-risk limitations and notes that personal property and services that are incidental to making real property available as living accommodations will be treated as part of the activity of holding such real property. This is intended to apply primarily to hotels and motels.

[59a] See Rev. Rul. 77-110, 1977-1 C.B. 58; Rev. Rul. 78-29, 1978-1 C.B. 62; Rev. Rul. 80-235, 1980-2 C.B. 229.

[60] I.R.C. § 465(e).

Proposed regulations under Section 465 have generally taken a hard line as to when amounts will be considered at risk. For example, Prop. Reg. § 1.465-6(e) states that if a taxpayer guarantees a liability of a business activity, his at-risk amount will not be increased until he actually repays the creditor and has no remaining legal rights against the primary obligor. It further states that the taxpayer is not at risk under Section 465(d)(4) to the extent that he is protected against the loss of his investment, whether such protection extends to amounts contributed to the activity, amounts borrowed in connection therewith, or amounts pledged as security for borrowing. Whether a borrower will be treated as being at risk for a contingent liability will depend on the likelihood of the contingency occurring or whether the protection against loss does not cover all likely possibilities.[61]

It also should be noted that there is a dichotomy between the proposed regulations under the at-risk limitations and the tax basis rules in regard to the amount that a limited partner has agreed to contribute to the partnership. Under Section 752, if a partnership uses recourse financing, a limited partner will be able to add the amount of his agreed-upon contribution to the limited partnership to his tax basis.[62] However, the proposed at-risk regulations state that a partner's at-risk amount will not include the amounts he is required to contribute to a partnership until such time as the contribution is actually made.[63] Where the additional contribution is evidenced by a promissory note payable to the partnership, the proposed regulations take the position that the partner's at-risk amount is increased only at such time as the proceeds of the note are actually devoted to the partnership's business activity.

If this position taken in the proposed regulations is ultimately sustained, a further limitation upon a limited partner's ability to take deductions in excess of his actual capital contribution will have been effectuated. Previously, where a tax shelter operation was required to use recourse financing (e.g., in the case of a guarantee by a general partner), the limited partnership agreement frequently provided for potential capital contributions (evidenced by a note) in excess of an amount reasonably expected to be required. This plan provided a means for the limited partners to deduct losses in excess of their actual capital contributions. The position taken in the at-risk regulations,

---

[61] Prop. Regs. § 1.465-6(c), 1.465-6(e), Ex. 3.

[62] Treas. Reg. § 1.752-1(e).

[63] Prop. Reg. § 1.465-22(a).

however, indicates that the amounts of potential capital contributions will not be treated as being at risk. Thus, for those activities subject to the at-risk limitations, losses in excess of the amount actually contributed to the partnership will not be allowed.

The 1981 Act added a provision that extended the at-risk limitations to the investment credit.[64] This provision limits the taxpayer's basis for investment credit purposes to the amount at risk at the close of the taxable year. The amount at risk is determined under a separate computation used solely for investment credit purposes. Unlike the at-risk limitations for losses, there is an exception from the investment credit at-risk limitation for nonrecourse financing from certain unrelated lenders such as banks or insurance companies. To qualify for this exception, the taxpayer must at all times be at risk for at least 20 percent of the basis of the property. Consequently, when financing is on a nonrecourse basis, there will be occasions when the at-risk rules may limit tax losses but not the investment credit. This limitation on investment credit may be especially significant for tax shelters in the equipment leasing area, which rely heavily on nonrecourse financing and are heavily promoted for the investment credit provided.[65] Section 46(c)(8) provides a clear road map for avoiding this limitation: Any nonrecourse financing must be from an unrelated institutional lender and cannot exceed 80 percent of the cost of the equipment.

¶ 8.04 Hobby Loss Provisions

A potential trap for tax shelter investments lies in the hobby loss provisions of the Code.[66] Section 183 provides that if an activity is not engaged in for profit, deductions attributable to that activity will be deductible only to the extent (1) they would be allowable under other sections of the Code without regard to whether that activity is engaged

---

[64] I.R.C. § 46(c)(8).

[65] It should be noted that Section 46(e)(3) of the Code greatly restricts the availability of the investment credit in the case of noncorporate lessors unless (other than in the case where the property was manufactured by the lessor) the term of the lease is less than 50 percent of the useful life of the property and during the first year of the lease, the sum of the deductions allowed to the lessor solely by reason of Section 162 exceeds 15 percent of the rental income produced by the property. Since most deductions produced by leased property arise under sections of the Code other than Section 162 (such as Section 163 interest, or cost recovery under Section 168), the 15 percent requirement is very difficult for noncorporate lessors to meet unless they are in the leasing business.

[66] I.R.C. § 183.

in for profit,[67] and (2) the deduction does not exceed an amount equal to the difference between the gross income derived from the activity plus the deductions allowable under item (1) above. Under Section 183(d) an activity is presumed to be engaged in for profit if the gross income from that activity exceeds the deductions attributable to that activity for two of the five taxable years ending with the current taxable year.

Because very few tax shelter operations derive a profit in two of the first five taxable years, they generally are not able to benefit from the Section 183 presumption that an activity is engaged in for profit. Consequently, most run the risk that Section 183 may be applied to deny the allocation of losses to investors. This problem is exacerbated by some tax shelters that have virtually no future profit potential. For example, at one time there was a good deal of concern among practitioners that the hobby loss provisions could be applied almost automatically to many low-income housing projects. Most of these projects have only limited potential for future appreciation. In addition, programs such as those developed under Section 236 of the National Housing Act provide for limitations on the amount of rent that can be received and a limitation of the return to the owners. In truth, most investors in such projects invested with the expectation of receiving tax losses and little else. Accordingly, there was a concern that Section 183 might be applied to most tax shelter partnerships owning low-income housing and, indeed, the government did attempt to make that argument in at least one case. Substantial political pressure was applied, however, and the Service finally ruled in 1979 that the construction and operation of an apartment project for low- and moderate-income housing under Section 236 of the National Housing Act is not an activity to which Section 183 of the Code applies.[68]

Consequently, in those types of shelters that encourage investment in other federally approved housing programs, there appears to be little present danger of the application of the hobby loss sections of the Code. The Service has clearly ruled, however, that Section 183 can be applicable to the activities of a partnership and that its provisions are applied at the partnership level.[69] Consequently, the potential is there for the application of this section — particularly to the most abusive tax shelter

---

[67] E.g., interest deductions under I.R.C. § 163 and the deduction for taxes under I.R.C. § 164.

[68] Rev. Rul. 79-300, 1979-2 C.B. 112.

[69] Rev. Rul. 77-320, 1977-2 C.B. 78.

schemes that have no purpose other than the production of tax losses. Because of this danger, most well-designed shelters at least attempt to create an impression that there is a long-range profit potential from the investment.

¶ 8.05 Retroactive Allocation of Losses

Prior to 1976, December was the busiest time of the year for tax shelter promoters. Many tax shelters were offered and developed during the latter part of the year, with the object being to provide losses to investors for that entire calendar year. The retroactive allocation of losses was often one of the major selling points for year-end tax shelter schemes. Although the Service had some success in litigating against the retroactive allocation of partnership losses,[70] the practice continued largely unabated until the enactment of the Tax Reform Act of 1976. The 1976 Act contained a provision that states, in essence, that the income or losses of a partnership will be allocable to a partner only for that portion of the year in which he is a member of the partnership, and not retroactively to periods prior to his entry.[71] This allocation to a partner must be based either on the basis of the number of days of the year in which an individual was a partner, or the partnership year must be divided into segments with income and losses allocated among the partners who were partners during that segment.

The Service has followed the enactment of this section with a ruling[72] that indicates the allocation of a partnership loss among partners according to their profit- and loss-sharing percentage as of the end of the taxable year in which the percentages were substantially changed one month before the taxable year due to a contribution of additional capital by the partners is not a proper method of allocation for purposes of Section 706(c)(2)(B) of the Code. The Service ruled that an acceptable method of allocation in such a case would be to allocate the partnership's items among the partners based on their differing percentages in the periods during the year in which each partner's differing percentage interest existed. The same rationale has been

---

[70] See Rodman v. Comm'r, 542 F.2d 845 (2d Cir. 1976).

[71] I.R.C. § 706(c)(2)(B).

[72] Rev. Rul. 77-310, 1977-2 C.B. 217. See also Rev. Rul. 77-119, 1977-1 C.B. 177, applying the no-retroactive-allocation-of-losses rule to pre-1976 partnerships. See Moore v. Comm'r, 70 T.C. 1024 (1978). But see Richardson v. Comm'r, 76 T.C. No. 45 (1981).

applied to members of a second-tier partnership.[73] Accordingly, the retroactive allocation of partnership losses has effectively been eliminated.[74] Any tax shelter that is being promoted as avoiding this rule is highly suspect.

¶ 8.06 Deductibility of Fees and Expenses

A factor that is often critical to the success of a tax shelter limited partnership in its early years is the successful deduction of many fees and expenses. As a general rule, most tax shelters attempt to maximize the deductible expenses arising from the capital contributions of the limited partners. In many cases, the deductions are statutorily provided, such as the deduction of intangible drilling expenses in oil and gas ventures.[75] In other cases, the deductions claimed are only limited by the ingenuity of the shelter promoters. Because of the wide variety of tax shelters and the unlimited possibility of types of deductions, it is not possible to discuss the merits of every deduction that might be claimed. There are, however, certain types of deductions common to many tax shelters. There are, in addition, statutory rules enacted in the 1976 Act that have had a significant impact on the deductions available through a tax shelter. These specific areas, basic to the taxation of tax shelters in general, are discussed in this section.

[1] Organizational Expenses

A major addition to the Code, created by the 1976 Act, is Section 709, relating to the treatment of organization and syndication fees of a partnership. It states that, except as provided therein, no deduction shall be allowed to any partnership or to any partner for the amounts paid or incurred to organize the partnership, or to promote the sale of or

---

[73] Rev. Rul. 77-311, 1977-2 C.B. 218. A second-tier partnership is when the limited partner in a partnership is itself a limited partnership.

[74] Another question relating to the allocation of losses arises in the context of allocation of the losses among the partners themselves. Section 704(b)(2) of the Code now provides that the allocation of losses under the partnership agreement may be disregarded if it does not have substantial economic effect. There have been numerous instances where partnerships have attempted to allocate all or a substantial portion of the losses to the individuals who could most effectively use the tax shelter, and there has been much resultant litigation on this point. See Orrisch v. Comm'r, 55 T.C. 395 (1970); Harris v. Comm'r, 61 T.C. 770 (1974); Holladay v. Comm'r, 649 F.2d 1176 (5th Cir. 1981); Boynton v. Comm'r, 649 F.2d 1168 (5th Cir. 1981).

[75] See generally I.R.C. § 263(c) and ¶ 8.06[3].

to sell an interest in the partnership.[76] Section 709(b) then provides that partnership organizational expenses may be amortized over a 60-month period, beginning with the month in which the partnership begins business.[76a] Organizational expenses are defined as those expenditures incident to the creation of the partnership, chargeable to the capital account and of a character that, if expended incident to the creation of a partnership having an ascertainable life, would be amortized over such life.[77] Syndication expenses, on the other hand, are not deductible. Consequently, those expenses incurred to promote the sale of the partnership interests, such as commissions to brokers and the like, will not be deductible at all by the partnership. Organizational expenditures, such as legal fees for the drafting of a partnership instrument, may be written off over a period of five years.[78]

This statutory rule relating to the deductibility of partnership organizational expenses can be thought of as both beneficial and detrimental to a tax shelter partnership. It is beneficial to a partnership inasmuch as it provides a definite useful life for the amortization of organizational costs. Previously, when partnership organizational expenses were required to be amortized, the deduction was often lost because of the indefinite life of most partnerships. Capitalization of the organizational expenditures meant, in most cases, that the deduction would never be allowed. On the other hand, the mere existence of Section 709 tends to encourage a revenue agent to classify questionable expenditures as organizational expenses rather than as currently deductible items. To the extent that such efforts are successful, they work against one of the basic purposes of tax shelters — the rapid deduction of expenditures to achieve a deferral of taxes.[79]

---

[76] I.R.C. § 709(a).

[76a] I.R.C. § 709(b)(1). The deductibility of certain start up costs is now governed by I.R.C. § 195, which provides for a 60-month amortization of eligible costs. See Rev. Rul. 81-150, 1981-1 C.B. 119.

[77] I.R.C. § 709(b)(2).

[78] The courts have also held that fees for attorneys' services rendered with respect to the organization of a partnership represent capital expenditures. Meldrum & Fewsmith, Inc., 20 T.C. 790 (1953), aff'd on other issue, 230 F.2d 283 (6th Cir. 1956). The I.R.S. has also ruled that payments to a general partner for organizing a partnership are capital expenditures. See Rev. Rul. 75-214, 1975-1 C.B. 185.

[79] It also should be noted that the I.R.S. is increasingly taking a hard line against what it has denominated as "pre-opening expenses." In this regard the I.R.S. has often taken a position that expenditures that occur prior to the active conduct of a trade or business must be capitalized and hence amortized over the

Another area that is often controversial relates to the deductibility of various fees paid to the organizers of a partnership who frequently serve as the general partner of that entity. This controversy often relates to whether such payments are indeed organizational expenditures [80] deductible under the statutory parameters just discussed as opposed to nondeductible syndication fees. A second aspect of this controversy is the deductibility of guaranteed payments made to a partner. Section 707(c) has long provided that payments to a partner for services rendered or for the use of capital, to the extent that such payments are determined without regard to the income of the partnership, may be deducted.[81] Accordingly, it was not uncommon to find substantial payments being made to the promoters or general partners of a tax shelter with a corresponding deduction claimed under Section 707(c) as a guaranteed payment. The Service had consistently maintained that such payments could not be deducted unless the payment also met the criteria for deductibility under Section 162.[82] This point was successfully litigated by the Service in the case of *Cagle v. Comm'r*.[83] In

---

useful life of that business. See Francis v. Comm'r, 36 T.C.M. 704 (1977), Richmond Television Corp. v. U.S., 345 F.2d 901 (4th Cir. 1965), rev'd on other grounds, 382 U.S. 68(1965); Madison Gas & Elec. Co. v. Comm'r, 72 T.C. 521 (1979), aff'd 633 F.2d 512 (7th Cir. 1980); Goodwin v. Comm'r, 75 T.C. 424 (1980); U.S. v. Manor Care, Inc., 490 F. Supp. 355 (D. Md. 1980); Blitzer v. U.S., 81-1 U.S.T.C. ¶ 9262 (Ct. Cl. 1981). On the whole, the I.R.S. has been relatively successful with this litigation although there is some variation in the decisions as to when a business commences and the precise test to be applied. Section 195 was added to the Code in 1980 so as to permit the taxpayer to elect a five-year amortization of start-up expenditures (as defined in Section 195(b)) incurred after July 29, 1980. If a taxpayer fails to make this election, however, and a deduction is denied upon audit under the *Richmond Television* line of cases, it will be too late to amortize these expenses.

[80] See Rev. Rul. 81-153, 1981-1 C.B. 387, where a promoter rebated an amount to an investor so that the investor could pay this sum to his tax advisor — purportedly for tax advice rendered. On the facts set forth in the ruling, the I.R.S. held that the payments were really for the sale of partnership interests and not for tax advice. Hence the payment was not deductible under Section 212 and could not be amortized by the partnership as an organizational expense.

[81] In Pratt v. Comm'r, 64 T.C. 203 (1975), management fees based on the gross rentals of a partnership were held not to be guaranteed payments under Section 707(c). In addition, since these payments were held to be to the partners acting in their capacity as partners, a deduction was denied under Section 707(e).

[82] That is, the payment had to be an ordinary and necessary business expense.

[83] 63 T.C. 86 (1974).

addition, the 1976 Act amended Section 707(c) to specifically provide a reference to Section 162(a). Accordingly, the payments made to a partner for services to the partnership or for the use of capital may be deducted by the partnership only if such payments would be deductible if they had been made to persons who were not members of the partnership. The designation of an expense as a guaranteed payment under Section 707(c) is not sufficient in and of itself to insure deductibility.

[2] Construction Period Interest and Taxes

The 1976 addition of a section relating to the amortization of real property construction period interest and taxes was also a major change. Prior to the enactment of Section 189, one of the major inducements for real property tax shelters involving new construction was the deductibility of interest and taxes arising during the construction period, prior to placing the newly constructed property in service. Section 189 changed this practice to require that construction period interest and real property taxes paid during the construction period must be amortized over the period of time set forth in the statute. After Section 189(b) is fully phased-in in 1983, all such expenditures must be amortized over a ten-year period.[84] The impact of this section is to reduce the tax deferral that could be achieved from shelters investing in new real estate construction by spreading out the time over which these construction period deductions can be taken.

The 1981 Act completely exempted low-income housing from Section 189,[85] and made it clear that real property that is not, and cannot reasonably be expected to be, held in a trade or business or in an activity conducted for profit is also excluded from that section. The exemption from Section 189, combined with other tax advantages for low-income housing,[86] such as the rapid amortization of low-income rehabilitation expenditures under Section 167(k) and the exemption of real estate from

---

[84] Section 189(b) provides for a phase-in of this section which varies depending upon the type of property being constructed. Nonresidential real property was subject to the most rapid phase-in, residential real property is to be fully phased in after 1983.

[85] I.R.C. § 189(d). Low-income housing previously was scheduled to be phased in by 1987.

[86] Low-income housing may also use a 200 percent declining balance cost recovery method as opposed to a 175 percent method for conventional real estate. I.R.C. § 168(b)(2)(A)(ii).

the at-risk rules, serves to increase the attractiveness of this type of real estate as a tax shelter.

[3] Intangible Drilling Expenses

A deduction critical to the operation of most oil and gas tax shelters is the write-off of intangible development costs for oil and gas wells, which is provided by Section 263(c) of the Code. This section, in essence, allows the immediate deductibility of amounts paid or incurred for labor, wages, fuel, and other items not having a salvage value in connection with the drilling of an oil and gas well. Because of this section, the bulk of the capital contributions made by an investor in an oil and gas shelter is usually allocated to the drilling of a well with the result that there is a very rapid deduction of the bulk of the investor's capital contribution. It is typical to see an immediate prepayment of such intangible drilling costs. The Service has ruled [87] that it will allow the deduction of prepaid drilling costs where the prepayment is required under a bona fide drilling contract, even though a substantial portion of the work is to be performed in the following year. These rulings appear to indicate that there must be a business purpose for the prepayments, such as providing the drilling contractor with funds needed for the drilling work or receiving a priority as to the use of the equipment.

¶ 8.07 Evaluating a Tax Shelter

The wide variety and scope of tax shelter schemes serves mainly to increase the difficulty of evaluating each proposed transaction. It is difficult to make a comparison, for example, when investigating such diverse areas as subsidized housing, oil and gas exploration, and growing fruit trees. Very few individuals, including those who regularly deal with and evaluate tax shelters, possess the expertise to evaluate such a wide variety of economic transactions. When this diverse economic character of tax shelter transactions is combined with increased amounts of legislative and ruling activity that has occurred in recent years, the task of weighing the merits of each program becomes exceedingly complex. There are, however, certain standard factors that must be evaluated in every tax shelter transaction. These factors, discussed

---

[87] Rev. Rul. 71-252, 1971-1 C.B. 146.

below, can give a potential investor a very good basis on which to weigh the merits of a particular tax shelter offering. The reader should be aware, however, that each offering raises additional questions and considerations to be factored into the equation. In other words, the list that follows will serve the intelligent investor or advisor only as a starting point in undertaking a complete analysis of each proposed transaction.

[1] Soundness of the Investment

The first and foremost rule in evaluating a tax shelter transaction is to ignore completely the promised tax benefits and to review the transaction in terms of economic soundness. In other words, does the transaction make economic sense absent the promised tax benefits? Although this rule sounds rather basic and straightforward, it is, unfortunately, frequently ignored in practice. It is not uncommon to see very astute businessmen who have reached a highly compensated status by virtue of their economic acumen completely ignore the proposed economics of a transaction once the magic words "tax shelter" appear on a syndicated offering. There is a tendency to take the attitude that, if the transaction fails, the investor can simply write off his loss. This attitude ignores the harsh reality that a tax write-off will never totally compensate an investor for a complete economic loss. A tax deduction only serves to ameliorate the loss to the extent of the tax dollars saved. If an individual is in the 50 percent tax bracket and suffers a $100,000 ordinary loss, the tax savings of $50,000 will reduce his out-of-pocket costs to $50,000, but will not recoup his entire investment. In addition, if a transaction is structured to require additional capital investments from the limited partners, the total amount of investor losses may not be readily apparent on the surface. Consequently, a tax shelter must be evaluated just as any other proposed business transaction would be — the economic rewards and risks must be weighed independently of the tax consequences involved.

The basic task in evaluating the economics of a transaction is to make a careful analysis of the underlying product or property to form a considered judgment as to its merits. For example, if the investment is being made in a newly constructed shopping center, what are the chances that the shopping center will be successful? Is it in a strong economic area? Is the area already saturated with shopping centers? What tenants has the management already attracted or are they simply trying to lease the property? If the offering relates to interest in an almond grove, what is the future market for almonds? Is the proposed grove in an area conducive to growing almonds?

Quite frequently, the private placement memorandum or offering circular accompanying a tax shelter investment provides information to enable the potential investor to evaluate the economic merits of the offering. It should be remembered, however, that the circular is usually prepared by the promoters of the offering or their counsel. Even though a wide variety of economic factors, including the negative ones, may be presented in the offering circular, these factors can often be slanted or the emphasis changed to present a more favorable picture than is really the case. Consequently, the analysis contained in these documents should be viewed with a highly critical eye. It is usually necessary to undertake an independent evaluation of these economic factors — often by contacting someone who is familiar with a particular area or industry.

No investment is risk-free. The potential investor in a tax shelter must be fully apprised of these economic risks, however, so that they may be weighed in comparison to the potential tax and economic benefits being offered. If information is not available to an individual or his advisors to enable them to fully weigh the economic consequences of a transaction, it is usually advisable not to invest in that particular deal. Very few people would invest in a nonsheltered transaction for which economic information was not available. Simply because a transaction is called a tax shelter, this basic rule should not be ignored.

[2] Review of Tax Risks

If a proposed investment appears to make economic sense, the next task is to carefully evaluate the tax consequences of this transaction. In theory, this task should be no different regardless of whether or not the investment is called a tax shelter. Any business transaction for individuals who have considerable wealth or income requires a careful analysis of the tax consequences. Since a tax shelter is heavily promoted because of the purported tax benefits involved, this analysis becomes even more critical. In addition, tax shelters are frequently based upon an aggressive tax posture that requires a relatively sophisticated analysis. Consequently, such investments often demand an extremely careful tax review and yet are structured in such a way as to make that review quite difficult for the layman.

Because of the critical importance of the tax analysis in a shelter type of investment, and because of the complexities of many of the offerings being promoted, the first rule of such analysis is that if the potential investor does not fully understand the tax consequences or risks, he should seek professional help. Although most highly salaried individuals have a basic understanding of the Code, and indeed, often have a relatively sophisticated understanding of its operation, very few people are true tax experts. Many tax shelter transactions are promoted by aggressive sales people whose surface explanations of the tax consequences sound quite plausible. Since the sales person or the promoter benefits if the highly salaried individual becomes a participant in a program, any tax analysis from a promoter must be viewed with a somewhat jaundiced eye. If a person is considering investment in tax shelters, he should rely upon an expert he can trust to give an objective tax analysis.

The tax analysis of a proposed shelter transaction concentrates on two basic areas. The first is whether the tax consequences of the investment will be as described by the promoter or the offering circular. In this regard, it is necessary to look not only at the overall tax benefits being presented, but at the specifics of the particular deal. For example, many tax shelters have a standard format that attempts to increase the ratio of first-year losses by accelerating as many deductions as possible into the early years of the investment. This may involve claiming dubious fees as first year deductions or seeking to write off payments that are in truth nondeductible organizational [88] or syndication fees. It is also common to find that the offering circular and/or tax projections accompanying the proposed investment tend to obscure the specific deductions being claimed. Thus, it is frequently necessary to ask very pointed questions regarding the tax projections in order to accurately evaluate their merits.

It is common to find that the tax opinion that accompanies most shelter investments is of only marginal help in evaluating the tax consequences. Many tax opinion letters confine themselves to the issue of partnership status and do not address the deductibility or nondeductibility of specific items. Even if the opinion does address deductibility, it may do so with equivocation.[89] Thus, the opinion letter may be of only limited help in evaluating the pertinent tax risks.

---

[88] Organizational fees are, however, subject to five-year amortization under Section 709.

[89] The I.R.S. has recently undertaken some controversial steps to regulate

The other important aspect of the tax analysis is the determination of the tax consequences of this transaction as applicable to the specific individual involved. For example, many tax shelter investments simply involve tax deferral. If the taxpayer is likely to be in the same or higher tax bracket in these later years, a calculated analysis will be necessary to determine if there are actually any tax benefits involved. It is often the case that a professional athlete or an artistic performer, who is in a high tax bracket for a limited period of time, will benefit far more than an executive whose high salary is more stable from a deferral created by a tax shelter investment. Another aspect is the effect of the indexing provisions effective in 1985 and thereafter. Since the same dollar amount of income will be taxed at a lesser rate in subsequent years, a deferral of income by accelerating deductions may often be beneficial.

Also, the effect of tax preference items upon a particular investor must be weighed. If the transaction creates substantial tax preference income,[90] it may have the effect of creating a liability for the alternative minimum tax imposed by Section 55 of the Code. Consequently, although the shelter may be creating tax losses for that individual, it may at the same time have the effect of subjecting portions of his income to the alternative minimum tax at a 20 percent rate. A very detailed arithmetic analysis is often necessary to determine if the tax "benefits" will actually be advantageous to a particular individual.

---

the scope of attorneys' opinions in tax shelter transactions. In the Federal Register dated September 4, 1980 (45 Fed. Reg. 58, 594), the Service issued proposed amendments to Circular 230, which governs practice before the I.R.S. In essence, these proposed rules would create strict standards for opinion letters to be distributed in prospective tax shelter transactions. These proposed rules would require the practitioner to exercise due diligence in ascertaining the facts of the transaction and in assuring that the opinion is accurately and clearly described in any discussion of the tax aspects appearing in the offering materials. These rules also would allow the practitioner only to provide an opinion if the opinion concluded that it was more likely than not that the bulk of the tax benefits on the basis of which a tax shelter had been promoted are allowable under tax law. Thus, these proposed rules not only would require a strict due diligence standard in discussing the tax benefits, but they require the attorney's evaluation of all major tax aspects of the transaction. As might be expected, these proposed rules are the subject of a good deal of controversy which is likely to continue into the indefinite future. In response to the Treasury's action, the American Bar Association has issued Ethics Opinion 346 (Jan. 29, 1982) relating to tax shelter opinion letters. Although this Opinion is not as far-reaching as the Treasury proposals, it does require the practitioner to look beyond the single issue of partnership status.

[90] The items of tax preference are set forth in Section 57(a). See ¶ 2.02. The most frequent items of preference income created by tax shelters are accelerated depreciation for real property, the oil depletion deduction, and capital gains.

[3] Real Cost of the Investment

When an individual elects to participate in a tax shelter, he is acquiring an interest in an investment property. Consequently, an important part of the analysis of a tax shelter investment is to ascertain how much of the investor's capital contribution will be applied to the acquisition of the investment property. Most tax shelters make provision for the payment of fees and commissions to the promoters of the transaction, as well as for the organizational expenses of the venture.[91] The amount, nature, and types of these fees are subject to a wide degree of variation. A careful analysis will frequently reveal that a syndicator is being paid several different fees under a multiplicity of categories, all of which have the effect of reducing the actual dollars going into the investment. This means, among other things, that it will be more difficult for the investor to benefit from the future appreciation of the investment inasmuch as the early appreciation in value, if any, will merely compensate the investor for the fees paid to the promoter at the inception of the transaction. Again, the amount and reasonableness of these items must be weighed in evaluating the transaction. Thus, an analysis of the fees being paid and/or the interest being given to the promoters usually reveals the real cost of the investment.

It is also necessary to evaluate the reasonableness of the acquisition costs of the property itself. Conflicts of interest are very common in these types of transactions. If the property is being acquired from the promoter or an affiliated entity, the acquisition price might be unduly inflated. If a related entity will manage the project, the fees being paid for these services should be compared against industry norms. Often an evaluation of these particular points requires a specific knowledge of the industry in question. Consequently, it is usually necessary to confer with someone who is familiar with the particular type of transaction or the particular geographic area in which the investment is located, in order to receive assurances on these points.

Most investors are counseled to avoid those transactions that are heavily loaded with front-end fees. These investments typically result in fewer real dollars going into the investment at the price of questionable front-end deductions. Conversely, it is often a signal that the promoter thinks highly of an investment if he is willing to forgo significant front-

---

[91] Organizational expenses might include legal and accounting fees, filing fees, appraisal fees and closing costs such as escrow fees, and loan points or title insurance. Points paid with respect to a loan, if in the nature of interest, must be amortized over the life of the loan.

end fees in favor of long-range equity participation. Although this cannot assure profit to an investor, it is an indication that the promoter thinks highly of the long-range prospects of the transaction.

Another step in determining the real cost of the investment is an analysis of the various guarantees, if any, that are being provided by the syndication promoters or the developers of a particular project. For example, many real estate syndications provide a negative cash-flow guarantee during the first few years of a project's operation.[92] Other typical guarantees may include occupancy guarantees or a promise to complete construction within a specified cost. The basic purpose of these covenants is to protect the investors against having to contribute additional cash to a project during the early years when it is just getting off the ground. If these guarantees are meaningful and are fulfilled, they can provide significant protection to the investor in terms of putting a cap on a project's cost. All too frequently, investors in a newly constructed project are faced with a cash bind in initial years of operation either because a real estate project is not fully rented in an expeditious fashion or because of construction cost overruns. Consequently, guarantees of the nature noted can be economically significant to investors.

The substance of any guarantees must be evaluated in the same manner as other economic considerations. A guarantee is only as good as the guarantor who makes it and/or the security provided to back up the guarantee. Consequently, it is important to determine the financial resources of the guarantor, his "track record" (see ¶ 8.07[4]), and the specific language of the guarantee. The security that is provided, if any, to back up the guarantee must also be evaluated. If the guarantor is involved in other projects or transactions, it is likely that he has made similar guarantees in those deals. Accordingly, an investigation of his ability to meet *all* of these obligations would be prudent. If, however, the guarantor does possess the financial strength to meet his obligations, the existence of such a promise can prove to be a very valuable and useful inducement towards investment.

[4] Promoter's "Track Record"

A factor that rivals the importance of the investment itself is the identity and record of the promoter or syndicator of a transaction.

---

[92] Such a guarantee is a covenant by the guarantor that the investment will not suffer a cash flow deficit in the years covered by the guarantee.

There are very few investments, no matter how prime, that will succeed on their own without successful management. A well-situated apartment project still requires management for rental and leasing purposes. The best cattle herd in the world is useless without someone familiar with the techniques of raising and breeding cattle. On the other hand, a promoter may have the finest managerial skills in the world and yet be unscrupulous or have no financial strength. Accordingly, it is imperative to analyze the promoter and his previous performance in evaluating the merits of any given investment.

The first aspect of this evaluation is an analysis of the promoter's past performance with similar ventures. An experienced syndicator should make available to investors a detailed record of past projects that he has sponsored. If he does not, claims of past success should be somewhat suspect. The potential investor must carefully scrutinize these records to determine how the performance matched projections given prior to the investment and how the performance compares with projections in the offer being considered. It is also pertinent to investigate the syndicator's past record with the Service. How have the previously syndicated offerings stood up under Service audit? If the projects have been frequently audited and considerable adjustments made, it is reasonable to assume that the present investment is likely to be a prime target for Service audit. It is also pertinent to ask whether the promoter has actual experience in managing the type of project being considered for investment. Just because a promoter has extensive experience managing commercial real estate does not mean that he can successfully manage an oil drilling venture.

To the extent possible, it is always advisable to assess the syndicator independently. Other investors should be interviewed, or other properties managed by this individual might be personally examined. Financial institutions or other references should be investigated and pertinent questions asked regarding the promoter's reputation. A personal meeting with the syndicator is always desirable. Frequently, syndicated offerings are distributed through brokers who have little or no direct contact with the syndicator himself. Most particularly, if the investor does not know the sales person or broker involved, attempts should be made to know the syndicator.

In many instances it will not be possible to evaluate many of these features independently. For example, if property is being offered in California by a midwestern syndicator and the potential investor resides in Philadelphia, a direct evaluation of the syndicator or the property itself may not be possible or economically feasible. If, however, very little information seems to be available concerning the offeror and if a direct investigation unearths little information, second thoughts should be given to the wisdom of the investment. This is particularly critical if the dollar amounts being considered for investment are substantial. It is well to bear in mind that a slick offering brochure often disguises the fact that the shelter investor is being asked to entrust a substantial investment to a complete stranger. If adequate information is not available regarding the stranger, great care should be exercised before investing.

[5] Ultimate Profit From the Transaction

A factor often overlooked in the evaluation of a tax shelter is a review of the ultimate profit from the transaction for the investors. If a tax shelter is thought of as an investment, a critical factor in analyzing any potential investment is to weigh the long-range rewards against the economic risk of investing. Quite obviously, the potential reward includes the tax shelter provided in the early years of the investment. However, since a shelter often results in only a deferral of taxes, it is imperative to weigh the long-range economic return that will be produced by the project at the time taxes are no longer being deferred. If a shelter produces deferral and nothing more, another similar type of investment may be required once the deferral ceases to exist if the taxpayer remains in a high income tax bracket. At the time the deferral ceases, that project may prove to be of little economic value.

This problem of little or no residual value frequently occurs in the area of low-income housing. Many low-income housing projects use rapid depreciation techniques [93] in order to provide large tax losses in early years to investors. Under such projects, the cash flow is frequently limited by regulations issued by the Department of Housing and Urban Development, with the consequence that the only significant incentive for the investors is the tax loss provided. Unfortunately, unless such projects are extremely well managed, they have a tendency to become run-down in a very short period of time and may not appreciate as do most real estate complexes. An investor in projects that have achieved

---

[93] An example of such rapid depreciation techniques would be the double declining balance method permitted under the Accelerated Cost Recovery System or five-year amortization of expenditures to rehabilitate low-income rental housing pursuant to Section 167(k).

this somewhat dubious status may be faced with declining or nonexistent tax losses, substantial depreciation recapture [94] if the project is sold, and a property with little or no economic worth in excess of the mortgage. Not all low-income projects fall into this category. However, many do, with unfortunate results to investors who failed to analyze the long-range profit potential from such an investment.

The long-range profit potential is also a function of the original price paid for the property. If the property is being purchased from a promoter at an inflated rate, the time required for a long-range gain is obviously increased.

An inquiry regarding the long-range profit potential of a project must not stop with an analysis of the economic potential of an investment. It is also critical to carefully review the syndication documents, most particularly the limited partnership agreement, to ascertain precisely who benefits from that long-range profit. Many syndications have a tendency to disproportionately reward their promoters for any long-range profit that is achieved. For example, offerings frequently appear wherein the limited partners invest virtually all the money, receive virtually all of the tax losses, and then only a third of the ultimate gain on sales. The truth is that in such instances the investors have taken all of the economic risk and, although they have received tax losses over a period of time as compensation, the rewards for taking this risk are severely limited by the partnership agreement. It is not uncommon, nor necessarily bad, for the syndicator to share in the long-range reward of a project. Investors in such transactions must expect to reward the syndicator for his successful management of a project. The investors must not, however, totally ignore the risk-reward ratio in analyzing the investment. If an investment is particularly risky,[95] the investors should rightfully expect to be rewarded for taking the economic risk of investment. If they are not to be so rewarded, they should not invest.

The foregoing analysis lists many critical factors to be weighed in evaluating a tax shelter investment. This list of critical factors should not be taken as a recommendation by the author to avoid all tax shelter investments. On the contrary, there are many such investments that are worthwhile for both the tax savings involved and the economic return

---

[94] I.R.C. § 1250. For low-income housing this recapture is phased out after 16⅔ years.

[95] Such as an oil exploration venture as opposed to a well development venture.

to the investors. These factors should, however, serve as points of caution for those who are weighing such investments. A tax shelter investment usually involves investing with a small group of strangers and entrusting control or management of that investment to another individual. In any case, where a person is investing his money with strangers and has virtually no control over the investment itself, it is imperative that factors such as those discussed in this section be evaluated prior to investing.

¶ 8.08 Estate Planning for Tax Shelters

Another component of tax planning relating to the use of tax shelters concerns the estate planning effects of such investments. A major factor is that tax shelters tend to be very illiquid in nature and accordingly increase the liquidity problems frequently found in the estates of many high-income individuals. Limited partnership agreements for tax shelter investments usually prohibit the sale or assignment of the partnership interests without consent of the general partners or a certain percentage of interests in the partnership. Thus, even if a purchaser is found, the sale of the partnership units may be prohibited. In addition, the limited partnership interest may be subject to Securities and Exchange Commission (SEC) restrictions that effectively prohibit its sale. Finally, many interests in tax shelter investments simply are not saleable. Because the amount of shelter produced by most of these investments tends to decrease after the first several years, those shelters that are held for a substantial period of time may "burn out" and have little attractiveness to other highly compensated individuals. Consequently, unless the shelter is producing substantial income or represents ownership in property that has appreciated substantially in value, such an interest may have little attractiveness to potential buyers.[96]

Generally speaking, a tax shelter investment will be an asset that is included in the gross estate of a deceased individual but that frequently cannot be disposed of in order to meet the estate's cash requirements. Consequently, when an estate is being evaluated, it is important to recognize the illiquid nature of tax shelter investments and to react accordingly. If the individual's portfolio is not balanced between liquid

---

[96] This serves to emphasize the point made throughout this chapter regarding the necessity of evaluating tax shelters as economic investments.

and illiquid investments, or if there is an excessive amount of tax shelter investments, severe liquidity problems may be indicated. It is also necessary to evaluate the income tax effect of retaining these investments. For example, if it is anticipated that the shelter will be producing a significant amount of deductions upon the death of its owner, the retention of that shelter interest may be desirable for high-income beneficiaries. If the highly compensated individual anticipates receiving substantial amounts of taxable income until his death, it may be desirable to specifically bequeath the tax shelter interest to the surviving spouse in order to have her benefit from the deductions directly or, in the alternative, to make specific provisions in the will to permit her to file a joint income tax return with the estate for the year of death. If it is likely that the shelter will have reached the crossover point, so that it is producing cash income in excess of available deductions, by the actuarially indicated time of death, it will be imprudent to bequeath the shelter interest to any high-income individual unless an equivalent amount of cash is also being produced.

If a shelter has reached the crossover point and is producing taxable income, it may be prudent to make a gift of the shelter interest to the taxpayer's children or to place it in trust for their benefit. This will enable the income to be taxed to lower-income recipients. A shelter that is particularly appropriate for this type of gift is an oil and gas shelter. Since most of the drilling expenses will be deducted in the first year or two, a gift immediately after the write-off of these expenses will enable the investor to retain the losses, but dispose of his interest prior to the receipt of income. If the gift is made prior to the venture having proven reserves, little or no gift tax will be involved. It also should be noted regarding a gift of real property that gifts are exempted from the recapture rules of Section 1250.[97] A gift of real estate after crossover has been reached will not trigger the recapture normally associated with the disposition of a partnership interest.

If the shelter will be producing income in excess of the cash available for distribution, it may not be wise to bequeath the interest to any individual. Under these circumstances, a reasonable alternative might be to bequeath the asset directly to a named charity so as to receive a deduction for the estate.[98] There is always some question as to whether the charity would be willing to accept the particular interest

---

[97] I.R.C. § 1250(d)(1).
[98] I.R.C. § 2055.

being bequeathed. If, however, the partnership interest does produce cash for the charity and entails little or no risk on its part for further capital contributions, the charity has little to lose by accepting such a donation.

Because it may not be possible to predict the tax status of the partnership interest upon someone's death at an uncertain date in the future, the tax shelter interest might be bequeathed to a named beneficiary with an alternate bequest to charity. In such a case, the desirability of retaining the tax shelter interest could be evaluated by the beneficiary upon the death of its present owner. If it were not advisable to retain the interest, the beneficiary could then disclaim interest in the property [99] and allow the shelter to pass to charity. Even if an individual did not have the foresight to include such an alternative request in his will, it might be possible to achieve the same result by having successive heirs disclaim interest in the property until it is escheated to the state. It is unwise, however, to rely on such a string of disclaimers because a multiplicity of heirs and statutory constraints may make the disclaimer process both time-consuming and expensive.

Accordingly, in evaluating the estate of an individual who is in the income tax bracket that makes the ownership of tax shelter interests attractive, it is imperative to realize that a large number of such interests may result in severe liquidity problems for the estate. In addition, if a particular investment has reached the crossover point so that it is producing taxable income in excess of cash distributions, a potential income tax problem will be created for the decedent's heirs. This is not to say that tax shelter investments should be completely discounted if they are attractive in nature. If however, they constitute a significant portion of someone's estate, they may create liquidity problems for the executor and/or income tax problems for the potential heirs.

---

[99] §§ 2046, 2518.

CHAPTER 9

Grantor Trusts *

		Page
¶ 9.01	Objectives for Creation of Trusts	9-2
¶ 9.02	Basic Trust Provisions	9-3
¶ 9.03	Revocable Trusts Created for Purposes Other Than Tax Savings	9-6
	[1] Lifetime Use of Revocable Trusts	9-6
	[2] Post-Death Benefits	9-6
	[3] Income Tax Considerations	9-8
	[4] Gift and Estate Tax Consequences	9-11
¶ 9.04	Relinquishment of Ownership of Trust to Reduce Tax Liability	9-11
	[1] Grantor Owns Entire Trust	9-11
	[2] Grantor Owns Part of Trust	9-12
	[3] Grantor Retains Only Corpus Interest	9-13
¶ 9.05	"Clifford" Trusts	9-13
¶ 9.06	Taxation of "Clifford" Trusts	9-14
	[1] Income Tax Benefits	9-14
	[2] Grantor's Gift Tax Liability on Creation	9-15
¶ 9.07	Current Distribution or Accumulation of Trust Income	9-16
¶ 9.08	Restriction on Grantor's Powers to Transfer Trust Ownership for Income Tax Purposes	9-17
	[1] Reversionary Interest Must Be Relinquished for a Sufficient Period of Time	9-17
	[a] Earliest Permissible Time for Reacquisition	9-17
	[b] Postponement of Reacquisition Date	9-18
	[2] Power to Control Beneficial Enjoyment Must Be Curtailed	9-19
	[a] Grantor as Trustee	9-19
	[i] Retained powers subjecting grantor to tax	9-20
	[ii] Permissible retained powers	9-20

---

* This chapter was researched and written by Israel G. Grossman, Esq. of Rosenman, Colin, Freund, Lewis and Cohen, New York.

		Page
	[b] Person Other Than Grantor as Trustee	9-23
	[c] Power to Remove Trustee	9-24
	[d] Reciprocal Trusts	9-25
	[3] Administrative Powers Exercisable by Grantor	9-25
	[a] Grantor's Use of Administrative Powers to Directly Control Beneficial Enjoyment	9-25
	[b] Offensive Administrative Powers Grantor Must Relinquish to Avoid Income Taxation	9-27
	[c] Borrowing From Trust by Grantor	9-27
	[4] Power to Revoke Subjecting Grantor to Tax	9-27
	[5] Use of Trust Income for Benefit of Grantor	9-28
	[6] Use of Trust Income for Support of Grantor's Dependents	9-29
¶ 9.09	Persons Other Than the Grantor as Owner of Trust	9-29
¶ 9.10	Grantor's Potential Estate Tax Liability	9-30
¶ 9.11	Alternative Methods of Achieving Income Tax Benefits From Transfer of Property	9-30
	[1] Irrevocable Trusts	9-31
	[2] Interest-Free Loans	9-31
	[3] Comparison of Grantor Trusts and Alternative Methods of Transfer	9-32
	[a] Outright Gifts	9-32
	[b] Irrevocable Trusts	9-33
	[c] Short-Term or "Clifford" Trusts	9-33
	[d] Interest-Free Loans	9-34
	[e] Interest-Free Loans to an Irrevocable Trust	9-35
¶ 9.12	Foreign Trusts	9-36

¶ 9.01 Objectives for Creation of Trusts

It is very common for wealthy individuals to transfer a substantial amount of their securities, real estate, or other investments into a trust.[1] One of the most important objectives of the grantor is to shift income from his high tax bracket to the beneficiary's lower bracket. If he is prepared to sufficiently relinquish control over the corpus and income of the trust, he will be able to save substantial federal and state income

---

[1] Under the Internal Revenue Code, an arrangement will be treated as a trust if it can be shown that its purpose is to vest in trustees responsibility for the protection and conservation of property for beneficiaries who cannot share in the discharge of this responsibility and, therefore, are not associates in a joint enterprise for the conduct of a business for profit. Treas.Reg. § 301.7701-4(a).

and estate taxes. However, the grantor may have other nontax objectives in creating a trust, including:

(1) Management of investments;

(2) Preservation of property for beneficiaries including the grantor who may be unable to manage property independently, presently or in the future because of advancing age, disability, impulsiveness, or the grasping hands of third parties;

(3) Provision for transfer to minors and to persons who are physically, mentally, or otherwise incapacitated, without being subject to local law impediments such as the need to appoint a guardian; and

(4) Avoidance of the disadvantages of probate, such as lack of privacy, additional costs, or delay in distribution, by transferring property outside the jurisdiction of the probate court.

From the tax standpoint, trusts can be a very useful vehicle for a highly compensated individual — to transfer assets so that he will no longer be treated as owner for tax purposes. Such a transfer may be either complete and irrevocable or temporary but for a sufficient period of time so that he will no longer be treated as the owner of all or a portion of the trust.

In addition to the tax savings, there are various nontax objectives that can be achieved through the creation of a trust. Therefore, even a revocable trust, which the grantor will be treated as owning for tax purposes, will be beneficial in a number of situations. However, if the only objective for creating a trust is to shift the income tax burden on certain assets for a limited period of time to lower bracket individuals, serious consideration should be given to the use of noninterest bearing demand loans as an alternative method of achieving such objectives.

¶ 9.02 Basic Trust Provisions

Any trust that the grantor creates will generally be in the form of a written agreement having the following provisions:

(1) *Trustee designation* — Specifying the individual(s) or institution(s) who will act as fiduciaries and the provision for the appointment of a successor trustee in the event of the death, resignation, or incapacity of the designated trustee.[2]

---

[2] A provision for a successor trustee is essential where the grantor has appointed himself as trustee.

(2) *Beneficiary designation* — Identifying the primary and contingent beneficiaries.

(3) *Corpus description and distributions* — Designating the property to be transferred to the trust initially and authorizing the trustee to receive additional contributions. With respect to the corpus the trustee may be:

> (a) Directed to make distributions of part or all of the corpus at one or several specified ages of the beneficiaries;
>
> (b) Given absolute discretion as to the time and manner of distribution;
>
> (c) Directed to make distributions in special circumstances, such as for special health, education, or support needs of the beneficiaries;
>
> (d) Required to distribute principal upon the exercise of a power of appointment granted to a beneficiary; or
>
> (e) Directed to retain principal during the lifetime of the first generation beneficiaries and make distributions to their children (i.e., a "generation skipping" trust).

(4) *Dispositive provisions* — Indicating the conditions under which the beneficiaries will receive income distributions from the trust. With respect to income the trustee can be:

> (a) Directed to make mandatory distributions to the beneficiaries of all or a portion of the income;
>
> (b) Given absolute discretion concerning the timing of distributions to designated beneficiaries and the right to "sprinkle" income among various beneficiaries based on their relative needs; or
>
> (c) Directed to make distributions subject to a reasonably ascertainable standard relating to the beneficiaries' health, education, and welfare.

(5) *Administrative provisions* — Listing the powers that can be exercised by the trustee in administering the trust. These powers can include the power to:

> (a) Retain, sell, abandon or exchange property;
>
> (b) Invest and reinvest trust assets in the trustee's discretion;

(c) Participate in joint ventures;

(d) Manage real property;

(e) Consent to and participate in corporate action (e.g., merger, liquidation, or reorganization);

(f) Appoint and employ agents, investment counsel, attorneys, etc.;

(g) Exercise or allow options to lapse;

(h) Allocate receipts and expenditures and make other adjustments between income and principal;

(i) Settle claims;

(j) Make loans;

(k) Distribute property in kind; and

(l) Any additional powers the grantor wishes to accord the trustee such as the power to make specific investments or types of investments.

(6) *Distribution to minors* — Providing for the appointment of a guardian who will receive distributions for the benefit of minors, permitting a distribution to a minor's parent or guardian on his behalf, or directing that any distribution to which a minor may be entitled be retained until he reaches maturity.[3]

(7) *Spendthrift clause* — Providing that the beneficiary cannot assign or transfer his interest and that it cannot be subject to the claim of his creditors.

(8) *Rule against perpetuities* — Providing that the trust shall terminate no later than twenty-one years after the death of the last surviving beneficiary who was alive at the time the trust was created, thereby protecting against inadvertent violation of the rule against perpetuities.

(9) *Trustee's fee* — Providing for the payment or waiving of fees determined on the basis of a statutory schedule or reasonable compensation considering the duties and responsibilities involved.

(10) *Bond* — Providing that no security or bond is necessary to assure the trustee's performance of his obligations. Otherwise the trust would be burdened with the annual cost of providing such bond or security.

---

[3] This provision will avoid the necessity of having a court-appointed guardian.

¶ 9.03 Revocable Trusts Created for Purposes Other Than Tax Savings

The creation of a trust that provides that the "grantor" (i.e., the person who furnishes the funds for the trust) reserves the power to revoke the trust will result in the grantor's being treated as the "owner" of the trust and, as a consequence, his being taxed on the income of the trust and the trust principal's being included in his estate for estate tax purposes. The grantor of such a revocable trust must report income and deductions of the trust on his own return as if the trust had not been created. For example, if the trust were to make a charitable contribution, it would be treated in the same manner as if the contribution were made by the grantor in his individual capacity and would be included with the grantor's other charitable gifts in computing his overall ceiling on charitable deductions. A revocable trust will, therefore, provide no income or estate tax savings to the grantor.

[1] Lifetime Use of Revocable Trusts

The primary motivation for the creation of a revocable trust is the nontax benefits that are available. For example, an individual who owns substantial amounts of stock, including listed securities or stock of closely held corporations, may find the burden of management of these properties to be too onerous, may not be available to manage the property because of a temporary medical disability, or may find it impractical to manage property in the United States during periods of travel or temporary residence in foreign countries. In any of the above situations, if the amount of property involved is substantial, the creation of a revocable trust, with the attendant costs and administrative burdens, may be justified.

Another situation where the revocable trust is sometimes, though not often, used is where a grantor is seeking a trial period during which he can ascertain the competence of an individual whom he is considering appointing as the trustee of his irrevocable lifetime or testamentary trust.

[2] Post-Death Benefits

An individual may also be interested in creating and funding a revocable trust in order to remove assets from his probate estate. Since the trust corpus is fully subject to estate tax under Sections 2036 and

2038 of the Code, the major advantages of such a testamentary vehicle are not tax-related. They include:

- Avoidance of state probate procedural requirements (e.g., restrictions in some states on the appointment of nonresident trustees, necessity for continuous court supervision of a testamentary trust, and the requirement of ancillary administration of assets, including real estate and, in some states, oil and gas or other mineral interests, located outside the decedent's domicile).
- Presence of competent management through professional trustees.
- Reduction of the estate's vulnerability to post-death contests, since, unlike a will, such trusts are not subject to the rules requiring testamentary proof and, additionally, their existence for some period before death will create a presumption of validity.
- Possible reduction in access to decedent's property.[4]
- Speedy transfer of property to trust beneficiaries in contrast to the delays inherent in the probate process.
- Uninterrupted trust administration after the death of the grantor.
- Reduction or elimination of costs usually based on the size of the probate estate including executor's commissions and attorney fees. However, where the trust requires management by a bank or third party trustee during the lifetime of the grantor, this expense may substantially offset the reduction in probate costs.
- Limitation of the disclosure of decedent's testamentary plan to his actual beneficiaries, trustees, and attorney, since the trust agreement and the trust assets, unlike a will and probate property, do not have to be identified in probate court records, which are subject to public inspection.
- Establishment of a nonprobate entity to which items payable by reason of the grantor's death — such as life insurance, distributions from a qualified profit sharing or pension plan, and other death benefits — may be made payable. Under Section 2042 of the Code, insurance made payable to the estate is automatically includable for estate tax purposes. Similarly, under Section 2039, employee death benefits from a qualified plan that are otherwise

---

[4] However, the Uniform Probate Code §§ 2-201 and 2-202 and most states (see, e.g., N.Y. State Powers & Trustee Law § 5-1.1 (McKinney 1981)) provide that the revocable trust be considered in calculating the spouse's share.

excludable from the gross estate will be includable if made payable to the estate. (See discussion at ¶ 14.05.) Therefore, by directing these funds to the pre-existing revocable trust, estate tax that would have been payable if the executor were the recipient of the payments can be avoided.[5] However, if the only objective in the use of a revocable trust is to avoid probate, significant consideration should be given to the use of other probate avoidance devices such as life insurance and joint tenancy.[6] Nevertheless, for a certain property with respect to which a step-up in basis to date-of-death value is desirable (e.g., tax shelter investments or substantially appreciated property), a trust would be preferable to joint tenancy, since only half of property jointly held with a spouse is now includable in an estate and, therefore, only half of the property would be given a step-up in basis.

[3] Income Tax Considerations

As previously indicated, the grantor of a revocable trust continues to be treated as the owner of its assets and taxed on all income as if earned individually. As a result, the transfer of certain assets to the trustee will usually not be considered a disposition for tax purposes. The following tax problems, with respect to certain assets, should therefore not be a cause for concern:

(1) The transfer to a revocable trust of investment credit property will not be considered a disposition that triggers recapture.[7]

(2) Neither the transfer to a revocable trust of unmatured installment notes receivable nor the distribution of such obligation to further trusts created under the trust instrument at the grantor's death will constitute a disposition under Section 453(d)(1), which accelerates the recognition of deferred gain on installment sales.[8]

(3) The transfer to a revocable trust of shares in a corporation subject to a Subchapter S election should not cause recapture.[9]

---

[5] See generally "The Revocable Living Trust as an Estate Planning Tool," 7 Real Prop., Prob. & Tr. J. 223, 234-238, 241-242 (1972).

[6] The appeal of joint tenancy between spouses has been increased by the 100 percent marital deduction now available for all property passing to a surviving spouse.

[7] Treas. Reg. § 1.47-3(f)(1)(ii)(b).

[8] See Rev. Rul. 76-100, 1976-1 C.B. 123; Rev. Rul. 74-243, 1974-1 C.B. 106.

[9] The Tax Reform Act of 1976 provided that any grantor trust, "all" of

(4) The transfer to a revocable trust of Section 1245 and Section 1250 property should not cause recapture.[10]

(5) The transfer to a trust of the grantor's personal residence will not cause the loss of the tax-free rollover privilege under Section 1034.[11]

When the revocable trust includes property that has a basis in excess of its fair market value, and the beneficiaries or new trusts resulting from a division of the principal trust have a right to receive from the trust a specific dollar amount, this amounts to the equivalent of a pecuniary bequest. Rather than satisfying such right with the property, the trustee should instead consider a sale to outsiders in order to establish a deductible loss and then distribute the proceeds. Such property should also not be sold to the grantor or the beneficiaries, even for its fair market value, because, under Section 267(b)(1), the loss will

---

which is owned by the grantor (i.e., the income and principal interest), or a voting trust can be a shareholder of an S corporation. Under the Revenue Act of 1978, a grantor trust is permitted to continue to be an eligible shareholder of an S corporation for two years after the grantor's death if the entire corpus is includable in the grantor's estate, and sixty days if it is not so includable. I.R.C. § 1361(c)(2). Also, the Code now provides that if a person other than the grantor is treated under I.R.C. § 678 as the complete owner of the trust, the trust (i.e., the deemed owner) may be a shareholder in an S corporation. The Act also provides that if the beneficiary of a trust that meets certain requirements (i.e., is a qualified Subchapter S trust) and he irrevocably elects to be treated as the owner of the trust for purposes of I.R.C. § 678, the trust is eligible to become a shareholder of an S corporation. A qualified Subchapter S trust is a trust with respect to which an election is made and that:

(A) owns stock in one or more electing S corporations,

(B) all of the income of which is distributed (or required to be distributed) currently to one individual who is a citizen or resident of the United States, and

(C) the terms of which require that:

  (i) at any time there shall be only one income beneficiary of the trust;

  (ii) any corpus distributed during the term of the trust may be distributed only to the current income beneficiary thereof;

  (iii) each income interest in the trust shall terminate on the earlier of the death of the income beneficiary or the termination of the trust; and

  (iv) upon the termination of the trust during the life of an income beneficiary, the trust shall distribute all of its assets to such income beneficiary. I.R.C. § 1361(d)(3).

On the other hand, only an "individual," defined by Section 1244(d)(4) to exclude a trust or estate or partnership, is allowed an ordinary loss deduction in certain small business corporation stock.

[10] A disposition is required for the recapture provisions to apply.

[11] See Rev. Rul. 66-159, 1966-1 C.B. 162.

be disallowed, as the disposition of the property will be considered a transaction between related parties, which includes a fiduciary of a trust and a beneficiary of such trust.[12] The loss will also be disallowed where the transaction is between a grantor and the fiduciary of any trust,[13] or between "a fiduciary of a trust and a fiduciary or beneficiary of another trust, if the same person is a grantor of both trusts."[14] A recoupment of the nondeductible loss would occur, however, in a case of a subsequent sale for gain by the transferee.[15]

After the death of the grantor, the trust becomes an independent tax entity. If the trust had been funded during the grantor's lifetime, the resulting advantage is that the income from the grantor's assets will be split between the taxpayers, the trust, and the grantor's estate. In a simple trust (i.e., a trust required to distribute all income currently) that has multiple beneficiaries, there is a further advantage in that the decedent's assets will be split between the estate and the numerous trust beneficiaries. On the other hand, if it is a complex trust (i.e., a trust not required to distribute income currently), the income from the grantor's assets will then be split between the trust and the grantor's estate, and later distributions by the trust to beneficiaries, or new trusts resulting from the principal trust, will be subject to the accumulation trust throwback rules.[16]

Therefore, the benefit of providing that the revocable trust be a simple trust during the post-death period is the elimination or minimization of the throwback problems while splitting the post-death income from the grantor's assets between the revocable trust beneficiaries and the estate, which is not likely to make significant distributions during the period of administration. Until recently, trust instruments often did

---

[12] I.R.C. § 267(b)(6).

[13] I.R.C. § 267(b)(4).

[14] I.R.C. §§ 267(b)(5), 267(b)(7).

[15] I.R.C. § 267(d).

[16] I.R.C. §§ 665-667. In contrast, the throwback rules are not applicable to distributions of accumulated estate income. The throwback rules generally provide that, at the time of the later eventual distribution of accumulated income, the beneficiary recipient will be taxed on the difference between (1) the tax he would have paid if the trust income, instead of being accumulated by the trust, had been distributed to him in the year it was earned, and (2) the tax actually paid by the trust. The major reason for the addition of the throwback rules to the Code was to preclude the use of lower tax bracket trusts to accumulate income in lieu of distributions to higher tax bracket beneficiaries.

not require current income distributions during the period immediately following the grantor's death. This was especially so in situations where a marital trust was to be established, and the revocable trust was to be divided into marital and nonmarital shares, which usually did not occur immediately upon the grantor's death and, in some circumstances, was purposely delayed.[17] With the reduction of the need to split trusts into marital and nonmarital shares, it is now more feasible to provide for simple trust status during the immediate post-death period.

[4] Gift and Estate Tax Consequences

The creation of a revocable trust by a grantor who retains the right to terminate the income interest and revest the property in himself will be considered an incomplete gift and, therefore, will not subject him to gift tax liability. On the other hand, since the grantor has, in effect, retained all rights of ownership, the trust assets will be fully includable in his estate.

¶ 9.04 Relinquishment of Ownership of Trust to Reduce Tax Liability

In many situations an important, if not major, objective of an individual with substantial taxable income is the savings of income or estate taxes. In order to achieve this objective, the grantor's identification with the trust must not be so complete as to cause him to be treated as the owner of the entire trust. The tax responsibility of the grantor increases or decreases in proportion to his ownership interest in the trust.

[1] Grantor Owns Entire Trust

If the grantor is treated as owner of the corpus as well as the income of the trust, he will be required to take into account, in computing his income tax liability, all items of income, deduction, and credit (includ-

---

[17] In light of the 100 percent marital deduction now available, the division of the revocable trust into separate marital and nonmarital shares is no longer necessary in many situations. But see "Estate Tax Unlimited Marital Deduction Has Limited Advantages in Larger Estates," 56 J. Tax. 236 (1982). See generally ¶ 15.02.

ing capital gains and losses) to which he would have been entitled had the trust not been in existence during the period he is treated as owner.[18]

In some situations it is to the grantor's benefit to be treated as owner. This is especially true if there are net operating and capital losses, tax credits, and other allowances attributed to the trust property that can be claimed by the grantor on his individual return if he is treated as owner of the trust. For example, an insurance trust that provides "sprinkling" powers to a trustee who is a related or subordinate party will be considered a trust owned by the grantor for income tax purposes, yet will not be includable in his estate for estate tax purposes under Section 2036 or Section 2038. As a result, interest deductions on borrowings of the cash surrender value to pay premiums will be available to the grantor, although he is not jeopardizing the exclusion of the insurance from his estate for estate tax purposes.

[2] Grantor Owns Part of Trust

The grantor can relinquish control over a part of a trust and retain an offending interest or power over the remaining corpus. He will then be treated as owning a pro rata share of both the income and corpus items of income, deduction, and credit, corresponding to the portion of the trust over which his power relates. For example, if he retains the power to revoke with respect to one half of the trust property, he will be treated for tax purposes as if he owned one half of the trust property. He may also retain a dollar amount of corpus. In this case, the portion he is treated as owning is a fraction, the numerator of which is the amount subject to the control of the grantor, and the denominator of which is normally the fair market value of the trust corpus at the beginning of the taxable year in question.[19] For example, assume the grantor creates an irrevocable trust with the income payable to his adult son for life and the remainder to his grandchildren, and the value of his entire corpus was $300,000 on January 1, 1983. If the grantor reserves the right to borrow up to $100,000 without adequate interest or security and does not exercise this power, he would be treated, under the grantor trust rules of Section 675(2), as owning one third ($100,000/$300,000) of each item of trust income, deduction, and credit falling within the 1983 calendar year.

---

[18] Treas. Reg. § 1.671-3(a)(1).
[19] Treas. Reg. § 1.671-3(a)(3).

[3] Grantor Retains Only Corpus Interest

The grantor can also retain ownership of the remainder interest of a trust, while sufficiently relinquishing control over the income portion so that he is not subject to income tax. For example, if he creates an irrevocable trust for a term of ten years and one day, with the income payable to his adult son and reversion on termination to himself, he will not be treated as owning the ordinary income portion. However, items of taxable income allocable to principal, under either the terms of the trust instrument or local law (generally capital gains), become part of the trust principal and, by reason of the grantor's reversion upon the trust's termination, are accumulated for future distribution to him. He is therefore treated as owner of the corpus portion [20] and will be taxed currently on items of gross income allocable to principal.[21] Normally this will involve only capital gains and losses, even though he will not actually receive any property from the trust until the termination of the ten-year term. If the trust provides that the beneficiary is entitled to all capital gains, he, rather than the grantor, will be liable for the capital gains tax.

¶ 9.05 "Clifford" Trusts

A trust created for the express purpose of relieving the grantor of income tax liability, while permitting him to retain a reversionary interest in the trust corpus, is commonly referred to as a short-term trust, ten-year trust, or Clifford Trust.

The derivation of the regulations relating to such grantor trusts or short-term trusts can be traced to the Supreme Court case of *Helvering v. Clifford*[22] and, on the basis of this case, such trusts have been denominated as Clifford Trusts. In *Helvering v. Clifford*, which was decided in 1940 (before joint returns were permissible), the grantor sought to make use of his wife as a second taxpayer earning a portion of the income on which he would otherwise be taxed. He was the trustee, and the assets were to return to him after five years. The Supreme Court refused to recognize this attempt to shift ownership because of the short

---

[20] I.R.C. § 677(a)(2); Treas. Reg. § 1.671-3(b); Rev. Rul. 58-242, 1958-1 C.B. 251.

[21] Treas. Reg. §§ 1.671-3(b)(2), 1.677(a)-1(g).

[22] 309 U.S. 331 (1940).

duration of the trust, the fact that the wife was the beneficiary, and the grantor's retention of control over the trust assets. Following its success in the *Clifford* case, the Service issued guidelines with respect to the requirements that had to be met in order for a grantor to avoid the fate of Mr. Clifford and to successfully shift his income tax burden to beneficiaries in a lower tax bracket. These rules, which became known as the Clifford regulations, were substantially adopted in Sections 673 through 678 of the Code of 1954.

¶ 9.06 Taxation of Clifford Trusts

[1] Income Tax Benefits

If funds or assets are placed in a Clifford Trust so that for a sufficient term, generally ten years, the income is irrevocably committed to a beneficiary other than the grantor, that income will be taxed to the beneficiary rather than the grantor. A taxable gift is created of the actuarial value of the income interest, and a corresponding amount (based on the actuarial value of the remaining term interest) is excludable from the estate of the grantor in the event of his death before the end of the trust term. At the end of the trust term, the property is returned to the grantor. This type of trust arrangement (i.e., a Clifford Trust) is especially useful for an individual who has a parent, adult child, or other relative to whom he is providing funds and reasonably expects to continue doing so for a period of at least ten years or during the lifetime of this beneficiary.[23]

For example, if a taxpayer who has reached the top 50 percent income tax bracket wishes to provide his elderly mother with $7,500 a year to supplement her resources, he must earn $15,000 from other assets to do so. Assuming a return of 15 percent on his investments, he would need $100,000 of principal in order to provide this $7,500 of after-tax dollars yearly income for his mother. On the other hand, if he were to set up a short-term trust for a period of ten years or the lifetime

---

[23] The gift tax cost to the grantor of such trust is minimal since the value of the trust income interest gifted is determined under the I.R.S. Regulations, which are based on an assumption of a 6 percent return. Additionally, the $10,000 per donee exclusion and the lifetime unified credit increasing to $600,000 by 1987 should eliminate or substantially reduce any gift tax liability. See generally ¶¶ 9.06[2], 9.10.

of his mother, only $50,000 of principal would be necessary to produce the same $7,500 of income annually. The grantor will, in effect, be shifting $7,500 of income annually from his high tax bracket to his mother, who ordinarily will be in a lower bracket and therefore would pay little or no tax. The result would be a federal income tax savings to the grantor of up to $3,750 per year.

[2] Grantor's Gift Tax Liability on Creation

The creation of a Clifford Trust will result in a taxable gift. The value of the gift, for gift tax purposes, is the present value of the right of the income beneficiary to receive the income for the term of the trust as determined under tables provided by the Service.[23a] Since such tables assume a 6 percent return, the actual fair market value of the gift will be greater than its value for gift tax purposes, resulting in substantially reduced gift tax expenses for the grantor.

The transfer to the Clifford Trust will qualify for the $10,000 annual exclusion to the extent that the transfer is a gift of a present interest. A transfer to a simple trust (i.e., one that requires current distribution of all income to the income beneficiary) is a gift of a present interest, which will qualify for the annual exclusion. On the other hand, if the trust is a complex trust (i.e., income can be accumulated or distributed to the income beneficiaries at the discretion of the trustee), it is considered to be a gift of a future interest. However, an exclusion will be allowed if the income of the trust is accumulated for the benefit of a minor beneficiary, provided the accumulated income must be paid to him no later than his reaching age 21. In addition, to the extent that the beneficiaries have the right to withdraw income from the trust each year, an exclusion is available even if the income of the trust is not currently distributed.

A transfer to a short-term trust that contains a power to sprinkle or accumulate income will be an incomplete gift if the income can be accumulated for the benefit of the grantor. However, if the accumulated income must ultimately be distributed to someone other than the grantor, the gift of the income interest will be complete; but there will be no annual exclusion available unless the holder of the power to sprinkle or accumulate is also the beneficiary.

[23a] Treas. Reg. § 25.2512-9(f), Table B.

¶ 9.07 Current Distribution or Accumulation of Trust Income

A grantor trust can provide that income is to be currently distributed or accumulated. If all income is required to be currently distributed to the grantor or his spouse, the grantor will be taxed on such income. On the other hand, if all income is currently distributable to the beneficiaries, it will be taxable to them rather than the grantor. Similarly, if all or part of a trust's income is required to be accumulated for future distribution to the grantor or his spouse, the portion accumulated will be taxable to the grantor. On the other hand, the grantor is not taxed if trust income is accumulated pursuant to a mandatory or discretionary power, even if such power is exercisable by the grantor or a nonadverse party, provided that the trust requires that accumulated income must ultimately be distributed to the current income beneficiaries in irrevocably specified shares; or to the income beneficiary from whom distribution is withheld, to his estate, or to his appointees (or to named takers in default of appointment) under a broad special power of appointment. However, any income accumulated for future distribution to the income beneficiary will be currently taxable to the trust and not the beneficiaries.[24] Subsequently, when the income is ultimately distributed to the beneficiary, he will be taxed under the throwback rules [25] as if the income had been received by him at the time it was earned, less a credit for the taxes paid by the trust. Income accumulated before the birth of the beneficiary or before he attains the age of 21 is excepted from the throwback rule.[26]

A provision for accumulation of income will be beneficial in only limited situations. For example, a trust for the benefit of a minor who is in a higher tax bracket than the trust will result in tax savings, since the throwback rules will not apply. Another situation where accumulation may result in savings is where a deferral of taxes is sought. If a beneficiary is in a higher tax bracket than the trust, accumulation of income will defer the payment of additional tax by this beneficiary until distribution. Additional income can then be earned by investing these tax monies, which do not have to be paid until a later period in time. Additionally, tax savings may result to a taxpayer who expects to be in a

---

[24] I.R.C. § 641(a)(1).
[25] I.R.C. §§ 665–667.
[26] I.R.C. § 665(b).

lower tax bracket for the three years preceding the termination of the Clifford Trust due to the application of the "short cut" Section 667(b) computation which, in this situation, will mitigate the impact of the throwback rule.[27]

In considering whether or not to accumulate trust income it should be remembered that the annual gift tax exclusion is not available if income must or may be accumulated by the trust. Additionally, in order to achieve the benefits of deferral, substantial sums of money will have to be tied up in the trust. It is therefore generally not advisable to provide for the accumulation of income in a "Clifford" Trust.

¶ 9.08 Restriction on Grantor's Powers to Transfer Trust Ownership for Income Tax Purposes

In order for a trust, or any portion thereof, to qualify under Section 671 through Section 677 of the Code so that the income will be taxed to the beneficiaries rather than the grantor, the grantor:

- Must sufficiently relinquish his reversionary interest as defined in Section 673 of the Code;
- May not retain the power to control the beneficial enjoyment of the trust assets as defined in Section 674 of the Code;
- May not retain certain prohibited administrative powers as defined in Section 675 of the Code;
- Must restrict his power to revoke the trust as defined in Section 676 of the Code;
- May not provide that trust income is to be distributed or accumulated for his benefit; and
- May not use any portion of the income of the trust to satisfy his support obligations. See Section 677 of the Code.

[1] Reversionary Interest Must Be Relinquished for a Sufficient Period of Time

[a] **Earliest Permissible Time for Reacquisition.** A grantor will be considered to have sufficiently relinquished his reversionary interest in both the corpus and income of the trust if (1) the possession or enjoyment of this interest will not revert to him until the expiration of a term

---

[27] I.R.C. § 667(b).

of at least ten years and one day from the time the property is transferred to the trust [28] or (2) the duration of the trust is to be the life of the income beneficiary. In the latter case, it does not matter whether the life expectancy of the income beneficiary is more or less than ten years. However, if the reversionary interest is to take effect on or after the death of an income beneficiary or upon the expiration of a specific term of years, whichever is earlier, the stated term of years must be for at least ten years.[29]

For example, suppose Taxpayer G creates an irrevocable trust for the benefit of his mother, age 95. The income is payable to her during her lifetime and, upon her death, is payable to G. The income paid to the mother is not taxed to G, even though the mother's life expectancy is less than ten years. However, if the trust provides that G's reversionary interest is to take effect on the earlier of his mother's death or a period of nine years, G will be treated as the owner of the entire trust and subject to income tax, since the alternative specific term is less than ten years. The likelihood of the alternative provision being invoked (i.e., his mother's living to age 104) is irrelevant.

Another alternative for qualification under the grantor trust rules is that the grantor's reversionary interest takes effect in possession or enjoyment by reason of some event other than the expiration of a specific term of years or the death of an income beneficiary, which event may not reasonably be expected to occur within ten years from that date. For example, the trust instrument can provide that the reversionary interest in any portion of the trust is to take effect on or after the death of the grantor (or any person other than the income beneficiary) if his life expectancy is at least ten years.[30]

[b] Postponement of Reacquisition Date. Any postponement of the date specified for the grantor's reacquisition of possession or enjoyment of the reversionary interest is considered a new transfer in trust, commencing with the date of the postponement, in determining whether there is a short-term trust. However, income that would not

---

[28] Treas. Reg. § 1.673(a)-1(a). The term of the trust should be slightly more than ten years to allow for any delay in transferring the assets to the trust after execution of the trust agreement.

[29] Treas. Reg. § 1.673(a)-1(b).

[30] Treas. Reg. § 1.673(a)-1(c).

have been taxed to grantor in the absence of the extension will not be taxed to him because of the postponement.[31]

For example, suppose taxpayer G places property in trust for his mother M, with a reversionary interest to G to take place after eleven years or upon the death of M, whichever is earlier. After the expiration of nine years, G extends the term of the trust for an additional three years. G is considered to have made a new transfer in trust for a period of five years (the remaining two years of the original transfer plus the three-year extension). He will be taxed on the trust income during the three-year extension period. However, the income of the first two years of such new term is not taxed to the grantor, since it would not have been taxed to him in the absence of the extension. Additionally, no additions should be made to the trust after its inception, at any time that may reasonably be expected to be within ten years of its ultimate termination.[32]

[2] Power to Control Beneficial Enjoyment Must Be Curtailed

In addition to giving up access to the property for a sufficient period of time, the grantor must also substantially relinquish direct or indirect control over the beneficial enjoyment of the trust property by persons other than himself during the trust period.

[a] **Grantor as Trustee.** Where the beneficial enjoyment of the corpus or income of any portion of the trust is subject to a power of disposition exercisable by the grantor or a nonadverse party, or both, without the approval or consent of any adverse party, the grantor is treated as the owner of that portion, and the income therefrom is taxable to him.

The powers that the grantor can retain without subjecting himself to tax on the income earned by the trust can be divided into two categories: first, a group of powers that result in no tax to the grantor, even if he or a related party is the trustee who can exercise such powers; second, a smaller but more important group of powers that result in no

---

[31] Treas. Reg. § 1.673(d)-1.
[32] Rev. Rul. 58-567, 1958-2 C.B. 365; Rev. Rul. 73-251, 1973-1 C.B. 324; Bibby v. Comm'r, 44 T.C. 638 (1965).

tax to the grantor only if held by persons considered to be sufficiently independent of the grantor.

[i] **Retained powers subjecting grantor to tax.** If the grantor or a related party as trustee has the power to control the identity of the beneficiaries after the creation of the trust, the grantor will be treated as the owner of the trust for income tax purposes.

For example, if the grantor creates an irrevocable trust with himself as trustee, which provides that the income is to be paid to *M*, his mother, and upon the earlier of the expiration of ten years or *M*'s death the principal is to pass to *B*, his brother, he will not be taxed on the income earned by the trust. This is because the identity of the beneficiaries is established in the trust instrument rather than by the grantor subsequent to the creation of the trust. However, if the grantor retains the right to add additional principal or income beneficiaries, to invade corpus for the benefit of *M*, or to accumulate income for the benefit of *B*, he will be treated as the owner of the trust for income tax purposes.

Another important power that cannot be retained by the grantor as trustee is to sprinkle the income at his discretion among various beneficiaries (e.g., his adult children) of a trust he created.[33]

[ii] **Permissible retained powers.** If the exercise of the powers described above will not take effect until more than ten years have passed since the creation of the trust, the grantor will be taxed only after the expiration of the period not affected by the power, and not at all if he relinquishes the power.[34]

The grantor may retain power to change corpus beneficiaries if such power is limited by a reasonably definite standard. If, in the example above, the grantor retained the power to make corpus distributions to *M*, but limited such power to a reasonably ascertainable standard, such power would not subject him to income taxation. An example of a reasonably ascertainable standard is one that is fixed in terms of the beneficiaries' customary standard of living, or their requirements for health, support, education, or maintenance.

The grantor can also retain the power to temporarily accumulate income, provided that the same income beneficiary from whom it was

---

[33] I.R.C. §§ 674(c), 674(d). See Laganas v. Comm'r, 281 F.2d 731 (1st Cir. 1960); United States v. Green, 176 F. Supp. 359 (S.D.N.Y. 1959).

[34] I.R.C. § 674(b)(2); Treas. Reg. § 1.674(b)-1(b)(2).

withheld will benefit from the accumulation. In order to meet this requirement, the accumulated income must ultimately be payable to the beneficiary from whom it was withheld, his estate, or appointees of the beneficiary who must be given a power of appointment that does not exclude from the class of possible appointees any person other than the beneficiary, his estate, his creditors, or the creditors of his estate.[35]

If, instead of creating a standard Clifford Trust with principal reverting to the grantor, the grantor provides for distributions of corpus, the requirement can also be met if the accumulated income is ultimately payable to the beneficiaries of current trust income. This applies only if the distribution occurs upon the distribution of corpus as augmented by the accumulated income or on termination of the trust and if the trust instrument irrevocably specifies their shares in such distributions.

For example, a trust provides that the income is to be paid in equal shares to the grantor's two adult sons, but the grantor reserves the power to withhold from either beneficiary any part of that beneficiary's share of income. The grantor also assumes the right to add the withheld portion to the trust corpus until the younger son reaches the age of 30 years, at which point the trust is to terminate and the corpus is to be divided equally between the two sons or their estates. Although exercise of this power may permit the shifting of accumulated income from one beneficiary to the other (since the corpus with the accumulations is to be divided equally), it is nevertheless permissible since the accumulation will ultimately inure to the benefit of current income beneficiaries in shares that have been irrevocably specified in the trust instrument. However, if the grantor of the trust reserves the power to distribute accumulated income to the beneficiaries in such shares as he chooses, he would be treated as the owner of the trust and taxed on its income, since the income accumulated is neither required to be payable only in conjunction with a corpus distribution nor required to be payable in shares specified in the trust instrument.[36]

If the trust designates in advance substitute recipients whose shares are irrevocably specified, the income accumulated for a particular beneficiary can be paid to these substitute recipients upon the premature death of the beneficiary, provided the income was initially accumu-

---

[35] Treas. Reg. § 1.674(b)-1(b)(6)(i)(a).

[36] Treas. Reg. § 1.674(b)-1(b)(6). However, the above powers, if exercisable only by independent trustees, would not subject the grantor to tax.

¶ 9.08[2][a]   NONCOMPENSATION PLANNING   9-22

lated and made payable to the initial beneficiary by a date that he reasonably could have been expected to survive. The designation of substitute beneficiaries in this manner is particularly appropriate in situations where the grantor is concerned with the welfare of a particular individual, but wants the benefits to be strictly limited to the individual's personal needs.

For example, a trust provides for the payment of income to the grantor's adult daughter, with the grantor retaining the power to accumulate the income until his death when all accumulations are to be paid to the daughter, if alive, otherwise to alternative takers (other than the grantor's estate) in specified shares. Since the date of distribution (the date of the grantor's death) can reasonably be expected to occur during the beneficiary's (the daughter's) lifetime, it is not necessary that the accumulations be payable to the daughter's estate for this exception to apply.[37]

The grantor can also reserve to himself a power exercisable during the period an income beneficiary is under age 21 or suffering from a legal disability to accumulate income and add it to corpus. In these situations, the amounts withheld do not have to ultimately be paid to the beneficiary from whom they were withheld, his estate, or his appointees. Thus, in the situation where the income beneficiary is a minor or has a legal disability, the grantor at least temporarily has considerable leeway to increase future distributions to corpus beneficiaries.

In the case of a charitable trust, the grantor can retain the power to change beneficiaries and still not be taxed on trust income, provided the benefits of corpus and income are irrevocably made payable to beneficiaries who are charitable or to similar tax-exempt organizations.[38]

The grantor can also retain the power to change beneficiaries by will without subjecting himself to tax. However, he will be taxed to the extent the power relates to income accumulated without the consent of an "adverse party."

For example, if all accounting net income is payable to a beneficiary for life and the grantor has a testamentary power to appoint the remainder, he will be taxed on the trust's capital gains and losses that are allocable to corpus.[39] The income of the trust will also be taxed to him if

---

[37] Treas. Reg. § 1.674(b)-1(b)(6)(ii), Ex. 3.
[38] I.R.C. § 674(b)(4); Treas. Reg. § 1.674(b)-1(b)(4).
[39] Treas. Reg. § 1.674(b)-1(b)(3).

he has the power to accumulate income without the consent of this beneficiary or another adverse party.

The grantor may also be able to accumulate income through the exercise of a permissible reserved power to allocate receipts and disbursements between corpus and income.[40] However, the allocations should be reasonable and be based on the generally accepted categorization of items as "income or corpus."

[b] Person Other Than Grantor as Trustee. When a grantor is not the trustee, or at least not the sole trustee, all of the above-permissible powers can be exercised, and a number of powers that would have caused the grantor to be taxed on the income of the trust can be granted to the trusteee without any ensuing adverse tax consequences to the grantor. Most significantly, although no trustee can retain the power to add additional beneficiaries, where a nongrantor is the trustee, the particular identity of the beneficiaries of the trust need not be so certain. One example of the advantages that can result from the availability of such additional power is the opportunity to distribute income to the lower tax bracket beneficiaries during each particular year of the trust's existence based on a current determination by the trustees.

As long as the trustees do not include the grantor or his spouse (if living with him), they can retain the power to distribute corpus to, for, or within a class of beneficiaries, provided the power is limited by a reasonably definite standard set forth in the trust instrument.[41] For instance, a power to distribute corpus for the education, support, maintenance, or health of the beneficiary, for his reasonable support and comfort, or to enable him to maintain his accustomed standard of living or to meet an emergency, would be characterized as a power limited by a reasonably definite standard. However, a power to distribute corpus from the pleasure, desire, or happiness of a beneficiary is not limited by a reasonably definite standard.[42]

A broader power to "sprinkle" or "spray" trust income or corpus that need not be restricted in advance by an external standard can be retained, provided the grantor is not a trustee and no more than half of

---

[40] I.R.C. § 674(b)(8). The grantor may also provide in the trust instrument for the automatic inclusion of after-born or after-adopted children as beneficiaries without being considered to have retained the power to control beneficial enjoyment. See Rev. Rul. 80-255, 1980-2 C.B. 272.

[41] Treas. Reg. § 1.674(d)-1.

[42] Treas. Reg. §§ 1.674(b)-1(b)(5)(ii), 1.674(b)-1(b)(5)(iii), Ex. 2.

the trustees vested with the power are "related or subordinate parties who are subservient to the wishes of the grantor."[43]

The term "related to or subordinate party" means any nonadverse party who is:

- The grantor's spouse if living with him;
- The grantor's father, mother, issue, brother, or sister, an employee of the grantor; a corporation or any employee of a corporation in which the stock holdings of the grantor and the trust are "significant" from the viewpoint of voting control; or a subordinate employee of a corporation in which the grantor is an executive.[44] The above parties are presumed to be subservient unless the contrary can be shown by a preponderance of the evidence.[45]

The sprinkling powers that can be exercised if less than half of the trustees are subservient or related include the power to:

- Distribute, apportion, or accumulate income to or for a beneficiary or beneficiaries, or to, for, or within a class of beneficiaries; or
- Pay out corpus to or for a beneficiary or beneficiaries (whether or not income beneficiaries).

The broad discretionary powers available to the trustees in this type of arrangement to sprinkle income or corpus without any advance restrictions, make it most suitable for planning purposes. A particular advantage of this type of trust is that the grantor's wife can be vested with the sprinkle or spray power, provided she shares it with one or more independent trustees such as *her* parents, sisters, or brothers, the grantor or his wife's uncle, nephew, cousin, or more remote relatives, their attorney, accountant, or friend. Therefore, the grantor, through his wife, would have the opportunity to retain substantial control over the trust assets without subjecting himself to income taxation.

[c] Power to Remove Trustee. If a grantor has an unrestricted power to remove an independent trustee and substitute any person, including himself, as trustee, he will, for all practical purposes, be

---

[43] I.R.C. § 674(c)(1).

[44] A director of a corporation is not considered to be a related or subordinate party. Rev. Rul. 66-160, 1966-1 C.B. 164.

[45] I.R.C. § 672(c).

considered to be the trustee; and if the trust instrument provides the trustees with sprinkling powers that can only be given to an independent trustee, the grantor would be subject to tax on the trust income. However, the grantor may reserve the right to remove, substitute, or add trustees in limited situations that do not occur during the taxable year, such as the death or resignation of, or breach of fiduciary duty by, an existing trustee, and he may also retain the power to remove or discharge an independent trustee, provided he must replace him with another independent trustee. However, for estate tax purposes the Service may take the position that such a retained power will result in the inclusion of the trust property in the grantor's estate.[46]

[d] Reciprocal Trusts. A device sometimes used for the purpose of circumventing the Code limitations on the ownership powers that can be retained by the grantor is the reciprocal trust. This arrangement generally involves two grantors, usually family members, who establish substantially identical trusts with the other as beneficiary and/or trustee. The effect is as though each grantor had created, in favor of himself, a trust that would otherwise be an invalid grantor trust. The Service and the courts have consistently held that such reciprocal trusts are an invalid method of circumventing the restrictions on retained control of beneficial enjoyment by the grantor.[47]

[3] Administrative Powers Exercisable by Grantor

[a] Grantor's Use of Administrative Powers to Directly Control Beneficial Enjoyment. Various administrative powers retained by the

---

[46] In Rev. Rul. 79-353, 1979-2 C.B. 325, the Service ruled that the corpus of a trust in which the grantor reserved such a power (and could not name herself trustee) was includable in her estate under Sections 2036(a)(2) and 2038(a)(1). In First Nat'l Bank of South Carolina v. U.S., 81-2 U.S.T.C. ¶ 13,422 (D.S.C. 1981), the Service's position was upheld in a situation where the grantor retained the power to appoint himself as successor trustee. However, in First Nat'l Bank of Denver, 648 F.2d 1286 (10th Cir. 1981), the Tenth Circuit clearly held that the mere power of the decedent to change corporate trustees (i.e., not to name himself as successor trustee) will not cause the trust corpus to be included in the decedent's estate.

[47] See, e.g., United States v. Estate of Grace, 395 U.S. 316 (1969); A.K. Krause v. Comm'r, 497 F.2d 1109 (6th Cir.) cert. denied, 419 U.S. 1108 (1974); Flato v. Comm'r, 195 F.2d 580 (5th Cir. 1952); Whitely v. Comm'r, 42 B.T.A. 316 (1940); Wyant v. Comm'r, 6 T.C. 565 (1946).

grantor may indirectly enable him to control the beneficial enjoyment of the trust income and corpus. For example, if the grantor or nonadverse party retains the power to purchase and sell such assets for the trust as he "deems appropriate," he, in effect, can substantially control how much should be distributed to the income beneficiaries and how much should be available to the remainderman by shifting from income-producing assets to investments with little or no income but substantial growth possibilities. Such investment powers, if retained by the grantor or nonadverse party and exercisable without the consent of an individual in a fiduciary capacity, will subject the grantor to tax in the situation where the trust funds consist of stock or securities of corporations in which the holdings of the grantor and trust reflect significant voting control.

The right to vote the controlling interest in a corporation whose stock is owned by the trust is another administrative power that, in effect, allows the grantor to control the extent of beneficial enjoyment. Therefore, where the combined holdings of the grantor and the trust of stock in a corporation are significant from the viewpoint of voting control, the income will be taxable to the grantor when the grantor or any nonadverse party retains the right to vote the shares without the approval or consent of any person in a fiduciary capacity.[48]

The right to vote or invest stock in a nonfiduciary capacity where only an insignificant percentage of stock is owned by the grantor and trusts, or the right to vote or to invest stock if exercised by the grantor or any other individual in a fiduciary capacity (even when the grantor and trust combined own a controlling interest), will not subject the grantor to tax.[49]

Therefore, the grantor who wishes to act as trustee may, through the exercise of the available administrative powers over investment and voting, indirectly achieve certain results, particularly the allocation of trust assets between income and corpus beneficiaries, which, if he retained directly as trustee, would subject him to tax.

---

[48] For example, in Moskin v. Johnson, 115 F. Supp. 565 (S.D.N.Y. 1953), aff'd, 217 F.2d 278 (2d Cir. 1954), trust income was taxed to the grantor who voted stock of the trust and commingled dividends with his own funds.

[49] However, if the grantor has a veto power with respect to the trustee's investment or voting decision, he, in effect, has the power to direct investments or vote the stock without the approval or consent of the fiduciary and will be taxed on the trust income if his holdings, when combined with that of the trust, are significant from the viewpoint of voting control.

[b] Offensive Administrative Powers Grantor Must Relinquish to Avoid Income Taxation. Certain administrative powers, if retained by the grantor or a nonadverse party, will subject the grantor to tax on the income of the trust. Such powers include the power to compel or direct the trustee to permit the grantor to reacquire the trust corpus by substituting other property of an equivalent value, or a power that enables the grantor or any person to deal with the trust property or income for less than an adequate consideration.

[c] Borrowing From Trust by Grantor. The grantor will not be subject to tax if he directly or indirectly borrows trust income or corpus if the loan provides for adequate interest and security and is made by a trustee other than the grantor or a related or subordinate trustee who is subservient to the grantor.[50] Even if the loan does not provide for adequate interest or security, the trust income will not be taxed to the grantor for that year (1) if he completely repays the loan (and interest) before the beginning of the succeeding year [51] or (2) in the situation where a trustee other than the grantor, acting alone, may, under a general lending power, lend to any person without adequate interest or security.

[4] Power to Revoke Subjecting Grantor to Tax

When a grantor does not have a substantial adverse interest and yet retains the power to revoke with respect to trust corpus or income, he is treated as the owner and will be taxed on the trust income if the power to revoke may result in the grantor's having a reversionary interest that can reasonably be expected to take effect in possession or enjoyment within ten years.

For example, Grantor *G* sets up a trust for eleven years for the benefit of his grandson, reserving to himself the right to revoke it at any

---

[50] A general lending power in the grantor acting alone as trustee, under which he has power to determine interest rates and the adequacy of security, is not in itself an indication that the grantor has power to borrow corpus or income without adequate interest or security. Treas. Reg. § 1.675-1(b)(2).

[51] However, if the grantor repays a loan before the end of the year and then proceeds immediately thereafter, at the beginning of the next year, to borrow substantially the same amount, the Service is likely to treat this transaction as one loan that has not been repaid, which will result in the inclusion of the trust income in that year and in the succeeding year in his taxable income.

time after five years, provided he gives the trustees notice of his intention to do so at least twelve months prior to the date of exercise. The income of the trust will be taxable to the grantor, not only after the expiration of the five-year term when his power to revoke would be available, but also during the first five years, since he has a vested right of revocation.[52]

The effect of a power to revoke is that the trust or that portion of the corpus to which the power applies is taxed as though the trust were not in existence. Where the grantor reserves a power to reacquire a portion of the property turned over to the trustees upon the payment of a small amount, the trust is revocable to the extent that the value of such portion of the corpus exceeds the amount required to be paid by him for its reacquisition.[53]

Even if the power to revoke is not exercised, the grantor will include all income and deductions of the trust on his personal return as if the trust had not been created. The beneficiaries will treat the amount received as nontaxable gifts. After 1981, the trust is no longer required to file a Form 1041, "Fiduciary Income Tax Return," in situations where it is the grantor to whom the income is taxable.

Where the exercise of the power to revoke is contingent on the happening of some future event that may never occur, the courts have held that the grantor will not be taxed on the trust income. For example, a trust that provided that income was to be distributed to the grantor's daughter until she reached age 40, at which time she would receive the corpus, was not considered to be revocable, although the grantor retained the right to terminate the trust in the event of the daughter's earlier death.[54]

[5] Use of Trust Income for Benefit of Grantor

If the income of the trust can, in the discretion of the grantor or a nonadverse party, be distributed or accumulated for future distribution to the grantor or his spouse or can be used to pay insurance premiums

---

[52] Beck v. Comm'r, 15 T.C. 642, (1950), aff'd, 194 F.2d 537 (2d Cir.), cert. denied, 344 U.S. 821 (1952).

[53] Fisher v. Comm'r, 28 B.T.A. 1164 (1933); Chandler v. Comm'r, 119 F.2d 623 (3d Cir. 1941).

[54] Rovensky v. Comm'r, 37 B.T.A. 702 (1938); see also Estate of Fish v. Comm'r, 42 B.T.A. 260 (1940); Milbank v. Comm'r, 41 B.T.A. 1014 (1940).

on the life of the grantor or his spouse, the grantor will be taxed on such income, even if it is not in fact so applied.

[6] Use of Trust Income for Support of Grantor's Dependents

Where the grantor creates a trust that provides that the income may be used to satisfy his obligation of support (e.g., for his minor child), he will be taxed on the income of such trust to the extent it is actually applied or distributed for such purposes. He will not, however, be taxed on the mere existence of a power in the hands of the trustee to apply trust income to satisfy the grantor's support obligations.[55]

In situations where a child is in college, the Service may take the position that the grantor should be taxed on trust income used to pay the child's tuition on one of two theories: (1) under state law the parent is obligated to pay for a child's tuition, or (2) under contract law the tuition bill is sent to the parent and he is discharging this bill or legal obligation with trust income.[56] An approach that would reduce income tax exposure would be to have the trustee make payments directly to the child and have the child arrange for the payment of his tuition and other expenses.

¶ 9.09 Persons Other Than the Grantor as Owner of Trust

A person other than the grantor will be treated as owner of a trust over which he has a power exercisable solely by himself to vest corpus or income in himself.[57] He will avoid taxation if there is a co-trustee who also has the power to manage the trust. The owner can also avoid taxation by renouncing the power within a reasonable time after he first became aware of its existence.[58]

---

[55] I.R.C. § 677(b).

[56] Morrill v. U.S., 228 F. Supp. 734 (D. Me. 1964). The law in some states providing that a child reaches majority at age 18 will not necessarily shelter the grantor paying his child's college tuition from taxation. See note 66 infra.

[57] I.R.C. § 678. A non-grantor trustee's discretionary power to distribute income or accumulate it for the benefit of his wife does not constitute a power to vest income in himself. The wife would also not be taxed even if she were a co-trustee of such a trust, provided she has no management authority.

[58] I.R.C. § 678(d); Treas. Reg. § 1.678(d)-1.

The power held by a trustee, or even a co-trustee, to apply the income of the trust to the support or maintenance of a person whom the holder of the power is obligated to support or maintain will result in the trust income being taxed to such trustee to the extent that the income is so applied.[59]

For example, a grandfather creates a trust with his two sons as co-trustees, which provides that they both, acting jointly, can apply the income for the support of the minor children of one of the co-trustees. To the extent income is so applied, the trustee parent will be subject to tax, since he is satisfying his legal obligation to support his children.

The power given a beneficiary to withdraw the greater of $5,000 or 5 percent of the value of the trust corpus will cause the holder to be taxed each year on the income from the withdrawable portion of the trust and on a proportionate part of the capital gains, whether or not the power is actually exercised in a particular year.[60]

¶ 9.10 Grantor's Potential Estate Tax Liability

If the grantor makes a completed gift of an income interest in trust, only the value of the reversionary interest will be included in his estate. The value of the reversionary interest is determined by consulting Regulations Section 20.2031-10(f), Table B. (This is discussed more extensively in Chapter 12.) In addition, if the grantor retains significant ownership powers (e.g., the power to accumulate income), the portion of the trust subject to such power will be includable in his estate.[61]

¶ 9.11 Alternative Methods of Achieving Income Tax Benefits From Transfer of Property

The above discussion relating to the creation of a trust for the purpose of saving income taxes emphasized the use of short-term or

---

[59] I.R.C. § 678(c).

[60] I.R.C. §§ 652, 678(a)(1); Rev. Rul. 67-241, 1967-2 C.B. 225.

[61] If the income is to be accumulated for the benefit of the grantor, he has retained enjoyment or possession under Section 2036(a)(1). If it must be distributed to the income beneficiary, it is taxable under Section 2036(a)(2), since he retains the power to designate who shall have possession or enjoyment, or under Section 2038(a)(1), since he retains a power to alter or amend the time of vesting. For a complete discussion of the retained powers that will result in includability in the estate, see Chapter 12.

Clifford Trusts to achieve such objective. However, similar income tax savings can be achieved by a direct transfer, the creation of an irrevocable trust, or the use of interest-free loans.

[1] Irrevocable Trusts

If an irrevocable trust is used, as opposed to a short-term grantor trust, the same restrictions on the grantor's powers will be necessary. The major difference is that the grantor will retain no reversionary interest. There will be a completed gift at the time of the transfer of the property into the trust, and the trust will be completely excluded from the grantor's estate. All trust income and capital gains will be taxed to the trust or the donee.

[2] Interest-Free Loans

A second alternative method for shifting the income tax burden from a high-bracket individual to his beneficiary is the use of non-interest-bearing demand loans. Such interest-free loans are commonly looked to as a simple alternative for trusts. The borrower, rather than the lender, is then taxed on the earnings from such loaned monies. The loan is generally made among family members for no interest. It is evidenced by a promissory note requiring repayment on demand. It is generally unsecured but can be secured. Unlike trusts, however, the interest-free loan arrangement has been challenged by the Service, and there is a risk that the tax-savings objectives may not be realized if the Service is successful in challenging the loan. There are no gift-tax consequences on the making of the loan as *Crown* illustrates.[62]

However, upon the expiration of the local statute of limitations period for collection, the loan will be treated as gifted in such year.[63] For estate tax purposes, the loan is an asset payable to the estate. However, the investment proceeds earned by the borrower are eliminated from the lender's estate. For income tax purposes, it is the borrower who is taxed on the income generated by investment of the loan proceeds. Interest-free loans are discussed more extensively at ¶ 11.09.

---

[62] Crown v. Comm'r, 67 T.C. 1060 (1977), aff'd, 585 F.2d 234 (7th Cir. 1978), nonacq., 1978-1 C.B. 2; Rev. Rul. 73-61, 1973-1 C.B. 408.

[63] Estate of Lang v. Comm'r, 64 T.C. 404 (1975), aff'd, 613 F.2d 770 (9th Cir. 1980).

[3] Comparison of Grantor Trusts and Alternative Methods of Transfer

The relative advantages and disadvantages of each of the above alternatives or an outright gift can be illustrated as in the examples below.

Assume John Donor is interested in embarking on a gift-giving program to provide for the education of his grandchildren, including the payment of their tuition for private secondary schools and colleges.[64] What are the advantages and disadvantages of the alternative methods available to accomplish such purpose?

[a] Outright Gifts. The 1981 Act provides an unlimited exclusion for tuition paid on behalf of an individual directly to the qualifying educational institution providing such services, provided the donor is not under an obligation under local law to pay such tuition.[65] This is in addition to the $10,000 annual exclusion. Although there is no gift tax

---

[64] Under state law, a grandfather is generally under no obligation to pay the tuition of his grandchildren.

[65] I.R.C. § 2503(e). For example, under New York law, which is looked to for federal tax purposes, whether such obligation exists must be determined on the basis of the facts and circumstances. New York Dom. Rel. L. § 236, Part B 7a(2) (effective July 1980), provides that in determining child support requirements, the educational needs of the child are considered in conjunction with the prior standard of living of the child and the financial resources of the parent. In Tannenbaum v. Tannenbaum, 50 A.D.2d 539, 375 N.Y.S. 2d 329 (1st Dep't 1975), and Ziran v. Ziran, 65 A.D.2d 514, 409 N.Y.S.2d 13 (1st Dep't 1978), the First Department held that, absent unusual circumstances, the furnishing of a private college education to one's children is not within the purview of necessities for which a father can be obligated. In Weyman v. Weyman, 51 A.D.2d 768, 379 N.Y.S.2d 717 (2d Dep't 1976) the Second Department felt that the father's income of $47,000 constituted a special circumstance making it incumbent on him to pay for his child's college education as a part of his support obligation. For a period of time it had been felt by some commentators that the First Department, unlike the Second Department, would hold that private school or college education was not a parental obligation in any situation. However, in a recent case, Connolly v. Connolly, 443 N.Y.S.2d 661 (1st Dep't 1981), the court, citing *Weyman,* held that under factual circumstances of the case they would not hesitate to direct the parent to pay private school or college expenses. The relevant facts in *Connolly* were that the child had been attending private schools since the age of 3 and the father, a physician, had an annual income of over $60,000. Therefore, it is now clear in New York that the issue of whether private school or college education is a support obligation of the father will be determined by the courts on the basis of facts and circumstances, rather than on a single uniform rule.

liability resulting from such a payment, these gifts are made with after-tax dollars. The following alternatives are, therefore, more advisable.

[b] Irrevocable Trusts. The advantages of irrevocable trusts are: (1) property and any appreciation thereon is excluded from the donor's estate and (2) all future income and capital gains are taxed to the trust or the beneficiaries and not to the donor. However, if trust assets are sold within two years of the transfer, the trust will be taxed at the rate that the grantor would have been taxed if he had realized the gain under Section 644 of the Code.[66]

On the other hand, there are distinct disadvantages: (1) The donor will irrevocably lose control over the property; and (2) a gift tax must be paid on the present value of the property placed in trust. However, no current payment will be due until the total gifts exceed the unified credit equivalent, which in 1982 was $225,000 and will increase gradually until it reaches $600,000 in 1987. There may, however, be a current state gift tax liability.

An irrevocable trust is advisable if (1) the property that is placed in the trust has substantial likelihood of appreciating in value, since the appreciation will not be subject to gift or estate tax or (2) the amount of the yearly gifts per donee will not exceed $10,000 ($20,000 if the spouse joins in the gift). There may, however, be some problem as to whether the gift in trust qualifies for the annual exclusion. See discussion at ¶ 11.02[3].

[c] Short-Term or "Clifford" Trusts. There are several advantages to these trust forms: (1) Donor is not taxed on trust ordinary income for 10 years; (2) trust income is usually taxed to lower bracket taxpayer; (3) trust corpus returns to the grantor at the expiration of the trust term; (4) the trust can permit invasion of principal for the beneficiaries, provided the invasion powers are limited by an ascertainable standard, such as health, support, education, or welfare; and (5) trust income can be used to pay the beneficiary's education expenses. However, the beneficiary's parents should not be the trustees unless under state law they are not obligated to pay such expenses as part of their support

---

[66] The purpose of Section 644 was to prevent people from transferring property they intended to sell to a trust, which would then sell it shortly thereafter and pay a lesser capital gains tax.

obligation.[67] If under a separation agreement or divorce decree the father assumes a contractual obligation to provide for private school and college education, he certainly should not be a trustee. If a person other than the parent is a trustee, the father will not be subject to income tax merely because the trust is fulfilling an obligation for which he otherwise would be responsible, and any gift tax payable or, alternatively, the reduction of unified credit is based on the actuarial present value of the gift under Treas. Reg. § 25.2512-9(f), Table B, which assumes a 6 percent interest return. For example, a ten-year-and-a-day transfer in trust of $100,000 is considered to be a gift with a value of only $44,161, which after the $10,000 annual exclusion is reduced to a gift of $34,161. The actual fair market value of the income interest in $100,000 for ten years and a day would have been substantially higher. At the end of ten years, the grantor has in his estate base the $34,161 gift plus the $100,000 trust assets, although the beneficiary may actually have received over $100,000 in income over the ten-year period.

The disadvantages of short-term or Clifford trusts are: (1) The grantor must be prepared to relinquish the income from the trust for a minimum period measured by the life of the beneficiary or ten years; (2) the grantor will give up the use and control of the principal transferred for the term of the trust; (3) the creation of the trust will result in a gift tax liability or, alternatively, will reduce the amount of the grantor's unified credit; and (4) capital gains realized by the trust are currently taxed to the grantor (income tax), even though they are added to trust corpus and are not available to the grantor during the term of the trust. However, if the trust provides that the beneficiary is to receive all the capital gains, the beneficiary, and not the grantor, will be taxed on the capital gains.

A short-term trust is advisable if the property to be transferred does not have a potential for substantial appreciation and the donor desires that it revert to him after a specified period of time (but not until the earlier of the expiration of ten years or the death of the beneficiary).

[d] Interest-Free Loans. An interest-free loan has many of the advantages of the short-term trust, without gift tax consequences or capital gains problems (i.e., the lender is not taxed on the loan income or the capital gains on the loan property). According to *Crown* and other

---

[67] See Rev. Rul. 81-98, 1981-1 C.B. 40.

litigated cases, [68] the courts hold that this is not a taxable gift, and the loan corpus is ultimately returned to the lender when he demands it. In addition, the costs of planning, drafting, and administering the transaction, as compared to short-term trusts, are substantially reduced or eliminated.

However, the Service is reluctant to concede the validity of the use of interest-free loans as a planning device, and such loans may trigger an audit. The Service takes the position that a taxable gift occurs in the year that the statute of limitations for collection of the demand loan expires under state law. A further significant disadvantage is that loan monies are often given directly to borrowers who may not be prepared to handle large sums of money or valuable assets. In the case of minors, who cannot enter into legally enforceable obligations, the monies properly should be loaned to a custodian account or trust created for the benefit of the minor. There is always a danger that the loan may not be repaid if the principal is squandered.

[e] Interest-Free Loans to an Irrevocable Trust. The use of interest-free loans in conjunction with an irrevocable trust may be a viable method of combining the advantages of each of the alternatives. By transferring money in the form of loans to the trust, the grantor will avoid paying income tax on the trust's earnings while not relinquishing control over the trust assets, since he can demand repayment at any time. The monies need not be tied up for ten years or longer in order to save income tax. There will also not be any gift tax liability since the monies are loaned to the trust instead of being given as an outright gift. Additionally, the monies are loaned to a trust having trustees who may be more capable of handling large sums of money than the beneficiaries, and where the beneficiaries are minors, a trust circumvents the otherwise incapacity of the minors to enter into enforceable loan transactions. To the extent the $10,000 per donee annual exclusion is available, monies can be given outright to the trust. The donor can terminate the lending program at any time should the Service be successful in challenging the validity of interest-free loans.

The problem with this suggestion is that the loan to the trust, which is payable on demand, bears no interest, and is not secured, may be challenged as a non-bona fide loan. The Service may argue that the

---

[68] Johnson v. U.S., 254 F. Supp. 73 (N.D. Tex. 1966). But see Estate of Berkman v. Comm'r, 38 T.C.M. 183 (1979).

lender should be taxed on the income earned by the borrower through the investment of the loan proceeds, especially if it is an intra-family loan, on an anticipatory assignment of income theory. The Service may also argue that since this is a demand loan, the grantor has the power to revest title in himself within ten years after the transfer of such property to the trust and, therefore, should be taxed on the trust income.[69]

While the arguments and challenges to interest-free loan arrangements discussed above have not yet been successfully advanced by the Service, the potential challenges make the use of loans as a planning device more risky. Therefore, unless the grantor is willing to assume these risks, he should avoid using loans if an alternative approach can be utilized to achieve a similar objective.

¶ 9.12 Foreign Trusts

A U.S. person who directly or indirectly transfers property to a foreign trust will be treated as the owner of the trust assets, the transfer notwithstanding, and will be taxable on the trust's income, including foreign source income, if there is a U.S. beneficiary of any portion of such trust.[70]

The character of a trust as "foreign" is based on a number of considerations, including the country under whose laws the trust was created, the nationality and residence of the trustee where the trust is being administered, and the nationality and residence of the grantor, and the nationality and residence of the beneficiaries. While each of the above factors is used in establishing the domestic or foreign character of a trust, the Service and the courts place particular emphasis on the location of the trustee and the trust administration.[71]

As a result of his gift to a foreign trust, the grantor may incur gift, income, and excise tax liability. He will be treated as having made a taxable gift to each of the trust's beneficiaries, rather than a single gift to the trust, and will have available a separate $10,000 per donee exclusion for each beneficiary with a present interest. For income tax purposes,

---

[69] I.R.C. § 673.

[70] I.R.C. § 679. The purpose of this section, which applies to trusts created after May 21, 1979, was to plug a loophole that had allowed U.S. persons to accumulate foreign source income free of tax.

[71] Rev. Rul. 60-181, 1960-1 C.B. 257. See Maximov v. United States, 373 U.S. 49 (1969), aff'g 299 F.2d 565 (2d Cir. 1962); B.W. Jones Trust v. Comm'r, 46 B.T.A. 531 (1941), aff'd, 132 F.2d 914 (4th Cir. 1943).

since the grantor is considered as the owner of the trust, he will be taxed on all its income.

In addition, if appreciated property is gifted to a foreign trust by a U.S. person, a 35 percent excise tax is imposed on the unrealized appreciation under Section 1491 of the Code. The rationale for this excise tax is to prevent a U.S. grantor from transferring appreciated assets (e.g., stock or securities) to a foreign trust that could dispose of the property without imposition of U.S. capital gains tax. Under Section 1492, there are two exceptions to the applicability of this penalty tax. One exception applies if the grantor can establish, to the satisfaction of the Secretary, that the transfer was not pursuant to a plan having as one of its principal purposes the avoidance of federal income tax. This exception cannot be relied upon in tax planning, since there are no precise guidelines for determining what is a "plan having as one of its principal purposes the avoidance of Federal income taxes." The second exception applies if the grantor files an election to recognize all of the unrealized appreciation or potential gain at the time of the transfer, under Section 1057. The amount of the potential gain is measured by the excess of the fair market value of the property transferred, over the adjusted basis of the property in the hands of the grantor.

The 35 percent excise tax rate was established in 1976 as an equivalent to the maximum tax rate on net long-term capital gains that would have been imposed had there been a sale of the property to the trust. However, the Revenue Act of 1978 increased the deductible portion of net long-term capital gains to 60 percent from 50 percent, and the 1981 Act reduced the maximum tax brackets to 50 percent, resulting in a maximum tax rate on net long-term capital gains of 20 percent. Therefore, the 35 percent excise tax is higher than the rate of tax if the taxpayer elects to recognize the gains under Section 1057. In addition, payment of the excise tax does not increase the grantor's basis in the property, while recognition of the gain does. However, if the property transferred is not eligible for long-term capital gain, e.g., inventory or a capital asset not held for more than one year, the 35 percent excise tax is less than the potential 50 percent income tax rate.

In summary, under current tax law there no longer are significant tax benefits to be attained by transferring assets to a foreign trust. If, for nontax business reasons, a foreign grantor trust is established with appreciated property, an election to currently recognize the potential gain (if capital gain) will produce a less onerous result than the 35 percent penalty tax otherwise imposed by Section 1491.

PART IV
Estate Planning

CHAPTER 10

Overview of Estate and Gift Taxation

		Page
¶ 10.01	Introduction	10-2
¶ 10.02	Basic Estate and Gift Tax Structure	10-5
	[1] Computation of Estate Tax	10-5
	[2] Unified Credit	10-7
	[3] Credit for Tax on Prior Transfers	10-7
	[a] Transfer of Property	10-8
	[b] Computation of the Credit	10-9
	[i] Value of the transferred property	10-9
	[ii] Estate tax paid on transferred property	10-10
	[iii] Decedent's estate tax attributable to transferred property	10-11
	[4] Credit for State Death Taxes	10-11
¶ 10.03	Deductions From the Gross Estate	10-13
	[1] Estate Administration Expenses	10-14
	[a] General Limitations	10-14
	[b] Allowable Deductions	10-15
	[i] Funeral expenses	10-15
	[ii] Probate and administration expenses	10-16
	[iii] Executor's commissions	10-16
	[iv] Other deductible expenses	10-17
	[c] Planning for Section 2053 Deductions	10-17
	[2] Claims Against the Estate	10-18
	[a] General Conditions for Deduction	10-19
	[b] Specific Types of Deductible Claims	10-20
	[i] Taxes	10-20
	[ii] Interest	10-21
	[iii] Charitable pledges	10-22
	[iv] Unpaid mortgages	10-22
	[c] Planning for Claims	10-22
	[i] Ascertaining potential claims	10-22
	[ii] Ensuring proper documentation	10-23
	[3] Losses During Administration	10-23

¶ 10.01   ESTATE PLANNING   10-2

		Page
¶ 10.04	Tax on Generation Skipping Transfers	10-24
	[1] Imposition of the Generation Skipping Tax	10-25
	[2] Planning With Respect to the Tax on Generation Skipping Transfers	10-26
	[a] Direct Bequests to Younger Generations	10-26
	[b] The Income Exception	10-27
	[c] The $250,000 Exclusion	10-29
¶ 10.05	Jointly Held Property	10-30
	[1] General Rule of Taxation	10-30
	[2] Joint Interests with Spouse	10-31

¶ 10.01 Introduction

The taxation of estates and gifts has undergone almost revolutionary change since 1976. The Tax Reform Act of 1976 and the Economic Recovery Act of 1981 (the 1981 Act) (when fully phased in) have instituted the following major changes in our estate and gift tax codes:

(1) Created a unified system of estate and gift taxation whereby lifetime gifts are cumulated with and taxed together with transfers occurring at death;

(2) Increased the amount that a person could transfer tax-free during his lifetime and at death from a total of $90,000 [1] to a total of $600,000;[2]

(3) Created a tax on generation skipping transfers whereby trust mechanisms that were designed to provide only an income interest to the next generation and thereby escape estate tax for that generation are now taxed as if an ownership interest had evolved upon that generation;

(4) Created an unlimited marital deduction so that an individual's entire estate can be passed free of tax to a surviving spouse; and

(5) Gradually reduced the maximum rate of taxation on estates from 70 to 50 percent, effective for deaths occurring in 1985 and thereafter.

---

[1] Prior to 1976, each individual had an exemption of $60,000 from the estate tax and $30,000 from the then separate gift tax.

[2] After the 1981 Act changes are fully phased in. This number does not include any amount transferred tax-free as a result of the Section 2503 annual gift tax exclusion or any other amount that may be transferred free of tax by virtue of deductions such as the marital deduction.

These changes have many profound estate planning implications. First, they drastically change the level at which an individual or a family needs to become concerned about federal estate tax planning. The increase in the level of exemptions has meant that many families of relatively moderate wealth need no longer be concerned about the federal estate tax. Depending on their domicile, state inheritance taxes may still constitute a considerable item, however. The magnitude of these inheritance taxes, on the other hand, is considerably less than the federal estate tax that was formerly faced.

These changes do not, however, eliminate the need for estate planning for most highly compensated individuals. Note that the unified credit, which will exempt estates of up to $600,000 from taxation when it is fully phased in, will not reach the level that exempts a $600,000 estate until 1987.[3] Thus, many estates below that level today will, in all likelihood, given our recent rates of inflation, be at or near the taxable level by the time the credit is fully phased in. In addition, many highly compensated individuals already have built or are building estates of that magnitude — particularly when the effect of life insurance is considered. Consequently, a substantial percentage of highly compensated individuals either remain at, or are likely to be at, taxable levels in regard to the federal estate tax. In addition, because the exemption from estate and gift taxation is available by means of a tax credit rather than a deduction, the initial federal taxation of estates commences at relatively high rates. Once the credit is fully phased in in 1987, the first dollar of an estate subject to taxation will be taxed at a rate of 37 percent. Because of these high rates, tax minimization becomes an important concern at initial levels of taxation.

The second major consequence of the changes brought about by the 1976 and 1981 Acts has been a rethinking of virtually all the standard estate planning techniques in effect prior to 1976. For example, by

---

[3] The unified credit is being phased in on the following schedule:

Year	Amount of Credit	Amount Exempt From Estate and Gift Taxes
1982	$ 62,800	$225,000
1983	79,300	275,000
1984	96,300	325,000
1985	121,800	400,000
1986	155,800	500,000
1987 (and thereafter)	192,800	600,000

creating a unified system of estate and gift taxation, the 1976 Act greatly reduces many of the previous advantages of making lifetime gifts. The 1981 Act counterbalanced this somewhat by increasing the per donee annual exclusion [4] to $10,000. These changes, combined with the unlimited marital deduction, have somewhat lessened the role of lifetime gifts in estate planning, although they do remain a viable alternative in many situations.[5]

Another area of drastic change has occurred in regard to marital deduction tax planning.[6] The enactment of the unlimited marital deduction means that federal estate taxes no longer have an impact upon an individual's ability to provide for a spouse. However, once these economic needs have been satisfied, tax planning to maximize the amount to be transferred to the succeeding generation becomes more important. Prior to these recent legislative changes, it was virtually axiomatic that the maximum transfers to the succeeding generation could be achieved by equalizing the estates of each spouse. Now, a combination of the greatly increased unified credit, the compression of estate tax rates into a relatively narrow range of 37–50 percent, and the continued impact of inflation has made decisions on how best to implement the marital deduction more complex.[7] In many instances it may now be more advantageous to have the first spouse to die make a nonmarital bequest in an amount equal to the deduction equivalent produced by the unified credit and to postpone taxation by leaving the remainder of the estate to the surviving spouse. In any event, the decisions in regard to the marital deduction are much more complex and individualized than prior to the 1976 and 1981 changes.

Similarly, transfers to succeeding generations have been greatly complicated by the tax on generation skipping transfers. The use of a trust or a trust equivalent in attempting to skip a generation invites the imposition of this tax.[8] Thus, the form and method of providing for children and grandchildren, particularly among the very wealthy, has been substantially modified.

This chapter outlines our basic system of estate taxation so as to set the stage for the discussion of the specific estate planning problems of

---

[4] I.R.C. § 2503(b).

[5] Lifetime gifts are discussed extensively in Chapter 11.

[6] See generally Chapter 15.

[7] See generally ¶ 15.02[1].

[8] See generally ¶ 10.04.

the highly compensated which are reviewed in the following chapters of Part IV. It first reviews the basic concepts of what is included in a gross estate and the primary deductions from the gross estate. Included in this review is a discussion of the two basic credits that affect estate and gift taxation [9] — the credit for tax paid on prior transfers and the credit for state inheritance taxes. A brief discussion of the tax on generation skipping transfers and the taxation of jointly held property then sets the stage for more detailed discussions in the succeeding chapters on estate planning.

¶ 10.02 Basic Estate and Gift Tax Structure

[1] Computation of Estate Tax

Section 2033 of the Code provides that the value of a decedent's gross estate shall include the value of all property to the extent of the interest therein of the decedent at the time of his death. Consequently, the essential concept of the estate tax is to use as the basis for taxation all property in whatever form owned by the decedent. As might be expected with such an inclusive concept, there are many disputes as to whether or not an item is includable in the gross estate of a decedent. The major items of dispute most relevant to the highly compensated individual are discussed throughout the succeeding chapters of this Part.[10] However, in reviewing these concepts, it is well to bear in mind the basic premise that the estate tax attempts to reach all property owned by the decedent at the time of death.

The value of a decedent's estate is the value of such property interests at the time of death. However, the estate may elect to value the property as of an alternate valuation date, which is six months after the date of the decedent's death.[11] In addition, there is a special valuation

---

[9] In addition to the unified credit.

[10] For example, the value of a gross estate will include certain property transferred in trust with varous "strings" attached that are statutorily covered in Sections 2036 through 2038 and that are discussed in Chapter 12. The retention of certain rights in a life insurance policy will result in the inclusion of the proceeds in the gross estate of a decedent. This topic is discussed in Chapter 13.

[11] See I.R.C. § 2032. If the property is sold or distributed prior to the alternate valuation date, the date of such sale or distribution shall constitute the alternate valuation date for that property.

procedure for certain family farms and other qualified real property.[12]

After the gross estate is determined, administration expenses, losses, and indebtedness [13] are deducted to arrive at the adjusted gross estate. From that number, the marital deduction [14] and the charitable deduction [15] are taken in order to calculate the taxable estate. The tentative estate tax liability is then determined by applying the unified rate schedule to the taxable estate. The taxable estate includes not only those items that were included in the decedent's adjusted gross estate but also "adjusted taxable gifts," which are essentially all lifetime transfers in excess of the annual exclusion made after December 31, 1976. Any gift taxes paid with respect to such lifetime transfers are then used to offset the tentative tax liability. Finally, the unified credit is subtracted from the tentative tax that is due as well as the other credits, such as the credit for taxes paid on prior transfers [16] and the credit for state death taxes paid.[17] The resulting figure indicates the estate tax liability.

The estate tax return is required to be filed within nine months after the date of the decedent's death.[18] After the 1981 Act is fully phased in by 1987, the estate tax return need only be filed if the decedent's gross estate exceeds $600,000. Prior to that time, the filing requirement is based on a phase-in schedule.[19]

This seemingly simple estate tax structure presents both a full range of complications for the uninitiated and a wide range of planning opportunities for the informed. The remainder of this Chapter discusses in somewhat more detail the basic concepts underlying the determina-

---

[12] I.R.C. § 2032A.
[13] See ¶ 10.03.
[14] See ¶ 15.02.
[15] See ¶ 15.02[2].
[16] See ¶ 10.02[3].
[17] See ¶ 10.02[4].
[18] I.R.C. § 6075(a).
[19] The schedule reads as follows:

Year	Gross Estate
1982	$225,000
1983	275,000
1984	325,000
1985	400,000
1986	500,000

tion of estate tax liability. The major planning emphasis will be on tax minimization for the highly compensated individual.

[2] Unified Credit

The effect of the unified credit discussed throughout this chapter should be briefly emphasized here. This credit, set forth in Section 2010, provides a direct dollar-for-dollar tax reduction in the amount of estate taxes due. When it is fully phased in,[20] the credit in an amount of $192,800 will shield an estate of $600,000 or less from taxation. The credit is limited to the amount of tax imposed by Section 2001.[21] Because Section 2010 provides a credit and not a deduction, the first dollars taxed in an estate (after 1987) will be at the rate for estates of $600,000 or more — i.e., 37 percent. To illustrate, a taxable estate of $600,100 (after 1987) would incur a tentative tax of $192,837. After reduction by the credit of $192,800, a tax of $37 would be due. Thus, the first $100 subject to tax would be taxed at the marginal rate of 37 percent. Consequently, although the 1981 Act increases in the unified credit do exempt many estates from taxation, those estates above the credit are initially taxed at relatively high rates.

[3] Credit for Tax on Prior Transfers

Section 2013 of the Code provides a credit for the federal estate taxes paid with respect to property transferred to the decedent from a person who died within ten years before or within two years after the decedent's death. The theory behind this section is that where multiple deaths have occurred in rapid succession, it would be onerous to subject the same property to repeated estate taxation.

Computation of the credit for tax paid on prior transfers is very significant in the case of decedents who had received considerable amounts of property from an individual who had recently died. There is very little planning that can be undertaken in regard to this section other than to note its existence — particularly when computing the potential estate taxes in regard to the estate of a seriously ill individual. The existence of the credit emphasizes the importance of looking

---

[20] The phase in schedule is set forth in note 3.
[21] I.R.C. § 2010(d).

closely at the source of assets that will be included in a client's estate. By carefully noting these sources on an estate planning questionnaire, the potential existence of this credit will be noted if the client should die within ten years of receiving assets from another decedent.

Generally speaking, the unlimited marital deduction will mean that there will be little utility arising from the credit for tax on prior transfers in a situation where the first spouse takes full advantage of the unlimited marital deduction. Typically, the credit will be most useful in the situation where there has been transfer from a nonspouse. In those situations where it is applicable, it may result in a considerable estate tax savings.

[a] Transfer of Property. Section 2013(a) provides that if the transferor died within two years of the death of the decedent, the decedent's estate will be allowed the full amount of the credit as provided by Sections 2013(b) and 2013(c). If the transferor predeceased the decedent by more than two years, the credit will be determined by applying the following percentages to the allowable credit:

Allowable Percentage	Years Transfer Preceded Decedent's Death
80%	three or four
60	five or six
40	seven or eight
20	nine or ten

The major requirement for the allowability of the credit is that there must have been a transfer of property from an individual who died within the requisite time limitations set forth in the statute. The regulations give a broad definition of property and include in the term such examples as annuities, life estates, estates for terms of years, vested or contingent remainders, and other future interests.[22] Thus, it is important to note that property that meets the requirements of Section 2013 is not necessarily the type of property that is included in the gross estate of the decedent.[23] For example, an individual may have transferred a life estate to a decedent and paid a significant estate tax on

---

[22] Treas. Reg. § 20.2013-5(a).
[23] Treas. Reg. § 20.2013-1(a).

the property so transferred. If the decedent died within the Section 2013 time frame, this property would not be included in his gross estate but could be eligible for the credit.[24] In addition, the decedent may have actually sold the property received but still could be eligible for the credit. Thus, it is not necessary to trace property into a decedent's estate. The critical factor is that a prior transferor had property included in his gross estate that was transferred to the decedent within the requisite time period.

The regulations similarly give a broad definition to the term "transfer."[25] Again, the critical factor is that the property interest was included in the gross estate of the transferor. For example, property may be received by the exercise or nonexercise of a power of appointment and, so long as it was includable in the gross estate of the holder of the power under Section 2041, it will be eligible for the credit. Property eligible for the credit may be transferred under a dower or curtesy law, by receipt as a surviving joint tenant or as a beneficiary under proceeds of a life insurance policy.

[b] Computation of the Credit. The credit that is allowed under Section 2013 is limited to the smaller of the federal estate tax attributable to the transferred property in the transferor's estate or the federal estate tax attributable to the value of the transferred property in the decedent's estate. The method of computing each of these limitations in regard to the two estates involved is entirely different.

[i] Value of the transferred property. The first stage in the computation of the credit is to determine the value of the transferred property. Section 2013(d) provides that the value of the property transferred to the decedent shall be the value used for determining the federal estate tax liability of the transferor, less certain deductions provided by that Section. In other words, if the property was valued in the estate of the transferor at $500,000 and, at the date of the decedent's death, it is worth $750,000, its value for Section 2013 purposes will be considered to be $500,000. This can be especially important in the case of appreciating property and in the situation where the decedent had

---

[24] See Rev. Rul. 59-9, 1959-1 C.B. 232; see also Rev. Rul. 66-271, 1966-2 C.B. 430.

[25] Treas. Reg. § 20.2013-5(b).

received a life estate. For example, if the decedent had a life estate in property resulting from a prior transfer and lived a far shorter period than his normal life expectancy, the value of the property eligible for the Section 2013 credit in his estate would be based on the value of his life estate as of the date of the prior transfer — irrespective of the fact that he lived for a much shorter period of time.

The value of the property transferred is then reduced by three deductions that are mandated by Section 2013(d). The first of these deductions is in the situation where the transferred property was subject to any estate, inheritance, legacy, or succession taxes that were payable out of the property transferred to the decedent.[26] In other words, this Section mandates that the credit be based on the net value (i.e., value at date of transfer, less estate taxes payable out of that property) of the property so transferred. If under the will of the transferor, the property was not chargeable with any estate or inheritance taxes, this reduction would be inapplicable. The second reduction is if the property was encumbered at the time of the transfer. For example, if the decedent had received real estate subject to a mortgage, the value of the property so transferred would be reduced by the amount of that mortgage. This limitation and the limitation in regard to estate and inheritance taxes are both based upon the theory that the value of the property so transferred will be considered to be its net amount. The final limitation of Section 2013(d) is that the value of the transferred property will be reduced by any marital deduction allowed with respect to such property.[27] Again, the theory is that if the property bore no taxes because of the marital deduction, no credit should be allowed for any estate tax that, in truth, was not paid with respect to this property.

[ii] Estate tax paid on transferred property. Once the adjusted value of the property is determined, the two limitations must be computed to determine the amount of the credit allowed. The first limitation is in regard to the estate tax paid by the transferor's estate on the transferred property. This limitation, which is set forth in Section 2013(b), attributes the estate tax paid by the transferor's estate based on the ratio of the value of the transferred property to the value of the

---

[26] Treas. Reg. § 20.2013-4(b)(1).

[27] I.R.C. § 2013(d)(3). See also Shedd v. Comm'r, 320 F.2d 638 (9th Cir. 1963). This limitation is especially significant in view of the unlimited marital deduction allowed by the 1981 Act.

transferor's taxable estate. The result is the estate tax attributable to the transferor's estate will be computed based on the *average* rate of tax paid by the transferor's estate. For example, if the value of the transferred property was $100,000 and if the decedent, who had a taxable estate of $500,000, paid a $100,000 estate tax, the limitation imposed by Section 2013(b) would be $100,000/$500,000 × $100,000 = $20,000.[28]

[iii] **Decedent's estate tax attributable to transferred property.** The second limitation is that the amount of credit cannot exceed the difference between the estate tax of the decedent otherwise payable and the net estate tax of the decedent that would be payable if the value of the transferred property were subtracted from the value of the decedent's estate.[29] In other words, the decedent's tentative estate tax is computed by calculating his estate tax and then recomputing his taxable estate by subtracting the value of the transferred property. The difference becomes the second limitation. Again, it is important to note that the transferred property need not actually be taxable in the decedent's gross estate in order to take advantage of the credit. The second limitation only refers to the "value" of the transferred property and requires that it be eliminated from the decedent's gross estate. It does not require that the property itself actually be included in the estate. Accordingly, the second limitation is computed by determining the *highest* marginal estate tax attributable to the inclusion of the value of the property in the estate of the decedent as compared to the first limitation, wherein the amount of tax attributable to the transferor's estate is computed based on the average rate of tax. After the two limitations are computed, the smaller of the two will determine the amount of the credit.

[4] Credit for State Death Taxes

Section 2011 of the Code provides a credit for inheritance, estate, legacy, or succession taxes paid to any state or territory of the United States or to the District of Columbia with respect to property included

---

[28] In truth, the computation of this limitation is somewhat more complex because various credits that are allowable under the Code must be included in the computations. See generally examples set forth in Treas. Reg. § 20.2013-6.

[29] I.R.C. § 2013(c)(1).

in the decedent's gross estate. The amount of credit is based on a graduated table set forth in Section 2011(b) and ranges from eight-tenths of one percent to 16 percent of the decedent's adjusted taxable estate. The adjusted taxable estate for purposes of Section 2011 is the taxable estate of the decedent reduced by $60,000. The credit is allowable only for such state taxes as were actually paid and the credit claimed, therefore, within four years after the filing of the estate tax return.[30] If, however, a timely petition for redetermination of a deficiency is filed with the Tax Court, then the statute of limitations for claiming the credit is the later of the previously mentioned four-year period or before the expiration of sixty days after the decision of the Tax Court becomes final.[31] The amount of credit is limited by Section 2011(f) to the amount of tax imposed by Section 2001, reduced by the amount of the unified credit provided by Section 2010. This Section will prevent any claim for refund based on zero federal estate taxes paid in those situations where the unified credit, which was greatly expanded by the 1981 Act, produces no net tax.

The regulations [32] require evidence of payment of the state inheritance tax in order to substantiate the claim for a credit. In practice, this requires obtaining a certificate from the state taxing authority that indicates the amount and time of payment. In those cases where there is a dispute as to the domicile of a decedent, two or more states may impose death taxes based on a claimed domicile. In those instances, the Service has ruled that, subject to the limitations of Section 2011, full credit will be allowed against both such taxes as actually paid.[33]

The practical effect of the credit in many instances is to cause the payment of those taxes represented by Section 2011 credit to be paid to the various states rather than to the federal government. Inasmuch as a state can enact an inheritance tax equivalent to the amount of the federal credit without increasing the total tax burden on its residents, virtually all states have done so. In fact, many states have added provisions to their inheritance taxes stating, in effect, that if the total amount of taxes imposed does not equal the federal credit, they will impose an additional tax up to that amount.

---

[30] I.R.C. § 2011(c).

[31] I.R.C. § 2011(c)(1). Section 2011(c)(3) provides that there is a similar sixty-day period for filing such a claim after a decision of any court of competent jurisdiction in a refund suit.

[32] Treas. Reg. § 20.2011-1(c)(2).

[33] Rev. Rul. 60-88, 1960-1 C.B. 365; Rev. Rul. 70-272, 1970-2 C.B. 187.

Consequently, the credit probably has an overall neutral effect on the tax burden imposed on an estate. It prevents double taxation up to the credited amount, but it also encourages states to enact an inheritance tax up to that same amount. If, however, a decedent was domiciled in a state that imposes an inheritance tax in excess of the federal credit, his estate will face an additional burden of taxation. Accordingly, it is imperative that the estate planner be fully cognizant of the state inheritance tax rates applicable to a client so as to be aware of its effect upon the client and its interplay with Section 2011.

The liberalization of the unified credit by the 1981 Act will mean that estates below the deduction equivalent provided by the credit need only be concerned about the effects of state inheritance taxes. This will be particularly true for those states that have not adopted a piggyback system, which automatically adjusts to changes in the federal estate tax code. In those states a significant inheritance tax burden is still being encountered, which, because of the lack of taxability on the federal level, will not produce an offsetting credit under Section 2011.

¶ 10.03 Deductions From the Gross Estate

After a calculation has been made to determine the decedent's gross estate, there are certain deductions that are specifically permitted by the Code. Foremost among these deductions are the marital deduction permitted by Section 2056 and the charitable deduction allowable by Section 2055. These deductions permit a considerable amount of tax planning and are discussed extensively elsewhere in this treatise.[34] Other deductions less susceptible to planning are the deductions permitted for funeral and administration expenses, indebtedness and taxes by Section 2053, and the deduction for losses during administration allowed by Section 2054. Although there is not a large amount of advance estate planning that can be undertaken in regard to these expenses, the estate planner must bear them in mind for two important reasons. First, he should be aware of the nature and types of deductions permitted so as to make a reasonable estimate of taxes likely to be due when undertaking advance planning for a decedent's estate. Secondly, the estate planning must be structured so as not to preclude the deductibility of these items that are often necessary and unavoidable expenses.

---

[34] See generally Chapter 15.

[1] Estate Administration Expenses

[a] General Limitations. Section 2053 permits an estate to deduct funeral expenses and expenses of administration that fall into two categories permitted by the regulations. The first category [35] includes amounts payable out of property, subject to claims allowable by the law of the jurisdiction where the estate is being administered, for funeral expenses, administration expenses, claims against the estate, unpaid mortgages, or any indebtedness in respect to the property, the value of the decedent's interest in which is included in the value of the gross estate undiminished by the mortgage or indebtedness. This category primarily consists of expenses in the above categories that are payable out of the probate estate.

The second category [36] includes those expenses incurred in administering property included in the gross estate but not subject to claims, and that would be allowable as deductions in the first category if the property being administered were subject to claims and the expenses were paid before the expiration of the date prescribed for the filing of a claim for refund with respect to the estate tax return. This second category essentially refers to properties that are not part of the probate estate, such as life insurance or jointly held property, and allows a deduction for expenditures incurred with respect to these items.

Both of these categories of deductible expenditures are subject to certain overall limitations. First, and perhaps most importantly, the expenditures must be permissible under the law of the local jurisdiction where the estate is being administered. Thus, for example, payments made for funeral expenses or executor's fees in excess of that permissible under state law will not be allowed as a deduction for federal estate tax purposes. Typically, the decision of a local probate court as to the amount of allowable expenditures will be accepted for federal tax purposes if that court passes upon the facts underlying the claim for deductibility.[37] If the local court does not pass upon these facts in its decree, the deduction may not be allowed. The Service will not accept a decree of a local court if it is in variance with the laws of the state.[38] The

---

[35] Treas. Reg. § 20.2053-1(a)(1).

[36] Treas. Reg. § 20.2053-1(a)(2).

[37] Treas. Reg. § 20.2053-1(b)(2).

[38] See, e.g. Rev. Rul. 77-443, 1977-2 C.B. 327, where the Service disallowed a claim for travel expenses allowed by a county court on the grounds that this determination was at variance with local law.

regulations do permit a deduction for estimated amount of payments in those situations where the exact amount is not known, provided that the estimate is ascertainable with reasonable certainty and will be paid.[39] Typically, these estimates are made with regard to such items as attorney's fees or executor's commissions which, although reasonably susceptible to close approximation, are not specifically determined as of the time of the filing of the estate tax return.

[b] Allowable Deductions. There are several clearly defined categories of expenses for which a deduction is allowable. These deductible expenses are subject to the overall limitations previously discussed. The discussion that follows briefly reviews each of the basic types of expenditures so as to provide a general outline of the allowable items. It is beyond the scope of this work to discuss exhaustively the specifics of each deduction, inasmuch as there is little inter vivos tax planning that can be done in regard to them. However, the estate planner must be generally aware of each of these items for the reasons outlined throughout this chapter.

[i] Funeral expenses. Deductible funeral expenses include the actual expenses of the funeral itself, such as the casket, undertaker's fees, flowers, embalming, and the transferring of the body. A deduction is also allowed for expenses relating to the burial site, such as the costs of purchasing a plot and tombstone or grave marker. The deductibility of expenses for perpetual care of the gravesite depends upon its allowability under local law. If such expenses are permitted under state probate law, a deduction will generally be permitted for federal estate tax purposes.[40]

In order to receive the deduction, the expense must actually be paid by the decedent's estate. Accordingly, if a distributee or a potential heir actually pays the expenses in order to avoid selling a specific item or items, it should be treated as a loan to the estate in order to preserve the deduction. In addition to the requirement that the expenditures must be allowable payments by the probate estate under local law, the regulations also impose a requirement that these expenses must be reasonable in amount.[41] Presumably, these two requirements will be

---

[39] Treas. Reg. § 20.2053-1(b)(3).
[40] See Treas. Reg. § 20.2053-2.
[41] Id.

parallel, although in theory they could be somewhat different. An executor may expect to get questioned upon audit if expenditures reach exceedingly high levels.[42]

[ii] Probate and administration expenses. Deductible administration expenses generally include the executor's fees, attorney's fees, and miscellaneous probate expenses, such as court fees, appraisal fees, expenses of bonds, and various filing fees. Again, these deductions are subject to the overall limitation that they must be permissible under state law and the Service tends to impose a reasonableness limitation. For example, in looking at the reasonableness of an attorney's fee, courts are likely to consider the results obtained or the experience and ability of the attorney.[43] The fees must also be shown to benefit the estate. Those fees incurred by beneficiaries as a result of litigating to improve their respective position with respect to the estate are considered to be personal expenses of those beneficiaries and not administration expenses.[44] In order for litigation expenses to be deductible, they must be incurred by the estate in the resolution of litigation that is essential to the proper settlement of the estate.

[iii] Executor's commissions. Similar considerations also underline the deductions of fees paid to executors. In addition to the question of deductibility, the payment of executor's commissions and the deduction thereof is often influenced by other planning factors. If the executor is also a primary beneficiary of the estate, it is necessary to weigh the question of whether it would be most beneficial from a tax standpoint to pay executor's commissions or to simply waive such commissions and receive equivalent amounts through the vehicle of a distribution from the estate. Inasmuch as the commissions receivable by an executor will represent taxable income to him, it is often necessary to compare his tax bracket from an individual income tax standpoint against the estate tax bracket. If, for example, the executor is in a 50 percent tax bracket and the estate is taxed at a rate of 37 percent, it may make no sense from a tax standpoint to pay an executor's commis-

---

[42] The Service takes the position that funeral expenses recovered under a wrongful death statute must reduce the deduction claimed on the decedent's estate tax return. Rev. Rul. 77-274, 1977-2 C.B. 326.

[43] See, e.g., First Nat'l Bank of Topeka v. U.S., 233 F. Supp. 19 (D. Kan. 1964); Schnorbach v. Kavanagh, 102 F. Supp. 828 (W. D. Mich. 1951).

[44] Treas. Reg. § 20.2053-3(c)(3).

sion to this individual since the tax benefit of the deduction will be far outweighed by the income tax disadvantage that results. If the same dollars would accrue to the benefit of the executor if the commission was not paid, prudent tax planning would require a waiver of the executor's commission in this case.

[iv] **Other deductible expenses.** Other types of expenses that are frequently deductible include the cost of storing or maintaining estate property, where immediate distribution is not feasible, and selling expenses for the sale of estate assets. The Service takes the position that where a sale of estate property is necessary in order to pay the decedent's debts, administration expenses or taxes, to preserve the estate or to distribute estate assets, the expenses of the sale are deductible.[45] Finally, it should be noted that amounts allowable as a deduction under Sections 2053 or 2054 shall not be allowed as a deduction or as an offset to the sales price of property in determining gain or loss in computing the taxable income of the estate or any other person.[46] This section of the Code disallows a double deduction; it prevents an estate from deducting the administration expenses just described for estate tax purposes and then deducting the same items on the estate's income tax return.

[c] **Planning for Section 2053 Deductions.** Although there is not an excessive amount of planning that can be done in regard to expected postmortem expenditures for funeral and administration expenses, there are certain basic planning strategies mandated by the statute. First, the estate planner must generally be aware of these deductions and have some estimates available as to their amount so as to be able to intelligently plan a decedent's estate. By estimating such expenses during the planning stages, the estate planner is able both to make a more intelligent estimate of the estate taxes potentially involved and to

---

[45] Treas. Reg. § 20.2053-3(d)(2). There is some conflict as to whether the regulations would be upheld in requiring one of these three purposes for sale in order to create a deduction. Both Estate of Swayne v. Comm'r, 43 T.C. 190 (1964) acq. 1965-2 C.B. 6 and Estate of Smith v. Comm'r, 510 F.2d 479 (2d Cir. 1975), cert. denied, 423 U.S. 827 (1976) have upheld the validity of these regulations while the Sixth Circuit in Estate of Park v. Comm'r, 475 F.2d 673 (6th Cir. 1973) has found that these regulations overstep the bounds of Section 2053 and looks more towards deductibility under local law.

[46] I.R.C. § 642(g).

assess the estate's liquidity position. An often overlooked fact of estate planning is the fact that these types of administrative expenses will impose a cash demand upon the estate in the period shortly after the decedent's death. Thus, the necessity for paying these expenses within the year after death must be included in any liquidity analysis.

In addition to using the expenditures for estate tax and liquidity estimates, it is important to make sure these expenditures are actually paid by the estate. If, for example, a decedent were to prepay funeral and burial expenses during his lifetime, no deduction would be available. Although the prepayment of such expenses during one's lifetime often provides some degree of comfort to an individual, it is counterproductive from an estate tax standpoint. An individual is well advised not to pay such expenses during his lifetime so as to not defeat the estate tax deduction. If a person is so inclined, he can make detailed plans for funeral arrangements without actually making payments for them.

The other major planning implication relating to Section 2053 arises from the fact that the deduction for nonprobate expenses (i.e., the so-called category two expenses) is only allowable if paid before the expiration of the statutory period of limitations on assessments as provided in Section 6501. In general, this means that they must be paid within the three-year period following the filing of the return for the estate tax. Consequently, if a prolonged estate administration period is contemplated, the potential executors of an estate should be well advised of this limitation and of the necessity to make such deductible expenditures within the time frame described. A failure to pay these expenses within the prescribed period may result in the loss of a deduction with respect to second category expenses.

[2] Claims Against the Estate

Section 2053(a)(3) permits a deduction for claims against the estate in the computation of the decedent's taxable estate. This deduction is limited to personal obligations of the decedent existing at the time of his death, whether or not matured, and interest thereon that had accrued at the time of his death. Only interest accrued at the date of the decedent's death is deductible, even though the executor elected the alternative valuation method provided under Section 2032.[47] Generally speaking, the allowance of a deduction for a claim founded upon a promise or an agreement is limited to the extent that the liability was contracted for,

---

[47] Treas. Reg. § 20.2053-4.

bona fide, and was for an adequate and full consideration in money or in monies worth. Liability imposed by law or arising out of torts is deductible.[48] Consequently, the basic concept behind this Section is one of netting the value of a decedent's estate. On the one hand, all property owned by the decedent is aggregated into the computation of his adjusted gross estate. On the other hand, obligations of the decedent are subtracted so as to provide, in effect, an accurate or true value of the estate's net worth.

[a] **General Conditions for Deduction.** The critical factor in determining the deductibility of a claim against the estate is that the claim was a valid and enforceable obligation against the decedent. As such, there is a good deal of dependence upon the law of the appropriate state in order to determine the enforceability of the claim. In the case of a joint and severable liability, the deduction is limited to the decedent's proportionate share of that liability. For example, where the decedent purchased a house as a joint tenant with rights of survivorship and was jointly liable on the mortgage with a spouse, the permissible deduction under Section 2053(a)(3) is one-half of the balance due on the mortgage.[49] The theory behind this limitation is that the decedent or his estate has a right of subrogation against the other joint tenant if he were to pay the entire debt. The regulations take the position that only enforceable claims against the decedent's estate may be deducted.[50] For example, no deduction was allowed for a payment of a debt by a decedent's executor to his wife's estate made after the statute of limitations had expired.[51]

If a claim is informally presented against the estate and paid, a deduction will be allowed provided it is an enforceable claim against the estate.[52] Similar factors of enforceability are considered in a case of alleged debts to relatives. Such intrafamilial transactions are closely

---

[48] Id.

[49] Rev. Rul. 79-302, 1979-2 C.B. 328; see also Estate of Atkins v. Comm'r, 2 T.C. 332 (1943).

[50] Treas. Reg. § 20.2053-4.

[51] Jones v. U.S., 424 F. Supp. 236 (E.D. Ill. 1976). See also, Estate of Lewis v. Comm'r, 49 T.C. 684 (1968); Estate of Wolfe v. Comm'r, 29 T.C. 441 (1957), aff'd on this issue, 264 F.2d 82 (3d Cir. 1959).

[52] Rev. Rul. 75-24, 1975-1 C.B. 306. See also Rev. Rul. 75-177, 1975-1 C.B. 307, where an informal claim in Florida for pre-October 1, 1973 estates was not allowed as a deduction because under local law at that time the claim was not enforceable.

scrutinized upon audit by the Service, but if the debt is genuinely incurred in a transaction, the deduction will be allowed.[53] In many instances, such alleged debts to relatives have been disallowed on the ground of lack of consideration (i.e., in reality a gift is being made).[54]

There have been many disputes over the deductibility of both contingent claims and guarantees of another's debts by a decedent. Generally speaking, if the estate is contingently liable for a debt and if it is indicated that there is a very real possibility that the liability will have to be paid, it has been held that the estate may take that contingency into account in valuing an asset.[55] Conversely, where the decedent was merely an endorsor or guarantor of another's debts, a deduction will be disallowed if it appears that the debtor has sufficient assets to pay the claim.[56] If an estate is secondarily liable and if there appears to be no real right of recovery against the primary obligor, a deduction will be allowed.[57]

[b] Specific Types of Deductible Claims

[i] Taxes. Taxes that have accrued as of the time of the decedent's death are generally deductible items.[58] For an accrued income tax to become deductible, the tax must be due and payable as a result of income earned by the decedent during his lifetime.[59] However, no deduction will be allowed for federal income taxes, absent proof that the tax was attributable to pre-death income.[60] If a joint return is filed,

---

[53] See Estate of Barlow v. Comm'r, 55 T.C. 666 (1971), acq. 1972-2 C.B. 1.

[54] Embry v. Gray, 52 A.F.T.R 1921 (D. Ky. 1956); Garrett v. United States, ¶ 53,329 P-H Memo. T.C., Lee M. Friedman, Exec. v. U.S., ¶ 44,072 P-H Memo. T.C.

[55] Guggenheim v. Helvering, 117 F.2d 469 (2d Cir. 1941), cert. denied, 314 U.S. 521.

[56] Estate of Lay v. Comm'r, 40 BTA 522 (1939). A similar result will obtain even when the estate pays a debt if it has a right of recovery against a solvent individual. See First Nat'l Bank of Pa. v. U.S., 398 F. Supp. 100 (W.D. Pa. 1975).

[57] Comm'r v. Wragg, Administrator (Lowe), 141 F.2d 638 (1st Cir. 1944).

[58] Treas. Reg. § 20.2053-6(a). State and foreign death taxes are generally not deductible, inasmuch as a credit may be had for these taxes under Section 2011 and Section 2014. I.R.C. § 2053(e). But see I.R.C. § 2053(d) with respect to an election to deduct certain foreign death taxes. See generally ¶ 10.02[4].

[59] Rev. Rul. 71-56, 1971-1 C.B. 404. See also Estate of Miles H. England v. Comm'r, ¶ 41,181 P-H Memo. T.C.

[60] Estate of Fred G. Adams v. Comm'r, ¶ 73,113 P-H Memo. T.C.

the portion of the joint liability for which the deduction is allowed is the amount for which the decedent's estate would be liable under local law as between the decedent and his spouse. Absent proof to the contrary, the deductible amount in the case of a joint return is computed by determining the ratio of the decedent's separate tax liability to the separate tax liability of his spouse.[61]

Deductibility of property taxes depends on whether or not the property tax liability was accrued at the time of the decedent's death. For example, when real property tax is accrued on a so-called tax day prior to the decedent's death, such amount was held to be deductible.[62] There are numerous rulings and cases as to the specific time of accrual of property taxes in various jurisdictions.[63] Consequently, it will be necessary to review the property tax mechanics in a state in order to determine if property taxes applicable to such property represent an accrued liability.

Gift taxes on gifts made by a decedent before his death are deductible.[64] If a gift is considered to be made one-half by a decedent and one-half by his spouse under Section 2513, the entire amount of the gift tax, unpaid at the decedent's death, attributable to a gift in fact made by the decedent is deductible. No portion of the gift tax attributable to a gift in fact made by a decedent's spouse is deductible unless such an obligation is enforced against the decedent's estate and unless the estate has no right of contribution against his spouse.

[ii] Interest. Interest on a mortgage or other indebtedness that had accrued prior to the date of death will be a deductible claim. The Service, however, will not allow an estate tax deduction for interest that accrues subsequent to the date of death. Even in those situations where installment payments are scheduled to fall due after death, the post death interest deductions will not be allowed.[65] It has been held, however, that the interest payable by an executor electing to pay the

---

[61] Treas. Reg. § 20.2053-6(f).

[62] Estate of Pardee v. Comm'r, 49 T.C. 140 (1967); Mack v. U.S., 160 F. Supp. 421 (E.D. Wis. 1958).

[63] Rev. Rul. 65-274, 1965-2 C.B. 377 (Cal.); Rev. Rul. 68-35, 1968-1 C.B. 190 (Wash.); Catalano v. U.S., 429 F.2d 1058 (5th Cir. 1969).

[64] Treas. Reg. § 20.2053-6(d). But see I.R.C. § 2035(c), which provides for the inclusion in the gross estate for gift taxes paid on any gift made within three years of the decedent's death.

[65] Rev. Rul. 77-461, 1977-2 C.B. 324.

estate tax in installments under Section 6166 is deductible by the estate as an administration expense.[66] The Service has also ruled that interest on an estate tax installment is a deductible administrative expense to the extent allowable under law.[67]

[iii] Charitable pledges. The regulations provide that a charitable pledge or subscription evidenced by a promissory note or otherwise, even though enforceable against the estate, will be deductible only to the extent that the liability therefore was contracted bona fide and for adequate and full consideration, in cash or its equivalent, or if it would have constituted an allowable deduction under Section 2055 if it had been made as a bequest.[68]

[iv] Unpaid mortgages. A deduction is allowed for unpaid mortgages or other indebtedness in respect of any property of the gross estate, provided the value of the property undiminished by the amount of mortgage or indebtedness is included in the value of the gross estate.[69] If the decedent's estate is liable for the amount of mortgage, the full value of property subject to the mortgage or indebtedness must be included in the gross estate, with a mortgage thereon being allowed as a deduction. If the estate is not liable, the value of the decedent's equity in the property need only be included in the adjusted gross estate. For example, in a situation where a decedent had conveyed one-half of the property of a ranch subject to a debt to his children prior to his death, only half of the indebtedness on the unpaid mortgage was held deductible.[70]

[c] Planning for Claims

[i] Ascertaining potential claims. The primary task of the estate planner in considering potential claims against the estate is to ensure that full cognizance is given to such claims in estate tax and

---

[66] Estate of Bahr v. Comm'r, 68 T.C. 74 (1977), acq. 1978-1 C.B. 1.

[67] Rev. Rul. 79-252, 1979-2 C.B. 333. Similarly, interest incurred on a deferred state death tax has been ruled deductible. Rev. Rul. 81-256, 1981-2 C.B. 183.

[68] Treas. Reg. § 20.2053-5.

[69] Treas. Reg. § 20.2053-7.

[70] Estate of Fawcett v. Comm'r, 64 T.C. 889 (1975).

liquidity calculations and to make sure that claims against the client that he acknowledges are fully documented. Consequently, in reviewing a decedent's estate in order to make estate tax predictions, all such claims or potential claims against the client should be reviewed in order to calculate accurately the estate tax that may be due. A review of potential claims is also significant in assessing an estate's potential liquidity situation. Many claims may fall due upon death, and, as such, will represent near-term cash demands upon the estate. Accordingly, in reviewing insurance coverage, or other liquid assets, the effect of such demands upon the estate must be calculated.

[ii] **Ensuring proper documentation.** The second task of the estate planner, who is trying to put the affairs of a client into order, would be to ensure that potential claims against him — particularly in intrafamilial claims — be properly documented. For example, in many cases it is common for a client to make a statement "I owe my brother ten thousand dollars, and it is my intention to have it paid upon death." If, however, there are no existing notes or other indications of this indebtedness, the estate tax deduction may be disallowed and the payment to the brother, even if honored, may be considered a bequest rather than a deductible payment. Consequently, it is important that those claims that the decedent acknowledges and wishes paid be properly documented. Intrafamilial debts and obligations are always closely scrutinized by estate tax auditors. Therefore, a lack of proper documentation is likely to lead to the denial of the deduction.

[3] Losses During Administration

Section 2054 provides a deduction for the value of losses incurred during the settlement of an estate arising when such losses are not compensated for by insurance or otherwise. In order for a loss to be deductible under this Section, the loss must be of the nature of a casualty type of loss and it must occur during a settlement of an estate.[71] For example, it has been held that a reduction in value of stocks because of a war is not a casualty loss within the meaning of the predecessor Section 2054.[72] On the other hand, the destruction of a house by a

---

[71] Treas. Reg. § 20.2054-1.

[72] Leewitz, Coex. v. U.S., 75 F. Supp. 312 (Ct. Cl. 1948); Lyman, Exrs. v. Comm'r, 83 F.2d 811 (1st. Cir. 1936).

tornado or an automobile by an accident are clearly casualty losses which, if not compensated by insurance, would be deductible. If loss occurs after property is distributed to beneficiaries, it may not be deducted. If the loss is partially compensated by insurance, the excess of the amount of loss over the insurance proceeds may be deducted.

¶ 10.04 Tax on Generation Skipping Transfers

The tax on generation-skipping transfers was added to the Code by the Tax Reform Act of 1976. The essential idea behind this tax was that transfers of property should be taxed on the average of at least once per generation. Accordingly, a tax was enacted [73] that would tax a deemed transfer of property placed in trust where the trust was established for the benefit of multiple generations. Prior to the enactment of Chapter 13 of Subtitle A of the Code, it was quite common for very wealthy families to establish a series of trusts that would provide only an income interest to children, with the remainder transferred to grandchildren. Inasmuch as a mere income interest would not be taxable in an individual's estate, this device would enable every other generation to escape the imposition of the estate tax while still retaining most of the benefits of the familial property. As a result, the generation skipping tax was enacted to attempt to eliminate this practice.

The essential idea behind the tax on generation skipping transfers is to impose a tax equivalent to the estate tax that would be imposed if the corpus had vested in the deemed transferor. Thus, the taxable base for the imposition of the tax is the value of the trust property for which an interest was terminated and the value of any property subject to a power, in such instances where the power had previously terminated. If the generation skipping transfer occurred at the time of the death of the deemed transferor, the trust would be entitled to the unused portion of the estate tax credit that the deemed transferor had not used.[74] This is especially important in light of the greatly increased amount of the unified credit brought forth by the 1981 Act. Similarly, the credits for taxes paid with respect to prior transfers and for state inheritance taxes are both available.[75]

The tax is typically paid directly out of the proceeds of the trust

---

[73] Chapter 13 of Subtitle A of the Code.

[74] I.R.C. § 2602(c)(3).

[75] I.R.C. §§ 2602(c)(4)-2602(c)(5)(B).

being distributed. The deemed transferor and his estate are not liable for the tax imposed. In the case of taxable distribution, however, the distributee of the property is personally liable for the tax to the extent of the fair market value of the property that he received.[76] The trustee is personally liable for the tax in a case of a taxable termination.[77]

[1] Imposition of the Generation Skipping Tax

The tax is imposed on the occurrence of a generation skipping transfer.[78] In order for the generation skipping transfer to be taxable, it must occur through either a generation skipping trust or a generation skipping trust equivalent.[79] A generation skipping trust is any trust having any younger generation beneficiaries who are assigned to more than one generation.[80] A younger generation beneficiary is a beneficiary who is assigned to a younger generation than a grantor's generation.[81] Generations are usually measured on the basis of lineal descendency so that, for example, a grantor, his wife, and his siblings would constitute one generation, his children a second generation, and his grandchildren a third generation. If these rules do not provide an answer to generation assignment, generations will be assigned on the basis of the relationship of an individual's age to the age of the grantor.[82] An individual born not more than 12½ years after the date of the grantor's birth will be assigned to his generation. An individual born between 12½ years and 37½ years after the grantor's birth will be assigned to the first younger generation.

The incidence of taxation will occur when a generation skipping transfer is considered to have been made by a deemed transferor. A

---

[76] I.R.C. § 2603(a)(1)(B).

[77] I.R.C. § 2603(a)(1)(A).

[78] The tax is effective for generation skipping transfers after April 30, 1976. Under the 1976 Act, the tax was not applicable in a case of transfers under irrevocable trusts in existence on April 30, 1976 or in the case of decedents dying before January 1, 1982 pursuant to a will or revocable trust that was in existence on April 30, 1976. The 1981 Act extended this so-called grandfather provision until January 1, 1983.

[79] I.R.C. § 2611(a).

[80] I.R.C. § 2611(b). The generation skipping trust equivalent might include an arrangement having a life estate with a remainder, an estate for years, or an annuity.

[81] I.R.C. § 2611(c)(1).

[82] I.R.C. § 2611(c)(5).

deemed transferor is the parent of the transferee of the property who is more closely related to the grantor of the trust than the other parent of such transferee. The taxable transfer will occur on either a taxable termination or a taxable distribution from a trust. Termination would typically occur by reason of the death of the first succeeding generation [83] or by lapse of time where the grantor had created an estate for years. A taxable distribution occurs when there is distribution from the trust, other than a distribution of income to a younger generation beneficiary of the trust, and that distribution skips an intermediate generation. For example, if the trustee had discretion to distribute the corpus to both a grantor's child and grandchild and exercise its discretion by distributing to the grandchild, this would constitute a taxable distribution.

The Code [84] provides an exclusion on transfers to grandchildren equal to $250,000 per deemed transferor. In the typical case (life estate to children with remainder to grandchildren), this would mean an exclusion of up to $250,000 per child. Thus, for example, if a grantor had four children and left each of them a life estate in trust with the remainder to their children, the total amount of exclusions available would equal $1 million.

[2] Planning With Respect to the Tax on Generation Skipping Transfers

The tax on generation skipping transfers is relatively easy to avoid, since when it applies is so precisely defined by the Code. The tax is only imposed on a transfer by trust or trust equivalent in those situations where the trust or trust equivalent involves beneficiaires assigned to more than one generation. Consequently, in order to avoid the tax, it is only necessary to design a transfer that does not fall within the above definition.

[a] Direct Bequests to Younger Generations. The first aspect of the generation skipping tax that is quite apparent is that the tax is only applicable to transfers in trust or trust equivalent. Consequently, a direct bequest that skips a generation will not be subject to the tax on generation skipping transfers. For example, if an individual has chil-

---

[83] Such as in the case of a life interest.
[84] I.R.C. §§ 2613(a)(4)(A), 2613(b)(6).

dren who are economically well-off, it would be possible to make direct bequests to his grandchildren. In such a case, the generation skipping tax would be avoided and the estate of his children would not be needlessly inflated with assets that they did not need. Such direct bequests could be made in any proportion that the individual saw fit.

If it were thought inadvisable to make a direct bequest to grandchildren because of their ages or lack of capacity to handle money, it would be possible to establish a trust for the benefit of the grandchildren that did not include their parents as beneficiaries. Since the tax is only applicable to a trust that benefits two or more succeeding generations, if a trust were established for the grandchildren only, the tax would not be applicable. In such a case, the trustee could be instructed to retain the property until the grandchildren reached a specified age and to distribute it directly to them. This trust would then have the effect of skipping a generation for estate tax purposes and yet retaining the management and control over the funds in the situation where the grandchildren themselves were too young to handle large sums of money.

In addition, the grantor could establish separate trusts for his children in which the grandchildren had no interest. So long as no member of the older generation had an interest or power in the trust for the benefit of the younger generation, a generation skipping tax would not be imposed. The concept of separate layers of trusts for different generations will allow a grantor to provide for multiple generations in trust without inflating the estate of the first younger generation any more than is economically necessary.

[b] The Income Exception. Another significant vehicle for utilizing a trust for the benefit of multiple generations without incurring the tax on generation skipping transfers is by prudent use of the income exception from the taxable distribution rules of Section 2613(a).[85] That Section provides, in essence, that distributions of current trust income will not be treated as a taxable distribution for purposes of the tax on generation skipping transfers regardless of the recipient of this income distribution. Consequently, a trust can be designed to permit the trustee to sprinkle trust income among various generations. If the trust was large enough, such a clause would enable significant transfers to

---

[85] A detailed discussion of this exclusion may be found in Egerton, "Current Planning Techniques for Generation Skipping," 39 N.Y.U. Institute § 53.02[3] (1981).

¶ 10.04[2][b] ESTATE PLANNING 10-28

younger generations without imposition of the generation skipping tax. The income distributions will, of course, be taxable to the younger generation beneficiaries. Since they are likely to be in a lower income tax bracket than the older generation, an income tax savings may result as well.

There are two caveats that should be noted in regard to the use of the income exclusion, since the Code has anticipated the most obvious means of abusing this exclusion. The first such means of expanding the use of this exclusion is to draft the trust instrument to give as broad as possible definition to the concept of trust income. In referring to the term "income," Section 2613(a) cross-references Section 643(b), which defines income as "determined under the terms of the governing instrument and applicable local law." Although this appears to give considerable leeway, the regulations do note that "Trust provisions that depart fundamentally from concepts of local law in the determination of what constitutes income are not recognized...."[86] Accordingly, the draftsman of the trust instrument seeking to use the income exception should give as broad a definition as possible under local law to the concept of income. Abusive definitions are not likely to be sustained.

A second possible abuse of the income exclusion would be to attempt to characterize all distributions to an older generation as distributions from corpus, while, at the same time, characterizing distributions to younger generations as being made from income. Section 2613(a)(2) attempts to restrict this possibility by providing that, for purposes of the taxable distribution rules only, if distributions from a trust are made in one year from both income and principal, distributions from income will be deemed to have been made in descending orders of beneficiaries beginning with those assigned to the oldest generation regardless of the income tax treatment of the distribution. The effect of this section would be to impose the tax on generation skipping transfers in those situations where a distribution of principal was deemed to have been made to a younger generation beneficiary. This problem could be avoided, however, by limiting trust distributions to income only or by not permitting distributions of income and principal in the same year. For example, distributions of income and principal could be made in alternate years with the alternating principal distributions in an amount necessary to cover economic need for two

---

[86] Treas. Reg. § 1.643(b)-1.

years being made to the older generation beneficiary. It is thus possible by careful draftsmanship to use the income exception to the taxable distribution rules to permit a trust to benefit multiple generations without the imposition of the generation skipping tax.

[c] The $250,000 Exclusion. Finally, it should be noted that a taxable generation skipping trust can be used to the extent of the $250,000 exclusion per deemed transferor. This will allow a fairly significant sum of money to be placed in a trust that can be made available, if necessary, to the first younger generation yet be excluded from their estate if it is not needed or consumed.

Generation skipping transfers are generally used only in those situations where either an individual has extremely large sums of money, so that it can be sprinkled among several generations, or in those cases where an individual's children have or will accumulate substantial amounts of wealth in their own right. In each of these situations, transfers to the second younger generation that will not be taxed in the estates of the first younger generation can significantly reduce the amount of familial wealth that will be subject to estate tax. In those instances where these conditions exist, multiple generation transfers are often advisable.

Although the tax on generation skipping transfers was enacted in order to provide the equivalent of an estate tax upon each generation, it is an imperfect vehicle for carrying out this goal. The tax on generation skipping transfers does not tax direct bequests to younger generations or transfers in trust that are solely to benefit the second succeeding generation. These factors, combined with the $250,000 exclusion per deemed transferor, can still make possible substantial transfers to a second younger generation in those situations where it is both advisable from a tax standpoint and financially possible from an economic standpoint to do so. Although the number of cases where such multiple generation transfers can be made is a relatively small proportion of all estates (even in the case of highly compensated individuals), those cases that permit such transfers will undoubtedly benefit by doing so. In such a situation, a familiarity with the mechanics of the tax on generation skipping transfers can enable generation skipping bequests to be made. The major difference from the situation that existed prior to the enactment of this tax is that the form of the transfer will be somewhat different than had traditionally been made.

¶ 10.05   Jointly Held Property

Estate taxation of jointly held property has always been one of the most confusing issues to the general populace. Many people have wrongfully assumed that property held in various forms of joint ownership would result in half the value of such property being included in the estate of a decedent. This assumption has proved to be wrong in most cases and has led to many unpleasant surprises.

[1]   General Rule of Taxation

Section 2040(a) of the Code provides that the value of the gross estate shall include the value of all property held by a decedent as joint tenants with right of survivorship, except to the extent that the survivor can prove that he or she furnished the consideration for the purchase of such property. In other words, the total value of all property jointly held with the rights of survivorship will be included in the estate of the first to die unless the survivor can demonstrate that he contributed to the purchase of such property. Because various forms of joint tenancy with rights of survivorship, particularly between spouses, have gained a good deal of popularity as a means of avoiding probate, many people have been affected by this section. For those who were unaware of the estate tax implications of joint ownership, a situation was frequently created whereby the executor would not have control over many of the assets since the property would pass directly to a survivor by virtue of the form of ownership. This, in turn, often left the executor short of cash to pay estate taxes or, on the other hand, resulted in the overfunding of the marital bequest.

Because of the phraseology of Section 2040(a), which includes jointly held property in a decedent's estate, unless proof is furnished to the contrary, there has been substantial litigation in regard to the question of whether a survivor had furnished consideration. The affirmative burden of proof upon the survivor to furnish such evidence has meant that there are numerous cases where it was found that the full value of jointly held property was includable in the estate.[87] Although there have been cases where the estate has been able to prove that a survivor had furnished consideration for the purchase of the jointly

---

[87] See Steen v. U.S., 195 F.2d 379 (9th Cir. 1952); English v. U.S., 270 F.2d 876 (7th Cir. 1959); Estate of Doyle v. Comm'r, 32 T.C. 1209 (1959); Estate of Dutcher v. Comm'r, 34 T.C. 918 (1960).

held property,[88] such cases tend to be in the minority. Generally speaking, where a decedent held property jointly, there is a difficult burden of proof for the estate to establish that a survivor furnished consideration for the property.

[2] Joint Interests with Spouse

Partially as the result of this situation, the 1976 Tax Reform Act created a term known as "qualified joint interests" in property that was applicable to property held as joint tenants by husbands and wives. If certain conditions were met,[89] only one-half of the value of the property included in the joint tenancy would be taxed in the decedent's gross estate regardless of who furnished the consideration therefor. Finally, the 1981 Act eliminated the qualified joint interest rules and provided that the estate of the first spouse to die will include only one-half of the value of the property held in joint tenancy with rights of survivorship regardless of the consideration furnished. Accordingly, there will be automatic exclusion of half of the value of jointly held property from the estate of the first spouse to die.[90] It is important to note, however, that this rule, which results in the inclusion of one half of the value of jointly held property in the decedent's estate, is only applicable in the case where the property is jointly held by spouses. Accordingly, in other situations, such as property jointly held by a father and son, the general rule of Section 2040(a) will be applicable and the full value will be included in the decedent's estate unless proof is furnished that the survivor furnished the consideration therefor.

Although the 1981 Act Amendments to Section 2040(b) have alleviated some of the harshness of the general rule regarding the taxation of the jointly held property, it remains inadvisable from a tax planning standpoint to overuse this form of ownership. There are two major tax disadvantages to the joint ownership of property with rights of survi-

---

[88] Harvey, Executor v. U.S., 185 F.2d 463 (7th Cir. 1950); First Nat'l Bank of Kansas City (Estate of Cline) v. U.S., 223 F. Supp. 963 (W.D. Mo. 1963).

[89] The conditions necessary were that (1) the interest must have been created by one or both of the joint tenants, (2) in the case of personal property, the creation of the joint interest must have been a completed gift for gift tax purposes, (3) in the case of real property, the donor must have elected to create the creation of the joint tenancy as a taxable gift, and (4) the joint tenants could only be the decedent and his spouse. See I.R.C. § 2040(b) as it existed prior to the 1981 Act.

[90] I.R.C. § 2040(b).

vorship. First, inasmuch as property that qualifies under Section 2040(b) will only be included in a decedent's estate to the extent of one-half of its value, only one-half of the property will receive the step-up in basis that occurs at death. Accordingly, if the surviving spouse desires to sell the property, this individual will recognize a gain on the one-half that was not included in the decedent's estate. Because the unlimited marital deduction results in all property being passed to a spouse on a tax-free basis, it is more advantageous to have the entire value included in a decedent's estate, pass it tax-free to a spouse, and receive a complete step-up in basis. In such a case, the surviving spouse can sell the property in the near future with little or no taxable gain.[91]

The other major disadvantage of the extensive use of joint ownership of property is that it may result in an overfunded marital bequest. As is discussed extensively throughout Chapter 15, in many instances it may be advisable not to take complete advantage of the marital deduction but rather to leave a portion of a decedent's estate to a person other than a surviving spouse. This course of action permits the decedent to take full advantage of his unified credit by making transfers to someone other than a spouse. If, however, a substantial portion of a decedent's assets are held jointly with a spouse, they will pass to the spouse regardless of the provisions of the decedent's will. Accordingly, an abundance of joint ownership will defeat the decedent's ability to make nonmarital transfers so as to take full advantage of his or her unified credit and any other estate splitting possibilities that are desired.

Joint ownership with rights of survivorship does have its advantages. In those estates that are no longer taxable, joint ownership can avoid the cost and delays of probate by facilitating an immediate transfer to a surviving spouse. Once a familial estate has reached the taxable magnitude, however, the limitations on joint ownership and its tax implications must be noted so that it is not overused.[92]

---

[91] The converse is, of course, true for property held jointly by a decedent and a person other than a spouse. In such a case it is to his disadvantage to have the entire value of property included in his estate because such a factor increases the estate's tax liability.

[92] Treas. Reg. § 20.2040-1(a)(2) provides that the amount includable in a decedent's estate where the survivor funished a portion of the consideration is that portion of the entire value of the property that the consideration furnished by the survivor bears to the total cost of acquisition and capital additions.

CHAPTER 11

Lifetime Gifts

		Page
¶ 11.01	Introduction	11-2
¶ 11.02	Outline of the Gift Tax Provisions	11-2
	[1] Unified System of Estate and Gift Taxation	11-2
	[2] Donee's Basis in Property	11-4
	[3] Annual Gift Tax Exclusion	11-4
	[4] Gift Tax Marital Deduction	11-7
	[5] Gifts in Contemplation of Death	11-8
¶ 11.03	What Is a Taxable Gift?	11-9
¶ 11.04	Estate and Income Tax Advantages of Making a Gift	11-14
	[1] Use of the Annual $10,000 Exclusion to Reduce the Estate	11-15
	[2] Removal of Subsequent Appreciation From Donor's Estate	11-17
	[3] Shifting the Incidence of Income Taxation	11-18
	[4] Removal of Gift Tax Paid From Decedent's Estate	11-19
	[5] Avoidance of Tax on Generation Skipping Transfers	11-19
¶ 11.05	Strategies for Gift Tax Reduction in General	11-20
¶ 11.06	Fractionalized Gifts	11-20
¶ 11.07	Net Gifts	11-23
¶ 11.08	Use of the Lifetime Credit	11-24
¶ 11.09	Interest-Free Loans	11-26
	[1] Gift Tax Consequences to the Lender	11-26
	[2] Income Tax Consequences to the Borrower	11-28
	[3] Tax Planning for Interest-Free Loans	11-30
¶ 11.10	Gifts to Minors	11-32
	[1] Section 2503(c) Trusts	11-33
	[a] Trustee's Discretion	11-33
	[b] Age of Distribution	11-35
	[c] Disposition on Death of Donee	11-38
	[2] Uniform Gifts to Minors Act — Custodial Transfer	11-40
	[3] Transfer to a Guardian	11-42
¶ 11.11	Gifts to Spouses	11-43

¶ 11.01 Introduction

The taxation of inter vivos gifts [1] was drastically changed by the Tax Reform Act of 1976. In that year, Congress adopted a so-called unified structure for estate and gift taxation and, in so doing, greatly reduced the advantages of making gratuitous inter vivos transfers of property. Despite these changes, there still are significant estate and income tax advantages to be derived by a highly compensated individual from lifetime gifts. This chapter reviews the basic parameters of gift taxation and explores many of the continuing advantages of a lifetime gift program, before delving into specific means of devising a gift program that incurs a minimum gift tax.

¶ 11.02 Outline of the Gift Tax Provisions

[1] Unified System of Estate and Gift Taxation

Section 2501(a)(1) of the Code imposes a gift tax upon the transfer of property by gift by an individual resident or nonresident. Pursuant to the Tax Reform Act of 1976, estate and gift taxes are computed from a single unified rate structure on the basis of cumulative lifetime and post mortem transfers. In other words, transfers made during one's lifetime are cumulated with transfers made at death in order to compute the estate and/or gift taxes due from a single rate table.[2] Prior to 1977, lifetime gifts were taxed from a separate rate table at rates that equaled 75 percent of the then-existing estate tax rates. At that time, not only were gift tax rates lower than estate tax rates, but it was also possible to progress up a separate cumulative rate structure with lifetime transfers. Post mortem transfers would then be taxed under a different rate table that ignored the effect of lifetime transfers other than gifts in contem-

---

[1] This chapter deals with general principles of gift taxation and specific problems relating to direct transfers of property by gift. Problems relating to transfers in trust are discussed in Chapter 12 relating to inter vivos trusts, and in ¶ 13.05 in regard to insurance trusts. Section 2503(c) trusts for minors are reviewed in ¶ 11.10[1] infra.

[2] The precise vehicle for cumulating lifetime taxable gifts with property held at death is by the addition of an item called "adjusted taxable gifts" to a decedent's estate by virtue of Section 2001(b)(1)(B). That section defines adjustable taxable gifts to be the "total amount of the taxable gifts (within the meaning of Section 2503) made by the decedent after December 31, 1976, other than gifts which are includable in the gross estate of the decedent."

plation of death. The net result of this prior tax structure was not only to imbue lifetime gifts with a significant tax advantage, but also to create a lower gross estate as a starting point for taxation after death.[3] Consequently, the Tax Reform Act of 1976 significantly reduced the advantage of making a lifetime gift, not only by taxing such transfers at the same rate as if they were held in a decedent's estate, but also by cumulating such transfers with those occurring at death.

The gift tax payable for any period of time is computed by applying the unified rate schedule[4] to cumulative lifetime transfers, and then by subtracting the taxes paid on lifetime transfers during previous periods. In making the computation of cumulative taxable gifts, the donor's pre-1977 taxable gifts are taken into account. However, in computing the taxes payable, the reduction for taxes previously paid is based on the current rate schedule, even though the gift tax imposed prior to January 1, 1977 may have been less than this amount.[5]

Another feature of the 1976 Act was the enactment of the unified credit against estate and gift taxes.[6] Section 2010 provides a tax credit[7] to be applied against gift taxes and/or estate taxes payable under the unified rate structure. To the extent the unified credit is utilized by an individual during his lifetime, it will be unavailable for application

---

[3] For example, if an individual owned $2 million worth of assets and made $1 million of taxable gifts, his gross estate (assuming no gifts in contemplation of death) would equal $1 million. The effect, of course, is to subject the estate to taxation at lower rate brackets.

[4] The uniform rate schedule is found in I.R.C. § 2001(c).

[5] For example, taxable gifts of $1 million under the unified rate schedule incur a tax (exclusive of credits) of $345,800. Under the prior gift tax schedule, the tax would be $244,275.

[6] See I.R.C. §§ 2505 and 2010.

[7] The original credit was phased in over a five-year period so that the full credit was not available for decedents who died prior to 1981. The 1981 Act (ERTA) increased the amount of credit according to the following schedule:

Year	Amount of Credit	Amount Exempt From Estate and Gift Taxes
1982	$ 62,800	$225,000
1983	79,300	275,000
1984	96,300	325,000
1985	121,800	400,000
1986	155,800	500,000
1987 (and thereafter)	192,800	600,000

against estate taxes upon his death.[8] This credit, which will be the equivalent to a deduction of $600,000 when fully phased in,[9] can thus be utilized against lifetime or post mortem transfers or any combination thereof.

[2] Donee's Basis in Property

The gift tax consequences to the donee remain the same as before the Tax Reform Act of 1976. The donee acquires the donor's basis in the property,[10] increased by any gift tax paid with respect to the gift.[11] If, however, the basis of the property exceeds its fair market value at the time of the gift, then, for purposes of determining loss, its basis will be its fair market value. Gifts thus do not receive the step-up in basis that occurs with assets held in a decedent's estate.[12] Consequently, if a sale of assets is contemplated by the donee, a gift of assets that are substantially appreciated may result in the donee facing a large capital gains tax upon sale.

[3] Annual Gift Tax Exclusion

One aspect of gift taxation that was not changed by the 1976 Tax Reform Act was the availability of the annual exclusion. Section 2503(b) of the Code provides that in computing taxable gifts for the calendar year the first $10,000 [13] of such gifts (other than gifts of future

---

[8] The Service has ruled that the credit must be applied against lifetime transfers when made. Rev. Rul. 79-398, 1979-2 C.B. 338. The taxpayer cannot elect to forgo use of the credit during his lifetime if the inter vivos transfers made are of a taxable magnitude.

[9] I.e., an estate of $600,000 would incur a tax of $192,800 under the unified rate structure.

[10] I.R.C. § 1015(a).

[11] I.R.C. § 1015(d).

[12] The 1981 Act adds a provision that requires a carryover basis rule for property received by a decedent by way of gift within one year of the decedent's death, where the property passes back to the original donor or the donor's spouse. I.R.C. § 1014(e). This section was added to curb an abuse whereby a donor could transfer low basis property to a donee with the expectation of reacquiring it with a stepped-up basis. The legislative sanctioning of the unlimited marital deduction made this section particularly crucial, since the transfer to a spouse would be tax-free.

[13] The amount of the exclusion was increased from $3,000 to $10,000 by the 1981 Act.

interests in property) to any person (less the aggregate amount of gifts to such person during the year) will not be included in the total amount of gifts made during such year. In other words, any donor may make a gift of a present interest in property to any individual or numbers of individuals of up to $10,000 per year without incurring any gift tax liability. If a donor's spouse joins in making a gift to that individual so that the gift will be considered as being one half of each,[14] up to $20,000 may be transferred to any donee annually without incurring gift tax liability and without utilizing the donor's unified estate and gift tax credit.

Three particular characteristics of the Section 2503(b) exclusion must be emphasized. The first is that the exclusion is applicable to each donee who happens to be the object of a particular donor's bounty. There are no limitations on the number of donees to which the $10,000 exclusion will apply. Second, the exclusion works, in effect, as a reduction in the value of taxable gifts made to each donee. Thus, for example, if an individual were to transfer $24,000 to a particular donee in a given calendar year, the utilization of $10,000 exclusion would have the effect of creating a $14,000 taxable gift to that donee.[15]

The Economic Recovery Tax Act of 1981 (the 1981 Act) added an unlimited exclusion for certain qualified transfers made after December 31, 1981.[16] "Qualified transfers" are defined to mean any amount paid on behalf of an individual as tuition to an educational organization described in Section 170(b)(1)(A)(ii) for the education or training of such individual or to any person who provides medical care [17] with respect to such individual as payment for such medical care. Thus, it is possible to transfer any amount for these specified purposes without any gift tax liability. These exclusions may be especially important in such situations as providing medical care for an aged relative or tuition for a college-age donee.

The other major aspect of the Section 2503(b) exclusion is that it is

---

[14] As provided in I.R.C. § 2513(a).

[15] If the taxpayer's spouse joined in making that gift, a $4,000 taxable gift would be made — one half by each spouse.

[16] I.R.C. § 2503(e). It should be noted that the medical expenses should be paid directly to the service provider in order to qualify under Section 2503(e). See Rev. Rul. 82-98, 1982-20 I.R.B. 10.

[17] As defined in Section 213(e).

¶ 11.02[3]

not applicable to gifts of future interests in property. The regulations define future interests as follows:

> (a) ...Future "interests" is a legal term, and includes reversions, remainders, and other interests or estates, whether vested or contingent, and whether or not supported by a particular interest or estate, which are limited to commence in use, possession or enjoyment at some future date or time. The term has no reference to such contractual rights as exist in a bond, note (though bearing no interest until maturity), or in a policy of life insurance, the obligations of which are to be discharged by payments in the future. But a future interest or interests in such contractual obligations may be created by the limitations contained in a trust or other instrument of transfer used in effecting a gift.
>
> (b) an unrestricted right to the immediate use, possession, or enjoyment of property or the income from property (such as a life estate or term certain) is a present interest in property....[18]

Generally, the concept of whether or not a gift constitutes a gift of a future interest in property is most critical when a transfer is made by trust. Many gifts in trust will not qualify as a present interest in property because the use or enjoyment of that property by the donee will not commence until some future date. It is clearly possible to design a trust that will qualify as a present interest in property.[19] It is also possible to design a trust so that the income interest given will qualify as a gift of present interest whereas the distribution of the principal will not.[20] The important point to note is that because of the present interest requirement of Section 2503(b), many transfers in trust will not qualify for the exclusion. If a transfer in trust is contemplated, the tax advisor either will have to use great care in designing the trust [21] so as to have it fit within the scope of the present interest rule or may have to recommend other gifts in order fully to use the Section 2503(b) exclusion.

---

[18] Treas. Reg. §§ 25.2503-3(a)-25.2503-3(b).

[19] See, e.g., discussion of the so-called Crummey Trust in Chapter 13. See also discussion of Section 2503(c) trusts at ¶ 11.10[1] infra.

[20] Herr v. Comm'r, 35 T.C. 732 (1961), aff'd, 303 F.2d 780 (3d Cir. 1962).

[21] Trusts, such as a Section 2503(c) trust or a Crummey Trust, may qualify for the annual exclusion.

[4] Gift Tax Marital Deduction

Another basic component of the gift tax is the deduction for lifetime gifts made to a spouse.[22] A donor making a gift to his or her spouse is allowed an unlimited deduction for such gifts.[23] The 1981 Act added the unlimited marital deduction provisions to the Code and included other technical changes in the gift tax marital deduction which conformed to similar changes in regard to the estate tax.

A provision was added so as to allow a qualified terminable interest to qualify for the marital deduction.[24] This section, meant to alleviate some of the harshness and complexities of the terminable interest rule, defines the term "qualified terminable interest in property" to mean any property transferred from a donor to his spouse which provides a qualifying income interest for life [25] and to which an election has been made.[26] The election to create qualified terminable interest property, which must be irrevocable, is made on the gift tax return for the calendar year for which the gift is made. If the election is made to create a qualifying income interest, the value of such interest will be included in the estate of the recipient.[27] In addition, a section was added to the Code [28] that makes it clear that any disposition of a qualifying income interest will be considered a transfer of such property — thereby creating a taxable gift. Thus, the spouse who is the recipient of such property will be subject to tax upon disposition of it, either at death or during life.

---

[22] I.R.C. § 2523.

[23] Prior to January 1, 1977, the gift tax marital deduction was a flat 50 percent of the amount of such gifts. From that date until December 31, 1981, a deduction was allowed for the first $100,000 of gifts made to such spouse after December 31, 1976, plus 50 percent of the amount by which such gifts exceed $200,000. Consequently, during this period the first $100,000 of gifts made to a spouse were tax-free, the second $100,000 of such gifts were subject to taxation, and for the remainder, a 50 percent deduction was allowed.

[24] I.R.C. § 2523(f).

[25] As defined in Section 2056(b)(7)(B)(ii). This requirement is discussed extensively in ¶ 15.03[3][d] relating to the estate tax marital deduction terminable interest rule.

[26] I.R.C. § 2523(f)(2).

[27] I.R.C. § 2044(a).

[28] I.R.C. § 2519.

[5] Gifts in Contemplation of Death

Another significant change in the principles of taxation of lifetime transfers was the 1981 change made to the gift in contemplation of death rule of Section 2035. Prior to 1982, that section provided that the value of a decedent's gross estate included the value of all property "to the extent of any interest therein of which the decedent has made a transfer, by trust or otherwise, during the three year period ending on the date of the decedent's death."[29] The only two exceptions to this rule were for any bona fide sales for adequate and full consideration in money or money's worth and for any gift to a donee during the calendar year if the decedent was not required by Section 2019 to file a gift tax return for the year in question.[30]

The 1981 Act eliminated the gift in contemplation of death rules for most transfers occurring after December 31, 1981.[31] Thus, except for those situations discussed below, a transfer made within three years of the date of death will not be included in the donor's taxable estate. The transfer will, of course, be considered an adjusted taxable gift which will be included in the calculation of the decedent's unified transfer taxes. Since the gift will not be included in the decedent's taxable estate, the donee will not receive a step-up in basis of the property.

This drastic change in the gift in contemplation of death rules is not applicable to certain specified transfers for which the decedent retained an interest. The types of transfers that still fall within the purview of this rule are transfers (either included in the decedent's gross estate or that would have been so included if the decedent had retained such an interest) with a retained life estate,[32] transfers taking effect at death,[33] revocable transfers,[34] powers of appointment,[35] or proceeds of life insurance, either receivable by the executor or for which the decedent had retained the incidents of ownership.[36] In addition, all gifts made within three years of the date of death are included in an estate for the

---

[29] I.R.C. § 2035(a).
[30] I.R.C. § 2035(b).
[31] I.R.C. § 2035(d).
[32] I.R.C. § 2036.
[33] I.R.C. § 2037.
[34] I.R.C. § 2038.
[35] I.R.C. § 2041.
[36] I.R.C. § 2042.

purposes of qualifying for current use valuation,[37] deferred payment of estate tax,[38] qualified redemptions to pay estate tax,[39] and estate tax liens.[40]

If a transfer falls within one of these specified categories, the gift in contemplation of death rules provide for the automatic inclusion of any gift made within three years of death, unless it falls within one of the exceptions set forth in Section 2035(b).[41] For those transfers, the only remaining aspect of gift planning that can be accomplished in a deathbed situation is to arrange for one or more transfers that fall within the exclusionary rule of Section 2503(b) and that do not require the filing of a gift tax return. By utilizing this exception in the deathbed situation, some modest estate tax savings can be achieved.

¶ 11.03 What Is a Taxable Gift?

The definition of a gift for gift tax purposes does not necessarily parallel the definition set forth under the laws of many states. The basic elements of a gift under the common-law definition used in virtually all jurisdictions are: (1) an intent to make the gift and (2) compliance with the formalities of transfer.

Perhaps the most comprehensive definition of a gift for tax purposes is found in the case of *Estate of Hite v. Commissioner*.[42]

> The essential elements of a bona fide gift *inter vivos* are (1) a donor competent to a gift; (2) a donee capable of taking the gift; (3) a clear and unmistakable intention on the part of the donor to absolutely and irrevocably divest himself of title, dominion, and control of the subject matter of the gift in *praesenti;* (4) the irrevocable transfer of the present legal title and of the dominion and control of the entire gift to the donee, so that the donor can exercise no further act of dominion or control over it; (5) a delivery to the donee of the subject of the gift or of the most effective means of commanding the dominion of it; and (6) acceptance of the gift by the donee....

---

[37] I.R.C. § 2032A.

[38] I.R.C. § 6166.

[39] I.R.C. § 303.

[40] Subchapter C of Chapter 64 of the Code.

[41] The exception in Section 2035(b)(1) for transfers made for adequate and full consideration is not a significant exception, since such a transfer would not constitute a gift in the first place.

[42] 49 T.C. 580, 594 (1968).

The regulations also note that "all transactions whereby property or property rights or interest are gratuitously passed or conferred upon another, regardless of the means or device employed, constitute gifts subject to tax."[43]

Although these definitions sound remarkably close to the common-law concepts of a gift, in practice there is substantial deviation from common-law definitions. Thus, for example, it is relatively clear that the requirement of intention to make a gift for tax purposes does not require an ascertainment of the donor's actual state of mind where such a factor is relevant under the common law.

The regulations take the position that "donative intent on the part of the transferor is not an essential element of the application of the gift tax to the transfer. The application of the tax is based on the objective facts of the transfer and the circumstances under which it is made, rather than on the subjective motives of the donor."[44] The classic case of *Commissioner v. Wemyss*[45] also took the position that donative intent is largely irrelevant for purposes of the gift tax. The *Wemyss* case indicated that where property is transferred for less than adequate and full consideration in money or money's worth, the excess of such money value will be deemed a gift for gift tax purposes. Consequently, the test under the Internal Revenue Code seems more a question of whether there has been adequate consideration for the transfer.[46]

An important exception to the gift tax is the ordinary business transaction concept. The regulations state that the "gift tax is not applicable to a transfer for a full and adequate consideration in money or money's worth, or to ordinary business transactions, described in Section 25.2512-8."[47] An "ordinary business transaction" is described in Regulations Section 25.2512-8 as "a sale, exchange or other transfer of property made in the ordinary course of business (a transaction which is bona fide, at arms length and free from any donative intent)

---

[43] Treas. Reg. § 25.2511-1(c).

[44] Treas. Reg. § 25.2511-1(g)(1).

[45] 324 U.S. 303 (1945).

[46] Transfers reached by the gift tax are not confined to those which, being without valuable consideration, accord with the common law concept of gifts, but embrace as well sales, exchanges, and other dispositions of property for a consideration to the extent that the value of the property transferred by the donor exceeds the value in money or money's worth of the consideration given therefor. Treas. Reg. § 25.2512-8.

[47] Treas. Reg. § 25.2511-1(g)(1).

will be considered as made for an adequate and full consideration in money or money's worth." Even though donative intent is not determinative of a gift for gift tax purposes, it is relevant to the question of whether an ordinary business transaction exists. If intent indicates that an ordinary business transaction is present, the gift tax will not be imposed solely because one of the parties made a less than favorable deal.

As might be expected, law books are replete with cases debating the question of whether or not particular transactions are gifts or ordinary business transactions. Generally speaking, if a transfer is between family members and involves less than adequate consideration, there is a substantial likelihood that a gift is involved. In addition, if a transfer is between an employer and employee, the Service tends to take the position that the transaction is compensatory rather than donative and will attempt to attribute gross income to the employee.[48] For example, the Service has ruled that a stock transfer by a corporation's majority shareholder to employees of that corporation constitutes gross income to the employees rather than a gift by the transferor stockholder.[49] In finding the transfer of an automobile to a business friend to be taxable income for the recipient, the Supreme Court, in the classic case of *Commissioner v. Duberstein*,[50] stated as follows:

> And conversely "[w]here the payment is in return for services rendered, it is irrelevant that the donor derives no economic benefit from it." Robertson v. United States, 343 U.S. 711, 714. A gift in the statutory sense, on the other hand, proceeds from a "detached and disinterested generosity," Commissioner v. LoBue, 351 U.S. 243, 246; "out of affection, respect, admiration, charity or like impulses." Robertson v. United States, supra, (343 U.S. at 714).

Just as the question of subjective intent has been given a relatively limited role, except in determining whether an ordinary business transaction is present, the formalities of transfer have largely been minimized in determining whether or not a gift has been made for federal tax purposes. To a great extent, these formalities of transfer have been more significant in determining the date of a gift for gift tax purposes than in

---

[48] If the transaction were a gift, it would not constitute income to the employee. I.R.C. § 102(a).

[49] Rev. Rul. 69-140, 1969-1 C.B. 46.

[50] 363 U.S. 278, 285 (1960).

¶ 11.03

ascertaining whether a gift has actually occurred. For example, the regulations state that where an endorsed stock certificate is delivered to the donee or his agent, a completed gift has been made.[51] When delivery is made to the donor's agent or to the issuing corporation or its transfer agent, the gift is not complete until the stock is transferred on the books of the corporation.

The Service has also issued rulings relating to the effective date of gifts of promissory notes and checks. In Rev. Rul. 67-396,[52] the donor delivered a check with the request that it not be deposited or cashed until a subsequent date. The ruling held that the gift of the check was completed when the check was actually cashed. In a second situation discussed in that ruling, the donor delivered a promissory note payable with interest after one year. The gift of the note was said to be completed when paid. If a promissory note or check held by a payee is endorsed and given to a donee, a gift will be completed at that time.[53] In essence, these cases and rulings and others of a similar nature look to the question of whether a taxpayer has parted with dominion and control over property so as to complete a gift. As such, they mainly affect the question of timing for gift tax purposes.

These questions of timing can be significant in planning for gift tax minimization. First, timing affects the availability of the $10,000 annual exclusion. If a donor had fully used the exclusion with respect to a given donee in a particular year, he may want to delay subsequent gifts to a future year. The converse is true if the exclusion has not been utilized. Timing is also significant with respect to the gift in contemplation of death rules that require a gift, in some circumstances, to have been made at least three years prior to death.

There is also an abundance of cases, rulings, and regulations relating to the question of whether a specific type of transaction constitutes a taxable gift.[54] If a person creates a joint bank account for himself and another in a form that allows the contributor to withdraw the entire fund without the consent of the other, there is a gift to the second person only when that person draws upon the account for his own benefit

---

[51] Treas. Reg. § 25.2511-2(h).

[52] 1967-2 C.B. 351.

[53] See Estate of Bartman v. Comm'r, 10 T.C. 1073 (1948).

[54] Certain specific transactions, such as interest-free loans, are discussed at ¶ 11.09 infra relating to strategies for the minimization of the gift tax.

without obligation to the original contributor.[55] The same rule also applies to joint brokerage accounts.[56] These types of joint accounts are somewhat "anti-planning" in nature in that they allow the donee, rather than the donor, to control the timing of a gift. When a tenancy in common is created, there is a gift valued by the difference between the value of the transferor's contribution and his proportionate interest in the property as a co-tenant. For example, if an individual purchased property entirely with his own funds and took title as a tenant in common with his son, a gift would have been made by him in an amount equal to one half of the value of the property.

The 1981 Act expanded the fractional interest rule in Section 2040 so as to provide if real or personal property is held jointly by a husband or wife with rights of survivorship, then for estate tax purposes it will be treated as belonging one half to each spouse.[57] Consequently, upon the death of the first spouse, only one half of the property will be included in the gross estate of the decedent, and only that one-half interest will receive a step-up in basis at death. In addition, the unlimited marital deduction makes it irrelevant whether or not a gift occurs at the time of creation of a joint tenancy with a spouse, since the property interest given to a spouse would pass free of tax in any event.

Other relatively common types of situations have been held to create taxable gifts. A gift may be created by the transfer of a partnership interest where the recipient partners furnish no consideration for their interests.[58] A gift may be made by the gratuitous forgiveness of a debt.[59] Similarly the payment of another's expenses, such as the payment of a mortgage for an adult son, will constitute a taxable gift.[60] Finally, it should be noted that where a husband and wife enter into a written agreement relative to their marital and property rights and are divorced within two years thereafter, any transfers made pursuant to that agree-

---

[55] See Treas. Reg. § 25.2511-1(h)(4).

[56] Rev. Rul. 69-148, 1969-1 C.B. 226.

[57] I.R.C. § 2040(b).

[58] Gross v. Comm'r, 7 T.C. 837 (1946), acq., 1946-1 C.B. 2.

[59] Treas. Reg. § 25.2511-1(a). In some situations the forgiveness of a debt may result in the realization of income to the debtor. See Crane v. Comm'r, 331 U.S. 1 (1947).

[60] Rev. Rul. 54-343, 1954-2 C.B. 318. There is an exception, of course, for qualified transfers as defined in Section 2503(e)(2), which relate to the payment of tuition or medical expenses for another. See ¶ 11.02[3] supra.

ment to a spouse in settlement of his or her marital or property rights, or to provide a reasonable allowance for the support of children of the marriage during minority, are statutorily deemed to be transfers made for a full and adequate consideration rather than a gift.[61] Thus, the typical property settlement made pursuant to divorce proceedings will be exempted from the gift tax.

In summary, unless there are specific statutory or regulatory exemptions, virtually any type of transfer made for less than a full and adequate consideration, except for the bad business deal, may become subject to a gift tax. Most particularly, in family situations, the absence of full consideration is likely to encourage the Service to take the position that a gift is involved regardless of the donor's intent. It is vitally important that the tax advisor understand these concepts and develop a "feel" for the situation where a taxable gift will result. As will be seen in the latter portions of this Chapter, a planned gift may be a very useful tax planning device. An unplanned gift can prove to be an unexpected nightmare.

¶ 11.04 Estate and Income Tax Advantages of Making a Gift

Although the Tax Reform Act of 1976 substantially reduced the tax advantages that can be derived from making gratuitous inter vivos transfers, there are significant estate and income tax advantages that remain. Because many of these advantages are of the type that will accrue only in the long run, a maximization of tax savings by the making of taxable gifts often requires a long-range coordinated program. Consequently, in undertaking tax planning for a highly compensated individual who has both a desire to mitigate the effects of his present high income tax bracket and to undertake an estate planning program that will minimize estate tax to the greatest extent possible, it is often advisable to consider a long-range gift giving program at an early age. Such a plan, if well thought out, can produce a very significant tax savings over a period of several years.

Before undertaking a long-range gift giving program, it is necessary to face the threshold question as to whether such a program is economically feasible for the taxpayer. Because, by definition, the making of a taxable gift results in the relinquishment of complete dominion and

---

[61] I.R.C. § 2516.

control of property, it first must be ascertained whether the taxpayer needs the property in question either now or at a later date. For example, a taxpayer, such as a professional athlete, may be in a high income tax bracket only for a limited number of years. In a case such as this, it is often necessary to build assets for later years when a substantial reduction in income is likely to occur. Consequently, it may not be appropriate for this person to completely relinquish ownership of substantial amounts of investment assets. Frequently, a solution such as a Clifford Trust [62] is more appropriate in a case where there is likely to be a significant downward fluctuation in earnings. On the other hand, an individual who is in a high income tax bracket with a very strong likelihood of remaining in this bracket until retirement, and who has already accumulated a substantial estate, may be a perfect candidate for a long-range gift giving program. If this person is also a participant in a generous qualified retirement plan and/or similarly has accrued substantial deferred compensation rights of one form or another, his retirement years may be of no real economic concern.

Many individuals are, quite naturally, reluctant to part with dominion and control over their assets. There is a tendency to fear the economic unknown of the future, which creates a disinclination to part with assets — no matter how substantial the estate. In such a case, it is usually necessary to review the following advantages of a long-range gift giving program and to demonstrate, in monetary terms, the magnitude of tax savings expected. Frequently, the shock of seeing the tax savings involved will create an incentive for the reluctant taxpayer to act.

[1] Use of the Annual $10,000 Exclusion to Reduce the Estate

The first major advantage of a long-range gift giving program is that a substantial amount of assets can be removed from a donor's estate completely tax free and without exhausting any of the unified credit simply by utilizing the $10,000 per donee annual exclusion provided in Section 2503(b). By fully utilizing this exclusion over a substantial number of years, a surprising amount of assets can be removed from the estate on a tax-free basis. Although a $10,000 gift does not sound like a staggering amount today, the continued use of this amount can produce very large numbers. For example, suppose a 30-

---

[62] This is discussed in Chapter 9.

year-old individual began giving $10,000 per year to each of his four children and continued this program until the age of 70. The result would be that $400,000 would given to each child, and a total of $1,600,000 would be removed from this individual's estate. If the taxpayer's spouse elected to join in the making of these gifts, the results could be doubled so that a total of $3,200,000 could be passed to the taxpayers' children by age 70 without incurring a single penny of gift tax and without using any of the taxpayers' unified lifetime credits. If the situation permitted, additional gifts could be made to grandchildren or the spouses of children so as to increase these amounts. If, in the example given, the taxpayers were in the 50 percent estate tax bracket, approximately *$1.6 million* of estate taxes could be saved on the death of the second spouse by an annual gift giving program within the exclusionary limits of Section 2503(b)! The estate tax reduction also positively impacts upon the estate's liquidity situation. By reducing taxes to this extent, the cash demands upon the estate are proportionately reduced. Of course, the amount that can be distributed under such a program will vary with the number of individuals who are the natural objects of the taxpayer's bounty, as well as the age at which such program commences. The basic point is, however, that the cumulative effect of commencing and continuing a $10,000 per donee gift giving program over a substantial period of time can be quite staggering. By itself, the use of the annual exclusion remains a very valuable estate planning device.

In weighing the factors to decide whether or not to commence such a program, the donor's economic situation is, of course, paramount. Before gifts of $10,000 per donee can be made, an individual has to be able to afford such gifts. Special emphasis should be given to retirement needs and the availability of other assets for emergencies. In addition, the effect of such a program upon the potential donee must also be weighed. Does the donee have the business experience or wisdom to manage the assets in question? Does the potential donee similarly have estate planning problems that will be exacerbated by receipt of these additional amounts? If the donee is the taxpayer's spouse, care must be taken to coordinate the amount distributed to the spouse under the taxpayer's will with these gifts. If the taxpayer's spouse does have substantial assets in his or her own name, the full utilization of the marital deduction [63] under the taxpayer's will may result in an imbal-

---

[63] See ¶ 15.02.

ance of the two estates and, thus, higher taxation than is necessary. Finally, if gifts are being given to a minor and the use of a trust is contemplated because of the minor's age, care must be taken to design the trust so that it will not be classified as a future interest that is ineligible for the Section 2503(b) exclusion. Such a situation may call for the use of a Section 2503(c) trust [64] or the institution of the so-called Crummey provisions [65] so as to ensure that a gift of a present interest is created.

[2] Removal of Subsequent Appreciation From Donor's Estate

A second significant — perhaps the most significant — advantage of a gift giving program is the removal from the donor's estate of all appreciation in the assets subsequent to the date of the gift. If an asset worth $100,000 is given away at age 30 and becomes worth $300,000 at age 50, the $200,000 of appreciation during that twenty-year period will never be included in the donor's estate. Even though the $100,000 [66] will be considered an adjustable taxable gift under Section 2001(b)(1)(B) to be included in the decedent's estate, the subsequent appreciation will never be taxed to him. Given the recent rates of inflation experienced in this country, the amount of estate and gift taxes that can be saved by allowing others to experience the inflationary gains can be highly significant.

The fact that subsequent appreciation in an asset will not be included in a donor's estate, either as an adjusted taxable gift or as part of the estate itself, suggests that the most appropriate objects of a long-range gift giving program are those assets that are likely to increase in value. Generally speaking, money or debt instruments are a poor choice for a gift giving program. Such property is not likely to increase in value and may itself be useful to the donor in order to provide liquidity to his estate. On the other hand, those types of property that have a high likelihood of appreciating in value will produce the greatest tax savings if made the subject of a gift. For example, if a taxpayer is starting a new business, a gift of a portion of the stock of that corporation or an interest

---

[64] Discussed at ¶ 11.10[1] infra.

[65] Crummey v. U.S., 397 F.2d 82 (9th Cir. 1968). This case is discussed in ¶ 13.05.

[66] Any deductions or exclusions would be subtracted from the amount of the taxable gift.

in a partnership may have little or no gift tax consequences. Because the business is new and has not yet started operations, the property transfered will have little or no value. If the business later becomes very successful, the stock or partnership interest that was transferred to the taxpayer's wife or children is likely to have appreciated substantially in value over that period of time. By making a transfer of this property at an early stage, the donor will have avoided significant amounts of gift and/or estate taxes. Of course, by making a transfer of property, the donor will not himself reap the benefits of the subsequent appreciation. Thus, as always, the decision must be made as to whether it is economically feasible to make this transfer. If the transfer is feasible, the tax savings can be large.

[3] Shifting the Incidence of Income Taxation

A further tax advantage of a gift giving program is that any taxable income produced by the assets that are given away will fall upon the donee rather than the donor. Consequently, if the donee is in a lower income tax bracket than the donor, an additional savings will result because of the reduced income taxation. The amount saved will be greater as the spread between the highest marginal tax brackets of the two taxpayers widens. In addition, since the income produced by the transferred asset will not accrue to the donor, his estate will not be inflated by the additional income produced.

It must be noted that it is not necessary to completely part with control over income-producing assets in order to shift the incidence of income taxation. Devices such as a Clifford Trust,[67] which, in essence, transfers assets to a trust for at least a ten-year period, or an interest-free loan [68] allow income to be shifted to a lower bracket taxpayer or taxpayers while permitting a reversion of the basic assets to the grantor. Such devices are most appropriate in those situations where the taxpayer is reluctant to relinquish complete control over certain income-producing assets and yet wishes to shift the incidence of current income taxation because of his high tax bracket. The reversionary type of transfer is often most appropriate for the taxpayer who is experiencing a limited number of high-income years with no assurance that this income level will continue. Thus, a professional athlete or an entertainer may wish to shift current income but retain long-range control

---

[67] This is discussed extensively in Chapter 9.

[68] This is discussed at ¶ 11.09 infra.

over the asset. On the other hand, a completed outright gift to a donee will accomplish the same income tax savings, but there will be no reversion of the asset.

[4] Removal of Gift Tax Paid From Decedent's Estate

A further advantage of an extensive gift giving program is that any gift taxes paid by the donor as a result of making such gifts will not be included in the decedent's estate at death. In contrast, if an individual dies owning the same assets and his estate pays an estate tax of the same amount, there is no deduction allowed to the estate for the estate taxes paid. The one major exception to this rule is that any gift taxes paid with regard to transfers made within three years of the decedent's death, that are subsequently included in the decedent's estate as a gift in contemplation of death, will also be included in the decedent's estate.[69] This gross-up rule, which was added by the Tax Reform Act of 1976, removes the substantial incentive that previously existed for making deathbed transfers. Previously, it was commonplace to make such transfers because, even if the transferred property was considered to be a gift in contemplation of death, the tax paid would not have been included in the decedent's estate and yet would have been credited against estate taxes. As noted above, the 1976 Tax Reform Act ended this practice. It did not, however, disturb the basic principle that a gift tax paid is not included in the decedent's estate. This is an additional incentive for making extremely large gifts if the donor has sufficient liquidity to pay the gift taxes involved.

[5] Avoidance of Tax on Generation Skipping Transfers

A direct inter vivos gift to grandchildren or other younger generations will avoid the tax on generation skipping transfers as set forth in Chapter 13 of the Code.[70] The Tax Reform Act of 1976 added this Chapter [71] to impose a tax on a deemed transferor when a generation skipping trust is established. The purpose of these provisions was to impose a tax, which is the equivalent of an estate tax, on those transfers that provided only an income interest to the next generation and did not vest the trust principal until the second or third succeeding generation. This tax, however, is only applicable to transfers in trust or trust

---

[69] I.R.C. § 2035(c).
[70] Discussed at ¶ 10.03.
[71] I.R.C. §§ 2601–2622.

equivalents.[72] Consequently, an outright gift to a second or third succeeding generation will avoid the imposition of this tax. A similar result flows from a direct bequest in a will to a younger generation. If the taxpayer's children have been well provided for or if they have independent sources of wealth, a direct gift to subsequent younger generations will produce this additional tax savings by avoiding the generation skipping tax. Moreover, the assets that were transferred will not be included in the estates of the generations that were skipped. Again, however, this type of tax planning is only appropriate where there is wealth of a sufficient magnitude to permit a complete skipping of generations.

¶ 11.05 Strategies for Gift Tax Reduction in General

As noted in the preceding section, it remains possible to achieve significant tax savings by the utilization of a well thought out long-range gift giving program. Despite these advantages, such transfers often incur a significant gift tax liability. If such a program appears feasible and if taxes are incurred, there are several possible courses of action that should be investigated in order to minimize the gift tax incidence upon the transfers of property. Consequently, the various strategies that are discussed in the remainder of this chapter are designed to reduce or eliminate the gift tax impact of a transfer upon the donor. These strategies typically involve the maximum utilization of the deductions, exclusions, and credits that are available to a taxpayer or the planning of a transfer so that it will not be characterized as a taxable gift. Another possible consideration is the making of a so-called net gift whereby the donee agrees to pay the donor's gift tax liability. By carefully utilizing and/or combining the techniques discussed below, a taxpayer can achieve the advantages of a gift giving program without actually paying significant gift tax dollars. This can be extremely important where the taxpayer's estate planning needs indicate considerable liquidity problems.

¶ 11.06 Fractionalized Gifts

It is not unusual for a taxpayer to agree to embark upon a gift giving program but only to the extent of fully utilizing his or her $10,000 per donee annual exclusion and not exhausting any of the unified lifetime

---

[72] I.R.C. § 2611(a).

credit. At the same time, however, the taxpayer's situation may indicate significant liquidity problems for his estate. Thus, the most appropriate assets to be given away are typically non-liquid assets that are likely to appreciate in value. It is not uncommon to find, however, that such assets are not readily divisible into $10,000 or $20,000 units. Assets such as real property or antiques often cannot be physically divided into such small units.

There are two possible solutions to this problem in order to make the transfers fall within the $10,000 annual exclusion. One approach would be to transfer an undivided fractionalized interest in such property on a yearly basis until title is completely transferred to the donee. Thus, if property was worth $80,000, an undivided one-quarter interest could be transferred to the donee annually for each of four years and still have the transfer fall within the confines of Section 2503(b).[73] This approach presents several practical problems and is only likely to work in a limited number of cases. First, there is the problem of the valuation of the undivided percentage interest. The fair market value of an undivided fractional interest in a building lot or antique dresser may be difficult to ascertain. Second, such a transaction may involve an inordinate amount of paper work because of the necessity of annual deeds or the like.

Finally, and most significantly, the property that is given away in increments is likely to be appreciating in value. If the property given away in Year 1 increased in value from $80,000 in that year to $96,000 in Year 2, the gift of a one-quarter interest in that property in Year 2 would be worth $24,000 rather than $20,000. Accordingly, the appreciation in value of the property may cause the donor to relinquish smaller and smaller increments of that property annually in order to stay within the $10,000 exclusion. If the property being transferred is valuable enough or increasing in value at a rapid pace, the donor simply may not be able to transfer the complete interest in this property and still remain within the confines of the Section 2503(b) exclusion.

An alternative approach to combat this problem, which is inherent in fractionalized gifts, would be for the potential donor to sell the property to the donee for its fair market value with the transferor taking back notes for all or a portion of the sales price. These notes could be secured by the property that is transferred, if necessary, and fall due in either $10,000 or $20,000 annual installments. When the notes become due, they can be forgiven annually in an amount that is equal to the gift

---

[73] This assumes that donor's spouse joined in making the gift.

tax exclusion. In this manner, the taxpayer is making a gift by forgiving the note so that the increase in value of the transferred property does not affect the amount of the gift.

This type of installment gift plan has been upheld by the Tax Court in *Haygood v. Commissioner,*[74] and *Estate of Kelley v. Commissioner.*[75] In the *Kelley* case, the taxpayers transferred property to their children and grandchildren in consideration for a stated cash payment and vendor lien notes. These notes in the face amounts of $6,000 and $3,000 were forgiven annually as they fell due. The Commissioner took the position in litigation that the taxpayers had made a gift of the entire value of the property in the year of transfer. The Tax Court, however, held that annual gifts were made each year as the notes were forgiven. The court stressed that a valid lien was created on the property that existed until the notes were forgiven annually. Consequently, the face amount of the notes was not subject to a gift until it was forgiven.

The Service has ruled that a transfer made pursuant to a plan such as this constitutes a taxable gift at the time of the transfer.[76] Thus, a taxpayer who is considering such a program must weigh the costs of potential litigation in order to achieve the desired result. Clearly, however, the weight of the case authority is with the taxpayer in such a situation and, in many cases, it may be worthwhile to take the litigation risk. The increase in the annual exclusion from $3,000 to $10,000 greatly increases the value of this exclusion, and this lends greater justification to the risks of litigation. In order to be successful, however, the taxpayer or his advisors should use extreme care in drafting legally enforceable notes that actually create a personal obligation upon the transferee. Another possibility might be for the donee to make one or two payments so that a clear pattern of complete forgiveness is not established.[77]

---

[74] 42 T.C. 936 (1964), acq. in result only, 1965-1 C.B. 4, acq. withdrawn and non-acq. substituted, 1977-2 C.B. 2.

[75] 63 T.C. 321 (1974), nonacq. 1977-2 C.B. 2.

[76] Rev. Rul. 77-299, 1977-2 C.B. 343.

[77] Another possible advantage of this type of plan is that payments could actually be made pursuant to the notes in later years if the cash was needed by the taxpayer. If, however, the property had a fair market value at transfer substantially in excess of its basis, the receipt of payment on these installment obligations could result in a taxable gain being realized by the taxpayer. It should be noted, however, that the Installment Sales Revision Act of 1980 contains a provision that would treat the cancellation of an installment obligation as a disposition of the obligation which is not a sale or exchange. As a consequence, the entire unreported gain of the seller would be taxable upon cancellation. I.R.C. § 453B(f). Accordingly, the installment sales approach may

¶ 11.07 Net Gifts

Another frequently encountered situation is where the taxpayer wishes to make a gratuitous transfer of a valuable asset but is either unable or unwilling to pay the gift tax involved. For example, if an individual has a significant liquidity problem in regard to his estate plan, the payment of a large gift tax would simply exacerbate the problem. Other individuals may be willing to make a substantial transfer of property but, at the same time, be unwilling to pay a large gift tax in regard to this transfer. In these and other similar cases, the solution to this dilemma may be to make a net gift. In such a case, the donor makes a transfer of the property subject to the condition that the donee pay the gift tax involved. The value of the net gift is determined by reducing the amount of the gift by the gift tax to be paid by the donee, and the gift tax liability is computed on the resulting amount.[78] Of course, in order to undertake a net gift plan, the donee must either have the cash available to pay the taxes or the transferred property must be capable of securing a loan of sufficient magnitude to pay the taxes.

A major disadvantage of a net gift program is that such gifts have been subject to a good deal of controversy between the Internal Revenue Service and taxpayers. The Service has taken the position in several litigated cases that the payment of gift taxes by a donee will result in taxable income to the donor where the amount of gift tax exceeds the donor's basis in the transferred property. Taxpayers initially had considerable success in litigating this issue.[79]

The Supreme Court recently put an end to this controversy by deciding the issue adversely to taxpayers in *Diedrich v. Commissioner*.[80] In *Diedrich* the donors transferred stock with a basis of $51,073 upon

---

no longer be appropriate if the property transferred is highly appreciated. See ¶ 14.02[2] for a more detailed discussion of this question in connection with the creation of income in respect of a decedent.

[78] See Rev. Rul. 71-232, 1971-1 C.B. 275, and Rev. Rul. 75-72, 1975-1 C.B. 310, for the Service's guidance as to how to compute the value of a net gift for gift tax purposes. The value of the gift is reduced only by the amount of gift tax liability actually assumed by the donee, and no consideration is deemed to flow from the donee to the taxpayer for the amount of tax attributable to the taxpayer's available unified credit. Rev. Rul. 81-223, 1981-2 C.B. 189.

[79] Hirst v. Comm'r, 572 F.2d 427 (4th Cir. 1978), aff'g 63 T.C. 307 (1974). See also Turner v. Comm'r, 410 F.2d 752 (6th Cir. 1969); Estate of Henry v. Comm'r, 69 T.C. 665 (1978); Owen v. Comm'r, T.C. Memo. 1978-51 (1978), aff'd, 652 F.2d 1271 (6th Cir. 1981). But see Johnson v. Comm'r, 59 T.C. 791 (1973), aff'd, 495 F.2d 1079 (6th Cir.), cert. denied, 419 U.S. 1040 (1974).

[80] — U.S. — (1982).

the condition that the donees pay the resulting gift tax of $62,992. On this set of facts, it was held that the donors realized taxable income by the donee's payment of a gift tax in excess of basis. It was reasoned that the donor incurred a liability to the United States upon the transfer and that the assumption of this liability resulted in an economic gain to the transferor. Following the rationale of *Crane v. Commissioner,*[81] this economic gain was treated as taxable income.

Although the Service has prevailed on this issue, in many circumstances the net gift may still result in an overall tax savings to the donee — even if an income tax does result. This is, of course, especially true if there is no gift tax liability in excess of basis. This principle holds true whether the transfer is made to a trust or to an individual.[82] Despite the holding in *Diedrich,* the net gift may be a valuable tax planning tool. It can enable the transfer of substantially appreciated property without demanding gift tax payments by the donor that may adversely affect his or her liquidity situation. For those individuals who are contemplating substantial gifts, but who are faced with a concern over the source of funds to pay estate taxes, the net gift approach may hold considerable promise. To undertake this course of action the taxpayer must be prepared to face an income tax where the gift tax due exceeds the basis of the property transferred. In such cases, the gift tax savings involved must be compared to the income tax costs to determine the feasibility of a transfer.[83]

¶ 11.08 Use of the Lifetime Credit

One question that will be frequently faced in considering a long-range inter vivos gift program is whether it is advisable to make gifts of such a magnitude as to utilize the taxpayer's lifetime unified estate and gift tax credit. This credit, when fully phased in, will allow the taxpayer

---

[81] 331 U.S. 1 (1947).

[82] If a transfer is made to a trust, the impact of Section 644 must be evaluated. This section provides that if appreciated property that is transferred to a trust is disposed of by the trust within two years of the transfer, the disposition will be taxed at the donor's rate rather than the rate applicable to the trust. Consequently, if the trustee were to sell the trust property or a portion of it to pay the taxes, the trust may be taxed in the same high tax bracket as the donor. In such cases, it may be preferable for the trust to borrow against the transferred property rather than selling the assets.

[83] This problem could, of course, be alleviated if high basis property is transferred. Property with a higher basis is generally preferable for a gift in any event, since the donee does not receive a step up in basis.

to make tax-free gifts above and beyond the annual exclusion in an amount equal to $600,000. However, to the extent that this credit is used during the taxpayer's lifetime, it will be unavailable at death.[84] The tax advisor is likely to find a natural reluctance on the part of many individuals to use the credit during their lifetime. There is a tendency to look at the credit as some form of bankable asset to be preserved until death.

Despite this common hesitancy to use the credit, it is often advisable to take full advantage of the credit as early as possible if the taxpayer has the assets and inclination to do so. By fully using the credit, the taxpayer is able to transfer assets to others and, in so doing, to remove the future appreciation of these assets from his estate. The taxpayer who transfers assets twenty years prior to his death will never be taxed on the twenty years of appreciation that occur in that interval. In addition, the income, if any, produced by those assets during the twenty-year period will accrue to the donee. The early use of the lifetime credit maximizes the amount of appreciation that will not be subject to estate or gift taxes on the taxpayer's part and similarly transfers the income stream produced by the asset to others. Furthermore, as noted above in ¶ 11.04[4], if the transfer requires the actual payment of gift taxes, the gift taxes paid will not be included in the donor's estate.

It also should be noted that, assuming no appreciation in the value of the asset,[85] the total taxes due upon the death of the taxpayer will be the same whether or not the asset was given away during the taxpayer's lifetime. The asset will be included in the decedent's estate either as part of his taxable estate or, if given away, as an adjusted taxable gift. Thus, unless the asset depreciated in value, there can be no added tax costs from an early utilization of the credit.[86] If, however, the property transferred does grow in value, the optimal tax posture can be achieved by the utilization of the credit at the earliest possible time. Given this fact, the decision as to the amount and extent of the credit to be used is largely dependent upon an economic judgment call relating to the taxpayer's ability to part with the property in question.

If, because of high tax rates or relatively young age, a taxpayer has

---

[84] Technically, the unified credit is not dissipated by making inter vivos gifts but rather adjusted taxable gifts made after December 31, 1976 during an individual's lifetime are added back into his taxable estate.

[85] This ignores the $10,000 annual exclusion.

[86] If the donor actually pays gift taxes above the credit, he will, however, lose the value of the use of the money between the date of the gift and the date of his death.

not accumulated a significant amount of assets, he may feel more comfortable in utilizing the credit over a substantial period of time. Each annual gift in excess of $10,000 per donee will expend a portion of the credit until it is finally exhausted.

¶ 11.09 Interest-Free Loans

Another means of assisting the natural objects of one's bounty is to make an interest-free demand loan to them. An interest-free loan enables an individual to assist children or other potential gift recipients, while providing that the principal sum will revert to him if needed. It is a particularly appropriate planning device for those individuals who feel that they are not in an economic position to make an outright substantial gift, or for those individuals who are concerned about possible estate liquidity problems at death. As might be expected, however, interest-free loans have created a good deal of judicial controversy both in the gift tax and income tax areas. Any taxpayer contemplating such a transaction would be well advised to scrutinize the existing case law carefully in structuring the transaction and also might reasonably anticipate a controversy with the Service.

[1] Gift Tax Consequences to the Lender

Although the concept of interest-free loans is being discussed in this book under the gift tax chapter, such a transaction, at least arguably, does not constitute a taxable gift. Thus, an interest-free loan is a means of tax minimization to the extent that taxpayers are successful in maintaining that such a loan does not constitute a taxable gift. Fortunately for the taxpayers and their advisors, there is a significant amount of case law to support the proposition that no taxable gift results from an interest-free loan.

The Service takes the position that an interest-free loan creates a taxable gift. In Rev. Rul. 73-61,[87] the Service ruled that the right to use money is an interest in property, the donative transfer of which is a taxable gift. In this ruling, the Service indicated that the right to use money for a term loan could be computed from IRS tables, which set forth present values of the interest-free use of money. For demand loans, the right to use the funds was not ascertainable at the time of the

---
[87] 1973-1 C.B. 408.

transaction. However, the value could be determined on a quarter-by-quarter basis as the lender allowed the borrower to continue usage of the money. It was indicated that the value of the interest-free loan could be determined on the last day of each calendar quarter. Consequently, to the extent an interest-free loan was made, this ruling took the position that a taxable gift was created.

This position has not been generally sustained in litigation. In *Crown v. Commissioner*,[88] the taxpayer was one of three brothers who were members of a partnership. This partnership made loans exceeding $18 million to twenty-four trusts established for relatives of the partners, most of whom were children of the brothers. The loans were entered on the partnership books as either open accounts or evidenced by demand notes. The demand notes made no provision for interest prior to demand, but did include a requirement for interest at the rate of six percent after demand was made. On this set of facts, the Commissioner took the position that the right to use the money without the payment of interest was a transfer of a valuable property right, requiring the assessment of a gift tax. The value of this gift was calculated to be $1,086,408, with the consequence that a gift tax deficiency of $46,085 was assessed against the petitioner. The Tax Court held for the petitioner and found that no taxable gift was made. The court found no favorable precedent for the Commissioner's action and, indeed, noted that there was one earlier case, *Johnson v. United States*,[89] where an interest-free loan had been held not to be subject to the gift tax. The court also indicated a reluctance to expand the scope of the gift tax without a clear congressional mandate, and expressed a concern that the principle being advanced by the Commissioner could be extended to a multiplicity of situations involving the gratuitous sharing of property among relatives. The Seventh Circuit upheld the Tax Court in a two-to-one decision. The Appellate Court emphasized the same factors as noted in the Tax Court opinion, and also stated that it had been furnished with no authority, suggesting that the recipient of the loan payable on demand had a legally protectable interest vis-à-vis the lender.

The Tax Court somewhat narrowed the scope of the *Crown* decision in *Estate of Berkman v. Commissioner*.[90] In *Berkman*, the taxpayer

---

[88] 67 T.C. 1060 (1977), nonacq. 1978-1 C.B. 2, aff'd, 585 F.2d 234 (7th Cir. 1978).

[89] 254 F. Supp. 73 (N.D. Tex. 1966).

[90] 38 T.C.M. 183 (1979).

had made substantial loans to his daughter in exchange for twenty-year, 6 percent notes. The court accepted the Commissioner's argument that the transfers were not at arm's-length within the meaning of the gift tax regulations, and, therefore, the difference between the amount of such transfer and the fair market value of each note constituted a taxable gift. The court rejected the application of the *Crown* decision in a case such as this and held that where the interest rate and term of the note are fixed, the market value for gift tax purposes can easily be determined. Consequently, this case was distinguishable from the situation in *Crown* where, because of the nature of the notes, the value at the time of the loan was both unknown and unknowable.

In regard to the question of whether an interest-free loan constitutes a taxable gift, the case law has thus produced a critical distinction between open-ended demand notes and notes made for a fixed term. If an individual is contemplating making an interest-free loan, there should be a bona fide note payable on demand. If a loan is made in that form, both the *Johnson* case and *Crown* case provide substantial support for the proposition that no taxable gift is being made. An adherence to this prescribed form is especially important, because, as noted above, the Service has indicated in a published ruling its position that such a transaction is a taxable gift, and has a tendency to litigate this question.

[2] Income Tax Consequences to the Borrower

A second aspect of the Service's attack on interest-free loans is an attempt to impute interest income to the borrower. Again, however, the Service has met with a distinct lack of success in this area. The cornerstone case in this area is *Dean v. Commissioner.*[91] In *Dean,* a husband and wife received interest-free loans in excess of $2 million from a controlled corporation. The Service argued that the taxpayers realized income to the extent of the economic benefit derived from the free use of funds. The Tax Court rejected this argument, relying heavily on the fact that if the taxpayers in *Dean* had borrowed the funds and paid interest, the payments of interest would have been deductible under Section 163 irrespective of the business purpose of the loans. In reaching this conclusion, the court explicitly stated that an interest-free loan results in no taxable gain to the borrower. In a subsequent case involving interest-free loans borrowed from a closely held corporation by a

---

[91] 35 T.C. 1083 (1961).

stockholder, the Tax Court indicated that it had reviewed its holding in the *Dean* case, and found it to be correct.[92] Consequently, again, no taxable income was to be imputed.

The Service has continued to press its attack on the income tax aspect of interest-free loans. Accordingly, in *Greenspun v. Commissioner*,[93] the Tax Court was presented with the situation where a preferential-rate loan was made to a taxpayer from a nonrelated corporation. Herman Greenspun had recieved a loan of $3 million from a corporation controlled by Howard Hughes on or about the same time he entered into an agreement to sell a television station and certain real estate to a Hughes-controlled corporation. Although Mr. Greenspun had refused to sell a newspaper owned by him to Mr. Hughes, the newspaper published several articles and editorials that, in a reversal of an earlier position, were favorable in tone to Hughes' interests. In its notice of deficiency, the Service took the position that the difference between the 3 percent rate of interest charged to Greenspun and a 6 percent rate represented consideration for future services. The Tax Court found that the loan was made at a favorable rate of interest in the expectation of receiving friendly press coverage from Greenspun, and also was intended to induce the sale of other property to Hughes. Despite this finding, the court held for the taxpayer, and held that no income was to be imputed from the below market rate loan.

In stating that it would follow the *Dean* decision, the Tax Court indicated some discomfort with its flat holding that an interest-free loan results in no taxable income to the borrower. The court stressed that under the circumstances in the *Greenspun* case, no deficiency would result even if taxable income were imputed, because a corresponding interest deduction would similarly have to be imputed.[94] The court did note, however, that not in all situations would the hypothetical loan transaction be taxed the same. For example, there are some cases in which the payment of interest would not give rise to a deduction under Section 163. Foremost among these situations is Section 265(2) of the Code, which disallows a deduction for interest paid with respect to

---

[92] Suttle v. Comm'r, 37 T.C.M. 1638 (1978), aff'd, 625 F.2d 1127 (4th Cir. 1980).

[93] 72 T.C. 931 (1979).

[94] The Service contended that the taxpayer would not be entitled to a corresponding deduction because no interest would have been paid by a cash basis taxpayer. The Tax Court felt that if it was going to impute interest income, it also must impute the deduction.

indebtedness incurred to purchase or carry tax-exempt obligations.[95] The court indicated that although it would continue to adhere to the *Dean* decision, it would look at the circumstances surrounding the hypothetical loan transaction to determine if it fell within the *Dean* rationale.[96]

Despite the repeated challenges of the Service, there is strong judicial support for the proposition that an interest-free loan does not result in taxable income to the borrower. The *Greenspun* case has indicated that this proposition is probably limited to those situations where the interest payment by the recipients of the loan would be wholly deductible. Consequently, the borrower should be cautioned against using the borrowed funds to purchase bonds on which the interest income is tax-exempt. This rule may also be limited in some situations where the loan is made with borrowed funds so that the corporation making the loan is deemed to be an agent of the taxpayer.[97] The Service has not ceased its attack on interest-free loans, however, and it continues to litigate the issue. There also have been judicial suggestions, particularly in the *Crown* case, that Congress should act to close this loophole. The magnitude of the favorable precedent, however, suggests that an interest-free loan, within the guidelines set forth in the decided cases, remains a viable planning tool unless such legislation if forthcoming.

[3] Tax Planning for Interest-Free Loans

If an interest-free loan is structured so as to comport with the case law outlined in the preceding discussion, it will not constitute a taxable gift by the lender and will not create taxable income to the borrower. As a consequence, the use of this device creates unique planning opportunities for the high-income taxpayer. An interest-free loan presents the lender with an opportunity in a situation where an outright gift may be either inappropriate or inadvisable, to provide a substantial economic benefit to an individual. In many situations, a highly compensated

---

[95] See discussion of Section 265(2) at ¶ 2.04[4][a][ii].

[96] In cases subsequent to *Greenspun,* the Tax Court indicated that it would continue to follow *Dean.* Zager v. Comm'r, 72 T.C. 1009 (1979), aff'd, 649 F.2d 1133 (5th Cir. 1981); Creel v. Comm'r, 72 T.C. 1173 (1979), aff'd, 649 F.2d 1133 (5th Cir. 1981); Baker v. Comm'r, 75 T.C. 166 (1980).

[97] See Creel v. Comm'r, note 96 supra, where a borrower corporation was held to be the taxpayers' agent, when it made interest payments on their behalf.

individual is desirous of assisting his children, or others, but feels that he cannot part with complete dominion and control over a considerable amount of assets. For example, although an executive may be highly salaried and have no present need for additional current income, he may not have created a substantial enough estate to enable a complete relinquishment of control over his investment assets. In these cases an interest-free loan might be appropriate, since the principal amount of the loan will be returned to the taxpayer.[98] Similar considerations may also be present in the case of an athlete or performer who is experiencing high income but is not sure how long the high-income status will last. In this situation, an interest-free loan enables a transfer of property but with a "string" attached if it ever becomes necessary to reclaim the property.

The interest-free loan can serve to shift income to a lower bracket taxpayer, as well as to make the funds available for the borrower's needs. Since the lender will not realize any income from the funds that are transferred, income is shifted away from the individual who is already in a high tax bracket. If the borrower is in a significantly lower bracket, a considerable tax savings can be realized on the income produced by the borrowed funds. In this respect, the interest-free loan serves many of the same purposes as a Clifford Trust,[99] but with a good deal more flexibility. In order to accomplish the same income-shifting goals in a short-term reversionary trust, the Code [100] imposes strict statutory requirements. Foremost among these requirements is that the reversionary trust be established for a minimum ten-year period. In contrast, the interest-free loan can accomplish the same purpose for a much shorter period, without the formalities and possible legal complications of a trust instrument, and without the costs inherent in establishing a trust. If there is a concern that the borrower will be unable to manage the funds, the interest-free demand loan can be made to a trust established for his benefit. So long as the trust is designed so that *its* income will not be taxable to the grantor, the interest-free loan would enable the grantor to move funds in and out of the trust as needed. The interest-free loan might be particularly attractive to the athlete or

---

[98] As is always the case in these situations, it is necessary to analyze whether the "borrower" can be trusted not to squander the money and return it when necessary.

[99] This is discussed in Chapter 9.

[100] I.R.C. § 673.

performer, who is experiencing a relatively short period of extremely high earnings, and who is unwilling to part with dominion and control over the fruits of this extremely lucrative period. Loans could be made to appropriate individuals during this high-income period, and then repaid to the taxpayer after his or her income has subsided and there is a greater need for the earnings from investment.

The major disadvantage of interest-free loans is that they do not offer the statutory security of a Clifford Trust. As was indicated above, the Service has frequently indicated its willingness to challenge these transactions from both an income tax and gift tax standpoint. To date, however, this attack has met with only a limited degree of success. A second concern relates to the use of the borrowed funds. If the borrower spends the principal on consumption-type items rather than investing it, the borrowed funds are not likely to be readily available for repayment upon demand. Thus, if there is a real expectation of repayment, the borrower and the lender should have a clear (but unwritten) understanding as to the use of the funds. This concern is, of course, greatly lessened if the borrower has other substantial assets from which to repay the loan. If potential repayment is a real and overriding concern, a Clifford Trust may be preferable to an interest-free loan.

¶ 11.10 Gifts to Minors

If a decision is made to undertake a long-range inter vivos gift program, it is not uncommon to find that the projected donees are the taxpayer's minor children and/or grandchildren. This normally presents additional problems for the donor. First, there is an understandable reluctance to turn a substantial amount of assets over to a minor child who does not possess either the money management skills or the maturity to handle significant sums of money. A gift giving program that only contemplates transfers within the scope of Section 2503(b) annual exclusion by itself may produce amounts of money that are far beyond the ability of a minor child to manage. For example, gifts of $20,000 per year over a twenty-year period would produce a total transfer of $400,000 — not including interest accumulations. Since gifts of $10,000 per year or less often represent a comfortable level of gift giving for many highly compensated individuals, they may find it necessary to devise a means of retaining control over the transferred funds, while still providing the donor with the benefits of the annual exclusion. Therein lies the peculiar problem of gifts to minors. Ordinarily, when significant gifts to minors are contemplated, a trust instrument is suggested. This provides both the money management skills needed on behalf of the minor, and also can direct the disposition of assets in the manner chosen by the parent or grandparent. However, as noted earlier in this chapter, in order to qualify for the annual exclusion, the gift must transfer a present interest in the property. Many trusts will not qualify for the annual exclusion because of the postponement of the enjoyment of the property transferred.[101] Fortunately, however, it is possible to make gifts to minors, in trust or otherwise, that qualify for the annual exclusion. This is particularly critical today because the utilization of the exclusion is one of the remaining major advantages of inter vivos gifts.

[1] Section 2503(c) Trusts

The Code itself specifically provides a means of establishing a trust for the benefit of a minor child that will qualify for the annual exclusion. Those trusts that meet the requirements of Section 2503(c) will qualify for the annual exclusion, and yet will provide the benefits of trust management for gifts to minors. This section of the Code creates three basic requirements in order to qualify for the exclusion:

(1) The property and income from the trust may be expended by or for the benefit of the donee, before he reaches age 21;

(2) The property, to the extent not so expended, must pass to the donee upon his attaining age 21; and

(3) In the event the donee dies before attaining age 21, such property must be payable to the donee's estate or as he may appoint under a general power of appointment.

The statute thus creates several specific requirements for a trust for the benefit of a minor to qualify for the annual exclusion. Despite the relative specificity contained in the statute, a Section 2503(c) trust allows a surprising degree of flexibility in the design of the trust instrument. Consequently, it is often a more useful vehicle for making gifts to minor children than is apparent on the face of the statute.

[a] Trustee's Discretion.
The first major requirement under Section 2503(c) is that the property and income from the trust may be

---

[101] Perhaps the most critical factor in the determination of whether or not a gift is a present interest is the postponement of enjoyment. See Fondren v. Comm'r, 324 U.S. 18 (1945).

expended by or for the benefit of the donee, before he attains age 21. Regulations Section 25.2503-4(b)(1) states that the trust can place no substantial restrictions on the exercise of the trustee's discretion to determine the amount, if any, of the income or property to be expended for the benefit of the minor. The cases and rulings tend to support the Service's position that no substantial restrictions can be placed on the scope of the trustee's discretion to distribution income and principal.

In Rev. Rul. 67-270,[102] the Service ruled that if

> "In addition to the provision for minor's health or education, the trust instrument provides that the trust property may be expended during the donee's minority for purposes which have no objective limitations (i.e., welfare, happiness and convenience) and which provision, when read as a whole approximate the scope of the term "benefit" as used in Section 2503(c) of the Code, the transfer is deemed to meet the requirements of Section 2503(c) that the property be expendable for the minor child's benefit."

In contrast, however, in Rev. Rul. 69-345,[103] the trustee's discretionary power was subject to the limitation that, in determining whether need existed, he was required to take into consideration other resources available to the beneficiary and other payments made to him or for his benefit. The beneficiary's parents were said to have considerable other resources with which to meet their support requirements, and the beneficiary held substantial property in his own name. On this set of facts, the Service ruled that the annual exclusion was not available, since the trust instrument and surrounding circumstances indicated that the trustee could not realistically be authorized to expend any portion of the trust for the benefit of the minor. In other words, the requirement that the trustee take into consideration the beneficiary's needs was held to be a substantial restriction on the exercise of his discretion given the surrounding circumstances of the family's economic position. Consequently, the standards for payment contained in the trust instrument should not reference the need of the minor child. This is particularly true for the children of the highly compensated who are unlikely to have any significant deprivations in any event.

Although the case law tends not to be quite as restrictive as the Service's rulings, it does follow the general proposition that there can be no substantial restrictions upon the trustee's discretion. For example, in

---

[102] 1967-2 C.B. 349.
[103] 1969-1 C.B. 226.

Pettus v. Commissioner,[104] the trust corpus could only be invaded for medical expenses of the beneficiaries. In this case, the gift of the trust corpus was considered to be a future interest. However, in *Williams v. United States*,[105] the Court of Claims held that a clause authorizing distribution only when, in the opinion of the trustee, the donee was in need of additional funds did not constitute a substantial restriction on the trustee's discretion, and, thus, the trust qualified under Section 2503(c). In *Duncan v. Commissioner*,[106] instructions to the trustee to apply available funds for the payment of insurance premiums did not preclude the availability of the Section 2503(c) exclusion. The case law has thus allowed some minor deviation from the general requirement that the trustee have discretion to distribute income and principal of the trust for the welfare and benefit of the minor. Clearly, however, any substantial restriction on the trustee's discretion will fail and relatively minor restrictions are likely to invite a challenge by the Service.

Consequently, to the extent the donor is willing to give the trustee broad discretion, it will increase the likelihood of qualification under Section 2503(c). This is often a wise course of action even without the statutory requirements. By giving the trustee the broadest possible discretion, he will be able to deal with any unexpected situation that may arise. Additionally, if the trustee is a close family member or confidant, he usually can be counted on to take cognizance of family wishes in exercising his discretion.

[b] Age of Distribution. The second major requirement under Section 2503(c) is that the property, to the extent not so expended, must pass to the donee on attaining age 21.[107] This requirement is often of particular concern to potential donors who would prefer to postpone the enjoyment of trust corpus beyond age 21.

There is, however, more flexibility in designing a trust to meet this requirement than might otherwise be expected from the face of the statute. The regulations [108] state that a trust will qualify as a present interest if the donee, upon reaching age 21, has the power to extend the term of the trust. Although this device may be satisfactory in many

---

[104] 54 T.C. 112 (1970).
[105] 378 F.2d 693 (Ct. Cl. 1967).
[106] 368 F.2d 98 (5th Cir. 1966).
[107] I.R.C. § 2503(c)(2)(A).
[108] Treas. Reg. § 25.2503-4(b)(2).

¶ 11.10[1][b]　　　ESTATE PLANNING　　　11-36

cases, it does require a positive act by the donee to extend a trust that would otherwise terminate at age 21. If there is a desire to extend the trust beyond this age, many donors would prefer that the trust continue by its own terms unless the trust beneficiary takes some specific action to terminate it.

Prior to 1974, the Service's position was that if a positive act was required by the donee to compel distribution of trust assets in order to terminate the trust at age 21, the trust would not qualify as a present interest.[109] The Service thereafter lost several cases on this point, and ultimately reconsidered its position. In *Heidrich v. Commissioner*,[110] the trust continued beyond the age of 21. The donees, however, had a continuing right to immediate possession of the trust corpus by making a simple written demand upon the trustee. The Tax Court held that the trust in question qualified as a present interest following a similar result in the earlier case of *Perkins v. Commissioner*.[111] In *Griffith v. Commissioner*,[112] the donor conveyed various properties in trust for the benefit of three minor children and gave them or their guardians a right to terminate the trust at any time. If the trusts were not terminated earlier, they would terminate automatically when the beneficiary reached age 30. These trusts were also held to be present interests in property.

As a consequence of losing these cases, the Service reevaluated its earlier position by issuing Rev. Rul. 74-43.[113] This ruling revoked Rev. Rul. 60-218 and set forth two instances where gifts to a minor under a Section 2503(c) trust would not be considered gifts of future interests, even though the minor was required to perform some positive act to terminate the trust at age 21. The ruling indicated that if a trust otherwise conforms to the requirements of Section 2503(c), it will not be considered a gift of a future interest, as long as the trust provides that the beneficiary, upon reaching 21, has either (1) a continuing right to terminate the trust by giving written notice to the trustee or (2) a right during a limited period to compel immediate distribution of the trust corpus by written notice to the trustee. In either case, the failure to so elect would result in the trust continuing for an additional period

---

[109] Rev. Rul. 60-218, 1960-1 C.B. 378.
[110] 55 T.C. 746 (1971).
[111] 27 T.C. 601 (1956).
[112] (D. Tex. 1962).
[113] 1974-1 C.B. 285.

11-37　　　　　　　　　　　LIFETIME GIFTS　　　　　　　　　¶ 11.10[1][b]

specified in the instrument. Consequently, a trust can be established that continues until the beneficiary reaches a later age, such as 30 or 35, unless within a reasonable period of time after his 21st birthday he formally elects to compel distribution of trust assets. Although a trust of this type does give the beneficiary the right to actually receive a corpus distribution, in many cases this right will not be exercised, and the trust can continue by its own terms for the period originally designated by the grantor.

It is also possible to restrict a trust further by providing differing treatment for the trust income and corpus. The regulations [114] require that both the property itself and the income may be expended for the benefit of the donee before he attains age 21. The word "both" does not appear in the statute, and is indicative of the Service's original position that both the income and corpus of the trust each had to meet Section 2503(c) requirements in order for the trust to qualify as a present interest. This position was not sustained in litigation. In *Herr v. Commissioner*,[115] the donor created the trust for the benefit of the minors who were to receive the principal at age 30. The trustees had discretion to retain, invest, or pay out income for the benefit of the minor. Any unexpended accumulated income had to be paid to the minor at the age of majority, or to his estate if he died before that time. The court held that the gifts of income to the beneficiary prior to the age of 21 qualified for the annual exclusion, whereas the gifts of the income payable from the ages of 21 to 30 and the corpus did not. Thus, it was possible to segregate the principal and income interests of a single trust for the purposes of determining Section 2503(c) qualification. The *Herr* case was affirmed on appeal and has been followed elsewhere.[116]

In Rev. Rul. 68-670,[117] a grantor established a ten-year income trust for a beneficiary, age 17. The trustee was directed, at his discretion, to pay the income of the trust to or for the benefit of the beneficiary until he reached age 21, whereupon all undistributed income was to be distributed to him. Thereafter, for the duration of the trust, all income was to be paid to the beneficiary. Upon termination, the corpus reverted to the grantor. On this set of facts, the Service ruled that the

---

[114] Treas. Reg. § 25.2503-4(a)(1).

[115] 35 T.C. 732 (1961), aff'd, 303 F.2d 780 (3d Cir. 1962).

[116] Weller v. Comm'r, 38 T.C. 790 (1962); Thebaut v. Comm'r, 1964-102 T.C.M., aff'd and rev'd on another issue, 361 F.2d 428 (5th Cir. 1966).

[117] 1968-2 C.B. 413.

right to receive trust income until the beneficiary reached the age of majority, or until his earlier death, met the requirements of Section 2503(c) and was not treated as a future interest, even though the beneficiary had no interest in the trust corpus. This ruling clearly indicates that the Service has acquiesced in the theory that the corpus can be considered a separate interest property for the purposes of Section 2503(c) qualification.

Segregation of income and corpus offers several planning possibilities where the grantor does not desire to distribute the corpus to the beneficiary at the age of 21 and is unwilling to allow a limited right to demand distribution at that age. For example, the income interest in the trust can be structured to meet Section 2503(c) requirements, with the distribution of corpus postponed until a later date. Of course, in order to fully utilize the Section 2503(b) exclusion, the income interest must be sufficiently large to be valued at $10,000 per donee per year. Accordingly, this approach is perhaps most relevant to trusts of a considerable magnitude. It is, however, precisely this type of trust that creates the greatest concern in regard to premature distribution of corpus. Accordingly, it is perhaps this large trust that will derive the greatest benefit from Rev. Rul. 68-670 and related cases.[118]

[c] **Disposition on Death of Donee.** The final requirement of Section 2503(c) is that in the event the donee dies before attaining age 21, such property must be payable to the donee's estate, or as he may appoint under a general power of appointment. Again, however, there is more flexibility in designating the distribution in the event of the donee's death than might otherwise appear on the surface of the statute.

The regulations [119] indicate that a trust will not fail to satisfy the conditions of Section 2503(c) where the governing instrument contains a disposition of the property or income not expended during the donee's minority, to persons other than the donee's estate, in the event of default of appointment by the donee. Consequently, if a trust provides the

---

[118] Another planning possibility where the trust income would not be valued at $10,000 per year would be to insert a so-called Crummey provision. See Crummey v. Comm'r, 397 F.2d 82 (9th Cir. 1968), discussed in detail in Chapter 13. This type of provision allows the beneficiary the right to demand a noncumulative distribution each year of an amount necessary to qualify for the exclusion. To the extent that this right is not exercised in any given year, it will then expire.

[119] Treas. Reg. § 25.2503-4(b)(3).

donee with the power to appoint unexpended corpus or income of the trust in the event of death, and in default of such appointment the assets will be distributable to a named contingent beneficiary, the trust will qualify under Section 2503(c).

The trust cannot, however, direct the disposition of unexpended income or corpus without, at the same time, granting a general power of appointment to the donee. For example, in the case of *Heath v. Commissioner*,[120] the trust instrument provided that if a beneficiary were to die before reaching age 21, his trust estate would continue for the benefit of his living decendents until they reached age 21. If the minor beneficiary were to die without having decendents, the corpus was to be divided equally among the trusts of his brothers and sisters. On this set of facts, the Tax Court held that the gifts in trust did not qualify for the annual exclusion because, in the event of the donee's death prior to age 21, his trust estate would not pass to his estate or as he might appoint. In *Clinard v. Commissioner*,[121] if the donee died prior to attaining age 21, the trust property was to be delivered to the donee's next of kin, other than donor. Such transfer was held not to qualify under Section 2503(c). Similarly, in *Messing v. Commissioner*,[122] the trust estates were to be paid to the surviving issue of the beneficiary, or to his estate if he died prior to reaching age 21. Since the trust estate passed contingently to the minor's estate, it was considered to be a gift of a future interest. Consequently, the cases have clearly indicated that a trust instrument cannot contain a disposition of trust assets (other than to the beneficiary's estate) that cannot be defeated by the donee's exercise of power of appointment. An alternate disposition can be used in the absence of the exercise of such power, which, practically speaking, will serve the same effect in most instruments.

The trust instrument also cannot limit the period of time in which the power of appointment can be exercised. In one frequently cited case,[123] the donees were prohibited from exercising the powers of appointment until they reached age 19. This limitation was said to be more restrictive than the limitation imposed by state law, and, consequently, it was held that the trust did not qualify for the annual

---

[120] 34 T.C. 587 (1960).

[121] 40 T.C. 878 (1963).

[122] 48 T.C. 502 (1967).

[123] Gall v. U.S., 521 F.2d 878 (5th Cir. 1975), cert. denied, 425 U.S. 972 (1976).

exclusion. Again, this emphasizes that although alternative dispositions can be used, the basic power of the donee to appoint the corpus in the event of death must not be restricted.

A Section 2503(c) trust can be a relatively flexible estate planning instrument, despite the rather specific language contained in that section of the Code. With careful drafting and adherence to the rulings and case law, a trust can be designed that can continue beyond age 21, that provides relatively broad discretion for the trustee, and that can provide for alternative dispositions of the trust corpus in default of the exercise of a general power of appointment by a donee who dies prior to reaching age 21. Extreme care must be exercised in drafting the instrument, however. It has been clearly held that retroactive reformation is not available to amend a trust to meet the annual gift tax exclusion requirements.[124] Thus, mistakes in drafting are not likely to be correctable. If, however, proper care is exercised, a relatively flexible instrument can be designed that enables the donor to use the annual gift tax exclusion. Because many high-income individuals find the level of gift giving that utilizes the annual exclusion to be quite comfortable, the availability of the annual gift tax exclusion is of considerable importance. For these individuals, a Section 2503(c) trust is a useful planning tool that should be given serious consideration when gifts to minors are being contemplated.

[2] Uniform Gifts to Minors Act — Custodial Transfer

A second useful means of transferring property to a minor child is to make a custodianship transfer under the Uniform Gift to Minors Act. This is a relatively simple and efficient means of making a transfer to a minor. All that is necessary is to draft a transfer instrument declaring that the properties transferred to a designated custodian "as custodian for a specified donee" under the appropriate state Uniform Gift to Minors Act. No other instrument need be executed. Thus, a Uniform Gifts to Minors Act is extremely easy to implement and avoids some of the complexities and inherent costs in drafting a trust instrument.

The custodian has broad powers to deal with the transferred property. The Act itself gives the custodian broad powers to exercise its discretion to accumulate or expend income or corpus and applies a relatively flexible prudent man standard towards the transferred prop-

---

[124] Van den Wymelenberg v. U.S., 397 F.2d 443 (7th Cir.), cert. denied, 393 U.S. 953 (1968); Davis v. Comm'r, 55 T.C. 416 (1970).

erty. The custodian is able to act with respect to the trust property without the necessity of frequent court approval, which often accompanies a guardianship. The custodianship property is distributed outright to the donee when he attains the age of majority. In those states that have lowered the age of majority, this means a mandatory distribution at age 18 or 19.

The tax effects of a Uniform Gifts to Minors Act transfer are, again, quite clear-cut and simple. A Uniform Gifts to Minors Act transfer will qualify for the Section 2503(b) annual exclusion.[125] Thus, such a transfer avoids the future interest problems that often accompany a trust that does not qualify under Section 2503(c) and preserves this important gift tax advantage. The donee reports income from the custodianship property on his or her own tax return, and the custodian is not required to file a fiduciary income tax return. If the donee has little or no income from other sources, a custodianship arrangement will mean that the transferred property will be subject to little or no income tax. There is, however, a potential estate tax problem if the donor himself acts as the custodian for the minor donee. Quite often a parent will transfer property to himself or herself as custodian for minor children. If this individual then predeceases the child, the custodianship property will be included in the donor's gross estate. It has been held in both rulings and cases that the retained rights to distribute or withhold distribution of the income and principal until the age of majority constitutes a retained power within the meaning of Section 2038(a)(1).[126] Accordingly, it is generally unwise to have the donor name himself as custodian. Prudent estate planning considerations require that an individual or institution other than the donor be named.

Although a Uniform Gifts to Minors Act custodianship transfer offers the advantages of simplicity and ease of administration, it does present two significant drawbacks. The first such drawback is the previously alluded to mandatory transfer at the age of majority, which can, in many states, mean an outright distribution at age 18. If the custodian is the recipient of considerable sums of money, this would mean that the donee will receive a distribution of these sums at a very young age. This will frequently be unacceptable to a donor, who would

---

[125] Rev. Rul. 56-86, 1956-1 C.B. 449; Rev. Rul. 59-357, 1959-2 C.B. 212.

[126] See Rev. Rul. 57-366, 1957-2 C.B. 619; Rev. Rul. 59-357, 1959-2 C.B. 212; Estate of Prudowsky v. Comm'r, 55 T.C. 890 (1971), aff'd, 465 F.2d 62 (7th Cir. 1972).

prefer to delay distribution until a later age or, at the very least, to stage the distribution in increments. Consequently, in the case of very large transfers, a Section 2503(c) trust with the income interest designed to meet the requirements of that section and the corpus distribution delayed beyond age 21, may be a better alternative. On the other hand, a distribution to a donee at age 18 or 19 can provide needed funds for a college education. Thus, if a relatively modest distribution is planned for these purposes, the Uniform Gifts to Minors Act transfer may prove to be a useful device. It will qualify for the annual gift tax exclusion, shift income to a lower bracket taxpayer, and turn over the needed funds for a college education.

The second major drawback of the custodianship transfer is that many states limit the types of assets that can be held by the custodian. Frequently, the state statutes only allow the transfer of securities, money, insurance policies, and annuity contracts. Accordingly, many types of assets that tend to be favored by investors today, such as gold, silver, antiques, real property, or other "hard goods," cannot be used for a custodianship type of transfer. Because these assets, which cannot be transferred, are of the type that have tended recently to appreciate the most in value, these are often the assets that are most appropriate for a gift giving program. The custodianship arrangement will permit, however, the utilization of income-producing assets, such as securities or money. The shifting of these assets from a highly compensated individual to a minor with little income adds to the utility of these arrangements, despite the limitations on the types of property that can be held. If there is a desire to expand the scope of the property to be transferred, it may be necessary to use a trust or some other type of arrangement.

[3] Transfer to a Guardian

Another alternative to deal with the inability of a minor to transfer or manage property is to cause the installation of a court-appointed guardian. The guardian is then able to manage the financial estate of a minor. This process is little used in practice because it is both time-consuming and expensive. The guardian is subject to the control of the court and generally is required to seek permission for most actions. Often the court-appointed guardian is restricted to a prescribed list of court-approved investments, and thus, has little flexibility in terms of the type of property that can be handled. The necessity and expense for frequent court appearances, as well as the restricted nature of the allowable investments, generally make the guardianship an unsatisfactory means of making a gift to a minor, except in a very unusual set of circumstances. The guardianship is most frequently used where the child suffers from a disability, such as mental retardation, and there is a desire for long-term supervision of the minor's assets. In such a case, particularly if the donor does not have a long life expectancy of if there is no trusted friend or relative to serve as trustee, long-term protection of a court may be desirable.

¶ 11.11 Gifts to Spouses

The 1981 Act drastically altered planning strategies in regard to lifetime transfers to spouses. As noted earlier, the Act provides for an unlimited marital deduction for both lifetime transfers and transfers at death. It also adopted the concept of "qualified terminable interest property" for both gift and estate transfers so as to allow certain terminable interests to qualify for the marital deduction.[127] Consequently, planning for the gift tax marital deduction starts with the proposition that virtually any transfer to a spouse, either during life or

---

[127] The gift tax marital deduction also contains a terminable interest rule similar to that found in regard to the estate tax marital deduction. Section 2523(b). This rule states that where on a lapse of time, on the occurrence of an event or contingency, or on the failure of an event or contingency to occur, such interest transferred to the spouse will terminate or fail, no deduction will be allowed with respect to such interest:

1. If the donor retains in himself or transfers or has transferred (for less than adequate and full consideration in money or money's worth) to any person other than such donee's spouse or the estate of such spouse, an interest in such property, and if by reason of such retention or transfer the donor (or his heirs or assigns) or such person (or his heirs or assigns) may possess or enjoy any part of such property, after the termination or failure of the interest transferred to the donee's spouse; or

2. If the donor immediately after the transfer to the donee's spouse has the power to appoint an interest in such property which he can exercise (either alone or in conjunction with any person) in such manner that the appointee may possess or enjoy any part of such property after such termination or failure of the interest transferred to the donee's spouse.

For purposes of this paragraph, the donor shall be considered as having, immediately after the transfer to the donee spouse, such power to appoint, even though such power cannot be exercised until after the lapse of time, upon the occurrence of an event or contingency, or on the failure of an event or contingency to occur. This rule may be avoided if an election is made with respect to qualified terminable interest property. Section 2523(f).

at death, will be tax-free. Since an inter vivos transfer will be tax-free upon both occasions, the question becomes, is there any advantage to making a transfer during one's life and to a spouse as opposed to waiting until death?

Before contemplating any transfer to a spouse, there are several factors in addition to the lack of an estate or gift tax that must be weighed. First, such a transfer is likely to produce no income tax consequences, since most married couples tend to file a joint return. Consequently, unless the two spouses are filing separate returns, a lifetime transfer to a spouse will result in no income tax consequences one way or the other. Second, consideration must be given to the effect of such a transfer upon the estate plan of the spouse. If it is assumed that the transferee spouse will be the second to die, an inter vivos gift to her (as well as a transfer to her at death) will have the effect of inflating her estate. Consequently, if the transferee spouse's estate is at or above taxable levels, it will be necessary to weigh the cost of additional tax upon her estate against her necessity to have the transferred assets for her economic well-being and the benefit of tax deferral arising from a tax-free transfer to a spouse.[128]

The most significant difference between a lifetime transfer to a spouse and a transfer at death is that property transferred at death will receive a step-up in basis to its date of death value, whereas the lifetime transfer is made with a carryover basis. Consequently, if there is any possibility of a surviving spouse selling an asset after the death of the first spouse, it is much more advantageous to pass the property at death, since it does receive this step-up in basis. Because the transfer tax consequences are the same whether or not there is a lifetime gift or transfer at death (that is, in either case there is a full deduction), there are very few circumstances in which a lifetime gift to a spouse will now be advisable. Such a transfer generally creates no estate tax or lifetime income tax advantage to the transferor and creates a post mortem income tax disadvantage for the surviving spouse in that the property will not receive a step-up in basis.

The one situation in which a lifetime transfer to a spouse may be most advantageous would be where one spouse owns substantially appreciated property and the other spouse is likely to die first. In such a case, if the first spouse transfers property to the other, and if the

---

[128] The concept and problems relating to over-funding the marital bequest are discussed extensively in Chapter 15.

transferee survives for at least one year,[129] a transfer back to the first spouse in the will of the transferee will result in a step-up in basis for the appreciated property. Quite obviously, there are a limited number of circumstances in which this set of facts will apply. In the proper case, however, such as the instance of a significant difference in the ages of the spouses, or if the one spouse is ill but not likely to die within one year, such a course of action may result in a significant tax advantage. In most cases, however, lifetime gifts to spouses, after 1981, will generally be inadvisable because they do not provide the stepped-up basis that occurs if the transfer is withheld until death.

---

[129] Survival for one year is necessary to avoid the rule of Section 1014(e).

CHAPTER 12

Irrevocable Lifetime Trusts *

		Page
¶ 12.01	Planning for the Use of Trusts	12-2
	[1] Definition of Irrevocable Trust	12-2
	[2] Transferor's Objectives	12-2
¶ 12.02	Grantor Trust as Alternative to Irrevocable Trust	12-3
	[1] Tax Consequences	12-3
	[2] Providing for Possibility of Grantor's Death During the Trust Term	12-4
	[3] Benefits of Grantor Trust vs. Irrevocable Trust	12-6
¶ 12.03	Estate Tax Considerations in Making Lifetime Irrevocable Gifts to Trusts	12-7
	[1] Current and Prior Law	12-7
	[2] Transfer of Non-Appreciating Property to Irrevocable Trust	12-8
	[3] Transfer of Potentially Appreciating Property	12-9
	[a] Examples of Tax Savings From Transfers to Irrevocable Trusts	12-9
	[i] Stock in closely held corporations	12-10
	[ii] Real estate	12-10
	[b] Exclusion of Transferred Property From Estate	12-11
¶ 12.04	Requirements for Removal of Transferred Property From Taxable Estate	12-11
¶ 12.05	Transfers for Consideration	12-12
¶ 12.06	Retention of Life Interest by Transferor	12-13
	[1] Includability in Transferor's Estate	12-13
	[2] Retention of Partial Interest	12-13
	[3] Retention of Implied Right	12-14
¶ 12.07	Use of Trust to Discharge Transferor's Obligations	12-15
	[1] Support Obligations	12-15
	[2] Obligations Other Than Support	12-16

---

* This chapter was researched and written by Israel G. Grossman, Esq. of Rosenman, Colin, Freund, Lewis and Cohen, New York.

		Page
¶ 12.08	Tax Consequences Affected by Identity of the Trustee	12-17
	[1] Transferor or Party Controlled by Transferor as Trustee	12-17
	[2] Power to Remove or Appoint Successor Trustees	12-19
	[3] Third Party as Trustee	12-21
	[4] Beneficiary as Trustee	12-21
¶ 12.09	Transferor's Retention of Administrative Powers	12-22
¶ 12.10	Transferor's Retention of Power to Alter, Amend, Revoke, or Terminate Trusts	12-24
	[1] Includability in Transferor's Estate	12-24
	[2] Permissible Retained Powers	12-25
	[3] General Rules	12-27
¶ 12.11	Transfers Taking Effect at Transferor's Death	12-27
	[1] Includability in Transferor's Estate	12-27
	[2] Avoiding Application of Section 2037	12-28
¶ 12.12	Advantages and Disadvantages of Irrevocably Transferring Property Out of One's Estate	12-30

¶ 12.01 Planning for the Use of Trusts

[1] Definition of Irrevocable Trust

An irrevocable trust is a trust that an individual creates to benefit persons other than himself, and to which he transfers property by gift. By definition, the grantor cannot alter, amend or revoke this trust instrument. In addition, the grantor must totally relinquish any income or reversionary interest in the trust in order for it to be irrevocable as required for tax purposes.

[2] Transferor's Objectives

Before creating such an irrevocable trust, an individual should be certain of the objectives he seeks to achieve, and whether he is prepared to relinquish the requisite amount of control over the trust property necessary to achieve such objectives.

The individual should determine if he seeks to:

(1) Relieve himself of the income tax on the income from such property for the rest of his life or for a certain period of time;

(2) Create a completed irrevocable gift and incur substantial gift tax liability on the transfer, or to make a gift for a stated

period of time and incur little or minimal current transfer tax liability; and/or

(3) Seek the exclusion of the property from his gross estate when he dies or to have the trust property or a part thereof included in his taxable estate.

Before making a transfer to an irrevocable trust, the income, and gift and estate tax ramifications of the transfer to the grantor and his beneficiaries should be carefully analyzed as noted in this chapter, and alternative transfer options considered. The irrevocable trust should also be compared to a direct gift, which is likely to produce the same estate tax consequences but not provide the normal trust advantages such as professional management of assets or protection for spendthrift beneficiaries.[1]

If it is then determined that an irrevocable trust should be created, the objectives of the grantor should be clarified and the trust terms carefully drafted to ensure that his objectives will be achieved without his being deemed to have retained any powers that would cause the trust to be included in his estate.

¶ 12.02 Grantor Trust as Alternative to Irrevocable Trust

[1] Tax Consequences

If a grantor's only objective is to relieve himself of the income tax liability on the income from property transferred for a certain number of years, for example, until he retires (at which time his income tax bracket will probably be lower), he could create a grantor trust for at least ten years or for the lifetime of the beneficiary, as discussed in Chapter 9. He would have to pay a gift tax in the year the trust is created based on the value of the income interest gifted (See ¶ 9.06[2]).

Since the property will return to the grantor after the specified period of time, it will be included in his gross estate upon his death. However, in the event he dies before the expiration of the term of the trust, the value of the income interest for the remaining term of the trust will be excluded from his estate.

For example, if grantor, *G,* creates a trust for ten years for the benefit of beneficiary, *B,* and dies after the fourth year, the following are the income, and gift and estate tax consequences:

G or his estate will not be subject to income tax during the ten-year

---

[1] See discussion at ¶ 9.01 of nontax objectives and tax objectives of trust creation.

period of the trust. *B* will have to include the trust income in his return for the ten-year period.

G will have to pay a gift tax at the time of the creation of the trust based on the actuarial value of the income interest irrevocably gifted. This amount is determined on the basis of the tables provided in the Gift Tax Regulations,[2] which assume a 6 percent growth rate. The value of a gift of income for a ten-year period would be 44.1605 percent of the principal amount gifted. In view of the fact that the current rate of return, even on an investment such as treasury notes or municipal bonds, is in excess of 6 percent, the actual value of the gift is in excess of the value ascribed to it by the Service, resulting in a significant gift tax savings.

[2] Providing for Possibility of Grantor's Death During the Trust Term

To the extent that the grantor does not survive the term of the trust (e.g., a ten-year period), the amount of gift tax savings is offset somewhat by a correspondingly inflated value ascribed to the remainder interest that is included in his estate. Therefore, in our example, when the grantor dies after four years, the remainder interest included in his estate is valued at 70.4961 percent of the principal on the basis of the I.R.S. Estate Tax Tables,[3] when in reality the fair market value of monies that are not to be received for a period of six years would certainly be discounted at greater than 30 percent. If the estate beneficiaries are the same as the income beneficiaries, then there is no concern that the value of the remainder interest included in the estate does not accurately reflect the true value of the income interest, since the income interest would otherwise have been fully includable in the grantor's estate.

However, if the beneficiaries of the grantor trust are not the same beneficiaries to whom the grantor wishes his estate to pass, the grantor may provide that in the event that he dies before the termination of the trust period the persons who should then be the income beneficiaries are the individuals to whom the grantor wishes his estate to pass. As a result, the beneficiaires of his estate will not be adversely affected, since they will receive both the income and the remainder of the trust, and

---

[2] Treas. Reg. § 25.2512-9(f), Table B.

[3] Treas. Reg. § 20.2031-10(f), Table B.

only the portion of the trust representing the value of the remainder interest will be included in the grantor's estate. Such a provision will not affect the exclusion from income tax liability enjoyed by the grantor and his estate for the period of the trust, since the trust will continue in existence for the full term. However, if the grantor's life expectancy at the time of the creation of the trust is greater than ten years or the term of the trust, then the provision described above is not advisable, since it would cause the entire value of the trust to be included in the grantor's estate under Section 2037. This section is likely to cause estate tax inclusion because (1) possession or enjoyment of the property can, through ownership of such interest, be obtained by the substitute beneficiaries only by surviving the decedent, and (2) since the grantor's life expectancy exceeded the term of the trust, it is likely that the value of his reversionary interest immediately before his death exceeded 5 percent of the value of such property. Therefore, if the grantor has a life expectancy of greater than ten years and he desires that his estate pass to beneficiaries other than the income beneficiaries of the trust, the trust should provide that, in the event of the grantor's death before the expiration of the term of the trust, the trust should terminate. Such a provision will not affect the exclusion of the income from the grantor's taxable income because the grantor's life expectancy at the time of the creation of the trust makes it unlikely that the reversionary interest will take effect within ten years from the creation of the trust.[4]

By including such a provision, the estate beneficiaries will be able to receive the trust property immediately, without having to wait until the expiration of the period of the trust term. Since the discount offered by the Service for their waiting until the expiration of the trust term is unrealistically low because of an assumption of a 6 percent return, it is in their interest to give up the discount in return for the receipt of the full value of the trust immediately.

If there is a surviving spouse, the unlimited marital deduction available allows estate tax on the trust property to be deferred until the death of the surviving spouse by providing, in the manner described above, that he or she is to receive the remainder on the death of the transferor,[5] who had a life expectancy greater than the term of the trust.

---

[4] I.R.C. § 673(a).

[5] However, it may not be advisable to provide that the surviving spouse be the beneficiary of the remainder interest if her estate is otherwise large and reduction of its size will produce significant estate tax savings on her ultimate death.

The unlimited marital deduction also allows the surviving spouse to receive the remaining income interest if the term of the trust exceeded the grantor's life expectancy.

[3] Benefits of Grantor Trust vs. Irrevocable Trust

In view of the fact that there is a unified gift and estate tax, there is little added advantage to creating a completely irrevocable trust, as opposed to a grantor or ten-year trust, in situations where it is not anticipated that the property transferred will appreciate in value between the time of the gift by the grantor and the date of his death, or where the taxable estate of the decedent or his surviving spouse will be minimal after utilization of the available unified credit.

Since under the 1981 Act an increased unified credit is being phased in over a period of five years until 1987, it in fact may be more advantageous not to create an irrevocable trust, since the same objective can often be achieved at a reduced current tax cost. For example, in 1983, when the unified credit is $79,300, the amount of total lifetime gifts that could be made without incurring a tax is $275,000.[6] If an individual wished to make a gift of $668,000 in trust for his two children, and provide that they are to receive the income from the trust during his lifetime and the principal upon his death, the federal gift tax would be $138,660 if this were a completely irrevocable gift. There would be no later estate taxes.

If he instead placed the monies into a ten-year grantor trust as discussed in the example at ¶ 12.02[2] above, in the year 1983 there would be no gift taxes payable, since the value of the ten-year income interest gifted would be less than the available $275,000 unified credit equivalent [7] and the two annual exclusions of $10,000 available for each donee. If he then dies four years after creating the trust, the value on the date of death of the remainder interest, which will pass to the estate after the expiration of the ten-year term, is included in the estate (i.e., 70.4961 percent or $470,847). The tax on this amount, assuming that this represents the bulk of his taxable estate, would be $145,800, less a state death tax credit of $9,067, or $136,774. Since by 1987 there will be an additional credit of $113,500 available, the estate tax payable would be approximately $24,000.

---

[6] If a spouse joins in the gift, lifetime gifts of $550,000 could be made since there would be two unified credits available.

[7] See note 6, supra.

Therefore, by not irrevocably gifting the monies during his lifetime, the grantor had the use of the $138,660 in gift taxes otherwise payable during his life. In addition, if he has only minimal additional assets in his taxable estate, or if the remainder of his estate qualifies for a marital deduction, he will also have reduced the total taxes on the transfer by the use of additional unified credit in 1987, which was not otherwise available to him in the earlier years when the initial transfer was made. Furthermore, by not creating a totally irrevocable trust, he retains the discretion to renew the trust at the expiration of the initial term or to make completely new provisions with respect to the assets without relinquishing any of the income tax benefits available [8] or incurring any additional estate or gift taxes.[9]

In summary, if the major objective is to transfer assets to a trust for the benefit of individuals in income tax brackets lower than grantor's, an irrevocable trust is not necessarily required since the same objectives can often also be achieved through the use of a "short term" grantor trust or the nonrecourse interest-free loans discussed in Chapter 9.

¶ 12.03 Estate Tax Considerations in Making Lifetime Irrevocable Gifts to Trusts

[1] Current and Prior Law

Prior to 1976, the transfer of assets to an irrevocable trust would produce an estate tax savings even if the assets did not appreciate between the time of the transfer and the individual's death, since the tax rates for gifts were lower than those for an estate. In addition, a lifetime gift tax exclusion was available and, if utilized, would not affect the

---

[8] Additional powers a grantor can retain under the grantor trust rules of Sections 673-678 without subjecting himself to income tax on trust income are discussed in Chapter 9.

[9] The absence of any additional estate or gift tax liability is based on the assumption that at the end of the initial trust term he will not create a new trust or, if a new trust is created, the increased unified credit equivalent then available (i.e., $600,000) will exceed the value of his estate or, if married, the estate of his surviving spouse. If a new trust is created and the value of the grantor's or, if married, his surviving spouse's estate exceeds the unified credit equivalent then available, there will be a gift tax liability incurred each time a new grantor trust is created based on the actuarial value of the interest gifted, and an estate tax liability on the remainder interest, as discussed earlier in this chapter.

estate tax rates. Also, by removing assets from the estate by payment of a gift tax, the estate would be in a lower tax bracket. However, the Tax Reform Act of 1976 equalized the estate and gift tax rates and provided a unified credit, which, if utilized to ease the gift tax burden, results in less credit being available to offset estate taxes on the death of the individual. Also, any gifts made after 1977 are added to the estate tax base, thereby pushing the remainder of the estate into a higher tax bracket. Therefore, the major estate planning goals under present law are to remove post-gift appreciation and the income earned by investment of the gifted property from the donor's estate. In an inflationary economy coupled with high interest rates, appreciation and interest income is likely to be more valuable than the property itself within a short period of time.[10]

Before the 1981 Act, a gift in trust of potentially appreciating assets to one's spouse would also be advantageous for estate tax purposes. However, as a result of the unlimited marital deduction now available, all property gifted or placed in a trust that provides the spouse with at least the right to its income for life will not be subject to estate tax. Therefore, there is no longer any federal gift or estate tax benefit to be derived by such interspousal transfers. In addition, where it is anticipated that all of an individual's assets in excess of the allowable unified credit will be left to the surviving spouse, there would have been no tax on that individual's estate in any event.

Therefore, an individual who wishes to leave assets of substantial value to persons other than his spouse will find it most advantageous to make gifts of potentially appreciating or income-producing assets via an irrevocable trust. By making certain lifetime transfers to an irrevocable trust, an individual may be able to stabilize the size of his estate or his surviving spouse's estate by passing all potential earnings and future appreciation to others.

[2] Transfer of Non-Appreciating Property to Irrevocable Trust

If the transferor is certain that he wishes to designate irrevocably particular beneficiaries of a trust, and the size of the gift is less than his unified credit equivalent or the combined credit equivalent of both himself and his spouse, it is more advantageous to create an irrevocable

---

[10] The advantages of lifetime gifts are discussed extensively in Chapter 11.

trust, since the income and remainder of the trust will then never be brought back into his estate and, unless the spouse is a beneficiary of the trust, it will also not be included in her estate. In 1982, gifts of $450,000 can be made tax-free if the spouse consents to making the gift; and by 1987, gifts of $1,200,000 can be made tax-free if the spouse joins in the gift. If, in addition to creating the irrevocable trust, each spouse provides in his will that substantially all his property will pass to the surviving spouse, then, under the marital deduction, there will be no estate tax on their remaining property until the death of the surviving spouse. If the surviving spouse had exhausted her unified credit in making the earlier transfer, all property remaining in her estate would be subject to federal estate tax.

As a result of the transfer, the income from the property transferred will not be part of either spouse's taxable income, and the accumulated earnings thereon will not be part of either spouse's estate. The advantage of the irrevocable trust as opposed to a trust for a period of time (e.g., ten years) is that the remaining principal is forever removed from the transferor's estate. In addition, the income that would be earned from investment of such principal, which would otherwise be building up the grantor's estate, is removed from his estate. It must be noted, however, that the same estate tax savings can be achieved by a direct gift to a donee. Consequently, if these estate tax savings are a paramount consideration, the advantages of a direct gift (see Chapter 11) versus a gift in trust must be weighed.

[3] Transfer of Potentially Appreciating Property

An irrevocable trust for the benefit of persons other than the spouse is a very valuable lifetime estate planning tool if the property that the transferor is contemplating transferring is potentially appreciating property. The most suitable assets to be placed in an irrevocable trust are those that are expected to substantially appreciate in value between the time of the transfer and the time of the transferor's death. These are assets such as life insurance (discussed in Chapter 13), real estate, stock of a closely held corporation, listed securities, partnership interests, patents, manuscripts, antiques, and lottery tickets.

[a] Examples of Tax Savings From Transfers to Irrevocable Trusts. The following examples illustrate the estate tax savings that can result from the placing of certain assets into an irrevocable trust.

[i] Stock in closely held corporations. For example, *A* is president and owns 70 of the 100 shares of the outstanding common stock of *ABC* Company, a newly organized corporation. His son, *B*, age 35, is vice president and owns the remaining 30 shares. *A* anticipates that the *ABC* Company will show substantial growth over the succeeding years. Upon his retirement or death, it is *A*'s expectation and desire that his son, *B*, will assume the management and control of the business. *A* also has two daughters, *C*, age 19, and *D*, age 27. At present he does not know what the future needs of *C* and *D* or his wife, *W*, will be upon his death. He has full confidence in the judgment of his son, *B*. It is *A*'s present intent that he and his son continue to retain control over the day-to-day activities of the corporation, but he wishes to transfer a substantial amount of the potential appreciation of the *ABC* stock to his wife and children in a manner that will minimize the estate taxes on his death and the subsequent death of his wife.

The procedure that may be followed to achieve this objective is the recapitalization of the *ABC* stock so that each current share of common stock is exchanged for one share of nonvoting common stock and one share of voting preferred stock. *A* would then transfer his 70 shares of common stock to an irrevocable trust, naming his son as trustee, which provides that the trustee has discretion to sprinkle income among *A*'s wife and daughters during his wife's life, and to distribute the remainder to his daughters upon his wife's death. The preferred stock would be devised by will or gradually gifted to *A*'s son when *A* is prepared to retire from *ABC*.

The creation of such a trust by *A* will insure that any appreciation in value of *ABC* stock will not be included in his or his wife's estate. He is able to accomplish this objective without losing control over the *ABC* Company during his lifetime.

[ii] Real estate. For example, *A* purchased Blackacre, a piece of undeveloped land he anticipates will become very valuable after he has completed the development of Whiteacre, which is adjacent to it. Currently, the property is rented for use as a farm, and the expenses, such as taxes and mortgage interest, exceed the income. *A* transfers the property into a trust that provides that the income may be distributed to his spouse, and upon his death, the trust property is to be distributed among his children in the trustee's discretion. For income tax purposes, *A*'s wife will be treated as the owner of the trust.[11] Therefore, on their

---

[11] I.R.C. § 677(a).

joint return, *A* and his wife will be able to continue to benefit from the income tax deductions generated by the property. However, for estate tax purposes, it is a sufficient transfer to remove the asset from his estate.

[b] Exclusion of Transferred Property From Estate. It is often advantageous to have tax shelter depreciable assets or investments whose basis is being eroded during the individual's lifetime as a result of other deductions claimed, included in one's estate so that a stepped up basis will be available upon the individual's death. However, with respect to assets that have substantial potential for appreciation, if the size of the estate passing to persons other than the spouse is large, a lifetime gift to an irrevocable trust may create estate tax advantages that exceed the income tax benefits that would otherwise flow from a step-up basis. This is especially true with respect to capital assets, such as real estate, provided there is no recapture of accelerated depreciation or other deductions, but instead all gain resulting from forgoing a step-up in basis is taxed at a maximum capital gain rate of 20 percent.[12] If such property became part of the estate, it would be taxed at a higher rate.

¶ 12.04 Requirements for Removal of Transferred Property From Taxable Estate

In order for a grantor to remove transferred assets from his gross estate successfully he must:

(1) Under Section 2036, not retain during his life:

   (a) The possession or enjoyment of, or the right to, income from the property; or

   (b) The right, either alone or in conjunction with any person, to designate the persons who will possess or enjoy the property or the income therefrom.

(2) Under Section 2038, not retain the power (alone or with another person) at the date of his death to alter, amend, revoke, or terminate the trust.

---

[12] There is also a possible exposure to the alternative minimum tax liability if the individual has other significant tax preference items (e.g., adjusted itemized deductions) in a particular year. Alternative minimum taxable income is generally taxed at a 20-percent rate and, therefore, may result in increased tax exposure. See generally ¶ 2.02; if the assets are nonappreciating, removal of the interest or earnings of the property from one's estate can also be achieved by alternative methods as discussed earlier.

(3) Under Section 2037, not provide that possession or enjoyment of the property can, through ownership of such interest, be obtained by the beneficiaries only by surviving him, if he also will retain a reversionary interest [13] in the property the value of which, immediately before his death, exceeds 5 percent of the value of the property.[14]

(4) Under Section 2041, not have a general power of appointment over trust property. Powers of appointment are extensively discussed at ¶ 16.03.

(5) Under Section 2035, survive by three years the transfer of property that otherwise would have been included under Section 2036, 2037, 2038, or 2042, or would have been included under any of those sections if the interest had been retained by the decedent.

¶ 12.05 Transfers for Consideration

If the transferor receives adequate consideration for the transfer of property in trust, the trust will not be included in his estate. Of course, in that situation the consideration received will presumably remain to be taxed in his estate. However, if he retains any of the proscribed powers of Sections 2036, 2037, and 2038, which would otherwise make the trust includable in his estate, the value of the property includable in his gross estate will be "the excess of the fair market value at the time of death of the property otherwise to be included on account of such transaction, over the value of the consideration received therefor by the decedent."[15]

Since the major estate planning objective in creating an irrevocable trust is to remove the potential appreciation from the transferor's estate, this objective will not be attained, even if adequate consideration is paid to the transferor at the time of the transfer, if he retains any of the rights described in Code Sections 2036, 2037, and 2038. For example, *G* transfers stock worth $10 to a trust that provides that *G* is to receive all

---

[13] Section 2037(b) provides that for purposes of Section 2037 the term "reversionary interest" includes a possibility that property transferred by the decedent may (1) return to him or his estate or (2) be subject to a power of disposition by him; but such term does not include a possibility that the income alone from such property may return to him or become subject to a power of disposition by him.

[14] Section 2037(b) of the Code and Treas. Reg. § 20.2037-1(c)(3) provide that the value of the reversionary interest is to be determined as of the moment before the decedent's death by usual methods of valuation including mortality and actuarial tables.

[15] I.R.C. § 2043(a).

dividends until his death and that upon his death the stock is to pass to *S. S,* in return for *G*'s creating the trust, gives *G* $10. There were, in fact, no dividends paid. If, when *G* dies, the stock is worth $1,000,000, $999,990 will be included in *G*'s estate (i.e., the value of the trust property at the time of his death, less the consideration he received at the time of the transfer).[16] This unfortunate result would not have occurred if *G* had not retained an income interest at the time of the transfer, which, under Section 2036, resulted in its being included in his estate.

¶ 12.06 Retention of Life Interest by Transferor

[1] Includability in Transferor's Estate

Under Section 2036 of the Code, transferred property is includable in the grantor's estate if, as trustee or otherwise, he retains "the right either alone or in conjunction with any other person to designate the person who shall possess or enjoy the property or the income therefrom." The rights that result in inclusion under Section 2036 are those that the grantor-decedent retained at the time of his transfer of the property. Such a right is deemed to have existed at the time of the transfer if there was then "an understanding, express or implied, that the interest or right would later be conferred."[17] If he received the right from someone else, his estate is not taxable.

[2] Retention of Partial Interest

At the time of the transfer the transferor cannot retain or reserve the use, possession, right to the income, or other enjoyment of the property that he has transferred for his life or for a period not ascertainable without reference to his death. If he retains such rights for a specified period only and he dies within that period, the entire trust will be included in his estate if the period is such as to evidence his intention that it should extend at least for the duration of his life.

---

[16] U.S. v. Allen, 293 F.2d 916 (10th Cir. 1961). In *Allen,* Maria Allen was receiving the income from a trust she created. She transferred this reserved life estate to her son in return for the value of the life estate. Although she no longer received any income from the trust, the Court held that the corpus of the reserved life estate was not removed from her estate by a transfer at the value of the reserved life estate.

[17] Treas. Reg. § 20.2036-1(a).

If the transferor retains the right to income, which does not take effect until after the death of another individual given a lifetime income interest, the entire value of the trust is includable, less the "carve-out" of the value of the outstanding life estate.[18]

For example, Father, F, transfers property in trust with the income payable to his son, S, during his lifetime; but if S should predecease F, then the income is to go to such beneficiaries as F designates. If F dies before S, the amount includable in F's gross estate under Section 2036 will be the excess of the value of the trust over the actuarial value of S's outstanding income interest.

[3] Retention of Implied Right

The retained right to income, use, possession or other enjoyment of property transferred need not be expressly provided for in the trust instrument. It may be inferred from the conduct of the parties. For example, in Rev. Rul. 78-409,[19] the Service has ruled that where the donor and donee are persons other than husband and wife,[20] for example a father and son, continued occupancy of the transferred realty by the donor father implies in itself the existence of an agreement of retained enjoyment by the donor father, even though the son paid all the upkeep costs and there was no express agreement that the father would continue to live in the house. Another example of an inferred power is a transfer of a painting by gift or trust with the painting remaining in the transferor's home. The full value of the painting on the date of the donor's death will be included in his estate.

If the decedent's power applies to only a part of the property, a proportionate part will be included in his estate. For example, in Rev. Rul. 79-117,[21] the Service ruled that where a decedent had transferred a vacation home to his adult children but reserved the right either to use

---

[18] Comm'r v. Nathan's Estate, 159 F.2d 546 (7th Cir. 1947).

[19] 1978-2 C.B. 234.

[20] With the introduction of the unlimited marital deduction by the 1981 Act, not only does a donor not benefit by the exclusion of a transfer to his wife although he continues to live in the residence, but in fact this may be a disadvantage. By excluding the property from his estate, his spouse does not get the benefit of a stepped-up basis for the property, which, because of the unlimited marital deduction, would not have been taxed in her estate in any event.

[21] 1979-1 C.B. 305.

or to rent the property for one month of each summer, 13.3 percent of the total value of the property (i.e., the percentage of annual rental value he retained) was includable in his gross estate under Section 2036(a)(1).

¶ 12.07 Use of Trust to Discharge Transferor's Obligations

[1] Support Obligations

If a grantor creates an otherwise irrevocable trust, appoints independent trustees, and provides in the trust agreement that the income or corpus is to be used to pay for the support of the beneficiaries who are his dependents, or to satisfy any other legal obligations of the grantor, the trust will be included in his gross estate under Section 2036 of the Code.[22] On the other hand, if the trustee's power to apply income or corpus in discharge of this obligation is merely discretionary, the trust would not be includable in the transferor's estate.[23] For example, in *Estate of Sessoms*,[24] where the trust provided that the income could be used by the wife for her and their children's maintenance, the trust was nevertheless not included in the transferor decedent's estate since he could not require that it be used for such purpose.

Similarly, in *Estate of Mitchell v. Commissioner*,[25] an irrevocable trust created by a decedent, which provided the trustee, decedent's son, with discretionary power to pay trust income and corpus for the support of decedent's wife, was not included in decedent's estate. The court found that the decedent's wife could not compel a distribution for her support under state law.

In *Townsend v. Thompson*,[26] decedent was the trustee of two identical trusts he had created for the benefit of his two minor sons until they each reached age 25. He retained the power to pay income to the

---

[22] Helvering v. Mercantile-Commerce Bank & Trust Co., 111 F.2d 224 (8th Cir.), cert. denied, 310 U.S. 654 (1940); First Nat'l Bank of Montgomery v. U.S., 211 F. Supp. 403 (D. Ala. 1962).

[23] In Estate of Barad v. Comm'r, 13 T.C.M. 223 (1954), the court held that where the decedent was not a trustee and the trustees alone could in their discretion determine whether the income from a trust for support and maintenance of decedent's minor son should be used for such support while the child was a minor, the trust was not includable in the decedent's estate.

[24] 8 T.C.M. 1056 (1949).

[25] 55 T.C. 576 (1970).

[26] 50-2 U.S.T.C. ¶ 10,780 (D. Ark. 1950).

beneficiary or his legal guardian, or to spend it for the education and maintenance of the boys while they were minors. Decedent died when only one of the sons had reached age 21. Only the trust for the benefit of that son was excluded from the decedent's gross estate.

In *Richards v. Commissioner*,[27] assets of a trust, which provided that income be used for the support of a beneficiary who was a legal dependent of the grantor, were included in the grantor's estate even though the assets had not in fact been producing income. In *Estate of Gokey v. Commissioner*,[28] a father created a trust that provided that the trustee, his wife, should use part or all of the income for the support, care, education, and welfare of his minor child. He died while the child was still a minor. The court held that the trust was not discretionary. The income had to be used for the support of the decedent's child, and, therefore, the trust was includable in the father's estate.

The above cases illustrate the importance of careful drafting and planning in creating an irrevocable trust. Where the beneficiaries of a trust are individuals whom the transferor has a legal obligation to support, he should be careful not to use any language including the word "support" unless he has absolutely determined that he wishes to require use of funds for support. For example, even if the grantor's only intent was that trust funds be used to pay for his son's entertainment, the use of "support" language will cause the trust to be included in his estate. Any language that directly or implicitly mandates that the trust be used to satisfy the transferor's legal obligation should be avoided, if this is not the grantor's intent, in order to avoid unnecessary estate taxes.

[2] Obligations Other Than Support

The answer to the question of whether a trust created by a grantor that provides that income is to be used to pay for the grantor's child's college education should be included in the grantor's estate depends on whether the use of such funds in this manner constitutes support.

In *Morrill v. United States*,[29] the district court held that when the colleges attended by the grantor's children sent bills to the grantor, they expected he would pay them. He, in effect, was considered to have assumed a contractual obligation. To the extent that trust funds were

---

[27] 375 F.2d 997 (10th Cir. 1967).
[28] 72 T.C. 721 (1979).
[29] 228 F. Supp. 734 (D. Me. 1964).

used to discharge this contractual tuition obligation, the trust income was held to be taxable to the grantor. The court did not reach the support issue.

In *Wyche v. United States*,[30] the court held that a trust that provided that the income was to be used to pay for the private school and certain dancing and music lessons for the grantor's children was not taxable to the grantor. The court determined that the grantor had no legal obligation to provide private school education, music lessons, or dancing lessons for his minor children. The case was distinguished from *Morrill* in that the father in *Wyche* had not assumed a contractual obligation. Therefore, if an irrevocable trust is created that provides that income is to be used to pay for a minor child's luxuries, such as travel to Europe, summer camp, tennis, horseback riding, music lessons, or private school, it will not be treated as a support trust.

With respect to payments by a trust for a child's college education, the most advisable approach would be to avoid the appearance that the income is being used to pay for college education. For example, instead of the trustee sending the college a check, as was done in *Morrill,* the monies should instead be paid to the trust beneficiaries without any stipulation that it must be used to pay tuition. The monies, of course, in fact can be so used by the beneficiary child to pay accumulated tuition bills. By following this approach, there is less of an indication that the trust monies are being used to pay for the child's college education, especially if the child has other assets that could have been used as a source of payment of the college tuition. In summary, any irrevocable trust created to reduce income taxes or estate taxes on post-transfer appreciation should be planned carefully to insure that the Service cannot take the position that under the trust instrument income is to be used to discharge the grantor's legal obligation of support.

¶ 12.08 Tax Consequences Affected by Identity of the Trustee

[1] Transferor or Party Controlled by Transferor As Trustee

If the trust instrument provides the trustee with discretion, with respect to either income or corpus, to do the following: name or change

---

[30] 749 C.C.H. ¶ 7911 (Ct. Cl. Commissioner's Report 1974).

¶ 12.08[1] ESTATE PLANNING 12-18

beneficiaries; change their shares of income or principal; decide whether income should be distributed immediately or accumulated and added to trust principal;[31] apply "sprinkling power" to determine which beneficiaries are to receive income;[32] or direct invasion of principal other than by following fixed and ascertainable standards[33]; or vote shares of stock in a controlled corporation transferred after June 22, 1976,[34] then the trust or a portion thereof will be included in the grantor's estate if he is a trustee or co-trustee who can exercise any of these powers, or if he retains the power to direct the trustee as to how such powers should be exercised.

Where the trustee's power to exercise his discretion is limited to applying funds for support, maintenance, comfort, welfare, education, care, necessity, illness, emergency and accident, the courts have generally held that the power is limited by an ascertainable standard.[35] Where

---

[31] In U.S. v. O'Malley, 383 U.S. 627 (1966), the Supreme Court ruled that a grantor's power, as co-trustee, to distribute or accumulate and add trust income to principal caused the value of the trust property and the accumulated income therefrom, although not part of the property originally transferred to the irrevocable trusts, to be included in his gross estate at death. The grantor's power as trustee to deny the income beneficiaries the immediate enjoyment of trust income was held to be a retention of power to designate the persons who would enjoy the income.

[32] Estate of McManus v. Comm'r, 172 F.2d 697 (6th Cir.), cert. denied, 337 U.S. 938 (1949).

[33] For example, a limitation on the grantor trustee's power to invade trust corpus for the income beneficiary's "comfortable care, maintenance and support" was considered to be an ascertainable standard. DeLancey v. U.S., 264 F. Supp. 904, 907 (D. Ark. 1967). Similarly, in Estate of Budd v. Comm'r, 49 T.C. 468, 469 (1968), the decedent's power as trustee to invade trust principal for the benefit of the income beneficiary to take care of expenses arising "in the event of sickness, accident, misfortune or other emergency," was considered to be limited by an ascertainable standard, and the trust was not includable in his gross estate.

[34] I.R.C. § 2036(b). A controlled corporation is defined as one in which the decedent and certain members of his family owned at least 20 percent of the total combined voting power of all classes of stock at any time after the transfer of the property within three years of the decedent's death. The constructive ownership rules of Section 318 of the Code apply in determining whether a corporation is controlled. Under Section 318, an individual is considered to constructively own stock owned directly or indirectly by his spouse, children, grandchildren, and parents, a proportionate part of a partnership or trust of which he is a beneficiary or member, and stock held by a corporation of which he is a 50-percent owner.

[35] See note 32, supra. See also State St. Trust Co. v. U.S., 263 F.2d 635 (1st Cir. 1959); Estate of Ford v. Comm'r, 53 T.C. 114 (1969), aff'd, 450 F.2d 878 (2d Cir. 1971); Merchant's Nat'l Bank v. Comm'r, 320 U.S. 256 (1943); Berry v. Kuhl,

the trustee is given discretion to use trust funds for the "best interests,"[36] "happiness,"[37] "benefit,"[38] or "pleasure or desire"[39] of the beneficiaries, the courts have held that there is no ascertainable standard, and the trust will be included in the grantor's estate if he retained such powers as trustee or otherwise.

The grantor's reserved power will result in inclusion in his gross estate, even if additional action by some other person is required to make the exercise effective.[40] For example, even if there are three trustees and a majority of the trustees are necessary to exercise any of the prescribed powers, nevertheless the trust is included in the grantor trustee's estate.[41] It is also immaterial whether the grantor retains any of the above prescribed powers as trustee or otherwise.[42]

[2] Power to Remove or Appoint Successor Trustees

Even if the decedent is not a trustee and under the trust instrument he does not specifically retain any of the discretionary powers described in Section 2036 or Section 2038, the entire trust would nevertheless be includable in his gross estate if the trustee was given such powers and the decedent had an unrestricted power to remove trustees and appoint himself as trustee. By virtue of his power of removal, he is considered to have the powers of the trustee.[43] Furthermore, even if the grantor

---

174 F.2d 565 (7th Cir. 1949); Leopold v. U.S., 72-1 U.S.T.C. ¶ 12,837 (C.D. Cal. 1972), aff'd, 510 F.2d 617 (9th Cir. 1975). However, a power to use funds for support will result in includability if the grantor can discharge a legal obligation through the use of such power. See discussion of discharge of support obligation at ¶ 12.07.

[36] See, e.g., Estate of Yawkey v. Comm'r, 12 T.C. 1164 (1949); Biscoe v. U.S., 148 F. Supp. 224 (D. Mass. 1957); Struthers v. Kelm, 218 F.2d 810 (8th Cir. 1955); Estate of Gleason v. Comm'r, 24 T.C.M. 1630 (1965).

[37] See, e.g., Estate of Boardman v. Comm'r, 20 T.C. 871 (1953).

[38] See, e.g., Estate of O'Connor v. Comm'r, 54 T.C. 969 (1970).

[39] See, e.g., Henslee v. Union Planters Nat'l Bank & Trust Co., 335 U.S. 595 (1949).

[40] Crile v. U.S., 76-2 U.S.T.C. ¶ 13,161 (Ct. Cl. 1976).

[41] Estate of Yawkey v. Comm'r, 12 T.C. 1164 (1949); DuCharme's Estate v. Comm'r, 164 F.2d 959 (6th Cir. 1947), modified, 169 F.2d 76 (6th Cir. 1948).

[42] I.R.C. § 2038(a)(1); Treas. Reg. § 20.2036-1(b)(3)(ii). See Estate of Carpenter v. U.S., 80-1 U.S.T.C. ¶ 13,339 (W.D. Wis. 1980).

[43] Treas. Reg. § 20.2038-1(a)(3). In Rev. Rul. 73-21, 1973-1 C.B. 405, the I.R.S. held that a trust in which the trustees had power to pay or accumulate income was includable where the grantor retained the right to name himself trustee should the original trustee be unable to serve by reason of death,

cannot appoint himself as trustee, if he can, without limit and in any event, remove a trustee and appoint a successor trustee, the trust will be includable in his estate. The Service has ruled in Rev. Rul 79-353 that even the power to change corporate trustees was sufficient to render the corpus includable.[44] The theory is that the retention of such power would assure the grantor that whatever changes he wanted made with respect to the disposition of the trust property would be made by the current corporate trustee, since it would be concerned that the grantor would exercise his power to change corporate trustees until he finds one willing to accede to his wishes.

In *First National Bank of Denver v. United States*,[45] the Tenth Circuit rejected the Service position that a trust that gave the trustees power to distribute corpus to the decedent should be included in the decedent's estate under Section 2041 as a power of appointment where the decedent who was the life beneficiary also had the power to name an individual, including himself, as trustee. The court interpreted the trust as providing only the decedent with a power to change corporate trustees, which it held does not cause inclusion under Section 2041. The Service, in *First National Bank of Denver*, did not argue that even a power to substitute corporate trustees should be construed as a general power of appointment. The failure of the Service to make such an argument and the court's clear holding that such power does not constitute a power of appointment are strong indications that in the analogous situation under Section 2036 and Section 2038, where the grantor retains the power to change corporate trustees, the trust should not be included in his estate. It is further arguable that the Service's position is untenable in view of the statutory provisions in Section 2036 and Section 2038, which require that the proscribed powers are those exercisable by the decedent "alone... or in conjunction with any other person," which would imply that the mere power to change corporate trustees should not result in includability. However, until the Service revokes Rev. Rul. 79-353, not only should the grantor not be a trustee, but he also should not retain the power to change corporate trustees, unless such power is limited to situations in which the original trustee resigns or is removed by judicial process.[46]

---

resignation, or incapacity. See also Estate of Farrel v. U.S. 553 F.2d 637 (Ct. Cl. 1977).

[44] 1979-2 C.B. 325.

[45] 648 F.2d 1286 (10th Cir. 1981).

[46] In Rev. Rul. 77-182, 1977-1 C.B. 273, the I.R.S. held that trust property was not includable in a decedent's gross estate where his power to appoint a

[3] Third Party as Trustee

If the grantor is not a trustee and does not retain the power to change trustees, then the trustee's power to change beneficial interests in the trust in the manner discussed above will not result in inclusion of the trust property in the grantor's gross estate, even if the trustee not only does not have an adverse interest to the grantor but in fact is subservient to the grantor. Therefore, a grantor could conceivably retain control over who will enjoy the beneficial interests of the irrevocable trust he creates by appointing an individual, attorney, or corporate trustee who he is confident will adhere to his wishes and direction. This "control," however, cannot be written into the trust instrument.

[4] Beneficiary as Trustee

As discussed above, if certain powers affecting beneficial enjoyment are retained, serious adverse consequences may result if the grantor is trustee. Since it is inadvisable for the grantor to be a trustee, who in fact should the trustee be? Can or should the beneficiaries be named as trustees? Suppose *A* creates a trust for his son; can his son, the sole income beneficiary, be the trustee? Under state law there generally is a prohibition against the sole beneficiary being the sole trustee. If there are two beneficiaries and they are both named as trustees, then there will be no problem under state law, since each of them owes a fiduciary obligation not only to himself but also to the other income beneficiary. However, upon the death of one of the beneficiaries, the trust will generally terminate. In addition, under Section 678, when the beneficiary as trustee has the power exercisable solely by himself to vest the corpus or the income therefrom in himself, he will be treated as the owner of the trust and will be taxed on all trust income. It is therefore inadvisable for a beneficiary to be the sole trustee.[47]

---

successor corporate trustee could arise only if the current trustee were to resign or be removed by judicial process. This was held not to be "a power that, in effect could have endowed the decedent with the trustee's discretionary power."

[47] Even if the income beneficiary is co-trustee with an outsider, there still may be adverse tax consequences in certain situations. For example, suppose the trust provides that the trustees, a son and an outsider, can distribute the income among a group that includes the son and his descendants. If the trustees have not paid out all the income on hand at the end of the year, the balance on hand will go to the son. The son, by abstaining or by veto power, can refuse to agree with the outside trustee on making payments. As a result, the income will pass to him. Therefore, under Section 678, the son has a power exercisable solely by himself to vest the income in himself. He will therefore be taxed on that trust income.

There are also adverse estate tax consequences from naming the beneficiary as trustee. If the trustees are given the right to invade principal, then the beneficiary as trustee has the power to invade principal for his benefit and, as a result, the trust will be included in his estate under Section 2041 as a general power of appointment. Even if the trustee is not a beneficiary but his child or spouse whom he has a legal obligation to support is a beneficiary, the Service may take the position that the trustee should be deemed to hold a general power of appointment under Section 2041 because his position as trustee affords him the opportunity to use trust assets to satisfy his support obligation.

It is often an express desire of the grantor that the beneficiary be a trustee. For example, in creating a trust for his son, the grantor may want the son to be able to participate in the management and investment of the trust so that he will develop a sense of responsibility and not feel that he is being coddled or treated as an incompetent. However, the grantor does not want the trust assets included in the beneficiary's estate. The technique that should be used to achieve these objectives is to appoint the beneficiary and another individual or corporation as co-trustees, and to provide that the nonbeneficiary trustee exclusively will exercise all of the discretionary powers such as payment of income or principal.

The grantor will then have to decide whether he wishes his wife, son, daughter, or whomever the beneficiaries of the trust are, to be dependent on an outsider trustee for income of the trust. He may decide that in lieu of creating a sprinkling trust, which provides the trustee with discretion as to which beneficiaries will receive income, it may be advisable to mandate that specific amounts of income must be distributed to each of the beneficiaries. With respect to principal, the grantor may decide to give the trustee discretion limited by an ascertainable standard, in which case the beneficiary can be a trustee. However, if the trustees will be given a general power of appointment with respect to principal, the beneficiaries should not be named trustees.

¶ 12.09 Transferor's Retention of Administrative Powers

If the powers the trust instrument provides the trustee are purely administrative, and if none of the powers discussed above that could directly affect the distribution of trust benefits are granted the trustee, then the fact that the grantor is trustee or can change trustees will not cause the trust property to be included in his gross estate.

The transferor as trustee, by retaining certain administrative and managerial powers, can, in effect, retain the right to designate the persons, i.e., income or principal beneficiaries, who will enjoy the trust. For example, the grantor-trustee can retain the power to allocate receipts to principal or income,[48] to determine investment policy,[49] or to take deductions for depreciation and amortization. These powers may not seem important but in fact could have a serious impact on the benefits of the income beneficiary. The trustee can tell the beneficiary that he will receive no income for a particular period because all receipts, dividends, and the like, were allocated to principal, or all assets were invested in non-income-producing property. The Service has argued that such powers are analogous to the right to accumulate or distribute and add trust income to trust principal, which was held by the Supreme Court in *United States v. O'Malley*[50] to result in inclusion of the trust and accumulated income in the grantor trustee's estate. The courts, however, have uniformly rejected this position.

In *State Street Trust Co. v. United States*,[51] the Service was able to win a temporary victory. The First Circuit held that the bundle of administrative powers retained by the trustee in conjunction with an exculpatory clause included in the trust instrument gave the trustees great latitude and removed them from the jurisdiction of a state court's supervision, which otherwise would assure that they were not acting arbitrarily or breaching their fiduciary obligation.

However, in *Old Colony Trust Co. v. United States*,[52] the First Circuit later reversed its position. The court held that despite the exculpatory clause in the trust, Massachusetts law protects the interest of all the beneficiaries, and that trustees are subject to the supervision of the state court in exercising their administrative powers. The court then stated that "we hold that no aggregation of purely administrative

---

[48] Estate of Peters v. Comm'r, 23 T.C.M. 994 (1964).

[49] U.S. v. Powell, 307 F.2d 821 (10th Cir. 1962). In Estate of Budd v. Comm'r, 49 T.C. 468 (1968), the administrative powers retained by the decedent trustee, including the right to invest in "nonlegal" investments, to classify receipts between income and principal, and to sell or purchase securities without accounting for any profits that might be realized on the transaction, did not result in the trust being included in his estate.

[50] 383 U.S. 627 (1966).

[51] 263 F.2d 635 (1st Cir. 1959).

[52] 423 F.2d 601 (1st Cir. 1970).

powers can meet the government's amorphous test of sufficient dominion and control so as to be equated with ownership."[53] Therefore, on the basis of case law precedent, a retention by the grantor of administrative powers alone will not cause a trust to be included in his estate, since as trustee he has a fiduciary duty to income beneficiaries and remaindermen under state law. However, as a practical matter it is nonetheless inadvisable for the grantor to act as trustee, unless the trustee's powers are clearly only administrative.

If possible, the grantor should consider not acting as trustee in order to preclude any possible argument by the Service that his being a trustee enabled him to designate who would enjoy the property or income of the trust, or to alter, amend, or revoke the trust.[54] This is especially so if the grantor can better achieve his objectives of retained control through the appointment of a cooperative party, such as a spouse or friend, as trustee. Since such outside subservient trustee can be granted not only administrative but also discretionary powers that can affect beneficial enjoyment, the grantor, as a practical matter, may have more control over the trust property than he would have had if he himself were the trustee with only retained administrative powers.

¶ 12.10 Transferor's Retention of Power to Alter, Amend, Revoke, or Terminate Trusts

[1] Includability in Transferor's Estate

Under Section 2038, if at the time of the transferor's death the enjoyment of the trust property was "subject to any change through the exercise of a power by the decedent alone or in conjunction with any other person to alter, amend, revoke or terminate," then it is includable under Section 2038 of the Code. The power that will result in inclusion under Section 2038 may have been retained at the time of the transfer or may have come into existence at a later date. A power in the grantor that relates only to the trust remainder would be included in his gross estate under Section 2038, although it may not otherwise have been includable under Section 2036.

The types of powers that result in includability under Section 2038 include:

---

[53] Id. at 603.

[54] See "Audit Techniques Handbook for Estate Tax Examiners," I.R.M. 4350 § (11)36, where the I.R.S. directs its examiners to carefully scrutinize retained administrative powers to determine if in fact they may be substantive.

(1) A power to change beneficiaries or vary the amounts distributable to income or corpus beneficiaries;

(2) Power to affect the interest of beneficiaries through control and management of trust corpus other than through the exercise of purely administrative powers;[55]

(3) Power to revoke or terminate the trust, whether such power results in return of the trust property to the grantor or acceleration of enjoyment by the remaindermen who were persons other than the income beneficiaries;

(4) Power to change or revoke a trust by will [56] or under state law;[57]

(5) Power to alter, amend, revoke, or terminate a trust created by another for whose benefit decedent created a similar reciprocal trust.

[2] Permissible Retained Powers

The trust may contain certain powers that will not result in taxability to the grantor under Section 2038. These powers include:

(1) A power held by decedent that was contingent on the happening of an event that did not yet occur at the time of his death. However, such retained power may result in inclusion under Section 2036.

For example, A transfers property in trust with income to B for life, remainder to B's surviving children. A retained the right to designate who should receive the remainder in the event B died without issue while A was still alive. If A in fact predeceased, the property would not be includable in his estate under Section 2038 since he had no retained power at the time of his death.[58] However, under Section 2036 the trust would be includable since A retained the right to designate the "persons who shall possess or enjoy the property...for...[a] period not ascertainable without reference to his death."[59]

In *Estate of Farrel v. United States*,[60] the trustees were given the power to vary beneficial interests. The decedent was not a trustee. However, the decedent reserved the right to fill vacancies and, under

---

[55] Schneider v. Comm'r, 35 B.T.A. 183 (1936).

[56] Estate of Cooper v. Comm'r, 7 T.C. 1236 (1946).

[57] Estate of Hill v. Comm'r, 64 T.C. 867 (1975).

[58] Treas. Reg. § 20.2038-1(b). Bank of New York v. U.S., 174 F. Supp. 911 (S.D.N.Y. 1957).

[59] Treas. Reg. § 20.2036-1(b)(3).

[60] 553 F.2d 637 (Ct. Cl. 1977).

state law, could appoint herself trustee. Since the contingent right to fill trustee vacancies had not arisen at the time of her death, the trust was not includable under Section 2038 by attributing the trustee's power to vary beneficial interests to the decedent. However, the court held that this trust was includable under Section 2036(a)(2), since the transferor retained a significant right at the time of the transfer and under Section 2036(a)(2) the moment of death is not exclusively important;

(2) Powers in persons other than the transferor to revoke the transfer or to return part of it to the transferor. However, such transfers may be taxed under Section 2037 as a transfer conditioned on survivorship;[61]

(3) Administrative powers that do not affect the rights of beneficiaries,[62] such as the right to allocate receipts to income or corpus, to determine investment policy for trust assets,[63] or to direct the issuance of voting proxies;[64] as discussed with respect to Section 2036, these powers taken together may in fact enable the grantor to have a significant impact on the relative rights of income and corpus beneficiaries;[65]

(4) Power over trusts not created by the decedent or with his funds[66] and not supported by similar reciprocal trusts created by decedent for others;[67]

(5) Power to add to corpus;[68] and

(6) A power reserved with respect to the property, which is subject in its exercise to a definite external standard such as "support, education, maintenance and general welfare."[69]

---

[61] See discussion at ¶ 12.11.

[62] U.S. v. Winchell, 289 F.2d 212 (9th Cir. 1961).

[63] Estate of Peters v. Comm'r, 23 T.C.M. 994 (1964).

[64] Estate of Downe v. Comm'r, 2 T.C. 967 (1943).

[65] See Old Colony Trust Co. v. U.S., discussed in ¶ 12.09 and note 52 supra.

[66] In Estate of Sinclaire v. Comm'r, 13 T.C. 742 (1949), the decedent gave her father money to create a trust fund that provided that decedent was to have the income for life and the power to appoint the remainder interests. Decedent was held to be the real settlor.

[67] See Estate of Newberry v. Comm'r, 201 F.2d 874 (3d Cir. 1953).

[68] Estate of Johnson v. Comm'r, 2 T.C.M. 299 (1943).

[69] Estate of Pardee v. Comm'r, 49 T.C. 140 (1967); U.S. v. Powell, 307 F.2d 821 (10th Cir. 1962); Leopold v. U.S., 72-1 U.S.T.C. ¶ 17,837 (C.D. Cal. 1972), aff'd, 510 F.2d 617 (9th Cir. 1975). See also similar discussion of ascertainable standard with respect to Section 2036 retained rights at ¶ 12.06.

[3] General Rules

Many of the powers and retained rights that will result in taxability under Section 2038 are taxable under Section 2036. In addition, Section 2038 is similar to Section 2036 in the following respects.

If a power involved is applicable to only a part of a trust, only that part is taxable.[70] If the power has expired, terminated, or been relinquished, the transferor will not be taxed unless the release of the power occurred within three years of his death.[71] If the transfer was made for adequate and full consideration in money or money's worth, it is not taxable. The proportion of trust assets valued at the date of death of the grantor that is taxed is a ratio of the part of the excess in value of the transferred property over the consideration to the total value of the transferred property at the time of the transfer.

A power that permits the grantor to affect the interests of beneficiaries will result in the trust assets being includable in the grantor's estate, even if the grantor cannot personally benefit by the exercise of the power,[72] and regardless of whether it was exercisable by the decedent as grantor or as trustee, alone or in conjunction with trustees, beneficiaries, or outsiders.[73]

¶ 12.11 Transfers Taking Effect at Transferor's Death

[1] Includability in Transferor's Estate

Under Section 2037 of the Code, a transfer by trust or otherwise is includable in the transferor's estate if:

(1) Possession or enjoyment of the property can, through ownership of such interest, be obtained only by surviving the decedent transferor;

(2) The decedent has retained a reversionary interest in the property, which includes a possibility that property transferred may

---

[70] Dravo v. Comm'r, 40 B.T.A. 309 (1939).

[71] Estate of Lloyd v. Comm'r, 47 B.T.A. 349 (1942); Estate of Burney v. Comm'r, 4 T.C. 449 (1944).

[72] Porter v. Comm'r, 288 U.S. 436 (1933).

[73] Struthers v. Kelm, 218 F.2d 810 (8th Cir. 1955); Union Tr. Co. of Pittsburgh v. Driscoll, 138 F.2d 152 (3d Cir. 1943); Estate of Hauptfuhrer v. Comm'r, 9 T.C.M. 974 (1950), aff'd, 195 F.2d 548 (3d Cir. 1952), cert. denied 344 U.S. 825.

(a) return to him or his estate or (b) be subject to a power of disposition by him; and

(3) The value of such reversionary interest immediately before the death of the decedent exceeds 5 percent of the value of the entire property. This value is determined (without regard to the decedent's death) by the use of actuarial tables and mortality tables prescribed in the Treasury Regulations.[74]

Before a transfer will be included, each of the above provisions must apply. The following example illustrates the type of transfer that would result in includability under Section 2037.

The decedent transfers property in trust with the income payable to his wife for life with the remainder payable to the decedent or, if he is not living at his wife's death, to his son or his estate. The son cannot obtain possession or enjoyment of the property without surviving the decedent. Therefore, if the decedent's reversionary interest immediately before his death exceeded 5 percent of the value of the property, the value of the property less the value of the wife's outstanding life estate is includable in the decedent's estate.[75]

The amount includable in the decedent-transferor's estate, if Section 2037 applies, is the value of the property transferred less any outstanding preceding interests in persons other than the transferor. Therefore, in the above example, the amount includable would be reduced by the wife's outstanding life estate.

[2] Avoiding Application of Section 2037

Since there are a number of conditions that must be present before a transfer will be considered includable under Section 2037, it is often possible for a grantor to achieve his transfer objectives without having the trust property, or at least a portion of it, included in his gross estate.

For example, *G* wishes to create a trust to provide for the needs of his children. However, during his lifetime he does not wish to have any monies expended by the trust. He can accomplish this objective by creating a trust that provides that income is to be accumulated for his life, and, at his death, principal and accumulated income is to be paid to his son if living, otherwise to *A* or *A*'s estate. Since he retained no reversionary interest in the property, no part of the property is includ-

---

[74] Treas. Reg. § 20.2031-10(f). These tables sometimes produce distorted results because they are based on a 6 percent interest return.

[75] Treas. Reg. § 20.2037-1(e), Ex. 3.

able in his gross estate, even though possession or enjoyment of the property could be obtained by the issue only by surviving the decedent.[76]

If, on the other hand, G did not wish to provide for an alternative disposition in the event of his son's prior death, then if the value of his reversionary interest that would arise by operation of law exceeded 5 percent of the value of the property at the time of his death, the entire trust would be includable in his gross estate. Even without making an alternative disposition, G could avoid includability of such trust in his estate if:

(1) He gives another person, for example his daughter, the unrestricted power to alter, amend, or revoke the trust. Assume that the daughter survived the decedent but did not, in fact, exercise her power during the decedent's lifetime. Since possession or enjoyment of the property could have been obtained by the daughter during the decedent's lifetime by the exercise of such general power of appointment, which was, in fact, exercisable immediately before the decedent's death, no part of the property will be includable in the decedent's estate;[77] or

(2) He provides that after a specified period of time, no less than his life expectancy at the time of the transfer, e.g., 15 years, the principal and accumulated income is to be paid to his son if then surviving. Assume that the decedent does in fact die before the expiration of the 15-year period. Since the son will be considered to have been able to possess or enjoy the property without surviving the decedent, the property will not be includable in the decedent's estate.[78]

If possession or enjoyment of the property is not conditioned on surviving the decedent, the property transferred will not be includable

---

[76] Id., Ex. 2. The problem with this plan, however, is that although there is no estate tax includability, gifts to such a trust will not be eligible for the $10,000 annual exclusion ($20,000 if spouse joins) since it is a gift of a future interest. In addition, the beneficiaries may be subject to additional income tax as a result of the accumulation throwback rules.

[77] I.R.C. § 2037; Treas. Reg. § 20.2037-1(e), Ex. 6. A grantor may wish to create a trust for each of his children giving each a general power of appointment over the other's trust in order to avoid application of Section 2037 to each trust.

[78] Treas. Reg. § 20. 2037-1(b). If, on the other hand, the income was to be accumulated for a period of 15 years or until the decedent's prior death, and the decedent's life expectancy at the time of this transfer was only 14 years, the son will not be conisdered able to possess or enjoy the property without surviving the decedent.

under Section 2037 even if the decedent retains a reversionary interest. For example, the decedent transferred property in trust with the income payable to his wife for life and, at her death, remainder passes to the decedent's then-surviving issue or, if none, to the decedent or his estate. Since each beneficiary can possess or enjoy the property without surviving the decedent, no part of the property is includable in the decedent's estate under Section 2037, regardless of the value of the decedent's reversionary interest. Therefore, by following the above procedure, a grantor who is certain of whom he wishes to enjoy the property he is transferring, at a minimal estate tax cost (i.e., the value of the reversionary interest), can provide that in the unlikely event that all his intended beneficiaries predecease him the trust property should be returned to him without causing the transferred property to be included in his estate under Section 2037. However, under Section 2033 of the Code, the value of the reversionary interest retained by the grantor (which generally should not be substantial) will be includable in his gross estate.

If, however, he is certain that he wishes particular beneficiaries to receive the trust property in all events but would prefer that one particular beneficiary not receive any of the property unless the grantor predeceases, he still will be able to minimize the estate tax exposure, since only the value of *that* individual's reversionary interest would be included in the grantor's estate.[79]

¶ 12.12 Advantages and Disadvantages of Irrevocably Transferring Property Out of One's Estate

Following the Tax Reform Act of 1976, gifts and estates are taxed at the same uniform rates and, in determining the tax bracket of an estate, all post-1976 taxable gifts [80] (other than gifts that are included in the gross estate of the decedent) are considered at their date of gift values.[81] Therefore, despite the changes made by the 1981 Act limiting the includability of transfers made within three years of death, the major federal estate tax savings achieved by the transfer of cash or nonappreciating property is the exclusion of the income earned on investment of

---

[79] Treas. Reg. § 20.2037-1(e), Ex. 4.

[80] Taxable gifts do not include gifts that were in amounts less than the applicable annual exclusion or otherwise not taxable as gifts, e.g., gifts qualifying for charitable or marital deductions.

[81] I.R.C. § 2001(b)(1)(B).

such property from a decedent's estate. Since there are other means of gifting such income (e.g., through the use of a grantor trust or nonrecourse loans), the transfer of cash or nonappreciating property to an irrevocable trust will, in most situations, produce little or no additional federal tax advantages.

However, lifetime transfers of even nonappreciating property to an irrevocable trust may produce a savings of state inheritance tax. Some states (e.g., New Jersey) impose an inheritance tax but have no gift tax. However, they may often apply a three-year contemplation of death rule similar to the pre-1982 federal law so that gifts made within three years of death are subject to state inheritance tax. Other states (e.g., New York) have both an estate tax and a gift tax. However, the gift tax rates are generally lower than the estate tax rates and pre-death gifts are not included in calculating the tax bracket of the estate. Therefore, the tax law in the state of residence of the grantor should be carefully examined to determine if significant state tax savings can be generated by lifetime transfers. In making any such determination, it may be significant to consider the federal tax consequences flowing from state gift, inheritance, or estate taxes paid. There is no gross-up of an estate for state gift taxes paid. The benefit of reducing one's estate by state gift taxes paid prior to death may be offset by the absence of a gift tax credit similar to the state death tax credit that can be taken on the federal estate tax return. However, often the state inheritance or estate taxes actually paid are far in excess of the credit provided against federal taxes. Therefore, a reduction in the size of the estate for state death tax purposes, as a result of lifetime transfers, will generally not reduce the federal death tax credit otherwise available. Therefore, lifetime transfers of even nonappreciating property can be used as a means of reducing state transfer taxes, while also reducing the size of the transferor's estate for federal estate tax purposes by the amount of state gift taxes paid.

Significant federal estate tax savings can be achieved with respect to irrevocable transfers of property that is expected to appreciate in value. Previously, transfers brought into the gross estate under the three-year rule were included in the gross estate at their date-of-death values (or alternative valuation date), thereby subjecting any appreciation in value of the transferred property between the date of gift and the date of death to estate taxation. As a result of the 1981 Act, which no longer automatically includes in the estate those transfers made within three years of death, the appreciation in the value of such transferred property will escape both gift and estate taxes.

However, a disadvantage of having the transfers excluded from the gross estate is the loss of the opportunity to achieve a step-up in basis to the estate tax value for income tax purposes.[82] Therefore, although no estate tax may be payable on the post-gift appreciation on such gifts, an income tax liability may result upon subsequent disposition of the gifted property due to the fact that the basis is not stepped-up for income tax purposes. As a result, transfers of potentially appreciating property are not advisable for tax purposes, unless it is anticipated that the transferor's estate will be subject to estate tax at an effective rate of at least the potential future capital gain tax liability, which may be as high as 20 percent.[83]

For example, in 1983 G transfers securities worth $260,000 into an irrevocable trust for the benefit of A. This results in a taxable gift of $250,000 ($260,000 less annual exclusion), which is covered by G's unified credit. G dies in 1984 when the securities are worth $750,000. Under Section 2035(d) the securities will not be included in G's gross estate as a transfer within three years of death. The securities will, however, be included at their $250,000 (after annual exclusion) date-of-gift value as an adjusted taxable gift for purposes of computing the estate tax on G's estate. The $500,000 appreciation will escape both gift and estate taxation. However, a subsequent sale of the securities for $750,000 will result in a capital gain of $500,000 subject to a maximum tax of 20 percent. Nevertheless, even if this were the sole asset includable in the transferor's estate, there would be a net tax savings as a result of the estate's being in a higher than 32 percent tax bracket for the amounts in excess of the unified credit equivalent available in 1984. But if the transferor had lived until 1987 when the exemption equivalent of the unified credit is $600,000, and these securities were the sole asset of his estate, there would be a net tax loss resulting from the transfer, since the estate tax savings on the appreciation excluded from the estate would be less than the potential income tax exposure on sale of the asset, which will not have a stepped-up basis.

If the property the grantor is considering transferring is real estate,

---

[82] I.R.C. § 1014(a).

[83] Assuming a maximum tax bracket of 50 percent, at which the capital gain, less the 60 percent capital gain deduction under Section 1202, is taxed. However, the 60 percent capital gain deduction is a tax preference item subject to alternative minimum tax which for certain presons with large capital gains or other tax preference items, e.g., adjusted itemized deductions in a particular year, may cause increased tax exposure. See I.R.C. § 55.

machinery, or other depreciable property to be used in a trade or business, in most situations it would be to the advantage of the beneficiaries that the property be includable in the grantor's estate so that they can achieve a stepped-up basis with concomitant additional depreciation deduction that can be used to offset ordinary income of the beneficiaries who are likely to be in higher tax brackets for income tax purposes than the estate is for estate tax purposes.

CHAPTER 13

Estate Taxation of Life Insurance

		Page
¶ 13.01	Significance of Life Insurance to the Estate	13-2
	[1] Liquidity	13-2
	[2] Building the Estate	13-3
	[3] Insurance for a Specific Purpose	13-3
¶ 13.02	General Principles of Estate Taxation of Life Insurance	13-4
	[1] Receivable by or for the Benefit of the Estate	13-4
	[2] Receivable by Other Beneficiaries	13-5
	[a] Incidents of Ownership in General	13-5
	[b] Incidents of Ownership Where Insured Is Trustee	13-6
	[c] Incidents of Ownership Where Policy Owned by Corporation	13-7
	[d] Controversy Regarding Incidents of Ownership	13-8
¶ 13.03	Removal of Life Insurance Proceeds from Decedent's Taxable Estate	13-11
	[1] In General	13-11
	[2] Gift Tax Consequences of Transfer of Life Insurance	13-11
	[3] Direct Transfer vs. Transfer in Trust	13-13
	[a] Direct Transfer to Other Individuals	13-13
	[b] Transfer in Trust	13-15
	[4] Gifts of Group Term Life Insurance	13-20
	[a] Requirements for an Effective Assignment	13-20
	[b] Incidents-of-Ownership Problems	13-20
	[c] Premium Payments as Gifts	13-21
¶ 13.04	Transfers of Life Insurance as Gifts in Contemplation of Death	13-22
	[1] Position of the Internal Revenue Service	13-23
	[2] Planning to Avoid Gifts in Contemplation of Death	13-26
¶ 13.05	Gifts of Present Interests — The *Crummey* Trust	13-28
	[1] Description of the Problem	13-28
	[2] The *Crummey* Case	13-29
	[3] Particular Problems With *Crummey* Provisions	13-30
	[a] Increase in Annual Exclusion	13-30

	Page
[b] Notice of Demand Provisions	13-31
[c] Length of Withdrawal Period	13-32
[d] Multiple Beneficiaries	13-32
[4] Planning for Use of the *Crummey* Provision	13-34

¶ 13.01 Significance of Life Insurance to the Estate

Because of the prevalence of life insurance as a fringe benefit,[1] it is rare to find a highly compensated individual who does not possess at least some employer-provided insurance. In addition, because of the liquidity provided by life insurance proceeds, as well as its use as an estate building device, it is typical to find that the highly compensated individual possesses a considerable amount of individual life insurance coverage. Before reviewing these estate tax consequences, however, it is well to review the basic purposes that induce the purchase of life insurance by a highly compensated individual.

[1] Liquidity

One of the major benefits of a life insurance policy is the liquid nature of the proceeds. The benefits of a policy are paid in cash and, at the option of the beneficiary, in one lump sum. Thus, life insurance can provide liquidity that is necessary for many estate planning purposes. Life insurance proceeds can be used to pay estate taxes or funeral and administration expenses, or to enable the exercise of valuable stock options or warrants. Life insurance on the life of a corporate executive that is owned by the corporation may enable that corporation to fund a buy-out agreement so as to purchase closely held stock from the executive's estate.

Life insurance may be especially significant if many of the highly compensated individual's investments are of a nonliquid nature. For example, if the individual has substantial investments in real estate, oil and gas, or closely held corporate entities, the estate may not have sufficient liquid assets available to pay estate taxes or administration expenses. In this situation, the presence of life insurance may enable the estate or the beneficiaries to retain valuable investments that otherwise

---

[1] See generally Chapter 6.

might have to be sold at an unfavorable price in order to raise money to pay estate taxes.[2]

[2] Building the Estate

Life insurance policies may also be used as a means of building an estate. This may be of particular significance to a young highly compensated individual who, despite having a considerable amount of earned income, has not yet reached the position of being able to accumulate significant assets. In this situation, additional life insurance may be necessary to protect his family in the event of his untimely death. Thus, life insurance can be used in order to build the estate of that individual to the point at which his family can maintain the standard of living to which they were accustomed by virtue of his highly compensated status. At some future time, as the individual is able to build an estate through various investments, it may be possible to cut back on the level of life insurance coverage.[3]

[3] Insurance for a Specific Purpose

Life insurance may also be purchased by the highly compensated individual for a specific purpose related to the peculiarities of his estate. The individual with a large mortgage or mortgages on his residence may purchase sufficient life insurance to repay the mortgage in the event of his untimely death. As mentioned earlier, corporations may purchase insurance on the lives of its stockholders in order to fund the corporate buy-out agreement. Life insurance may also be maintained as a result of specific contractual requirements in various business contracts, such as when an executive is exceedingly important to a successful venture, or as the result of a separation agreement with a former spouse.

---

[2] In a situation where the decedent owns substantial interests in closely held businesses, the provisions for extended payment of estate taxes provided by Section 6166 may prove beneficial. In order to qualify under this Section, the interest in the closely held business must equal at least 35 percent of the decedent's adjusted gross estate. I.R.C. § 6166(a)(1).

[3] If an individual is purchasing insurance for estate building purposes with a view of dropping it at a later time, it is usually preferable to purchase the cheapest type of term insurance. This will enable coverage during the desired period and the insurance can be dropped as the individual's estate reaches a higher plateau and as the rates for the insurance increase.

¶ 13.02 General Principles of Estate Taxation of Life Insurance

Section 2042 of the Code requires that life insurance on a decedent be included in the decedent's estate if (1) the proceeds of the policy are receivable by or for the benefit of his estate or (2) the proceeds are receivable by other beneficiaries, and the decedent possessed, either alone or in conjunction with others, the incidents of ownership on the policy. Consequently, although this frequently comes as a surprise to many clients who are not aware of the intricacies of the Code, the proceeds of a life insurance policy on the life of a decedent will normally be subject to the federal estate tax unless certain steps are undertaken to avoid the two broad inclusionary rules just mentioned.

[1] Receivable by or for the Benefit of the Estate

The payment of life insurance proceeds directly to the decedent's executor or administrator will make these proceeds includable in the decedent's taxable estate.[4] Similarly, the proceeds will be taxable even if the estate is not directly named as a beneficiary under the terms of the policy if the economic benefits of the policy accrue to the estate. For example, if the proceeds of the policy are receivable by another beneficiary but are subject to a legally binding obligation to pay taxes, debts, or other charges enforceable against the estate, then the amount of the proceeds required for payment in full of such taxes, debts, or charges is includable in the gross estate.[5] Similarly, if the decedent purchased an insurance policy in favor of another person or a corporation as collateral security for a loan or other accommodation, its proceeds are considered to be receivable for the benefit of an estate.[6]

Accordingly, if there is to be any hope of removing life insurance proceeds from the decedent's estate, the estate cannot be named as beneficiary of the policy and another named beneficiary cannot be encumbered with an obligation running in favor of the estate. For example, if the proceeds are made payable to an insurance trust, the trustee of that trust cannot be obligated to pay the decedent's estate taxes or debts. Any transfers made by the trustee of this type must be

---

[4] I.R.C. § 2042.
[5] Treas. Reg. § 20.2042-1(b)(1).
[6] Id.

made as a result of the exercise of the trustee's "voluntary" discretion.[7] If the terms of the trust instrument specifically prohibit the trustee from paying the debts or taxes of the estate, the insurance proceeds clearly would not be includable in the decedent's gross estate.

[2] Receivable by Other Beneficiaries

[a] Incidents of Ownership in General. The decedent's estate will similarly include the proceeds of insurance, which are receivable by other beneficiaries if the decedent retained, at the time of his death, any incidents of ownership in the life insurance policy. As might be expected, the Service has given a relatively broad definition to the term "incidents of ownership."[8] The regulations take the approach that the term has reference to the right of the insured or his estate to the economic benefits of the policy. The regulations state that the possession of *any* of the following powers requires the inclusion of the insurance proceeds in the insured's gross estate.[9] These powers are to:

(1) Change the beneficiary;

(2) Surrender or cancel the policy;

(3) Assign the policy;

(4) Revoke an assignment;

(5) Pledge the policy for a loan;

(6) Obtain from the insurer a loan against the cash surrender value of the policy.

The term "incidents of ownership" also includes a reversionary interest in the policy or its proceeds if the value of this reversionary interest immediately before the death of the decedent exceeded 5 percent of the value of the policy.[10] The terms "reversionary interest" and "incidents

---

[7] This is discussed extensively in the section on insurance trusts. See ¶ 13.03[3][b] supra.

[8] Treas. Reg. § 20.2042-1(c)(2).

[9] Id.

[10] Treas. Reg. § 20.2042-1(c)(3). The term "reversionary interest" includes the possibility that the policy or its proceeds may return to the decedent or his estate and the possibility that the policy or its proceeds may become subject to a power of disposition by him.

of ownership" do not include the possibility, however, that the decedent might receive the policy or its proceeds by inheritance through the estate of another person or as a surviving spouse under a statutory right of election.[11]

[b] Incidents of Ownership Where Insured Is Trustee. The regulations also attempt to expand the definition of ownership in two particular cases. First, they indicate that the decedent is considered to have an incident of ownership in an insurance policy on his life held by a trust if, under the terms of the policy, the decedent, either alone or in conjunction with another person, has the power as trustee or otherwise to change the beneficial ownership in the policy or its proceeds or the time and manner of enjoyment thereof.[12] This particular regulation has been the subject of considerable litigation. In *Estate of Fruehauf v. Commissioner*,[13] the Sixth Circuit held that the mere possession of powers in the nature of incidents of ownership with no beneficial interest in the proceeds does not in and of itself require inclusion of the proceeds in an insured's estate where the powers were held in a fiduciary capacity. Opposite views have been taken by the Fifth Circuit in *Rose v. United States*[14] and *Terriberry v. United States*.[15] The Service follows the views set forth in the regulations and has reaffirmed this in Rev. Rul. 76-261.[16] Consequently, unless an individual resides in the Sixth Circuit, it appears prudent to name someone else as trustee if the use of an insurance trust is contemplated. Even if an individual resides in the jurisdiction where the precedent is favorable, it is always prudent to consider the possibility of future migrancy. Highly compensated individuals are likely to be highly mobile individuals and it is possible that they may move into another jurisdiction after execution of an insurance trust. Although such a trust may contain choice-of-law provisions designed to use the favorable precedent, one can never be certain that these provisions will be controlling.

The amount of litigation on this topic and the fact that the Service has expressed opposition would indicate that the appointment of the

---

[11] Id.
[12] Treas. Reg. § 20.2042-1(c)(4).
[13] 427 F.2d 80 (6th Cir. 1970).
[14] 511 F.2d 259 (5th Cir. 1975).
[15] 517 F.2d 286 (5th Cir. 1975), cert. denied, 424 U.S. 977 (1976).
[16] 1976-2 C.B. 276.

insured as trustee is an invitation to costly litigation. Accordingly, prudence dictates the use of an independent trustee.

[c] Incidents of Ownership Where Policy Owned by Corporation. The second instance where the regulations make a particular effort to expand the meaning of the term incidents of ownership relates to the situation where a life insurance policy is owned by a corporation owned or controlled by the decedent. If the economic benefits of a policy on the decedent's life are reserved to the corporation that the decedent controls, the incidents of ownership in the policy will *not* be attributed to the decedent through his stock ownership of the corporation.[17] These proceeds will, however, be taken into consideration in valuing the stock of the corporation. Thus, for example, the payment of $100,000 of life insurance proceeds to a corporation controlled by the decedent would presumably increase the net worth of that corporation by $100,000 and would be reflected in the value of the stock owned by the decedent at his death. Similarly, this would be the case if the proceeds were payable to a third party for a valid business purpose, such as satisfaction of debt of a corporation.

If any part of the proceeds of the insurance policy are not payable to or for the benefit of the corporation, and are thus not taken into account in valuing the decedent's stockholdings in the corporation, any incidents of ownership held by the corporation will be attributed to the decedent through his stock ownership where the decedent is a sole or controlling stockholder. Consequently, if the decedent was a sole stockholder of a corporation and the corporation owned a policy on his life, the proceeds of which were payable to the decedent's spouse, the incidents of ownership held by the corporation will be attributed to the decedent through his stock ownership and the proceeds will be included in his gross estate under Section 2042. The decedent will not be deemed to be a controlling stockholder of the corporation unless, at the time of his death, he owns stock possessing more than 50 percent of the total combined voting power of the corporation.[18] In the case of group term life insurance under Section 79, the power to surrender or cancel a

---

[17] Treas. Reg. § 20.2042-1(c)(6).

[18] Id. The decedent will be considered to be the owner of only the stock with respect to which legal title was held at the time of death by the decedent, the decedent and another person jointly, and as trustee of a voting trust or any other trust with respect to which the decedent was treated as owner under Subpart E, Part 1, Subchapter J of the Code immediately prior to his death.

policy held by a corporation will not be attributed to any decedent through his stock ownership.

Consequently, in the situation where a decedent is the sole or controlling shareholder of a corporation, the Service will attempt to reach the proceeds of the life insurance policies on his life owned by the corporation either through the valuation of the stock of the corporation or through attribution of incidents of ownership of the policies by virtue of his control of the corporation.

The Tax Court has upheld the validity of the regulations that require the inclusion of insurance proceeds from a policy owned by a corporation in the gross estate of the decedent in the situation where the decedent is a controlling but not the sole shareholder of a corporation. In *Estate of Levy v. Commissioner*,[19] the decedent owned 80.4 percent of the issued and outstanding voting stock of the corporation and all of the issued and outstanding nonvoting stock. The corporation owned two split-dollar insurance policies on the decedent's life, both of which named his widow as beneficiary. The Tax Court upheld the inclusion of the policies in decedent's estate. The Tax Court stated that it saw no distinction between the sole shareholder and a controlling shareholder and noted that in either case the shareholder had the power to effect the disposition of the insurance proceeds. Accordingly, the validity of Treas. Reg. § 20.2042-1(c)(6) was upheld.[20]

[d] Controversy Regarding Incidents of Ownership. The Service has taken an extremely hard line as to when a decedent possesses the incidents of ownership in a life insurance policy with the result being that there has been a substantial amount of litigation on this topic. In general, if a decedent has retained any form of control over the economic consequences of a life insurance policy, the Service has contended that the proceeds thereunder are includable under Section 2042. For example, the proceeds of an employer owned split-dollar life

---

[19] 70 T.C. 873 (1978).

[20] See also Rev. Rul. 76-274, 1976-2 C.B. 278, where the I.R.S. presents certain factual illustrations to set forth its position as to when a corporation controlled by the decedent possessed incidents of ownership in an insurance policy on his life under a split-dollar arrangement. Situation 3 in that ruling was modified by Rev. Rul. 82-145, 1982-31 I.R.B. 7, which held that where the decedent's controlled corporation held at the time of his death the right to borrow against the cash surrender value of the policy, the portion of the policy proceeds payable other than to or for the benefit of the corporation was includable in the decedent's gross estate.

insurance policy were held to be includable in the decedent's gross estate when the owner of the policy could not change the beneficiary without the written consent of the decedent.[21] When a decedent assigned all interest in a life insurance policy to his wife as owner and beneficiary, but retained the power to prevent the change of beneficiary to or assignment of the policy to anyone not having an insurable interest in his life, the Service ruled that he had retained the incidents of ownership in the policy and the proceeds thereunder were includable in his gross estate.[22]

The courts, on the whole, have followed the lead of the Service in broadly defining incidents of ownership. In determining whether the decedent possessed incidents of ownership with respect to a policy, the court said "the relevant question is whether decedent had the capacity to do something to effect the disposition of the proceeds if he had so wanted."[23] The court continued: "The very phrase 'incident of ownership' connotes something partial, minor, or even fractional in its scope. It speaks more of possibility than of probability."[24] The Tax Court has spoken of "fractional" powers that can bring a policy within the gross estate of a decedent.[25] If, however, one of these "fractional" powers is contingent upon an event over which the insured does not have control, that same court has found the policy proceeds not includable.[26]

---

[21] Schwager v. Comm'r, 64 T.C. 781 (1975). See also Rev. Rul. 79-129, 1979-1 C.B. 306, where a decedent assigned a life insurance policy to an irrevocable trust but retained a right to borrow against the cash surrender value of the policy and to receive the proceeds to this same extent. This split-dollar arrangement between the decedent and his own insurance trust was held to be sufficient to include the entire amount of insurance proceeds in the decedent's gross estate.

[22] Rev. Rul. 75-70, 1975-1 C.B. 301. See also Rev. Rul. 76-261, 1976-2 C.B. 276, where a decedent had purchased life insurance and transferred complete ownership to his wife. Upon her death, he became trustee of a residuary trust for the benefit of his children that included the policy as an asset. Under the terms of the trust he could use the loan value of the policy to pay the premiums, elect to receive annual dividends, borrow on the policy, assign or pledge the policy, and determine how the proceeds were to be paid. On this set of facts, the I.R.S. ruled that the decedent possessed sufficient incidents of ownership to require inclusion of the policy proceeds in his estate.

[23] U.S. v. Rhode Island Hosp. Trust Co., 355 F.2d 7, 11 (1st Cir. 1966).

[24] Id. at 10.

[25] Estate of Smead v. Comm'r, 78 T.C. No. 3 (1982).

[26] See Estate of Smith v. Comm'r, 73 T.C. 307 (1979) (could purchase policy in the event the employer stopped paying policy premiums); Estate of Beauregard v. Comm'r, 74 T.C. 603 (1980) acq. 1981-1 C.B. 1 (power to change beneficiaries effectively removed by property settlement and court order).

There are numerous other cases and rulings where the decedent retained one or more incidents of ownership of a policy and the proceeds were held includable in his gross estate.[27] Even in those situations where the Service has lost in litigation, it has still attempted to expand the definition of incidents of ownership as far as possible. For example, the Service unsuccessfully contended that the ability of a decedent to give a trustee investment advice made the proceeds of an insurance policy taxable.[28] Thus, the lesson to be learned is that in an attempted assignment of a life insurance policy to remove the proceeds from an individual's estate, the insured must exercise extreme caution so as not to retain any power that might be construed as an incident of ownership. To retain any such power is surely to invite litigation with uncertain results.

An interesting case on the topic of retention of the incidents of ownership in a life insurance policy is *Estate of Margrave v. Commissioner.*[29] In *Margrave,* the decedent's spouse bought an insurance policy on his life, naming as the beneficiary the trustee of a revocable trust created by the decedent. Under this arrangement, as long as the trustee remained the beneficiary of the insurance policy, the decedent had the power to control the ultimate disposition of the insurance proceeds. On this set of facts, the Tax Court held that the decedent did not possess the incidents of ownership in the policy and similarly did not hold a general power of appointment over the policy or its proceeds. In essence, it was decided that the decedent did not have any incidents of ownership over the policy because his ability to direct the proceeds was only a hope — subject to the policy owner's absolute whim.[30] Moreover, inasmuch as the trustee's rights to the policy proceeds did not vest until the decedent's death, there was no property to which a power of appointment could attach.

Although *Margrave* presents an interesting means of removing the proceeds of a life insurance policy from a decedent's estate while, at the same time, retaining a modicum of control over the disposition of the proceeds, reliance on this case at this time seems somewhat premature.

---

[27] See Kearns v. U.S., 399 F.2d 226 (Ct. Cl. 1968); St. Louis Union Trust Co. (Orthwein) v. U.S., 262 F. Supp. 27 (D. Mo. 1966); Caldwell v. Jordan, 119 F. Supp. 66 (D. Ala. 1953); Comm'r v. Karagheusian's Est., 233 F.2d 197 (2d Cir. 1956).

[28] Estate of Mudge v. Comm'r, 27 T.C. 188 (1956), nonacq. 1964-1 C.B. 6.

[29] 71 T.C. 13 (1978), aff'd, 618 F.2d 34 (8th Cir. 1980).

[30] Id. at 17 (1978).

There was a strong dissent in the Tax Court opinion and the Service has not acquiesced in the decision. Consequently, it can be expected that the Service will continue to litigate this question, at least until other circuits have similarly spoken.

¶ 13.03 Removal of Life Insurance Proceeds From Decedent's Taxable Estate

[1] In General

Inasmuch as Section 2042 specifically defines the situations in which the proceeds of insurance on a decedent's life will be taxable, the methods of avoiding taxation are also similarly clear. If an insurance policy can be arranged so that the proceeds are not payable to the decedent's estate (or mandated to be used for the benefit of the estate), and if the decedent retains no incidents of ownership over the life insurance policy itself, the proceeds will not be included in his gross estate.[31] Although this sounds relatively simple, it is easier said than done. As has been shown in the preceding section, there is frequent dispute as to when the incidents of ownership of a policy have been effectively assigned because this is an area upon which the Service casts a wary eye. In addition, there are other problems that frequently arise regarding the attempted assignment of the incidents of ownership of a life insurance policy. This section explores those other problems.[32]

[2] Gift Tax Consequences of Transfer of Life Insurance

A transfer of a life insurance policy, either outright to another individual or to a trust, is a gift for gift tax purposes.[33] The amount of the gift for tax purposes is not the face value of the policy but is, in essence, its replacement value at the time of the gift. The value of the gift is normally determined by the price charged by the company for comparable contracts, or if that price is not available, "by adding to the interpolated terminal reserve at the date of the gift, the proportionate part of the gross premium last paid before the date of the gift which

---

[31] I.R.C. § 2042.

[32] Problems relating to gifts of life insurance policies in contemplation of death are explored in ¶ 13.04 supra.

[33] Treas. Reg. § 25.2511-1(a).

covers the period extending beyond that date."[34] Translated into easily understood terms, this usually means that the value of the policy equals the cash surrender value of the policy plus any unearned premium at the time of the gift. For term insurance policies, the replacement value will be the unearned premium from the date of the gift until the date at which the next premium is due. For example, if annual premiums are paid on the term insurance policy on January 1 of each year and if a gift was made of that policy on December 20 of a year prior to the payment of the next premium, the value of the gift for tax purposes would be virtually nothing.[35]

The potentially large discrepancy between the gift tax value of a transfer of a life insurance policy and the face amount of the proceeds thereof illustrates why the removal of life insurance proceeds from an estate is such an important and popular estate planning device. A gift of a life insurance policy produces minimal gift tax consequences and, at the same time, removes a significant asset from the decedent's taxable estate. This can be true even in the situation where a whole life policy is involved. For example, if an individual withdrew the cash surrender value of a whole life policy just prior to making a transfer by taking a large loan against this cash surrender value, the gift tax cost of making a transfer would be relatively minimal. Thus, in most situations, it is possible to make a gift of a life insurance policy without incurring a gift tax [36] or without using a significant portion of an individual's unified estate and gift tax credit.

A gift of the life insurance policy will qualify for the $10,000 per donee annual exclusion if the transfer is a gift of a present interest.[37] A direct transfer of a policy to another individual will be a gift of a present interest in that policy. Although transfers in trust frequently do not qualify as a gift of a present interest, there are means of making a transfer so qualify. This is discussed in ¶ 13.05.

It also should be noted that the payment of insurance premiums by

---

[34] Treas. Reg. § 25.2512-6(a).

[35] The value of a gift of a split-dollar arrangement is the interpolated terminal reserve of the policy plus the proportionate part of the premiums paid before the date of the gift reduced by the employer's interest in the policy. Rev. Rul. 81-198, 1981-2 C.B. 188.

[36] Most such gifts would fall within the confines of the $10,000 per donee annual exclusion.

[37] I.R.C. § 2503(b).

someone other than the owner of the policy constitutes a gift for gift tax purposes.[38] Thus, if an individual transfers a life insurance policy to his spouse and continues to make the annual premium payments, he will be making a gift in the amount of the premium payments each year. Again, the normal questions of whether or not the gift is of present interest will be involved.

[3] Direct Transfer vs. Transfer in Trust

Because the removal of life insurance policy proceeds from an estate constitutes such a significant tax saving device, the question that is most frequently faced is not whether such a transfer should be undertaken, but rather in what form should such a transfer be made. Generally speaking, if an individual's estate is in the taxable category and unless there is a compelling reason to pay the proceeds directly to that individual's executor, there is usually a significant tax advantage in making an assignment of the life insurance policy. In this case, the tax advisor is faced with the question of whether the transfer should be made outright to another individual, such as the spouse of the insured, or to a trust that will benefit the spouse and other potential beneficiaries. Inasmuch as both of these devices will remove the policy proceeds from the estate of the insured,[39] other reasons that create a preference for one form of transfer versus another assume greater importance.

[a] Direct Transfer to Other Individuals. The most significant advantages of a direct transfer to another individual are the ease and simplicity of transfer and the minimal cost of doing so. Because no trust need be drafted, the transfer can usually be accomplished simply by filling out a document that is readily available in preprinted form from virtually every insurance company. The transfer can be accomplished quickly and without many of the complexities that usually accompany a trust instrument.

The insured must realize, however, that in order for a transfer, either directly to another individual or in trust, to become effective, it must be complete and unequivocal. Accordingly, such a transfer must

---

[38] See Comm'r v. Boeing, 123 F.2d 86 (9th Cir. 1941).

[39] This assumes that there are no gift-in-contemplation-of-death problems under Section 2035. See ¶ 13.04 supra.

be viewed in light of the stability of the insured's relationship to the transferee. For example, the insured may make a transfer to his spouse and the marriage may later become unstable. A transfer could be made to children who later have a falling-out with their parents. Although this problem is inherent in any outright gift, it is magnified in the situation of an insurance policy where an extremely large amount of insurance proceeds may be involved. Of course, if the insured continues to make the annual premium payments personally, he could simply stop making payments if his relationship with the transferee became untenable. In such a situation, if the individual was still insurable, a replacement insurance policy could be obtained to provide the requisite amount of coverage.[40]

If the insured who had transferred a policy was no longer insurable, his ability to redirect policy proceeds as he desired by the purchase of a new policy may have been irretrievably lost. In this respect, however, it must be noted that a direct transfer of an insurance policy to an individual does offer certain benefits over transfers to an irrevocable trust. As long as the new policy owner continues to maintain a cordial relationship with the insured, it is likely that changes in beneficiaries will continue to be made according to the insured's wishes. If a transfer is made to the insured's spouse and it becomes necessary to adjust the beneficiary designation, such a change is likely to be made as long as a spouse is in agreement with the plan that is adopted. If, for example, one of the insured's children developed special needs for medical care or education, the spouse could merely change the beneficiary designation of the policy in an attempt to provide for these needs. The trust situation might not, in many instances, afford this same degree of flexibility.

A further problem with a direct transfer of an insurance policy may arise in a situation where the new owner predeceases the insured individual. If a contingent owner had not been previously named, it is possible that the policy might revert back to the insured. Thus, if the insured had made a gift of an insurance policy to his spouse and she predeceased him, the policy could return to the insured if the spouse's will left all of her assets to her husband. Accordingly, if a direct transfer is contemplated, it is always necessary to either name a contingent owner, such as the insured's children, or to make a direct bequest of all insurance policies in the will of the spouse to someone other than the

---

[40] It should be noted, however, that the transferee could continue to make the premium payments himself so as to continue the original policy in force.

insured. Such a relatively simple course of action will prevent the original purpose of the transfer — removal of the assets from the estate of the insured — from being defeated.

[b] Transfer in Trust. A life insurance trust offers several advantages over a direct gift of an insurance policy. First, and most significantly, the trust may be established so that, in addition to removing the life insurance proceeds from the estate of the insured, the proceeds will not be taxable in the estate of his spouse. For example, if the trust terms specified that a surviving spouse was to be paid income for life and, upon her death, the proceeds were to be distributed to the insured's children, the proceeds would not be taxable in the estate of the insured's spouse. Consequently, death taxes on both members of the same generation could be avoided. In addition, the proceeds would not pass through the probate estate of either spouse, thus avoiding additional probate and administrative costs. Unexpected emergencies or changes in a spouse's financial situation could be provided for by granting the trustee discretionary authority to pay the principal over to the surviving spouse, if necessary, for her health or welfare.

The insurance trust established in the manner previously described allows the insured to control the ultimate disposition of the trust proceeds. In this respect, the insurance trust offered a significant advantage over the pre-1981 Act marital deduction trust, which, in order to qualify for the marital deduction, required the surviving spouse to be given a general power of appointment over the trust corpus.[41] The 1981 Act amendments, which added the so-called qualified terminable interest property [42] to the Code, now permit a transfer in trust to qualify for a marital deduction even though a general power of appointment is not present. Depending upon the personal situation of the insured, however, this ability to control the ultimate disposition of the trust assets can be very significant in the insurance trust.[43]

As noted earlier, one of the principal purposes for the purchase of

---

[41] I.R.C. § 2056(b)(5).

[42] I.R.C. § 2056(b)(7).

[43] For example, an insured individual whose spouse is substantially younger may have a concern that his wife might remarry and disinherit his children. This type of concern is also present when one or both spouses have been previously married and the surviving spouse would not be the natural parent of the insured's children.

life insurance is to enable the estate to have sufficient liquid assets in order to pay debts, taxes, and funeral and administration expenses. If, however, the proceeds of an insurance policy are payable to the trustee, they technically will not be available to the executor to serve these purposes.[44] In addition, if the trustee is under a legally binding obligation to pay these expenses or to make loans to the estate for these purposes, the insurance proceeds will be considered payable for the benefit of the estate and thus will be includable in the insured's gross estate.[45] Such a direction would defeat a major purpose behind the establishment of the insurance trust — the removal of the proceeds from the estate of the insured. The recommended method for dealing with this problem is to grant the trustee the discretionary authority to purchase assets from the estate of the insured and to make loans to the estate. The cash generated either by a purchase of assets [46] or by a loan can be used for the payment of taxes or for other cash requirements of the estate. If the estate is likely to possess assets that are normally not considered as prudent trustee investments (such as stock in a closely held corporation), the trustee should be specifically authorized to purchase these particular assets from the estate.[47]

Because the trustee cannot be mandated to make such a purchase or to make loans to the estate, there is always the danger that the insurance proceeds will not be used in the manner in which the insured had hoped. In most cases, however, if a close family member or friend is selected as the trustee, the decedent's wishes in this regard will be carried out despite the discretionary nature of the authority granted to the trustee. It is prudent to warn the insured of this danger and to take care to see that this topic is discussed with a trustee prior to the funding of the trust with the insured's life insurance policies.

The other significant advantage underlying the use of an insurance

---

[44] The proceeds will be owned by the trustee rather than by the executor and thus will not be part of the probate estate.

[45] Treas. Reg. § 20.2042-1(b)(1).

[46] Because of the step-up in basis of these assets at death, little or no taxable gain will be incurred by the estate because of such a purchase. Accordingly, the sale of these assets to the trustee will in most instances be free of any tax.

[47] If a decedent already possesses a significant amount of stock in his employer corporation or options to purchase the same stock, it would also be prudent to relieve the trustee of diversification requirements in the event of purchase of additional stock in that corporation. In the appropriate instance, the stock of a particular employer corporation should be mentioned by name if this diversification problem seems to be particularly acute.

trust is that the trust offers the usual trust advantages of professional management of the assets and the ability to use spendthrift clauses to shield the insurance proceeds from creditors of the beneficiaries. In addition, if there is a considerable amount of insurance proceeds that will eventually be transferred to the trust, the trust vehicle serves as a means of protecting younger beneficiaries from themselves by not having huge sums of money placed directly into their hands at an early age. The typical trust devices of staggering the age for distribution of the trust proceeds can be used in an insurance trust as well as in any other trust vehicle.

The question of professional management is somewhat more difficult to deal with in an insurance trust than in other irrevocable trusts because such a trust is typically funded only with insurance policies prior to the death of the insured. Consequently, the only duties of the trustee prior to the death of the insured consist of receiving sufficient proceeds to pay the premiums on the insurance policy and making the payments. Because of this, many financial institutions are not overly interested in serving as trustees during that period or, if they are, they charge a fee of the magnitude that most grantors are not willing to pay. In addition, many individuals have a concern that, if a financial institution is selected as trustee, the institution will not be sufficiently flexible in terms of making loans to the decedent's estate or purchasing assets from it. In other words, there is the underlying concern that the financial institution will exercise the discretionary authority given in these situations in a manner contrary to what the decedent had desired. On the other hand, there is frequently a danger that the individual selected as trustee does not have sufficient financial management expertise to carry out a long-term investment of the trust proceeds. Moreover, the individual selected as trustee may himself die prior to termination of the trust.

There are several approaches for dealing with these conflicts between naming an individual or an institution as trustee. First, an institution can be named as successor trustee in the event of the death of the original trustee or if he is unable to serve for some reason. Secondly, it is possible to name an institution to be added as a trustee at some point subsequent to the death of the insured. Thus, for example, an institution could be appointed as an additional co-trustee at a period commencing one year after the death of the insured. This would allow the individual trustee sufficient time to make loans to the estate for estate tax purposes or to purchase assets from the estate without being encumbered by the often rigid approach of an institution. At the same time, if the trust was to continue for an extended period of time, professional management of the assets could be provided.

The trust does offer several disadvantages as compared to a direct gift of an insurance policy. The first such disadvantage is the cost and complexity of establishing the trust. Unlike the direct assignment of an insurance policy, there are generally costs involved in drafting and establishing the trust. In addition, the trust vehicle is somewhat more cumbersome to deal with in that transfers must be made to the trust every year in order to pay the premiums on the insurance policies.[48] A tax identification number must be obtained for the trust. On the other hand, none of these complexities or costs are so great that they should unduly discourage the establishment of an insurance trust. The complexities are no more than those that the typical highly compensated individual must deal with on a daily basis. Although there are certain legal costs in having a trust instrument drafted, the amount of savings generated — particularly by bypassing the estate of the surviving spouse — will frequently more than justify this relatively minimal outlay.

The other, and perhaps most significant, disadvantage of the insurance trust stems from its irrevocable nature. Because the insurance trust must be irrevocable in order to remove the proceeds from the estate of the insured, it cannot, by definition, be altered, amended, or changed. Accordingly, the insurance trust, just as any other irrevocable trust instrument, creates the potential that changed circumstances will make its terms obsolete. For example, if the decedent should divorce his present wife, or if certain of the beneficiaries should die prior to the insured, there is the danger that the dispositive scheme in the trust instrument may be directly contrary to the insured's wishes.

However, many contingencies can be provided for in the trust instrument. For example, alternate beneficiaries can be named in the event of the death of the insured's spouse and/or children. Changed marital circumstances can be provided for to some degree by referring to a particular familial relationship rather than to a named individual. For instance, the bequest upon the decedent's death could be made to the insured's "wife" rather than by referring to his wife by name. For

---

[48] A trust could be funded so as to provide sufficient income in order to pay the annual premium. If this was the case, the income of the trust would be taxable to the grantor under the grantor trust provisions of the Code. See I.R.C. § 677(a)(3).

this reason, it is not uncommon to see an insurance trust also define the term "wife" as "the woman to whom I am married at the time of my death." Similarly, children can be referred to as a class of individuals rather than being named individually. This allows for the inclusion of after-born children as well as for the situation caused if one of the children should predecease the insured. Alternate trustees can be named to serve in the event of the death or inability to serve of the chosen individual trustee. It is frequently advisable to name an institution as the ultimate backup trustee in the event that a string of unfortunate circumstances makes it impossible for all individual trustees or their alternates to serve.

Although many contingencies can be provided for by careful drafting of the trust instrument, there is always the possibility that circumstances will arise that were unforeseen at the time the insurance trust was implemented.[49] In these cases, the trust instrument may be obsolete.

There are essentially two ways to deal with the obsolete irrevocable insurance trust. The first such method is to simply stop paying premiums on the life insurance policies that are owned by the trust. However, as noted in the discussion of direct gifts (see ¶ 13.03[2]), this may result in the loss of insurance coverage if the insured individual is no longer insurable. Consequently, if the grantor is no longer insurable, this method of dealing with the irrevocable trust would prove feasible only where the trust terms are so contrary to the insured's current wishes that a continuation of them would be totally impractical.

The second method of dealing with the obsolete trust is to draft the instrument so as to give the trustee discretionary authority to make a distribution of any insurance policies contained in the trust directly to a beneficiary. If such a clause is inserted, a cooperative trustee would be able to distribute the policies to a beneficiary, who could then deal with them in an appropriate manner. Of course, if the beneficiary who might receive this distribution is for some reason an inappropriate individual to deal with the policies, such a bail-out clause might not be effective.

---

[49] One such change, for example, could be a substantial revision of the Estate and Gift Tax provisions of the Code. It is highly likely that many trusts that were drafted prior to 1976 may have been made unnecessary by the Tax Reform Act of 1976 and the 1981 Act changes, which will have the effect of exempting many estates from taxation. It is conceivable that many insured individuals who drafted trusts during the pre-1976 era may no longer have a need for such trusts as a means of avoiding estate taxation.

[4] Gifts of Group Term Life Insurance

[a] Requirements for an Effective Assignment. The assignment of group term life insurance presents special problems that must be faced by the estate planner. Assignment of such life insurance policies is occasionally prohibited, both under the terms of the policy and by state law. Accordingly, there is this additional level of concern relative to the insured's ability to assign the policy.

Although historically there has been a certain amount of confusion as to the Service's position on the assignment of group term life insurance, this position has largely been clarified by a series of rulings. In Rev. Rul. 69-54,[50] as later modified by Rev. Rul. 72-307,[51] the Service has indicated that the following requirements must be met in order for an employee to completely divest himself of incidents of ownership of group term life insurance. These requirements are:

(1) The insured must have the right to convert his group insurance to individual coverage;

(2) The insured must irrevocably assign all rights in the policy, including the right to convert to individual insurance; and

(3) Both state law and the policy must permit the insured to make such an assignment.

Rev. Rul. 72-307 modified the original ruling so as to indicate that the right of the insured to cancel his policy by terminating employment is not considered to be an incident of ownership.[52] Accordingly, it is no longer necessary for the insured to have the right to convert to individual coverage upon cessation of employment in order to make a valid and complete transfer. If this right does exist, however, it must be assigned along with all other rights in the group term policy in order for the transfer to be effective.

[b] Incidents-of-Ownership Problems. Although the right to assign group term life insurance is now clearly established under the guidelines set forth above, there is always the potential for controversy

---

[50] 1969-1 C.B. 221.

[51] 1972-1 C.B. 307.

[52] See also Landorf v. U.S., 408 F.2d 461 (Ct. Cl. 1969), which reached the same conclusion in a judicial forum and which led to the issuance of Rev. Rul. 72-307.

over whether the insured has completely assigned all of the incidents of ownership of the policy. The Tax Court has ruled, in a case of first impression, that the ability of an insured to convert a group policy to an individual policy upon the termination of his employment will not be considered an incident of ownership so as to bring the policy within his estate.[53] The court noted that the act of terminating employment created such adverse economic consequences that it could not be an incident of ownership. It also found itself unable to distinguish Rev. Rul. 72-307, where the power to terminate employment merely cancelled the policy.

The Service has ruled that the decedent did not possess any incidents of ownership in a group term policy owned by a third party under an employer's plan that provided that optional insurance could be purchased by qualified third parties if the employee initially rejected such coverage. It also ruled that the employee may later apply for insurance coverage if the third party ceases, for reasons other than death, to qualify as an eligible owner.[54] There has also been a continuing controversy when the employee retains certain settlement options under a policy. For example, in the *Connelly* case, where an assigned group term insurance contract permitted the decedent to elect to have reduced monthly payments made to his beneficiary for a longer period, the proceeds were held not to be includable in the decedent's gross estate.[55] The Service had indicated that it will not follow the *Connelly* decision, which holds that the employee-decedent's right to elect optional settlement modes in conjunction with the employer was not an incident of ownership.[56] Accordingly, further controversy can be expected in this area.

[c] **Premium Payments as Gifts.** A transfer of the group term life insurance policy is a gift similar to the transfer of any other life insurance policy. If a policy is assigned and the employer continues to pay premiums on the policy, it will be considered as if the employee had made a gift each year in an amount equal to the premium payments. In

---

[53] Estate of Smead v. Comm'r, 78 T.C. No. 3 (1982).

[54] Rev. Rul. 76-421, 1976-2 C.B. 280.

[55] Connelly v. U.S., 551 F.2d 545 (3d Cir. 1977); but see Lumpkin v. Comm'r, 474 F.2d 1092 (5th Cir. 1973), rev'ing 56 T.C. 815 (1971), nonacq. 1973-2 C.B. 4.

[56] Rev. Rul. 81-128, 1981-1 C.B. 469.

Rev. Rul. 76-490,[57] it was held that a group term policy transferred to an irrevocable insurance trust had no ascertainable value for gift tax purposes since the employer could have simply failed to make further premium payments each year and that the transfer was a gift of a present interest. In Rev. Rul. 79-47,[58] however, an assignment to an irrevocable life insurance trust was considered to be a gift of a future interest. This question of whether or not an assignment to a trust will constitute a gift of a future interest is dealt with extensively in ¶ 13.05 relating to the use of *Crummey* provisions in life insurance trusts.

Accordingly, unless there is a prohibition under state law or in the master group contract, employee group term life insurance can be assigned to either an individual or an insurance trust just as any other life insurance policy can.[59] Particular care must be taken to ascertain that the policy is truly assignable and to insure that additional incidents of ownership, such as the conversion privilege, are similarly assigned. Just as with the assignment of individually owned policies, any attempt to retain control over the policy is likely to be vigorously resisted by the Service. Accordingly, although there is some favorable authority, such as *Connelly*, that allows the retention of a right to select optional settlement modes without the policy being considered a retained incident of ownership, such a course of action is sure to invite controversy with the Service. Inasmuch as there is a clearly prescribed path to remove a group term life insurance policy from a decedent's estate, it is generally not advisable to attempt reliance on an isolated case in order to retain certain controls over the policy.

¶ 13.04 Transfers of Life Insurance as Gifts in Contemplation of Death

Although Section 2035(d) virtually eliminated the gift-in-contemplation-of-death rules for transfers occurring after 1981, these rules remain applicable to transfers of life insurance policies. Section 2035(d) is inapplicable to property subject to Section 2042 (i.e., life insurance) as well as to property that would have been included under this section if the property had been retained until death. Accordingly, a transfer of a

---

[57] 1976-2 C.B. 300.

[58] 1979-1 C.B. 312.

[59] Group term policies also present certain additional problems relative to the controversy surrounding gifts in contemplation of death. See ¶ 13.04.

life insurance policy that would have been includable in a decedent's estate if retained until death [60] will remain subject to the gift-in-contemplation-of-death rules.[61] Thus, it is necessary to become familiar with these rules as they apply to transfers of life insurance policies.

For these types of transfers that remain subject to the rules of Section 2035, any transfer within three years of death will automatically be included in a decedent's estate.[62] Generally speaking, any transfer of a life insurance policy by gift within three years of a decedent's death will subject the proceeds of that policy to taxation in the transferor's gross estate. Section 2035(b) creates two major exceptions to the automatic inclusion rule. The first exception is for a bona fide sale for adequate and full consideration in money or money's worth. Since, however, a transfer of a life insurance policy for valuable consideration will frequently make the proceeds of such policy subject to income tax,[63] a transfer for consideration is usually an inadvisable means of removing the policy proceeds from an individual's estate. The second major exception to Section 2035 is for transfers for which a gift tax return does not have to be filed by the donee — i.e., transfers that fall within the annual exclusion of Section 2503(b). This particular exception is specifically made inapplicable to the transfer of a life insurance policy. Conseqently, if a gift of a life insurance policy is within the confines of the $10,000 per donee annual exclusion, it still remains subject to the gift-in-contemplation-of-death rules.

[1] Position of the Internal Revenue Service

The Service's basic position as to the interrelationship of Section 2035 and the assignment of life insurance policies is set forth in Rev. Rul. 71-497.[64] In that ruling, a decedent, four years prior to his death, purchased and transferred to his wife all incidents of ownership in a whole life insurance policy and a five-year term policy on his life. He

---

[60] See generally ¶ 13.02 supra.

[61] See Rev. Rul. 82-141, 1982-29 I.R.B. 10. This ruling also held that when a decedent's will controlled, within three years of the decedent's death, all incidents of ownership in a life insurance policy on his life, the value of the life insurance proceeds will be includable in the decedent's gross estate.

[62] Prior to the Tax Reform Act of 1976, Section 2035 only created a presumption that property transferred within three years of death was a gift in contemplation of death.

[63] I.R.C. § 101(a)(2).

[64] 1971-2 C.B. 329.

¶ 13.04[1] ESTATE PLANNING 13-24

continued to pay the premiums on the policies until the time of his death. It was held that no part of the proceeds of either of the life insurance policies was includable in the decedent's gross estate. However, with respect to both policies, the value of any premiums paid by the decedent within three years of his death was includable in his gross estate.

In the second situation described in that ruling, the decedent had purchased an accidental death policy on his life for a one-year term designating his children as owners and beneficiaries, and continued to pay the full premium on this policy. After his death by accidental means, it was held that the decedent had in substance transferred to his children, not the use of the cash amount of the premium payment, but the right to the insurance coverage for the one-year period of the policy. Accordingly, the proceeds of the accidental death policy were includable in his gross estate. It is clear that if an individual divests ownership of either a whole life policy or a term policy whose term extends more than three years beyond the transfer date and then lives more than three years after the time of the transfer, the policy proceeds will avoid the gift-in-contemplation-of-death rules of Section 2035. This result will be true even if the transferor continues to make the premium payments.[65] Any premiums paid by the decedent within the three-year period prior to his death will, however, be includable in his estate under Section 2035. If ownership of the policy is assigned within three years of death, the entire amount of the policy proceeds will be includable in the decedent's gross estate.[66]

The status of an assignment of group term life insurance policies was left somewhat unclear by Rev. Rul. 71-497, inasmuch as the ruling held that the proceeds of a one-year accidental death policy were includable in the decedent's gross estate. Recent rulings have alleviated this concern somewhat. In Rev. Rul. 82-13,[67] the decedent was covered by a renewable group term life insurance policy obtained by his employer upon which all premiums were paid by the company. The policy was renewable annually upon payment of the premium at standard rates without the necessity of showing insurability. The decedent had assigned all rights under this policy more than three years prior to

---

[65] See also Estate of Coleman v. Comm'r, 52 T.C. 921 (1969).
[66] See, e.g., Rev. Rul. 81-14, 1981-1 C.B. 456.
[67] 1982-2 I.R.B. 9.

his death. Upon this set of facts, the Service held that the value of the policy is not includable in the decedent's gross estate under Section 2035 even though the decedent, through his employer, is considered to have made premium payments. The Service reasoned that the payment of premiums at the time of policy renewal did not create new rights nor was the payment of premiums a repurchase of insurance. Consequently, each payment was not considered a new transfer for purposes of Section 2035 and the proceeds were held not to be includable in the decedent's estate. Accordingly, a transfer of automatically renewable term insurance more than three years prior to the decedent's death will not be considered to fall within Section 2035.

A further problem relating to the interaction of Section 2035 and the assignment of group term life insurance policies concerned the situation where the employer changed insurance carriers. For example, what if an employee had made an assignment of all rights under a group term life insurance policy and five years later the employer changed insurance carriers? In this situation a new assignment would be necessary. If the employee then died within three years of the second assignment, would the proceeds be includable in his gross estate under Section 2035? On this set of facts, the Service has reversed its earlier position [68] and has held that a second assignment required only because of the employer's change of insurance carriers will not bring the policy proceeds into the decedent's gross estate when the original assignment was made more than three years prior to his death.[69] This ruling and the aforementioned Rev. Rul. 82-13 should provide greater flexibility to individuals who desire to assign the incidents of ownership in a group term life insurance policy.[70] If such an assignment is made more than three years prior to the decedent's death, in most situations the inclusionary rule of Section 2035 can clearly be avoided. However, any premiums paid by the employer within three years of death will be

---

[68] See Rev. Rul. 79-231, 1979-2 C.B. 323.

[69] Rev. Rul. 80-289, 1980-2 C.B. 270. The ruling also requires that the new insurance arrangement be identical in all relevant aspects to the employer's previous insurance arrangement.

[70] Rev. Rul. 82-13, 1982-2 I.R.B. 9 also provides greater flexibility to the employer to change carriers as lower price policies are made available. Because the trend in recent years has been toward lower priced term policies, the desire to change policies or carriers is fairly widespread. Such a change can now be accomplished without fear of negating any previous policy assignments by employees.

considered a gift by the employee. If they do not exceed the amount of the annual exclusion, no gift tax consequences will result.[71]

[2] Planning to Avoid Gifts in Contemplation of Death

Inasmuch as Section 2305 provides an automatic rule of inclusion if the gift is made within three years of death, planning the transfer of life insurance policies to avoid Section 2035 is difficult. The advice frequently given to clients who are contemplating such a transfer is to live for three years. In actuality, the continued impact of Section 2035 upon the transfers of life insurance policies suggests that the major planning implication for the highly compensated individual or his advisors is to consummate the transfer of the incidents of ownership of a life insurance policy at the earliest possible date. The earlier that a transfer is made, the greater the probability that the individual transferor will survive for the requisite three-year period so as to avoid Section 2035.

If a new policy is being purchased, rather than an existing policy being transferred, it can be contended that the direct purchase of the new policy by the intended owner may avoid the dictates of Section 2035 if the insured dies within three years of the purchase of the policy. If, however, the insured pays the premiums on the policy during that period, there is a substantial chance that the policy proceeds will be includable in his gross estate. Although there is some split of authority on this point, several cases have held that where another individual purchases a life insurance policy, the premiums of which are paid by the insured, the proceeds will be includable in the insured's gross estate if he dies within three years from the original purchase of the policy.[72] Consequently, in many situations, even a direct purchase of the policy

---

[71] It will be very rare that the premiums paid by the employer exceed the amount of the annual exclusion. Inasmuch as Section 79 limits the amount of group term life insurance that can be provided an employee on a tax-free basis to $50,000, many corporate employers limit their individual coverage to this amount. In such a situation, the annual premium payments will be well below the $10,000 annual exclusion. Even if the amount of coverage exceeds the $50,000 level, group term rates are low enough that the premium payments will almost always be below the amount of the annual exclusion.

[72] See Estate of Silverman v. Comm'r, 521 F.2d 574 (2d Cir. 1975), acq. 1978-1 C.B. 2; Detroit Bank & Trust Co. v. U.S., 467 F.2d 964 (6th Cir. 1972); First Nat'l Bank of Oregon v. U.S., 488 F.2d 575 (9th Cir. 1973); but see Mercantile Trust Co. Nat'l Assoc. v. U.S., 312 F. Supp. 108 (E.D. Mo. 1970); Gorman v. U.S., 288 F. Supp. 225 (E.D. Mich. 1968).

by the intended owner will be ineffective to avoid Section 2035 if the insured pays the premium.

The cases cited above support two planning implications if the policy to be transferred is one that is newly purchased. First, since there is some slight split of authority in this area, the newly purchased policy should always be directly obtained by the intended owner, even if the grantor intends to pay the premiums. In this situation, if the insured does not live in an area where adverse case authority already exists, there is an argument supported by reported cases that the policy proceeds are excludable if the insured should die within the three-year period.[73] Secondly, these cases clearly indicate that the preferable situation would be for the intended owner of the policy to make the premium payments from his own funds, if at all possible. For example, if a wife purchases a new life insurance policy on the life of her husband, the optimal position would be for her to purchase the policy with funds that were in her own name and to continue to make premium payments with her own funds. Although it is not clear that such a course of action would avoid Section 2035, there is at least a strong argument that it would.[74]

In summary, Section 2035 continues to have an impact upon the transfers of life insurance policies made within three years of the death of the decedent. If an individual transfers a policy and then dies within a three-year period, the policy proceeds will automatically be included in his gross estate. Since there is very little that can be done to avoid this inclusionary rule, prudent planning suggests that transfers of policies be made as early as possible and as rapidly as possible if it is thought

---

[73] See cases cited at note 72, supra.

[74] If, however, a beneficiary of an insurance trust were to make the annual premium payment, the I.R.S. may argue that the beneficiary had made a transfer with a retained life interest, which is taxable under Section 2036 in the estate of the beneficiary. In Goodnow v. U.S., 302 F.2d 516 (Ct. Cl. 1962), the I.R.S. made this argument to attempt to include the policy proceeds in the estate of a widow-beneficiary who had admittedly paid the premiums on the policies owned by an insurance trust. The taxpayer prevailed because she had not transferred the policies to the trust — her husband had. Thus, it is imprudent for an owner of a policy on the life of another to transfer it to an insurance trust under which he is the beneficiary of a life estate. If the policy is purchased by the trust and if a future beneficiary pays the premiums, it may well be considered an indirect purchase and transfer and be treated as if directly purchased by the beneficiary. In such a case, an attempt to avoid the gift-in-contemplation-of-death rules by the insured may result in taxation of the policy in the estate of the surviving spouse or other life beneficiary.

desirable to remove the policy proceeds from the decedent's estate and if other considerations permit such a transfer. If a new policy is being purchased with a view towards naming either another individual or an insurance trust as the owner, the intended owner should directly make the purchase of the new policy — preferably with his own funds. Although in many cases a direct purchase will not avoid Section 2035 if the insured pays the premiums on the policy, a slight possibility does exist that this tactic will be successful. The possibilities of success increase if the new owner of the policy is able to pay premiums directly from his own financial resources.

¶ 13.05 Gifts of Present Interests — The *Crummey* Trust

[1] Description of the Problem

A problem that had long impeded the use of insurance trusts was the fact that many gifts in trust simply were not gifts of a present interest and did not qualify for the annual exclusion provided by Section 2503(b). This was particularly true for insurance trusts whose assets frequently consisted only of bare title to insurance policies until the death of the grantor. In this situation, there would be no current distributions of income or other assets that qualified for the annual exclusion.

The effect of an insurance trust not qualifying for the annual exclusion meant that the annual payment of premiums by the grantor, which were taxable gifts themselves, would serve to consume a portion of the grantor's lifetime unified credit or to necessitate a payment of gift tax if the credit had been consumed. If the insurance trust was in effect for a substantial period of time prior to the grantor's death, a significant percentage of his lifetime credit would have been consumed by the payment of premiums. Thus, while the insurance proceeds that were payable to the trust would escape estate taxation, the estate itself would be subject to greater taxation because of the utilization of all or a portion of its lifetime credit.[75] The unavailability of the annual exclusion

---

[75] With the increase in the unified credit to a level that will equal a $600,000 deduction in 1987, it might be argued that the utilization of a portion of this credit is irrelevant to many grantors. The fact remains, however, that if an individual and his spouse have combined estates that are significantly below the deduction equivalent produced by the unified credit, a device, such as an insurance trust, is probably unnecessary. In other words, most, if not all, individuals who are using an insurance trust are those types of individuals whose estates are in the taxable category and who must be concerned about frivolously wasting a portion of their unified credit.

caused, in many instances, an individual seeking to remove the proceeds of life insurance from his gross estate to make direct gifts of such policies to other individuals rather than utilizing the trust vehicle. Inasmuch as the insurance trust also provides a means of bypassing the estate of the surviving spouse,[76] the use of a very valuable estate planning vehicle was frequently restricted.

[2] The *Crummey* Case

Practitioners developed a means of qualifying an insurance trust for the annual exclusion that was judicially sustained in the well-known case of *Crummey v. Commissioner.*[77] In *Crummey,* the grantors had established an irrevocable trust for the benefit of their four children, two of whom were minors and two of whom were adults. The trust granted each child the right to demand from the trust at any time during the year the lesser of $4,000 or the amount of any annual transfer made by the grantor. If the child made such a demand, it was to be paid immediately in cash. If a demand was not made in any particular year, that right would extinguish and not cumulate from year to year. In addition, if the child were a minor at the time of the gift, his guardian could make a demand on behalf of the child. On this set of facts, the Commissioner denied the annual exclusion for those gifts with respect to children who were minors at the time of the gift, and the Tax Court sustained this rationale. On appeal, the Ninth Circuit reversed and held that all gifts, including those to minor children, qualified for the annual exclusion. The court reasoned that both state law and the trust instrument permitted the guardian to make the requisite demand on behalf of the minor, which was found to be sufficient to qualify for the exclusion.

Although the *Crummey* case has never been specifically acquiesced in by the Service, there have been no further significant challenges on this point and most practitioners feel that the utilization of a *Crummey*-type of provision is a relatively safe way to qualify an irrevocable insurance trust for the annual exclusion. Thus, most insurance trusts drafted today include a *Crummey* clause that gives each beneficiary the right to demand a distribution each year in an amount equal to the lesser of the grantor's annual contributions to the trust or the annual exclusion.[78] If this demand is not made in any given year, the right

---

[76] See ¶ 13.03[3][b] supra.

[77] 397 F.2d 82 (9th Cir. 1968).

[78] See, however, the discussion that follows in ¶ 13.05[3][a] relative to the problems potentially created by the increase in the annual exclusion to $10,000.

lapses on December 31 of that year.[79] Of course, the fact that a demand right exists does create a potential concern that it will be exercised by the beneficiary. If the right were exercised, the ability of the trustee to pay premiums on the insurance policies could be defeated, inasmuch as most insurance trusts contain nothing in the way of assets other than the insurance policies and since grantors typically contribute only that amount necessary to pay the annual premium on the policies. In practice, however, this demand right is rarely, if ever, exercised and merely represents a means of qualifying the trust for the exclusion.

[3] Particular Problems With *Crummey* Provisions

Although the general parameters of a *Crummey* provision are quite clear and simple, there are several details that deserve the careful attention of the practitioner before inserting such a provision in an insurance trust. Although, as noted above, there has been a paucity of litigation on this topic, most experienced practitioners pay careful attention to the problems discussed below in the hope of avoiding the possibility of litigation with respect to their trust instruments.

[a] Increase in Annual Exclusion. The increase in the annual exclusion to $10,000 by the 1981 Act has created a danger than an improperly drawn *Crummey* provision might create a taxable power of appointment with respect to an unsuspecting beneficiary. A *Crummey* provision is, in essence, a general power of appointment granted to the beneficiary. If such a power is allowed to lapse (as it almost always will), such lapse will be taxable only to the extent that it exceeds in value the greater of $5,000 or 5 percent of the aggregate value of the assets out of which the lapsed power could have been satisfied.[80] Consequently, to avoid a potential tax problem for an unsuspecting beneficiary, the *Crummey* power should be limited to the greater of $5,000 or 5 percent of the aggregate value of the trust assets. In other words, simply because

---

[79] It is usually preferable to place *Crummey* trusts on a calendar year. This will prevent a bunching of rights into a single calendar year which, in very large trusts, could cause the amount received by a beneficiary in that year to exceed the annual exclusion.

[80] I.R.C. §§ 2041(b)(2), 2514(e). It should be noted that the lapse provisions for purposes of the "5 + 5" powers are measured on a calendar-year basis. This is a further reason to place the insurance trust on a calendar year for accounting and lapse purposes.

the annual exclusion has been increased to $10,000, a practitioner should not draft a *Crummey* clause that increases the withdrawal right to the full amount of the annual exclusion.

In almost all cases, a limitation of the *Crummey* demand power to $5,000 will satisfy the grantor's needs, since it is rare, if ever, that the annual premium payments exceed this amount. It also should be remembered that this particular right can be given to each beneficiary. Accordingly, if there are four beneficiaries of the trust, the total of the premium payments that would qualify for the annual exclusion under *Crummey* provisions would equal $20,000. This should be more than sufficient in most situations.

[b] Notice of Demand Provisions. If the grantor gives a beneficiary the right to demand a yearly distribution by the insertion of a *Crummey* provision in an insurance trust, care should be taken to ensure that the beneficiary is notified of his rights of withdrawal. The Service has taken the position that if a grantor does not inform a competent donee of his rights so as to give him a reasonable opportunity to exercise his power, the withdrawal power will not constitute a present interest for gift tax purposes and consequently will not qualify for the annual exclusion.[81] Although generally speaking, a person who is incapable of exercising a general power of appointment will still be deemed to possess that power for estate tax purposes, even though he is unaware of that power,[82] it is preferable to similarly notify such a beneficiary. Accordingly, the trust should contain a provision requiring the trustee to notify each beneficiary in writing of the existence of the power granted by the *Crummey* provision. It also appears to be good practice to have the trust give notice annually of additions to the trust so as to put the beneficiary on notice each year. Most practitioners will draft a notice letter to all beneficiaries at the time of execution of the trust and see that the trustee mails such a notice to the beneficiaries. Presumably, if the grantor of the trust is also a guardian of the minor children (as is usually the case), the grantor has actual knowledge of annual additions to the trust corpus and no real notification is necessary. The safest course of action, however, is for the trustee to simply mail a notice annually to the beneficiaries of additions to the trust corpus and the period for exercise of the withdrawal rights.

---

[81] Rev. Rul. 81-7, 1981-1 C.B. 474.
[82] Rev. Rul. 75-350, 1975-2 C.B. 366.

[c] Length of Withdrawal Period. *Crummey* provisions are typically drafted so that the period of time in which the withdrawal can be made during any given year is limited. In practice, this period usually corresponds to the length of time in which the amount representing the premium payments that are due is part of the trust assets prior to payment by the trustee of the insurance premiums. By limiting the length of time for withdrawal, the practical possibility of withdrawal is somewhat limited.

It is advisable to have the full amount available for withdrawal actually under the trustee's control during the period in which the withdrawal right exists. If the trustee does not actually possess the funds that the beneficiary can withdraw during the withdrawal period, it remains vulnerable to the Service's argument that the withdrawal right is more illusory than real. For this reason, and to restrict somewhat the practical possibilities of withdrawal, most trust instruments are drafted to limit the period for withdrawal. The grantor then makes an annual contribution to the trust prior to the commencement of the withdrawal period and the premium payments are made shortly after the expiration of this annual period.

There is very little in the way of specific guidance as to how long to make the withdrawal right to withstand Service scrutiny. The practical answer to the problem is that the length of the withdrawal period must be sufficient so that the beneficiary has some reasonable opportunity to actually exercise his rights. In other words, a trust instrument that limits the beneficiary's withdrawal rights to between 1 a.m. and 3 a.m. on December 14 of each year is not likely to be sustained. One author has suggested that two weeks is the minimum period of time required to represent a safe period for the existence of the withdrawal right.[83] Although such a period of time is probably sufficient, most *Crummey* provisions seem to be drafted to allow a withdrawal period of at least one month. The existence of such a withdrawal period, plus adherence to the notification requirements mentioned above, should clearly permit the *Crummey* provision to withstand scrutiny.

[d] Multiple Beneficiaries. If there is more than one trust beneficiary, the question may arise as to the amount of the annual exclusion that is being used with respect to each beneficiary. In addition, because multiple beneficiaries may be able to demand the same sums of money,

---

[83] See Henszey, "*Crummey* Power Revisited," 59 Taxes 76 (Feb. 1981).

the amount that each beneficiary may obtain is somewhat speculative if the amount contributed to the trust is insufficient to satisfy all demands. For example, assume that a grantor has two children and inserts a *Crummey* provision in the trust giving each of them a right to demand the greater of $5,000 or 5 percent of the trust assets annually. Assume further that the trust owns one life insurance policy on the life of the grantor, the annual premiums on which are $4,000. In the typical course of events, the grantor will contribute $4,000 to the trust and, subsequent to the expiration of the demand period, the trustee will pay the premium. On this set of facts, does the grantor claim two $2,000 annual exclusions or one $4,000 annual exclusion?

Although the answer to this question will in some cases be irrelevant, in others it will not. For example, if the grantor wished to give $8,000 in cash to each of his children annually in addition to the life insurance premium payment, it would be important (in the previous example) that an amount of $2,000 be considered the annual exclusion with respect to each child arising as a result of the *Crummey* provisions. Moreover, if one child could theoretically demand the entire $4,000, the other child's right to any amount from the trust would be somewhat speculative. Since this same argument could be applied in reverse, it is conceivable that the Service could take the position that the speculative nature of both rights would mean that neither child had a present interest that qualified for the annual exclusion.

This problem was addressed somewhat in Rev. Rul. 80-261.[84] In this ruling, the grantor transferred $13,000 to an irrevocable trust in which each of five beneficiaries had a demand right to receive $4,000 from the trust corpus. The trust provided that if the corpus was insufficient to satisfy the demands of all beneficiaries, it would be distributed on a pro rata basis among those beneficiaries who made a demand. On this set of facts, the Service concluded that if a beneficiary is assured of receiving a minimal amount of trust corpus, then the exclusion provided by Section 2503(b) will be allowable in an amount the donee could receive with certainty, notwithstanding the fact that the donee must first make a demand for the corpus. Consequently, it was concluded that since each of the donees was assured of receiving only one fifth of $13,000, or $2,600, then the amount of the annual exclusion for such beneficiaries was limited to that amount.

This ruling suggests that when there are multiple trust beneficiaries

---

[84] 1980-2 C.B. 279.

one of two approaches should be followed in drafting a *Crummey* provision so as to assure that the proper amount of annual exclusion is received. One such alternative would be to create a separate trust share for each beneficiary so that the trustee would automatically divide the annual contribution into shares for each beneficiary. If this is too cumbersome, a clause could be inserted to grant each beneficiary a right to receive a pro rata share of the annual additions to the trust. By inserting such a provision, a grantor can fully ascertain the amount of the annual exclusion that is available for each beneficiary and will eliminate any possible contention that the amount each beneficiary can demand is too speculative to qualify for the annual exclusion.

[4] Planning for Use of the *Crummey* Provision

The effect of the *Crummey* technique is to make the annual exclusion available for insurance trusts as well as for direct gifts of an insurance policy. As such, the availability of the annual exclusion becomes a neutral factor in making a choice between a direct gift and an insurance trust. Consequently, the *Crummey* provision should be inserted in virtually all insurance trusts, with the exception of a situation where there is an overriding concern that the beneficiary would actually make annual withdrawals, which would make the funds unavailable for payment of insurance premiums. Since such a course of action could have the effect of cancelling an insurance policy unless the grantor made another contribution in the same year, the likelihood of a withdrawl occurring is relatively minimal.

By neutralizing the availability of the annual exclusion as a factor to weigh when choosing between the direct gifts and the insurance trust, the *Crummey* provision has greatly expanded the use of insurance trusts in recent years. Because the trust provides a means of bypassing the estates of both spouses, it is frequently a preferable solution in the case of many highly compensated individuals. In addition, because large sums of money are likely to be involved, the professional management provided by the trust vehicle is often favored.

CHAPTER 14

Estate Planning for Compensation Plans

		Page
¶ 14.01	Introduction	14-2
¶ 14.02	Income in Respect of a Decedent (IRD)	14-3
	[1] Purpose of IRD Rules	14-3
	[a] Definition of IRD	14-4
	[b] Timing and Character of IRD Income	14-5
	[c] Specific Examples of IRD Receivables	14-7
	[i] Noncompensation IRD items	14-7
	[ii] Compensation-related IRD items	14-8
	[2] Deductions in Respect of a Decedent	14-10
	[3] Income Tax Deduction for Estate Tax Attributable to IRD	14-12
	[a] General Method of Computation	14-12
	[b] Specific Computational Problems	14-13
	[i] Marital deduction	14-13
	[ii] Capital gain	14-15
	[iii] Lump-sum distributions from qualified plans	14-16
	[4] General Planning	14-16
¶ 14.03	Estate Planning for Deferred Compensation	14-17
	[1] Tax Consequences Under Section 2039(a)	14-18
	[2] Avoiding Estate Taxation — Death-Benefit-Only Plans	14-20
	[a] Early Cases Exclude Death-Benefit-Only Plans	14-20
	[b] The "Combination" Controversy	14-21
	[i] Early cases	14-21
	[ii] The *Schelberg* case	14-23
	[iii] The *Siegel* case	14-24
	[c] The Problem of the Power to Amend	14-26
	[d] The Gift Tax Problem	14-28
	[e] Planning to Avoid Taxability	14-28
	[i] Separate plans	14-29
	[ii] Restriction on other post-retirement plans	14-29

	Page
[iii] No power to amend	14-29
[3] Review of Beneficiaries' Needs	14-29
¶ 14.04 Estate Planning for Stock Options and Section 83 Plans	14-31
¶ 14.05 Estate Planning for Qualified Retirement Plans	14-35
[1] $100,000 Exclusion for Annuities	14-35
[a] Requirements for Exclusion	14-35
[i] Specifically enumerated type of plan	14-35
[ii] Not payable to participant's executor	14-36
[iii] Contributions must be made by employer	14-37
[iv] Not applicable to lump-sum distributions	14-38
[v] Benefits must be "receivable" under a plan	14-38
[b] Additional Planning Considerations	14-40
[i] Exclusion from spouse's estate	14-40
[ii] Income tax status of beneficiary	14-42
[2] Lump-Sum Distributions	14-43
[3] Individual Retirement Accounts	14-45

¶ 14.01 Introduction

Inasmuch as the vast majority of highly compensated individuals are participants in one or more employment-related compensation plans, tax planning with respect to these plans becomes a major component of the overall estate plan for such individuals. Lifetime income tax planning in regard to compensation plans has been reviewed extensively in Part II of this treatise. It is also imperative that the individual's estate plan integrate the various compensation arrangements in which he may participate. Frequently, substantial time will be spent reviewing the income tax aspects of a particular compensation planning proposal while, at the same time, its estate planning ramifications are ignored. This can cause serious difficulties — most particularly if the compensation plan represents an asset subject to federal estate tax and yet is unavailable to the executor for the payment of estate taxes because it is a nonprobate asset.[1]

---

[1] Compensation plans will not frequently be a probate asset, since the employee usually names a beneficiary under the provisions of the plan who is thereby designated to receive any postdeath benefits that are available. The beneficiary designation will mean that the employee's entitlements under the plan will pass directly to the beneficiary by operation of law as opposed to being an item that becomes part of the probate estate.

In addition, if careful estate planning is not undertaken with respect to the income tax consequences of the compensation plan to the named beneficiaries, a substantial amount of the proceeds may be wasted in the payment of income taxes. Consequently, the well-devised estate plan for an individual's compensation arrangements will include not only a review of the plan's estate tax consequences, but also an understanding of the income tax consequences of the plan to either the estate or the named beneficiary. This chapter discusses the estate planning concepts involved with respect to the major types of compensation plans that have been reviewed in Part II.

¶ 14.02 Income in Respect of a Decedent (IRD)

Any review of estate planning for compensation plans must begin with an understanding of the concept of income in respect of a decedent (hereinafter IRD). This troublesome and often confusing concept, which is contained in Section 691 of the Code, presents problems that are common to virtually every type of compensation-related asset found in a decedent's estate. Accordingly, the first step in formulating an estate plan with respect to compensation-related items is to review and understand this concept.

[1] Purpose of IRD Rules

Section 691(a)(1) of the Code provides that the amount of all items of gross income in respect of a decedent that is not properly includable in the decedent's final return shall be included in the gross income for the taxable year when received by the decedent's estate, a distributee of the estate, or the person who acquires from the decedent the right to receive the amount by bequest, devise, or inheritance. In other words, if a decedent had an accrued right to receive income prior to his death, but had not actually received such income, it would not be reportable on the final return of a cash-basis taxpayer.[2] When that income is subsequently received, however, it will represent income in respect of a decedent and be taxable to the recipient. Income in respect of a decedent is thus created in the situation where the decedent has a receivable of one form or another that has not yet been paid. The IRD will be taxable when

---

[2] This return would only include income received through the date of death.

payment is made with respect to that receivable. Accordingly, an IRD item will typically represent an asset that is taxable in the decedent's estate and will also be subject to income tax when received.

An understanding of the basic purpose of Section 691 is a critical factor in comprehending its operation. The purpose of the IRD section is to keep the step-up in basis rule of Section 1014(a) from preventing the income taxation of a decedent's receivables. Section 1014(a) of the Code operates to step up the basis of property that is taxable in a decedent's estate to its fair market value at the date of the decedent's death or the alternate valuation date — i.e., its estate tax value. The application of this rule to a receivable would mean that much of the income being generated by that receivable could escape income taxation, inasmuch as payments to the recipient would merely represent a recovery of basis until the amount equal to the date of death value was received. Accordingly, payments that would represent income for a decedent's services or the taxable proceeds from a sale of assets would not, if this basis step-up rule was applicable, be subject to income taxation.

The statutory vehicles to prevent such income from escaping taxation are embodied in Sections 691 and 1014(c). Section 1014(c) states that Section 1014(a) will not apply to property that constitutes a right to receive income in respect of a decedent under Section 691. Section 691 then, in tandem, provides that an item of IRD when received will be subject to income taxation. The IRD scheme thus prevents pre-death receivables of a cash-basis taxpayer from escaping income taxation.

[a] **Definition of IRD.** The statute itself does not define the term "income in respect of a decedent." The regulations [3] attempt to provide a general definition by stating that the term "income in respect of a decedent"

> refers to those items to which a decedent was entitled as gross income but which were not properly includable in computing the taxable income for the taxable year ending with the date of his death or for a previous taxable year under the method of accounting employed by the decedent. Thus, the term includes: (1) all accrued income of a decedent who reported his income by use of the cash receipts and disbursements method; (2) income accrued solely by reason of the decedent's death in case of a decedent who

---

[3] Treas. Reg. § 1.691(a)-1(b).

reports his income by use of an accrual method of accounting; and (3) income to which a decedent had a contingent claim at the time of his death.

This definition of IRD attempts to tax a decedent's right to income which, because of its status relative to the decedent's method of accounting, will not have been taxable on his final return. Specific examples of what does or does not constitute IRD are discussed somewhat later in this chapter.[4]

[b] Timing and Character of IRD Income. Although the existence of an item such as accrued vacation pay will create an IRD receivable in a decedent's estate, the existence of such an item in and of itself does not produce taxable income. In order for taxable income to be recognized by a recipient specified in Section 691(a)(1), it is necessary for a triggering event to occur so that the IRD will be considered to have been received by the recipient. An IRD item thus represents the potential for the receipt of taxable income rather than taxable income in and of itself. When such taxable income is received, it will retain the same character that it would have had in the hands of the decedent had he lived and received the income.[5] Thus, capital gain that creates an IRD item will be taxed as capital gain in the hands of the recipient. Compensation which has accrued, but has not been received, will be taxed as ordinary income when received.

The recognition of IRD will typically be precipitated by the receipt of the IRD income or the transfer of the IRD receivable. However, the death of a decedent, which thereby transfers the IRD receivable to an estate, is not a triggering event. Similarly, the distribution of an IRD receivable to a beneficiary who has inherited it is not considered to be a transfer requiring the recognition of income.[6] The regulations state that "if a right to income in respect of a decedent is transferred by an estate to a specific or residuary legatee, only the specific or residuary legatee must report such income in gross income when received."[7]

Consequently, in the typical situation where an IRD receivable is transferred from a decedent to his estate and then subsequently

---

[4] See ¶ 14.02[1][c]

[5] I.R.C. § 691(a)(3).

[6] I.R.C. § 691(a)(2).

[7] Treas. Reg. § 1.691(a)-4(b)(2).

transferred to a beneficiary, income recognition will not result. The general concept is that these types of so-called involuntary transfers that merely pass the receivable to a potential recipient are not the type of triggering events that require recognition of income. It should be noted, however, that the transfer of an IRD receivable to a beneficiary to satisfy a pecuniary bequest will require the recognition of income on behalf of the estate.[8] This presents a potential trap for the executor who might unwittingly precipitate the premature recognition of income by transferring an IRD receivable in order to satisfy a pecuniary bequest. Prudent post mortem estate planning usually requires the use of assets other than IRD receivables to satisfy pecuniary bequests so as to avoid the recognition of income by the estate on the transfer.[9] Prudent lifetime estate planning will often require the arrangement of the assets of the client so as to enable the estate to pay any pecuniary bequests with an asset other than an IRD receivable.

The events that trigger the recognition of income with respect to an IRD receivable are the collection of the receivable (i.e., the receipt of cash) or a transfer of the receivable other than the types previously described. Thus, the sale or exchange of an IRD receivable will require the recognition of income.[10] Similarly, an inter vivos gift of this receivable will trigger IRD recognition. Generally speaking, any other type of disposition of the receivable other than by transfer to a beneficiary of the estate, will also trigger the recognition of income.

In the case of IRD receivables resulting from an installment sales obligation, Section 691(a)(5), which was added to the Code by the Installment Sales Revision Act of 1980, has established a revised set of guidelines. In essence, this section provides that a transfer of the installment obligation to the obligor no longer qualifies as an exempt transfer, with the result that a transfer to such a person will immediately cause the recognition of income. For example, if a father sold property to his son taking back installment sales notes, a transfer of these notes to the son by the estate would require the recognition of income in respect

---

[8] See Estate of Noel v. Comm'r, 50 T.C. 702 (1968); Findlay v. Comm'r, 332 F.2d 620 (2d Cir. 1964).

[9] If, however, the estate was in a significantly lower *income* tax bracket than the beneficiary, the use of an IRD receivable to satisfy a pecuniary bequest may result in an overall tax savings to the family, despite the acceleration of taxation caused by the pecuniary transfer.

[10] I.R.C. § 691(a)(2).

of a decedent by the estate.[11] In addition, a cancellation of the obligation is treated as a transfer [12] as is any cancellation of the obligation occurring at the death of the decedent. If an obligation becomes unenforceable it will be treated as if it were cancelled. This section further provides that if the decedent and the obligor are related persons within the meaning of Section 453(f)(1), the obligation must be valued at least at its face value for the recognition of income. Thus, in a situation where there are related parties involved, the estate will not be able to claim a discount from the face value of the notes in order to reduce the amount of income that is recognized. Although Section 691(a)(5) does create several ambiguities, the basic thrust of this section will be to require the recognition of IRD income when installment sales receivables are transferred to the obligor. This may result in the unintended creation of income in respect of a decedent in those situations where neither the estate planner nor the executor is unaware of the existence of this section.

[c] Specific Examples of IRD Receivables

[i] **Noncompensation IRD items.** Because the topic of this chapter is compensation planning for the estate, the discussion of specific items that do or do not result in the creation of IRD will be focused on compensation-related items. It is important to recognize, however, that there are many noncompensation types of receivables that create income in respect of a decedent. A very typical item is installment sales obligations with respect to a sale that took place prior to the decedent's death. Another very common IRD item that may be found in the estate of a highly compensated individual is interest that

---

[11] Installment sales of property to a relative with the annual cancellation of the installment notes is a device frequently used to enable the transfer of valuable property to an individual while restricting the size of the donor's gifts to the amount of the annual exclusion. (See the discussion of this technique in ¶ 11.06 on inter vivos gifts.) If the decedent died prior to the cancellation of all notes, the notes would typically either be transferred to the obligor or cancelled at death. The enactment of Section 691(a)(5) means that such a transfer to the obligor or such a cancellation will result in recognition of income in a situation where this income recognition was previously avoided. It still may be possible to avoid recognition of income by creating obligations which, by their own terms, cease to exist upon the death of a decedent. See Estate of Moss v. Comm'r, 74 T.C. 1239 (1980), acq. 1981-1 C.B. 2.

[12] I.R.C. § 691(a)(5)(A)(ii).

was earned but not received prior to death that would have been recognized if the decedent had been using the accrual method of accounting.[13] In addition, the right to receive a dividend, if death occurred on or after the record date but prior to the payment date, will also be considered IRD.[14] In the case of royalties, receivables that are attributable to the period prior to death will be considered IRD receivables and royalties accruing subsequent to death will not.[15] The same rule is presumably true for rents and crop shares.[16]

[ii] Compensation-related IRD items. It is in the compensation area, however, that the concept of income in respect of a decedent has been given its broadest definition. It is quite easy to surmise, in those situations where a decedent had a fully enforceable right to certain income that had accrued prior to his death, that income in respect of a decedent will be created. For example, salary that had not been paid for the decedent's final month of work, or accrued vacation pay for the period worked prior to the decedent's death, are clearly IRD items. The concept has been extended, however, in the compensation area beyond those compensation items to which the decedent had an accrued right at the time of his death to potential payments for which the decedent merely had an expectancy. There has been a tendency to declare that when the genesis of a payment is the decedent's personal services, income in respect of a decedent will result, irrespective of the precise legal status of the IRD receivable at death.

The leading and most frequently cited case in this area is *O'Daniel's Estate v. Commissioner*.[17] In *O'Daniel's*, the decedent was employed by a corporation, and, upon his death, his employer's discretionary bonus for the year of his death had not been designated. When the bonus was paid in the year after his death, it was held to be income in respect of a decedent, even though the decedent had no legally enforceable right to the monies upon his death. Similarly, in *Brausch's Estate v.*

---

[13] See Levin v. U.S., 373 F.2d 434 (1st Cir. 1967); Rev. Rul. 79-340, 1979-2 C.B. 320; Rev. Rul. 76-153, 1976-1 C.B. 180.

[14] See Estate of Cooper v. Comm'r, 291 F.2d 831 (4th Cir. 1961); Rev. Rul. 64-308, 1964-2 C.B. 176.

[15] Rev. Rul. 60-227, 1960-1 C.B. 262, modifying Rev. Rul. 57-544, 1957-2 C.B. 361.

[16] Rev. Rul. 64-289, 1964-2 C.B. 173.

[17] 173 F.2d 966 (2d Cir. 1949).

Commissioner,[18] the decedent's employer voluntarily continued to pay salary to the decedent's estate for a period of twelve months subsequent to his death. The Second Circuit noted that, despite the fact that the payments were voluntary and could not have been enforced, they were not gifts being made by the employer. Accordingly, this fact, plus the fact that the employer had a practice of making such payments, created an inference that they were payments for services that should be considered income in respect of a decedent. It is thus apparent that income in respect of a decedent in regard to compensation-related rights is likely to be created in those areas wherein a decedent merely had an expectancy of reward based upon past services, in addition to those particular instances where the decedent had an accrued legal right to a specific payment upon his death.

There are many specific rulings and regulations that create IRD in the compensation area. Salary or wages that had not been actually received by a decedent prior to this death or entitlement to fringe benefits, such as vacation pay or taxable sick pay, are clearly IRD.[19] The regulations similarly take the position that unpaid deferred compensation that the employee was entitled to receive prior to his death will be considered IRD when received by a beneficiary.[20] If the payments are being made pursuant to a plan under which they *never* would have been payable to the employee, but only to his designated beneficiaries (a so-called death-benefit-only plan), it is arguable that no IRD is created since the decedent never would have had an entitlement or right to the specific payment. This conclusion is consistent with the cases that have held that a taxable asset is not created in the estate by the existence of such a plan.[21] Because such a benefit is clearly employment-related, however, the possibility does exist that the courts would find IRD in such a situation.

It also seems clear that payments from a qualified pension or profit-sharing plan are considered IRD.[22] Because the income taxation of these distributions is specifically covered by special provisions of the Code,[23] the classification of this distribution or distributions as income

---

[18] 186 F.2d 313 (2d Cir. 1951).

[19] Treas. Reg. § 1.691(a)-2(b), Ex. 1; Rev. Rul. 59-64, 1959-1 C.B. 31.

[20] Treas. Reg. § 1.691(a)-2(b), Ex. 1.

[21] See discussion at ¶ 14.03[2] supra.

[22] Hess v. Comm'r, 271 F.2d 104 (3d Cir. 1959).

[23] See the discussion in ¶ 5.04.

in respect of a decedent will not impact upon the manner of income taxation of the distribution. It may, however, enable the distributee to be entitled for a Section 691(c) deduction [24] if the distribution was taxable for estate tax purposes.[25] The regulations also take the position that the value for estate tax purposes of stock options, which are includable in gross income under various sections of the Code,[26] will be considered to be income in respect of a decedent under Section 691(a).[27]

Accordingly, it is fair to state that income in respect of a decedent will be created by most compensation-related items. The effect of this conclusion is that if the particular item of compensation is also taxable for estate tax purposes,[28] a double tax burden will result, in that the same compensation-related receivable will be subject to both estate tax and income taxation. Although this fact may be ameliorated somewhat by the availability of the Section 691(c) deduction,[29] this deduction does not provide complete relief from the double taxation that results. Accordingly, applicability of Section 691(a) to compensation-related items does create an overall estate taxation problem.

[2] Deductions in Respect of a Decedent

As we have seen, the perceived legislative necessity for Section 691(a) was created by the fact that income accrued, but not received, during the lifetime of a decedent could possibly escape income taxation altogether. A similar need was felt to prevent the potential loss of deductions that had accrued but that had not been paid by the decedent during his lifetime. As a result, Congress also enacted Section 691(b), which provides for a deduction in respect of a decedent.

The type of deductions that may be allowed under Section 691(b) are statutorily specified to be Section 162, business expenses; Section 163, deduction for interest; Section 164, deduction for taxes; Section 212,

---

[24] See the discussion in ¶ 14.02[3] supra.

[25] The estate taxation of distributions from qualified plans is discussed in ¶ 14.05.

[26] Specifically referred to are Section 421(b) prior to the amendment by Section 221(a) of the Revenue Act of 1964, in the taxable years ending before January 1, 1964, or under Sections 422(c)(1), 423(c) or 424(c)(1), whichever is applicable.

[27] See Treas. Reg. § 1.691(c)-1(c)(1).

[28] This is discussed extensively in ¶¶ 14.03–14.05 supra.

[29] See ¶ 14.02[3] supra.

expenses for the production of income; Section 511, deductions for depletion; and Section 33, foreign tax credits. Because of the specificity of Section 691(b), there are many items that normally might be deducted by a decedent during his lifetime that will not qualify as a deduction in respect of a decedent. Included among these items that are not specifically mentioned are medical expenses, alimony payments, charitable deduction carryovers, or losses under Sections 165 and 166. Although some of these items may be deductible by the estate, despite their exclusion from Section 691(b), the lack of classification as a deduction in respect of a decedent can be quite significant. Pursuant to Section 642(g) of the Code, an estate must file a waiver with respect to its right to claim deductions under Sections 2053 or 2054 for certain items in order to claim the same items on the estate's fiduciary income tax return. This Section has the effect of preventing a double deduction — an item may be deducted on the estate tax return or on the estate's income tax return, but not both. Section 642(g) is, however, inapplicable on its face to deductions in respect of a decedent. Thus, an item that qualifies as a deduction in respect of a decedent, may be deducted on both the estate's (or beneficiary's) income tax return and the estate tax return.

A deduction in respect of a decedent may be claimed when paid. The thrust of this rule is similar to that relating to income in respect of a decedent, which recognizes such an item in the income of a taxpayer when received or disposed of by transfer. The right to claim a deduction in respect of a decedent rests with the estate but, if the estate is not liable to discharge, the obligation to which the item relates, the right to deduct the item, will pass to the person who "by reason of death of the decedent or by bequest, devise, or inheritance acquires, subject to such obligation, from the decedent an interest in the property of the decedent."[30]

It should be noted that the deduction need not actually be paid by the person entitled to it.[31] The critical factor in regard to the Section 691(b) deduction (other than that the payment relate to one of the specifically deductible items mentioned therein) is that the deductible expense must be attributable to the period prior to the decedent's death. Thus, guardian fees and legal expenses in connection with an incompetent decedent, which had accrued prior to his death, have been held to constitute a deduction in respect of a decedent as related to the produc-

---

[30] I.R.C. § 691(b)(1)(B).

[31] See Estate of Hooks v. Comm'r, 22 T.C. 502 (1954).

¶ 14.02[3]   ESTATE PLANNING   14-12

tion of income.[32] Similarly, commissions paid by the estate of a decedent to the trustee of the decedent's grantor trust were deductible for both income tax and estate tax purposes to the extent that they were attributable to income producing assets and represented a fee for services rendered prior to the decedent's death.[33]

There is little planning that can be undertaken with respect to Section 691(b) deductions, since they largely represent items that by happenstance are accrued, but unpaid, at the decedent's death. An estate planner should be aware of the specific types of deductions allowable under Section 691(b) so as to be able to properly categorize such deductions and obtain the double tax benefit involved.

[3] Income Tax Deduction for Estate Tax Attributable to IRD

Because income in respect of a decedent is both taxable in a decedent's estate and subject to income taxation, it can be subject to a very onerous double tax burden. In order to reduce this burden somewhat, Section 691(c) of the Code was enacted to provide an *income* tax deduction for the estate tax payable with respect to the IRD. Although the purpose of this Section is to mitigate against the double burden of taxation often borne by IRD, in practice its operation has been often confusing and controversial. This confusion, coupled with the frequent amendment to the law during the past couple of decades, has meant that the specific parameters of the Section 691(c) deduction are still somewhat unclear.

[a] General Method of Computation. It should be noted at the onset of this discussion that the Section 691(c) deduction does not provide complete relief against the double taxation that is frequently encountered by IRD. Because this section provides a deduction rather than a credit, its value is limited to the highest marginal income tax bracket of the IRD recipient. Thus, if the recipient of the IRD is in the 50 percent tax bracket, the deduction will provide a net savings of $.50 on the dollar for each dollar of estate tax paid. Consequently, although the Section 691(c) deduction is valuable, it can never provide complete relief against the double taxation of IRD.

---

[32] Rev. Rul. 71-423, 1971-2 C.B. 255.
[33] Rev. Rul. 76-498, 1976-2 C.B. 199.

The Section 691(c) deduction is computed by comparing the estate taxes attributable to an estate both with and without the net value of the IRD items.[34] The difference between the two calculations then represents the amount of estate tax which is considered to be attributable to the inclusion of IRD in the gross estate and forms the basis for the Section 691(c) deduction. The amount of the deduction thus is computed by reference to the highest marginal estate tax bracket to which the estate is subject. The Service has ruled that this deduction must be claimed as an itemized deduction on a taxpayer's return rather than as a deduction from gross income in arriving at adjusted gross income.[35]

[b] Specific Computational Problems. There are several specific computational problems that relate to the calculation of the Section 691(c) deduction. Because of the importance of the Section 691(c) deduction in those situations where both an estate tax and an income tax are involved, it is important to understand the nature of these problems in order to be able to maximize the Section 691(c) deduction.

[i] Marital deduction. Because the purpose of the Section 691(c) deduction is to alleviate somewhat the double burden of taxation that is faced by IRD, it appears logical to conclude that when an item of IRD is not subject to estate taxation (such as when it is part of a marital bequest), no Section 691(c) deduction should be allowed. In truth, the conclusion is somewhat more complex — particularly in those situations where a formula type of marital bequest is involved. Although the use of formula bequests will undoubtedly be reduced by the enactment of the unlimited marital deduction, many of the computational problems prevalent when such formula bequests were regularly used remain. If the estate planner is not aware of these complexities, the effect may be to reduce the size of the Section 691(c) deduction by an improper allocation of IRD items to the marital bequest.

The regulations under Section 691 take the position that "in computing the estate tax without including the net value in the gross estate (of the IRD), any estate tax deductions (such as the marital deduction)

---

[34] Note that the Section 691(c) deduction is based on the net value of the IRD items. Thus, deductions in respect of a decedent provided by I.R.C. § 691(b) must first be subtracted from I.R.C. § 691(a) items when computing the income tax deductions under I.R.C. § 691(c).

[35] Rev. Rul. 78-203, 1978-1 C.B. 199.

¶ 14.02[3][b]   ESTATE PLANNING   14-14

which may be based upon the gross estate shall be recomputed so as to take into account the exclusion of such net value from the gross estate."[36] The regulations thus clearly take a position that the marital deduction must be recomputed under a formula-type bequest [37] so as to take cognizance of the exclusion of the IRD from the decedent's estate. Although it is clear that a recomputation of the marital deduction is required in the situation where there is a formula bequest, the precise method of making such a recomputation is not equally clear.

What is evident is that the size of the Section 691(c) deduction is affected by both the funding or nonfunding of the marital bequest by the IRD and the type of marital bequest that is used in the will. For example, if the only assets that pass to the surviving spouse are IRD items, they will be eligible for the unlimited marital deduction and will also generate no Section 691(c) deduction, inasmuch as the computation of the federal estate tax would be the same with or without the items of IRD. Conversely, if the marital bequest consists of a fixed dollar amount, and if the IRD is bequeathed to a nonmarital portion of a decedent's estate, a maximum Section 691(c) will be produced equal to the full increment in federal estate tax caused by the inclusion of the IRD in the estate. If, however, a formula marital bequest is used and if the *entire* amount (rather than, for example, one-half the amount) of IRD is considered to be funding the marital bequest, it is possible that the entire Section 691(c) deduction would be lost.[38]

Although the precise method of calculation of the Section 691(c) deduction is unclear in the situation where a formula marital bequest is used, it is evident that the use of an IRD item to fund a marital bequest, where the surviving spouse is receiving less than the entire estate, may result in the loss of the Section 691(c) deduction. Of course, if the entire estate is left to the surviving spouse, this factor becomes irrelevant because there will be no Section 691(c) deduction.

---

[36] Treas. Reg. § 1.691(c)-1(a)(2); see also Rev. Rul. 67-242, 1967-2 C.B. 227 for a fuller explanation of the Service's view on how to compute the I.R.C. § 691(c) deduction.

[37] The various types of bequests that may be utilized in a will are described in ¶ 15.04.

[38] This is because the estate tax both with and without the marital deduction, if such assumption were made, would be precisely equal. An example of such calculations may be found in *Cleary,* "Revisions In Deduction for IRD Items Create New Planning Possibilities," 53 J. Tax'n 70 (1980).

There may be other valid reasons for not bequeathing IRD items to the surviving spouse. As noted earlier, if the marital bequest is a pecuniary bequest, the use of an IRD item to satisfy the pecuniary bequest may result in the acceleration of income taxation.[39] Additionally, if the surviving spouse is in a high income tax bracket, it may be advisable to allocate the IRD items to a nonmarital beneficiary, such as a child who may be in a lower income tax bracket. An allocation such as this may serve not only to minimize the income tax on the IRD item itself, but also to maximize the Section 691(c) deduction that might otherwise be reduced by bequeathing this asset to the marital portion of the estate.

[ii] **Capital gain.** The question of how to compute the Section 691(c) deduction when the IRD consists of long-term capital gain has long been a subject of controversy. Generally speaking, it is to the taxpayer's advantage to use the deduction to reduce other income (i.e., other than the capital gain), inasmuch as the capital gain is subject to a more favorable rate of taxation. The Revenue Act of 1978 ended this controversy by specifically resolving this question in Section 691(c)(4), which is applicable to persons receiving IRD items as the result of death occurring subsequent to November 6, 1978. This section provides that the Section 691(c) deduction must be used to reduce the amount of long-term capital gain before the capital gain deduction is applied. Thus, if a taxpayer had received $5,000 of long-term capital gain and was eligible to receive a Section 691(c) deduction of $1,000, the computation of taxable income would be made as follows:

Gross income–capital gain	$5,000
Less: 691(c) Deduction	1,000
	$4,000
Less: Capital gain Deduction (60%)	2,400
Net taxable income	$1,600 [40]

---

[39] It must be noted, however, that any income taxes paid will ultimately reduce the gross estate of the surviving spouse.

[40] For decedents dying prior to the effective date of the statute, the Internal Revenue Service has conceded to the prior litigation and has allowed taxpayers to use I.R.C. § 691(c) deductions after the application of the capital gain deduction. Rev. Rul. 79-185, 1979-1 C.B. 221.

[iii] Lump-sum distributions from qualified plans. Another controversy surrounding the calculation of the Section 691(c) deduction related to the calculation of such deduction in connection with the lump-sum distribution from a qualified pension or profit sharing plan. The calculation of the income tax consequences of such a distribution may be made under a special ten-year forward averaging provision found in Section 402(e)(1) of the Code.[41] Again, the question is whether the Section 691(c) deduction is used to reduce the total taxable amount calculated under Section 402(e)(1) or is to be applied subsequent to the computation of the total taxable amount. Similarly, to the situation with the capital gain, Section 691(c)(5) now requires the total taxable amount to be reduced by the Section 691(c) deduction. Thus, the total amount of income is reduced prior to applying the favorable method of taxation permitted by Section 402(e)(1).

[4] General Planning

Because a highly compensated individual is likely to be the owner of several assets that produce IRD, estate planning with respect to these items becomes extremely important. Proper planning in regard to these items requires a realization of the tax consequences of these items from both an estate and income tax planning standpoint. The typical task involved is to calculate the effect of both the estate and the income tax on the IRD items and to allocate them in such a manner as to minimize these taxes. Thus, for example, if an IRD item is contained in the decedent's estate, it is likely, with certain exceptions that will be discussed later in this chapter, to produce both an income and an estate tax. Assuming that economic needs of potential beneficiaries have been adequately provided for, the following factors should then be considered in planning to minimize the total tax impact of the IRD:

(1) What is the income tax bracket of the recipient of the IRD income? Generally, the lowest income tax will be produced if the IRD is allocated to a recipient in a lower tax bracket.

(2) What is the amount of the Section 691(c) deduction? If the IRD

---

[41] If an election is made to exclude the first $100,000 of a lump-sum distribution from the decedent's gross estate, the recipient of the distribution must elect to forego the favorable tax consequences permitted by I.R.C. § 402(e). See generally, I.R.C. § 2039(f)(2). This is discussed extensively in ¶ 14.05[2] supra.

is allocated to the marital share or a charitable beneficiary, in many cases a Section 691(c) deduction will either be reduced or eliminated. This will impact on the total taxable amount due with respect to the IRD.

(3) Conversely, an allocation of an IRD to the marital share may eliminate the estate tax with respect to the IRD because of the unlimited marital deduction. This must be counterbalanced against the potential reduction or loss of the Section 691(c) deduction.

(4) The use of IRD to fulfill a pecuniary bequest may result in the unwanted acceleration of income with consequent bunching of income and unfavorable income tax consequences.

(5) A bequest of an IRD item to charity will produce a charitable deduction for the estate and the beneficiary will not be taxed on receipt of the IRD income.[42]

Planning with respect to the distribution of IRD requires an analysis of the above factors. After such an analysis is completed, it may be possible to attempt to allocate the IRD items so as to minimize the total tax impact of them. Because of the prevalence of IRD items in the estates of many highly compensated individuals, it is imperative that this analysis be made.

¶ 14.03 Estate Planning for Deferred Compensation

Most deferred compensation plans provide for the payment of benefits to an employee's survivor after his death. If a plan makes no provision for post death benefits, there are no estate tax consequences, inasmuch as no asset remains after death for possible estate tax inclusion. Since very few employees would want their deferred compensation rights to terminate if they were to die prior to receipt of all deferred benefits, a deferred compensation plan that makes no provision for payment to survivors is almost never found. Because the typical plan does provide some form of survivors' benefits, there is a compelling necessity to integrate an individual's deferred compensation into his estate plan.

The necessity for integrating the deferred compensation into an estate plan usually arises in one of two basic contexts. First, if the tax

---

[42] Of course if all of the estate's IRD is left to charity, there will be no I.R.C. § 691(c) deduction.

advisor or compensation planner is designing a deferred compensation plan, the estate tax consequences of this plan to the employee should be weighed. In the alternative, if a compensation plan is already in existence, the beneficiary of the plan will want to weigh the various elective options that are available in light of estate planning considerations and may also want to make other adjustments in his estate plan in view of the existence of the deferred compensation. In other words, an adequately prepared estate plan cannot ignore compensation plans that exist now or may shortly thereafter be in existence. Because most highly compensated individuals tend to develop an estate of the magnitude where tax planning is a significant consideration, the estate tax consequences of these compensation plans cannot be ignored.

[1] Tax Consequences Under Section 2039(a)

The estate tax consequences of a deferred compensation plan are governed essentially by Section 2039(a) of the Code.[43] Although the Service has relied on other sections of the Code in an attempt to include death benefits payable under a deferred compensation arrangement in a decedent's gross estate,[44] most of the parameters of estate tax includability are governed by Section 2039(a).[45] There are four basic requirements for estate tax includability under Section 2039(a):

(1) An annuity or other payment must be received by a beneficiary.[46]

---

[43] I.R.C. § 2039(a) reads as follows:

(a) GENERAL — The gross estate shall include the value of an annuity or other payment receivable by any beneficiary by reason of surviving the decedent under any form of contract or agreement entered into after March 3, 1931 (other than as insurance under policies on the life of the decedent), if, under such contract or agreement, an annuity or other payment was payable to the decedent, or the decedent possessed the right to receive such annuity or payment, either alone or in conjunction with another for his life or for any period not ascertainable without reference to his death or for any period that does not in fact end before his death.

[44] See, e.g., Estate of Tully v. U.S., 528 F.2d 1401 (Ct. Cl. 1976) and Estate of Siegel v. Comm'r, 74 T.C. 613 (1980), discussed in ¶ 14.03[2][b].

[45] The estate tax consequences of qualified plans are largely governed by I.R.C. § 2039(c) of the Code and are discussed in ¶ 14.05 supra.

[46] These payments can be conditional or unconditional and may include one or more payments extending over any period of time. Treas. Reg. § 20.2039-1(b).

(2) The payment must be receivable under any form of contract or agreement entered into after March 3, 1931.

(3) Under this contract or agreement, an annuity or other payment must be payable to the employee for his life or for any period not ascertainable without reference to his death or for any period that does not in fact end before his death.

(4) The purchase price of the annuity must be contributed by the decedent.[47] However, any contributuion by the decedent's employer or former employer toward the purchase price of the contract or agreement is considered to have been contributed by the decedent if made by reason of his employment.

Consequently, the basic thrust of Section 2039(a) is to require the inclusion in the decedent's gross estate of a nonqualified joint and survivor annuity payable to beneficiaries of the decedent. Under the typical deferred compensation arrangement, if payments under the plan are made to a former employee's surviving spouse or other beneficiary, the value of this annuity will be included in the decedent's estate. In estimating the size of an individual's estate for estate planning purposes, any deferred compensation rights possessed that fall within the scope of Section 2039(a) should not be overlooked.

In undertaking a tax planning assignment for a highly compensated individual, a significant factor to weigh in evaluating whether or not to institute a deferred compensation arrangement is the possible estate tax includability under Section 2039(a). If the type of nonqualified plan is adopted that provides for payments to the employee for life and for survivor's payments to another individual, it is highly likely that a taxable estate asset will have been created. Whether or not this will cause a significant problem depends upon a myriad of factors. For example, if the value of the deferred compensation for estate tax purposes is high in relation to the cash payments that will be made under the plan for the first year or so, the existence of this plan may create liquidity problems for the estate, despite the fact that the plan is designed to provide an annual income supplement to the survivor.[48] If the highly compensated individual already is faced with significant estate tax problems, it might be wise to place more emphasis on other

---

[47] I.R.C. § 2039(b).

[48] This may be particularly true if the survivor has a long life expectancy or if payments are guaranteed for a substantial period of time.

¶ 14.03[2][a]   ESTATE PLANNING   14-20

compensatory schemes that will not require estate tax inclusion.[49] This is particularly true if the deferred income is of little more than marginal significance to the survivor. On the other hand, if the taxable asset is left to the surviving spouse, it may qualify for the unlimited marital deduction and thus incur no real estate tax consequences. In this situation, there will be no significant estate tax problem created.

Accordingly, the first step in estate planning for deferred compensation is to recognize that the typical deferred compensation arrangement that provides lifetime payments to an executive and survivor benefits to a beneficiary is likely to be included in the decedent's estate. If the deferred compensation arrangement is thought to be desirable for other reasons, the estate planning response to this potential estate tax inclusion can take one of two forms. First, the advisor can react and respond to the estate tax includability by undertaking other estate planning measures and by assuring himself that there will be sufficient liquidity in the estate to pay the estate tax attributable to inclusion of this item in the gross estate. This liquidity may be inherent in other estate assets or may have to be provided by other means, such as the purchase of additional insurance.[50] The second possible response would be to design a deferred compensation arrangement that would not require estate tax inclusion under Section 2039(a).

[2] Avoiding Estate Taxation — Death-Benefit-Only Plans

[a] **Early Cases Exclude Death-Benefit-Only Plans.** It is possible to design a deferred compensation arrangement that will fall outside of the scope of Section 2039(a). As was indicated above, for an annuity or other payment to be includable under that section, the annuity or payment must be paid or payable to the decedent. Thus, if no payments are to be paid or are payable to the employee, Section 2039(a) will not be applicable. If a plan provides for payments to a decedent's widow or other survivors and makes no further provision for payments of any sort whatsoever to the employee, one of the basic requirements of Section 2039(a), at least on the surface, is missing. This is the so-called death-benefit-only type of arrangement. Generally speaking, if taxpayers have been able to demonstrate that a plan provides death

---

[49] Qualified plans, for example, may qualify for an estate tax exclusion of up to $100,000.

[50] The role of insurance in providing estate liquidity is discussed in ¶ 13.01[1].

benefits to a surviving spouse or child and nothing more, they have been successful in avoiding includability under Section 2039(a).

In *Estate of Fusz*,[51] the decedent's contract provided for salary payments for his services as an employee and made provision for further payments to his wife in the event of his death. The Tax Court held that the death benefit payable to the widow was not includable as part of the decedent's taxable estate, inasmuch as Section 2039(a) does not apply where no provisions are made for post-retirement benefits to the decedent or anyone else. The *Fusz* rationale thus limited the phrase "other payment" in Section 2039(a)(2) to post-employment benefits during the decedent's lifetime. Similarly, where a plan provided for a death benefit to surviving beneficiaries of the decedent, but did not provide for any post-employment benefits to the decedent himself, a taxpayer has been successful in avoiding includability.[52]

[b] The "Combination" Controversy. The Service's response to a claimed exclusion as a death-benefit-only plan has been to attempt to combine various other types of plans maintained by an employer into a single plan, so as to contend that payments made or potentially made to a decedent under such other plans, must be considered together with a survivor's benefit plan to constitute an annuity payable to a decedent within the meaning of Section 2039(a). By so combining various other plans with a separate survivor's plan, the Service is able to argue that all the requirements for includability under Section 2039(a) have been met. The regulations adopt such a "combination" approach.[53] They specifically state that the contract or arrangement "includes any arrangement, understanding or plan, *or any combination of arrangements, understandings or plans* arising by reason of the decedent's employment." (emphasis added) This position of the Service in attempting to combine various employee benefit plans for the purpose of Section 2039(a) has led to frequent litigation with varying degrees of success for the Service.

[i] Early cases. For example, in *Bahen v. United States*,[54] the Court of Claims sustained the includability of certain survivor's bene-

---

[51] Estate of Fusz v. Comm'r, 46 T.C. 214 (1966), acq. 1967-2 C.B. 2.
[52] See Estate of Tully v. U.S., 528 F.2d 1401 (Ct. Cl. 1976).
[53] Treas. Reg. § 20.2039-1(b).
[54] 305 F.2d 827 (Ct. Cl. 1962).

fits paid to a widow of a deceased Chesapeake and Ohio Railroad executive. Under the deferred compensation plan adopted by the company, it would pay a stated maximum sum on the employee's death, either before or after retirement, to his widow or to surviving children under the age of 21 in sixty equal monthly installments. If, however, the officer became totally incapacitated for further performance of duty while still employed, the payment could be made to him in sixty equal monthly installments as long as he survived, with any unpaid installments payable to his widow or minor children. When Mr. Bahen died, he was neither receiving any payments under the deferred compensation plan nor was he eligible to receive such payments. The court found, however, that he did possess the right to receive disability payments in the future if certain conditions were fulfilled and, consequently, all the requirements for includability under Section 2039 had been met.

The Commissioner was similarly successful in the case of *All v. McCobb*.[55] The *All* case sustained the includability of a death benefit plan maintained by the Standard Oil Company (New Jersey), under which twelve equal monthly payments were made to certain survivors of deceased annuitants with benefits equal to twelve times the monthly retirement allowance paid to the annuitant. Although a lower court had excluded the death benefit payments from the decedent's gross estate as being the functional equivalent of insurance, the Second Circuit reversed and found the death benefit plan to be includable under Section 2039 [56] — presumably because of a combination with the retirement income plan.

As noted earlier, the taxpayer was successful in excluding payments under a death benefit type of plan in *Estate of Fusz v. Commissioner*,[57] where no post-employment benefits were payable to the decedent. Consequently, the principal developed that payments which, in effect, represented wage continuation payments, would not be combined with death benefit payments for the purpose of finding includability under Section 2039(a). The Service acquiesced in the *Fusz* case and also issued a ruling, which held that the benefits accruing under an employment sickness and accident income plan cannot be combined with a survi-

---

[55] 321 F.2d 633 (2d Cir. 1963).

[56] Other successfully litigated cases by the Service include Gray v. U.S., 410 F.2d 1094 (3d Cir. 1969) and Estate of Wadewitz v. Comm'r, 39 T.C. 925 (1963), aff'd, 339 F.2d 980 (7th Cir. 1964).

[57] Supra note 51.

vor's income plan for the purpose of determining the includability of survivor's benefit in the decedent's gross estate under Section 2039(a).[58] The Service reasoned that the rights and benefits of different plans that will be considered together for purposes of the Section 2039 regulations are limited by the *Fusz* rationale to rights and benefits accruing to an employee, other than the rights to receive compensation for services rendered or to be rendered. On the facts set forth in this ruling, the Service considered the payments under the sickness and accident income plan to be a continuation of wage or salary payments that were thus not in the nature of an annuity.

The Service has also ruled that benefits accruing under a qualified employee's retirement benefit plan, such as a pension plan or profit sharing plan, cannot be considered together with benefits under a nonqualified survivor's income plan for purposes of determining the includability of the survivor's benefit in the decedent's gross estate under Section 2039(a).[59] These cases and rulings have thus established certain parameters as to when plans maintained by the same employer could be combined for purposes of Section 2039(a). Quite clearly, actual wage payments, such as those being received in the *Fusz* case, sickness or accident plans *of a limited duration,* or payments under a qualified retirement plan, would not be combined with a survivor's benefit plan so as to force the includability of such a plan under Section 2039(a). Other payments, such as long term disability payments, remained a source of continuing controversy.

[ii] **The *Schelberg* case.** The case of *Schelberg v. Commissioner* has shed some further light on the parameters of the combination approach.[60] In *Schelberg,* the decedent died while employed by the International Business Machines Corporation (IBM). Among the benefit plans maintained by his employer was an uninsured and unfunded survivor's income benefit plan that would make monthly payments to Schelberg's widow at the rate of ¼ of his regular monthly compensation until his allotted total benefit was received. In addition, IBM main-

---

[58] Rev. Rul. 77-183, 1977-1 C.B. 274.

[59] Rev. Rul. 76-380, 1976-2 C.B. 270; see also, Treas. Reg. § 20.2039-1(b), Ex. 6.

[60] Schelberg v. Comm'r, 612 F.2d 25 (2d Cir. 1979), reversing 70 T.C. 690 (1978).

tained a sickness and accident plan that would provide salary to an employee absent from work due to sickness for a period of up to fifty-two weeks in any twenty-four month period. In extraordinary cases, this plan could be extended for more than fifty-two weeks at the employer's discretion. Finally, the employer maintained a long term disability program for employees with more than five years of service. If an employee was found to be totally and permanently disabled, he would be eligible to receive periodic benefits under this plan. Such benefits would begin upon the expiration of the fifty-two-week period under the separate accident and sickness plan.

At the time of Schelberg's death he was not receiving payments under any of the aforementioned plans. His widow, however, became eligible upon his death to receive a survivor's income benefit of $1,062.50 per month. The Service contended that the payments to which the decedent might have become eligible under the long term disability plan constituted an annuity or other payment payable to the decedent, so as to allow it to combine this plan with the survivor's benefit plan, and thus include the survivor's benefit plan in the decedent's gross estate under Section 2039(a). The Second Circuit reversed the Tax Court and held that the rights of the decedent Schelberg under the disability plan were too dissimilar in nature from an annuity and too contingent to meet the conditions of Section 2039(a). The court stated that the basic purpose of Section 2039(a) was to deal with the nonqualified joint and survivor annuity situation, which was totally unlike the instance where a deceased employee might have received disability payments if he had lived. It reasoned that the disability payments that might have been received by Schelberg had he survived were closer to the sickness and accident payments under a health and accident plan than a post retirement payment under an annuity. Cases such as *Bahen* were distinguished on the ground that the taxpayers' rights in those cases were created pursuant to the *same* deferred compensation plan and that Mr. Bahen would have received the payments in any event — either post or preretirement.

[iii] The *Siegel* case. In *Estate of Siegel v. Commissioner,*[61] the decedent entered into an agreement with his employer whereby, in addition to his annual compensation, he would receive, in the event of disability, certain payments for the remaining terms of the contract. In

---

[61] 74 T.C. 613 (1980).

the event of his death, the remaining payments would be paid to the decedent's children. The agreement further provided that the decedent and his employer could mutually consent to modify the children's rights and interests under the agreement. Mr. Siegel died while he was a full time employee and his children became entitled to payments under the agreement with a commuted value of $811,362. On this set of facts the Tax Court held that the right to these payments was not an annuity or other payment so as to be includable within a decedent's gross estate under Section 2039(a) but that the decedent did retain a power to alter, amend, revoke, or terminate a transfer under Section 2038(a)(1). Each of these conclusions is of particular significance in terms of estate planning for the survivors' benefits and thus each deserves separate analysis.

The specific issue under Section 2039(a) in the *Siegel* case was whether the disability benefits to which the decedent was potentially entitled constituted an annuity or other payment within the meaning of that section. The agreement provided that payments would be made to the decedent after "his employment is duly terminated because of disability" but at the same time contemplated a continuing obligation to work for the employer. Apparently it was the customary practice with the decedent's employer that management employees, such as the decedent, would continue to render services to the company to the extent possible during a period of disability. The Tax Court concluded that if disability payments were made under the agreement, they would constitute wages for services rendered or payments in lieu of wages during a period of absence from work because of sickness or other incapacity following which the decedent would have been expected to return to work. Accordingly, the court held that these payments were not post-employment benefits and therefore could not be combined with the survivor's payments under Section 2039(a).

In considering the impact of the *Schelberg* case, upon the case at hand, the Tax Court noted that, in *Schelberg,* the decedent would have had a right to disability payments with no continuing obligation to his employer once the corporate panel determined his total and permanent disability. In contrast, Mr. Siegel had no right to disability payments free from an obligation to perform services to the best of his ability. Inasmuch as these payments were said to be distinguishable from those in *Schelberg,* the court stated that it did not need to reconsider its *Schelberg* holding in light of the subsequent reversal by the Second Circuit. Accordingly, a conclusion of nonincludability under Section 2039(a) was reached without facing up to the specific issue of whether the Tax Court would adhere to its original *Schelberg* position.

What conclusions can be drawn from *Siegel* in regard to the Tax Court's stated position under the Section 2039(a) issue? Does it represent an attempt to narrow or restrict the rationale of *Schelberg,* or is *Siegel* merely indicative of judicial attitude not to reach an issue that is deemed unnecessary by a court? Clearly, the *Siegel* case represents a continuation of the trend, exemplified by the *Schelberg* decision, of the Service being unsuccessful in combining other types of employment benefits with a survivor's benefit plan for purposes of Section 2039(a).

Although the Tax Court did not adopt the *Schelberg* rationale, it did reach the same conclusion that a long term disability plan should not be combined with a survivor's benefit plan for purposes of Section 2039(a). It should also be noted that the Tax Court reached this conclusion despite the fact that the disability plan and the survivor's benefit plan emanated from the same contract, as opposed to the *Schelberg* case, where the disability plan and the survivor's benefit plan were separate written plans. This separateness of plans was one factor noted by the Circuit Court in *Schelberg* in supporting its rationale of estate tax exclusion. In this respect the *Siegel* case can be said to be a liberalization of *Schelberg.*

On the other hand, the Tax Court, in *Siegel,* gave a great deal of emphasis to the fact that the disability plan created a continuing employment obligation, as opposed to *Schelberg,* where no such obligation was found. In this respect, the long-term disability plan in *Siegel* was likened more to a sickness and accident plan than one that compensated permanent disability. This can be construed as an attempt to narrow the scope of the *Schelberg* rationale to those cases in which the disability plan fits this particular fact pattern. It should be noted, however, by distinguishing the *Schelberg* case, Judge Chabot reached the same conclusion as the Second Circuit while avoiding the necessity of saying that a colleague on the bench (Judge Raum) had wrongly decided the Tax Court opinion in *Schelberg.* Consequently, it is not possible at this time to predict the position of the Tax Court if it were faced with a non Second Circuit disability plan that clearly imposed no further work requirement. The *Siegel* case might best be described as half a step toward adopting the *Schelberg* rationale.

[c] **The Problem of the Power to Amend.** The second important aspect of the *Siegel* case is that the court adopted the Service's position

that the value of the payments to the decedent's children is includable in his gross estate by reason of Section 2038(a)(1). The contract between the decedent and his employer stated that "no right or interest is hereby granted to the children of Siegel except as set forth herein and such rights or interests are subject to any modification of this agreement by mutual consent of Siegel and the Corporation." The court held that this clause reserved the power, in connection with the employer, to modify the rights of the beneficiary by subsequent agreement so as to create includability under Section 2038(a)(1). The court noted that in previous cases that had considered the Section 2038 issue,[62] there was no express reservation of a power to amend. The court also concluded that by reserving the right to amend, the decedent had reserved greater rights than under local contract law. Consequently, this reservation of power to amend was held to be sufficient to bring the survivor's benefits within the scope of Section 2038(a)(1).

The *Siegel* case has two definite planning implications under Section 2038(a)(1). First, it evidences a renewed effort on the part of the Service to use this Section as well as Section 2033 to find estate tax includability for survivor's benefits. This approach is not particularly surprising in view of the Service's limited success under Section 2039(a) in recent years and its traditional skepticism regarding the excludability of nonqualified survivors' benefits. Consequently, this approach, especially given its success of the *Siegel* case, is likely to represent a trend of the future. In future cases that challenge the excludability of nonqualified survivors' benefits, the Service is likely to increase its reliance upon this section as opposed to its more traditional combination approach under Section 2039(a).

The second major point in regard to Section 2038 relates to the Tax Court's relatively broad interpretation of that section. The Court of Claims in the *Tully* case had found that the decedent did not possess any power to alter, amend, revoke, or terminate the survivors' benefits within the meaning of Section 2038(a)(1). Although the agreement in *Tully* contained no express provision to permit modification, the Court of Claims in that case did specifically address the possibility of bilateral modification. In so doing, it held that the word "owner," as used in Section 2038(a)(1), does not extend to powers of persuasion. Thus, the fact that an individual might persuade his employer to change a con-

---

[62] See Estate of Tully v. U.S., 528 F.2d 1401 (Ct. Cl. 1976); Kramer v. Comm'r, 406 F.2d 1363 (Ct. Cl. 1969).

tract was held to be irrelevant by the Court of Claims. The court further found in *Tully* that the language "in conjunction with" in Section 2038(a)(1) does not extend to the possibility of bilateral contract modification. If the language used in the *Siegel* contract was found in the *Tully* case, it appears quite clearly that the Court of Claims would have still found Section 2038(a)(1) inapplicable. Consequently, the interpretation given by the Tax Court in the *Siegel* case creates the possibility of relatively broad extension of Section 2038. Although the court placed a good deal of emphasis upon the reserved power to mutually amend, which was absent in *Tully*, the thrust of this holding appears to go far beyond the *Tully* case.

[d] The Gift Tax Problem. Another approach of the Service to combat its lack of success under Section 2039(a) has been to attempt to classify the payment of death benefits to a survivor as a taxable gift from the employee to the survivor. In Rev. Rul. 81-31,[63] an employee entered into a contract which promised to pay a death benefit to his surviving spouse, but only if he was employed at the time of death. The Service held that the employee made an inter vivos transfer, the value of which became ascertainable at the time of his death. Consequently, it was ruled that there was a taxable gift in the quarter in which death occurred.[64] It remains to be seen whether or not this position will be sustained in litigation. The employee never had any rights to a benefit during his lifetime and any rights accruing to the widow did not mature until the employee died while employed. The "gift" was thus perfected by death. This attempt to impose a gift tax upon death-benefit-only plans undoubtedly will be a future battleground between the IRS and corporate executives.

[e] Planning to Avoid Taxability. The cases and rulings just discussed create very clear planning implications for the design of a death-benefit-only program which will be excluded from the decedent's estate. If it is desirable to implement a plan that will provide no lifetime

---

[63] 1981-1 C.B. 475.

[64] In its generosity the Service noted that the gift qualified for the annual exclusion. It also must be noted that if this "gift" was made to the surviving spouse (as it typically the case), the unlimited marital deduction may effectively eliminate the tax consequences of this transfer.

payment to the employee, but will, as the consequence, be excludable from his estate, the design parameters are quite clearly circumscribed.

[i] Separate plans. The first lesson that is emphasized by the *Schelberg* case is that the survivor's benefit plan must be established by the employer as a separate plan in and of itself. Although the employer may offer other benefit programs for its executives, the survivor's plan should constitute a separate written document whether it is for one individual executive or for a group of them. Any descriptions of benefit plans that are distributed to executive employees should list separately and describe separately the survivor's benefit plan.

[ii] Restriction on other post-retirement plans. Second, the other types of plans that can be maintained in combination with a survivor's income plan must be carefully restricted. It seems quite obvious that if the employer maintains a nonqualified plan that provides post-employment annuity type payments to the employee, it will be combined with the survivor's income plan for purposes of Section 2039(a). Qualified plans clearly create no problem in this regard.

[iii] No power to amend. Finally, as suggested by the *Siegel* case, it would appear to be inadvisable to include in the survivor's income plan an express provision that would allow changes to the benefits provided to beneficiaries, either with or without the employer's consent.[65] In the alternative, if the conditions so warrant, a clause in the plan prohibiting the change of beneficiaries might also help to alleviate potential Section 2038 problems. Although the parameters of the estate tax excludability are not precisely drawn, if the guidelines set forth in the preceding cases and rulings are followed, it does appear possible to design a survivor's income plan that will not be included in the decedent's estate.

[3] Review of Beneficiaries' Needs

Another factor that weighs heavily in devising an estate plan for deferred compensation is the income tax status and economic needs of the contingent beneficiary. For example, if an executive's spouse is

---

[65] An examination should be made of the relevant state law to determine if the contingent income beneficiary under such a plan acquires rights that might later be enforced if the beneficiaries or the plan itself were changed.

likely to be in a high income tax bracket, regardless of the receipt of deferred income rights, it may be more advantageous from a tax standpoint to either name the executive's children as the contingent beneficiaries of the deferred income rights [66] or to spread out the payments over a greater number of years. The same basic principle that governs the decision to enter into a deferred compensation arrangement also comes into play in selecting the contingent income beneficiary. If the contingent income beneficiary is in the same or higher tax bracket than the individual who created the deferred compensation, little or no income tax savings will result from the deferral itself. A bequest to children might be a particularly appropriate planning move if the spouse has no real economic need for the income. This will often be the case because the widow will typically have substantial rights under a qualified retirement plan and is also likely to receive a substantial tax-free inheritance because of the unlimited marital deduction. Consequently, a transfer of deferred compensation rights to children will also serve to reduce the size of the widow's own estate.

Finally, the question of timing of receipt should not be overlooked. Care should be taken to coordinate the potential receipt of the deferred compensation with other benefits and/or income likely to be received by the same recipient. For example, it might be advisable to plan deferred compensation payments so that they will be received in those years in which the beneficiary is receiving a nontaxable return of contributions made under a qualified plan.[67] In summary, the entire compensation package, including qualified plans, stock options, survivor's income plans, and deferred compensation, should be coordinated to the maximum possible extent in attempting to minimize the income tax impact upon the recipient.

The economic needs of both the employee and the potential beneficiary must always be paramount. It is often easy to place so much emphasis on the tax planning that the recipient's financial requirements are not properly analyzed. For example, although a death-benefit-only plan that is excludable from the estate may be attractive for tax planning purposes, it makes sense only if the employee has the economic ability

---

[66] This may also increase the size of the I.R.C. § 691(c) deduction. See ¶ 14.02[3] supra.

[67] If all of the employee's contributions will be recovered within a three-year period from the annuity starting date, no tax will be imposed until all such contributions have been recovered. See I.R.C. § 72(d)(1) discussed in ¶ 5.04[1].

to forego a post-retirement annuity. Similarly, generation skipping (i.e., avoiding the spouse as a contingent beneficiary) for the contingent beneficiary is feasible only if the surviving spouse can afford to pass up the income. As noted throughout this chapter, there are many estate planning opportunities relating to deferred compensation. As with any tax generated planning, they are appropriate only if economically advisable.

¶ 14.04 Estate Planning for Stock Options and Section 83 Plans

The coordination of a restricted stock plan or a stock option [68] (either an incentive option or a nonqualified option) into an estate plan generally creates two specific additional tasks for the tax advisor. The first task is to deal with the liquidity problems that are frequently presented to the estate by the existence of a stock plan. The second problem is to carefully draft the dispositive instruments so that the executor or testamentary trustee has adequate powers to deal with those equity interests that are likely to be held by the estate.

Restricted stock and options both represent nonliquid assets held by an estate. As such, their existence will create an estate tax liability without representing the cash necessary to pay such a liability. The restricted stock will be valued in the estate at its fair market value per share [69] by any one of a number of means, depending on the nature and character of the stock. If the employer is a closely held corporation, whose shares are not publicly traded, estate tax valuation may present a significant practical problem unless there is a requirement that the employee resell the stock to the corporation at a price fixed by formula. Unexercised options will be included in the gross estate at a value equal to the spread between the fair market value of the stock on the valuation date over the option price.[70] Thus, to the extent of the value of these assets, the taxable estate will be increased and an additional tax liability may result.

In addition, if the decedent's estate includes a number of option rights, there will be a further liquidity demand if it is thought desirable to exercise the options. Moreover, incentive stock options create a

---

[68] The income taxation of options is discussed in Chapter 4.

[69] See generally Treas. Reg. § 20.2031-2.

[70] Rev. Rul. 53-196, 1953-2 C.B. 178.

statutory requirement that the options be exercised within a three-month period after the decedent's death.[71] Consequently, for this type of option, the liquidity demands are relatively immediate. Section 83, in contrast, creates no such requirement. However, despite this statutory flexibility in Section 83, the option plans of most employers are likely to contain some requirement as to the period in which options can remain outstanding after death.

Consequently, if an option is valuable, the executor is generally faced with the problem of providing the liquidity to exercise his option within a relatively short period of time after the decedent's death. Because the exercise of a non-qualified option is in and of itself a taxable event,[72] the exercise of the nonqualified option imposes an additional liquidity demand in the form of income taxes due with respect to the exercise itself. Accordingly, in preparing an estate plan for an individual possessing a significant amount of stock options, the tax advisor must remain cognizant that the existence of such options will create a liquidity requirement for estate taxes and the exercise of the option itself. If the option is nonqualified, the income taxes due with respect to the exercise of the option will create an additional cash demand.

The basic means of providing estate tax liquidity are discussed elsewhere in this book.[73] However, a discussion of a few specific techniques is appropriate here. Many plans, particularly those established by closely held corporations, include provisions whereby the employee is required to sell his corporate stock (or to exercise an option and then sell the stock) back to the employer at a formula price within a certain period after death. This alleviates the liquidity problem inherent in restricted stock plans or options, but it also means that the employee's heirs will not be able to share in any future appreciation of the corporate stock. If, however, a restricted stock plan is viewed as a means of rewarding the employee for appreciation in value of the corporation while he is productively employed by it, the buy-back approach is consistent with this theory. Also, as noted in Chapter 4, many corporations combine a stock option plan with a program of

---

[71] I.R.C. § 422A(a)(2) requires that incentive stock options must be exercised within three months after termination of employment.

[72] The exercise would be taxable unless there was a previous I.R.C. § 83(b) election.

[73] See Chapter 13 on estate planning for life insurance.

financing the exercise of the option. If the financing benefits are also available to the employee's heirs, liquidity needs are somewhat alleviated. It should be noted that in a case of a closely held corporation, a buyback or buyout type of arrangement may be almost mandatory if the employee or his estate is to realize the full value for the stock. In such cases, the sale of a minority interest in a closely held corporation is virtually impossible but for the corporately created market. Because of the lack of market and the liquidity problems discussed above, most stock plans for closely held corporations contain a mechanism to create a market for the restricted stock.

Another commonly used technique to provide the liquidity needs resulting from restricted stock or nonqualified options is to attempt to balance the estate so as to ensure the existence of substantial liquid assets to meet these cash requirements or to provide adequate life insurance coverage to create the needed funds. Finally, if the decedent's interest in the closely held corporation constitutes a significant portion of his estate, it may be possible for the estate to elect the extended payment of the estate taxes provided by Section 6166 of the Code.[74] In order to qualify under this Section, however, the rather restrictive definition of a closely held business in the Code must be met.[75] Thus, the extended payment provisions will only be available in a limited number of cases where the decedent's interest in the corporation is quite substantial. The basic problem is to recognize that a restricted stock plan or a stock option will create the liquidity needs just discussed and will necessitate plans to provide for these needs. Each of the approaches discussed, or a combination of them, will be available to help resolve these problems. The critical task is to recognize the existence of the problem so that planning can be undertaken at an early enough stage to mitigate its development.

The other major estate planning tasks created by the existence of a

---

[74] I.R.C. § 6166 provides for the payment of estate taxes over a fifteen-year period if the decedent's interest in a closely held business constitutes at least 35 percent of the value of his gross estate. Under this section, payments may be deferred for five years and then paid in installments over the remaining ten-year period.

[75] A closely held business is defined in I.R.C. § 6166(b)(1)(C) (as amended by the 1981 Act) to be the stock in a corporation carrying on a trade or business if 20 percent or more in value of the voting stock of such corporation is included in determining the gross estate of the decedent or if the corporation has fifteen or fewer shareholders.

restricted stock plan or a stock option is to ensure that the executor and/or trustees have the appropriate power to effectively deal with these securities. Primarily, this is a task of carefully drafting the will or trust instrument to ensure an adequate fiduciary powers clause. The well-drafted instrument should provide the fiduciary with the power to exercise any stock options outstanding at death without regard to any diversification requirements that may be imposed by law. This latter requirement may be particularly significant, inasmuch as a typical corporate executive is likely to own considerable amounts of stock of his employer or options to purchase such stock. Even if the executive is not the owner of a controlling interest, employer-related securities are likely to constitute a significant portion of his estate. In such cases it may even be advisable to specifically mention the employer securities as being the proper subject for purchase or for exercise of an option without regard to diversification.

It is also advisable to grant specific power to the fiduciary to borrow money for the exercise of a stock option or for the exercise of a right under a stock purchase plan. This is particularly critical because of the liquidity problems relating to restricted stock or stock options. If an option or a stock right is valuable, it would be tragic to see such a right expire because there were questions in regard to the fiduciary's power to borrow money for these purposes or because the resulting construction question was tied up in probate court beyond the expiration date of the option. It may also be useful to insert a specific clause granting the fiduciary the power to *retain* such investments, despite a lack of diversification. The fiduciary will still be required to exercise his discretion to evaluate the wisdom of exercising options or retaining holdings in the employer corporation, but the empowering instruments should be drafted in such a manner as to allow him to undertake such course of action if it is advisable.

Because of the wide variety of restricted stock plans and because the nonqualified options does not have to conform to a particular statutory structure, an estate planner who is dealing with preexisting employer plans will be faced with the task of individually reviewing each plan so as to note its particular characteristics. Although the problems discussed in this section tend to be common to all such plans, the unique and individual design inherent under Section 83 demands a careful analysis of each plan's peculiar characteristics. Once this analysis is made, any individual problems inherent in a specific plan can be

14-35 COMPENSATION PLANS ¶ 14.05[1][a]

addressed in integrating that plan into the client's overall estate planning picture.

¶ 14.05 Estate Planning for Qualified Retirement Plans

As noted throughout Chapter 5, qualified retirement plans of various forms provide significant income tax advantages in the form of deductibility of employer contributions, lack of current taxation to the employee, both for employer contributions and for earnings of the trust, and in terms of taxation distributions. In addition to these income tax advantages, qualified plans also contain significant estate tax advantages that often exceed the benefits available to other types of plans. These estate tax advantages will be reviewed in this section.

[1] $100,000 Exclusion for Annuities

Section 2039(c) of the Code provides an estate tax exclusion for the value of an annuity receivable by a beneficiary under qualified plans. The value of this exclusion is limited to $100,000 for the estates of decedents dying after December 31, 1982.[76] Consequently, if an annuity payment meets the requirements of Section 2039(c), the typical recipient of a survivor's annuity under a qualified plan will find that the first $100,000 in value of the annuity is not subject to any estate tax burden.

[a] Requirements for Exclusion

[i] **Specifically enumerated type of plan.** The first major requirement for qualifying for the estate tax exclusion is that the payments made must be made under one of the specified types of plans set forth in Section 2039(c). The four types of plans that are listed as qualifying under that section are:

(1) "An employee's trust (or under a contract purchased by an employees' trust) forming part of a pension, stock bonus, or profit sharing plan which, at the time of the decedent's separation from employment (whether by death or otherwise) or at the time of termination of the plan, if earlier, met the various requirements of Section 401(a);

---

[76] I.R.C. § 2039(g).

(2) "A retirement annuity contract purchased by an employer (and not by an employees' trust) pursuant to a plan which, at the time of the decedent's separation from employment (by death or otherwise) or at the time of termination of the plan, if earlier, was a plan described in Section 403(a);

(3) "A retirement annuity contract purchased for an employee by an employer which is an organization referred to in section 170(b)(1)(A)(ii) or (vi), or which is a religious organization (other than a trust), and which is exempt from tax under section 501(a); or

(4) "Chapter 73 of Title 10 of the United States Code."[77]

Only the specifically enumerated plans set forth above can qualify for the estate tax exclusion. The requirement that the plan be a qualified plan must be met at the time of separation of service or at the time the plan terminated in the case of a Section 401(a) or Section 403(a) plan. For tax sheltered annuities referred to in Section 403(b), the requirement, with respect to the plan, must be met at the time the annuity is purchased.

[ii] Not payable to participant's executor. A second basic requirement is that the exclusion under Section 2039(c) will not be available if the beneficiary of the annuity is the decedent's executor. In determining whether or not the benefits are receivable by the decedent's executor, the regulations under Section 2039 refer to the Section 2042 regulations relating to the includability of life insurance proceeds in the estate of a decedent.[78] This reference means that the exclusion will be denied if the benefits are reserved for the benefit of the estate even if the executor is not specifically designated as the beneficiary. Thus, if the beneficiary was required to use the payments received under the plan to pay obligations of the estate, such as estate taxes or administration expenses, the Section 2039(c) exclusion would be lost. In Rev. Rul. 73-404,[79] a testamentary trust established under a decedent's will had discretion to use the corpus of the trust to satisfy various obligations of the estate. This trust was also named a beneficiary under the decedent's qualified profit-sharing plan, but was specifically prohibited from using

---

[77] I.R.C. § 2039(c). Requirement number (4) refers to a retired serviceman's protection plan or survivor benefit plan.

[78] Treas. Reg. §§ 20.2039-2(b), 20.2042-1(b).

[79] 1973-2 C.B. 319.

any of the proceeds from the qualified plan for the benefit of the estate. On this set of facts, the Service concluded, because of this preclusion, that the payments under the plan were not receivable by the executor.

A similar conclusion was reached in the situation where a state law exempted these benefits from liability for estate expenses and debts.[80] Although the trustee of the trust was permitted to use trust funds to pay estate obligations, the assets of the estate were sufficient to satisfy its debts. The ruling went on to hold that unless the beneficiary is subject to a binding obligation to pay estate obligations, funds received from the qualified plan were not considered to be receivable by or for the benefit of the estate.[81] Thus, it seems relatively clear that if the decedent uses the criteria that have long been in existence in the insurance area [82] so as to allow the beneficiary to assist the estate, if necessary, but not mandate it, the benefits will not be considered to have been received by the executor.

[iii] Contributions must be made by employer. The third requirement for a Section 2039(c) exclusion is that the exclusion is only applicable to amounts which are not attributable to contributions or payments made by the decedent. If the plan was contributory, the exclusion is determined by multiplying the amount payable to a beneficiary by a fraction that compares the decedent's contributions to the total contributions made under the plan.[83] It should be noted, however, that, unlike the situation with Section 2039(b), payments made by the decedent's employer will not be deemed to be made by the decedent.[84]

---

[80] Rev. Rul. 77-157, 1977-1 C.B. 279.

[81] See also Estate of Salisbury, 34 T.C.M. 1441 (1975).

[82] See Chapter 13.

[83] The specific formula set forth in the Treas. Reg. § 20.2039-2(c)(1) is as follows: "The amount to be excluded from a decedent's gross estate under Section 2039(c) is an amount which bears the same ratio to the value at the decedent's death of an annuity or other payment receivable by the beneficiary as the employer's contribution (or a contribution made on the employer's behalf) on the employee's account to the plan or towards the purchase of the annuity contract bears to the total contributions on the employee's account to the plan or towards the purchase of the annuity contract."

[84] I.R.C. § 2039(c). When a decedent under a contributory plan elected at retirement to take a lump-sum refund of his contributions, plus accrued interest, the survivor annuity paid was held to be attributable to employer contributions and thus was excludable under Section 2039(c). Rev. Rul. 78-151, 1978-1 C.B. 291.

In the situation where the employer's contributions to the plan on the employee's account cannot be readily ascertained, the regulations provide a method for determining the amount of the exclusion.[85] In this situation, the total contributions to the plan on the employee's account is the value of the annuity or other payment payable to the decedent and his survivor computed as of the time the decedent's rights first mature. This creates the total contributions to the plan, and, by subtracting from this amount the amount of the employee's contribution, the amount of the employer's contributuion on the employee's behalf may be obtained. Since it is possible, if not likely, that this method will produce a much less favorable exclusion ratio, it is usually recommended that an employer keep careful records that set forth its contributions and the employee's separate contributions in a readily ascertainable form.

[iv] Not applicable to lump-sum distributions. A final major requirement for qualification for the Section 2039(c) exclusion is that the payments must be made in a form other than a lump-sum distribution as referred to in Section 2039(f).[86] Accordingly, the Section 2039(c) exclusion is basically applicable to annuity type payments received from a qualified plan.

[v] Benefits must be "receivable" under a plan. The statute requires that, in order to be exempt under Section 2039(c), the benefits must be "receivable" under one of the types of plans that are specified in that section. Although this requirement seems rather straightforward, controversy has developed in the situation where the employee is considered to have been in constructive receipt of the plan benefits so that they were not deemed to have been paid from the plan itself. In these situations, the Service has taken the position that the Section 2039(c) exclusion from the estate tax is not available.

The regulations describe the situation where an employee had the option to leave his plan benefits with the trustee under an arrangement whereby interest would be paid to him during his lifetime, with the principal to be paid at death to his designated beneficiary.[87] Under this settlement option, the employee could retain the right to have the principal paid to himself in a lump sum up to the time of his death. The regulations take the position that the employee selecting this option is

---

[85] Treas. Reg. § 20.2039-2(c)(2).

[86] Treatment of lump-sum distributions is discussed in ¶ 14.05[2] supra.

[87] Treas. Reg. § 20.2039-2(b), Ex. 4.

considered to have constructively received the amount credited to his account upon retirement. As a consequence, the amount that remains at death is not considered to be receivable by the designated beneficiary under the profit-sharing plan and the exclusion of Section 2039(c) is not applicable.

In order for the doctrine of constructive receipt to be applicable, it appears that the employee must have unrestricted control over the plan proceeds. For example, in Rev. Rul. 55-423,[88] the Service indicated that there would not be constructive receipt if there was a penalty for withdrawal and a prior irrevocable election to defer distribution to a fixed or determinable time had been made. A similar conclusion was reached in the situation where an employee would suffer an economic penalty in that the surrender of certain guaranteed payments required the acceptance of the commuted value of guaranteed payments that would have been less than the amount required to purchase an annuity of comparable value.[89] When an employee's account was segregated in a plan and subject to his recommended investments, constructive receipt was not found because the assets remained subject to control by the trustees and thus were not considered to be subject to his unfettered command.[90] However, when a decedent elected a deferred life annuity beginning at age 95, but retained the right to surrender it or convert it into a deferred annuity, the court held that the cash surrender value of his deferred annuity was includable in his estate so that the amounts received by his beneficiary were receivable from the decedent rather than his qualified plan.[91] Where retirement contracts were purchased and assigned to a decedent upon termination of employment, they were held to be not "under a contract purchased by an employee's trust." They therefore ceased to be part of a pension plan after assignment and were not excludable under Section 2039(c).[92]

The doctrine of constructive receipt does remain a weapon in the government's arsenal in an attempt to defeat the Section 2039(c) exclusion. Although this extension of the income tax doctrine of constructive receipt to defeat an estate tax exclusion for qualified plans has

---

[88] 1955-1 C.B. 41.

[89] Rev. Rul. 80-158, 1980-1 C.B. 196. See also Rev. Rul. 77-34, 1977-1 C.B. 276, where employer contributions were held not to be constructively received despite a plan that permitted employee withdrawals because such withdrawals resulted in a twelve-month suspension from plan participation.

[90] Estate of Brooks v. Comm'r, 50 T.C. 585 (1968), acq. 1969-1 C.B. xxiv.

[91] Northern Trust Co. v. U.S., 389 F.2d 731 (7th Cir. 1968).

[92] Estate of Silverman v. Comm'r, 61 T.C. 605 (1974).

been applied in a limited number of cases, it clearly does represent a threat to the estate tax exclusion when the plan proceeds are subject to the employee's complete and unfettered control. It is interesting to note that the "made available" language of Section 402(a)(1), which imposed an income tax upon an employee when proceeds were considered to have been constructively received by him, has been repealed for taxable years beginning after 1981.[93] Inasmuch as there were no corresponding changes made to Section 2039(c), it is to be assumed that the Service can continue to apply the doctrine of constructive receipt to defeat the estate tax exclusion. Because of the fact that very significant amounts of assets can be accumulated in a qualified plan for the benefit of an employee, Section 2039(c) is an extremely valuable estate tax exclusion. The potential use of the constructive doctrine does create a cautionary note to plan designers. Settlement options under the plan must be carefully reviewed so that an employee who has not actually received the proceeds will not, by virtue of loosely drawn settlement provisions, be considered to have constructively received them.

[b] Additional Planning Considerations

[i] **Exclusion from spouse's estate.** If an annuity form of payment is elected under a qualified plan, the benefits thereunder will typically be payable to a surviving spouse. If we assume that the various requirements for excludability under Section 2039(c) have been met, the question arises as to whether any benefits will be taxable in the estate of the surviving spouse if additional payments remain to be paid to contingent beneficiaries after her death. In other words, is it possible to use the $100,000 Section 2039(c) exclusion to avoid the estates of both spouses? In *Estate of Kleemeier v. Commissioner*,[94] the Tax Court stated that the Section 2039(c) exclusion is only available to the estate of a decedent who was an employee covered by the retirement plan under which the benefit is paid. Thus, in order for the exclusion to be applicable, the decedent must be the employee who was a participant in the plan that accrued the benefits. In Rev. Rul. 79-190,[95] the Service confirmed that the Section 2039(c) exclusion is inapplicable when benefits were paid on a survivor's death to a contingent beneficiary *to be designated by the survivor.* Under this set of facts, the Service held

---

[93] I.R.C. § 402(a).
[94] 58 T.C. 241 (1972).
[95] 1979-1 C.B. 299.

that the value of the remaining benefits should be included in the survivor's estate under the provisions relating to general powers of appointment.[96]

Although this case and ruling does limit the availability of the Section 2039(c) exclusion to the estate of the participant in the plan, they do illustrate a means of utilizing proper planning to avoid liability in the estate of a survivor. Once the Service had found Section 2039(c) inapplicable in Rev. Rul. 79-190, it was necessary for them to find another handle upon which to find estate tax includability on behalf of the survivor. This handle was the fact that the surviving beneficiary had the power to name a contingent beneficiary and thus, in effect, possessed a general power of appointment over the remaining benefits.[97] It is submitted that if this power had not resided in the surviving beneficiary, the Service would have had no means to include the contingent benefit in her estate. If the plan participant had selected both a surviving beneficiary and a contingent beneficiary, this power would not have resided in the surviving beneficiary, who would have possessed no control over the ultimate disposition of the plan proceeds. Under this set of circumstances, it would have been difficult, if not impossible, for the Service to include the guaranteed benefits in her estate.

Consequently, a proper planning tool in a situation where an annuity payout is selected is for the plan participant to select the contingent beneficiary. If the basic requirements of Section 2039(c) are met by the estate of a participant, this should enable the plan proceeds to avoid taxation in the estate of both spouses. Another means of achieving the same end would be for the plan participant to name a nonmarital trust established under his will as the primary beneficiary of remaining proceeds upon his death. Since the nonmarital trust is not taxable in the estate of the surviving spouse,[98] this method will also avoid taxation in the estates of both spouses, at least up to the $100,000 limit.

---

[96] I.R.C. § 2041(a)(2).

[97] Since the survivor could have named her estate as the contingent beneficiary, a general power of appointment was created.

[98] See generally Chapter 15. If a nonmarital trust is named as the primary beneficiary, the bequest will not qualify for the marital deduction. In such a case, the $100,000 limit on the I.R.C. § 2039(c) deduction may become an important factor to weigh. If the value of the annuity is in excess of $100,000, the availability of the unlimited marital deduction may create an incentive for a bequest to the spouse rather than to the nonmarital trust.

[ii] **Income tax status of beneficiary.** In addition to planning the Section 2039(c) exclusion, and also possibly to avoid estate taxation in the estate of the surviving spouse, a further consideration in the designation of survivor benefits is the income tax status of the beneficiary. Because the benefits paid from the qualified plan will be taxable upon receipt (except to the extent of employee contributions), an additional income tax savings can be achieved if the benefits are directed to lower tax bracket beneficiaries. Quite obviously, the first consideration in choosing the recipient of survivor benefits is the economic needs of the spouse. Many times, however, the surviving spouse of a highly compensated individual will be more than adequately provided for because of the wealth that has been accumulated during her lifetime. In addition, because of the unlimited marital deduction, it is possible for the decedent to leave any assets that he chooses to the surviving spouse without incurring any estate tax on this transfer of assets. Furthermore, the surviving spouse may be a contingent beneficiary under other employment-related plans, such as a deferred compensation plan, stock appreciation plan, or the like. Accordingly, it is prudent to review the spouse's economic needs and her possible income tax situation with a consideration to diverting the survivor's benefits under a qualified plan to lower income beneficiaries, such as the decedent's children. It should also be noted that such a beneficiary designation will not disturb the Section 2039(c) exclusion. This exclusion is available if the basic requirements discussed above are met and is not dependent upon the designation of the surviving spouse as the beneficiary.[99] Thus, if the economic review of the decedent's estate reveals that the surviving spouse does not require the benefits that will flow from the qualified plan, a designation of an alternate beneficiary may achieve both an estate tax exclusion and a taxation of income of the benefits at a lower rate of tax.[100]

---

[99] If the value of the benefits exceeds $100,000, the availability of the marital deduction for a transfer to the surviving spouse will, however, be a significant tax consideration.

[100] A method of making these benefits available to the surviving spouse only if needed and yet achieving a lower rate of income taxation would be to designate a nonmarital trust established under the decedent's will as the beneficiary of the survivor's benefits. Typically, such a trust will grant the trustee discretionary authority to pay income and/or principal to the surviving spouse if necessary for her health, maintenance, or comfort. If a nonmarital trust was the beneficiary under a plan, the trustee could divert funds to the spouse if she should need them, and if she did not, he could achieve preferential income tax treatment by distributing benefits to the surviving children.

[2] Lump-Sum Distributions

As noted earlier, the Section 2039(c) exclusion is only applicable to annuity payments. The treatment of the other major form of qualified plan distribution — lump-sum payments — is governed by Section 2039(f). That section provides a general rule that the estate tax exclusion of Section 2039(c) is not applicable in the situation where there is a lump-sum distribution. This exclusion will be available for a lump-sum distribution, however, if the recipient elects irrevocably not to be taxed under the ten-year forward averaging provisions that are otherwise applicable to lump sum distributions for a qualified plan.[101] Consequently, the recipient of a lump-sum distribution has a choice of electing either favorable income tax treatment for the distribution or a $100,000 estate tax exclusion, but not both.[102]

The election to forego or not to forego the favorable income tax treatment is made on the income tax return of the recipient. This can cause some potential problems if the recipient is not also a beneficiary under the decedent's will. In this situation, the recipient would be solely concerned with the income tax treatment of the plan proceeds and would presumably not have the same interest or concern as to the estate tax effect of the distribution. This would be particularly so in a situation where either the state law or the decedent's will do not require the plan proceeds to be charged with their ratable portions of the estate tax. In order to avoid conflicts of this type, some plans are now being drafted so as to allow the plan participant to make the choice between the favorable estate tax treatment or favorable income tax treatment. This can be useful in the somewhat unusual situation where the plan beneficiary is not also a beneficiary under the decedent's last will and testament.

The choice between the $100,000 estate tax exclusion or favorable income tax treatment thus becomes a question of calculating the tax consequences of each choice and determining the choice that is most favorable. If the beneficiary of the lump-sum distribution is the dece-

---

[101] I.R.C. § 402(e)(4)(A). The taxation of lump-sum distributions and the definition thereof are reviewed extensively in ¶ 5.04[2].

[102] It should be noted that the caption of I.R.C. § 2039(f)(2) states "exception where recipient elects not to take ten year averaging," thus raising the inference that the recipient need not elect to forego the favorable capital gains treatment permitted with respect to pre-1974 contributions. The language of the statute makes no such distinction, however, and it is generally accepted at this time that the recipient must irrevocably elect to forego both forms of favorable taxation in order to achieve the estate tax exclusion.

dent's spouse, the choice will almost be to opt for the most favorable income tax treatment, inasmuch as the estate tax includability brought about by the favorable income tax election will be counterbalanced by the unlimited marital deduction available for property passing to the decedent's spouse. In this situation, there will be no net estate tax attributable to the inclusion of the plan proceeds in the decedent's estate and the favorable income tax treatment will still be received. If the recipient of the distribution is someone other than a decedent's spouse, it will be necessary to calculate the dollar effect of one choice versus another. The limitation of the estate tax exclusion to $100,000 by the 1982 Act will be a factor that will weigh more heavily in favor of opting for the favorable income tax treatment in the situation where there are nonmarital beneficiaries and an extremely large account under a qualified plan.

Quite often a more difficult choice is whether or not to take a lump-sum distribution together with the favorable income tax treatment or to accept an annuity with the concomitant Section 2039(c) exclusion. The lump-sum distribution has the advantage of allowing the beneficiary to receive the entire amount of the proceeds for possible investment or use, subject to a relatively low rate of taxation provided by the ten-year forward averaging provisions. If the distribution was taxed in the decedent's estate and if the beneficiary is someone other than a surviving spouse, a Section 691(c) income tax deduction is likely to be available to ameliorate somewhat the taxation in the estate.[103] It should also be noted that, as the provisions of the 1981 Act are fully phased-in, fewer and fewer estates will be subject to taxation. Thus, after 1987, estates of less than $600,000 will not be subject to any taxation. For those estates below the taxable figure, the question of estate tax excludability (limited to $100,000) versus favorable income taxation treatment will be clearly answered in favor of the income tax benefits.

On the other hand, the annuity payment clearly provides a $100,000 estate tax exclusion and deferral of income tax until the payments are actually received. If the beneficiary is likely to be in a situation where retirement years will produce declining income, this deferral will mean that the income is subject to tax at a lesser rate with corresponding tax savings. Also, if a lump-sum distribution is received by a surviving spouse, the remaining proceeds will clearly be taxed in

---

[103] The calculation of the I.R.C. § 691(c) deduction in connection with a lump-sum distribution is discussed at ¶14.02[3][b][iii] supra.

her estate upon her death. As was noted in the discussion of Section 2039(c), the designation of contingent beneficiaries by the plan participant, or the use of a nonmarital trust as a recipient of the survivor's benefits, may enable the estate tax to be avoided in the estates of both spouses.

The choice between various settlement options, with their different estate tax and income tax treatment, presents an interesting question of balance that must be weighed in each individual situation in order to determine the proper choice. The highly compensated individual has an additional advantage in this situation in that the benefits that have been built up in a qualified plan may not be critical to the economic well being of his surviving spouse. In this situation, prudent tax planning may enable that individual to avoid estate taxation of the first $100,000 of plan proceeds and to have the plan proceeds distributed in such a manner that income taxation will be minimized. Even if the surviving spouse does have a need for the plan proceeds, they will not be taxed in the decedent's estate and, with a minimal amount of planning, any proceeds that remain after the spouse's death can be distributed without being taxable in her estate. This favorable treatment from an estate tax standpoint of qualified plans is merely another of the many benefits that attaches to this type of plan. The estate tax treatment further emphasizes why a qualified plan is the most favorable benefit that can be provided for a highly compensated individual and is usually the first such benefit so adopted as part of the employer's compensation package.

[3] Individual Retirement Accounts

The $100,000 estate tax exclusion with respect to qualified plans has been extended to Individual Retirement Accounts (IRAs) in the case of decedents dying after December 31, 1976. Section 2039(e) provides an exclusion from the decedent's gross estate for the value of a qualifying annuity receivable by a beneficiary under an individual retirement plan. The term individual retirement plan is defined in the Code to mean: (1) an individual retirement account described in Section 408(a); (2) an individual retirement annuity described in Section 408(b); or (3) a retirement bond described in Section 409(a). The regulations list two specific limitations upon his exclusion.[104] First, the

---

[104] Treas. Reg. § 20.2039-5(a)(2).

Section 2039(e) exclusion applies only with respect to the gross estate of a decedent on whose behalf an individual retirement plan was established. Thus, the exclusion does not apply to the estate of a decedent who is only a beneficiary under the plan. Secondly, the exclusion does not apply to an annuity receivable by or for the benefit of the decedent's estate. This exception, which is similar to the exception under Section 2039(c), also defines the term "receivable by or for the benefit of the decedent's estate" with reference to the regulations under Section 2042.[105]

The Section 2039(e) exclusion is only available for qualifying annuities receivable by a beneficiary. The term qualifying annuity is defined in the regulations an an annuity contract or other arrangement providing a series of substantially equal periodic payments to be made to such beneficiary for his life for over a period ending at least thirty-six months after the decedent's death.[106] The term "annuity contract" also includes an annuity purchased for a beneficiary and distributed to the beneficiary if, under Section 408 of the Code, the contract is not included in the gross income of the beneficiary upon distribution. Payments will be considered periodic if they are made to the beneficiary at regular intervals. The payments will be considered substantially equal, even though the amounts receivable by the beneficiary may vary. The regulations take the position, however, that payments will not be considered substantially equal if more than 40 percent of the total amount payable to the beneficiary under the IRA determined as of the date of the decedent's death, and excluding any post mortem increases, is payable to the beneficiary in any twelve-month period.[107] Thus, a distribution that bunches a substantial proportion of the payments into a one-year period will cause the payments not to be considered a qualifying annuity and not to be eligible for the $100,000 exclusion.

The amount of the qualifying annuity that is excludable from the decedent's gross estate is limited to $100,000.[108] In addition, the Code does provide certain limitations upon this exclusion. If a payment to

---

[105] Treas. Reg. § 20.2039-5(a)(2)(i).

[106] Treas. Reg. § 20.2039-5(b).

[107] Id.

[108] I.R.C. § 2039(g). The amount to be excluded under I.R.C. § 2039(e) is aggregated with the amount excluded under I.R.C. § 2039(c) for the purposes of the $100,000 limitation. Thus, there are not two $100,000 exclusions available — only one.

one of the excludable type of accounts was not allowable as a deduction under Section 219 (i.e., was an excess contribution), or was not a rollover contribution described in Sections 402(a)(5), 403(a)(4), and 403(b)(8) (but only to the extent that such contribution is attributable to a distribution from a contract described in Subsection (c)(3)), Section 405(d)(3), Section 408(d)(3) or Section 409(b)(3)(c), the exclusion does not apply. The exclusion is thus not applicable to excess contributions and to amounts that were not the rollover contributions described in the various sections just referenced.

An annuity payable from an IRA account, which is funded with tax-free rollover contributions from a qualified plan, will also qualify for the Section 2039(e) exclusion. It should be noted, however, that a spouse who receives a lump-sum distribution at the death of a deceased employee is allowed to roll over this distribution into an IRA pursuant to Section 402(a)(7) and defer the taxation on the amount received. Because Section 402(a)(7) is not referenced in Section 2039(e), this type of rollover distribution will not qualify for IRA exclusion. Thus, it appears that this exclusion is not available to the estates of both spouses in such a situation.[109]

Although the double estate tax exclusion does not appear to be available to Section 402(a)(7) rollovers, the section which allows spousal rollovers does present a unique tax planning device. First, the income tax deferral allowed by a rollover may be very valuable to a high income spouse who may remain in a high income tax bracket for those years immediately following the death of her spouse. In addition, it appears that the spouse may be able to obtain this income tax deferral and still qualify for the Section 2039(f)(2) exclusion available for lump-sum distributions. This section, as noted earlier,[110] provides an estate tax exclusion, where the recipient elects not to take advantage of the ten-year forward averaging provisions available for lump-sum distributions. Section 2039(f)(2) indicates that this exclusion is available where the recipient elects irrevocably to "treat the distribution as taxable under Section 402(a) (without the application of Paragraph (2) thereof)." Inasmuch as the spousal rollover provisions are contained in Section 402(a)(7), this language apparently does not preclude the avail-

---

[109] The use of rollover contributions to defer income taxation was discussed at ¶ 5.05.

[110] See ¶ 14.05[2].

ability of the $100,000 estate tax exclusion to a spouse making the rollover. Consequently, a spouse, by utilizing the section, may be able to both obtain a $100,000 estate tax exclusion and defer the income tax on the lump-sum distribution from a qualified plan. As noted above, however, the Section 2039(e) exclusion with respect to IRAs will not then be available on the death of the surviving spouse.

Despite this one limitation on Section 2039(e), the availability of $100,000 estate tax exclusion further illustrates the advantage of establishing an IRA, either on a contributory basis during one's lifetime or as a means of receiving a rollover distribution from a qualified plan. The participant will receive deductions for lifetime contributions and will be taxed on the proceeds only when received. In addition, Section 2039(e) will allow a $100,000 estate tax exclusion from the estate of the participant in the plan if the relatively simple requirements of that section are met. Consequently, the establishment of an IRA can be one of the most beneficial tax planning devices to the highly compensated individual.

CHAPTER 15

Tax Planning With Wills

		Page
¶ 15.01	The Need for a Last Will and Testament	15-2
	[1] The Marital Deduction	15-3
	[2] Disposition of Decedent's Assets	15-3
	[3] Grant of Powers to Fiduciaries	15-4
¶ 15.02	Planning for the Use of the Marital Deduction	15-5
	[1] Tax Planning With Marital Deduction Provisions	15-5
	[a] General Principles	15-5
	[b] Economic Needs of the Spouse	15-9
	[c] Use of Unified Estate and Gift Tax Credit by Both Spouses	15-9
	[d] Effect of Progressive Rate Structure	15-11
	[e] Time Value of Money Saved by Use of Marital Deduction	15-11
	[f] Other Factors in Determining Size of Marital Bequest	15-14
	[2] Qualification for Marital Deduction	15-15
	[a] Decedent Must Be Survived by Spouse	15-15
	[i] Marital status	15-16
	[ii] Survival	15-17
	[b] Property Must Pass From Decedent to Spouse	15-18
	[c] Property Must Be Included in Decedent's Gross Estate	15-19
	[d] Citizenship or Residency	15-19
¶ 15.03	Terminable Interests and Transfers in Trust	15-20
	[1] Definition of Terminable Interest	15-20
	[2] Factors Making Terminable Interest Nondeductible ...	15-21
	[a] Statutory Requirements	15-21
	[b] Transfer of the Same "Property"	15-21
	[c] Interpretation of State Law	15-22
	[d] Contingent Interests	15-23
	[3] Exceptions to Terminable Interest Rule	15-24
	[a] Survival for a Limited Period of Time	15-24
	[b] Life Estate With General Power of Appointment ..	15-26

		Page
	[c] Life Insurance With Power of Appointment	15-32
	[d] Qualified Terminable Interest Property	15-34
¶ 15.04	Drafting the Marital Deduction Provision	15-36
	[1] Fractional Share Provisions	15-37
	[2] Pecuniary Bequests	15-38
	[3] Equalization Clauses	15-40
¶ 15.05	Other Tax Planning Devices Available by Will	15-43
	[1] Disclaimers	15-43
	[a] Requirements for Qualified Disclaimers	15-44
	[b] Complete vs. Partial Disclaimers	15-47
	[2] Charitable Bequests	15-48
	[a] Estate Taxation of Charitable Bequests	15-48
	[i] Eligible recipients	15-48
	[ii] Allowable methods of charitable transfer	15-49
	[iii] Additional requirements for charitable bequests	15-52
	[b] Planning for the Charitable Deduction	15-53
	[3] Income Tax Planning Considerations	15-54
	[a] Heirs' Tax Situation	15-55
	[b] Potential Sale of Bequeathed Property	15-55
	[c] Estate and Spouse Filing Joint Return	15-56

¶ 15.01 The Need for a Last Will and Testament

A will is the cornerstone of an estate plan. Although this statement sounds patently obvious, the will's importance is frequently overlooked in practice. This oversight takes two very common forms. First, there are a surprising number of people, highly compensated or otherwise, who simply forget to make a will, who mean to do so but do not get around to making one, or who choose not to make one. If such a person dies without a valid last will and testament, he must rely on the intestacy laws of his state of domicile to make a distribution of assets and to appoint someone to handle the estate's affairs. At the other extreme are those individuals who do have a will, but whose document is so simplistic or so poorly drawn as to create probate or tax problems. These individuals, or the advisors they have retained, frequently view the execution of the last will and testament as a rather mechanical process to be concluded with only a minimal amount of thought. Although any will at all is usually better than having no will, this is not always the case. There are many instances where a poorly drawn will may create more problems than it solves. Each of these situations — the death with no will or the death with a poorly drawn will — tend to suffer the same deficiency from a tax standpoint. In each case, the decedent has probably failed to take advantage of the significant tax planning opportunities to save both estate taxes and income taxes when executing a will. This chapter illustrates the tax planning opportunities that are available by will, and guides the advisor on how to draft an instrument to achieve these savings.

[1] The Marital Deduction

The first and most important topic for discussion is estate and tax planning relating to the marital deduction. The marital deduction, and its integration with the unified estate and gift tax credit, provides the basic tax planning device available in the will. More often than not, the proper use or lack of use of the marital deduction will, in and of itself, justify whatever amount was expended to draft the will. There are, however, many other tax planning opportunities that can be effectuated by will. Proper draftsmanship can permit the post mortem use of disclaimers for effective tax planning. The will may or may not utilize charitable bequests as a tax reduction device and may enable the estate or the surviving heirs to effectively reduce the income tax burden on estate assets. Consequently, there are many tax planning opportunities available when drafting this basic instrument.

[2] Disposition of Decedent's Assets

Although the focus of this chapter will be on tax planning through the use of the will, it is well to bear in mind the many other benefits accorded by having a well-drafted will. First, to the extent possible, this document controls the disposition of the decedent's assets.[1] Thus, the will can define who will receive certain items of property and when they will receive them. The will also appoints designated individuals to handle the decedent's affairs. By appointing executors, trustees, or guardians, the will can ensure that the individuals or institutions

---

[1] The ability of the will to direct disposition of assets is, of course, limited by other statutory provisions. For example, state dower or curtesy laws give the surviving spouse a specified minimum interest in the decedent's estate. Many forms of joint ownership or preexisting contract rights may limit a decedent's ability to bequeath certain property.

chosen by the decedent to handle a specified function are actually appointed to do so. A failure to name such individuals in a will [2] can result in unknowns being intimately involved in the decedent's affairs. Although a court appointed executor, trustee, or guardian may in many instances prove to be satisfactory, it also may result in excessive costs, actions taken that would be contrary to the decedent's intentions, and a lack of understanding of a family situation. These risks alone argue forcefully against any reliance on state intestacy laws to distribute a decedent's assets.

[3] Grant of Powers to Fiduciaries

The last will and testament also defines the powers to be accorded to these various appointees and contains certain guidelines for their actions. Consequently, if a decedent wishes his estate to sell or to retain a particular piece of property, he can state these instructions in his will. Within the parameters set by the estate and trust codes of the various states, the decedent can effectively set the scope for the future course of action taken by his trustees or executors. The will can also relate funeral and burial instructions and may directly reduce probate costs by permitting the executor and/or trustees to serve without bond. Most importantly, however, a will provides a sense of security to an individual by setting forth a personalized arrangement for the disposition of his assets. Despite any future changes that may occur in the state laws of intestate distribution, the person who has executed the will has the certainty of knowing his assets will be distributed, by whom they will be distributed and in what manner this will occur.

Although there are advocates of avoiding probate by the use of joint interests in property, and although a state's current intestacy laws [3] may provide a reasonable approximation of an individual's plans for distribution of his assets, no highly compensated individual should even consider either approach. As will be seen in the discussion of the use of the marital deduction, an over-reliance on joint forms of ownership will result in the loss of the estate-splitting and tax-planning opportunities created by the marital deduction. Reliance on the state

---

[2] Or a failure to have a last will and testament.

[3] A further danger of relying on intestacy laws is that they may be amended — unknown to a particular individual. Even if the current laws provide a satisfactory distribution scheme, there is no assurance that this scheme will remain constant until death.

intestacy laws means that no tax planning has been undertaken. Consequently, these factors, when combined with the other benefits from having a last will and testament, make it imperative that the highly compensated individual have such an instrument. An individual who has achieved a highly compensated status will acquire too many assets and have too compelling a need for tax planning to leave his estate planning to the vagaries of the laws of the intestate distribution and the false promise of joint ownership.

¶ 15.02 Planning for the Use of the Marital Deduction

[1] Tax Planning With Marital Deduction Provisions

[a] **General Principles.** The most widely used tax planning device that is available to the draftsman of a will is the estate tax marital deduction. This deduction, which permits assets to pass from decedent to a surviving spouse on a tax-free basis, was originally enacted for two primary purposes: (1) to equalize the estate tax treatment of those individuals who resided in common-law states with those who resided in community property states; and (2) to permit a decedent to transfer assets to his spouse undiminished by tax as if they were a single taxpaying entity.

Under the laws of community property states,[4] property acquired by a married couple during their marriage would be considered as belonging half to each spouse. Accordingly, the spouses who died in a community property state would only have half of the accumulated marital wealth attributable to each of them for estate tax purposes. In contrast, in common-law jurisdictions, property would be wholly attributed to the spouse who earned it for tax purposes. Accordingly, prior to the enactment of the marital deduction, the residents of community property states received a significant advantage in the calculation of estate taxes by virtue of the automatic estate-splitting feature of the community property laws. Consequently, the marital deduction provisions were enacted in 1948 to provide some form of equality for the residents of these two legal systems.[5] In addition, as the marital deduction provisions have evolved, the notion has grown that it is desirable to

---

[4] The community property states are California, Washington, Texas, Idaho, Louisiana, Nevada, New Mexico, and Arizona.

[5] The marital deduction was originally equal to one-half of a decedent's adjusted gross estate.

permit a decedent to leave his estate to a surviving spouse on a tax-free basis. With these two concepts in mind, the marital deduction provisions, as most recently amended by the Tax Reform Act of 1976 and the Economic Recovery Tax Act of 1981 (the 1981 Act) have come into being.

Section 2056 of the Code now permits an unlimited estate tax deduction for property that actually passes to a surviving spouse, but only to the extent that such interest is included in determining the value of the gross estate.[6]

Accordingly, the marital deduction provisions permit a decedent to pass his entire estate to a surviving spouse on a tax-free basis. When this deduction is combined with the unified estate and gift tax credit [7] which, when fully phased in by 1987, will be equivalent to a deduction of $600,000, a decedent who has made no lifetime gifts in excess of the $10,000 annual exclusion can transfer an unlimited amount to a surviving spouse plus $600,000 to other beneficiaries without incurring any estate tax.[8] Whether or not it is desirable to fully use the unlimited marital deduction and the precise requirements for qualifying for the marital deduction are discussed throughout this chapter.

The marital deduction provisions offer perhaps the most signifi-

---

[6] I.R.C. § 2056(a). After the enactment of the Tax Reform Act of 1976, but prior to the 1981 Act, the maximum allowable deduction was equal to the greater of $250,000 or 50 percent of a decedent's adjusted gross estate.

[7] I.R.C. § 2010.

[8] The unified credit against estate and gift taxes, when fully phased in by 1987, will exempt all estates below $600,000 from taxation irrespective of any other deductions. The phase in schedule for the increase in the unified estate and gift tax credit is as follows:

Year of Death	Amount of Credit	Amount Exempt From Estate and Gift Tax
1982	$ 62,800	$225,000
1983	79,300	275,000
1984	96,300	325,000
1985	121,800	400,000
1986	155,800	500,000
1987 and thereafter	192,800	600,000

For convenience of discussion throughout this book, the credit will often be referred to numerically as the equivalent of a $600,000 deduction. For those years prior to 1987, the reader should substitute the appropriate amount in the third column above in order to determine the deduction equivalent if an individual should die in that year.

cant tax planning opportunity available in conjuncton with preparation of a will. This potential goes far beyond the ability of a decedent to transfer his entire estate to his surviving spouse on a tax-free basis. Although the marital deduction certainly makes possible a substantial bequest to a surviving spouse without incurring any estate tax, the other significant tax planning opportunity created by Section 2056 is to enable the couple's estate to be split between two spouses so as to maximize the total amount of assets that can be transferred to the next generation. The tax planning utility of the marital deduction thus centers around the ability of the tax planner to design a will that significantly increases the amount of assets that will pass to the children, in addition to providing a direct benefit to the surviving spouse.

A simple example will illustrate this point. If an individual has a taxable estate of $2,000,000 and bequeaths the entire estate to his [9] surviving spouse, he will receive a marital deduction of $2,000,000 and his estate will incur no tax. He will not, however, use any of his lifetime unified estate and gift tax credit, which would have enabled him to pass assets to others on a tax-free basis. If, however, he had bequeathed $1,000,000 to his spouse and the remainder of his estate to his children,[10] he would receive a marital deduction of $1,000,000 and his estate would incur a federal tax of approximately $153,000.[11] A far more significant difference in taxation will occur upon the death of the surviving spouse. In the first example, the surviving spouse would have received a taxable estate of approximately $2,000,000. On her subsequent death, her estate would incur taxes of approximately $587,200.[12] In the second example, however, the surviving spouse would have a taxable estate of only $1,000,000 and would incur an estate tax of approximately $153,000. Thus, by bequeathing an amount equal to approximately one half of the estate to the surviving spouse, the decedent in the second example was able to greatly increase the total

---

[9] For convenience of discussion throughout this Chapter, it will be assumed that the male dies first. The same principles, of course, are applicable to the reverse situation.

[10] The portion passing to the children could also be bequeathed to a trust for their benefit.

[11] This example assumes death in 1987 or thereafter.

[12] Assuming death in 1987 and thereafter, and also assuming that the second spouse had no assets in her own name, that there was no appreciation or depreciation in these assets and assuming that no dissipation or consumption of the assets. The effect of a credit for any death taxes paid by the husband's estate is also ignored.

¶ 15.02[1][a]   ESTATE PLANNING   15-8

assets that would pass to the next generation by saving estate taxes (for both spouses combined) of approximately $281,200. Splitting the estate of the first spouse to die between the surviving spouse and the children enabled each spouse to fully utilize the unified estate and gift tax credit and to move separately up the progressive rate structure. This form of estate splitting, which directs the nonmarital portion of the estate of the first spouse to die away from the estate of the second spouse, is the most commonly used vehicle to reduce estate taxes in wills of highly compensated individuals.

The ability to bequeath a nonmarital share, either in trust or outright, is also dependent upon the extent to which the spouses have taken title to property as joint owners with rights of survivorship. If there is an excessive amount of joint ownership of property, the jointly-owned property will pass to the surviving spouse automatically by operation of law, and the ability of a decedent to bequeath such property to a trust or someone other than a surviving spouse will be defeated. Since a family residence is typically held in joint names, the placement of other property in joint names will often preclude the estate-splitting possibilities created by the interplay of the marital deduction and the unified estate and gift tax credit. The fear of probate, which often induces many married couples to take virtually all property in joint names, will often lead to excessive estate taxes. Consequenlty, it is the rare case where joint ownership with rights of survivorship makes sense for the highly compensated.[13]

The 1981 Act added several complexities to marital deduction tax planning. The Act both substantially increased the amount of unified estate and gift tax credit and reduced the maximum estate and gift tax rates to 50 percent. These changes, however, are phased in over a substantial period of time with the rate reductions not being fully effective until 1985 and the phase-in of the credit not being fully effective until 1987. Consequently, the numerical parameters facing an

---

[13] Another disadvantage of joint ownership is that the half of the asset that will not be included in the estate of the first spouse to die pursuant to Section 2040 will not receive a step-up in basis. For example, if a married couple jointly owned a vacation home with a basis of $40,000 and a fair market value of $200,000, the property would be considered as owned one half by each spouse. On the death of the first spouse, one half of the property would be considered as passing to the survivor and qualifying for the marital deduction. The basis for this half of the property would be stepped-up to $100,000, making a total basis of $120,000. In contrast, if the entire property had been included in the estate of the first spouse to die, it similarly would pass to the survivor tax-free, but the basis of the property wuld be stepped-up to $200,000.

estate planner will be changing on a yearly basis, at least until 1987. In addition, the fact that the marital deduction is no longer limited to the greater of $250,000 or one half of a decedent's adjusted gross estate means that there is greater flexibility than ever before in determining the amount of the marital deduction. Acordingly, there are now several factors that should be considered in determining the amount of marital deduction. These factors are discussed below.

[b] Economic Needs of the Spouse. The first and foremost consideration in determining the amount of the marital bequest must always be the economic needs of the spouse. Because it is often desirable from a tax standpoint not to bequeath more than a specified portion of a decedent's estate to the surviving spouse, there is a natural tendency on the part of many tax planners to automatically adopt such an approach. This, however, may be undesirable from an economic standpoint if the surviving spouse is not provided for adequately. Because of this concern for the surviving spouse, it is possible (and indeed it is quite common) to devise the nonmarital portion of the estate to a trust for the benefit of the decedent's children while, at the same time, giving the trustee discretion to distribute income or principal to the spouse if necessary for her support or medical care. The practical disadvantage of this type of will is that it does require the surviving spouse to deal with the trustee in order to obtain access to these funds and may prove to be cumbersome or expensive in modest-sized estates. However, a nonmarital trust may provide some assurance to an individual that his spouse is adequately cared for while, at the same time, undertaking the tax planning advantages that are available through estate splitting. In any event, the primary consideration must be the economic well-being of the surviving spouse.

[c] Use of Unified Estate and Gift Tax Credit by Both Spouses. A second important consideration in determining the amount of the marital bequest is the maximum utilization of the unified estate and gift tax credit by each spouse. If the total combined estate of both spouses is below the amount of the unified credit, there is no need for tax planning in this regard since the estate of the second spouse to die will not be taxed even if she inherits everything.[14] However, once the total com-

---

[14] This assumes no substantial appreciation in assets occurred subsequent to the death of the first spouse.

bined assets of both spouses exceeds the amount of the available credit, a tax savings can always be achieved [15] by bequeathing a portion of the assets of the first spouse to die to someone other than the surviving spouse. By making such a bequest, each spouse will be able to use all or a portion of the unified estate and gift tax credit so as to split the estate for estate tax purposes. These principles can be illustrated in the following examples.

If an individual had a $600,000 taxable estate and bequeathed his estate to the surviving spouse, the entire bequest will qualify for the marital deduction. On the death of the second spouse, no tax will be incurred because the unified estate and gift tax credit will exempt the estate from taxation.[16] Consequently, for estates below the current level of the unified credit, there is no tax advantage to estate splitting.

If, however, an individual had a taxable estate of $1.2 million and bequeathed one half of this estate to the surviving spouse and one half to a nonmarital trust, no tax would be incurred on his death because of a combination of the marital deduction and the unified estate and gift tax credit. On the death of the second spouse, no tax would be incurred because her $600,000 estate would be fully exempted by the unified credit. If this individual had bequeathed his entire $1.2 million taxable estate to the surviving spouse, there would be no tax on his death because of the unlimited marital deduction. On the death of the second spouse, however, a tax of approximately $245,000 would be incurred. Consequently, by splitting his estate so as to allow both spouses to take advantage of the unified credit, the decedent was able to achieve a tax savings of $245,000.[17]

Consequently, a principle that should always be considered is the full use of the unified credit by each spouse. To the extent that one of the spouses' estates exceeds the amount of the unified credit that is currently in force, there usually will be a tax advantage to not fully using the marital deduction and bequeathing some amount to a person other than the spouse so that the first spouse's estate takes some advantage of the unified credit.

---

[15] This assumes that the 1981 increases in the credit have been fully phased in.

[16] This example would be applicable in 1987 and thereafter.

[17] All of these examples again assume that the phase-in of the unified credit had been completed. The same principles apply in earlier years but with the numbers reduced to correspond to the phase-in schedule.

[d] Effect of Progressive Rate Structure. The next factor to be considered in determining the amount of the marital bequest is the tax savings to be achieved from estate splitting so that each spouse fully uses the lower rates that result from working up the progressive rate structure. This factor has been greatly diminished by the 1981 Act, which had the effect of compressing estate tax rates from a range of 37 percent to 50 percent.[18] When this Act is fully phased-in, estates of $600,000 or more will be taxed at an initial rate of 37 percent and will reach the maximum 50 percent bracket at a taxable amount of $2.5 million. Consequently, once the combined estates of both spouses exceeds $1.2 million, the family unit can still achieve additional tax savings by splitting the incidents of the estate tax between both spouses so as to allow each spouse to progress up the rate bracket structure.

For example, if an individual left his entire $5 million taxable estate to his surviving spouse, his estate would incur no tax, but the spouse's estate (assuming she owned no other assets) would incur a tax of $2,083,000 upon her death. If he had left one half of his estate to the spouse with the remainder to a nonmarital trust, his estate would incur a tax of $833,000 on his death. The surviving spouse would incur a similar tax, making a total tax of $1,666,000. In this instance, by the effect of a combination of both spouses fully using the unified credit and each spouse working his or her way up the progressive rate structure, a total tax savings of $417,000 will be obtained.[19]

The 1981 changes have somewhat reduced the advantages of estate splitting once the combined estates exceed the level that is exempted by the unified credit since the maximum differential in rates is now limited to 13 percent. This means that the maximum amount that can be saved by estate splitting above the amount of the unified credit will be $117,000. This amount does, however, still represent a significant amount of savings that can be achieved by not fully using the unlimited marital deduction once both estates exceed the amount of the unified credit.

[e] Time Value of Money Saved by Use of Marital Deduction. Weighed against this potential savings arising from complete estate

---

[18] The 37 percent rate will be the minimum rate once the unified credit of $192,800 becomes effective in 1987. The 50 percent maximum rate becomes effective in 1985.

[19] This example again assumes the 1981 changes have been fully phased-in.

¶ 15.02[1][e]   ESTATE PLANNING   15-12

splitting so that each spouse fully uses the progressive nature of the tax brackets should be the time value of the taxes saved by a more extensive usage of the marital deduction. If the total combined estates of both spouses is more than double the amount of the unified credit, once the estates have been planned so that each spouse fully utilizes the unified credit, *some* tax will be incurred on the death of one of the spouses. By a more extensive usage of the unlimited marital deduction, the payment of all federal estate taxes can be delayed until the death of the second spouse. Thus, the time value of the delay in payment of taxes must be counterbalanced against the savings engendered by each spouse fully using the progressive nature of the tax brackets. If the first spouse makes a greater use of the marital deduction, the taxes saved upon his death may be invested by the surviving spouse. The second spouse, in effect, has the use of this money interest-free during the interval between her husband's death and hers. The longer this interval, the greater the advantage of deferring payment of taxes by a more extensive utilization of the marital deduction.

Consequently, in those instances where there is a great dissimilarity in ages between the two spouses, the tax advantage of making nonmarital bequests in excess of the unified credit may be greatly diminished. In such a case, it may make sense to make a nonmarital bequest in the amount of the unified credit and then to leave the remainder to the surviving spouse.[20] Another situation where the possibility of time delay becomes more significant is when both spouses are relatively young. If one of the spouses were to die at a relatively young age, the odds are that the second spouse would survive for an extended period of time. In such a case, the advantages of making a nonmarital bequest in excess of the amount of the unified credit are greatly diminished.[21]

Balanced against the benefits of deferral must be the fact that any appreciation in assets subsequent to the death of the first spouse and any income received from these assets will be included in the estate of

---

[20] A clause that is often used to bequeath the maximum amount to the nonmarital trust that is sheltered by the unified credit reads as follows, "the maximum amount which, considering all credits available to my estate (without causing or increasing a state death tax based on the federal credit for state death taxes) which will result in no federal estate tax payable at my death."

[21] If both spouses were to die simultaneously in a joint disaster, this factor, of course, would not be present. In such a case, it might be possible to make an alternative bequest in the event of a joint disaster so as to more fully utilize the estate splitting that arises from the progressive rate structure.

the second spouse unless consumed or made the subject of a gift within the confines of the annual gift tax exclusion. In other words, if an asset is made the subject of a nonmarital bequest, any appreciation subsequent to the death of the first spouse will be removed from the estates of both spouses. Consequently, if an asset is likely to appreciate substantially in value over time, this appreciation and growth may more than counterbalance the effect of deferral obtained from the use of the unlimited marital deduction. An estate tax deferral from a marital bequest, unlike an income tax deferral, does not automatically produce a tax benefit to the family inasmuch as all of the growth of the asset will be taxed in the estate of the second spouse. Quite obviously, this potential for growth is very difficult to predict, as is the time interval that is likely to occur between the death of both spouses. The potential for the asset to appreciate and obviate the effects of deferral does illustrate the principal that it is typically advantageous to leave assets to the nonmarital portion of a will that are thought most likely to appreciate in value.

Another factor that is difficult to evaluate when assessing the benefits of deferral is the future legislative climate as it will impact upon estate taxes on the death of the second spouse. In recent years, there has been a tendency to greatly liberalize the federal estate tax. If this trend were to continue, the advantages of deferral would increase inasmuch as the second spouse would be likely to face an estate tax code that is more generous than the one that is applicable on the death of the first spouse. The converse would be true if the legislative climate were to change. Again, it is very difficult to predict. In 1976, few estate tax experts would have freely predicted that by 1986 estates of $600,000 or less would be exempted from federal estate taxation. Even though this is a very difficult factor to predict, it is one that must be considered when weighing the question of whether or not to maximize deferral of estate taxes by making greater use of the unlimited marital deduction.

Because (beginning in 1985) the maximum estate tax rate of 50 percent will be effective for taxable estates of 2.5 million, there is no further tax rate advantage of splitting estates once the combined estates of both spouses exceeds $5 million. In other words if the first spouse to die arranged his affairs so that his taxable estate equalled $2.5 million and his spouse's equalled the same amount, no further tax savings would flow from estate splitting above that level. The maximum tax advantage above that level would seem to arise from making a $2.5 million nonmarital bequest and leaving everything else to the surviving spouse. By limiting the nonmarital bequest in estates of $5 million or more to $2.5 million, the family achieves both the maximum advantages of estate splitting, and the time delay permitted by increasing the marital deduction above 50 percent of the adjusted gross estate. If factors such as an age dissimilarity are present, the estate planner may want to reduce the nonmarital bequest even further.

[f] Other Factors in Determining Size of Marital Bequest. There are several other factors that will impact upon the estate planner's decision as to the extent to which he will recommend his clients use the maximum marital deduction. Perhaps the most significant of these factors is the fact that the use of the unlimited marital deduction will mean that all income from the estate will be directed to the surviving spouse. This is true whether or not the marital bequest is made in the form of an outright bequest or in the form of a trust that qualifies for the marital deduction.[22] Because the spouse of a highly compensated individual is likely to have considerable income from various sources, a will that takes complete advantage of the unlimited marital deduction may result in much of this income being subject to taxation at the highest marginal rate bracket. Consequently, overuse of a marital bequest may contain income tax disadvantages as well as estate tax disadvantages.

Another factor to consider may be the impact of state death taxes. Not all states automatically adopt the federal system of estate taxation. Consequently, full use of the marital deduction could possibly mean that a significant portion of the marital bequest is not shielded from state taxation. In addition, if a state imposes taxes at a rate in excess of the federal credit, the use of the unlimited marital deduction may result in no state death tax credit being available on the death of the first spouse to offset state death taxes payable at that time or the wasting of state death taxes on the death of the second spouse.[23]

Finally, other personal factors such as the testator's desire to make direct bequests to someone other than the surviving spouse will influence the decisions made as to the size of the marital bequest. This multiplicity of factors clearly illustrates that the determination of the amount of the marital bequest, given the 1981 changes, is a rather

---

[22] See generally ¶ 15.03[3] infra.

[23] A good article discussing the interrelationship between the use of the unlimited marital deduction and the federal credit for state death taxes is Garlock, "Estate Tax Unlimited Marital Deduction Has Limited Advantage In Larger Estates," 56 J. Tax. 236 (1982).

complex decision requiring the weighing of numerous factors. Often there will be no one clear answer since such considerations as date of death of the surviving spouse and future appreciation of assets cannot be predicted with any degree of accuracy. The estate planner must carefully consider all of these factors and review them with his client so that the client is aware of the impact of these decisions.

[2] Qualification for Marital Deduction

Once a decision is made as to the proper usage of the marital deduction, it is the estate planner's task to ensure that the particular transfers made to or for the benefit of the surviving spouse are arranged in such a manner that they will qualify for the deduction. Essentially, a deduction is allowed to the estate for the value of any interest in property that passes or has passed from the decedent to his [24] surviving spouse, but only to the extent that such interest is included in determining the value of the gross estate.[25] No deduction will be allowed for transfers of a life estate or other terminable interests.[26] Consequently, in order for a transfer to qualify for the marital deduction, the following basic requirements must be met:

(1) The decedent must be survived by a spouse;
(2) Property must pass to such spouse;
(3) The value of the properties so passing must be included in the gross estate of the decedent; and
(4) The decedent must be a citizen or resident of the United States.

If a transfer meets these basic requirements and if the property so transferred does not fall within the definition of the terminable interest rule, a marital deduction will be allowed to the extent permitted by statute.

[a] Decedent Must Be Survived by Spouse. The first requirement for qualification for the marital deduction is that the decedent must be

---

[24] For convenience of discussion, it will be assumed that the male spouse dies first. Obviously, the same principles prevail if the reverse is true.

[25] I.R.C. § 2056(a).

[26] I.R.C. § 2056(b). Terminable interests are discussed in detail in ¶ 15.03 infra.

survived by a spouse. This necessitates a finding of both the proper marital status at the time of death and a finding of survivorship.

[i] **Marital status.** Generally speaking, the marital status of the purported surviving spouse will be determined according to the laws of the decedent's domicile. A common-law marriage will be recognized for federal income tax purposes if applicable state law recognizes such marriages.[27] Presumably, this same rule is also applicable to determine eligibility for the marital deduction. Most controversy relating to the question of whether or not someone is survived by a spouse generally arises in the context of an individual who has died and is survived by both a purported ex-spouse and a questionable divorce decree. The Service has indicated that it generally will not question the validity of any divorce decree until a court of competent jurisdiction declares divorce to be invalid.[28] If a state court proceeding, where there is proper jurisdiction over the parties or the subject matter, declares a prior divorce to be invalid, the Service will generally follow the later court decision rather than abide by the divorce decree.[29] Generally speaking, however, these questions as to whether or not there is a valid marriage do not arise in most planning situations.[30] The major exceptions, which undoubtedly will require an incursion into the laws of the state in question, are where there is a common-law living arrangement [31] or where there is a questionable divorce decree. Because of a general easing of our divorce laws in the past decade, there tend to

---

[27] Rev. Rul. 58-66, 1958-1 C.B. 60.

[28] Rev. Rul. 67-442, 1967-2 C.B. 65.

[29] There has been a fair amount of litigation on this topic. See Borax v. Comm'r, 349 F.2d 666 (2d Cir. 1965), cert. denied, 383 U.S. 935 (1966); Wondsel v. Comm'r, 350 F.2d 339 (2d Cir. 1965), cert. denied, 383 U.S. 935 (1966); Estate of Steffke v. Comm'r, 64 T.C. 530 (1975); Estate of Goldwater v. Comm'r, 64 T.C. 540 (1975); Estate of Spalding v. Comm'r, 34 T.C.M. 1074 (1975) rev'd, 537 F.2d 666 (2d Cir. 1976). Generally speaking, the Tax Court takes the position that if the divorce had been ruled invalid by a court in the state having jurisdiction over the administration of the estate, the marital deduction will be disallowed. The Second Circuit seems to see as critical whether or not the estate is being administered in a state other than that which had decreed the divorce invalid and whether or not the decedent whose estate taxes were at issue had been a party to the first marriage or the invalid divorce.

[30] Very few individuals who have been through a divorce proceeding turn around and leave a substantial bequest to their former spouse.

[31] The recent "palimony" suits whereby "live in" arrangements were held to create certain legal rights might be relevant in this context.

be fewer and fewer situations that may be affected by the validity of a "quickie" foreign divorce.

[ii] Survival. The second aspect of the requirement that the decedent be survived by a spouse is, of course, that of survival. Because survival is typically a factual question, one's initial reaction might be that there is little that can be done about this question from a planning standpoint. Although this is generally true, certain steps can be undertaken to ensure the availability of the marital deduction in the event of a common disaster. It is not unusual to find that because of the circumstances surrounding the death of both spouses, it is impossible to determine which of the spouses survived the other. In this situation, the regulations take the position that a presumption, whether supplied by local law, the decedent's will, or otherwise, that the decedent was survived by his spouse will be recognized in satisfying the survivorship requirements of the statute, but only to the extent that it has the effect of giving the spouse an interest in the property includable in her gross estate.[32] In these circumstances, if an estate tax return is required to be filed for the estate of the decedent's spouse, the marital deduction will not be allowed on the final audit of the estate tax return of the decedent's estate with respect to any property interest that has not been finally determined to be includable in the gross estate of his spouse. Under the Uniform Simultaneous Death Act, a presumption is created that each spouse survived the other. However, a maker of a will may create a different presumption as to the order of the death in order to preserve the marital deduction.

Consequently, it is the responsibility of an estate planner to address in a will the question of which spouse will be deemed to be the survivor in the common death situation. Typically, if for tax purposes one of the spouses will be considered to be the owner of the bulk of the familial assets and the other spouse will be considered to own very few assets, the will of the spouse with the large estate should contain a clause to the effect that in a common disaster situation, he or she will be deemed to be survived by his or her spouse. The other spouse's will should contain complementary language to the effect that he or she will be deemed to have survived the other. The net effect of this language will be to enable a splitting of the assets between the two spouses (assuming that only a portion of the larger estate was bequeathed to the surviving spouse) and

---

[32] Treas. Reg. § 20.2056(e)-2(e).

a likely estate tax savings. The use of the common disaster clause should parallel the desirability of fully funding the marital deduction. For example, if the taxable estates of both spouses are likely to be equal prior to death, a presumption that each survived the other may be the most beneficial.[33] In such a case, an insertion of language that made it clear which was to be the survivor could have a negative tax impact. In any event, in drafting the will, the estate planner must exercise care to address himself to the simultaneous death situation and then properly plan the wills of both spouses to provide for this contingency if such an unfortunate event should occur.

[b] Property Must Pass From Decedent to Spouse. The second major requirement for the marital deduction is that the property must "pass" from the decedent to his surviving spouse. Quite obviously, a direct bequest from a decedent to his surviving spouse will satisfy this requirement. The regulations, however, list numerous other instances in which property will be considered to have passed to a surviving spouse.[34] Included in this list is property passing by operation of law, such as joint ownership, property passing pursuant to a power of appointment, a dower or curtesy interest, proceeds of insurance upon the life of a decedent, property passing during the decedent's lifetime which is includable in the decedent's estate,[35] and a survivor's interest in an annuity or other payment described in Section 2039 to the extent that it is includable in the decedent's gross estate under that section.

Property is considered as passing to the surviving spouse only to the extent that it is transferred to her as a beneficial owner.[36] Thus, for example, if property passed to a surviving spouse as a trustee where she had no beneficial interest in the trust corpus, a marital deduction would not be allowed. If a surviving spouse elects to take against the will, the dower or curtesy interest retained by her is considered as having passed to her, but that property left to her under the will is not considered as having so passed. Similarly, if as a result of a will contest additional property will pass to the surviving spouse, that interest so acquired will

---

[33] This would allow each spouse to take maximum advantage of the Unified Estate and Gift Tax Credit.

[34] Treas. Reg. § 20.2056(e)-1(a).

[35] An example of such property would be a gift in contemplation of death under I.R.C. § 2035.

[36] Treas. Reg. § 20.2056(e)-2(a).

be considered as having passed to her for purposes of the marital deduction. The converse will be true if property must be transferred by the spouse to others as a result of such contest.

[c] Property Must Be Included in Decedent's Gross Estate. The requirement that the property interest that is passed to the spouse must be included in the decedent's gross estate is taken directly from the statute and is derived from the same logic that requires the value of an item to be included in the estate before a deduction related to it will be permitted. To do otherwise would permit a double tax benefit to the estate. The regulations denominate property that is not included in the decedent's gross estate and which passes to a surviving spouse as a nondeductible interest.[37] These regulations also further define the term "nondeductible interest" to refer to those situations under which the estate might conceivably receive a multiple deduction for the same item. For example, if a transfer to a surviving spouse will result in the estate receiving a deduction under Section 2053 for expenses or indebtedness, it will be considered a nondeductible interest for purposes of the marital deduction provisions. Similarly, if during the settlement of an estate, a loss deductible under Section 2054 occurs with respect to a property interest, then the interest to the extent of that deductible loss is conversely nondeductible for the purposes of the marital deduction.[38]

[d] Citizenship or Residency. The requirement that the decedent must be a citizen or resident of the United States at the time of his death relates back to the basic statutory provision imposing the estate tax upon the taxable estate of any individual who was a citizen or resident of the United States.[39] The marital deduction regulations further amplify this requirement by specifically stating that the marital deduction is not allowed in the case of an estate of a nonresident who is not a citizen of the United States at the time of his death.[40] However, if the decedent was a citizen or resident, his estate is entitled to the marital deduction irrespective of the fact that his surviving spouse was neither a resident nor a citizen. Consequently, it is the citizenship or residency of

---

[37] Treas. Reg. § 2056(a)-2(b)(1).
[38] Treas. Reg. § 20.2056(a)-(b)(3).
[39] I.R.C. § 2001.
[40] Treas. Reg. § 20.2056(a)-1(a).

the decedent that is critical in determining the eligibility for the marital deduction — not the citizenship or residence of the surviving spouse. This is both fair and logical since it is the citizenship or residence of the decedent that is initially determinative of taxation.

Generally speaking, the basic requirements for qualification for the marital deductions are rather straightforward and easy to achieve. With the exception of the terminable interest rule discussed below in ¶ 15.03, most planning decisions in regard to the marital deduction relate to the extent to which it should be used and the type of provision to be inserted in the will to achieve the planned use. The qualification requirements set forth in this section of the chapter are clearly defined and should not be overlooked. A failure to recognize and meet these basic requirements can cause the more complex planning related to other questions to be entirely wasted.

¶ 15.03 Terminable Interests and Transfers in Trust

One of the most difficult aspects of qualifying for the marital deduction is to ensure that the bequest or transfer does not fall within the definition of the terminable interest rule. This rule, which is basically found in Section 2056(b) of the Code, denies the marital deduction to certain terminable interests in property that pass to a surviving spouse. The basic concept behind this rule is to preclude a marital deduction for those interests in property that pass to a spouse that would not, unless consumed or dissipated during her lifetime, be taxed in her estate upon death. With this concept in mind, a rather complex set of principles have developed governing the taxation of terminable interests in property. Unless these concepts are closely followed, many transfers to a spouse — particularly transfers in trust — will not qualify for the marital deduction.

[1] Definition of Terminable Interest

A terminable interest is an interest in property "which will terminate or fail on a lapse of time or on the occurrence or the failure to occur of some contingency."[41] Life estates, terms for years, annuities, patents, and copyrights are therefore terminable interests. However, a bond, note, or similar contractual obligations, the discharge of which would

---

[41] Treas. Reg. § 20.2056(b)-1(b).

not have the effect of an annuity or a term for years, are not terminable interests.[42]

[2] Factors Making Terminable Interest Nondeductible

[a] Statutory Requirements. Section 2056(b) denies a marital deduction for a terminable interest but only in certain circumstances. Such an interest will be nondeductible if (a) an interest in such property passes or has passed (for less than an adequate and full consideration in money or monies' worth) from the decedent to any person other than such surviving spouse (or the estate of such spouse) and (b) by reason of such passing, such person (or his heirs or assigns) may possess or enjoy any part of such property after such termination or failure of the interest so passing to the surviving spouse. In addition, no deduction will be allowed with respect to a terminable interest if such interest is to be acquired for the surviving spouse pursuant to direction of the decedent, by his executor or the trustee of a trust.[43] Thus, for terminable interests to be nondeductible, the interest in property must pass to someone other than the surviving spouse and this other person must possess or enjoy some part of the property after the termination of the spouse's interest. As will become apparent later,[44] there are certain exceptions whereby terminable interests that would otherwise be nondeductible within the meaning of these rules may, despite this apparent infirmity, qualify for a deduction.

[b] Transfer of the Same "Property." In determining whether a terminable interest is nondeductible, it is critical to make the distinction between the terms "property" and "interest." The transfer is only nondeductible if another interest in the *same* property is passed from the decedent to some other person. Thus, for example, if a decedent left a life estate in each of two oil wells to his spouse with the remainder interest to his children, a terminable interest would have been created because the spouse's interest in this property would fail upon her death and an interest in this *same* property would pass to the decedent's children at that time. If, however, the decedent bequeathed one oil well in fee simple to his surviving spouse and his interest in the other well to

---

[42] Id.
[43] I.R.C. § 2056(b)(1)(c).
[44] See ¶ 15.03[3] infra.

his children, there would be no terminable interest because another person would not have an interest in the same property as the spouse. In considering the status of an annuity, the property is the fund from which the payments are made.[45] Consequently, when another person acquires a right to the annuity payments after the termination of the spouse's interest, no marital deduction is allowable for the value of the spouse's interest in that annuity. If, however, two separate annuity payments arose on the death of the decedent, the share of the proceeds used in funding the surviving spouse's annuity would be considered to be one property interest, and the share of the fund that constituted the other person's annuity would be considered an additional separate property. In such a case, a marital deduction would be allowed for the surviving spouse's annuity.[46]

[c] Interpretation of State Law. Upon many occasions, the question as to whether or not an interest in property is terminable will depend upon an interpretation of local law. For example, if property passes to a surviving spouse subject to a contract by that spouse to dispose of the interest in property in favor of a specified person, the interest does not qualify for the marital deduction.[47] In such a case, the critical question relates to the amount of control the spouse has over the property she receives under the decedent's will.[48] Where under local law the widow only had a life estate in property passing to her under her husband's joint and mutual will, no marital deduction is allowed.[49] Similarly, questions of whether a dower or curtesy interest qualify for the marital deduction have turned on interpretations of state law.[50] There also has been considerable controversy relating to the deductibil-

---

[45] Rev. Rul. 76-404, 1976-2 C.B. 294.

[46] Rev. Rul. 77-130, 1977-1 C.B. 289.

[47] Treas. Reg. § 20.2056(e)-2(a). Estate of Siegel v. Comm'r, 67 T.C. 662 (1977).

[48] See for example, Batterton v. U.S., 406 F.2d 247 (5th Cir. 1968).

[49] Elson v. Comm'r, 28 T.C. 442 (1957).

[50] Rev. Rul. 72-8, 1972-1 C.B. 309 specifically related to a dower interest obtained under Florida law, which was said to qualify for the marital deduction. See also Rev. Rul. 72-7, 1972-1 C.B. 308; First Nat'l Exch. Bank of Roanoke (Will of Pell) v. U.S., 335 F.2d 91 (4th Cir. 1964) (Virginia dower right not a terminable interest); Dougherty v. U.S., 292 F.2d 331 (6th Cir. 1961) (cash in lieu of dower received by Kentucky estate not terminable interest); Hawaiian Trust Co. v. U.S., 412 F.2d 1313 (Ct. Cl. 1969) (lump sum paid to widow as commuted value of dower for Hawaiian estate qualified for marital deduction).

ity or nondeductibility of widow's allowances. This issue has been litigated in the United States Supreme Court, which has ruled that the character of the widow's allowance must be determined as of the date of death of the decedent. The Court held that if the interest is not vested until awarded by the appropriate court having jurisdiction over the estate, the interest is nondeductible.[51] Consequently, state law must again be consulted to determine the characterization of such an allowance.

[d] Contingent Interests. Those interests that are found to be contingent are of the type that will not qualify for the marital deduction. It is critical that the marital transfer vests in the surviving spouse. For example, a bequest to a surviving spouse of a portion of the proceeds of the sale of certain property "if and when" the property was sold was found to be a terminable interest.[52] No marital deduction was allowed for a bequest to a surviving spouse on the condition that he file with the probate court an agreement to bequeath an equivalent amount to his daughter within four months after decedent's death.[53]

The act of electing will not necessarily render an interest terminable. In *Estate of Tompkins v. Comm'r,*[54] the decedent's will gave his surviving spouse a life estate in trust, but in a codicil he provided that in lieu of the trust interest she should take $40,000 outright, in which event the trust provision was to be null and void. To obtain the $40,000, the spouse had to file a written election with the executor of the decedent's estate "within 60 days after his qualification as...executor." The spouse made a timely election, and the estate deducted the $40,000 paid to the spouse. It was held that the surviving spouse received the $40,000 pursuant to a testamentary right of election, not a power of appointment, and that such right was an "interest in property" within

---

[51] Jackson v. U.S., 376 U.S. 503 (1964). Under California law, the right to the allowance would have terminated if the widow had died or remarried prior to the court award. See also Kliban v. U.S., 37 A.F.T.R.2d 1567 (D. Conn. 1976) (Connecticut awarded terminable interest because of probate court discretion); Estate of Avery v. Comm'r, 40 T.C. 392 (1963), acq. 1971-2 C.B. 1 (Missouri widow's allowance qualified for deduction); Stephens v. U.S., 270 F. Supp. 968 (D. Mont. 1967) (Montana widow's allowance terminable); Rev. Rul. 76-166, 1976-1 C.B. 287 (Arizona allowance in lieu of homestead not a terminable interest).

[52] Casey v. U.S., 23 A.F.T.R.2d 1839 (D. Ill. 1964).

[53] Estate of Ray v. Comm'r, 54 T.C. 1170 (1970).

[54] 68 T.C. 912 (1977). See also Neugass v. Comm'r, 555 F.2d 322 (2d Cir. 1977).

the meaning of Section 2056(a) and the act of electing is not a contingency that would render the interest received terminable under Section 2056(b)(1).

These particular areas of controversy clearly point out that if a gift of less than an entire interest in property to a spouse is being contemplated, there must be a very careful consideration of the law of the appropriate jurisdiction to review that jurisdiction's characterization of the interest being passed. Unless the particular interest in property being passed falls within one of the exceptions of the terminable interest rules discussed below, there is a clear and present danger of disqualification of the marital deduction. A careful review of the situation is needed before the estate planner is able to assure himself that the particular transfer will qualify.

[3] Exceptions to Terminable Interest Rule

There are four basic situations where an interest in property passing to a surviving spouse will be deductible even though it might normally be denominated a terminable interest. These situations are where an interest is terminable only because (1) it is conditioned upon the spouse surviving the decedent for a limited period of time, (2) there is a right to income for life coupled with a general power of appointment in the surviving spouse or (3) there are insurance or annuity payments held by an insurer with a general power of appointment in the surviving spouse. In addition, the 1981 Act added a fourth exception for so-called Qualfied Terminable Interests in Property (often called a "Q-Tip"). Each of these exceptions is commonly used in the estate planning process and is an important tax planning device. Because of the critical importance of the marital deduction in most estate planning situations, it is imperative that these exceptions be fully understood.

[a] Survival for a Limited Period of Time. Section 2056(b)(3) provides an exception to the terminable interest rule so as to allow a marital deduction if the only condition under which the surviving spouse's interest will terminate is the death of the surviving spouse within six months after the decedent's death or her death as a result of a common disaster that also resulted in the decedent's death and the death does not, in fact, occur.[55] The regulations take the position that if

---

[55] See Treas. Reg. § 20.2056(b)-3(a).

the only condition that will cause the surviving spouse's interest to terminate is of such a nature that it can *only* occur within six months following the decedent's death, the Section 2056(b)(3) exception will apply if the condition does not in fact occur. If, however, the condition is one that may occur either within the six month period or thereafter, this exception will be inapplicable.[56]

Judicial opinion has generally followed the position taken by the regulations when reviewing these so-called survival clauses. If the clause is drafted in such a manner that the condition upon which it is predicated can occur subsequent to the six-month period, the marital deduction has been disallowed. For example, marital transfers conditioned upon survival to the date of distribution have been held not to qualify for the marital deduction, since the distribution could, in fact, occur more than six months after the decedent's death.[57] Similarly, the marital deduction has been disallowed when the bequest in the decedent's will is conditioned upon the spouses' survival until probate of the will.[58] In each of these cases, it was possible for the bequest to terminate subsequent to the six-month period. If a survivorship clause is being contemplated, it is imperative that it be specifically limited to six months and not be conditioned upon some event which, while it might normally take place within a six-month period, could conceivably occur after that date.[59]

It is quite routine to see a six-month survivorship clause inserted in wills and, indeed, such clauses are frequently employed without a good deal of consideration having been given to their utility. As is the case with many planning devices, the proper usage of a survivorship clause may be beneficial from both a tax and administrative standpoint. In other cases, an attempt to use these survivorship exceptions can have a detrimental effect. In many respects, the desirability of using the survivorship exception to the terminable interest rule parallels the desirability of funding the marital bequest in the first place. The

---

[56] Treas. Reg. § 20.2056(b)-3(b).

[57] Estate of Street v. Comm'r, 25 T.C. 673 (1955); Estate of Sbicca v. Comm'r, 35 T.C. 96 (1960); Farrell v. U.S., 198 F. Supp. 461 (S.D. Cal. 1961). Very few estates are completely distributed within a six-month period.

[58] Hansen v. Vinel, 413 F.2d 882 (8th Cir. 1969); Estate of Fried v. Comm'r, 445 F.2d 979 (2d Cir. 1971), cert denied, 404 U.S. 1016 (1972).

[59] The service has ruled that the six-month survivorship period terminates on the day of the sixth calendar month after the decedent's death, numerically corresponding to the day of the calendar month on which the death in fact occurred. Rev. Rul. 70-400, 1970-2 C.B. 196.

advantage of using the survivorship clause in a will is that those assets that would otherwise be bequeathed to a person who died shortly after the decedent will not be subject to a second probate — thereby presumably saving administrative and probate costs, as well as estate taxes in the second estate. If, however, the marital bequest was being made for estate-splitting purposes (i.e., the decedent possesses substantial assets and the surviving spouse, none), there could be a significant tax advantage in using a survivorship clause in regard to the marital bequest. If, on the other hand, a marital bequest is being made to a spouse who has substantial assets in her own name with the knowledge that she ultimately would have a significantly larger estate than the decedent, the use of the Section 2056(b)(3) exception would prevent the surviving spouse's estate from being needlessly inflated if her death shortly followed shortly after the decedent's. The administrative and probate costs of having the same assets pass through a second estate in a particular jursidiction must also be weighed.

Consequently, it is necessary to carefully evaluate the desirability from a tax standpoint of using a survivorship clause in regard to the marital bequest. In many instances, the most desirable course of action may be to insert a survivorship clause in the will, but to except the marital bequest from that clause. In any event, the decision on whether or not to use such a clause must be made on the basis of informed tax and administrative planning rather than blindly inserting or not inserting such a clause in a standard form will.

[b] Life Estate With General Power of Appointment. Prior to the enactment of the 1981 Act the most commonly used exception to the terminable interest rule was the bequest of a life estate with a power of appointment to the surviving spouse.[60] Although this exception is

---

[60] I.R.C. § 2056(b)(5) reads as follows:

LIFE ESTATE WITH POWER OF APPOINTMENT IN SURVIVING SPOUSE — In the case of an interest in property passing from the decedent, if his surviving spouse is entitled for life to all the income from the entire interest, or all the income from a specific portion thereof, payable annually or at more frequent intervals, with power in the surviving spouse to appoint the entire interest, or such specific portion (exercisable in favor of such surviving spouse, or of the estate of such surviving spouse, or in favor of either, whether or not in each case the power is exercisable in favor of others), and with no power in any other person to appoint any part of the interest, or such specific portion, to any person other than the surviving spouse —

(A) the interest or such portion thereof so passing shall, for pur-

applicable to a legal life estate coupled with a general power of appointment, it typically takes the form of a so-called marital deduction trust, which encompasses the marital portion of a decedent's estate. In order to qualify for this exception, the trust must meet all of the following requirements:[61]

(1) The surviving spouse must be entitled for life to all of the income of the entire interest or a specific portion of the entire interest, or to a specific portion of all the income from the entire interest.

(2) The income payable to a surviving spouse must be payable annually or at more frequent intervals.

(3) The surviving spouse must have the power to appoint the entire interest or a specific portion to either herself or to her estate (i.e., a general power of appointment).

(4) The power in the surviving spouse must be exercisable by her alone and (whether exercisable in a will or during her lifetime) must be exercisable in all events.

(5) The entire interest or the specific portion must not be subject to a power in any other person to appoint any other part to a person other than the surviving spouse.

In determining whether these conditions have been met, the regulations provide that the applicable provisions of the law of the jurisdiction under which the interest passes and, if the transfer is in trust, the applicable provisions of the law governing the administration of the trust must be weighed.[62] For example, if the will or trust is silent as to one of these five requirements, that particular gap may be overcome by the applicable provisions of state law. In making a determination of what is the applicable state law, the Supreme Court has held that the federal tax authorities are not bound by a determination of the property

---

poses of subsection (a), be considered as passing to the surviving spouse, and

(B) no part of the interest so passing shall, for purposes of paragraph (1)(A), be considered as passing to any other person other than the surviving spouse.

This paragraph shall only apply if such power in the surviving spouse to appoint the entire interest, or such specific portion thereof, whether exercisable by will or during life, is exercisable by such spouse alone and in all events.

[61] Treas. Reg. § 20.2056(b)-5(a).
[62] Treas. Reg. § 20.2056(b)-5(e).

interest by a state trial court, but rather are only bound by a decision of the highest court of the state. If there is no decision by the highest court of the state, the federal authorities must apply what they find to be the state law after giving "a proper regard" to the rulings of lower state courts.[63]

The question of whether the surviving spouse is entitled for life to all of the income from the entire interest or a specific portion of the entire interest depends on whether the effect of the trust is to give her substantially that degree of beneficial enjoyment of the trust property during her life that the principles of the law of trusts accord to a person who is unqualifiedly designated as the life beneficiary of a trust. Such enjoyment is given only if it was a decedent's intention, as manifested by the terms of the trust instrument and the surrounding circumstances, that the trust should produce for the surviving spouse during her life such an income, or that the spouse should have such use of the trust property as is consistent with the value of the trust corpus.[64] The Service takes the position that an interest passing in trust will not satisfy this requirement if the primary purpose of the trust is to safeguard property without providing the spouse with the required beneficial enjoyment. If the trust corpus consists of property that is not likely to be income producing, and the spouse cannot compel the trustee to convert or otherwise deal with the property to provide income, the interest passing to the spouse may not qualify.[65] Thus, the trust cannot by its terms or composition evidence an intention to deprive the surviving spouse of a right to income from the corpus.

If the trust requires or allows the trustee to accumulate income, the trust will fail to qualify. For example, the Service has ruled that where the decedent's will established a trust under which all income was payable to the surviving spouse, except that the trustee was required to accumulate $40,000 during the first two years of the trust's existence to pay for the education of the decedent's grandchildren, the trust did not qualify for the marital deduction.[66] Where the trust provided that income for the past year was to be paid quarterly during the year following that in which the income was earned, the marital deduction

---

[63] Commissioner v. Bosch, 387 U.S. 456 (1967).
[64] Treas Reg. § 20. 2056(b)-5(f)(1).
[65] Treas. Reg. § 20.2056(b)-5(f)(5).
[66] Rev. Rul 77-444, 1977-2 C.B. 341.

was similarly denied.[67] The marital deduction has also been disallowed where the trustee had the power to divert income toward the maintenance and education of others.[68]

Although there have been many cases that have upheld the marital deduction where the trust instrument on its face did not conclusively require the payment of all income to the surviving spouse,[69] the mere fact that litigation was required in those cases illustrates the dangers of poorly worded or ambiguous provisions relating to the distribution of trust income. Any language in a marital deduction trust other than that which clearly entitles the surviving spouse to all of the income from the entire interest or a specific portion of the entire interest, or to a specific portion of all income from the entire interest, is simply not recommended.[70] Any direction to the trustees other than a clear instruction to distribute all income to the spouse is ill advised.

The requirement that the surviving spouse must have a power of appointment can be fulfilled by a power that falls within one of three categories: (1) the power to appoint must be fully exercisable in her own favor at any time following the decedent's death; or (2) a power to appoint must be exercisable in favor of her estate; or (3) a combination of the previously two mentioned powers.[71] These powers must be exercisable in all events, irrespective of when she may die.[72]

The basic thrust of the power of appointment requirement is that the surviving spouse must have a power of appointment over the

---

[67] Rev. Rul. 72-283, 1972-1 C.B. 311. See also Rev. Rul. 75-128, 1975-1 C.B. 308 disallowing a marital deduction where the trustee had accumulation powers. But see, Merchants Nat'l Bank of Cedar Rapids v. U.S., 326 F. Supp. 384 (N.D. Iowa 1971), where the trustee could exercise his discretion to use, apply, expend, or accumulate the income for the wife's benefit in the event that she became ill or unable to manager her own affairs. The court held that the testator's general intent was to merely authorize the trustee to accumulate income during the quarter and to pay the same over at the end of the quarter.

[68] Estate of Weisberger v. Comm'r, 29 T.C. 217 (1957).

[69] See Estate of Todd, Jr. v. Comm'r, 57 T.C. 288 (1971); Estate of Mittleman v. Comm'r, 522 F.2d 132 (D.C. Cir. 1975).

[70] See Rev. Rul. 69-56, 1969-1 C.B. 224 where the Service illustrates those administrative powers or directions conferred upon fiduciaries that will not result in the disallowance of the marital deduction.

[71] Treas. Reg. § 20.2056(b)-5(g)(1).

[72] The Service has ruled that unless the language of the trust instrument expressly confers the right to appoint to the surviving spouses' estate, no marital deduction is permitted. Rev. Rul. 76-502, 1976-2 C.B. 273.

interest or property to dispose of it to whomever she pleases without the consent of any other person and with such power being exercisable in all events. The requirement that the surviving spouse have the power to dispose of the property to whomever she pleases [73] cannot be defeated in any way. For example, if the state law construed a power of appointment to not allow the holder of the power to appoint to her own estate, the deduction may be lost.[74] A preexisting binding contract to dispose of property in a certain manner may also defeat the deduction. If, however, the power of appointment is construed under state law to be an absolute power of disposition, the requirements of the Code will be satisfied.[75] Naming alternate takers in the absence of the exercise of the power of appointment is quite common and is permissible.[76] Most marital deduction trusts provide for a distribution to children (or a nonmarital trust for their benefit) in the absence of the exercise of a power of appointment. Indeed, it is even permissible to grant an unqualified power of appointment followed by language expressing a desire that the property should be appointed in a specific manner.[77] The existence of the requirement that the surviving spouse have the power to appoint to whomever she pleases plus the frequency of litigation on this topic points out the dangers of not drafting exceedingly clear language into the trust instrument giving the surviving spouse the power to so appoint. The absence of clear language both invites litigation and may make the qualification for the marital deduction dependent upon the vagaries of state law.

Adherence is also necessary to the requirement that the exercise of the power of appointment cannot require the joinder or consent of any other person.[78] Similarly, care must be taken to ensure that the power is exercisable in all events. The case law is replete with instances where the marital deduction has been denied because the power of appointment was not exercisable in all events. For example, where a testator had bequeathed two residences to his wife with the power to sell them and

---

[73] Treas. Reg. § 20.2056(b)-5(g)(2).

[74] Estate of Allen v. Comm'r, 29 T.C. 465 (1957).

[75] See Rev. Rul. 77-30, 1977-1 C.B. 291; Salter v. Comm'r, 545 F.2d 494 (5th Cir. 1977).

[76] Rev. Rul. 55-394, 1955-1 C.B. 458.

[77] Estate of Holland v. Comm'r, 64 T.C. 499 (1975), acq. 1975-2 C.B. 1.

[78] See generally, Treas. Reg. § 20.2056(b)-5(g)(3).

use the proceeds to acquire the fee simple in another residence, the deduction was denied on the ground that the power of appointment was for a limited purpose and was not exercisable in all events.[79] In *Estate of Hollingshead v. Commissioner*,[80] the surviving spouse was given a life estate in property with the remainder left to the children and a discretionary "5 + 5" power to appoint the principal to himself.[81] Inasmuch as the surviving spouse's power of appointment could not exceed 5 percent of the trust corpus per year, only that amount was considered to be "exercisable in all events" for purposes of the marital deduction. A wife's life estate, coupled with the power of appointment predicated upon survival until the will was probated, was held not to be exercisable in all events.[82] A power to demand corpus conditioned upon a surviving spouse remaining competent and not requiring the appointment of the guardian was similarly held not exercisable in all events and not qualified for the Section 2056 deduction.[83] Thus, again it is critical that the trust instrument not even create the appearance of placing restrictions on the spouse's power of appointment. To do so only invites litigation and the potential loss of the marital deduction.

The marital deduction trust is a very valuable and frequently used estate planning vehicle. By placing the marital bequest in trust, the decedent can provide the usual advantages of professional trust management and avoid having the trust assets probated in the surviving spouse's estate. The decedent may also use the trust provisions to ensure that the assets are distributed in a manner he chooses if the power of appointment granted to the surviving spouse is not exercised (as it is

---

[79] U.S. v. First Nat'l Trust & Sav. Bank of San Diego (Estate of Vajen) 335 F.2d 107 (9th Cir. 1964).

[80] 70 T.C. 578 (1978).

[81] A "5 + 5" power allows an individual to appoint the greater of $5,000 or 5 percent of the aggregate value of a trust corpus. The usage of this power derives from the language of Section 2041(b)(2), which states that the lapse of a power of appointment will be considered a release of such power. This rule is, however, only applicable to the extent that the property that would have been appointed by the exercise of the lapsed power exceeds the greater of the "5 + 5" amount. See ¶ 16.03[2][c] infra.

[82] Silvey Ex'x. v. U.S., 265 F. Supp. 235 (N.D. Ala. 1966).

[83] Starrett (Estate of Tingley) v. Comm'r, 223 F.2d 163 (lst Cir. 1955). The Service has ruled, however, that mental incompetency of the surviving spouse to exercise an unrestricted power over the trust principal during her lifetime does not preclude the trust from qualifying for the marital deduction. Rev. Rul. 55-518, 1955-2 C.B. 384.

not in most cases). The power of appointment granted to the spouse does create the danger that the ultimate disposition of the assets will not be in accordance with the decedent's wishes. If this is a concern and the trust vehicle appears preferable to a direct bequest, a qualified terminable interest trust [84] should be considered.

Since the basic concept of the marital deduction trust is that the surviving spouse has the essential equivalent of ownership over the assets, those assets will be taxable in her estate. Consequently, the marital deduction trust is more of an asset management vehicle than a tax saving device per se. The same estate tax consequences will be achieved by a direct bequest of the assets to the spouse. Accordingly, the critical question determining whether to use a trust for the marital bequest typically involves weighing the advantages previously discussed against the expenses of establishing and maintaining the trust and the wisdom of forcing the surviving spouse to deal with the trustee in regard to these assets. If, however, the trust vehicle is chosen, careful adherence to the five basic requirements set forth in the regulations is mandatory. The danger lies in improper usage of the trust, which may cause the marital deduction to be lost.

[c] Life Insurance With Power of Appointment. Section 2056(b)(6) provides an additional major exception to the terminable interest rule for an interest passing to a surviving spouse that consists of the proceeds held by an insurer under the terms of a life insurance, endowment, or annuity contract that meets certain specified conditions to enable it to become a deductible interest. Because the taxable estate of highly compensated individuals frequently includes life insurance that passes to the surviving spouse,[85] it is imperative that those proceeds that pass to the surviving spouse qualify for the marital deduction. If the proceeds are paid in a lump sum directly to the spouse, there is absolutely no question as to the deductibility.[86] If the proceeds are paid in any other manner, however, there is a concern as to their deductibility. The regulations [87] set forth five basic requirements for qualification:

---

[84] Discussed in ¶ 15.03[3][d], infra.

[85] The general topic of taxability of life insurance proceeds and methods of removing them from the taxable estate are discussed in Chapter 13.

[86] Treas. Reg. § 20.2056(e)-2(b)(3)(ii).

[87] Treas. Reg. § 20.2056(b)-6(a).

(1) The proceeds must be held by the insurer subject to an agreement either to pay the entire proceeds or a specific portion thereof in installments or to pay interest thereon during the life of the surviving spouse and only to her.

(2) The installments must be payable annually or more frequently, beginning not later than thirteen months after the decedent's death.

(3) The surviving spouse must have the power to appoint all or a specific portion of the amount held by the insurer to either herself or her estate.

(4) The power exercisable by the surviving spouse must be exercisable by her alone (whether exercisable by will or during life) and must be exercisable in all events.

(5) The amounts payable under the contract must not be subject to a power in any other person to appoint any part thereof to any person other than the surviving spouse.

It should be evident from reviewing these requirements that there is a very close parallel between these qualifications and the requirements for a marital deduction trust. The major additional factor is the specific requirement that payments must commence within thirteen months after the decedent's death. Because of this similarity, there is no need to extensively discuss these requirements. The regulations do note that an insurance contract that requires the insurer to make annual or more frequent payments will not be disqualified merely because the surviving spouse must comply with certain formalities such as furnishing proof of death subsequent to the insurer.[88]

The Tax Court, in *Estate of Fiedler v. Commissioner*,[89] held that where the surviving spouse, rather than the decedent, has the choice of settlement options, and where each of these settlement options meets the requirements of Section 2056(b)(6), the marital deduction will be allowable. In the *Fiedler* case, the surviving spouse actually made the election more than thirteen months after the decedent's death and was required under the terms of the policy to revoke a contingent beneficiary designation before he could appoint the proceeds to his estate. The Tax Court held, however, that the fact that the proceeds were payable within the thirteen-month period meant that the policy qualified. In

---

[88] Treas. Reg. § 20.2056(b)-6(d). See also Estate of Cornwell v. Comm'r, 37 T.C. 688 (1962).

[89] 67 T.C. 239 (1976), acq. 1977-1 C.B. 1.

addition, the requirement of revoking the contingent beneficiary designation was likened to a formal requirement for the convenience of the insurer and held to be of no substantive importance.

It is important to review these requirements for qualification of life insurance for the marital deduction when the proceeds payable to a surviving spouse will be includable in the decedent's estate. If the decedent policy owner selects a settlement option providing for anything other than a direct lump-sum payment to the spouse, he or his advisors must be aware of these requirments that so closely parallel the requirement for a marital deduction trust. In truth, most insurance companies design their policies so that these requirements will be met. This qualification cannot be assumed, however, and the policy provisions must be reviewed with the insurer so that the marital deduction is not lost.

[d] Qualified Terminable Interest Property. The 1981 Act added a fourth exception to the terminable interest rule for so-called Qualified Terminable Interests in Property.[90] "Qualified terminable interest property" is defined as property that passes from the decedent in which the surviving spouse has a "qualifying income interest for life" and for which an election is made by the executor on the estate tax return. A qualifying income interest for life exists if the surviving spouse is entitled to all of the income from the property payable annually or at more frequent intervals, and if no person has a power to appoint any part of the property to any person other than the surviving spouse.[91] Thus, the Qualified Terminable Interest Property Rule allows a decedent to leave a life estate providing income to his spouse and to have that income interest qualify for the marital deduction.

The price paid for obtaining the marital deduction for qualified terminable interest property is the inclusion of such property in the taxable estate of the spouse. Such property will be taxable to the spouse on the earlier of (1) a disposition during her lifetime [92] or (2) in her gross estate at death.[93] Consequently, the tax consequences of qualified termi-

---

[90] See generally § 2056(b)(7).

[91] I.R.C. § 2056(b)(7)(B)(ii). The power of appointment condition does not apply to a power exercisable only at or after the death of the surviving spouse. This language would seemingly preclude a general power of appointment in favor of the surviving spouse.

[92] I.R.C. § 2519(b)(1).

[93] I.R.C. § 2044.

nable interest property are similar to those of property transferred outright to the spouse — exclusion from the first estate and inclusion in the second.

The planning implications for the establishment of qualified terminable interest property are relatively similar to those considerations underlying any other gift or postmortem transfer to a spouse. If the surviving spouse's estate is considerably larger than that of the transferor, it may make sense to devise the property to others and not needlessly inflate the larger estate. Additionally, if the spouse were to receive qualified terminable interest property and then make a lifetime transfer of it, the entire value of the property less amounts received by the spouse on its disposition is treated as a taxable gift. Moreover, there would be no annual gift tax exclusion for the transfer of the remainder interest because the remainder interest would be a gift of a future interest. Accordingly, there appears to be little to gain from creating qualified terminable interest property if the spouse is likely to make a gift of such property during her lifetime.

The major planning opportunity offered by qualified terminable interest property is that this concept allows a testator to establish a trust for the benefit of his spouse without granting the spouse a power of appointment. One of the primary disadvantages of the traditional marital trust is that the power of appointment granted to the surviving spouse could allow her to defeat the testator's wishes as to the ultimate disposition of his assets. This is particularly critical in a second marriage situation where an individual wishes to provide an income interest for his current spouse but is concerned that she might exercise the power of appointment to disinherit his children from a prior marriage. The so-called Q-Tip trust eliminates this fear by eliminating the power of appointment requirement and thus allowing the testator to control the ultimate disposition of property.

Another unique planning opportunity that arises from qualified terminable interest property is due to the fact that its tax treatment as a marital deduction item can be elected by the executor. Accordingly, it would be possible to make a bequest to a surviving spouse in a form that would qualify under Section 2056(b)(7) and to leave the determination as to the tax consequences to the executor. At the time of death, the executor could make a determination as to whether it would be most beneficial to claim the marital deduction and have the property included in the taxable estate of the surviving spouse or to have no marital deduction claimed and the property taxed in the estate of the decedent. The flexibility accorded by a bequest of this nature might be especially useful for those estates where it is unclear whether or not the marital deduction is going to be overfunded, and where it is unclear when the will is being drafted precisely where the greatest tax benefit will lie.

As noted earlier in the discussion relating to planning for the marital deduction,[94] tax planning for the marital deduction is in a state of transition because of the phase-in of the increase in the unified estate and gift tax credit and the reduction in the maximum rate of tax. Consequently, for those individuals whose estates are on the borderline of taxability, or those estates that might suffer divergent tax results depending on the year of death, a bequest which, if elected by the executor, would qualify as qualified terminable interest property offers needed and very useful flexibility. It, in effect, allows the executor to choose which spouse will be taxed on the property in question.

¶ 15.04 Drafting the Marital Deduction Provision

After the decision has been made as to the extent to which the marital deduction should be utilized and whether or not the marital and nonmarital shares will pass in trust, the estate planner is then faced with the task of drafting the marital deduction clause to correspond to these planning decisions. In addition to questions relating to the amount of the marital deduction and the manner of making such a bequest, there are also important decisions relating to the specific type of property to be transferred. For example, it may be desirable for income tax or other reasons that a specific piece of property be transferred or not be transferred to the surviving spouse; or there may be certain types of property that cannot be readily divided between the marital and nonmarital shares.

The estate planner is also faced with the problem that, although he is evaluating the estate at a particular moment in time, the will or trust instrument will become operative at death, which may be several years in the future. In the interim, the property being held by his client may appreciate or depreciate in value or may be sold and replaced with other very different types of property. The estate planner is thus faced with the necessity of developing a marital deduction provision that will not only accurately reflect today's planning decisions, but that will also adequately serve his client in the future. Because there is a tendency on the

---

[94] See ¶ 15.02 supra.

part of most individuals not to review their estate plan on an annual basis, the need for a future protection in the drafting of a will or trust instrument becomes critically important. For this reason, various types of formula or equalization provisions have become quite popular in drafting the marital deduction clause where estate splitting is a desirable goal. These various types of provisions all share the common trait of attempting to automatically adjust the marital and nonmarital bequests as the assets that comprise the decedent's estate either change or fluctuate in value. This section discusses some of the more popular marital deduction provisions and the variations that have developed.

[1] Fractional Share Provisions

A fractional formula provision bequeaths a fractional share or a percentage of all assets of the residuary estate to the surviving spouse. If the complete estate splitting is desired, this type of provision will generally bequeath one half of the estate to the spouse. Although a fractional share provision can take many forms, it typically bequeaths a fraction to the surviving spouse whose numerator being 50 percent of the value of the adjusted gross estate as finally determined for federal estate tax purposes, minus the aggregate value of all properties includable in the adjusted gross estate for federal estate tax purposes that qualify for the marital deduction; and whose denominator is the aggregate value as finally determined for federal estate tax purposes of the assets comprising the decedent's residuary estate. This fractional amount is then bequeathed to the spouse either outright or in trust with the remainder bequeathed to a nonmarital trust or to specified beneficiaries.

In theory, at least, the fractional share formula bequeaths the surviving spouse a fraction of each item of property in the residuary estate. This can potentially cause a problem in those estates in which an executor has an obligation to actually fractionalize each asset. Although state law or the will itself may permit the executor to select assets of sufficient value to fund the bequest, there is the potential that the fiduciary may have to divide each asset in the residue between the marital and nonmarital shares. The other disadvantage of the fractional formula provision is that the executor may not know the amount of the marital deduction until the completion of the administration of the estate. Since the fraction is based on a specified percentage of the residuary estate, the surviving spouse will be entitled to receive an

¶ 15.04[2] ESTATE PLANNING 15-38

amount based on values at the time of distribution. Consequently, there may be a delay in calculating the precise amount of marital deduction.[95] On the other hand, since the surviving spouse receives a specified percentage of the residue, she will share in the appreciation or depreciation of the value of the estate during the administration. Consequently, if the original intent was to equalize the marital and nonmarital shares, the fractional formula share will continue to provide this type of equality.

Finally, it should be noted that the fractional formula marital deduction provision results in no recognition of gain or loss during the funding of the marital bequest since the fractional share is not a bequest of a specific dollar amount.[96] Thus, the fractional formula bequest will result in relatively favorable income tax treatment for the estate.

[2] Pecuniary Bequests

A pecuniary bequest is a bequest of a specific dollar amount. The pecuniary formula bequest means "an amount equal to" a fraction of the entire gross estate. Rather than leaving a part of each asset to the marital or nonmarital portions, it is considered a bequest of a specific dollar amount which may, if the will or state law permits, be satisfied either in kind or in cash. Because the pecuniary bequest is a bequest of a specified dollar amount, the marital portion will not share in the appreciation or the depreciation of the estate during administration. A typical pecuniary formula provision might read as follows: "I give and bequeath to my wife *an amount equal to* 50 percent of the value of my adjusted gross estate as finally determined for estate tax purposes, minus the value of those assets which qualify for the marital deduction allowable in determining the federal estate tax payable with respect to my estate."

Because the pecuniary bequest is considered a bequest of a specific dollar amount, the estate will recognize a taxable gain or loss upon funding the bequest unless there has been no change in value in the property between the date of death and the day of distribution or unless date of death values are used to determine the amount of property

---

[95] As a consequence, the executor may have to seek an extension of time to file the estate tax return.

[96] Treas. Reg. § 1.661(a)-2(f)(1).

which funds the bequest.[97] Thus, the pecuniary formula provision may produce unfavorable income tax consequences to the estate — particularly in those situations where a substantial period of administration is likely, with assets that may appreciate in value. On the other hand, the pecuniary bequest is somewhat easier to administer than the fractional share provision since the executor will know the amount of the marital deduction as of the date of death or the alternate valuation date.

The pecuniary formula bequest is typically coupled with a specific power granted to the executor to satisfy the bequest either in cash or kind or partly in cash and partly in kind. This so-called pick-and-choose clause originally caused a great deal of consternation to the Service. Such a bequest, when not coupled with other restrictions in either the instrument or the applicable state law, would allow the executor to either distribute depreciated assets to the marital share or to concentrate the distribution of appreciated assets to the nonmarital share. The result of this type of selection would be to decrease the estate of the surviving spouse and reduce the total estate taxes to be paid upon her subsequent death.

In response to the popularity of this type of provision, the Service issued Rev. Proc. 64-19 [98] relating to those situations where a pecuniary bequest provided that the executor or trustee may satisfy the bequest in kind with assets at the value as finally determined for federal estate tax purposes. That revenue procedure (which is applicable to both formula pecuniary bequests or those of a fixed dollar amount) indicates that the full amount of the pecuniary bequest or transfer to trust will be allowed as a marital deduction if under the appropriate state law or terms of the governing instrument one of two conditions are met: (1) if the fiduciary must distribute assets, including cash, having an aggregate fair market value on the date or dates of distribution amounting to no less than the amount of the pecuniary bequest or transfer as finally determined for federal estate tax purposes or (2) where the fiduciary must distribute

---

[97] See Rev. Rul. 60-87, 1960-1 C.B. 286. See also Rev. Rul. 82-4, 1982-1 I.R.B. 14 where a will required that in dividing an estate equally between decedent's two children, the executor was to take into account the date of death value of shares of stock transferred to one child during the testator's life. On this set of facts, the Service ruled that the bequest was one of a specific sum of money and the estate would realize gain on the distribution of any appreciated stock.

[98] 1964-1 C.B. 682.

assets, including cash, fairly representative of appreciation or depreciation in the value of all property available for distribution in satisfaction of the pecuniary bequest or transfer. If the governing instrument or applicable state law does not impose one of these two requirements, the bequest will be considered as unascertainable in amount and thus a nondeductible terminable interest.

Although many states have passed laws to ensure that pecuniary bequests will be interpreted to comply with the requirements of Rev. Proc. 64-19, in those situations to which the procedure is applicable,[99] care should be taken to insert a clause which requires that the fiduciary comply with one of the two requirements set forth in Rev. Proc. 64-19. Thus, it is very typical to see a pecuniary formula provision coupled with a requirement that the distribution in satisfaction of the bequest shall consist of assets, including cash, fairly representative of the appreciation or the depreciation in the value of all property available for distribution. The failure to include such an instruction or a request that the assets when distributed aggregate in value no less than the amount of the pecuniary bequest or transfer as determined for federal estate tax purposes may cause the disallowance of the marital deduction.

[3] Equalization Clauses

Because the maximum familial tax savings from the use of the marital deduction may arise in those cases where the estates of both spouses are equal,[100] it is not surprising that draftsmen of testamentary instruments began the search for a clause which would devise that amount to a surviving spouse that was necessary to equalize the estates of both spouses at the time of the death of the first spouse. The result of these efforts has been the so-called equalization clause which has gained some popularity with many estate planners, has received a certain

---

[99] The revenue procedure is not applicable to fractional share bequests under which each beneficiary shares proportionally in the appreciation or depreciation of the value of assets, to bequests of specific assets, or to pecuniary bequests in which the bequest must be satisfied in cash, to which the fiduciary has no discretion in the selection of the assets to be distributed in kind, or to which the bequest must be satisfied with assets selected by the fiduciary based on a valuation on the date or dates of their distribution.

[100] The same savings may arise if both estates are at least in the same marginal tax bracket.

amount of court approval and until recently, has attracted significant and continued opposition from the Service.

A typical example of such a clause is found in *Estate of Smith v. Commissioner*,[101] which is the primary judicial interpretation of this question:

> There shall be allocated to the Marital Portion that percentage interest in the balance of the assets constituting the trust estate which shall...obtain for the settlor's estate a marital deduction which would result in the lowest Federal estate taxes in the settlor's estate and settlor's wife's estate, on the assumption that settlor's wife died after him, but on the date of his death and that her estate were valued as of the date on (and in the manner in) which settlor's estate is valued for Federal Estate tax purposes; settlor's purpose is to equalize insofar as possible, his estate and her estate for Federal Estate tax purposes, based upon said assumptions.

The equalization clause thus requires a valuation of both spouses' estates and bequeaths to the survivor only that amount necessary to equalize both of them. The Service took the position in the *Smith* case that the use of the equalization clause resulted in a nondeductible terminable interest since, if the decedent's executor chose to value his estate on the alternate valuation date, the surviving spouse could conceivably have a larger estate at that time. If this was the case, no property would pass to her and her interest in the decedent's estate would fail. The Tax Court held that the surviving spouse's interest indefeasibly vested as the date of the decedent's death and that the problems alluded to by the Service were problems of valuation rather than vesting. The Seventh Circuit in affirming the Tax Court decision agreed and noted that the purpose of the terminable interest rule which was to limit the marital deduction to interests in property that, unless consumed or disposed of, would be taxed in the surviving spouse's estate, as was the situation in the *Smith* case. The Tax Court has also upheld the use of the equalization clause in the *Estate of Meeske v. Commissioner*,[102] and *Estate of Laurin v. Commissioner*.[103]

---

[101] 66 T.C. 415 (1976), aff'd, 565 F.2d 455 (7th Cir. 1977), nonacq. 1978-1 C.B. 3, nonacq. withdrawn and acq. substituted, 1982-4 I.R.B. 5.

[102] 72 T.C. 73 (1979), aff'd, 645 F.2d 8 (6th Cir. 1981).

[103] ¶ 79,145 P-H Memo. T.C., aff'd, 645 F.2d 8 (6th Cir. 1981).

There are many factors that must be carefully weighed before making any decision to utilize any equalization clause. Although, in theory, the utilization of an equalization clause could frequently result in the lowest combined taxes for both spouses' estates, several other factors require serious consideration. First, it should be noted that after years of opposition the Service has finally withdrawn its opposition to the use of equalization clauses and has acquiesced in the above noted cases.[104] Thus the threat of potential litigation over the use of these clauses has receded.

The tax savings achieved by using this clause may not be as great as might otherwise appear on the surface. The trade-off in using the equalization clause (as well as other clauses which do not fully fund the marital deduction) is a relinquishment of the deferral of taxes that is achieved by full utilization of the marital deduction. In addition, because of the compression of estate tax rates by the 1981 Act into a relatively narrow range, the actual dollar savings from precise estate splitting in many cases may be insignificant. If the tax savings achieved by equalizing two estates is relatively minimal, it may be more advantageous to fully fund the marital deduction under the premise that the earnings achieved on the tax that is deferred will outweigh the potential estate tax savings arising from equalization.

On the other hand, if both spouses have substantial assets in their own name, an equalization clause may be a useful way of minimizing the combined taxation on both estates. Such a clause could take maximum advantage of both spouses' unified credit and the graduation in rates up to the 50 percent bracket. If, however, both spouses' taxable estates already exceed $2.5 million, nothing will be saved by further equalization since each estate will be in the maximum rate bracket.[105]

Finally, the possible administrative problems arising from the use of the equalization clause must be considered. The usage of this clause requires the executor of the decedent's estate to not only value the estate of the decedent but also to make an evaluation of the estate of the surviving spouse. If the estate of the survivor contains many difficult to value items, such as closely-held stock, antiques or the like, the difficulties and costs of making such a valuation may be too burdensome to

---

[104] Rev. Rul. 82-23, 1982-4 I.R.B. 13.

[105] This assumes that the 1981 rate reductions are fully phased in. In such a case, any bequest to the surviving spouse would be taxed at the maximum rate upon the death of the surviving spouse.

justify the estate tax savings involved. Despite these drawbacks, the equalization clause may produce significant estate savings in the proper circumstance. The advisor may also want to consider other alternatives such as the use of disclaimers by the surviving spouse [106] to achieve the same result.

¶ 15.05 Other Tax Planning Devices Available by Will

Although the Marital deduction represents the most significant tax planning device that is available through the last will and testament, there are several other tax planning actions that can be undertaken when drafting that document. These additional courses of action, which affect both the estate tax liability and the income tax of the estate and the heirs, can present a significant tax savings opportunity to the highly compensated. Consequently, when drafting this instrument, these other opportunities should not be overlooked.

[1] Disclaimers

A disclaimer is an action whereby an heir or legatee renounces his interest in property to which he was entitled from the estate of the decedent. By renouncing this interest, the property typically passes to another individual either by operation of law or by a specific alternate bequest in the governing instrument. For example, if a will makes a specific bequest of property to a surviving spouse with an alternate bequest to the testator's son, a disclaimer by the surviving spouse would, under the laws of most states, result in the property being passed to the son. Consequently, although the disclaimer must be made by a beneficiary or legatee rather than the testator, the draftsman of the will can place a beneficiary in a position to make such a disclaimer (or make it virtually impossible to make one) when drafting the will instrument. Thus, the drafting of the will directly affects the ability of the heirs to use the disclaimer as a tax planning device.

Although the disclaimer has been available to estate planners for many years, the interest in it as a tax planning tool was heightened by the code amendments made by the enactment of the Tax Reform Act of 1976. Prior to the enactment of the 1976 amendments, the Gift Tax Regulations set forth certain basic requirements for making a dis-

---

[106] Discussed at ¶ 15.05[1] infra.

claimer free of gift tax [107] which were heavily dependent on the local law of the donor's domicile. Problems were frequently created, however, because the variation in the laws of many states created greatly different tax treatment throughout the country. Accordingly, the Tax Reform Act of 1976 added Section 2518 to the Code in an effort to provide uniformity to the law of disclaimers. That section provides that if a so-called "qualified disclaimer" is made, the federal estate and gift tax provisions will apply to the property as being disclaimed as if the interest had never been transferred to the person making the disclaimer. By making a disclaimer that meets the requirements of a qualified disclaimer set forth in Section 2518(b), a person will be treated as never having owned the disclaimed property and a gift tax will not be assessed with respect to its transfer.

The use of disclaimers thus permits, for example, a legatee under a will who has sufficient assets of his own, to disclaim an interest in property and pass it to his children without incurring any gift tax. If a marital deduction is overfunded, a surviving spouse may disclaim interest in property so as to take title only to those assets which are sufficient to place her own estate in the optimal tax position. By doing so, the surviving spouse may substantially reduce the estate taxes that will ultimately be imposed upon her estate. Conversely, if the marital deduction is underfunded, the beneficiaries of the nonmarital portion may be able to disclaim interest in property passing to them so that it will pass to the surviving spouse.[108] Such a course of action will directly decrease the taxes being imposed upon the estate of the decedent. The qualified disclaimer thus has many estate planning uses which can result in a substantial savings of estate and gift taxes. These savings can only be achieved if the requirements for a qualified disclaimer are met and if proper draftsmanship of the last will and testament permits the disclaimed property to pass to the appropriate person or persons.

[a] Requirements for Qualified Disclaimers. Section 2518(b) sets forth four basic requirements for a qualified disclaimer. The qualified disclaimer is defined to be an irrevocable and unqualified refusal by a person to accept interest in property, but only if:

---

[107] See Treas. Reg. § 25.2511-1(c).

[108] These types of disclaimers might be particularly useful during the phase in of the 1981 Act when the amount of the unified credit is being adjusted annually.

(1) The refusal is in writing;

(2) The writing is received by the transferor of the interest, his legal representative, or the holder of the legal title to the property to which the interest relates not later than the date which is nine months after the later of (a) the date on which the transfer creating the interest in such person is made, or (b) the date on which such person attains age 21;

(3) Such person has not accepted the interest or any of its benefits; and

(4) As a result of such refusal, the interest passes without any direction on the part of the person making the disclaimer and passes either (a) to the spouse of the decedent, or (b) to a person other than the person making the disclaimer.

A disclaimer of an undivided portion of an interest which meets the requirements of Section 2518(b) will be treated as a qualified disclaimer of that portion of the interest.[109]

Proposed regulations under Section 2518 have attempted to clarify the basic statutory requirements. As with any new statute, however, there remains a good deal of ambiguity and uncertainty. Consequently, unless the situation demands otherwise, there is a good deal of wisdom in taking a straight-forward and conservative course of action in order to achieve a qualified disclaimer. For example, the legislative history of Section 2518 clearly indicates that Congress intended to create a national system of disclaimer rules and avoid the differing effect of local laws.[110] Despite this attempt, however, the proposed regulations create a good deal of dependence upon local law. The proposed regulations state that if the disclaimer does not divest title in the property under state law, it is not a qualified disclaimer within the meaning of Section 2518(b).[111] In addition, the proposed regulations provide that a qualified disclaimer can be made only with respect to an interest which can be the subject of disclaimer under local law.[112]

Partially in response to these proposed regulations, "the 1981 Act" added a section which specifically makes it clear that the disclaimer need not meet local law requirements in order to be valid.[113] Although

---

[109] I.R.C. § 2518(c).

[110] See, e.g., H.R. 94-1380, 94th Cong., 2d Sess. 66 (1976).

[111] Prop. Reg. § 25.2518-1(c)(1).

[112] Prop. Reg. § 25.2518-1(c)(3).

[113] I.R.C. § 2518(c)(3).

¶ 15.05[1][a] ESTATE PLANNING 15-46

local law will determine who is a valid transferee, this new section will presumably effectuate the original congressional intent of making federal law determinative of the effectiveness of a disclaimer.

As noted earlier, one of the requirements of the statute is that renunciation be made within nine months of the date of the transfer creating the interest or on which the disclaimant attains the age of 21. The proposed regulations do provide that Section 7502 that treats timely mailing as meeting a filing requirement is inapplicable in this situation.[114] Consequently, actual delivery within the specified time frame is required for the disclaimer to be effective. Because this is a deviation from the normal rule in tax matters that mailing by a specified date is sufficient, extra care must be taken to comply with this particular provision.

The area in which the will's draftsman can provide the most assistance to beneficiaries who may potentially disclaim property relates to the last two requirements of Section 2518(b)(4). That section requires that the property, which is the subject of the disclaimer, must pass either to the surviving spouse or to someone other than the disclaimant without any direction upon the part of the person making the disclaimer. Thus, a qualified disclaimer differs from a power of appointment in that the disclaimant cannot specifically direct who will receive the property. The draftsman of a will can make possible disclaimers which will benefit logical secondary recipients of property by providing alternate beneficiaries in the will. For example, if there is a concern that the marital deduction may be overfunded by the time of the testator's death, the testator can draft his will so as to provide alternate beneficiaries for specific items of property. The surviving spouse would then have the ability to disclaim interest in those items of property so that they will pass to the logical secondary beneficiaries, such as the children. Another possibility might be to draft a marital bequest with an alternate bequest to a named charity. In such a case, if the surviving spouse did not need the particular property or if the marital deduction was overfunded, a disclaimer would result in the property passing to charity with the estate receiving the resulting deduction. The absence of such an alternate bequest may result in either the property passing under the state intestacy laws or the necessity for a long series of disclaimers in order to achieve a desired result. By careful advance planning which anticipates the possibility of certain items of

---

[114] Prop. Reg. § 25.2518-2(c).

property being disclaimed, the will draftsman can set the stage for the proper utilization of this tax planning vehicle.

[b] Complete vs. Partial Disclaimers. In order for a disclaimer to be effective, the interest in the property must pass completely to a person other than the individual making the disclaimer. It is possible, however, to make a disclaimer of a partial interest in the property. The proposed regulations specifically note that if the requirements of those regulations are met, the disclaimer of an entire interest in property may make a qualified disclaimer even though the disclaimant has another interest in the same property.[115] In order to make such a disclaimer, it must relate to severable property with the disclaimant making a qualified disclaimer with respect to specific items.[116] Severable property is property which can be separated from other property which is joined and which, after severance, maintains a complete and independent existence. This means that a legatee of shares of corporate stock may accept some shares of the stock and make a qualified disclaimer of the remaining shares. On the other hand, if a person had an income interest for life from particular securities, he could not make a qualified disclaimer of the income interest for only a ten year period.[117] A person may make a disclaimer of an undivided portion of interest in property such as a fraction or percentage of every interest owned by him. A person cannot, under the proposed regulations, disclaim certain specific rights with respect to the property and retain other rights. For example, the Service indicates that a disclaimer cannot be made in fee simple of real property with a retention of a life estate.[118]

With these caveats and areas of concern noted in the proposed regulations and the requirements of the statute in mind, it is possible to utilize a qualified disclaimer either for the reduction of estate taxes for the decedent or for the surviving spouse to effect a transfer to a subsequent generation without incurring a gift tax. By drafting the will so as to provide alternate beneficiaries so as to easily make possible such a disclaimer, the estate planner can set the stage for effective post mortem estate planning. Although the last will and testament is not the instrument which initiates the disclaimer, the drafting of this instru-

---

[115] Prop. Reg. § 25.2518-3(a)(1)(i).
[116] Prop. Reg. § 25.2518-3(a)(1)(ii).
[117] Prop. Reg. § 25.2518-3(a)(1)(i).
[118] Prop. Reg. § 25.2518-3(b).

ment may enable such an action to be undertaken or may have the effect of precluding it. Thus, the estate planner must attend to this possibility when drafting the last will and testament.

[2] Charitable Bequests

An additional tax planning opportunity that is available to the draftsman of the last will and testament is the possible inclusion of a charitable bequest in that instrument. The charitable bequest can provide an effective means of reducing a testator's estate taxes and, at the same time, enable that individual to support the philanthropic organization of his choice. Thus, the charitable bequest has a good deal of utility to the highly compensated and most particularly for those who are either in an extremely high estate tax bracket or who have no (or a limited number of) heirs or other natural recipients of their estate.

[a] Estate Taxation of Charitable Bequests. Section 2055 provides an unlimited charitable deduction for bequests, legacies, devises, or transfers made to qualified charities which are made in the manner that is set forth in the Code. An individual could, in theory, leave his entire estate to a qualified charitable organization and receive a deduction (subject to a few limitations to be discussed) for the entire bequest. Unlike the income tax charitable deduction, there are no percentage limitations on the amount that can be deducted.

[i] Eligible recipients. The Code [119] specifies four particular types of recipients which would qualify for the charitable deduction. These are:

(1) Governmental units for exclusively public purposes;

(2) A corporation, trust, or community chest organized and operated exclusively for religious, charitable, scientific, literary, or educational purposes, or for the prevention of cruelty to children or animals, no part of the net earnings of which inures to the benefit of any private stockholder or individual and which is not disqualified for exemption under Section 501(c)(3) by reason of attempting to influence legislation and which does not participate or intervene in any political campaign on behalf of any candidate for public office;

---

[119] I.R.C. § 2055(a).

(3) A trust or trustee or fraternal society, order or association operating under the lodge system if the contribution is to be used by such recipient exclusively for religious, charitable, scientific, literary, or educational purposes, or for the prevention of cruelty to children or animals, which similarly does not engage in the activities prescribed in number 2 above; and

(4) Any veteran's organization incorporated by an act of Congress or its departments or local chapters or posts, no part of the net earnings which inures to the benefit of any private shareholder or individual.

As a review of this list should indicate, the eligible recipients of charitable transfers which qualify for the estate tax deduction are essentially, with minor differences in wording, similar to those qualified for the income tax deduction under Section 170.

[ii] **Allowable methods of charitable transfer.** In addition to the requirement that the charitable transfer be made to a statutorily specified recipient, the transfer must also be made in the prescribed manner. Quite obviously, a direct bequest of property to charity will qualify. A qualified disclaimer by a primary beneficiary may also result in a direct bequest to charity if the charity had been named as alternate beneficiary. The type of transfer that causes the most difficulty in regard to qualification, however, relates to the so-called split-interest transfer where the transferee or other individuals retain some form of interest in the property which is transferred to charity. The Tax Reform Act of 1969 made radical changes which strictly limited the types of transfers that would be considered deductible in those instances where a private individual retained an interest in property which was transferred to an exempt organization. The regulations denominate these qualifying transfers as "deductible interests."[120] Those transfers which qualify as deductible interests are as follows:[121]

(1) *Undivided portion of decedent's interest.* The regulations take the position that such an interest must consist of a fraction or percentage of each and every substantial interest or right owned by the decedent

---

[120] Treas. Reg. § 20.2055-2(e)(2).

[121] In addition, the 1981 Act added Section 2055(e)(4), which treats a contribution of a work of art with a retention of its copyright as separate interests for purposes of the charitable deduction. Consequently, a deduction will be allowed for a transfer of a work of art without a transfer of its copyright, provided the use of the property by the organization is related to its function.

¶ 15.05[2][a] ESTATE PLANNING 15-50

in the property and must extend over the entire term of the decedent's interest in the property. For example, if the decedent transfers his interest in an office building to his spouse for life and retains a reversionary interest in that building, the bequest by the decedent of one half of that reversionary interest to charity would not be considered a deductible transfer because interest in the same property has already passed from the decedent for private purposes and the reversionary interest will not be considered the decedent's entire interest in the property. If on the other hand, he had been given a life estate in property for the life of his wife and if the decedent had no other interest in the property, the bequest by the decedent by one half of that life estate to charity would be considered a transfer of a deductible interest because he would have transferred a percentage or fraction of his entire interest.

(2) *Remainder interest in personal residence or remainder in farm.* This type of transfer typically involves a devise of a life estate to a spouse with the remainder to charity. The regulations take the position that a personal residence is any property that was used by the decedent as a personal residence even though it was not his principal residence.[122] A farm is defined to mean any land used by the decedent or his tenant for the production of crops, fruits, or other agricultural products or for the sustenance of livestock.

(3) *Charitable remainder trusts and pooled income funds.* The type of charitable remainder trusts which qualify for the estate tax charitable deduction are charitable remainder annuity trusts as defined in Section 664(d)(1), a charitable remainder unitrust as defined in Section 664(d)(2) and a pooled income fund as defined in Section 642(c)(5). In essence, a charitable remainder annuity trust is a trust from which a sum certain (which is not less than 5 percent of the initial net fair market value of all property placed in a trust) is to be paid, not less than annually, to one or more persons who are not a charitable organization living at the time of the creation of the trust for a term of years in excess of twenty or for the lives of such individuals, from which no amount other than the previously described payments may be paid to or for the use of a person other than a charitable organization and following the termination of which the remainder interest will be transferred to a charitable organization.[123]

A charitable remainder unitrust is a trust for which a fixed *percent-*

---

[122] Treas. Reg. § 20.2055-2(e)(2)(ii). The personal residence exception does not extend to furnishings in the decedent's residence. Rev. Rul. 76-165, 1976-1 C.B. 279.

[123] I.R.C. § 664(d)(1).

age, not less than 5 percent of the net fair market value of the assets, will be paid to an individual who is not a charitable organization for his life or a term not in excess of twenty years and from which no other payment will be made to a noncharitable individual and following the termination of which the remainder interest is transferred to a charity.[124] The pooled income fund, which is defined in Section 642(c)(5), is a trust which is frequently created by a public charity from which an income interest is paid to a private beneficiary and upon the extinction of which, the remainder interest in the property so transferred is severed from the trust corpus and either paid or retained for the use of the designated public charity.[125] All of these vehicles have

---

[124] I.R.C. § 664(d)(2). A trust otherwise qualifying as a unitrust will fail where a portion of a specified trustee's fee will be charged against the unitrust. Rev. Rul. 74-19, 1974-1 C.B. 155.

[125] The full text of that section reads as follows:

(5) DEFINITION OF POOLED INCOME FUND — For purposes of paragraph (3), a pooled income is a trust —

(A) to which each donor transfers property, contributing an irrevocable remainder interest in such property to or for the use of an organization described in section 170(b)(1)(A) (other than in clauses (vii) or (viii)), and retaining an income interest for the life of one or more beneficiaries (living at the time of such transfer),

(B) in which the property transferred by each donor is commingled with property transferred by other donors who have made or make similar transfers.

(C) which cannot have investments in securities which are exempt from taxes imposed by this paragraph,

(D) which includes only amounts received from transfers which meet the requirements of this paragraph,

(E) which is maintained by the organization to which the remainder interest is contributed and of which no donor or beneficiary of an income interest is a trustee, and

(F) from which each beneficiary of an income interest receives income, for each year for which he is entitled to receive the income interest referred to in subparagraph (A), determined by the rate of return earned by the trust for such year.

For purposes of determining the amount of any charitable contribution allowable by reason of a transfer of property to a pooled fund, the value of the income interest shall be determined on the basis of the highest rate of return earned by the fund for any of the three taxable years immediately preceding the taxable year of the fund in which the transfer is made. In the case of funds in existence less than three taxable years preceding the taxable year of the fund in which a transfer is made, the rate of return shall be deemed to be 6 percent per annum, except that the Secretary may prescribe a different rate of return.

the common trait of attempting to precisely define the value of the interest bequeathed to charity. In each case, a specified portion or percentage of either the income or assets are paid to the noncharitable lifetime beneficiary with the remainder bequeathed to charity upon termination of this private use.

[iii] **Additional requirements for charitable bequests.** In addition to the requirements that the charitable transfer be made to a specified beneficiary and in the proper form, the Code imposes certain other limitations on the charitable deduction. First, it is specifically provided that the deduction under Section 2055 may not exceed the value of the transferred property required to be included in the gross estate.[126] This requirement merely follows the fundamental concept that before a deduction is allowable, the property must be included in the decedent's gross estate.[127] The Code also provides that where either by terms of the will or by operation of law, any state succession, legacy, or inheritance taxes are payable out of the charitable bequest, the charitable deduction will be correspondingly reduced.[128] Consequently, in those instances where it is required that the charitable bequest proportionately bear part of the state inheritance taxes, the charitable deduction will be decreased accordingly. If there is an intention to maximize the charitable deduction, the draftsman should provide that the taxes will be paid disproportionately by other beneficiaries or allocated to other portions of the estate. Similarly, the charitable deduction may be reduced by administrative expenses chargeable against the bequest.[129] These requirements are generally aimed at limiting the charitable deduction to the amount actually received by the qualified beneficiary and prohibiting a double deduction for the same item. As such, they represent relatively logical and easily understood concepts. From a drafting standpoint, they create the necessity of inserting carefully drawn allocation clauses in the will or trust instrument.

Finally, the charitable bequest should be drafted in such a manner so as not to be contingent on the occurrence of some event or the actions

---

[126] I.R.C. § 2055(d).

[127] Treas. Reg. § 20.2055-1(a).

[128] I.R.C. § 2055(c). These taxes may qualify for the credit for state death taxes under I.R.C. § 2011.

[129] Alston v. U.S., 349 F.2d 87 (5th Cir. 1965); Rev. Rul. 73-98, 1973-1 C.B. 407.

of a third person. Generally speaking, a contingent bequest to charity will not qualify for the deduction unless the possibility that the charity will not take is so remote as to be negligible.[130] For example, the Service has ruled that no deduction is allowable for a testamentary bequest to charity contingent on the approval of a third party.[131] No deduction was allowed for a charitable remainder contingent on the life tenant's death without children in a situation where it was biologically possible that the life tenant could have children.[132] No deduction was allowed for a charitable bequest to a university contingent upon a daughter's death before age 50.[133] Although there are instances where the Service has found that the possibility of the charity not taking the bequest is so remote as to be negligible,[134] these cases and rulings are the exception and are difficult to predict. As a general rule, if there is a desire to obtain the charitable deduction, the bequest should not be contingent.

[b] Planning for the Charitable Deduction. Because the charitable deduction is unlimited in scope, it obviously provides a great potential for the reduction of estate taxes. For example, if one-half of the decedent's adjusted gross estate was left to the surviving spouse and the remainder to charity, the combination of the charitable and the marital deduction would mean that no taxes would be paid by the decedent. If the surviving spouse then left her entire estate to charity, the transfer would again be nontaxable. It is a fundamental concept, however, that a gift to charity ultimately means a complete relinquishment of ownership of the asset and a transfer of it outside the family situation. Thus, in essence, a decision to transfer property to charity (with perhaps a retained life interest) means that the decedent has made a decision to turn the assets over to a designated charitable institution rather than pay a percentage of it to the federal or state government by means of an estate or inheritance tax. The decedent must essentially make a decision whether he wishes to pay a specified percentage of the value of the

---

[130] Treas. Reg. § 20.2055-2(b).

[131] Rev. Rul. 64-129, 1964-1 C.B. 329.

[132] Rev. Rul. 71-442, 1971-2 C.B. 336. See also Rev. Rul. 59-143, 1959-1 C.B. 247 where a charitable bequest contigent on a 54-year old daughter remaining childless was allowed.

[133] Underwood v. U.S., 407 F.2d 608 (6th Cir. 1969), aff'g 270 F. Supp. 389 (E.D. Tenn. 1967).

[134] See, e.g., Rev. Rul. 67-229, 1967-2 C.B. 335.

property to state and federal governments or completely transfer control of that property over to a designated charity. The charitable deduction, quite obviously, becomes more valuable as the size of the estate increases. Thus, the charitable deduction will save more tax dollars for the estates in the 50 percent bracket [135] than it will for estates in the 37 percent bracket.

If a deduction is made to utilize charitable bequests as a means of estate tax reduction, the draftsman must use extreme care to ensure that the objective of obtaining the deduction will be met. It first must be determined that the potential charitable recipient or recipients qualify for the deduction and that, particularly if a split interest is contemplated, the method of transfer chosen complies with the requirements for that type of transfer. The apportionment of taxes and other expenses must be considered so that the bequest, and hence, the deduction, is not reduced by these items. If there is a desire to make a charitable bequest but the individual is unsure as to whether his surviving spouse or other beneficiaries will have the economic need for certain assets, one possible approach would be to make a bequest to the beneficiary with an alternate bequest to charity. If the beneficiary, at the time of the decedent's death, did not require or desire those assets, a qualified disclaimer could then be made which would entitle the estate to the charitable deduction. Of course, such an approach is dependent upon the beneficiary actually making the disclaimer subsequent to the decedent's death and is beyond the control of the decedent. By drafting the will or appropriate trust instrument in such a manner, however, the decedent can make possible use of the disclaimer if it is either appropriate or desired.

[3] Income Tax Planning Considerations

Although the primary thrust of the will from a tax planning standpoint is, by necessity, directed towards the reduction of estate taxes, there are certain income tax planning opportunities that should not be overlooked. These planning possibilities can greatly increase the likelihood of both the estate and selected heirs reducing their income tax.

---

[135] When the 1981 Act is phased in this tax rate will be applicable to taxable estates in excess of 2.5 million dollars.

[a] Heirs' Tax Situation. Perhaps the most basic, but frequently overlooked, income tax planning opportunity lies in the testator's ability to direct income producing properties among various heirs according to their income tax effect. In planning a will, consideration should always be given to the income tax status of the potential recipients of the bequeathed property. For example, if it is anticipated that the surviving spouse will be receiving a large amount of income either from her own assets, from the spouse's compensation plans, or from jointly owned property which will pass to her by operation of law, it may be foolish to bequeath to her substantial amounts of income producing property. The result of such an action would be to subject this income to taxation at extremely high rates because of the spouse's already substantial income. In such a case, it might be advisable to bequeath such property either directly to the children or to a nonmarital trust.[136] On the other hand, if the decedent owns substantial amounts of property which either throw off tax shelter or produce income that is partially tax sheltered, these may be appropriate vehicles to leave to the surviving spouse with substantial amounts of income. The converse is, of course, true. If the surviving spouse has little or no income, economic necessity as well as prudent tax planning should result in income producing property being transferred to her.

[b] Potential Sale of Bequeathed Property. Consideration must also be given to the potential appreciation or depreciation of the properties relative to its basis subsequent to the death of the testator. Because the basis of all property will be stepped up to the value that is reported on the decedent's estate tax return, such property may typically be sold immediately subsequent to the decedent's death so as to incur little or no capital gain. As time progresses, many of the assets which were held in the decedent's estate will appreciate in value and thus carry the potential for creating a capital gains tax when sold. If there is a likelihood that the surviving spouse will be selling assets from

---

[136] If a marital trust is established, care must be taken to comply with the requirements in the regulations that the spouse receive the enjoyment from the property in the trust. Consequently, if a will is designed to leave only nonincome-producing items to a marital trust, there is the potential that the marital deduction will be disallowed. If there is a conscious effort to leave nonincome-producing items to the surviving spouse, it may be better to handle it by means of a direct bequest rather than a marital trust.

the decedent's estate, it may be more advisable to bequeath assets to her with little or no potential to appreciate, so as to minimize the capital gain upon sale.[137] Such items as certificates of deposit, stable blue chip stocks, or corporate bonds may provide a ready income and asset base to insure the surviving spouse's economic well being, yet, at the same time, carry little potential capital gain possibility if sold.

[c] Estate and Spouse Filing Joint Return. Finally, the draftsman of the last will and testament should insert a provision in the will which would give the executor permission to file a joint return with the surviving spouse if desirable. In the absence of such a provision, it may be impossible to do so under the law of the appropriate jurisdiction or the expense and hassle of a court proceeding may be necessary to get such permission to undertake this filing. The ability to file a joint return with the surviving spouse may be very valuable — particularly if the estate has substantial amounts of income and the surviving spouse has little or no such income of her own. In such a case, a filing of a joint return would produce a substantial income tax savings. Accordingly, the will draftsman should make provision for this possibility.

---

[137] This is also advantageous from an estate tax standpoint because the appreciation in the value of assets subsequent to the decedent's death will ultimately increase the estate of the surviving spouse. It is typically more beneficial from an estate planning standpoint to leave the appreciating assets either directly to a subsequent generation or to a nonmarital trust.

CHAPTER 16

Private Annuities, Powers of Appointment

		Page
¶ 16.01	Introduction	16-2
¶ 16.02	Private Annuities	16-2
	[1] Taxation of Private Annuities	16-3
	[2] Special Tax Problems for the Annuitant	16-5
	[a] Retention of Security	16-6
	[b] Retained Life Estate	16-7
	[c] Value of the Annuity Promise	16-8
	[d] Foreign Trusts	16-9
	[3] Tax Consequences to Transferee	16-10
	[4] Tax Planning With Private Annuities	16-12
	[a] Removal of Assets From the Estate	16-12
	[b] Liquidity	16-12
	[c] Disadvantages of the Private Annuity	16-13
	[d] Alternatives to the Private Annuity — Installment Sale of Property	16-14
¶ 16.03	Powers of Appointment	16-16
	[1] Definition of General Power of Appointment	16-16
	[2] Exclusions From Definition of General Power of Appointment	16-17
	[a] Ascertainable Standard Exclusion	16-17
	[b] Joint Power Exclusion	16-20
	[c] "5 + 5" Power	16-21
	[3] Factors Affecting Taxation of Powers of Appointment	16-22
	[a] Capacity to Exercise Power	16-23
	[b] Release of Power	16-23
	[c] Gift Tax Consequences	16-24
	[4] Planning Objectives for Powers of Appointment	16-24
	[a] Shifting of Assets	16-24
	[b] Access to Trust Corpus	16-25
	[c] Marital Deduction Qualification	16-25

¶ 16.04   Inflation Planning 16-25

Appendix   Present Worth of Annuity, Life Interest, Remainder Interest 16-29

¶ 16.01   Introduction

Previous chapters of Part IV have discussed the various estate planning techniques that have greatest applicability to the highly compensated individual. The major focus has been on estate planning necessitated by compensatory devices, and on planning vehicles that have the greatest use to individuals with large amounts of earned income. Other standard, but less widely useful, estate planning techniques are also appropriate for use by some highly compensated individuals, and in particular circumstances, may prove to be quite valuable. This chapter reviews these techniques, including private annuities and powers of appointment, and concludes with some general comments on inflation planning for the highly compensated individual.

¶ 16.02   Private Annuities

A private annuity is an arrangement whereby a person transfers property to another individual or to a corporation in exchange for that individual's or corporation's promise to pay the transferor specified amounts for the duration of the transferor's life. The private annuity is distinguished from a commercial annuity in the sense that the promissor of the payments is not in the business of selling annuities on a commercial basis. Consequently, the issuer of a private annuity does not have the actuarial diversification of risk sought by a commercial issuer such as an insurance company.

The private annuity in estate planning is useful because it removes an asset or assets from an individual's estate in exchange for a promise to pay a fixed sum of money that expires at death. Since this promise to pay expires at death, nothing remains to be included in the transferor's estate. The private annuity is frequently given consideration by estate planners for individuals, such as the highly compensated, who have acquired a significant amount of assets over a lifetime. There are, however, a variety of estate planning and income tax considerations that must be weighed before a decision can be made to use a private annuity in a particular case.

[1] Taxation of Private Annuities

The Service's present position as to the taxation of private annuities is set forth in Rev. Rul. 69-74.[1] That ruling recognizes the dual nature of a private annuity in that it contains both an element of a sale of property and a lifetime annuity. Based on that concept, the annuity transaction is taxed as follows:

(1) The taxpayer first calculates his exclusion ratio in the contract, which is the ratio of the taxpayer's investment in the contract to the expected return under the contract. The investment in the contract is described in Section 4 of that ruling as being the transferor's basis in the property transferred. The expected return under the contract is determined by multiplying the annual or monthly payments by the taxpayer's life expectancy. This exclusion ratio thus represents a fraction or percentage that when multiplied by the dollar amount of each payment will indicate that portion of the payment that will not be taxable until the taxpayer's basis has been recovered in full.

(2) The taxpayer then determines the portion of each payment that will be considered as capital gain. The capital gain is the difference between the taxpayer's adjusted basis in the property being transferred and the present value of the annuity promise.[2] This capital gain is reported on an installment basis over the period of years measured by the annuitant's life expectancy. Consequently, the gain will be realized ratably over the expected remainder of the annuitant's life and will be paid in full only if he lives to his actuarially determined life expectancy.

(3) Finally, the excluded amount and the capital gain portion are subtracted from the amount of each payment. The remainder is considered to be an annuity that is taxed at ordinary income rates for the transferor's entire life. If the transferor outlives his life expectancy as outlined in the tables, the portion of the gain that was formerly taxed as capital gain will be taxed at ordinary rates for the remainder of transferor's life. Any excess of the fair market value of the property transferred over the present value of the annuity promise is considered to be a gift for federal gift tax purposes and must be reported as such.

---

[1] 1969-1 C.B. 43.

[2] The present value of the annuity promise is determined under the estate and gift tables set forth in Treas. Reg. § 20.2031-10(f), and Treas. Reg. § 25.2512-9(f). See Appendix.

¶ 16.02[1] ESTATE PLANNING 16-4

These steps may be illustrated with the following example:[3] Suppose a 74-year-old male transferred property with a fair market value of $42,748.56 and an adjusted basis of $20,000 in exchange for a promise to receive an annuity of $7,200 in $600 monthly installments for the remainder of his lifetime. Under this set of facts, the fair market value of the property transferred equals the value of the annuity promise as determined under the regulations,[4] so that no taxable gift will result. The taxpayer's expected return under the annuity is $72,720.[5] This would result in the following tax consequences:

(1) The exclusion ratio equals the investment in the contract ($20,000) divided by the expected return ($72,720) or 27.5 percent. Thus, $1,980 of each annual payment is excluded from income throughout the life of the contract.

(2) The taxpayer realizes a capital gain of $22,748.56 ($42,748.56 − $20,000) to be reported ratably over the taxpayer's life expectancy of 10.1 years or at the rate of $2,252.33 per year.

(3) The remainder of each annual payment ($2,967.67) is taxed at ordinary income rates. Thus, if the taxpayer paid capital gains taxes at a rate of 20 percent and was in the 50 percent ordinary income tax bracket, the total taxes with respect to each $7,200 payment would be $1,934.30.

(4) After 10.1 years, the capital gain portion would be taxed as ordinary income.

Rev. Rul. 69-74 adopts a taxation concept that is somewhat similar to the installment sales provisions of the Internal Revenue Code. Any gain accruing to the taxpayer by reason of the transfer of property is to be taxed ratably over the transferor's lifetime, rather than permitting him to recoup his basis in the property prior to paying any tax. Consequently, unless the transferor under a private annuity arrangement has a high basis in the property that is the subject of the contract, he will realize taxable income, albeit partially at capital gain rates,[6]

---

[3] This example is taken from the facts set forth in Rev. Rul. 69-74 as updated with the current annuity tables promulgated in Treas. Reg. § 20.2031-10. These tables are reproduced in Appendix 1 at the end of this Chapter. This same example was used in Ellis, "Private Annuities," 195-2d T.M. at A-7.

[4] The value of the annuity equals $7,200 times 5.9373.

[5] 10.1 years life expectancy times $7,200.

[6] Which are limited by the 1981 Act to 20 percent.

throughout his lifetime. In addition, if the taxpayer outlives the life expectancy tables, he will realize ordinary income on that portion that had formerly been taxed as capital gain once the entire gain has been reported.

It should be noted that the rules of taxation set forth in Rev. Rul. 69-74 are only applicable in the true private annuity situation. That ruling is inapplicable in the case of a commercial annuity. In addition, the Service has issued a ruling relating to annuities from organizations that issue annuities "from time to time." In the case of annuities issued by such an organization, the Service takes the position that the transferor realizes an immediate gain on the transfer of the property equal to the difference between the adjusted basis in the property and the present value of the annuity promise.[7] In the case of annuities issued by organizations that fall within the definition of Rev. Rul. 62-136, the Service seems to regard the annuity promise as the equivalent of cash, so as to require the immediate recognition of gain.[8] Presumably, the principal application of Rev. Rul. 62-136 is to those large charitable organizations that issue annuities with some degree of regularity. Frequently, individuals will make transfers to a university or other public charity in exchange for a lifetime annuity, and those instances would appear to be governed by the aforementioned revenue ruling.[9]

[2] Special Tax Problems for the Annuitant

Although Rev. Rul. 69-74 outlines the Service's basic position regarding the tax consequences of a private annuity transaction, there are several other factors that can radically alter or effect the consequences outlined in that ruling. In structuring the private annuity, it is

---

[7] Rev. Rul. 62-136, 1962-2 C.B. 12.

[8] In Rev. Rul. 62-137, 1962-2 C.B. 28, the Service promulgated tables for determining the present value of an annuity governed by Rev. Rul. 62-136, which then becomes the transferor's investment in the contract for Section 72 purposes. Rev. Rul. 72-438, 1972-2 C.B. 38 sets forth new actuarial valuation rates to be used in lieu of those contained in Rev. Rul. 62-137.

[9] There is some question as to the effect of Treas. Reg. § 1.1011-2(c), Ex. 8 upon Rev. Rul. 62-136. That example in the regulations deals with a bargain sale of property to a charity in return for a private annuity and suggests that the Service may be developing a new means of taxing a private annuity — at least when issued by a charitable organization. At the same time, however, the Service has not revoked Rev. Rul. 62-136 and, indeed, seemingly reaffirmed it with the issuance of Rev. Rul. 72-438. Thus, the precise status of this question remains unresolved.

important to consider these other variables, which frequently enter the picture. These variables can present unexpected traps that can dramatically alter the tax posture outlined above.

[a] Retention of Security. The typical private annuity transaction involves the transferee making an unsecured and unfunded promise to pay a specified amount to the transferor for his lifetime. As such, the promise to pay the annuity closely resembles the promise made in a deferred compensation arrangement where, in order to obtain deferral, the promise must be both unsecured and unfunded.[10] If, in the annuity situation, the transferor retains a security interest in the property that is transferred, immediate taxation is likely to result.

In *Estate of Bell v. Comm'r*,[11] the stock that was transferred in return for the annuity promise was placed in escrow as security for the promise of the transferee. In addition, the annuity agreement provided for a cognovit judgment against the transferee in the event of default.[12] On this set of facts, the Tax Court determined that the gain on the transfer of the stock must be reported in full currently, as opposed to spreading the gain over the expected life of the annuity promise. Thus, in the case where the private annuity was secured, the installment-sale-like principals of Rev. Rul. 69-74 were found to be inapplicable. This decision of the Tax Court was followed in the case of *212 Corporation v. Comm'r*.[13] Consequently, it is clear that if the taxpayer is desirous of designing a private annuity that results in the tax consequences set forth in Rev. Rul. 69-74, no security interest can be retained in the transferred property. Indeed, one risk that a potential annuitant must weigh in the private annuity situation relates precisely to this requirement. Inasmuch as the transferor is not allowed to retain a security interest if the previously described tax consequences are to be received, the risk of nonpayment must be carefully weighed before deciding whether a private annuity represents a viable economic arrangement.

---

[10] See generally ¶ 5.03.

[11] 60 T.C. 469 (1973).

[12] A cognovit judgment is a confession of judgment by the debtor whereby he gives written authority for entry of judgment against him in the event of default.

[13] 70 T.C. 788 (1978). See also by way of contrast Fehrs Finance Co. v. Comm'r, 58 T.C. 174 (1972), aff'd, 487 F.2d 184 (8th Cir. 1973), where an unsecured private annuity was allowed to be reported on a deferred basis.

[b] Retained Life Estate. When income-producing property is transferred to an individual in exchange for a promise to pay a private annuity, there is, if the transaction is improperly structured, a danger that the property will be considered by the Service to have been transferred with a retained life estate. If such a position were sustained, the property would be included in the transferor's estate under the provisions of Section 2036 of the Code, and one of the basic estate planning purposes relating to the use of private annuities would be defeated. This danger is particularly acute if the value of the annuity promise is exactly equal or almost equal to the income that will be produced by the transferred property. In such a case the impression is created that the decedent had transferred property to another individual or a trust entity and retained a lifetime income interest in it.

The Service has issued two rulings that emphasize this danger. In Rev. Rul. 68-183,[14] the grantor of a trust sold stock in a corporation having a fair market value of seven hundred × dollars in exchange for the trust's contractual obligation to pay him forty × dollars each year for the rest of his life. The current income yield of the property held in the trust was said to equal forty × dollars per year. The only funds available for making the annual payment to the grantor were those payments received as income by the trust. On this set of facts, the Service ruled that although the transaction purported to be a sale of the stock to the trust by the grantor, in substance it was a contribution of stock to the trust with the reservation of an income interest in the trust for life. Since all of the income of the trust was used to make payments to the grantor, he was considered to be the owner of the trust under Section 677(a) of the Code. In addition, the trust corpus would be included in his estate under Section 2036.

In Rev. Rul. 79-94,[15] an individual transferred the right to income from an irrevocable trust to his children in return for the children's agreement to make annuity payments that were not less than the trust income or an amount certain that was less than the average trust income. It was held that the fair market value of the trust corpus on the date of the individual's death was includable in his gross estate under Section 2036(a) because the likelihood was that the children would never have to make payments from their own funds and because the decedent had received no consideration for the transfer.

---

[14] 1968-1 C.B. 308.
[15] 1979-1 C.B. 296.

These rulings indicate the necessity for caution in avoiding the Section 2036(a) argument. The annuity agreement should create a personal liability to the transferee that exists without regard to whether or not the property transferred produces income. It is preferable to have the annuity payments made in an amount that substantially differs from any income that is produced by the transferred property. It is also preferable that the payor of the annuity have assets in addition to those that were transferred in exchange for the annuity promise. This, again, indicates that there is a strong likelihood of payment. Accordingly, it is definitely not recommended that a private annuity be funded by income-producing property transferred to a trust for which the sole source of income was the transferred property. It is certainly advisable that the annuity be paid by an individual or corporation who possesses resources from which to make the annuity payments above and beyond the transferred property.

[c] Value of the Annuity Promise. As noted in the discussion of Rev. Rul. 69-74, the value of the annuity promise is required to be taken from the tables set forth in the Estate and Gift Tax Regulations. The Service's use of these tables has been sustained in the typical annuity situation.[16] In certain instances, however, the use of these tables may be inappropriate. For example, in Rev. Rul. 76-491,[17] an annuity was to be paid exclusively from the assets of a trust that could be distributed at any time through the exercise of the trust beneficiaries' power of appointment. On this set of facts, the Service held that the annuity had no fair market value and the entire value of the property transferred by the donor to the trust in exchange for the purported annuity promise was a gift for gift tax purposes. Quite obviously, the uncertainty of the value of the annuity promise led the Service to reject the usage of the annuity tables in this situation. Similarly, in Rev. Rul. 80-80,[18] the Service ruled that the actuarial tables in the regulations shall be applied unless the individual is known to have been afflicted, at the time of the transfer, with an incurable physical condition that is in such an advanced stage that death is clearly imminent. Death was said not to be

---

[16] See Estate of Bartman v. Comm'r, 10 T.C. 1073 (1948) acq. 1948-2 C.B. 1; Estate of Hart v. Comm'r, 1 T.C. 989 (1943).

[17] 1976-2 C.B. 301.

[18] 1980-1 C.B. 194.

clearly imminent if there is a reasonable possibility for survival for more than a very brief period.[19]

The use, or lack thereof, of the tables contained in the Regulations will significantly affect the question of whether a taxable gift has been made at the time of the annuity transfer. The use of the tables has the advantage for the estate planner of providing a certain valuation for the annuity promise. As such, it is relatively easy to structure the transaction so that no gift is being made. This may be particularly critical if contemplation of death is an issue.[20] A similar problem would arise in in the situation outlined in Rev. Rul. 76-491, where the promise cannot be valued. Of course, there may be several annuity situations where the transferor is intentionally making a gift by transferring property above and beyond the value of the promised annuity. In such a case, it might be advisable to actually make two transfers — one for the gift element and one in exchange for the annuity promise. Such a procedure might be useful in limiting the exposure of the property transferred in exchange for the annuity to any possible contemplation of death arguments.

[d] **Foreign Trusts.** There was period of time when it became very popular to establish a foreign trust to be the payor of an annuity.[21] However, Section 1491 of the Code, as most recently amended in 1975, may effectively eliminate the advantages of such a transaction. If appreciated property is transferred to a foreign trust, Section 1491 imposes an excise tax equal to 35 percent of the excess of the fair market value of the property so transferred over the sum of the adjusted basis of such property in the hands of the transferor plus the amount of gain recognized to the transferor at the time of transfer. For this tax not to apply, it must be established to the satisfaction of the Secretary that the transfer is not in pursuance of a plan having one of its principal purposes being the avoidance of federal income tax.[22] If this tax is

---

[19] See also Continental Illinois Nat'l Bank & Trust Co. v. U.S., 504 F.2d 586 (7th Cir. 1974); Miami Beach First Nat'l Bank v. U.S., 443 F.2d 116 (5th Cir. 1971).

[20] The 1981 Act repealed the gift in contemplation of death rules of I.R.C. § 2035, except in certain specified instances. See ¶ 11.01[5].

[21] See, e.g., Kanter, "Recent Tax Decisions Shed Further Light on Private Annuity Transactions," 42 J. Tax'n 66 (1975).

[22] I.R.C. §§ 1492(2) and 1494(b).

applicable, the 35 percent rate would be applied at the time of transfer and, in addition, gain would be recognized as received pursuant to principals of Rev. Rul. 69-74. Consequently, it would be inadvisable to make a transfer to a foreign trust without receiving an advance ruling that Section 1491 is inapplicable.

The Service has issued two rulings relating to the applicability of Section 1491 to the transfer of appreciated stock to a foreign entity in exchange for an annuity. In Rev. Rul. 78-356,[23] the Service ruled that Section 1491 of the Code does not apply to the transfer of appreciated stock by a U.S. citizen to a foreign corporation in an arm's-length exchange for an annuity, the present value of which was equal to the fair market value of the stock. In Rev. Rul. 78-357,[24] a U.S. citizen transferred appreciated stock to a foreign partnership in exchange for an annuity with a present value less than the fair market value of the stock. The Service ruled that the excess of the stock's fair market value over the annuity's present value was a nontaxable contribution of property to the partnership. Therefore, the transferor was liable at the time of the transfer for the tax imposed by Section 1491 on the stock's value in excess of its adjusted basis. Although both of these rulings were applicable to transactions consummated before October 3, 1975, when Section 1491 of the Code was amended, it appears that the principles enunciated by them would be equally applicable to the present Section. If such is the case, the use of a foreign trust when the annuity promise equals the value of the property transferred would not trigger the application of Section 1491. Because of the uncertainty of this situation, if the use of a foreign trust is contemplated, the transferor would be well advised to be certain of his valuation of the transferred property and to obtain an advance ruling as to the inapplicability of Section 1491.

[3] Tax Consequences to Transferee

In making a determination as to the wisdom of entering into a private annuity transaction, it is necessary to consider the tax consequences of the transaction to the transferee who will be the payor of the annuity. This is particularly critical if the transferee is a related party or corporation, as is usually the case. Cognizance first must be given to the fact the payments made by the transferee will not be deductible.

---

[23] 1978-2 C.B. 226.
[24] 1978-2 C.B. 227.

Consequently, all payments will be made with after-tax dollars. Thus, the transferee with a high income tax bracket will be faced with the burden of making recurring nondeductible payments when he is probably in need of additional deductions.

The other major tax issues relating to the tax consequences to the transferee involve the basis for determining gain or loss if the property is sold or otherwise disposed of and for taking depreciation if the property is depreciable. The Service's position regarding basis and depreciation questions is set forth in Rev. Rul. 55-119.[25] That ruling first notes that it is not until the death of the annuitant that the fixed cost of the property acquired in exchange for the annuity in promise can be determined. Once the annuitant has died and the payments have terminated, the cost of the property for federal tax purposes is the total of the annuity payments made. However, the Service takes the position that the basis of the property for determining the allowance for depreciation prior to the death of the annuitant shall be the value of the prospective payments under the annuity contract until such time as the payments equal the value set forth in the tables. Subsequent payments will then be added to the basis of the property as made. If disposition of the property occurs after the death of the annuitant, the basis for determining gain or loss shall again be the total of the payments actually made under the contract.

If the disposition of the property occurs prior to the death of the annuitant, the basis for determining gain shall be the total of the annuity payments made under the contract up to the date of disposition, plus the value of the prospective payments remaining to be paid in accordance with the annuity tables. The basis for determining loss shall be the total of the annuity payments actually made. Of course, in such a situation the taxpayer may realize a gain or loss for federal tax purposes as a result of events occurring subsequent to the disposition. For example, if the total of the payments made under the contract exceeds the basis of the property used in determining the gain or loss on a disposition, the excess is treated as a loss in the year or years in which paid. On the other hand, in the case of a recognized gain upon disposition of the property prior to the death of the annuitant, if the total of the annuity payments ultimately made is less than the basis for computing such gain, the excess of such basis over the total of the annuity payments will constitute income in the year that the annuitant dies.

---

[25] 1955-1 C.B. 352.

Consequently, Rev. Rul. 55-119 basically adopts the position that gain or loss created by the disposition of the property prior to the death of the annuitant can be adjusted in subsequent years as annuity payments are made. This fact may make the tax planning of the payor difficult because of uncertainties as to the ultimate tax consequences. These uncertainties may be more critical if the transferred property is to be used in a trade or business where the depreciation factor is critical or where the property is more likely to be sold over time.

If the transferor is an individual, there may be a tendency on the part of such an individual to retain the property transferred in exchange for a private annuity because of this ultimate tax uncertainty. On the other hand, if there is no real intention of disposing of the transferred property, as is the case with items such as vacation home or family residence, these questions may prove to be immaterial. In any event, these considerations should be reviewed in an overall family context prior to making the private annuity arrangement.

[4] Tax Planning With Private Annuities

[a] **Removal of Assets From the Estate.** The major advantage of private annuity from an estate planning standpoint is the removal of the transferred assets from the estate of the transferor. In return for this transfer, the individual will receive an income stream that will cease upon his death. Consequently, if the annuity payments are not merely accumulated and saved by the transferor or, in the alternative, if the transferor does not reach his life expectancy as defined in the annuity tables, there will be a net decrease in his estate. In addition, any appreciation in the value of the asset subsequent to the transfer will not be in the annuitant's estate.

[b] **Liquidity.** A further advantage of the private annuity is that it is a means of providing liquidity to the annuitant during the remaining years of his life while, at the same time, removing a nonliquid asset from his estate. For example, if the potential annuitant transfers stock in a closely held corporation in exchange for an annuity from either the corporation or his children, he has succeeded in removing from his estate a nonliquid asset that could create a substantial estate tax liability without any corresponding means of producing cash to pay for that liability. This factor might be particularly advantageous if the asset was difficult to sell or if the maintenance of familial control was an overrid-

ing consideration. Also, in such a case, a commercial annuity may not be readily available.

[c] Disadvantages of the Private Annuity. On the other hand, the transfer of appreciated property in exchange for private annuity is a taxable event that will trigger the imposition of a capital gains tax as well as the receipt of ordinary income on the annuity portion. If the transferred assets had been retained until death, they would receive a stepped-up basis and could be sold without incurring any (or a negligible amount of) capital gain. Thus, if the assets are readily salable, it may be necessary to balance the estate tax savings involved against the capital gains tax that may be encountered as well as the income tax on the annuity portion.

If the potential annuitant retains his highly compensated status, either post- or preretirement, the income tax cost of private annuity may counterbalance any potential estate tax savings. In those cases where the individual remains in the 50 percent income tax bracket and is subject to a 20 percent capital gains rate, there may be absolutely no tax incentive for undertaking such an arrangement. This may also be the case if the annuitant is in such an economic position that he is likely to accumulate the funds received through the annuity payments. Such a course of action could build the transferor's estate up to the same level as prior to transfer, with the only real difference being that the annuitant is in a more liquid position. In a situation such as this, unless there is a real concern over the annuitant's liquidity position, a combination of little estate reduction (particularly if the annuitant survives to or beyond his mortality table life expectancy) plus the income tax paid, may mean that there is no tax advantage from the private annuity.

The economic risks and burdens of the private annuity must also be weighed. Inasmuch as it is not possible to retain any security interest in the transferred property if the Rev. Rul. 69-74 treatment is to be sustained, the transferor bears the risk of nonpayment. Although most closely knit family situations offer a high degree of assurance in this regard, this is not always the case. If the transferee's economic position should change, the annuity payments may prove to be too great a burden. This problem might be particularly acute if the transferee was a corporate entity that suffered a reversal of its economic fortunes.

Concern must also be given to the economic burden being placed on the transferee. In those situations where valuable property is being transferred by a very old individual, the annuity required to avoid the imposition of a gift tax will be substantial because of this individual's limited life expectancy. In this case, the annuity payment may place too great a burden upon the transferee. This problem would become acute if the transferor lives far beyond his life expectancy as set forth in the mortality tables. In such a case, the transferee who would have paid far more for the property than its value as of the date of transfer and would retain the economic burden of making the payments for a substantial period of time. In addition, these payments must be made by the transferee with after-tax dollars since no deduction is available with respect to any portion of the annuity payments.[26] Consequently, the economic burdens and risks on both sides must be weighed before undertaking to execute an annuity arrangement.

Despite these many drawbacks and risks, the private annuity does have a place in the estate planning situation, and its use must be considered when reviewing the estate of the highly compensated individual. The private annuity is perhaps most useful in the case of older individuals whose income has declined (or is expected to decline in retirement years) and who are concerned about the liquidity of their estate. For example, a perfect candidate for a private annuity might be an individual who has accumulated very valuable non-income-producing assets, such as art, antiques, or real estate. If these factors are combined with the potential heirs having the economic ability to make substantial annuity payments and assets that are likely to appreciate in value, the situation may be perfect for the use of the private annuity. Under this set of facts, a valuable and appreciating asset would be removed from the decedent's estate, the estate's liquidity difficulty might be alleviated or at least substantially improved, and the income tax burden of the annuity would be more than offset by the estate tax savings involved.

[d] Alternatives to the Private Annuity — Installment Sale of Property. A possible alternative to the use of the private annuity is to enter into an installment sale of property with the unpaid installment obligation to be extinguished at the transferor's death. Although a transaction so structured with a preexisting cancellation of the debt upon the death of the transferor remains a somewhat uncharted area of the law, it does offer an interesting possibility for taxpayers in poor

---

[26] Bell v. Comm'r, 76 T.C. 232 (1981); Dix v. Comm'r, 46 T.C. 796 (1966), aff'd, 392 F.2d 313 (4th Cir. 1968).

health or at an advanced age. The Tax Court has held that an unpaid installment obligation extinguished at death according to the terms of an installment sales contract (and accompanying note) were excluded from the decedent's adjusted gross estate.[27] Thus, the cancellation device achieves the same estate tax purpose (i.e., exclusion) as a private annuity. It should be noted that the cancellation must not occur in a will or other testamentary instrument, but rather must be part of the instruments governing the transaction. In addition, the length of the note should be equal or less than the transferor's actuarially determined life expectancy.[28] Thus, if the transferor achieves his life expectancy, full payment would be received in the properly structured transaction. An important distinction between the self-cancelling installment sale and the private annuity is that if there is an unexpectedly long life span, the installment sale obligor will not be burdened by payments that continue for an indefinite period of time. There is a definite limit to the obligation.

The income tax effects of a preexisting cancellation clause are somewhat less clear. The Installment Sales Revision Act of 1980 added certain provisions to the Code that were designed to make the cancellation of an installment obligation at death a taxable event.[29] Because, however, the extinguishment of an installment obligation by a preexisting contract term does not result in the extinguishment of a right that is already in existence, the argument can be made that this falls outside the scope of the 1980 revisions. On the death of the transferor, no right remains to be canceled. Quite obviously, the Service can be expected to resist this argument, which would mean that a transaction would escape both estate and income taxation. Consequently, the issue is likely to be litigated with uncertain results. If such a technique were successful, it would result in substantial income tax benefits to the transferee [30] — particularly if death occurred long before the normal life expectancy.

---

[27] Estate of Moss v. Comm'r, 74 T.C. 1239 (1980), acq. 1981-1 C.B. 2; Cain v. Comm'r, 37 T.C. 185 (1961), acq. 1962-2 C.B. 4. Note that in the Moss case the stock that was transferred was secured by a pledge agreement — a device that could result in immediate taxation of a private annuity sale.

[28] See Pinzur & Peaskin, "Installment Sales for Estate Planning Purposes under the New Act," 59 Taxes 407 (1981).

[29] I.R.C. § 691(a)(5)(C) treats an obligation that becomes unenforceable as if it were cancelled. This means that it will be treated as a taxable transfer.

[30] The transferee also receives an income tax deduction for the interest that is actually paid. Whether or not this results in more or less ordinary income to the transferor than an equivalent private annuity depends upon the facts of the specific situation.

¶ 16.03 Powers of Appointment

Section 2041 of the Code makes a general power of appointment held by a decedent includable in the decedent's gross estate.[31] Similarly, the exercise or release of a general power of appointment is deemed to be a transfer of property subject to the gift tax by virtue of Section 2514. Despite this basic rule of includability, it is possible to design a power of appointment that will not be taxed in a decedent's estate. Also, because of the flexibility provided by a power of appointment, the vehicle remains a useful estate planning device in many instances where it will be included in a decedent's estate. Accordingly, the power of appointment is one of the standard estate planning techniques that must be considered when reviewing the estate plan of the highly compensated individual.

[1] Definition of General Power of Appointment

A general power of appointment is a power by which the decedent has the authority to appoint property in favor of (1) himself, (2) his estate, (3) his creditors, or (4) creditors of his estate.[32] For example, if an income beneficiary of a trust has the power to appoint the trust corpus to himself, his estate, his creditors, or creditors of his estate, the power would be considered to be a general power of appointment. A general power of appointment will be includable in the decedent's estate if he has the power to appoint the underlying property to any one of the four previously mentioned categories.[33] Thus, a power to appoint underlying property in favor of any one of those four categories will result in estate tax includability.

In contrast, a limited power of appointment will not be included in

---

[31] Throughout this section, the discussion will relate to powers of appointment created after October 21, 1942. Somewhat different statutory rules are applicable to powers created on or before that date. Because of the limited applicability of these rules, however, they will not be discussed in this paragraph. Consequently, the reader should assume that the entire discussion relates to powers created after October 21, 1942.

[32] I.R.C. § 2041(b)(1).

[33] See, e.g., Estate of Edelman v. Comm'r, 38 T.C. 972 (1962); Pennsylvania Co. v. U.S., 69 F. Supp. 577 (E.D. Pa. 1946). Note, however, that the Service has ruled that a widow's right to elect against her husband's will is not a general power of appointment if she dies prior to making an election, Rev. Rul. 74-492, 1974-2 C.B. 298.

a decedent's estate. Essentially, a limited power is any power of appointment that does not fall within the above-noted definition of a general power of appointment. In practice, however, a limited power of appointment for federal estate tax purposes is generally a power that is exercisable only in favor of one or more designated persons or a class of persons other than the decedent, his estate, his creditors, or creditors of his estate. For example, a decedent may have had a power to appoint certain assets to one or more specific individuals, or among a class of individuals such as his children. In either case, because the decedent did not have the power to appoint the property to any of the four prohibited classes, the power would be considered to be a limited power of appointment and not includable in the decedent's taxable estate.

[2] Exclusions From Definition of General Power of Appointment

In addition to limiting the taxation of powers of appointment to general powers, the Code also contains statutory exceptions so as to exclude certain powers from the definition of a general power of appointment.

[a] Ascertainable Standard Exclusion. The Code provides that a power to consume, invade, or appropriate property for the benefit of the decedent, which is limited by an ascertainable standard relating to the health, education, support, or maintenance, of the decedent, shall not be deemed to be a general power of appointment.[34] The regulations list certain limitations on the exercise of a power that meet the statutorily prescribed ascertainable standard. This approved list includes the following terms: support, support in reasonable comfort, maintenance in health and reasonable comfort, support in his accustomed manner of living, education, including college and professional education, health, medical, dental, hospital and nursing expenses, and expenses of invalidism.[35] An ascertainable standard may also be imposed by state law.[36]

It is clear that the terms "support and maintenance" are not

---

[34] I.R.C. § 2041(b)(1)(A).

[35] Treas. Reg. § 20.2041-1(c)(2).

[36] See Rev. Rul. 76-502, 1976-2 C.B. 273 (Maryland); Rev. Rul. 77-194, 1977-1 C.B. 283 (New Jersey).

limited to the bare necessities of life. However, the basic thrust of the ascertainable exclusion is that the power granted to an individual must be limited by the standards set forth so as not to vest in that individual an unlimited right to consume for his own benefit. If such an unlimited power is granted to an individual, the result will be the estate tax inclusion. If it is thought desirable to grant a completely discretionary power to distribute trust corpus for the benefit of an individual, prudent estate planning requires that this power be given to an independent trustee rather than to that individual. The Service has ruled that a completely discretionary power to distribute corpus to an individual will not render that power taxable to his estate under Section 2041, where the trustee was a completely independent bank.[37] Accordingly, if this type of complete discretion is desired, the discretion must be given to an independent party or the result will be an estate tax inclusion for the individual who is the holder of this power.

As might be expected, there has been frequent litigation and controversy relating to whether or not the limitations set forth in various will and trust instruments truly establish an ascertainable standard within the meaning of the Code. For example, a Texas life tenant's power to "use, occupy, enjoy, convey, or expend" property during her lifetime was held to be a general power of appointment not limited by an ascertainable standard.[38] In another case, a surviving spouse was given a life estate in certain stock with the right to dispose, sell, trade, or use the stock during her lifetime for her comfort and care as she saw fit. Upon her death, this was held under Virginia law not to be limited by an ascertainable standard and therefore was a general power of appointment includable in her estate.[39] A trust in which the decedent income beneficiary has a right to principal as she "from time to time may require" was includable in her gross estate as a trust over which she had a general power of appointment not limited by an ascertainable standard.[40] The Service has also ruled that a life beneficiary of a trust with a power to invade corpus if desired to continue in an accustomed standard of living, possessed a general power of appointment, since

---

[37] Rev. Rul. 76-368, 1976-2 C.B. 271.

[38] Phinney v. Kay, Executor (Rosenman), 275 F.2d 776 (5th Cir. 1960).

[39] First Virginia Bank v. United States, 490 F.2d 532 (4th Cir. 1974).

[40] People's Trust Company of Bergen County (Will of O'Brien) v. United States, 412 F.2d 1156 (3d Cir. 1969).

power to invade was not limited by an ascertainable standard relating to the decedent's health, education, support, or maintenance.[41]

As should be apparent from the preceding discussion, state law is of paramount importance in determining whether or not a power is limited by an ascertainable standard. For example, in one case the seemingly broad language, "the right to use all or any part of the principal as she may see fit," was found to be a nongeneral power of appointment because it was limited to the extent necessary for support under the applicable state law.[42]

The frequency of litigation under this section and the tenor of the previously discussed cases and rulings creates several clear planning implications for the design of a power of appointment limited by an ascertainable standard. First, because of the frequency of litigation on this point and a wide variety of decisions reached thereunder, it is strongly advisable to use language or standards that have been approved by the Service in the regulations. In other words, to deviate from the statutorily approved terms set forth in Regulations Section 20.2041-1(c)(2) [43] is both an invitation to litigate a matter and a creation of a danger that the power of appointment may be held to be a general power of appointment. Consequently, unless a draftsman of a will or trust instrument is willing to limit the power of appointment language to these prescribed terms, it is generally preferable to use a vehicle other than a grant of a power of appointment to the income beneficiary.

The second planning implication from these cases is that if more flexibility is desired to distribute a trust corpus to an individual, it is preferable to give this power to an independent, but friendly, trustee rather than creating a power of appointment in the income beneficiary that runs a danger of being included in his estate as a general power of appointment. Another potential solution would be to grant a general power of appointment but limit it to a so-called "5 + 5" power.[44] If it is

---

[41] Rev. Rul. 77-60, 1977-1 C.B. 282. In another case, the word enjoyment was held to connote contentment, ease, happiness, and pleasure and thus was not limited to the requisite ascertainable standard. Stafford v. United States, 236 F. Supp. 132 (E.D. Wis. 1964).

[42] Barritt v. Tomlinson, 129 F. Supp. 642 (S.D. Fla. 1955). See also Lehman v. United States, 448 F.2d 1318 (5th Cir. 1971) (no ascertainable standard created under Texas law).

[43] These terms are paralleled in the gift tax Regulations. Treas. Reg. § 25.2514-1(c)(2).

[44] See ¶ 16.03[2][c].

thought desirable to grant an income beneficiary of a trust, a power to appoint property to himself limited by an ascertainable standard, the wording of that standard must be precisely drawn. To do otherwise is only to invite litigation with uncertain results.

[b] Joint Power Exclusion. Another situation, whereby a power that is exercisable in favor of a decedent, his estate, his creditors, or the creditors of his estate be considered a non-general power of appointment, is in the situation where certain joint powers are exercisable only in conjunction with another person. If the power is not exercisable by the decedent, except in conjunction with the creator of the power, the power is not deemed a general power of appointment.[45] If the power is not exercisable by the decedent, except in conjunction with a person having a substantial interest in the property subject to the power that is adverse to the exercise of the power in favor of the decedent, such power will also not be deemed a general power of appointment.[46] The regulations [47] indicate that an adverse interest is considered to be substantial if its value in relation to the total value of the property subject to the power is not insignificant. Thus, for example, an adverse interest in a $1 million trust, whereby the coholder of a joint power of appointment had a power to appoint one cent to himself, would be considered insignificant so as to bring that power within the joint power exclusion.

The effect of creating a joint power of appointment that falls within the parameters of these exceptions is somewhat similar to the creation of an independent trustee, in that the other party must make an affirmative decision to distribute the property to the joint power holder. As such, it is an effective way to keep a general power of appointment out of an individual's estate. The danger in utilizing the joint power route is that, again, the power clause must be precisely drawn. If the interest of the joint power holder is found not to be adverse to the second holder of the power, the other holder would be faced with the situation where the property would be considered to be a general power of appointment includable in his estate and yet obtainable only with the consent of another person. If this other person was

---

[45] I.R.C. § 2041(b)(1)(C)(i).

[46] I.R.C. § 2041(b)(1)(C)(ii).

[47] Treas. Reg. § 20.2041-3(c)(2).

not "friendly" or was non-cooperative, the other power holder could be taxed on this property and yet have no practical means of obtaining its benefits. Accordingly, if the joint power route is contemplated with someone other than the creator of the power, that power must be structured so that both of the holders of the power clearly have an adverse interest.

If a joint power is created with a nonadverse party, the Code provides that the power will be deemed to be a general power of appointment only with respect to a fractional part of the property subject to that power.[48] In such an instance, the fraction will be determined by dividing the value of the property by the number of individuals who may exercise the power in favor of themselves. Thus, in effect, a possessor of such joint power with a nonadverse party is treated as a fractional owner of the property with the others who are the permissible appointees.

[c] **"5 + 5" Power.** A third exception, whereby a power in a decedent to appoint property to himself will not be considered to be a general power of appointment, is where the possessor's power to appoint property to himself, to his estate, to creditors of his estate, or to his creditors is limited to the greater of $5,000 or 5 percent of the aggregate value of the property subject to the power in any given year. This so-called "5 + 5" power is one of the estate planning devices most frequently used to permit an individual to have access to a trust corpus without including the entire value of that corpus in his or her estate. The decedent's estate does include the value that the holder of the power could appoint himself in the year of death. If the power is not cumulative and had lapsed in previous years, such lapsed amounts will not be includable in his estate.[49] For example, if an income beneficiary of a trust with an aggregate value of $1 million had the power to appoint to himself in any given year the greater of $5,000 or 5 percent of the aggregate value of the trust, he would have the power in any such year to appoint $50,000 to himself. In the year of death, $50,000 would be includable in his adjusted gross estate, but his estate would not include a similar value for previous years when this power had lapsed or had not been exercised.

---

[48] I.R.C. § 2041(b)(1)(C)(iii).

[49] See generally I.R.C. § 2041(b)(2).

The planning value of the "5 + 5" power lies in the fact that it can provide flexibility to an income beneficiary so as to allow that beneficiary access to a portion of the trust corpus and yet, at the same time, keep the bulk of a trust's assets out of that income beneficiary's estate. That beneficiary has the unequivocal power to obtain funds in the event of emergencies or increased expenditure requirements but will not, unless the power is exercised repeatedly over a number of years, find the value of a substantial portion of the trust corpus included in his estate.

The "5 + 5" power in many ways is preferable to the ascertainable standard exception in that it is much easier to draft and is less subject to vague interpretations and frequent court battles. It is thus a somewhat safer exception to the general power of appointment rules. It is also preferable, in many situations, to the joint power exclusion in that the income beneficiary has an unfettered right to obtain a limited portion of the trust corpus without seeking the consent of another person. It offers greater flexibility and is less prone to the danger that the two joint power holders may reach loggerheads over the potential exercise of a power. The disadvantage of a "5 + 5" power is that it automatically includes the value of that power in the beneficiary's estate on the date of death. If the power is never exercised, the holder will be taxed on property that he did not actually use or enjoy. This is often a small price to pay, however, for the flexibility accorded — especially when a trust is likely to remain in existence over a number of years. The "5 + 5" power, in effect, provides a safety net to an income beneficiary, which protects him against unforeseen economic changes or developments that occur subsequent to the creation of a trust or will.[50]

[3] Factors Affecting Taxation of Powers of Appointment

As a general rule, the fact that a decedent possessed a general power of appointment is sufficient to include the property subject to the power in his estate pursuant to Section 2041. The critical factor is possession of such a power. Typically, the exercise of the power, or the lack thereof, is irrelevant to estate taxation. Essentially, if a decedent had a general power of appointment at the time of his death, or if he exercises or releases a power in his will, property subject to the power will be includable in his gross estate.[51]

---

[50] A "5 + 5" power could be combined with a discretionary power in an independent trustee to distribute corpus. This will afford an even greater protection against unforeseen economic difficulties.

[51] I.R.C. § 2041(a)(2).

[a] **Capacity to Exercise Power.** The question of whether the possession of a general power of appointment without the mental capacity to exercise that power should result in inclusion in a decedent's estate has been litigated on several occasions. It is the position of the Service that incompetency of a power holder to exercise that power will not allow the power of appointment to be removed from the holder's estate.[52] In general, the courts have tended to follow the Service's position and have held that incompetency or lack of mental capacity to exercise a general power of appointment will not bar inclusion in a decedent's gross estate.[53] Although there have been some recent cases that have held that lack of mental incapacity will bar inclusion of a power of appointment in a decedent's gross estate,[54] these cases are definitely in the minority. In the bulk of the litigation to date, the courts have generally followed the Service's position that lack of mental capacity to exercise the power will not defeat the inclusion of a general power of appointment in a decedent's gross estate. Similar results have followed, where a decedent possessed a general power of appointment and the capacity to exercise it, but had no knowledge of the existence of the power.[55] Consequently, the critical factor in virtually all of these cases appears to be the fact that the existence of a general power of appointment will result in inclusion in a decedent's estate.

[b] **Release of Power.** It should be noted that a power of appointment released by a decedent at the time of his death is subject to estate tax. In addition, such a power released by a decedent is subject to tax under Section 2041 if the release is of the type that if it were a transfer of property owned by the decedent, the property would be includable in the decedent's estate under Sections 2035 to 2038 of the Code.[56] Generally, a lapse of a power of appointment is considered a release of a power of appointment. Consequently, if the lapse occurs at the time of the decedent's death, the power is subject to the estate tax. If the lapse

---

[52] See Rev. Rul. 75-351, 1975-2 C.B. 368; Rev. Rul. 55-518, 1955-2 C.B. 384.

[53] See Estate of Hurd v. Comm'r, 160 F.2d 610 (1st Cir. 1947); Fish v. U.S., 432 F.2d 1278 (9th Cir. 1970); Williams v. U.S., 634 F.2d 894 (5th Cir. 1981), reversing 78-2 T.C. ¶ 13,264 (W.D. Tex. 1978); Pennsylvania Bank and Trust Co. v. U.S., 597 F.2d 382 (3d Cir. 1979).

[54] See Boeving v. U.S., 493 F. Supp. 665 (E.D. Mo. 1980); Finley v. U.S., 404 F. Supp. 200 (S.D. Fla. 1975), rev'd on other grounds, 612 F.2d 166 (5th Cir. 1980).

[55] Estate of Freeman v. Comm'r, 67 T.C. 202 (1976).

[56] I.R.C. § 2041(a)(2).

occured during the decedent's lifetime, in such a manner that the property would be includable under Sections 2035 to 2038, then the property is similarly included in the decedent's adjusted gross estate. There is an exception, of course, for lapses within the parameter of the "5 + 5" power. Such lapses are not treated as general powers and are not included in the decedent's estate.

[c] Gift Tax Consequences. Section 2514 provides the gift tax consequences for general powers of appointment and basically parallels the estate tax treatment under Section 2041. Thus, the exercise or release of a general power of appointment is deemed a transfer of property by the donee at the time of the exercise or release. This transfer would be a taxable gift unless the transfer or release fell within the parameters of the "5 + 5" provision.

[4] Planning Objectives for Powers of Appointment

[a] Shifting of Assets. The basic planning utility of powers of appointment to the highly compensated individual is to permit the shifting of assets and their tax consequences among a variety of individuals subsequent to the death of the creator of the power. Thus, for example, an individual may leave a trust to provide income to his surviving spouse for life, with the remainder to be divided equally among the children and, at the same time, he may grant the wife a limited power of appointment to change the distribution among the children. This limited power of appointment would not be includable in the surviving spouse's estate and would allow her the flexibility to change the proportion of distribution of the remainder as economic circumstances or tax considerations evolved. During her lifetime, if the economic circumstances of the children became greatly different, it would be possible to change the proportion of distributions from the trust to take cognizance of this difference. In addition, if the tax posture of the children differed, the surviving spouse could direct the disposition of specific assets so as to minimize the income tax consequences to the children. She could, for example, appoint income producing property to children in lower tax brackets and property producing shelter to those children in the higher brackets. Since the decedent may not have been able to foresee these circumstances at the time of his death, the grant of a limited power of appointment to the surviving spouse enables post mortem estate and tax planning that he could not have undertaken.

[b] Access to Trust Corpus. Similar planning flexibility flows from the grant of a "5 + 5" power to an individual.[57] Such a power will not result in the trust corpus being included in the holder's estate, and yet will allow unrestricted access to a certain portion of the trust assets without the consent of the trustee or any other party. The "5 + 5" power thus provides additional protection to an income beneficiary without needlessly inflating that beneficiary's estate.

[c] Marital Deduction Qualification. A general power of appointment, although it results in inclusion in a decedent's estate, is necessary when a trust for the benefit of a surviving spouse is designed to qualify for the marital deduction.[58] Consequently, the use of a general power of appointment enables a decedent to have the benefits of trust management and conservation of assets and yet allows a bequest in trust to qualify for the marital deduction. Other uses of a general power of appointment in an estate planning device are somewhat limited because of the fact that such a power creates estate tax inclusion. It would be counterproductive from a tax standpoint, for example, to allow an individual to appoint a trust corpus in favor of his or her estate,[59] since such a power would result in estate tax inclusion without allowing the decedent to have any use of the property during his or her lifetime. Accordingly, most planning involving the use of powers of appointment involves (1) creation of a general power of appointment in a trust so as to qualify it for the marital deduction, (2) assuring that a power of appointment is a limited power of appointment so as to avoid estate tax inclusion or (3) assuring that an otherwise general power of appointment falls within the stated exceptions to that categorization so as to avoid inclusion in a decedent's estate.

¶ 16.04 Inflation Planning

The one common theme that has permeated the preceding sections of this treatise has been the compelling necessity to undertake both tax

---

[57] See discussion at ¶ 16.03[3][c].

[58] See Treas. Reg. § 20.2056-(b)5(a). This is discussed more extensively in ¶ 15.03[3][b]. The general power of appointment is not necessary for a transfer in trust to qualify as a qualified terminable interest that was added by the 1981 Act. I.R.C. § 2056(b)(7). See ¶ 15.03[3][d].

[59] Such a power would be a general power of appointment and thus includable in the estate.

and economic planning in order to combat the effects of inflation. Many of the tax planning recommendations that have been given were made with the assumption that a significant degree of inflation is likely to continue for at least the near term. The economic effect of inflation has been to erode the value of assets providing a fixed rate of return while, at the same time, increasing the value of many of the assets owned by the highly compensated individual. This increase in value has raised the potential of a substantial capital gains tax on the sale of such assets during an individual's lifetime or, in the alternative, has significantly increased the size of that individual's estate if the assets are held until death. In either case, the result of inflation is the need for sophisticated tax planning.

In the income tax area, the impact of inflation upon tax planning has always been significant. Inflation pushes salaries of highly compensated individuals to higher levels, keeping their marginal rates at or near 50 percent. It was not until the passage of the Economic Recovery Tax Act of 1981 that there was any significant attempt to combat the effects of this inflationary induced bracket creep upon an individual. Presumably, the indexing provisions adopted by the 1981 Act will help counteract the effect of income increases that do no more than keep pace with inflation. There is always the potential, however, that subsequent Congresses of a different political persuasion may repeal or alter the indexing provisions.

The impact of inflation upon compensation planning devices has been discussed throughout this book. For example, the discussion of deferred compensation noted in several places that the value of tax deferral created by such a plan would be largely negated if the plan did not make an attempt to increase the deferred amount under some formula that took cognizance of inflation. Similarly, many types of stock appreciation plans or stock options have gained in popularity, inasmuch as they represent a vehicle for adjusting a compensatory device to the effects of inflation without subjecting the executive to current taxation.

Qualified retirement plans have proven to be a very popular vehicle in the executive compensation area inasmuch as they allow a tax-free accumulation of earnings during the employee's working career. This accumulation, which is not subject to current income taxation, permits the employee to save for his retirement years without being taxed on inflationary induced earnings. In addition, many pension plans attempt to counteract the effects of inflation by basing their benefit formula on the employee's earnings during the period immediately preceding retirement when, presumably, earnings will be the highest. This mitigates against the effects of inflation by not subjecting the retirement income formula to those earlier years when salaries would have been at lower dollar levels. Other types of fringe benefits, such as insurance coverage, require a constant review to make sure that they remain adequate in an inflationary economy.

From an estate planning standpoint, much of the tax planning that is undertaken is done so with the assumption that inflation will continue to increase the value of the assets that are owned by the highly compensated individual. As inflation increases the value of many of the assets owned by this individual, the result is an increase in potential estate tax liability. In undertaking an inter vivos gift program, the appropriate response to inflationary tendencies is to make gifts of those assets that are most likely to appreciate in value while retaining income producing assets of a fixed value that will not be subject to appreciation. From an estate planning standpoint this both removes any subsequent appreciation from the donor's estate and is likely to improve the estate's liquidity position. A further estate planning response necessitated by inflation is to constantly review an individual's insurance coverage to make sure that there is sufficient liquidity to pay estate taxes. This is particularly critical if a sale of an individual's other assets would produce a serious disruption to the affairs of his desired beneficiaries.

Inflation also has a significant impact upon the marital deduction tax planning. The implementation of the unlimited marital deduction by the 1981 Act means that the family now has the ability to completely postpone tax upon the death of the first spouse. This necessitates a weighing of the potential time value of the use of the postponed tax payments as opposed to any additional tax that might be incurred by both increasing the estate of the second spouse and having these assets appreciate in value. The fear of inflation may also create a perceived economic necessity to leave more assets to the surviving spouse than may otherwise be desirable for optimal tax planning. Inflation always creates the concern that adequate provision will not have been made for the spouse.

It is not accurate to say that inflation induces the need for tax planning — it merely exacerbates it. The necessity for tax planning would exist even if we lived in a society that experienced a zero rate of inflation. Since our economy has a tax structure that subjects both income and transfers of property to high rates of tax at graduated rates and also suffers a significant rate of inflation, the need for tax planning for the individual who has high amounts of earned income becomes particularly acute. The failure to undertake this planning will result in significant proportions of that individual's earnings and accumulations being taxed by the federal and state governments. Proper planning can, however, serve to mitigate these effects. It is unlikely that the highly compensated individual will reach a position so as to be able to completely eliminately both the estate tax and the income tax. This individual can, by proper planning, reduce both of these taxes to somewhat more manageable proportions. It is the author's hope that the planning devices detailed throughout this treatise will guide both the highly compensated individual and his advisors toward the achievement of this goal.

APPENDIX: Present Worth of Annuity, Life Interest, Remainder Interest

Table, single life male, 6 percent, showing the present worth of an annuity, of a life interest, and of a remainder interest

1 Age	2 Annuity	3 Life Estate	4 Remainder	1 Age	2 Annuity	3 Life Estate	4 Remainder
0	15.6175	0.93705	0.06295	40	13.1538	0.78923	0.21077
1	16.0362	.96217	.03783	41	12.9934	.77960	.22040
2	16.0283	.96170	.03830	42	12.8279	.76967	.23033
3	16.0089	.96053	.03947	43	12.6574	.75944	.24056
4	15.9841	.95905	.04095	44	12.4819	.74891	.25019
5	15.9553	.95732	.04268	45	12.3013	.73808	.26192
6	15.9233	.95540	.04460	46	12.1158	.72695	.27305
7	15.8885	.95331	.04669	47	11.9253	.71552	.28448
8	15.8508	.95105	.04895	48	11.7308	.70385	.29615
9	15.8101	.94861	.05139	49	11.5330	.69198	.30802
10	15.7663	.94598	.05402	50	11.3329	.67997	.32003
11	15.7194	.94316	.05684	51	11.1308	.66785	.33215
12	15.6698	.94019	.05981	52	10.9267	.65560	.34440
13	15.6180	.93708	.06292	53	10.7200	.64320	.35680
14	15.5651	.93391	.06609	54	10.5100	.63060	.36940
15	15.5115	.93069	.06931	55	10.2960	.61776	.38224
16	15.4576	.92746	.07254	56	10.0777	.60466	.39534
17	15.4031	.92419	.07581	57	9.8552	.59131	.40869
18	15.3481	.92089	.07911	58	9.6297	.57778	.42222
19	15.2918	.91751	.08249	59	9.4028	.56417	.43583
20	15.2339	.91403	.08597	60	9.1753	.55052	.44948
21	15.1744	.91046	.08954	61	8.9478	.53687	.46313
22	15.1130	.90678	.09322	62	8.7202	.52321	.47679
23	15.0487	.90292	.09708	63	8.4924	.50954	.49046
24	14.9807	.89884	.10116	64	8.2642	.49585	.50415
25	14.9075	.89445	.10555	65	8.0353	.48212	.51788
26	14.8287	.88972	.11028	66	7.8060	.46836	.53164
27	14.7442	.88465	.11535	67	7.5763	.45458	.54542
28	14.6542	.87925	.12075	68	7.3462	.44077	.55923
29	14.5588	.87353	.12647	69	7.1149	.42689	.57311
30	14.4584	.86750	.13250	70	6.8823	.41294	.58706
31	14.3528	.86117	.13883	71	6.6481	.39889	.60111
32	14.2418	.85451	.14549	72	6.4123	.38474	.61526
33	14.1254	.84752	.15248	73	6.1752	.37051	.62949
34	14.0034	.84020	.15980	74	5.9373	.35624	.64376
35	13.8758	.83255	.16745	75	5.6990	.34194	.65806
36	13.7425	.82455	.17545	76	5.4602	.32761	.67239
37	13.6036	.81622	.18378	77	5.2211	.31327	.68673
38	13.4591	.80755	.19245	78	4.9825	.29895	.70105
39	13.3090	.79854	.20146	79	4.7469	.28481	.71519

* Treas. Reg. § 20.2031-10(f).

Appendix

1 Age	2 Annuity	3 Life Estate	4 Remainder	1 Age	2 Annuity	3 Life Estate	4 Remainder
80	4.5164	0.27098	0.72902	95	2.0891	0.12535	0.87465
81	4.2955	.25773	.74227	96	1.9997	.11998	.88002
82	4.0879	.24527	.75473	97	1.9145	.11487	.88513
83	3.8924	.23354	.76646	98	1.8331	.10999	.89001
84	3.7029	.22217	.77783	99	1.7554	.10532	.89468
85	3.5117	.21070	.78930	100	1.6812	.10087	.89913
86	3.3259	.19955	.80045	101	1.6101	.09661	.90339
87	3.1450	.18870	.81130	102	1.5416	.09250	.90750
88	2.9703	.17822	.82178	103	1.4744	.08846	.91154
89	2.8052	.16831	.83169	104	1.4065	.08439	.91561
90	2.6536	.15922	.84078	105	1.3334	.08000	.92000
91	2.5162	.15097	.84903	106	1.2452	.07471	.92520
92	2.3917	.14350	.85650	107	1.1196	.06718	.93282
93	2.2801	.13681	.86319	108	.9043	.05426	.94574
94	2.1802	.13081	.86919	109	.4717	.02830	.97170

* *Table, single life female, 6 percent, showing the present worth of an annuity, of a life interest, and of a remainder interest*

1 Age	2 Annuity	3 Life Estate	4 Remainder	1 Age	2 Annuity	3 Life Estate	4 Remainder
0	15.8972	0.95383	0.04617	40	14.0468	0.84281	0.15719
1	16.2284	.97370	.02630	41	13.9227	.83536	.16464
2	16.2287	.97372	.02628	42	13.7940	.82764	.17236
3	16.2180	.97308	.02692	43	13.6604	.81962	.18038
4	16.2029	.97217	.02783	44	13.5219	.81131	.18869
5	16.1850	.97110	.02890	45	13.3781	.80269	.19731
6	16.1648	.96989	.03011	46	13.2290	.79374	.20626
7	16.1421	.96853	.03147	47	13.0746	.78448	.21552
8	16.1172	.96703	.03297	48	12.9147	.77488	.22512
9	16.0901	.96541	.03459	49	12.7496	.76498	.23502
10	16.0608	.96365	.03635	50	12.5793	.75476	.24524
11	16.0293	.96176	.03824	51	12.4039	.74423	.25577
12	15.9958	.95975	.04025	52	12.2232	.73339	.26661
13	15.9607	.95764	.04236	53	12.0367	.72220	.27780
14	15.9239	.95543	.04457	54	11.8436	.71062	.28938
15	15.8856	.95314	.04686	55	11.6432	.69859	.30141
16	15.8460	.95076	.04924	56	11.4353	.68612	.31388
17	15.8048	.94829	.05171	57	11.2200	.67320	.32680
18	15.7620	.94572	.05428	58	10.9980	.65988	.34012
19	15.7172	.94303	.05697	59	10.7703	.64622	.35378
20	15.6701	.94021	.05979	60	10.5376	.63226	.36774
21	15.6207	.93724	.06276	61	10.3005	.61803	.38197
22	15.5687	.93412	.06588	62	10.0587	.60352	.39648
23	15.5141	.93085	.06915	63	9.8118	.58871	.41129
24	15.4565	.92739	.07261	64	9.5592	.57355	.42645
25	15.3959	.92375	.07625	65	9.3005	.55803	.44197
26	15.3322	.91993	.08007	66	9.0352	.54211	.45789
27	15.2652	.91591	.08409	67	8.7639	.52583	.47417
28	15.1946	.91168	.08832	68	8.4874	.50924	.49076
29	15.1208	.90725	.09275	69	8.2068	.49241	.50759
30	15.0432	.90259	.09741	70	7.9234	.47540	.52460
31	14.9622	.89773	.10227	71	7.6371	.45823	.54177
32	14.8775	.89265	.10735	72	7.3480	.44088	.55912
33	14.7888	.88733	.11267	73	7.0568	.42341	.57659
34	14.6960	.88176	.11824	74	6.7645	.40587	.59413
35	14.5989	.87593	.12407	75	6.4721	.38833	.61167
36	14.4975	.86985	.13015	76	6.1788	.37073	.62927
37	14.3915	.86349	.13651	77	5.8845	.35307	.64693
38	14.2811	.85687	.14313	78	5.5910	.33546	.66454
39	14.1663	.84998	.15002	79	5.3018	.31811	.68189

* Treas. Reg. § 20.2031-10(f).

Appendix ESTATE PLANNING

1 Age	2 Annuity	3 Life Estate	4 Remainder	1 Age	2 Annuity	3 Life Estate	4 Remainder
80	5.0195	0.30117	0.69883	95	2.0891	0.12535	0.87465
81	4.7482	.28489	.71511	96	1.9997	.11998	.88002
82	4.4892	.26935	.73065	97	1.9145	.11487	.88513
83	4.2398	.25439	.74561	98	1.8331	.10999	.89001
84	3.9927	.23956	.76044	99	1.7554	.10532	.89468
85	3.7401	.22441	.77559	100	1.6812	.10087	.89913
86	3.5016	.21010	.78990	101	1.6101	.09661	.90339
87	3.2790	.19674	.80326	102	1.5416	.09250	.90750
88	3.0719	.18431	.81569	103	1.4744	.08846	.91154
89	2.8808	.17285	.82715	104	1.4065	.08439	.91561
90	2.7068	.16241	.83759	105	1.3334	.08000	.92000
91	2.5502	.15301	.84699	106	1.2452	.07471	.92529
92	2.4116	.14470	.85530	107	1.1196	.06718	.93282
93	2.2901	.13741	.86259	108	.9043	.05426	.94574
94	2.1839	.13103	.86897	109	.4717	.02830	.97170

Table of I.R.C. Sections

[*References are to paragraphs (¶) and notes (n.).*]

I.R.C. §	
1(f)	2.01[4] n.3, 3.02[1] n.6
1(f)(4)	2.01[4] n.4
22(a)	7.08[1]
31	2.02[1] n.11
33	14.02[2]
39	2.02[1] n.11
43	2.02[1] n.11
44G(a)(1)	5.02[8] n.31
44G(a)(2)	5.02[8] n.31
44G(b)(1)	5.02[8] n.31
44G(c)	5.02[8] & n.30
44G(c)(4)	5.02[8] n.32
44G(c)(5)	5.02[8] n.32
46(c)(8)	8.03[3] & n.64
46(e)(3)	8.03[3] n.65
55	2.02 n.5, 2.02[1] & n.11, 3.02[1] n.5, 8.07[2] n.90, 12.12 n.82
55(b)	2.02[1]
55(e)	2.01[1] n.8
55(e)(3)	2.02[1] n.9
56	2.02, 8.07[2]
57	2.02[2][a], 3.02[1] n.5
57(a)	2.02[2], 8.07[2] n.90
57(a)(1)	2.02[2][i] n.20
57(a)(2)	2.02[2][a]
57(a)(5)	2.02[2][i] n.21
57(a)(6)	2.02[2][i] n.22
57(a)(7)	2.02[2][i]
57(a)(11)(B)	2.02[2][f]
62(10)	5.06[2][a] n.167
72	5.04[1] & ns. 98, 105, 7.04[1], 16.02[1] n.8
72(b)	5.04[1] n.96
72(d)	5.04[1] n.97, 6.05[3] n.81
72(d)(1)	14.03[3] n.67
72(f)	5.04[1] n.99
72(m)(3)	6.03[1][b][iii]
72(m)(3)(b)	6.05[2] n.74

I.R.C. §	
72(m)(7)	5.04[2][a], 5.04[2][a][iii] n.111, 5.04[2][b] n.122, 6.03[1][b][i] & n.34
72(o)(5)	5.05[1]
72(p)	5.04[1] n.98
79	6.01, 6.03, 6.03[1][a], 6.03[2], 6.03[3], 6.03[4], 6.03[5], 6.05, 6.05[2], 6.05[4], 6.06[2], 13.02[2][c], 13.04[2]
79(b)	6.03[1][b][ii], 6.03[1][b][iii], 6.05[2]
79(b)(1)	6.06[2], 6.06[3] n.88
79(b)(2)(D)	6.03[1][b][ii]
79(c)	4.03[1][b], 6.03[1][a] n.31
79(d)(1)	6.03[2] n.41
79(d)(3)	6.03[2] n.42
79(d)(3)(B)	6.03[2] n.44
79(d)(5)	6.03[2]
83	3.03[2] & n.25, 3.05[2], 3.05[3], 4.01 & ns. 1, 2, 4.01[1][a], 4.02 & ns. 3, 4, 6, 4.02[1], 4.02[2] & n.19, 4.02[3], 4.02[3][b], 4.02[3][c], 4.03, 4.03[1] & n.36, 4.03[3], 4.04[2], 4.04[3], 14.04
83(a)	4.02 n.5, 402[2], 4.02[3][a], 4.02[3][c], 6.06[2]
83(b)	4.02[2], 4.02[3][a], 4.02[3][b], 14.04 n.72
83(c)(3)	4.02 n.5
101(a)	6.03[2]
101(a)(1)	6.02[1], 6.05[3], 6.07 n.92
101(a)(2)	6.02[1] n.2, 13.04 n.63
101(a)(2)(A)	6.02[1] n.3
101(a)(2)(B)	6.02[1] n.3
101(b)	6.05[3], 7.06 & ns. 43, 45
101(b)(2)	7.06 n.44
101(b)(2)(B)	7.06 n.46
101(b)(2)(C)	7.06 n.45

T-1

TABLE OF I.R.C. SECTIONS

[References are to paragraphs (¶) and notes (n.).]

I.R.C. §	
101(b)(3)	7.06 n.43
101(c)	6.02[1] & n.6
101(d)	6.02[1]
101(d)(1)(B)	6.02[1]
102(a)	11.03 n.48
103	2.04[4][a][ii]
103(a)	2.04[4][a][i]
103(b)	2.04[4][a][i]
103(b)(2)(A)	2.04[4][a][i] n.54
103(b)(4)	2.04[4][a][i] n.55
103(b)(6)(D)	2.04[4][a][i] n.56
103(b)(6)(I)	2.04[4][a][i] n.56
104(a)(1)	7.04[2]
105	7.03[3]
105(a)	7.03[1]
105(b)	7.02 n.3, 9.03[2]
105(d)	7.04[1]
105(d)(3)	7.04[1] n.22
105(d)(4)	7.04[1] n.23
105(d)(5)(A)	7.04[1] n.25
105(d)(6)	7.06 n.45
105(h)	7.03[2], 9.03[3]
105(h)(2)	7.03[2] n.9
105(h)(3)(A)(i)	7.03[2] n.12
105(h)(3)(B)	7.03[2] n.13
105(h)(5)	7.03[2] n.16
106	7.02 & n.2
116	2.02[2][i]
117	2.04[5][a]
119(a)	7.08[3][d] n.80
120	7.07 n.51
121	2.04[4][c][ii]
121(b)(2)	2.04[4][c][ii] n.75
121(d)(1)	2.04[4][c][ii] n.76
125	6.03[2], 7.07 & n.52
125(b)	7.07 ns. 53, 57
125(d)(2)	7.07 n.56
125(e)(1)	7.07 n.54
125(g)(2)	7.07 n.55
125(g)(4)	7.07 n.53
127	7.05 & ns. 33, 42
127(b)	7.05 n.40
127(b)(3)	7.05 n.41
127(c)(1)	7.05 n.39
127(c)(3)	7.05 n.42
127(c)(6)	7.05 n.38
127(d)	7.05 n.33
128	2.02[2][i]

I.R.C. §	
162	3.02[2][c] n.12, 4.02[3][c] n.31, 5.02[8] n.32, 7.05, 8.03[3], n.65, 8.06[1], 14.02[2]
162(a)	8.06[1]
163	2.01, 8.03[3] n.65, 8.04 n.67, 14.02[2]
163(d)	2.04[2][b], 8.01[2][c] n.8
163(d)(2)	2.04[2][b] n.48
163(d)(3)(B)	2.04[2][b] n.47
164	8.04 n.67, 14.02[2]
165	5.04[2][d], 14.02[2]
166	14.02[2]
167	2.02[2][c], 2.03[1]
167(k)	2.02[2][a] n.13, 8.06[2], 8.07[5] n.93
167(m)(1)	2.02[2][b]
168	2.02[2][g], 2.04[2] n.39, 8.03[3] n.65
168(a)	2.02[2][g]
168(b)(2)(A)(ii)	8.06[2] n.86
169	2.02[2][c]
170	6.03[1][b][ii] n.37, 15.05[2][a][i]
170(b)	2.04[2][b]
170(b)(1)	2.04[2][b] n.44
170(b)(1)(A)	15.05[2][a][ii] n.125
170(b)(1)(A)(ii)	7.06, 11.02[3], 14.05[1][a][i]
170(b)(1)(A)(vi)	14.05[1][a][i]
170(b)(1)(C)	2.04[2][b] n.45
170(c)	6.03[1][b][ii]
173	2.02[2][i]
174(a)	2.02[2][i]
183	8.04 & n.66
183(d)	8.04
184	3.02[1] n.5
189	8.06[2]
189(b)	8.06[2] & n.84
189(d)	8.06[2] n.85
195	8.06[1] n.79
195(b)	8.06[1] n.79
212	4.02[3][c] & n.31, 5.02[8] n.32, 7.08[3][b], 8.06[1] n.80, 14.02[2]
212(3)	7.08[3][b] n.74
213	2.01, 7.02, 7.03[1], 7.03[3] & n.21
213(a)(1)	7.02

TABLE OF I.R.C. SECTIONS

[References are to paragraphs (¶) and notes (n.).]

I.R.C. §	
213(a)(2)	7.02 n.1
213(e)	7.03[1], 11.02[3] n.17
215(i)(2)(A)	5.03[2][a]
219	5.02[6], 14.05[3]
219(b)(1)	5.06[2][a] n.165
219(c)	5.06[2][a] n.168
219(f)(3)	5.06[2][a] n.166
221	2.01[1] n.2
221(a)	14.02[1][c][ii] n.26
263(c)	2.02[2][f] n.19, 8.06 n.75, 8.06[3]
264(a)(1)	3.04 n.44, 6.02[2], n.9, 6.04[2] n.66, 6.07 n.91
264(a)(2)	6.02[4][a] n.14
264(a)(3)	6.02[2] n.10, 6.02[4][a], 6.02[4][b][i], 6.02[4][b][iii], 6.02[4][b][iv]
264(c)	6.02[4][b]
264(c)(1)	6.02[4][b][i] & n.18
264(c)(2)	6.02[4][6][ii] n.21
264(c)(3)	6.02[4][b][iii] & n.23
264(c)(4)	6.02[4][b][iv]
265(2)	2.04[4][a][ii], 8.01[2][c] n.8, 11.09[2] n.95
267(b)(1)	9.03[3]
267(b)(4)	9.03[3] n.13
267(b)(5)	9.03[3] n.14
267(b)(6)	9.03[3] n.12
267(b)(7)	9.03[3] n.14
267(d)	9.03[3] n.15
274(a)	7.08[3][a] n.73, 7.08[3][d]
274(a)(1)	7.08[3][d]
274(e)(1)	7.08[3][d] & n.86
274(h)	7.08[3][c] n.76
303	11.02[5] n.39
318	7.03[2] n.15, 12.08[1] n.34
401(a)	3.05, 5.02[5], 5.02[7], 5.02[8], 5.03[3] n.79, 5.06[2][b] n.170, 14.05[1][a][i]
401(a)(4)	5.02[6], 5.02[9], 5.03[1]
401(a)(5)	5.03[1] & n.53
401(a)(8)	5.02[2] n.8
401(a)(11)(G)(iii)	5.03[2][a]
401(a)(17)	5.03[2][d] n.68
401(a)(17)(B)(i)	5.03[2][d] n.69
401(a)(17)(B)(ii)	5.03[2][d] n.73

I.R.C. §	
401(a)(23)	5.02[5] n.12
401(c)(1)	5.02[9] n.38, 5.04[2][b] n.122
401(c)(3)	5.02[9] n.41
401(c)(4)	5.02[9] n.38
401(d)(2)(A)	5.02[9] n.43
401(d)(2)(B)	5.02[9] n.42
401(d)(3)	5.02[9] n.44
401(d)(6)	5.02[9] n.46
401(j)	5.03[2][d]
401(j)(1)	5.03[2][d] n.70
401(j)(2)	5.03[2][d] n.72
401(j)(3)	5.03[2][d]
401(j)(3)(A)	5.03[2][d] n.72
401(j)(4)	5.02[9] n.45
401(j)(5)(A)	5.03[2][d] n.71
401(k)	5.02[6]
401(k)(2)	7.07
401(k)(2)(B)	5.02[6] n.18
401(k)(2)(C)	5.02[6] n.20
401(k)(3)	5.02[6]
401(k)(3)(A)(i)	5.02[6] n.21
401(k)(3)(A)(ii)	5.02[6] n.23
401(k)(4)	5.02[6] n.22
402(a)	3.03[1] & n.18, 5.05[2] n.159, 14.05[1][a][v] n.93
402(a)(1)	5.04[1], 5.04[2][d] & n.135, 14.05[1][a][v]
402(a)(2)	5.04[2][b] n.121
402(a)(3)	5.04[2][d]
402(a)(3)(A)	5.04[2][d] n.143
402(a)(3)(B)	5.04[2][d] n.143
402(a)(5)	3.05[1], 5.04[2][a][iii], 14.05[3]
402(a)(5)(C)	5.05[1] n.153
402(a)(5)(D)	5.05[1] n.155
402(a)(5)(D)(iv)	5.05, 7.05[1] n.156
402(a)(6)(B)	5.04[2][a][iii]
402(a)(6)(C)	5.05[1] n.158
402(a)(6)(D)	5.05[1] n.152
402(a)(7)	5.05[2] & n.159, 14.05[3]
402(a)(8)	5.02[6]
402(e)	5.04[2][a][iii], 5.04[2][c], 14.02[3][b][iii] n.41
402(e)(1)	5.04[2][a][iii], 14.02[3][b][iii]

TABLE OF I.R.C. SECTIONS

[*References are to paragraphs (¶) and notes (n.).*]

I.R.C. §	
402(e)(1)(C)	5.04[2][c] n.124
402(e)(1)(D)	5.04[2][c] n.127
402(e)(4)	5.02[6], 4.05[3]
402(e)(4)(A)	5.04[2], 5.04[2][a], 5.04[2][a][i] n.106, 5.04[2][a][ii], 5.04[2][a][iii], 5.04[2][d] n.146, 5.06[2][b], 14.05[2] n.101
402(e)(4)(D)	5.04[2][c] n.124
402(e)(4)(D)(ii)	5.04[2][d] n.133
402(e)(4)(H)	5.04[2][a][iii] n.119, 504[2][d]
402(e)(4)(J)	5.04[2][d] n.134
402(e)(4)(K)	5.04[2][d] n.142
402(e)(4)(L)	5.04[2][c] n.131
403(a)	5.05[1], 7.06, 14.05[1][a][i]
403(a)(4)	14.05[3]
403(b)	7.06 n.46, 14.05[1][a][i]
403(b)(8)	14.05[3]
404	5.02[8] n.32
404(a)	6.06[2] n.85
404(a)(3)(A)	5.02[1] n.6
404(a)(3)(B)	5.02[5]
404(e)(1)	5.03[2][d] n.67
405(d)(3)	14.05[3]
408	14.05[3]
408(a)	5.06[1], 5.06[1][a] & n.160, 14.05[3]
408(a)(6)	5.06[1][a] n.161
408(a)(7)	5.06[1][a] n.161
408(b)	5.05[1], 5.06[1], 5.06[1][b] n.162, 5.06[1][b] & ns. 162, 163, 14.05[3]
408(b)(3)	5.06[1][b] n.163
408(d)(3)	14.05[3]
408(d)(3)(D)	5.05[1] n.157
408(f)(1)	5.06[2][b] n.171
408(f)(3)	5.06[2][b] n.172
408(n)(1)	5.06[2][b] n.170
408(n)(2)	5.06[2][b] n.170
409	7.05[1], 5.06[1], 3.06[1][c]
409(a)	5.06[1][c] n.164, 14.05[3]
409(b)(3)(c)	14.05[3]
409A	5.02[8]
409A(a)	5.02[8] n.30
409A(b)(1)	5.02[8] n.33

I.R.C. §	
409A(b)(2)	5.02[8] n.33
409A(c)	5.02[8] n.34
409A(d)	5.02[8] n.34
409A(e)	5.02[8]
409A(h)	5.02[5] n.13, 5.02[8] n.36
409A(h)(1)(B)	5.02[8] n.37
409A(h)(2)	5.02[5] n.14
409A(h)(3)	5.02[5] n.14
409A(h)(4)	5.02[5] n.15
409A(l)	5.02[7] n.25
409A(l)(3)	5.02[7] n.26
410	5.02[9]
410(a)(1)	5.03 n.48
410(b)	5.03[1] n.51
410(b)(3)(A)	5.03[1] n.52
411(a)	5.03 n.49
411(b)	5.03 n.50
415	5.02[6], 5.03[2], 5.03[3], 5.03[4]
415(b)	5.03[2][a]
415(b)(1)	5.03[2][a]
415(b)(2)(C)	5.03[2][a] n.58
415(b)(3)	5.03[2][a] n.54
415(b)(4)	5.03[2][a]
415(b)(5)	5.03[2][a] n.60
415(c)(1)	5.03[2][b], 7.03[3]
415(c)(2)	5.03[2][b] n.61
415(c)(2)(B)	5.03[3]
415(d)(1)	5.03[2][a] n.56
415(d)(3)	5.03[2][a] n.55
415(e)(1)	5.03[2][c] n.64
415(e)(2)	5.03[2][c] n.65
415(e)(2)(B)	5.03[4] n.93
415(e)(3)	5.03[2][c] n.66
415(e)(3)(B)	5.03[4] n.93
416	5.03[4] n.85
416(b)(1)	5.03[4] n.88
416(c)(1)	5.03[4] n.89
416(c)(2)	5.03[4] n.90
416(d)(1)	5.03[4] n.92
416(e)	5.03[4] n.91
416(g)(1)	5.03[4] n.86
416(h)(2)	5.03[4] n.93
416(i)(1)	6.03[2] n.40
416(i)(1)(A)	5.03[4] n.87
421(b)	14.02[1][c][ii] n.26
422	4.04, 6.04[3]

TABLE OF I.R.C. SECTIONS

[References are to paragraphs (¶) and notes (n.).]

I.R.C. §
422(b) 4.04 n.48
422(c)(1) ...... 14.02[1][c][ii] n.26
422(c)(7) .... 3.05[3] n.58
422A .. 2.02[2][d], 2.04[3], 3.05[3] n.58, 4.01, 4.02[2], 4.04 n.47, 4.04[2]
422A(a)(2) 14.04 n.71
422A(b) .... 4.04[3]
422A(c)(1) .... 4.04[2] n.50
422A(c)(4)(A) .... 4.04[2] n.53
422A(c)(5)(A) .... 4.04[2] n.60
422A(c)(5)(B) .... 4.04[2] n.55
422A(c)(8) .... 4.04[2] n.51
423(c) .... 14.02[1][c][ii] n.26
424(c)(1) ...... 14.02[1][c][ii] n.26
425(f) .... 5.04[2][d] n.143
446(b) .... 2.04[2][a] n.40
453(d)(1) .... 9.03[3]
453(f)(1) .... 14.02[1][b]
453B(f) 11.06 n.77
461(g) .... 2.04[2][a] n.43
465 ..... 8.01[2][c] n.7, 8.02[3][b], 8.03, 8.03[2], 8.03[3]
465(a)(1) .... 8.03[3] n.56
465(b) .... 8.03[3] n.57
465(b)(4) .... 8.03[3] n.58
465(c)(3)(D) .... 8.03[3] n.59
465(d)(4) .... 8.03[3]
465(e) .... 8.03[3] n.60
482 .... 2.04(5)(a)
501(a) .... 7.06, 14.05[1][a][i]
501(c)(3) .... 15.05[2][a][i]
501(c)(9) .... 6.06[3]
511 .... 14.02[2]
611 .... 2.02[2][e], 8.03[1]
617 .... 2.02[2][i]
616(a) .... 2.02[2][i]
641(a)(1) 9.07 n.24
642(c)(5) .... 15.05[2][a][ii]
642(g) .... 10.03[1][b][iv] n.46, 14.02[2]
643(b) .... 10.04[2][b]
644 .... 9.12[3][b] & n.67, 11.07 n.82
652 .... 9.09 n.60
664(d)(1) ... 15.05[2][a][ii] & n.123
664(d)(2) ... 15.05[2][a][ii] & n.124

I.R.C. §
665 .... 4.07 n.25, 9.03[3] n.16
665(b) 9.07 n.26
666 .... 4.07 n.25, 9.03[3] n.16
667 .... 2.02[1], 9.03[3] n.16, 9.07 n.25
667(a) .... 2.04[5][a] n.89
667(b) 9.07, 9.07 n.27
671 .... 9.08
672 .... 9.08
672(c) .... 9.08[2][b] n.45
673 .... 9.05, 9.08, 9.08[1][a], 9.12[3][e] n.69, 11.09[3] n.100, 12.02[3] n.8
673(a) .... 12.02[2] n.4
674 .... 9.08, 9.08[2], 12.02[3] n.8
674(b)(2) .... 9.08[2][a][ii] n.34
674(b)(4) .... 9.08[2][a][ii] n.38
674(b)(8) .... 9.08[2][a][ii] n.40
674(c) .... 9.08[2][a][i] n.33
674(c)(1) .... 9.08[2][b] n.43
674(d) .... 9.08[2][a][i] n.33
675 ..... 9.08, 9.08[3], 12.02[3] n.8
675(2) .... 9.04[2]
676 .... 9.08, 12.02[3] n.8
677 .... 9.08, 9.08[5], 12.02[3] n.8
677(a) .... 12.03[3][a][ii] n.11, 16.02[2][b]
677(a)(2) .... 9.04[3] n.20
677(a)(3) .... 13.03[3][b] n.48
677(b) .... 9.08[6] n.55
678 ... 9.03[3] n.9, 9.05, 9.09 n.57, 12.02[3] n.8, 12.08[4] & n.47
678(a)(1) 9.09 n.60
678(c) 9.09 n.59
678(d) 9.09 n.58
679 .... 9.13 n.70
691 .... 2.04[4][d], 14.02[1], 14.02[3][b][i]
691(a) .... 14.02[1][c][ii], 14.02[2], 14.02[3][a] n.34
691(a)(1) .... 14.02[1], 14.02[1][b]
691(a)(2) ..... 14.02[1][b] ns. 6, 10
691(a)(3) .... 14.02[1][b] n.5
691(a)(5) ...... 14.02[1][b] & n.11
691(a)(5)(A)(ii) ... 14.02[1][b] n.12
691(a)(5)(C) ...... 16.02[4][d] n.29
691(b) ... 14.02[2], 14.02[3][a] n.34
691(b)(1)(B) .... 14.02[2] n.30

TABLE OF I.R.C. SECTIONS

[References are to paragraphs (¶) and notes (n.).]

I.R.C. §
691(c) ..... 2.02[1], 14.02[1][c][ii],
    14.02[3], 14.02[3][a] & n.34,
    14.02[3][b], 14.02[3][b][i] &
    n.36, 14.02[3][b][ii] & n.40,
    14.02[3][b][iii], 14.02[4] n.42,
    14.03[3] n.66, 14.05[2],
    14.05[2] n.103
691(c)(4) .... 14.02[3][b][ii]
691(c)(5) .... 14.02[3][b][iii]
701 .... 8.02[1] n.11
701(y) .... 9.03[3] n.9
704(b)(2) 8.05 n.74
704(d) 8.03 n.42
705 .... 8.03[1] n.44
706(c)(2)(B) .... 8.05 & n.71
707(c) .... 8.06[1] & n.81
707(e) .... 8.06[1] n.81
709 .... 8.06[1], 8.07[2] n.88
709(a) .... 8.06[1] n.76
709(b) .... 8.06[1]
709(b)(1) .... 8.06[1] n.76
709(b)(2) .... 8.06[1] n.77
722 .... 8.03[1] n.43
752 .... 8.03[3]
752(a) .... 8.03[2] n.46
752(b) .... 8.03[2] n.47
752(c) .... 8.03[2] n.48
752A .... 8.03[2]
911 .... 2.04[5][a]
931 .... 2.04[5][a]
1014(a) .... 2.04[4][d] n.80, 12.12
    n.82, 14.02[1]
1014(c) .... 14.02[1]
1014(e) .. 11.02[2] n.12, 11.11 n.129
1015(a) .... 11.02[2] n.10
1015(d) .... 11.02[2] n.11
1031 .... 2.04[4][b]
1034 ... 2.04[4][c][i], 2.04[4][c][ii],
    9.03[3]
1034(a) .... 2.04[4][c][i] n.68
1034(e) .... 2.04[4][c][i] n.74
1035 .... 6.02[3]
1036(a) .... 4.03[1]
1057 .... 9.13
1091 .... 2.03[2]
1091(d) .... 2.03[2]
1202 .... 2.02[2][h], 12.12 n.83
1202(a) .... 2.03[1] n.24
1211(b)(1) .... 2.03[1] n.27

I.R.C. §
1212(b) .... 2.03[1] n.28
1221 .... 2.03[1]
1231 .... 2.03[1] n.25
1244(d)(4) .... 9.03[3] n.9
1245 .... 2.02[2][b], 2.04[3],
    8.01[2][b], 9.03[3]
1250 .... 2.02[2][a], 2.02[2][b],
    2.04[3] & n.50, 8.01[2][b],
    8.07[5] n.94, 8.08, 9.03[3]
1250(a)(1)(B) .... 2.04[3] n.52
1250(d)(1) 8.08 n.97
1301 .... 2.04[5] n.82
1302 .... 2.04[5] n.82
1303 .... 2.04[5] n.82
1303(a) .... 2.04[5][a] n.83
1303(b) .... 2.04[5][a] n.84
1303(c) .... 2.04[5][a]
1304 .... 2.04[5] n.82
1305 .... 2.04[5] n.82
1361(c)(2) .... 9.03[3] n.9
1361(d)(3) .... 9.03[3] n.9
1372(e)(5) .... 8.02[1] n.12
1491 .... 9.13, 16.02[2][d]
1492 .... 9.13
1492(2) .... 16.02[2][d] n.22
1494(b) .... 16.02[2][d] n.22
1504(a) .... 8.02[3][a] n.32
2001 .... 10.02[2], 10.02[4],
    15.02[2][d] n.39
2001(b)(1)(B) .... 11.02[1] n.2,
    11.04[2], 12.12 n.81
2001(c) .... 11.02[1] n.4
2010 .... 10.02[2], 10.02[4],
    11.02[1] & n.6, 15.02[1][a] n.7
2010(d) .... 10.02[2] n.21
2011 .. 10.02[4], 10.03[2][b][i] n.58,
    15.05[2][iii] n.128
2011(b) .... 10.02[4]
2011(c) .... 10.02[4] n.30
2011(c)(1) .... 10.02[4] n.31
2011(c)(3) .... 10.02[4] n.31
2011(f) .... 10.02[4]
2013 .... 10.02[3], 10.02[3][a],
    10.02[3][b], 10.02[3][b][i]
2013(a) .... 10.02[3][a]
2013(b) .. 10.02[3][a], 10.02[3][b][ii]
2013(c) .... 10.02[3][a]
2013(c)(1) .... 10.02[3][b][iii] n.29
2013(d) .... 10.02[3][b][i]

TABLE OF I.R.C. SECTIONS

[References are to paragraphs (¶) and notes (n.).]

I.R.C. §	
2013(d)(3)	10.02[3][b][i] n.27
2014	10.03[2][b][i] n.58
2019	11.02[5]
2032	10.02[1] n.11, 10.03[2]
2032A	10.02[1] n.12, 11.02[5] n.37
2033	10.02[1], 12.11[2], 14.03[2][c]
2035	11.02[5], 12.04, 13.03[3] n.39, 13.04 & n.62, 13.04[1], 13.04[2], 15.02[2][b] n.35, 16.02[2][c] n.20, 16.03[3][b]
2035(a)	11.02[5] n.29
2035(b)	11.02[5] & n.30, 13.04
2035(b)(1)	11.02[5] n.41
2035(c)	10.03[2][b][i] n.64, 11.04[4] n.69
2035(d)	11.02[5] n.31, 12.12, 13.04
2036	9.02[2], 9.04[1], 10.02[1] n.10, 11.02[5] n.32, 12.04, 12.05, 12.06[1], 12.02[2], 12.07[1], 12.08[2], 12.10[1], 12.10[2] & n.68, 12.10[3], 13.04[2] n.74, 16.02[2][b], 16.03[3][b]
2036(a)	16.02[2][b]
2036(a)(1)	9.11 n.62, 12.06[3]
2036(a)(2)	9.08[2][c] n.46, 9.11 n.62, 12.10[2]
2036(b)	12.08[1] n.34
2037	10.02[1] n.10, 11.02[5] n.33, 12.02[2], 12.04 & n.13, 12.05, 12.11[1], 12.11[2] & n.77, 16.03[3][b]
2037(b)	12.04 ns. 13, 14
2038	9.03[2], 9.04[1], 10.02[1] n.10, 11.02[5] n.34, 12.04, 12.05, 12.08[2], 12.10[1], 12.10[2], 12.10[3], 14.03[2][e][iii], 16.03[3][b]
2038(a)(1)	9.08[2][c] n.46, 9.11 n.62, 11.10[2], 12.08[1] n.42, 14.03[2][b], 1403[2][c]
2039	9.03[2], 14.03[2][b], 14.05[1][a][ii]
2039(a)	14.03[1] & n.43, 14.03[2][a], 14.03[2][b], 14.03[2][d], 14.03[2][e][ii]

I.R.C. §	
2039(a)(2)	14.03[2][a]
2039(b)	14.03[1] n.47, 14.05[1][a][iii]
2039(c)	4.05[4] n.83, 14.03[1] n.45, 14.05[1], 14.05[1][a][i] n.77, 14.05[1][a][ii], 14.05[1][a][iii] & ns. 83, 84, 14.05[1][a][iv], 14.05[1][a][v], 14.05[1][b][i], 14.05[1][b][ii], 14.05[2], 14.05[3] & n.108
2039(e)	14.05[3] & n.108
2039(f)	5.04[3] n.149, 14.05[1][a][iv], 14.05[2]
2039(f)(2)	14.02[3][b][iii] n.41, 14.05[2] n.102, 14.05[3]
2039(g)	14.05[1] n.76, 14.05[3] n.108
2040	11.03
2040(a)	10.05[1], 10.05[2]
2040(b)	10.05[2] & ns. 89, 90, 11.03 n.57
2041	10.02[3][a], 11.02[5] n.35, 12.04, 12.08[2], 12.08[4], 16.03, 16.03[2][a], 16.03[3], 16.03[3][b], 16.03[3][c]
2041(a)(2)	14.05[1][b][i] n.96, 16.03[3] n.51, 16.03[3][b] n.56
2041(b)(1)	16.03[1] n.32
2041(b)(1)(A)	16.03[2][a] n.34
2041(b)(1)(C)(i)	16.03[2][b] n.45
2041(b)(1)(C)(ii)	16.03[2][b] n.46
2041(b)(1)(C)(iii)	16.03[2][b] n.48
2041(b)(2)	13.05[3][a] n.80, 15.03[2][b] n.81, 16.03[2][c] n.49
2042	11.02[5] n.36, 12.04, 13.02, 13.02[1] n.4, 13.02[2][c], 13.02[2][d], 13.03[1] & n.31, 13.04, 14.05[1][a][ii], 14.05[3]
2043(a)	12.05 n.15
2044	15.03[2][d] n.93
2044(a)	11.02[4] n.27
2045	8.08 n.99
2046	8.08 n.99
2053	10.03, 10.03[1][a], 10.03[1][b][iv] & n.45, 10.03[1][c], 14.02[2]
2053(a)(3)	10.03[2]
2053(d)	10.03[2][b][i] n.58

TABLE OF I.R.C. SECTIONS

[References are to paragraphs (¶) and notes (n.).]

I.R.C. §
2053(e) .... 10.03[2][b][i] n.58
2054 .... 10.03[3], 14.02[2], 15.02[2][c]
2055 .... 8.08 n.98, 10.03, 15.05[2][a], 15.05[2][a][iii]
2055(a) ...... 15.05[2][a][i] n.119
2055(c) ..... 15.05[2][a][iii] n.128
2055(d) ..... 15.05[2][a][iii] n.126
2055(e)(4) .... 15.05[2][a][ii] n.121
2056 .... 10.03, 15.02[1][a], 15.03[2][b]
2056(a) .... 15.02[1][a] n.6, 15.02[2] n.25
2056(b) ..... 15.02[2] n.26, 15.03, 15.03[2][a]
2056(b)(1) .... 15.03[2][d]
2056(b)(1)(C) .... 15.03[2][a] n.43
2056(b)(3) .. 15.03[2][a], 15.03[3][a]
2056(b)(5) ...... 13.03[3][b] n.41, 15.03[2][b] n.60
2056(b)(6) .... 15.03[2][c]
2056(b)(7) ...... 13.03[3][b] n.42, 15.03[2][d] & n.90, 16.03[4][c] n.58
2056(b)(7)(B)(ii) .... 11.02[4] n.25, 15.03[2][d] n.91
2305 .... 13.04[2]
2501(a)(1) .... 11.02[1]
2503 ...... 10.01 n.2, 11.02[1] n.2
2503(b) ...... 10.01 n.4, 11.02[3], 11.02[5], 11.04[1], 11.06, 11.10, 11.10[1][b], 11.10[2], 13.03[2] n.37, 13.04, 13.05[1], 13.05[3][d]
2503(c) ... 11.02[3] n.21, 11.04[1], 11.10[1], 11.10[1][a], 11.10[1][b], 11.10[1][c], 11.10[2]
2503(c)(2)(A) ... 11.10[1][b] n.107
2503(e) .... 9.12[3][a] n.66, 11.02[3] n.16
2503(e)(2) 11.03 n.60
2505 .... 11.02[1] n.6
2513 .... 10.03[2][b][i]
2513(a) .... 11.02[3]
2514 ...... 16.03, 16.03[3][c] n.56

I.R.C. §
2514(e) .... 13.05[3][a] n.80
2516 .... 11.03 n.61
2518 .... 8.08 n.99, 15.05[1]
2518(b) .... 15.05[1]
2518(b)(4) .... 15.05[1]
2518(c) .... 15.05[1] n.109
2518(c)(3) ...... 15.05[1] n.113
2519 .... 11.02[4] n.28
2519(b)(1) ...... 15.03[2][d] n.92
2523 .... 11.02[4] n.22
2523(b) 11.11 n.127
2523(f) .. 11.02[4] n.24, 11.11 n.127
2523(f)(2) 11.02 n.26
2602(c)(3) 10.04 n.74
2602(c)(4)–2602(c)(5)(B) 10.04 n.75
2603(a)(1)(A) 10.04 n.77
2603(a)(1)(B) 10.04 n.76
2611(a) .... 10.04[1] n.79, 11.04[5] n.72
2611(b) .... 10.04[1] n.80
2611(c)(1) .... 10.04[1] n.81
2611(c)(5) .... 10.04[1] n.82
2613(a) .... 10.04[2][b]
2613(a)(2) .... 10.04[2][b]
2613(a)(4)(A) ...... 10.04[1] n.84
2613(b)(6) .... 10.04[1] n.84
3402 .... 4.02[3][c]
4972(c) .... 5.03[3] n.77
4975(c)(1)(B) .... 5.02[7] n.27
4975(d)(3) .... 5.02[8] n.28
4975(e)(7) .... 5.02[7]
4975(e)(8) .... 5.02[7] n.25
6075(a) .... 10.02[1] n.18
6166 ..... 10.03[2][b][ii], 11.02[5] n.38, 13.01[1] n.2, 14.04 & n.74
6166(a)(1) .... 13.01[1] n.2
6166(b)(1)(C) 14.04 n.75
6501 .... 10.03[1][c]
6694(a) .... 2.02[1]
7502 .... 15.05[1]
7701(a)(2) ...... 8.02[2] ns. 16, 22
7701(a)(3) ...... 8.02[2] ns. 17, 22

Table of Treasury Regulations

[References are to paragraphs (¶) and notes (n.).]

TREAS. REG. §	
1.47-3(f)(1)(ii)(b)	9.03[3] n.7
1.57-1(b)(1)	2.01[2][a] n.15
1.57-1(b)(6)	2.01[2][a] n.14
1.57-1(d)(4)	2.01[2][c] n.16
1.57-1(f)(7)	2.01[2][d] n.18
1.61-1(a)	7.08[1] n.58
1.61-2(d)(2)(ii)(b)	6.03[5] n.55
1.72-2(a)(3)	7.04[1] n.103
1.72-8(a)(1)	6.05[3] n.81
1.72-16(b)(4)	5.04[1] ns. 100, 102, 6.05[3] n.80
1.72-16(c)(2)(ii)	6.05[3] n.78
1.72-16(c)(3), Ex. (1)	6.05[3] n.80
1.79-1(a)	6.03[2] n.38
1.79-1(b)(1)	6.03[4] n.53
1.79-1(c)(1)	6.03[3] n.45, 8.03[3] n.46
1.79-1(c)(2)(iii)	6.03[3] n.48
1.79-1(c)(4)	6.03[3] n.49
1.79-1(d)	6.03[4] n.52
1.79-2(b)(2)	6.03[1][b][i] n.35
1.79-2(b)(3)	6.03[1][b][i] n.36
1.79-2(c)(3)(i)	6.03[1][b][ii] n.37
1.79-3(d)(2)	6.03[1][a] n.32, 6.03[5] n.56
1.83-1(a)(1)	4.02 n.6
1.83-2	4.02[3][a] n.26
1.83-2(a)	4.02[3][a] n.25
1.83-2(b)	4.02[3][a] n.26
1.83-2(e)	4.02[3][a] n.26
1.83-2(f)	4.02[3][a] n.27
1.83-3(a)(2)	4.02[1][a] n.8, 4.02[2] n.23
1.83-3(a)(3)	4.02[[1][a] n.10
1.83-3(a)(4)	4.02[1][a] n.10
1.83-3(a)(5)	4.02[1][a] n.10
1.83-3(a)(6)	4.02[1][a] n.10
1.83-3(b)	4.02[1][b] n.12
1.83-3(c)(1)	4.02[1][b] n.13
1.83-3(c)(3)	4.02[1][b] n.14

TREAS. REG. §	
1.83-3(d)	4.02[1][c] n.15
1.83-3(e)	3.03[2] n.25, 3.05[2] n.57, 6.01 n.1
1.83-4(a)	4.02[3][b] n.29
1.83-5(a)	4.02[1][a] n.11, 4.03[3] n.45
1.83-6(a)(2)	4.02[3][c] n.32
1.83-7	4.02[2]
1.83-7(b)	4.02[2]
1.83-7(b)(1)	4.02[2] n.17
1.101-1(a)(1)	6.02[1] n.1
1.101-1(b)(2)	6.02[1] n.4
1.101-1(b)(5)	6.02[1] n.5
1.101-2(a)(2)	7.06 n.47
1.104-1(b)	7.04[2]
1.105-11(a)	7.03[2] n.17
1.105-11(b)(1)(ii)	7.03[3] n.20
1.105-11(c)(2)(iii)(C)	7.03[2] n.14
1.105-11(c)(3)(i)	7.03[2] ns. 10, 11
1.105-11(d)(1)(ii)	7.03[3] n.20
1.105-11(g)(1)	7.03[2] n.18, 9.03[3] n.19
1.119-1(d)	7.08[3][d] n.81
1.121-1(c)	2.04[4][c][ii] n.78
1.121-1(d),	2.04[4][c][ii] n.79
1.162-5(a)	7.05 n.34
1.162-5(b)(2)-(3)	7.05 n.35
1.264-4(b)	6.02[4][a] n.15
1.264-4(c)(1)(i)	6.02[4][a] n.16
1.264-4(c)(2)	6.02[4][a] n.17
1.264-4(d)(1)(i)	6.02[4][b][i] n.19
1.264-4(d)(1)(iv)	6.02[4][b][i] n.20
1.264-4(d)(2)	6.02[4][b][ii] n.22
1.264-4(d)(3)	6.02[4][b][iii] n.24
1.264-4(d)(4)	6.02[4][b][iv] n.26
1.264-4(d)(4)	6.02[4][b][iv] n.27
1.401-1(a)(2)(iii)	5.02[5] n.10
1.401-1(b)(1)(i)	6.05[1] n.70
1.401-1(b)(1)(ii)	6.05[1] n.70

T-9

TABLE OF TREASURY REGULATIONS

[References are to paragraphs (¶) and notes (n.).]

TREAS. REG. §
1.401-1(b)(1)(iii) ..... 5.02[5] n.11
1.401-1(b)(2) .... 5.02[1] n.5
1.401-10(b)(3)(ii) .... 5.02[9] n.39
1.401-12(e)(1) .... 5.03[3] n.81
1.402(a)-1(b)(1)(i) .... 5.04[2][d] ns. 136, 137
1.404(a)-1(a)(2) ...... 6.06[2] n.85
1.415-6(b)(5) ...... 5.03[2][b] n.62
1.415-6(b)(7)(iii) ... 5.03[2][b] n.63
1.451-2 .... 2.04[1] n.37
1.451-2(a) .... 3.03[1] n.14
1.501(c)(9)-1 .... 6.06[3] n.90
1.501(c)(9)-2 .... 6.06[3] n.89
1.501(c)(9)-2(b)(1)(i) ...... 6.06[3] n.91
1.643(b)-1 .... 10.04[2][b] n.86
1.661(a)-2(f)(1) ..... 15.04[1] n.96
1.671-3(a)(1) .... 9.04[1] n.18
1.671-3(a)(3) .... 9.04[1] n.18, 9.04[2] n.19
1.671-3(b) .... 9.04[3] n.20
1.671-3(b)(2) .... 9.04[3] n.21
1.673(a)-1(a) ..... 9.08[1][a] n.28
1.673(a)-1(b) ..... 9.08[1][a] n.29
1.673(a)-1(c) ..... 9.08[1][a] n.30
1.673(d)-1 .... 9.08[1][b] n.31
1.674(b)-1(b)(2) .. 9.08[2][a][ii] n.34
1.674(b)-1(b)(3) ...... 9.08[2][a][ii] n.39
1.674(b)-1(b)(4) ...... 9.08[2][a][ii] n.38
1.674(b)-1(b)(5)(ii) ..... 9.08[2][b] n.42
1.674(b)-1(b)(5)(iii) ..... 9.08[2][b] n.42
1.674(b)-1(b)(6) ...... 9.08[2][a][ii] n.36
1.674(b)-1(b)(6)(i)(a) .. 9.08[2][a][ii] n.35
1.674(b)-1(b)(6)(ii) .... 9.08[2][a][ii] n.37
1.674(d)-1 .... 9.08[2][b] n.41
1.675-1(b)(2) ...... 9.08[3][c] n.50
1.677(a)-1(g) .... 9.04[3] n.21
1.678(d)-1 .... 9.09 n.58
1.691(a)-1(b) ...... 14.02[1][a] n.3
1.691(a)-2(b) .... 14.02[1][c][ii] ns. 19, 20
1.691(a)-4(b)(2) .... 14.02[1][b] n.7

TREAS. REG. §
1.691(c)-1(a)(2) .... 14.02[3][b][i] n.36
1.691(c)-1(c)(1) .... 14.02[1][c][ii] n.27
1.752-1(e) .... 8.03[2] n.52, 8.03[3] n.62
1.1011-2(c), ... 16.02[1] n.9
1.1031(a)-1(b) ..... 2.04[4][b] n.63
1.1031(d)-2 ... 2.04[4][b] ns. 64, 65
1.1035-1(c) .... 6.02[3] n.12, 8.02[3] n.13
1.1091-2(a) .... 2.03[2] n.30
1.1302-2(b)(1) ..... 2.04[5][a] n.91
1.1303-1(a) ... 2.04[5][a] ns. 83, 88
1.1304-3(b)(1) ..... 2.04[5][a] n.93
20.2011-1(c)(2) ..... 10.02[4] n.32
20.2013-1(a) ..... 10.02[3][a] n.23
20.2013-4(b)(1) ..... 10.02[3][b][i] n.26
20.2013-5(a) ..... 10.02[3][a] n.22
20.2013-5(b) ..... 10.02[3][a] n.24
20.2013-6 ..... 10.02[3][b][ii] n.28
20.2031-2 .... 14.04 n.69
20.2031-10 .... 12.02[2] n.2, 12.11[1] n.73, 16.02[1] n.3
20.2031-10(f) ...... 9.11, 12.02[2] n.3, 12.11[1] n.74, 16.02[1] n.2
20.2036-1(a) .... 12.06[1] n.17
20.2036-1(b)(3) .... 12.10[2] n.59
20.2036-1(b)(3)(ii) ...... 12.08[1] n.42
20.2037-1(b) .... 12.11[2] n.78
20.2037-1(c)(3) 12.04 n.14
20.2037-1(e) .... 12.11[1] n.75, 12.11[2] ns. 76, 77, 79
20.2038-1(a)(3) ......12.08[2] n.43
20.2038-1(b) .... 12.10[2] n.58
20.2039-1(b) .... 14.03[1], n.46 14.03[2][b] ns. 53, 59
20.2039-2(b) .... 14.05[1][a][ii] n.78, 14.05[1][a][v]
20.2039-2(c)(1) .... 14.05[1][a][iii] n.83
20.2039-2(c)(2) .... 14.05[1][a][iii] n.85
20.2039-5(a)(2) .... 14.05[3] n.104

TABLE OF TREASURY REGULATIONS

[References are to paragraphs (¶) and notes (n.).]

Treas. Reg. §	
20.2039-5(a)(2)(i)	14.05[3] n.105
20.2039-5(b)	14.05[3] ns. 106, 107
20.2040-1(a)(2)	10.05[2] n.92
20.2041-1(c)(2)	16.03[2][a] & n.35
20.2041-3(c)(2)	16.03[2][b] n.47
20.2042-1(b)	14.05[1][a][ii] n.78
20.2042-1(b)(1)	13.02[1] ns. 5, 6, 13.03[3][b] n.45
20.2042-1(c)(2)	13.02[2][a] ns. 8, 9
20.2042-1(c)(3)	13.02[2][a] ns. 10, 11
20.2042-1(c)(4)	13.02[2][b] n.12
20.2042-1(c)(6)	13.02[2][c] & ns. 17, 18
20.2053-1(a)(1)	10.03[1][a] n.35
20.2053-1(a)(2)	10.03[1][a] n.36
20.2053-1(b)(2)	10.03[1][a] n.37
20.2053-1(b)(3)	10.03[1][a] n.39
20.2053-2	10.03[1][b][i] ns. 40, 41
20.2053-3(c)(3)	10.03[1][b][ii] n.44
20.2053-3(d)(2)	10.03[1][b][iv] n.45
20.2053-4	10.03[2] ns. 47, 48, 10.03[2][a] n.50
20.2053-5	10.03[2][b][iii] n.68
20.2053-6(a)	10.03[2][b][i] n.58
20.2053-6(d)	10.03[2][b][i] n.64
20.2053-6(f)	10.03[2][b][i] n.61
20.2053-7	10.03[2][b][iv] n.69
20.2054-1	10.03[3] n.71
20.2055-1(a)	15.05[2][a][iii] n.127
20.2055-2(b)	15.05[2][a][iii] n.130
20.2055-2(e)(2)	15.05[2][a][ii] n.120
20.2055-2(e)(2)(ii)	15.05[2][a][iii] n.122
20.2056(a)-1(a)	15.02[2][d] n.40

Treas. Reg. §	
20.2056(a)-2(b)(1)	15.02[2][c] n.37
20.2056(a)-2(b)(3)	15.02[2][c] n.38
20.2056(b)-1(b)	15.03[1] ns. 41, 42
20.2056(b)-3(a)	15.03[a] n.55
20.2056(b)-3(b)	15.03[3][a] n.56
20.2056(b)-5(a)	15.03[2][b] n.61, 16.03[4][c] n.58
20.2056(b)-5(e)	15.03[2][b] n.62
20.2056(b)-5(f)(1)	15.03[2][b] n.64
20.2056(b)-5(f)(5)	15.03[2][b] n.65
20.2056(b)-5(g)(1)	15.03[2][b] n.71
20.2056(b)-5(g)(2)	15.03[2][b] n.73
20.2056(b)-5(g)(3)	15.03[2][b] n.78
20.2056(b)-6(d)	15.03[3][c] n.88
20.2056(e)-1(a)	15.02[2][b] n.34
20.2056(e)-2(a)	15.02[2][b] n.36, 15.03[2][c] n.47
20.2056(e)-2(b)(3)(ii)	15.03[2][c] n.86
20.2056(e)-2(e)	15.02[2][a][ii] n.32
25.2503-3(a)-(b)	11.02[3] n.18
25.2503-4(a)(1)	11.10[1][b] n.114
25.2503-4(b)(1)	11.10[1][a]
25.2503-4(b)(3)	11.10[1][c] n.119
25.2511-1(a)	11.03 n.59, 13.03[2] n.33
25.2511-1(c)	11.03 n.43, 15.05[1] n.107
25.2511-1(g)(1)	11.03 ns. 44, 47
25.2511-1(h)(4)	11.03 n.55
25.2511-2(h)	11.03 n.51
25.2512-6(a)	13.03[2] n.34
25.2512-8	11.03 & n.46
25.2512-9	9.10 n.61
25.2512-9(f)	9.06[2] n.23, 9.12[3][c], 12.02[1] n.2
25.2514-1(c)(2)	16.03[2][a] n.43
25.2531-9(f)	16.02[1] n.2

TABLE OF TREASURY REGULATIONS

[References are to paragraphs (¶) and notes (n.).]

TREAS. REG. §
301.7701-2 ...... 8.02[2] & n.18, 8.02[4] n.37
301.7701-2(a)(1) ..... 8.02[2] n.19
301.7701-2(a)(3) ..... 8.02[2] n.20
301.7701-2(b)(1) ... 8.02[2][a] n.23
301.7701-2(c)(3) ... 8.02[2][b] n.26
301.7701-2(d)(1) ... 8.02[2][c] n.29
301.7701-2(e)(1) ... 8.02[2][d] n.30
301.7701-2(g) ..... 8.02[a][b] n.28
301.7701-3(b)(2) ... 8.02[2][b] n.27, 8.02[2][d] n.30
301.7701-4(a) 9.01 n.1

PROPOSED REGULATIONS

PROP. REG. §
1.61-16 .... 3.03[3][a] n.33, 3.03[3][b] n.40
1.61-16(b) .... 7.08[2] n.68
1.61-17 .... 7.08[2] n.71
1.61-18 .... 7.08[2] n.71
1.61-19 .... 7.08[2] n.71
1.61-20 .... 7.08[2] n.71
1.61-21 .... 7.08[2] n.71
1.61-22 .... 7.08[2] n.71
1.83-6(e) .... 4.02[2] n.19
1.83-6(f) .... 4.02[2] n.19
1.105-9(a)(2) .... 7.04[1] n.24
1.402(e)-2(d)(1)(ii)(A)
.... 5.04[2][a][ii] n.107

PROP. REG. §
1.402(e)-2(d)(1)(ii)(B)
.... 5.04[2][a][ii] n.108
1.402(e)-2(d)(1)(iii)
.... 5.04[2][a][ii] n.109
1.402(e)-2(d)(3)(ii) ..... 5.04[2][b] n.122
1.402(e)-2(e)(3) ...... 5.04[2][a][iii] n.120
1.402(e)-3(a) ...... 5.04[2][c] n.130
1.402(e)-3(c)(2) ... 5.04[2][c] n.129
1.402(e)-14(b) .... 5.04[2][c] n.132
1.465-6(c) .... 8.03[3] n.61
1.465-6(e) .... 8.03[3] & n.61
1.465-22(a) .... 8.03[3] n.63
25.2518-1(c)(1) .... 15.05[1][a] n.111
25.2518-1(c)(3) .... 15.05[1] n.112
25.2518-2(c) ...... 15.05[1] n.114
25.2518-3(a)(1)(i) ..... 15.05[1][b] ns. 115, 117
25.2518-3(a)(1)(ii) .... 15.05[1] n.116
25.2518-3(b) ...... 15.05[1] n.118
301.7701-2 .... 8.02[5] n.38
301.7701-3 .... 8.02[5] n.38

TEMPORARY REGULATIONS

TEMP. REG. §
14a.422A-1 .... 4.04[1] ns. 49, 52, 53, 54, 57, 58, 59

Table of Revenue Rulings, Revenue Procedures, and Other IRS Releases and Guidelines

[References are to paragraphs (¶) and notes (n.).]

REVENUE RULINGS

Rev. Rul.
53-196 .... 14.04 n.70
54-343 .... 11.03 n.60
55-119 .... 16.02[3] & n.25
55-228 .... 7.06 n.48
55-394 .... 15.03[2][b] n.76
55-423 .... 3.03[1] & n.19, 14.05[1][a][v] & n.88
55-424 .... 3.03[1] n.21
55-518 .... 15.03[2][b] n.83 16.03[3][a] n.52
55-747 .... 6.04[2] n.59, 6.05[2] n.75
55-749 .... 2.04[4][b] n.67
56-86 .... 11.10[2] n.125
56-406 .... 2.03[2] n.32
57-163 .... 5.03[3] n.81
57-260 .... 3.03[1] n.21
57-366 .... 11.10[2] n.126
57-544 .... 14.02[1][c][i] n.15
58-66 .... 15.02[2][a][i] n.27
58-211 .... 2.03[2] n.36
58-242 .... 9.04[3] n.20
58-567 .... 9.08[1][b] n.32
59-9 .... 10.02[3][a] n.24
59-64 .... 14.02[1][c][ii] n.19
59-143 ...... 15.05[2][a][iii] n.132
59-357 ...... 11.10[2] ns. 125, 126
60-31 .... 3.02[2][b] n.9, 3.03[3][a] & n.33, 3.03[3][b]
60-31 .... 3.03[3][a] n.32
60-87 .... 15.04[2] n.97
60-88 .... 10.02[4] n.33
60-181 .... 9.13 n.71
60-195 .... 2.03[2] n.34
60-218 ...... 11.10[1][b] & n.109
60-227 .... 14.02[1][c][i] n.15

Rev. Rul.
60-323 .... 3.03[3] n.79
61-212 .... 6.05[1] n.71
62-136 ...... 16.02[1] & ns. 7, 8, 9
62-137 .... 16.02[1] n.8
62-199 .... 7.02 n.5
63-144 .... 7.08[3][d] & n.87
64-129 ...... 15.05[2][a][iii] n.131
64-279 .... 3.03[3][b] n.37
64-289 .... 14.02[1][c][i] n.16
64-308 .... 14.02[1][c][i] n.14
64-328 .... 6.04[2] & ns. 58, 66
65-21 .... 5.02[9] n.47
65-274 .... 10.03[2][b][i] n.63
66-110 ...... 6.04[2] & ns. 58, 59, 62, 6.05[2] n.75
66-143 .... 6.05[1] n.72
66-159 .... 9.03[3] n.11
66-160 .... 9.08[2][b] n.44
66-271 .... 10.02[3][a] n.24
66-114 .... 2.04[4][c][i] n.69
67-154 .... 6.04[2] ns. 58, 61, 6.05[2] n.76
67-229 ...... 15.05[2][a][iii] n.134
67-241 .... 9.09 n.60
67-242 .... 14.02[3][b][i] n.36
67-270 .... 11.10[1][a] & n.102
67-336 .... 5.04[1] n.104
67-396 .... 11.03 & n.52
67-442 .... 15.02[2][a][i] n.28
68-31 .... 6.05[1] n.72
68-35 .... 10.03[2][b][i] n.63
68-99 .... 3.04 n.43
68-124 .... 7.06 n.49
68-183 .... 16.02[2][b] & n.14
68-647 .... 5.04[1] n.105
68-670 ...... 11.10[1][b] & n.117
69-54 .... 13.03[4][a] & n.50

T-13

TABLE OF REVENUE RULINGS

[References are to paragraphs (¶) and notes (n.).]

Rev. Rul.	
69-56	15.03[2][b] n.70
69-74	16.02[i] & ns. 1, 3, 16.02[2], 16.02[2][a], 16.02[2][c], 16.02[2][d], 16.02[4][c]
69-148	11.03 n.56
69-154	7.02 n.3
69-345	11.10[1][a] & n.103
69-382	6.06[2] n.84
69-408	6.05[1] n.73
69-434	2.04[4][c][ii] n.73
69-478	6.06[2] n.85
69-627	5.03[3] n.78
69-647	5.04[2][a][iii] n.114
69-650	3.03[3][a], 3.03[3][a] n.36
70-272	10.02[4] n.33
70-400	15.03[2][a] n.59
70-435	3.03[3][a] & ns. 32, 35
70-658	5.03[3] n.82
71-56	10.03[2][b][i] n.59
71-58	7.05 n.37
71-232	11.07 n.78
71-251	5.04[2][d] n.139
71-252	8.06[3] n.87
71-419	3.05[2]
71-423	14.02[2] n.32
71-442	15.05[2][a][iii] n.132
71-497	13.04[1] & n.64
72-7	15.03[2][c] n.50
72-8	15.03[2][c] n.50
72-15	5.04[2][d] n.140
72-25	3.04 & n.47
72-44	7.04[2] n.27
72-45	7.04[2] n.27
72-135	8.03[2] n.54
72-275	5.03[3] n.80
72-283	15.03[2][b] n.67
72-291	7.04[2] n.30
72-307	13.03[4][a] & ns. 51, 52, 13.03[4][b]
72-328	5.04[2][d] n.141
72-400	7.04[2] n.28
72-438	16.02[1] ns. 8, 9
72-440	5.04[2][d] n.146
72-579	8.07 n.87
73-13	7.08[3][b] n.74
73-21	12.08[2] n.43
73-29	5.04[2][d] & n.144
73-61	9.12[2] n.63, 11.09[1] & n.87
73-98	15.05[2][a][iii] n.129
73-251	9.08[1][b] n.32
73-312	5.04[2][d] n.145
73-404	14.05[1][a][ii] & n.79
73-599	6.06[2] n.85
74-19	15.05[2][a][iii] n.124
74-43	11.10[1][b] & n.113
74-61	2.04[5][a] n.92
74-243	9.03[3] n.8
74-250	2.04[4][c][i] n.70
74-492	16.03[1] n.33
75-24	10.03[2][a] n.52
75-40	2.04[5][a] n.86
75-70	13.02[2][d] n.22
75-72	11.07 n.78
75-128	15.03[2][b] n.67
75-177	10.03[2][a] n.52
75-214	8.06[1] n.78
75-241	7.02 n.4
75-350	13.05[3][b] n.82
75-351	16.03[3][a] n.52
75-481	5.03[2][a] n.57, 5.03[3] n.84
75-500	7.04[2] n.27
75-528	6.03[3] n.50
75-539	7.02 n.6
76-100	9.03[3] n.8
76-153	14.02[1][c][i] n.13
76-165	15.05[2][a][ii] n.122
76-166	15.03[2][c] n.51
76-261	13.02[2][b] & n.16, 13.02[2][d], n.22
76-346	2.03[2] n.35
76-368	16.03[2][a] n.37
76-380	14.03[2][b] n.59
76-404	15.03[2][b] n.45
76-421	13.03[4][b] n.54
76-490	13.03[4][c] & n.57
76-491	16.02[2][c] & n.17
76-498	14.02[2] n.33
76-502	15.03[2][b] n.72, 16.03[2][a] n.36
77-24	5.03[2][a] n.57
77-30	15.03[2][b] n.75
77-34	14.05[1][a][v] n.89
77-60	16.03[2][a] n.41
77-110	8.03[2] n.53
77-119	8.05 n.72
77-130	15.03[2][b] n.46

TABLE OF REVENUE RULINGS T-15

[*References are to paragraphs (¶) and notes (n.).*]

REV. RUL.
77-157 .... 14.05[1][a][ii] n.80
77-182 .... 12.08[2] n.46
77-183 .... 14.03[2][b] n.58
77-194 .... 16.03[2][a] n.36
77-201 .... 2.03[2] n.33
77-235 .... 7.04[2] n.29
77-274 .... 10.03[1][b][i] n.42
77-299 .... 11.06 n.76
77-310 .... 8.05 n.72
77-311 .... 8.05 n.73
77-320 .... 8.04 n.69
77-443 .... 10.03[1][a] n.38
77-444 .... 15.03[2][b] n.66
77-461 .... 10.03[2][b][ii] n.65
78-29 .... 8.03[2] n.53
78-57 .... 5.03[3] n.84
78-151 .... 14.05[1][a][iii] n.84
78-203 .... 14.02[3][a] n.35
78-357 .... 16.02[2][d] & n.24
78-356 .... 16.02[2][d] & n.23
78-409 .... 12.06[3] & n.19
78-420 .... 6.04[2] & n.63
79-1 .... 5.03[2][a] n.57
79-5 .... 5.03[2][a] n.57
79-47 .... 13.03[4][c] & n.58
79-50 .... 6.04[2] & n.65
79-90 .... 5.03[2][a] n.59
79-94 .... 16.02[2][b] & n.15
79-106 .... 8.02[4] n.38
79-117 .... 12.06[3] & n.21
79-129 .... 13.02[2][d] n.21
79-185 .... 14.02[3][b][iii] n.40
79-190 ...... 14.05[1][b][i] & n.95
79-231 .... 13.04[1] n.68
79-252 .... 10.03[2][b][ii] n.67
76-274 .... 13.02[2][c] n.20
79-300 .... 8.04 n.68
79-302 .... 10.03[2][a] n.49
79-336 ...... 5.04[2][a][iii] & n.115
79-340 .... 14.02[1][c][i] n.13
79-353 .... 9.08[2][c] n.46,
                   12.08[2] & n.44
79-398 .... 11.02[1] n.8
80-14 .... 7.04[2] n.30
80-28 .... 2.02[1] n.12
80-42 .... 8.03[2] n.53
80-80 .... 16.02[2][c] & n.18
80-129 .... 5.04[2][a][iii] n.117
80-137 .... 7.04[2] n.31

REV. RUL.
80-158 .... 14.05[1][a][v] n.89
80-172 .... 2.04[4][c][ii] n.77
80-220 .... 6.03[3] n.51
80-244 ...... 4.03[1], 6.03[1] n.37,
                            4.04[2]
80-255 .... 9.08[2][a][ii] n.40
80-261 .... 13.05[3][d] & n.84
80-289 .... 13.04[1] n.69
80-300 .... 4.03[2] n.40
80-350 ...... 5.03[3], 7.03[3] n.76
81-7 .... 13.05[3][b] n.81
81-14 .... 13.04[1] n.66
81-31 .... 14.03[2][d] & n.63
81-47 .... 7.04[2] n.31
81-98 .... 4.12[3][c] n.68
81-121 .... 7.06 n.45
81-122 .... 5.04[2][d] n.138
81-128 .... 13.03[4][b] n.56
81-141 ...... 5.04[2][a][iii] n.117
81-153 .... 8.06[1] n.80
81-198 .... 13.03[2] n.35
81-223 .... 11.07 n.78
81-255 .... 6.02[4][b][iv] n.28
81-256 .... 10.03[2][b][ii] n.67
82-1 .... 2.04[4][c][ii] n.76
82-4 .... 15.04[2] n.97
82-13 .... 13.04[1] & ns. 67, 70
82-23 .... 15.04[3] n.104
82-98 .... 11.02[3] n.16
82-121 .... 4.03[2] n.43
82-141 .... 13.04 n.61
82-145 .... 13.02[2][c] n.20

REVENUE PROCEDURES

REV. PROC.
64-19 .... 15.04[2] & n.98
71-19 .... 3.03[3][b] & n.38
72-13 ... 8.02[3][a] & n.31, 8.02[6]
72-18 .... 2.04[4][a][iii] n.58
74-8 .... 2.04[4][a][ii] n.58
74-17 .... 8.02[3][b] & n.33
79-29 .... 6.03[4] n.53
82-18 .... 4.04[2] n.62

OFFICE DECISIONS

O.D.
514 .. 7.08[1] n.67, 7.08[3][d] n.84
946 .... 7.08[1] n.66

Table of Cases

[References are to paragraphs (¶) and notes (n.).]

A

Acacia Mut. Life Ins. Co. v. U.S. 272 F. Supp. 188 (D. Md. 1967)	7.08[3][c] n.75
Adams, Fred G., Estate of v. Comm'r ¶ 73,113 P-H Memo T.C.	10.03[2][b][i] n.60
All v. McCobb 321 F.2d 633 (2d Cir. 1963)	14.03[2][b] & n.55
Allen, U.S. v. 293 F.2d 916 (10th Cir. 1961)	12.05 n.16
Allen, Estate of v. Comm'r 29 T.C. 465 (1957)	15.03[2][b] n.74
Alston v. U.S. 349 F.2d 87 (5th Cir. 1965)	15.05[2][a][iii] n.129
American Body & Equip. Co. v. U.S. 511 F.2d 649 (5th Cir. 1975)	4.02[4][b][iv] & ns. 29, 30
Andrews v. Comm'r ¶ 81,247 P-H Memo T.C.	2.04[4][c][i] n.71
Atkins, Estate of v. Comm'r 2 T.C. 332 (1943)	10.03[2][a] n.49
Avery, Estate of v. Comm'r 40 T.C. 392 (163), acq., 1971-2 C.B. 1	15.03[2][c] n.51

B

Bahen v. U.S. 305 F.2d 827 (Ct. Cl. 1962)	14.03[2][b] & n.54
Bahr, Estate of v. Comm'r 68 T.C. 74 (1977), acq., 1978-1 C.B. 1	10.03[2][b][ii] n.66
Baker v. Comm'r 75 T.C. 166 (1980)	11.09[2] n.96
Bank of N.Y. v. U.S. 174 F. Supp. 911 (S.D.N.Y. 1957)	12.10[2] n.58
Barad, Estate of v. Comm'r 13 T.C.M. 223 (1954)	12.07[1] n.23
Barlow, Estate of v. Comm'r 55 T.C. 666 (1971), acq., 1972-2 C.B. 1	10.03[2][a] n.53
Barritt v. Tomlinson 129 F. Supp. 642 (S.D. Fla. 1955)	16.03[2][a] n.42

TABLE OF CASES

[References are to paragraphs (¶) and notes (n.).]

Bartman, Estate of v. Comm'r .... 11.03 n.53, 16.02[2][c] n.16
  10 T.C. 1073 (1948)
Batterton v. U.S. .... 15.03[2][c] n.48
  406 F.2d 247 (5th Cir. 1968)
Bayley v. Comm'r .... 2.04[4][c][i] n.73
  35 T.C. 288 (1960)
Beauregard, Estate of v. Comm'r ..... 13.02[2][d] n.26
  74 T.C. 603 (1980), acq., 1981-1 C.B. 1
Beck v. Comm'r .... 9.08[4] n.52
  15 T.C. 642 (1950), aff'd, 194 F.2d 537
  (2d Cir.), cert. denied, 344 U.S. 821
  (1952)
Beckman v. U.S. .... 2.04[5][a] n.91
  396 F. Supp. 44 (D. Kan. 1975)
Bell v. Comm'r .... 16.02[4][c] n.26
  76 T.C. 232 (1981)
Bell, Estate of v. Comm'r .... 16.02[2][a] & n.11
  60 T.C. 469 (1973)
Berkman, Estate of v. Comm'r ...... 9.11[3][d] n.68, 11.09[1] & n.90
  38 T.C.M. 183 (1979)
Berry v. Kuhl .... 12.08[1] n.35
  174 F.2d 565 (7th Cir. 1949)
Bibby v. Comm'r .... 9.08[1][b] n.32
  44 T.C. 638 (1965)
Biggs v. Comm'r .... 2.04[4][b] n.66
  632 F.2d 1171 (5th Cir. 1980)
Biscoe v. U.S. .... 12.08[1] n.36
  148 F. Supp. 224 (D. Mass. 1957)
Blitzer v. U.S. .... 8.06[1] n.79
  81-1 U.S.T.C. ¶ 9262 (Ct. Cl. 1981)
Boardman, Estate of v. Comm'r ...... 12.08[1] n.37
  20 T.C. 871 (1953)
Boeing, Comm'r v. .... 13.03[2] n.38
  123 F.2d 86 (9th Cir. 1941)
Boeving v. U.S. .... 16.03[3][a] n.54
  493 F. Supp. 665 (E.D. Mo. 1980)
Borax v. Comm'r .... 15.02[2][a][i] n.29
  349 F.2d 666 (2d Cir. 1965), cert.
  denied, 383 U.S. 935 (1966)
Bosch, Comm'r v. .... 15.03[2][b] n.63
  387 U.S. 456 (1967)
Bowers, Corliss v. .... 3.03[1] & n.15
  281 U.S. 376 (1930)
Boynton v. Comm'r 8.05 n.74
  649 F.2d 1168 (5th Cir. 1981)

TABLE OF CASES

[References are to paragraphs (¶) and notes (n.).]

Brausch's Estate v. Comm'r 186 F.2d 313 (2d Cir. 1951)	14.02[1][c][ii] & n.18
Brooks, Estate of v. Comm'r 50 T.C. 585 (1968), acq., 1969-1 C.B. 20	14.05[1][a][v] n.90
Budd, Estate of v. Comm'r 49 T.C. 468 (1968)	12.08[1] n.33, 12.09 n.49
Burney, Estate of v. Comm'r 4 T.C. 449 (1944)	12.10[3] n.71

C

Cagle v. Comm'r 63 T.C. 86 (1974)	8.06[1] & n.83
Cain v. Comm'r 37 T.C. 185 (1961), acq., 1962-2 C.B. 4	16.02[4][d] n.27
Caldwell v. Jordan 119 F. Supp. 66 (D. Ala. 1953)	13.02[2][d] n.27
Campbell Sash Works v. U.S. 217 F. Supp. 74 (N.D. Ohio 1963)	7.08[3][c] n.76
Carpenter, Estate of v. U.S. 80-1 U.S.T.C. ¶ 13,339 (W.D. Wis. 1980)	12.08[1] n.42
Casey v. U.S. 13 A.F.T.R.2d 1839 (D. Ill. 1964)	15.03[2][d] n.52
Catalano v. U.S. 429 F.2d 1058 (5th Cir. 1969)	10.03[2][b][i] n.63
Century Elec. Co. v. Comm'r 192 F.2d 155 (8th Cir. 1951)	2.04[4][b] n.67
Chandler v. Comm'r 119 F.2d 623 (3d Cir. 1941)	9.08[4] n.53
Clifford, Helvering v. 309 U.S. 331 (1940)	9.05 & n.22
Clinard v. Comm'r 40 T.C. 878 (1963)	11.10[1][c] & n.121
Coca v. Comm'r 35 T.C.M. 1454 (1976)	2.04[5][a] n.92
Coleman, Estate of v. Comm'r 52 T.C. 921 (1969)	13.04[1] n.65
Connelly, Sr. v. U.S. 551 F.2d 545 (3d Cir. 1977)	13.03[4][b] & n.55, 13.03[4][c]
Connolly v. Connolly 443 N.Y.S.2d 661 (1st Dep't 1981)	9.12[3][a] n.66
Continental Ill. Nat'l Bank & Trust Co. v. U.S. 504 F.2d 586 (7th Cir. 1974)	16.02[2][c] n.19

TABLE OF CASES

[References are to paragraphs (¶) and notes (n.).]

Cooper, Estate of v. Comm'r 291 F.2d 831 (4th Cir. 1961)	14.02[1][c][i] n.14
Cooper, Estate of v. Comm'r 7 T.C. 1236 (1946)	12.10[1] n.56
Corliss v. Bowers 281 U.S. 376 (1930)	3.03[1], 3.03[1] n.15
Cornwell, Estate of v. Comm'r 67 T.C. 239 (1976), acq., 1977-1 C.B. 1	15.03[2][c] n.89
Cowden v. Comm'r 289 F.2d 20 (5th Cir. 1961)	3.03[2] & ns. 26, 27, 28
Crane v. Comm'r 331 U.S. 1 (1947)	3.03[2] & n.49, 11.03 n.59, 11.07 & n.81
Crashley v. Comm'r ¶ 79,513 P-H Memo T.C.	7.05 n.36
Creel v. Comm'r 72 T.C. 1173 (1979), aff'd, 649 F.2d 1133 (5th Cir. 1981)	11.09[2] ns. 96, 97
Crile v. U.S. 76-2 U.S.T.C. ¶ 13,161 (Ct. Cl. 1976)	12.08[1] n.40
Crown v. Comm'r 67 T.C. 1060 (1977), aff'd, 585 F.2d 234 (7th Cir. 1978), nonacq., 1978-1 C.B. 2	9.11[2] & n.62
Crummey v. U.S. 397 F.2d 82 (9th Cir. 1968)	11.04[1] n.65, 11.10[1][b] n.118, 13.03[4][c], 13.05[2] & ns. 77, 79, 13.05[3], 13.05[3][a], 13.05[3][c], 13.05[3][d], 13.05[4]

D

David Centre v. Comm'r 55 T.C. 16 (1970)	3.04 n.46
Davis v. Comm'r 55 T.C. 416 (1970)	11.10[1][c] n.124
Dean v. Comm'r 35 T.C. 1083 (1961)	11.09[2] & ns. 91, 96
DeLancey v. U.S. 264 F. Supp. 904 (D. Ark. 1967)	12.08[1] n.33
Detroit Bank & Trust Co. v. U.S. 467 F.2d 964 (6th Cir. 1972)	13.04[2] n.72
Diedrich v. Comm'r —U.S.— (1982)	11.07 & n.80
Disney, U.S. v. 413 F.2d 783 (9th Cir. 1969)	7.08[3][c] n.78

TABLE OF CASES

[References are to paragraphs (¶) and notes (n.).]

Dix v. Comm'r .... 46 T.C. 796 (1966), aff'd, 392 F.2d 313 (4th Cir. 1968)	16.02[4][c] n.26
Dougherty v. U.S. .... 292 F.2d 331 (6th Cir. 1961)	15.03[2][c] n.50
Downe, Estate of v. Comm'r .... 2 T.C. 967 (1943)	12.10[2] n.64
Doyle, Estate of v. Comm'r .... 32 T.C. 1209 (1959)	10.05[1] n.87
Dravo v. Comm'r .... 40 B.T.A. 309 (1939)	12.10[3] n.70
Driscoll, Union Trust Co. of Pittsburgh v. .... 138 F.2d 152 (3d Cir. 1943)	12.10[3] n.73
Duberstein, Comm'r v. .... 363 U.S. 278 (1960)	7.08[1] & ns. 63, 64, 11.03 & n.50
DuCharme's Estate v. Comm'r .... 164 F.2d 959 (6th Cir. 1947), modified, 169 F.2d 76 (6th Cir. 1948)	12.08[1] n.41
Duncan v. Comm'r .... 368 F.2d 98 (5th Cir. 1966)	11.10[1][a] & n.106
Dutcher, Estate of v. Comm'r .... 34 T.C. 918 (1960)	10.05[1] n.87

E

Edelman, Estate of v. Comm'r ...... 38 T.C. 972 (1962)	16.03[1] n.33
Elson v. Comm'r .... 28 T.C. 442 (1957)	15.03[2][c] n.49
Embry v. Gray .... 52 A.F.T.R. 1921 (D. Ky. 1956)	10.03[2][a] n.54
England, Estate of v. Comm'r .... ¶ 41,181 P-H Memo T.C.	10.03[2][b][i] n.59
English v. U.S. .... 270 F.2d 876 (7th Cir. 1959)	10.05[1] n.87
E.T. Sproull v. Comm'r .... 16 T.C. 244 (1951), aff'd, 194 F.2d 541 (6th Cir. 1952)	3.03[3][a] & n.34, 3.04 & n.41

F

Farrell v. U.S. .... 198 F. Supp. 461 (D. Cal. 1961)	15.03[2][a] n.57
Farrel, Estate of v. U.S. .... 553 F.2d 637 (Ct. Cl. 1977)	12.08[2] n.43, 12.10[2] & n.60

TABLE OF CASES

[References are to paragraphs (¶) and notes (n.).]

Fawcett, Estate of v. Comm'r 64 T.C. 889 (1975)	10.03[2][b][iv] n.70
Fehrs Fin. Co. v. Comm'r 58 T.C. 174 (1972), aff'd, 487 F.2d 184 (8th Cir. 1973)	16.02[2][a] n.13
Fenstermaker v. Comm'r 37 T.C.M. 898 (1978)	7.08[3][d] n.85
Fiedler, Estate of v. Comm'r 67 T.C. 239 (1976), acq., 1977-1 C.B. 1	15.03[2][c] & n.89
Findlay v. Comm'r 332 F.2d 620 (2d Cir. 1964)	14.02[1][b] n.8
Finley v. U.S. 404 F. Supp. 200 (S.D. Fla. 1975), rev'd on other grounds, 612 F.2d 166 (5th Cir. 1980)	16.03[3][a] n.54
First Nat'l Bank of Denver v. U.S. 648 F.2d 1286 (10th Cir. 1981)	12.08[2] & n.45
First Nat'l Bank of Kansas City [Estate of Cline] v. U.S. 223 F. Supp. 963 (D. Mo. 1963)	10.05[1] n.88
First Nat'l Bank of Montgomery v. U.S. 211 F. Supp. 403 (D. Ala. 1962)	12.07[1] n.22
First Nat'l Bank of Or. v. U.S. 488 F.2d 575 (9th Cir. 1973)	13.04[2] n.72
First Nat'l Bank of Pa. v. U.S. 398 F. Supp. 100 (W.D. Pa. 1975)	10.03[2][a] n.56
First Nat'l Bank of S.C. v. U.S. 81-2 U.S.T.C. ¶ 13,422 (D.S.C. 1981)	9.08[2][c] n.46
First Nat'l Bank of Topeka v. U.S. 233 F. Supp. 19 (D. Kan. 1964)	10.03[1][b][ii] n.43
First Nat'l Exch. Bank of Roanoke [Will of Pell] v. U.S. 335 F.2d 91 (4th Cir. 1964)	15.03[2][c] n.50
First Nat'l Trust and Sav. Bank of San Diego [Estate of Vajen], U.S. v. 355 F.2d 107 (9th Cir. 1964)	15.03[2][b] n.79
First Va. Bank v. U.S. 490 F.2d 532 (4th Cir. 1974)	16.03[2][a] n.39
Fish v. U.S. 432 F.2d 1278 (9th Cir. 1970)	16.03[3][a] n.53
Fisher v. Comm'r 28 B.T.A. 1164 (1933)	9.08[4] n.53
Fish, Estate of v. Comm'r 42 B.T.A. 260 (1940)	9.08[4] n.54

TABLE OF CASES

[References are to paragraphs (¶) and notes (n.).]

Flato v. Comm'r 195 F.2d 580 (5th Cir. 1952)	9.08[2][d] n.47
Fondren v. Comm'r 324 U.S. 18 (1945)	11.10 n.101
Ford, Estate of v. Comm'r 53 T.C. 114 (1969), aff'd, 450 F.2d 878 (2d Cir. 1971)	12.08[1] n.35
Francis v. Comm'r 36 T.C.M. 704 (1977)	8.06[1] n.79
Freeman, Estate of v. Comm'r 67 T.C. 202 (1976)	16.03[3][a] n.55
Fried, Estate of v. Comm'r 445 F.2d 979 (2d Cir. 1971), cert. denied, 404 U.S. 1016 (1972)	15.03[2][a] n.58
Friedman, Lee M., Ex'r v. U.S. ¶ 44,072 P-H Memo T.C.	10.03[2][a] n.54
Frost v. Comm'r 61 T.C. 488 (1974)	2.04[5][a] n.86
Fruehauf, Estate of v. Comm'r 427 F.2d 80 (6th Cir. 1970)	13.02[2][b] & n.13
Fry, Estate of v. Comm'r 19 T.C. 461 (1952), aff'd, 205 F.2d 517 (3d Cir. 1953)	5.04[2][a][iii] & n.113
Fusz, Estate of v. Comm'r 46 T.C. 214 (1966), acq., 1967-2 C.B. 2	14.03[2][a] & n.51, 14.03[2][b] & n.57

G

Gall v. U.S. 521 F.2d 878 (5th Cir. 1975), cert. denied, 425 U.S. 972 (1976)	11.10[1][c] n.123
Garrett v. U.S. ¶ 53,329 P-H Memo T.C.	10.03[2][a] n.54
Garwood v. Comm'r 62 T.C. 699 (1974)	7.05 n.37
Gegax v. Comm'r 73 T.C. 329 (1979)	5.04[2][a][iii] n.116
Gleason, Estate of v. Comm'r 24 T.C.M. 1630 (1965)	12.08[1] n.36
Glensder Textile Co. v. Comm'r 46 B.T.A. 176 (1942)	8.02[2][a] n.24
Gokey, Estate of v. Comm'r 72 T.C. 721 (1979)	12.07[1] & n.28
Goldsmith v. U.S. 586 F.2d 810 (Ct. Cl. 1978)	3.03[1] n.17, 3.03[2] & n.29, 3.04 n.45

TABLE OF CASES

[References are to paragraphs (¶) and notes (n.).]

Goldwater, Estate of v. Comm'r 64 T.C. 540 (1975)	15.02[2][a][i] n.29
Goodnow v. U.S. 302 F.2d 516 (Ct. Cl. 1962)	13.04[2] n.74
Goodwin v. Comm'r 75 T.C. 424 (1980)	8.06[1] n.79
Gorman v. U.S. 288 F. Supp. 225 (E.D. Mich. 1968)	13.04[2] n.72
Gotcher, U.S. v. 401 F.2d 118 (5th Cir. 1968)	7.08[3][c] n.75
Grace, Estate of, U.S. v. 395 U.S. 316 (1969)	9.08[2][d] n.47
Gray, Embry v. 52 A.F.T.R. 1921 (D. Ky. 1956)	10.03[2][a] n.54
Gray v. U.S. 410 F.2d 1094 (3d Cir. 1969)	14.03[2][b] n.56
Green, U.S. v. 176 F. Supp. 359 (S.D.N.Y. 1959)	9.08[2][a][i] n.33
Greenspun v. Comm'r 72 T.C. 931 (1979)	11.09[2] & ns. 93, 96
Griffith v. Comm'r (D. Tex. 1962)	11.10[1][b] & n.112
Gross v. Comm'r 7 T.C. 837 (1946), acq., 1946-1 C.B. 2	11.03 n.58
Guggenheim v. Helvering 117 F.2d 469 (2d Cir. 1941), cert. denied, 314 U.S. 521	10.03[2][a] n.55

H

Hanlin v. Comm'r 38 B.T.A. 811 (1938), aff'd, 108 F.2d 429 (3d Cir. 1939)	2.03[2] n.31
Hansen v. Vinel 413 F.2d 882 (8th Cir. 1969)	15.03[2][a] n.58
Harris v. Comm'r 61 T.C. 770 (1974)	8.06[1] n.74
Hart, Estate of v. Comm'r 1 T.C. 989 (1943)	16.02[2][c] n.16
Harvey, Ex'r v. U.S. 185 F.2d 463 (7th Cir. 1950)	10.05[1] n.88
Hauptfuhrer, Estate of v. Comm'r 9 T.C.M. 974 (1950), aff'd, 195 F.2d 548 (3d Cir. 1952), cert. denied, 344 U.S. 825	12.10[3] n.73

TABLE OF CASES

[References are to paragraphs (¶) and notes (n.).]

Hawaiian Trust Co. v. U.S. 412 F.2d 1313 (Ct. Cl. 1969)	15.03[2][c] n.50
Haygood v. Comm'r 42 T.C. 936 (1964), acq. in result only, 1965-1 C.B. 4, acq. withdrawn and nonacq. substituted, 1977-2 C.B. 2	11.06 & n.74
Heath v. Comm'r 34 T.C. 587 (1960)	11.10[1][c] & n.120
Heidel v. Comm'r 56 T.C. 95 (1971)	2.04[5][a] n.86
Heidrich v. Comm'r 55 T.C. 746 (1971)	11.10[1][b] & n.110
Henry, Estate of v. Comm'r 69 T.C. 665 (1978)	11.07 n.79
Henslee v. Union Planters Nat'l Bank & Trust Co. 335 U.S. 595 (1949)	12.08[1] n.39
Herr v. Comm'r 35 T.C. 732 (1961), aff'd, 303 F.2d 780 (3d Cir. 1962)	11.02[3] n.20, 11.10[1][b] & n.115
Hess v. Comm'r 271 F.2d 104 (3d Cir. 1959)	14.02[1][c][ii] n.22
Hill, Estate of v. Comm'r 64 T.C. 867 (1975)	12.10[1] n.57
Hite, Estate of v. Comm'r 49 T.C. 580, 594 (1968)	11.03 & n.42
Holladay v. Comm'r 649 F.2d 1176 (5th Cir. 1981)	8.05 n.74
Holland, Estate of v. Comm'r 64 T.C. 499 (1975), acq., 1975-2 C.B. 1	15.03[2][b] n.77
Hollingshead, Estate of v. Comm'r 70 T.C. 578 (1978)	15.03[2][b] & n.80
Hooks, Estate of v. Comm'r 22 T.C. 502 (1954)	14.02[2] n.31
Horwith v. Comm'r 71 T.C. 932 (1979)	4.02 n.5
Houlette v. Comm'r 48 T.C. 350 (1967)	2.04[4][c][i] n.72
Hurd, Estate of v. Comm'r 160 F.2d 610 (1st Cir. 1947)	16.03[3][a] n.53

J

Jackson v. U.S. 376 U.S. 503 (1964)	15.03[2][c] n.51

[*References are to paragraphs (¶) and notes (n.).*]

Jacuzzi v. Comm'r .... 61 T.C. 262 (1973)	3.04 & n.42
Johnson v. Comm'r .... 59 T.C. 791 (1973), aff'd, 495 F.2d 1079 (6th Cir.), cert. denied, 419 U.S. 1040 (1974)	11.07 n.79
Johnson, Moskin v. .... 115 F. Supp. 565 (S.D.N.Y. 1953), aff'd, 217 F.2d 278 (2d Cir. 1954)	9.08[3][a] n.48
Johnson v. U.S. .... 254 F. Supp. 73 (N.D. Tex. 1966)	9.11[3][d] n.68, 11.09[1] & n.89
Johnson, Estate of v. Comm'r .... 2 T.C.M. 299 (1943)	12.10[2] n.68
Jones v. U.S. .... 424 F. Supp. 236 (E.D. Ill. 1976)	10.03[2][a] n.51
Jones, B.W., Trust v. Comm'r ...... 46 B.T.A. 531 (1941), aff'd, 132 F.2d 914 (4th Cir. 1943)	9.13 n.71
Jordan, Caldwell v. .... 119 F. Supp. 66 (D. Ala. 1953)	13.02[2][d] n.27

K

Karagheusian, Estate of, Comm'r v. ... 233 F.2d 197 (2d Cir. 1956)	13.02[2][d] n.27
Kavanagh, Schnorbach v. .... 102 F. Supp. 828 (W.D. Mich. 1951)	10.03[1][b][ii] n.43
Kay, Ex'r [Rosenman], Phinney v. .... 275 F.2d 776 (5th Cir. 1960)	16.03[2][a] n.38
Kearns v. U.S. .... 399 F.2d 226 (Ct. Cl. 1968)	13.02[2][d] n.27
Kelley, Estate of v. Comm'r .... 63 T.C. 321 (1974), nonacq. 1977-2 C.B. 2	11.06 & n.75
Kelm, Struthers v. .... 218 F.2d 810 (8th Cir. 1955)	12.08[1] n.36, 12.10[3] n.73
Kintner, U.S. v. .... 216 F.2d 418 (9th Cir. 1954)	8.02[2] n.21
Kleemeier, Estate of v. Comm'r ...... 58 T.C. 241 (1972)	14.05[1][b][i] & n.94
Kliban v. U.S. .... 37 A.F.T.R. 26, 76-1567 (D. Conn. 1976)	15.03[2][c] n.51
Kowalski, Comm'r v. .... 434 U.S. 77 (1977)	7.08[3][d] n.82

[*References are to paragraphs (¶) and notes (n.).*]

Kramer v. Comm'r .... 406 F.2d 1363 (Ct. Cl. 1969)	14.03[2][c] n.62
Krause, A.K. v. Comm'r .... 497 F.2d 1109 (6th Cir. 1974), cert. denied, 419 U.S. 1108 (1974)	9.08[2][d] n.47
Kuhl, Berry v. .... 174 F.2d 565 (7th Cir. 1949)	12.08[1] n.35

L

Laganas v. Comm'r .... 281 F.2d 731 (1st Cir. 1960)	9.08[2][a][i] n.33
Lage v. Comm'r .... 52 T.C. 130 (1969), acq., 1969-2 C.B. xxiv	7.05 n.36
Landorf v. U.S. .... 408 F.2d 461 (Ct. Cl. 1969)	13.03[4][a] n.52
Lang, Estate of v. Comm'r .... 64 T.C. 404 (1975), aff'd, 613 F.2d 770 (9th Cir. 1980)	9.12[2] n.64
Laramy v. Comm'r .... 25 T.C.M. 809 (1966)	3.03[1] n.16
Larson v. Comm'r .... 66 T.C. 159 (1976)	8.02[4] & n.36, 8.02[5], 8.02[6]
Laurin, Estate of v. Comm'r .... ¶ 79,145 P-H Memo T.C., aff'd, 645 F.2d 8 (6th Cir. 1981)	15.04[3] & n.103
Lay, Estate of v. Comm'r .... 40 B.T.A. 522 (1939)	10.03[2][a] n.56
Leavens v. Comm'r .... 467 F.2d 809 (3d Cir. 1972), rev'g 44 T.C. 623 (1965)	3.03[1] & n.20
Leewitz, Coex'r v. U.S. .... 75 F. Supp. 312 (Ct. Cl. 1948)	10.03[3] n.72
Lehman v. U.S. .... 448 F.2d 1318 (5th Cir. 1971)	16.03[2][a] n.42
Leopold v. U.S. .... 72-1 U.S.T.C. ¶ 12,837 (C.D. Cal. 1972), aff'd, 510 F.2d 617 (9th Cir. 1975)	12.08[1] n.35, 12.10[2] n.69
Levin v. U.S. .... 373 F.2d 434 (1st Cir. 1967)	14.02[1][c][i] n.13
Levy, Estate of v. Comm'r .... 70 T.C. 873 (1978)	13.02[2][c] & n.19
Lewis, Estate of v. Comm'r .... 49 T.C. 684 (1968)	10.03[2][a] n.51

TABLE OF CASES

[References are to paragraphs (¶) and notes (n.).]

Lloyd, Estate of v. Comm'r .... 12.10[3] n.71
   47 B.T.A. 349 (1942)

LoBue, Comm'r v. .... 7.08[1] & ns. 61, 62, 11.03
   351 U.S. 243 (1956)

Lumpkin v. Comm'r .... 13.03[4][b] n.55
   474 F.2d 1092 (5th Cir. 1973) rev'g
   56 T.C. 815 (1971), nonacq. 1973-2
   C.B. 4

Lyman, Exrs. v. Comm'r .... 10.03[3] n.72
   83 F.2d 811 (1st Cir. 1936)

M

Mabley, Jr., Comm'r v. .... 7.08[3][d] n.83
   24 T.C.M. 1794 (1965)

Mack v. U.S. .... 10.03[2][b][i] n.62
   160 F. Supp. 421 (E.D. Wis. 1958)

Madison Gas and Elec. Co. v. Comm'r   8.06[1] n.79
   72 T.C. 521 (1979), aff'd, 633 F.2d 512
   (7th Cir. 1980)

Manor Care, U.S. v. .... 8.06[1] n.79
   490 F. Supp. 355 (D. Md. 1980)

Margrave, Estate of v. Comm'r ...... 13.02[2][d] & ns. 29, 30
   71 T.C. 13 (1978), aff'd, 618 F.2d 34
   (8th Cir. 1980)

Maximov v. U.S. 9.13 n.71
   373 U.S. 49 (1969), aff'd, 299 F.2d
   565 (2d Cir. 1962)

McCann v. U.S. .... 7.08[3][c] n.76
   81-2 U.S.T.C. ¶ 9689 (Ct. Cl. Trial
   Div. 1981)

McCobb, All v. .... 14.03[2][b] & n.55
   321 F.2d 633 (2d Cir. 1963)

McDonough v. U.S. .... 2.04[4][a][ii] n.61
   577 F.2d 234 (4th Cir. 1968)

McManus, Estate of v. Comm'r ...... 12.08[1] n.32
   172 F.2d 697 (6th Cir. 1949), cert.
   denied, 337 U.S. 938 (1949)

Meeske, Estate of v. Comm'r .... 15.04[3] & n.102
   72 T.C. 73 (1979), aff'd, 645 F.2d 8
   (6th Cir. 1981)

Meldrum & Fewsmith, Inc. v. Comm'r   8.06[1] n.78
   20 T.C. 790 (1953), aff'd on other
   issue, 230 F.2d 283 (6th Cir. 1956)

TABLE OF CASES

[References are to paragraphs (¶) and notes (n.).]

Mercantile Commerce Bank & Trust Co., Helvering v. .... 111 F.2d 224 (8th Cir. 1940), cert. denied, 310 U.S. 654 (1940)	12.07[1] n.22
Mercantile Trust Co. Nat'l Ass'n v. U.S. 312 F. Supp. 108 (E.D. Mo. 1970)	13.04[2] n.72
Merchant's Nat'l Bank v. Comm'r .... 320 U.S. 256 (1943)	12.08[1] n.35
Merchants Nat'l Bank of Cedar Rapids v. U.S. .... 326 F. Supp. 384 (N.D. Iowa 1971)	15.03[2][b] n.67
Merians v. Comm'r .... 60 T.C. 187 (1973)	7.08[3][b] n.74
Messing v. Comm'r .... 48 T.C. 502 (1967)	11.10[1][c] & n.122
Miami Beach First Nat'l Bank v. U.S. 443 F.2d 116 (5th Cir. 1971)	16.02[2][c] n.19
Milbank v. Comm'r .... 41 B.T.A. 1014 (1940)	9.08[4] n.54
Millar v. Comm'r .... 67 T.C. 656 (1977), aff'd, 577 F.2d 212 (3d Cir. 1978)	8.03[2] n.51
Mitchell, Estate of v. Comm'r .... 55 T.C. 576 (1970)	12.07[1] & n.25
Mittleman, Estate of v. Comm'r ...... 522 F.2d 132 (D.C. Cir. 1975)	15.03[2][b] n.67
Moore v. Comm'r .... 70 T.C. 1024 (1978)	8.05 n.72
Morrill v. U.S. .... 228 F. Supp. 734 (D. Me. 1964)	9.08[6] n.56, 12.07[2] & n.29
Morris, Estate of .... ¶ 81,368 P-H Memo T.C.	2.04[4][a][ii] n.60
Morrissey v. Comm'r .... 296 U.S. 34 (1935)	8.02[2] n.19
Moskin v. Johnson .... 115 F. Supp. 565 (S.D.N.Y. 1953), aff'd, 217 F.2d 278 (2d Cir. 1954)	9.08[3][a] n.48
Moss, Estate of v. Comm'r .... 74 T.C. 1239 (1980), acq., 1981-1 C.B. 2	14.02[1][b] n.11, 16.02[4][d] n.27
Mudge, Estate of v. Comm'r .... 27 T.C. 188 (1956) nonacq. 1964-1 C.B. 6	13.02[2][d] n.28

TABLE OF CASES

[References are to paragraphs (¶) and notes (n.).]

N

Nathan's Estate, Comm'r v. .... 12.06[2] n.18
159 F.2d 546 (7th Cir. 1947)

Neugass v. Comm'r .... 15.03[2][d] n.54
555 F.2d 322 (2d Cir. 1977)

Newberry, Estate of v. Comm'r ...... 12.10[2] n.67
201 F.2d 874 (3d Cir. 1953)

Noel, Estate of v. Comm'r .... 14.02[1][b] n.8
50 T.C. 702 (1968)

Northern Trust Co. v. U.S. .... 14.05[1][a][v] n.91
389 F.2d 731 (7th Cir. 1968)

O

O'Connor, Estate of v. Comm'r ...... 12.08[1] n.38
54 T.C. 969 (1970)

O'Daniel's Estate v. Comm'r .... 14.02[1][c][ii] & n.17
173 F.2d 966 (2d Cir. 1949)

Old Colony Trust Co. v. U.S. .... 12.09 & ns. 52, 53, 12.10[2] n.65
423 F.2d 601 (1st Cir. 1970)

O'Malley, U.S. v. .... 12.08[1] n.31, 12.09 & n.50
383 U.S. 627 (1966)

Orrisch v. Comm'r 8.05 n.74
55 T.C. 395 (1970)

Owen v. Comm'r 11.07 n.79
T.C. Memo 1978-51 (1978), aff'd, 652 F.2d 1271 (6th Cir. 1981)

P

Pardee, Estate of v. Comm'r .... 10.03[2][b][i] n.62, 12.10[2] n.69
49 T.C. 140 (1967)

Park, Estate of v. Comm'r .... 10.03[1][b][iv] n.45
475 F.2d 673 (6th Cir. 1973)

Penn Cent. Transp. Co., In re .... 3.02[2][b] & n.10
484 F.2d 1300 (3d Cir. 1973)

Pennsylvania Bank and Trust Co. v.
U.S. .... 16.03[3][a] n.53
597 F.2d 382 (3d Cir. 1979)

Pennsylvania Co. v. U.S. .... 16.03[1] n.33
69 F. Supp. 577 (D. Pa. 1946)

People's Life Ins. Co. v. U.S. .... 7.08[3][c] ns. 75, 77
373 F.2d 924 (Ct. Cl. 1967)

People's Trust Co. of Bergen County
(Will of O'Brien) v. U.S. .... 16.03[2][a] n.40
412 F.2d 1156 (3d Cir. 1969)

TABLE OF CASES

[References are to paragraphs (¶) and notes (n.).]

Perkins v. Comm'r 27 T.C. 601 (1956)	11.10[1][b] & n.111
Peters, Estate of v. Comm'r 23 T.C.M. 994 (1964)	12.09 n.48, 12.10[2] n.63
Pettus, Jr. v. Comm'r 54 T.C. 112 (1970)	11.10[1][a] & n.104
Phinney v. Kay, Ex'r (Rosenman) 275 F.2d 776 (5th Cir. 1960)	16.03[2][a] n.38
Pledger v. Comm'r 71 T.C. 618 (1979)	4.02 n.5
Porter v. Comm'r 288 U.S. 436 (1933)	12.10[3] n.72
Powell, U.S. v. 307 F.2d 821 (10th Cir. 1962)	12.09 n.49, 12.10[2] n.69
Pratt v. Comm'r 64 T.C. 203 (1975)	8.06[1] n.81
Prudowsky, Estate of v. Comm'r 55 T.C. 890 (1971), aff'd, 465 F.2d 62 (7th Cir. 1972)	11.10[2] n.126
Pulver v. Comm'r T.C. Memo 1982-437	5.02[9] n.39

R

Ray, Estate of v. Comm'r 54 T.C. 1170 (1970)	15.03[2][d] n.53
Resnick v. Comm'r 66 T.C. 74 (1976), aff'd, 555 F.2d 634 (7th Cir. 1977)	2.04[2][a] n.42
Rhode Island Hosp. Trust Co., U.S. v. 355 F.2d 7, 11 (1st Cir. 1966)	13.02[2][d] ns. 23, 24
Richards v. Comm'r 375 F.2d 997 (10th Cir. 1967)	12.07[1] & n.27
Richardson v. Comm'r 76 T.C. 45 (1981)	8.05 n.72
Richmond T.V. Corp. v. U.S. 345 F.2d 901 (4th Cir. 1965), rev'd on other grounds, 382 U.S. 68 (1965)	8.06[1] n.79
Riff, Sr., Comm'r v. 368 F.2d 965 (10th Cir. 1966)	7.08[3][c] n.79
Robertson v. U.S. 343 U.S. 714	11.03
Robinson v. Comm'r 44 T.C. 20 (1965), acq., 1970-2 C.B. xxiii, acq. corrected, 1976-2 C.B. 2	3.04 & n.49

[*References are to paragraphs (¶) and notes (n.).*]

Rodman v. Comm'r .... 542 F.2d 845 (2d Cir. 1976)	8.05 n.70
Rose v. U.S. .... 511 F.2d 259 (5th Cir. 1975)	13.02[2][b] & n.14
Rovensky v. Comm'r .... 37 B.T.A. 702 (1938)	9.08[4] n.54

S

St. Louis Union Trust Co. (Orthwein) v. U.S. .... 262 F. Supp. 27 (D. Mo. 1966)	13.02[2][d] n.27
Sakol v. Comm'r .... 67 T.C. 986 (1977), aff'd, 574 F.2d 694 (2d Cir. 1978), cert. denied, 439 U.S. 859 (1978)	4.02 n.4
Salisbury, Estate of .... 34 T.C.M. 1441 (1975)	14.05[1][a][ii] n.81
Salter v. Comm'r .... 545 F.2d 494 (5th Cir. 1977)	15.03[2][b] n.75
Sandor v. Comm'r .... 62 T.C. 469 (1974), aff'd, 536 F.2d 874 (9th Cir. 1976)	2.04[2][a] n.41
Sbicca, Estate of v. Comm'r .... 35 T.C. 96 (1960)	15.03[2][a] n.57
Schelberg v. Comm'r .... 612 F.2d 25 (2d Cir. 1979) rev'g 70 T.C. 690 (1978)	14.03[2][b] & n.60, 14.03[2][e][i]
Schneider v. Comm'r .... 35 B.T.A. 183 (1936)	12.10[1] n.55
Schnorbach v. Kavanagh .... 102 F. Supp. 828 (W.D. Mich. 1951)	10.03[1][b][ii] n.43
Schwager v. Comm'r .... 64 T.C. 781 (1975)	13.02[2][d] n.21
Sessoms, Alexander, Estate of .... 8 T.C.M. 1056 (1949)	12.07[1] & n.24
Sharvy v. Comm'r .... 67 T.C. 630 (1977), aff'd per curiam, 566 F.2d 1118 (9th Cir. 1977)	2.04[5][a] n.86
Shedd v. Comm'r .... 320 F.2d 638 (9th Cir. 1963)	10.02[3][b][i] n.27
Siegel, Estate of v. Comm'r .... 74 T.C. 613 (1980)	14.03[1] n.44, 14.03[2][b] & n.61, 14.03[2][c], 14.03[2][e][iii]
Siegel, Estate of v. Comm'r .... 67 T.C. 662 (1977)	15.03[2][c] n.47

TABLE OF CASES

[References are to paragraphs (¶) and notes (n.).]

Silverman, Estate of v. Comm'r 521 F.2d 574 (2d Cir. 1975), acq., 1978-1 C.B. 2	13.04[2] n.72
Silverman, Estate of v. Comm'r 61 T.C. 605 (1974)	14.05[1][a][v] n.92
Silvey Ex'x v. U.S. 265 F. Supp. 235 (N.D. Ala. 1966)	15.03[2][b] n.82
Sinclaire, Estate of v. Comm'r 13 T.C. 742 (1949)	12.10[2] n.66
Smead, Estate of v. Comm'r 78 T.C. No. 3 (1982)	13.02[2][d] n.25, 13.03[4][b] n.53
Smith, Comm'r v. 324 U.S. 177 (1945)	7.08[1] & ns. 59, 60
Smith, Estate of v. Comm'r 510 F.2d 479 (2d Cir. 1975), cert. denied, 423 U.S. 827 (1976)	10.03[1][b][iv] n.45
Smith, Estate of v. Comm'r 66 T.C. 415 (1976), aff'd, 565 F.2d 455 (7th Cir. 1977), nonacq. 1978-1 C.B. 3, nonacq. withdrawn and acq. substituted, 1982-4 I.R.B. 5	15.04[3] & n.101
Smith, Estate of v. Comm'r 73 T.C. 307 (1979)	13.02[2][d] n.26
Spalding, Estate of v. Comm'r 34 T.C.M. 1074 (1975) rev'd, 537 F.2d 666 (2d Cir. 1976)	15.02[2][a][i] n.29
Sproull, E.T. v. Comm'r 16 T.C. 244 (1951), aff'd, 194 F.2d 541 (6th Cir. 1952)	3.03[3][a] & n.34, 3.04 & n.41
Stafford v. U.S. 236 F. Supp. 132 (E.D. Wis. 1964)	16.03[2][a] n.41
Stanley v. Comm'r 33 T.C. 614 (1959)	2.04[4][c][i] n.73
Starker v. U.S. 602 F.2d 1341 (9th Cir. 1979)	2.04[4][b] n.66
Starrett (Estate of Tingley) v. Comm'r 223 F.2d 163 (1st Cir. 1966)	15.03[2][b] n.83
State St. Trust Co. v. U.S. 263 F.2d 635 (1st Cir. 1959)	12.08[1] n.35, 12.09 & n.51
Steen v. U.S. 195 F.2d 379 (9th Cir. 1952)	10.05[1] n.87
Steffke, Estate of v. Comm'r 64 T.C. 530 (1975)	15.02[2][a][i] n.29
Stephens v. U.S. 270 F. Supp. 968 (D. Mont. 1967)	15.03[2][c] n.51

TABLE OF CASES

[References are to paragraphs (¶) and notes (n.).]

Stolk v. Comm'r 40 T.C. 345 (1963), aff'd, 326 F.2d 760 (2d Cir. 1964)	2.04[4][c][i] n.72
Street, Estate of v. Comm'r 25 T.C. 673 (1955)	15.03[2][a] n.57
Struthers v. Kelm 218 F.2d 810 (8th Cir. 1955)	12.08[1] n.36, 12.10[3] n.73
Suttle v. Comm'r 37 T.C.M. 1638 (1978), aff'd, 625 F.2d 1127 (4th Cir. 1980)	11.09[2] n.92
Swayne, Estate of v. Comm'r 43 T.C. 190 (1964), acq., 1965-2 C.B. 6	10.03[1][b][iv] n.45

T

Tannenbaum v. Tannenbaum 50 A.D.2d 539, 375 N.Y.S.2d 329 (1st Dep't 1975)	9.12[3][a] n.66
Tebon v. Comm'r 55 T.C. 410 (1970)	2.04[5][a] n.91
Terriberry v. U.S. 517 F.2d 286 (5th Cir. 1975), cert. denied, 424 U.S. 977 (1976)	13.02[2][b] & n.15
Thebaut v. Comm'r 1964-102 T.C.M., aff'd and rev'd on another issue, 361 F.2d 428 (5th Cir. 1966)	11.10[1][b] n.116
Thompson, Townsend v. 50-2 U.S.T.C. ¶ 10,780 (D. Ark. 1950)	12.07[1] & n.26
Todd, Jr., Estate of v. Comm'r 57 T.C. 288 (1971)	15.03[2][b] n.69
Tomlinson, Barritt v. 129 F. Supp. 642 (S.D. Fla. 1955)	16.03[2][a] n.42
Tompkins, Estate of v. Comm'r 68 T.C. 912 (1977)	15.03[2][d] & n.54
Towne v. Comm'r 78 T.C. 791 (1982)	6.03[2] n.39
Townsend v. Thompson 50-2 U.S.T.C. ¶ 10,780 (D. Ark. 1950)	12.07[1] & n.26
Trisko v. Comm'r 29 T.C. 515 (1957)	2.04[4][c][i] n.71
Tufts v. Comm'r 651 F.2d 1058 (5th Cir. 1981), rev'g 70 T.C. 756 (1978)	8.03[2] n.51

TABLE OF CASES

[References are to paragraphs (¶) and notes (n.).]

Tully, Sr., Estate of v. U.S. . . . . 528 F.2d 1401 (Ct. Cl. 1976)	14.03[1] n.44, 14.03[2][a] n.52, 14.03[2][c] n.62
Turner v. Comm'r . . . . 410 F.2d 752 (6th Cir. 1969)	11.07 n.79
212 Corp. v. Comm'r . . . . 70 T.C. 788 (1978)	16.02[2][a] & n.13

U

Underwood v. U.S. . . . . 407 F.2d 608 (6th Cir. 1969), aff'g 270 F. Supp. 389 (E.D. Tenn. 1967)	15.05[2][a][iii] n.133
Union Planters Nat'l Bank & Trust Co., Henslee v. . . . . 335 U.S. 595 (1949)	12.08[1] n.39
Union Trust Co. of Pittsburgh v. Driscoll . . . . 138 F.2d 152 (3d Cir. 1943)	12.10[3] n.73
Unser v. Comm'r . . . . 59 T.C. 528 (1973)	2.04[5][a] & n.92

V

Van den Wymelenberg v. U.S. . . . . 397 F.2d 443 (7th Cir.), cert. denied, 393 U.S. 953 (1968)	11.10[1][c] n.124
Vinel, Hansen v. . . . . 413 F.2d 882 (8th Cir. 1969)	15.03[2][a] n.58

W

Wadewitz, Estate of v. Comm'r . . . . . . 39 T.C. 925 (1963), aff'd, 339 F.2d 980 (7th Cir. 1964)	14.03[2][b] n.56
Warren Jones Co. v. Comm'r . . . . 524 F.2d 788 (9th Cir. 1975)	3.03[2] n.31
Watson v. Comm'r . . . . 31 T.C. 1014 (1959), nonacq. 1963-1 C.B. 5	7.05 n.36
Weisberger, Estate of v. Comm'r . . . . 29 T.C. 217 (1957)	15.03[2][b] n.68
Weller v. Comm'r . . . . 38 T.C. 790 (1962)	11.10[1][b] n.116
Welsh v. U.S. . . . . 210 F. Supp. 597 (N.D. Ohio 1962), aff'd, 329 F.2d 145 (6th Cir. 1964)	7.05 n.36

TABLE OF CASES

[References are to paragraphs (¶) and notes (n.).]

Wemyss, Comm'r v. .... 324 U.S. 303 (1945)	11.03 & n.45
Weyman v. Weyman .... 51 A.D.2d 768, 379 N.Y.S.2d 717 (2d Dep't 1976)	9.12[3][a] n.66
Whitely v. Comm'r .... 42 B.T.A. 316 (1940)	9.08[2][d] n.47
Williams v. U.S. .... 634 F.2d 894 (5th Cir. 1981), rev'g 78-2 T.C. ¶ 13,264 (W.D. Tex. 1978)	16.03[3][a] n.53
Williams v. U.S. .... 378 F.2d 693 (Ct. Cl. 1967)	11.10[1][a] & n.105
Willits v. Comm'r .... 50 T.C. 602 (1968), acq., 1969-1 C.B. 21	3.03[1] n.16
Winchell, U.S. v. .... 289 F.2d 212 (9th Cir. 1961)	12.10[2] n.62
Wisconsin Cheeseman v. U.S. .... 388 F.2d 420 (7th Cir. 1968)	2.04[4][a][ii] n.59
Wolfe, Estate of v. Comm'r .... 29 T.C. 441 (1957), aff'd on this issue, 264 F.2d 82 (3d Cir. 1959)	10.03[2][a] n.51
Wondsel v. Comm'r .... 350 F.2d 339 (2d Cir. 1965), cert. denied, 383 U.S. 935 (1966)	15.02[2][a][i] n.29
Woodsam Assoc. v. Comm'r .... 16 T.C. 649 (1951), aff'd, 198 F.2d 357 (2d Cir. 1952)	8.03[2] n.51
Wragg, Adm'r (Lowe), Comm'r v. ... 141 F.2d 638 (1st Cir. 1944)	10.03[2][a] n.57
Wyant v. Comm'r .... 6 T.C. 565 (1946)	9.08[2][d] n.47
Wyche v. U.S. .... 749 C.C.H. ¶ 7911, Ct. Cl. Commissioner's Report (1974)	12.07[2] & n.30

Y

Yawkey, Estate of v. Comm'r .... 12 T.C. 1164 (1949)	12.08[1] ns. 36, 41

Z

Zager v. Comm'r .... 72 T.C. 1009 (1979), aff'd, 649 F.2d 1133 (5th Cir. 1981)	11.09[2] n.96

TABLE OF CASES

[References are to paragraphs (¶) and notes (n.).]

Ziran v. Ziran .... 9.12[3][a] n.66
   65 A.D.2d 514, 409 N.Y.S.2d 13
   (1st Dep't 1978)

Zuckman v. U.S. .... 8.02[4] & n.35, 8.02 [6]
   524 F.2d 729 (Ct. Cl. 1975)

Index

[References are to paragraphs (¶) and notes (n.).]

A

Alternate valuation date, estate tax, 10.02[1]
Alternative minimum tax, 2.02
  alternative minimum taxable income, 2.02[1]
  computation, 2.02[1]
  generally, 2.02
  penalties for ignoring, 2.02[1]
  planning, 2.02[3]
  preference items, 2.02[2]
    accelerated cost recovery deduction, 2.02[2][g]
    accelerated depreciation
      leased personal property, 2.02[2][b]
      real property, 2.02[2][a]
    amortization, pollution control, 2.02[2][c]
    capital gain, 2.02[2][h]
    depletion, 2.02[2][e]
    incentive stock options, 2.02[2][d]
    intangible drilling costs, 2.02[2][f]
    mining exploration and development, 2.02[2][i]
    miscellaneous, 2.02[2][i]
Annual exclusion, gift tax, 11.02[3], 11.04[1]
  See also Gift tax
Annuities. *See* Private annuities; Qualified plans
Athletes, 1.02[3]
At-risk rules
  definition of, 8.03[3]
  generally, 8.03[3]
  investment credit, 8.03[3]
Averaging. *See* Income averaging

B

Basis
  death, basis after, 2.04[4][d]
  gifts, 11.02[4]
  joint property, at death, 15.02[1][a] n.13
  loss limitation, partnerships, 8.03
  partnership interest, 8.03[1]
    loans to partnership, 8.03[2]
    nonrecourse liabilities, 8.03[2]
  property transferred for services, 4.02[3][b]
  step-up at death, 2.04[4][d]
Bequests and devises
  See also Wills
  charitable, 15.02[2]
  fractional share, 15.04[1]
  pecuniary, 15.04[2]

C

Cafeteria plans, 7.07
  antidiscrimination requirements, 7.07
Capital gain
  capital assets, definition, 2.03[1]
  deduction, 2.03[1]
  generally, 2.03
  income in respect of decedent, 14.02[3][b][ii]
  losses, limitation on, 2.03[1]
  preference item, 2.02[2][h]
  private annuities, 16.02[1]
  wash sales, 2.03[2]
    basis, 2.03[2]
    generally, 2.03[2]
    substantially identical, 2.03[2]
Cash or deferred plans, 5.02[7]
  qualification requirements, 5.02[7]

INDEX

[References are to paragraphs (¶) and notes (n.).]

Charitable bequests, estate tax
  contingent bequests, 15.05[2][a][iii]
  donees, permissible, 15.05[2][a][i]
  methods of transfer, 15.05[2][a][ii]
  planning for, 15.05[2][b]
  pooled income fund, 15.05[2][a][ii]
  remainder interests, 15.05[2][a][ii]

Clifford Trusts, 9.05, 9.06[1]
  See also Grantor trusts

Compensation, deferred. *See* Deferred compensation

Constructive receipt, deferred income, 3.03[1]

Contemplation of death, gifts
  generally, 11.02[5]
  insurance gifts, 13.04

Conventions, taxability of, 7.08[3][c]

Corporate executives, 1.02[1]

Credit on prior transfers, 10.02[3]
  allowable percentage, 10.02[3][a]
  computation of, 10.02[3][b]
  transfer of property, 10.02[3][a]
  value of transferred property, 10.02[3][b][i]

Credit, state death taxes, 10.02[4]

Custodians
  gifts to, 11.10[1]

D

Death-benefit-only plans, 14.03[2]
  amend, power to, 14.03[2][c]
  beneficiaries' needs, 14.03[3]
  combination of plans, 14.03[2][b]
  disability plan with, 14.03[2][b]
  gift tax consequences, 14.03[2][d]
  planning, 14.03[2][e]
  power to amend, 14.03[2][c]
  qualified plan with, 14.03[2][b]
  separate plans, 14.03[2][e][i]

Death benefits, 7.06
  See also Survivor's death benefits

Decedents estates. *See* Estate planning; Estate tax; Wills

Deductions
  borrowing cash value of life insurance, 6.02[4]
  charitable, estate tax, 15.05[2]
  decedent, deduction in respect, 14.02[2]
  educational assistance programs, 7.05
  estate tax, 10.03
  gross estate, from, 10.03
  income in respect of decedent, 14.02[2], 14.02[3]
  individual retirement accounts, 5.06[2][a]
  life insurance premiums, 6.02[2]
  marital deduction, 15.02
  property transferred for services, 4.02[3][c]
  split-dollar insurance, 6.04[2]

Deferred compensation
  advance rulings, 3.03[3][b]
  advantages, 3.02
  constructive receipt, 3.03[1]
  economic benefit theory, 3.03[2]
  economics of deferral, 3.02[2]
    alternative investments, 3.02[2][a]
    cash flow, 3.02[2][c]
    risks of deferral, 3.02[2][b]
  escrow arrangements, 3.03[3][a]
  estate planning, 14.03
  forfeiture conditions, 3.02[2][b]
  funding, 3.04
  guarantee, third party, 3.04
  how to defer, 3.03
  income in respect of decedent, 14.02[1][c][ii]
  indexing, 3.02[1]
  investments, choice of, 3.04
  life insurance funding, 3.04
  phantom stock plans, 3.05[2]
  risks of deferral, 3.02[2][b]
  Service's position, 3.03[3]
  tax savings, 3.02[1]
  trust arrangements, 3.04
  types of plans, 3.05
    investment type plans, 3.05[1]
    phantom stock plans, 3.05[2]
  unsecured promise, 3.03[3][a]

INDEX

[References are to paragraphs (¶) and notes (n.).]

Depreciation, recapture, 2.04[3]
Disability plans, 7.04[1]
   definition of disability, 7.04[1]
   exclusion from income, 7.04[1]
   workmen's compensation, 7.04[2]
Disclaimers, renouncing bequeathed property, 15.05[1]
   requirements for, 15.05[1]
   time for making, 15.05[1]

E

Educational assistance programs, 7.05
   antidiscrimination requirements, 7.05
   deductibility, 7.05
Education trusts, 12.07
Employee benefits. *See* Fringe benefits; Pension plans; Profit sharing plans; Qualified plans
Employee stock ownership plans (ESOPs), 5.02[7]
   PAYSOPs, 5.02[8]
Entertainers, 1.02[4]
Equalization clause, marital deduction, 15.04[3]
ESOPs. *See* Employee stock ownership plans
Estate planning
   See also Estate tax; Estate tax, deductions; Life insurance, estate tax
   annuity, qualified, 14.05[1]
      payable to executor, 14.05[1][a][ii]
      spouse's estate, 14.05[1][b][i]
   annuity, nonqualified, 14.03[1]
   beneficiaries' needs, 14.03[3]
   changes in recent years, 10.01
   charitable bequests, 15.05[2]
   death-benefit-only plans, 14.03[2]
   deferred compensation, 14.03
   disclaimers, 15.05[1]
   generation skipping tax, 10.04
   individual retirement accounts, 14.05[3]
   inflation planning, 16.04
   Keogh plans, 14.05
   lump-sum distributions, 14.05[2]
   marital deduction, 15.02
   nonqualified options, 14.04
   options, 14.04
   pension plans, 14.05
   powers of appointment, 16.03
   private annuities, 16.02
   profit-sharing plans, 14.05
   qualified plans, 14.05
   restricted stock, 14.04
   Section 83 plans, 14.04
   tax shelters, 8.08
Estate tax
   See also Estate tax, deductions
   adjusted taxable gifts, 10.02[1]
   alternate valuation date, 10.02[1]
   charitable bequests, 15.05[2]
   Clifford Trusts, 9.10
   credit, prior transfers, 10.02[3]
   disclaimers, 15.05[1]
   grantor trusts, 9.10
   irrevocable trusts, tax savings, 12.03
      removal from estate, 12.04
   jointly held property, 10.05[1]
   marital deduction requirements, 15.02[2]
   options, 14.04
   powers of appointment, 16.03
   qualified plans, 14.05
   revocable trusts, 9.03[4]
   state death tax credit, 10.02[4]
   tax return, 10.02[1]
   unified credit, 10.02[2]
   value of estate, 10.02[1]
Estate tax, deductions
   administration expenses, 10.03[1]
      planning for, 10.03[1][c]
      state law, 10.03[1][a]
      types, 10.03[1][b]
   charitable bequests, 15.05[2]
   claims against estate, 10.03[2]
      charitable pledges, 10.03[2][b][iii]
      conditions for deduction, 10.03[2][a]
      contingent claims, 10.03[2][a]
      planning, 10.03[2][c]

[References are to paragraphs (¶) and notes (n.).]

Estate tax, deductions *(cont'd)*
  claims against estate *(cont'd)*
    types, 10.03[2][b]
    executor's commissions, 10.03[1][b][iii]
    funeral expenses, 10.03[1][b][i]
    generally, 10.03
    interest, 10.03[2][b][ii]
    losses during administration, 10.03[3]
    marital deduction, 15.02
    mortgages, 10.03[2][b][iv]
    probate expenses, 10.03[1][b][ii]
    sales expenses, 10.03[1][b][iv]
    taxes, 10.03[2][b][i]
Exclusion, annual. *See* Gift tax
Executives, 1.02[1]

F

Financial counseling, 7.08[3][b]
"5 + 5" powers, 16.03[2][c]
Foreign trusts, 9.12
  excise tax, 9.12
  private annuities, 16.02[2][d]
Fringe benefits
  business meals, 7.08[3][d]
  cafeteria plans, 7.07
  conventions, 7.08[3][c]
  death benefits, 7.06
  disability plans, 7.04[1]
  educational assistance programs, 7.05
  financial counseling, 7.08[3][b]
  fringe benefits, statutory, 7.01
  meals and lodging, 7.08[3][d]
  nonstatutory benefits, 7.08
    income taxation generally, 7.08[1]
    planning for, 7.08[3]
    Treasury proposals re, 7.08[2]
  planning, 7.08[3]
  Treasury proposals re, 7.08[2]
Future interest gifts, 11.02[3]

G

General power of appointment. *See* Powers of appointment

Generation skipping tax
  avoidance by gift, 11.04[5]
  deemed transferor, 10.04[1]
  direct bequests, 10.04[2][a]
  exclusion for grandchildren, 10.04[1], 10.04[2][c]
  income exception, 10.04[2][b]
  outline of tax, 10.04[1]
  planning, 10.04[2]
Gifts
  See also Gift tax; Minors, gifts to
  advantages of making, 11.04
  business transactions, 11.03
  contemplation of death, 11.02[5]
  contemplation of death, insurance, 13.04
    IRS position, 13.04[1]
    planning, 13.04[2]
  death-benefit-only plans, 14.03[2][d]
  definition of, 11.03
  divorce, 11.03
  fractionalized gifts, 11.06
  generation skipping tax, avoiding, 11.04[5]
  installment gifts, 11.06
  intent to make, 11.03
  interest-free loans, 11.09[1]
  irrevocable trusts, 12.03
  life insurance, 13.03[2]
  minors, gifts to, 11.10
  net gifts, 11.07
  saving income tax, 11.04[3]
  spouses, gifts to, 11.11
  subsequent appreciation, 11.04[2]
  time of, 11.03
Gift tax
  See also Gifts
  adjusted taxable gifts, 10.02[1]
  annual exclusion, 11.02[3], 11.04[1]
    future interests, 11.02[3]
    qualified transfers, 11.02[3]
  basis to donee, 11.02[2]
  Clifford Trusts, 9.06[2]
  contemplation of death, 11.02[5]
  credit, using by gift, 11.08
  death-benefit-only plans, 14.03[2][d]

[References are to paragraphs (¶) and notes (n.).]

disclaimers, 15.05[1]
exclusion, 11.02[3]
future interests, 11.02[3]
general principles, 11.02
interest-free loans, 11.09[1]
life insurance transfer, 13.03[2]
marital deduction, 11.02[4]
powers of appointment, 16.03[3][c]
present interests, 11.02[3]
removal from estate, 11.04[4]
revocable trusts, 9.03[4]
strategies to reduce, 11.05
unified credit, 11.02[1]
using lifetime credit, 11.08

Gifts to minors. *See* Minors, gifts to

Grantor trusts
 accumulations of income, 9.07
 administrative powers retained, 9.08[3]
 alternatives to, 9.11
 beneficial enjoyment, control of, 9.08[2]
  reciprocal trusts, 9.08[2][d]
  removal powers, 9.08[2][c]
  trustee
   grantor as, 9.08[2][a]
   others as, 9.08[2][b]
 borrowing by grantor, 9.08[3][c]
 clauses, basic, 9.02
 Clifford Trusts, 9.05
  gift on creation, 9.06[1]
 control over benefits, 9.08[2]
 distributions of income, 9.07
 estate tax liability, 9.10
 foreign trusts, 9.12
 grantor's death during term, 12.02[2]
 income tax if grantor is owner, 9.04
  corpus only, 9.04[3]
  entire trust, 9.04[1]
  part of trust, 9.04[2]
 income to grantor, 9.08[5]
 interest-free loan comparison, 9.11[2], 9.12[3][d]
 irrevocable trust comparison, 9.11[1], 12.02[1], 12.02[3]
 loans to, 9.11[3][e]

 objectives in creating, 9.01
 owners, other than grantor, 9.09
 powers, retained as taxable, 9.08
  administrative, 9.08[3]
  beneficial enjoyment control, 9.08[2]
  permissible, 9.08[2][a][ii]
  revoke, 9.08[4]
 provisions, basic, 9.02
 reversionary interests, 9.08[1]
  postponement of reversion, 9.08[1][b]
 revocable trusts, 9.03
 revoke, power to, 9.08[4]
 rule against perpetuities, 9.02
 spendthrift clause, 9.02
 spouse, income to, 9.08[5]
 sprinkling powers, 9.08[2][b]
 support of dependents, 9.08[6]
 ten-year requirement, 9.08[1][a]
 throwback rules, 9.07
 transfers of ownership, 9.08
 trustee, grantor as, 9.08[2][a]

Group term insurance
 See also Life insurance
 generally, 6.03

Guardian, gift to, 11.10[3]

H

Health insurance, 7.02
 deduction by individuals, 7.02
 disability plans, 7.04[1]
 exclusion for premiums, 7.02
 medical reimbursement plans, 7.03

Highly compensated individuals
 inflation, effects, 1.01
 tax problems, 1.03
 types, 1.02

Hobby losses, 8.04

H.R. 10 plans. *See* Keogh plans

I

Incentive stock options
 comparison with nonqualified, 4.04[3]
 dollar limitations on, 4.04[2]

I-6 INDEX

[References are to paragraphs (¶) and notes (n.).]

Incentive stock options (*cont'd*)
  estate planning for, 14.04
  generally, 4.04
  planning, 4.04[3]
  qualification requirements, 4.04[2]
  sequencing rule, 4.04[2] n.52
  stock appreciation right with, 4.04[2]
  tandem option with, 4.04[2]
  taxation, 4.04[1]
Income averaging
  computation, 2.04[5][a]
  generally, 2.04[5]
  planning for, 2.04[5][b]
  support test, 2.04[5][a]
Income in respect of decedent (IRD)
  compensation items, 14.02[1][c][ii]
  deduction in respect of decedent, 14.02[2]
    claimed when paid, 14.02[2]
    types, 14.02[2]
  deferred compensation, 14.02[1][c][ii]
  definition, 14.02[1]
  estate tax, deduction, 14.02[3]
  income tax deduction (estate taxes), 14.02[3]
    capital gains, 14.02[3][b][ii]
    computation, 14.02[3][a]
    lump-sum distributions, 14.02[3][b][iii]
    marital deduction, 14.02[3][b][i]
  income, when realized, 14.02[1][b]
  installment sales
    as IRD, 14.02[1][c][i]
    transfer of obligation, 14.02[1][b]
  pecuniary bequests of, 14.02[1][b]
  pension plan, 14.02[1][c][ii]
  planning, 14.02[4]
  profit-sharing plan, 14.02[1][c][ii]
  purpose, 14.02[1]
  timing of recognition, 14.02[1][b]
  triggering events, 14.02[1][b]
Income tax
  See also Deferred compensation; Income averaging; Income in respect of decedent
  generally, 2.01

income averaging, generally, 2.04[5]
income in respect of decedent, 14.02
indexing, 2.04[1]
  effect deferred compensation, 3.02[1]
  individual retirement accounts, 5.06[2]
  interest-free loans, 11.09[2]
  life insurance proceeds, 6.02[1]
  medical reimbursement plans, 7.03[1]
  ownership of trust, 9.04
  pecuniary bequests, 15.04[2]
  planning strategies, 2.04
    accelerating deductions, 2.04[2]
    avoiding taxable income, 2.04[4]
    capital gain, ordinary income, 2.04[3]
    deferral of income, 2.04[1]
    limitations accelerating deductions, 2.04[2][a], 2.04[2][b]
  private annuities, 16.02[1]
  rates of taxation, 2.01[1]
    effect on credits, 2.01[3]
    effect on deductions, 2.01[2]
  residence, sale, 2.04[4][c]
  revocable trusts, 9.03[3]
  sale of residence
    generally, 2.04[4][c]
    replacement of, 2.04[4][c][i]
    sale, age 55, 2.04[4][c][ii]
  saving through gifts, 11.04[3]
  will, income tax planning, 15.05[3]
Indexing. *See* Income tax
Individual retirement accounts (IRAs)
  annuities, retirement, 5.06[1][b]
  bonds, retirement, 5.06[1][c]
  deductibility of contributions, 5.06[2][a]
  distributions, taxation, 5.06[2][b]
  estate planning, 14.05[3]
  income taxation, 5.06[2]
  individual retirement annuities, 5.06[1][b]

INDEX

[References are to paragraphs (¶) and notes (n.).]

planning, 5.06[3]
qualification requirements, 5.06[1]
spousal IRAs, 5.06[2][a]
types, 5.06[1]
Inflation, estate planning, 16.04
Installment sales
  as IRD, 14.02[1][c][i]
  transfer of obligation, 14.02[1][b]
Insurance. *See* Health insurance; Life insurance; Workmen's compensation
IRAs. *See* Individual retirement accounts
Interest-free loans, 11.09
  Clifford Trust comparison, 9.11[2], 9.12[3][d]
  gift tax consequences, 11.09[1]
  income tax consequences, 11.09[2]
  irrevocable trust, loans to, 9.11[3][e]
  planning, 11.09[3]
  shifting income, 11.09[3]
Inter vivos gifts. *See* Gifts
Irrevocable trusts
  administrative powers, retention, 12.09
  advantages, 12.12
  amend, power to, 12.10
  appreciating property, transfer, 12.03[3]
  Clifford Trust, comparison, 9.11[1]
  closely held stock, transfer of, 12.03[3][a][i]
  consideration, transfer for, 12.05
  death, transfers effective, 12.11
    included in estate, 12.11[1]
  definition, 12.01[1]
  discharge of transferor's obligations, 12.07
  educational expenses, 12.07
  estate tax savings, 12.02[2], 12.02[3]
  foreign trusts, 9.12
  grantor trust comparison, 12.02[1], 12.02[3]
  life estate, retention, 12.06
    implied right, 12.06[3]
    included in estate, 12.06[1]
    partial interest, 12.06[2]
  nonappreciating property, transfer, 12.03[2]
  objectives of transferor, 12.01[2]
  obligations, discharge, 12.07
    college, 12.07[2]
    support, 12.07[1]
  real estate transfer, 12.03[3][a][ii]
  removal from estate, 12.04
  removal of trustee, 12.08[2]
  retained powers, 12.10
    permissible retained powers, 12.10[2]
  revoke, power to, 12.10
  state inheritance taxes, 12.12
  terminate, power to, 12.10
  transfers effective at death, 12.11
  trustee, effect on tax, 12.08
    beneficiary as trustee, 12.08[4]
    grantor as, 12.08[1]
    removal powers, 12.08[2]
    third party trustee, 12.08[3]

J

Jointly held property
  estate taxation, 10.05[1]
  marital bequests, 10.05[2]
  spouse, jointly held with, 10.05[2]

K

Keogh plans, 5.02[9]
  See also Qualified plans
  contribution limits, 5.03[2][d]
  estate planning, 14.05
  limits on contributions, 5.03[2][d]
  owner-employees, 5.02[9]
Key-man insurance, 6.07

L

Life insurance
  See also Life insurance, estate tax
  borrowing cash value, 6.02[4]
    denial of deduction, 6.02[4][a]
    exceptions to denial, 6.02[4][b]

INDEX

[References are to paragraphs (¶) and notes (n.).]

Life insurance (cont'd)
  borrowing cash value (cont'd)
    trade or business, 6.02[4][b][iv]
    unforeseen events, 6.02[4][b][iii]
  cash value, borrowing, 6.02[4]
  corporation as beneficiary, 6.02[2]
    deduction for premiums, 6.02[2]
    interest deduction, 6.02[4]
  deferred compensation, 3.04
  exchanges of policies, 6.02[3]
  exclusion from income tax, 6.02[1]
  group term insurance, 6.03
    antidiscrimination, 6.03[2]
    exceptions to taxability, 6.03[1][b]
    income taxation, 6.03[1][a]
    permanent insurance with, 6.03[4]
    qualification, 6.03[2]
    small groups, 6.03[3]
    spouse or children, 6.03[5]
    terminated, retired employees, 6.03[1][b][i]
  income tax, proceeds, 6.02[1]
    interest on proceeds, 6.02[1]
  installment payment of proceeds, 6.02[1]
  interest on proceeds, 6.02[1]
  key-man insurance, 6.07
  premiums, deductibility, 6.02[2]
  qualified plans, 6.05
    comparison with group term, 6.05[4]
    death benefit, income tax, 6.05[3]
    income taxation, 6.05[2]
    limitations on coverage, 6.05[1]
    planning for, 6.05[4]
    retired employees, 6.05[2]
  retired lives reserve, 6.06
    description of, 6.06[1]
    funding, 6.06[3]
    income taxation, 6.06[2]
  split-dollar insurance, 6.04
    deduction, 6.04[2]
    description, 6.04[1]
    income taxation, 6.04[2]
    planning, 6.04[3]
    P.S. 58, 6.04[2]
  spouse, group coverage, 6.03[5]
  transfer for consideration, 6.02[1]

Life insurance, estate tax
See also Life insurance trusts
  corporate owned policies, 13.02[2][c]
  Crummey trust, 13.05
    how to draft, 13.05[3]
    planning, 13.05[4]
    problems, 13.05[3]
  estate, receivable by, 13.02[1]
  general principles, 13.02
  gift in contemplation of death, 13.04
    IRS position, 13.04[1]
    planning, 13.04[2]
  gift to individuals, 13.03[3][a]
  gift tax on transfer, 13.03[2]
    group term, premium payments, 13.03[4][c]
  group term insurance, 13.03[4]
    assignment, 13.03[4][a]
    incidents of ownership, 13.03[4][b]
    premium payments, gifts, 13.03[4][c]
  incidents of ownership, 13.02[2][a]
    corporate ownership, 13.02[2][c]
    group term insurance, 13.03[4][b]
    corporate ownership, 13.02[2][c]
  purposes of, 13.01
    buyout, 13.01[3]
    estate building, 13.01[2]
    liquidity, 13.01[1]
    mortgage insurance, 13.01[3]
  removal from estate, 13.03
    direct gifts, 13.03[3][a]
    trusts, 13.03[3][b]
  retained ownership of policy, 13.02[2][d]
  taxable to estate, 13.02
  trust, transfer to, 13.03[3][b]

Life insurance trusts
  annual exclusion, 13.05
  contingencies, 13.03[3][b]

[*References are to paragraphs (¶) and notes (n.).*]

Crummey trust, 13.05
  how to draft, 13.05[3]
  planning, 13.05[4]
  problems, 13.05[3]
  length, withdrawal period,
    13.05[3][c]
  multiple beneficiaries, 13.05[3][d]
  notice, demand provisions,
    13.05[3][b]
  transfers to, 13.03[3][b]
  trustee choice, 13.03[3][b]

Like-kind exchanges, generally,
  2.04[4][b]

Limitations on losses
  at-risk rules, 8.03[3]
  hobby losses, 8.04
  partnership basis, 8.03[1]

Limited powers of appointment. *See* Powers of appointment

Loans, interest free, 11.09[1]

Losses, wash sales, 2.03[2]

Lump-sum distributions
  See also Qualified plans
  capital gain taxation, 5.04[2][b]
  corporate reorganizations,
    5.04[2][a][iii]
  definition, 5.04[2][a]
    balance to credit, 5.04[2][a][ii]
    one taxable year, 5.04[2][a][i]
  employer securities, 5.04[2][d]
    definition, 5.04[2][d]
  estate planning, 14.05[2]
  income in respect of decedent,
    14.02[3][b][iii]
  minimum distribution allowance,
    5.04[2][c]
  participation requirement,
    5.04[2][a][iv]
  planning for taxation, 5.04[3]
  rollovers, 5.05
  securities, appreciation, 5.04[2][d]
  separation from service,
    5.04[2][a][iii]
  ten-year averaging, 5.04[2][c]
    election re, 5.04[2][c]
    minimum distribution
      allowance, 5.04[2][c]

M

Marital deduction
  bequests, amount, 15.02[1]
  citizenship or residency,
    15.02[2][d]
  drafting of provisions, 15.04
    equalization clause, 15.04[3]
    fractional shares, 15.04[1]
    pecuniary bequests, 15.04[2]
  gift tax, 11.02[4]
  income in respect of decedent,
    14.02[3][b][i]
  marital trust, 15.03[3][b]
  planning, 15.02[1]
  power of appointment trust,
    15.03[3][b]
  powers of appointment,
    16.03[4][c]
  qualification requirements,
    15.02[2]
    citizenship, 15.02[2][d]
    included in estate, 15.02[2][c]
    property passes to spouse,
      15.02[2][b]
    survival by spouse, 15.02[2][a]
  qualified terminable interests,
    15.03[3][d]
  survivorship clause, 15.03[3][a]
  terminable interests, 15.03
    contingent interests, 15.03[2][d]
    definition of, 15.03[1]
    exceptions to, 15.03[3]
    life insurance, 15.03[3][c]
    nondeductible, 15.03[2]
    power of appointment trust,
      15.03[3][b]
    qualified terminable interests,
      15.03[3][d]
    state law, effect of, 15.03[2][c]
    survival for stated time,
      15.03[3][a]
  trust, marital, 15.03[3][b]
  trusts, qualified terminable
    interest, 15.03[3][d]
  unified credit, use of, 15.02[1][c]
  unlimited deduction, 15.02[1][a]

Meals and lodging
  deductibility, 7.08[3][d]
  taxability, 7.08[3][d]

[References are to paragraphs (¶) and notes (n.).]

Medical reimbursement plans, 7.03
  antidiscrimination requirement, 7.03[2]
  diagnostic tests, 7.03[2]
  income taxation, 7.03[1]
  planning, 7.03[3]
Minors, gifts to
  custodial transfer, 11.10[2]
  generally, 11.10
  guardian, 11.10[3]
  present interest trusts, 11.10[1]
    age of distribution, 11.10[1][b]
    death of donee, 11.10[1][c]
    trustee's discretion, 11.10[1][a]
    trust for minor, 11.10[1]
  uniform gift to minor, 11.10[2]
Money purchase pension plans, 5.02[3]

N

Net gifts, 11.07
Nonqualified deferred compensation. *See* Deferred compensation
Nonqualified options, 4.02[2]
  description of plans, 4.03[1]
  estate planning, 14.04
  readily ascertainable value, 4.02[2]
  value, 4.02[2]

O

Options. *See* Incentive stock options; Nonqualified options

P

Partnerships
  See also Tax shelters, subhead: deductions
  organizational expenses, 8.06[1]
    fees deductibility, 8.06[1]
    real cost, 8.07[3]
  retroactive allocation losses, 8.05
  syndication fees, 8.06[1]
  tax classification, 8.02
    centralization of management, 8.02[2][b]
    continuity of life, 8.02[2][a]
    court cases re, 8.02[4]
    free transferability, 8.02[2][d]
    Kintner regulations, 8.02[2] n.21
    limited liability, 8.02[2][c]
    net worth requirement, 8.02[2][a]
    planning to achieve, 8.02[6]
    regulations re, 8.02[2]
    ruling requirements, 8.02[3]
Payroll-based stock ownership plans, (PAYSOPs), 5.02[8]
Pecuniary bequests, 15.04[2]
Pension plans, 5.02[2]
  See also Qualified plans
  benefit limits, 5.03[2][a]
  contribution formulas, 5.02[2]
  estate planning, 14.05
    annuities, exclusion, 14.05[1]
    lump-sum distributions, 14.05[2]
  income in respect of decedent, 14.02[1][c][ii]
  limitation on benefits, 5.03[2][a]
  loans from plan, 5.04[1] n.98
  money purchase plans, 5.02[3]
  rollovers, 5.05
  target benefit plans, 5.02[4]
  voluntary contributions, 5.03[3]
Phantom stock plans, 3.05[2]
Planning, income tax. *See* Income tax, planning strategies
Powers of appointment, 16.03
  adverse interests, 16.03[2][b]
  ascertainable standard exclusion, 16.03[2][a]
  beneficiary of trust as trustee, 12.08[4]
  disclaimers, comparison to, 15.05[1]
  "5 + 5" powers, 16.03[2][c]
  general power of appointment, 16.03[1]
    definition, 16.03[1]
    exclusions from definition, 16.03[2]
  gift tax consequences, 16.03[3][c]
  incompetent persons, 16.03[3][a]

INDEX

[References are to paragraphs (¶) and notes (n.).]

joint power exclusion, 16.03[2][b]
knowledge of, 16.03[3][a]
limited power of appointment, 16.03[1]
marital deduction, 16.03[4][c]
planning, 16.03[4]
release of power, 16.03[3][b]
support or maintenance, 16.03[2][a]
Preference items, 2.02[2]
See also Alternative minimum tax
Private annuities
  alternatives, 16.02[4][d]
  basis to transferee, 16.02[3]
  capital gain, 16.02[1]
  charitable organizations, 16.02[1]
  disadvantages, 16.02[4][c]
  escrow arrangements, 16.02[2][a]
  foreign trusts, 16.02[2][d]
  installment sales vs., 16.02[4][d]
  life estate retained, 16.02[2][b]
  planning, 16.02[4]
  private annuity, transferee's basis, 16.02[3]
  removal from estate, 16.02[4][a]
  security interest, 16.02[2][a]
  taxation, 16.02[1]
  transferee, taxation, 16.02[3]
  trust arrangements, 16.02[2][b]
  value of annuity, 16.02[2][c]
Professionals, 1.02[2]
Profit-sharing plans, 5.02[1]
  See also Incentive stock options; Nonqualified options; Qualified plans
  cash or deferred plans, 5.02[6]
  contribution formulas, 5.02[1]
  contribution limits, 5.03[2][b]
  estate planning, 14.05
    annuities, exclusion, 14.05[1]
    lump-sum distributions, 14.05[2]
  income in respect of decedent, 14.02[1][c][ii]
  limits on contributions, 5.03[2][b]
  loans from plan, 5.04[1] n.98
  profit requirement, 5.02[1]
  rollovers, 5.05
  stock bonus plans, 5.02[5]
  voluntary contributions, 5.03[3]

Property transferred for services
  bargain sales, 4.03[3]
  basis, 4.02[3][b]
  deduction for, 4.02[3][c]
  election as income, 4.02[3][a]
  estate planning, 14.04
  forfeiture risk, 4.01[1][b]
  generally, 4.01
  holding period, 4.02[3][b]
  incentive stock options, generally, 4.04
  nonlapse provisions, 4.03[3]
  nonqualified options, generally, 4.01[2]
  property, definition, 4.01 n.1
  restricted stock plan, 4.03[3]
  stock appreciation rights, 4.03[2]
  transferability under regulations, 4.01[1][c]
  transfer, when occurs, 4.01[1][a], 4.01[1][c]
  types of plans, 4.03
  vested, substantially, 4.01[1][b]
  withholding, 4.02[3][c]

Q

Qualified disclaimers, 15.05[1]
Qualified plans
  annuities, taxation, 5.04[1]
    investment in contract, 5.04[1]
    three-year rule, 5.04[1]
  antidiscrimination, 5.03[1]
  cash or deferred plans, 5.02[6]
  employee stock ownership plans, 5.02[7]
  distributions, taxation of, 5.04
    annuities, 5.04[1]
    lump sums, 5.04[2]
  estate planning, 14.05
    annuities, exclusion for, 14.05[1]
    individual retirement accounts, 14.05[3]
    lump-sum distributions, 14.05[2]
  income tax, generally, 5.01
  individual retirement accounts, 5.06
  Keogh plans, 5.02[9]

[*References are to paragraphs (¶) and notes (n.).*]

Qualified plans (*cont'd*)
  life insurance, 6.05
    income taxation, 6.05[2]
    limitation on coverage, 6.05[1]
    planning, 6.05[4]
  limitation on benefits, 5.03[2]
    Keogh plans, 5.03[2][d]
    multiple plans, 5.03[2][c]
    pension plans, 5.03[2][a]
    profit-sharing plans, 5.03[2][b]
  loans from plan, 5.04[1] n.98
  lump-sum distributions, taxation, 5.04[2]
    capital gains, 5.04[2][b]
    definition, 5.04[2][a]
    ten-year averaging, 5.04[2][c]
  mandatory contribution limits, 5.03[3]
  money purchase plans, 5.02[3]
  PAYSOPs, 5.02[8]
  pension plans, generally, 5.02[2]
  profit-sharing plans, 5.02[1]
  qualification requirements, 5.03
  rollovers, 5.05
    partial rollovers, 5.05[1]
    requirements, generally, 5.05[1]
    spousal rollovers, 5.05[2]
  stock bonus plans, 5.02[5]
  target benefit plans, 5.02[4]
  top-heavy plans, 5.03[4]
  types of qualified plans, 5.02
  voluntary contributions, 5.03[3]
Qualified terminable interests, 15.03[3][d]

R

Residence, sale
  See also Income tax, subhead: sale of residence
  age 55, 2.04[4][c]
  generally, 2.04[4][c]
  replacement, 2.04[4][c]
Restricted stock plan, 4.03[3]
Retired lives reserve, generally, 6.06
  See also Life insurance
Retirement accounts. *See* Individual retirement accounts

Revocable trusts, 9.03
  estate taxation, 9.03[4]
  gift taxation on creating, 9.03[4]
  income taxation, 9.03[3]
  postmortem benefits, 9.03[2]
  recapture considerations, 9.03[3]
  uses of, 9.03[1]
Rollovers. *See* Qualified plans

S

Salesman, 12.02[5]
Section 83. *See* Property transferred for services
Section 2503(c) trust. *See* Minors, gifts to
Short term trusts. *See* Grantor trusts
Split-dollar insurance, generally, 6.04
  See also Life insurance
State death tax credit, 10.02[4]
Stock appreciation rights, 4.03[2]
  incentive option with, 4.04[2]
  taxability, 4.03[2]
  with nonqualified option, 4.03[2]
Stock bonus plans, 5.02[5]
  employee stock ownership plans, 5.02[7]
  put option requirement, 5.02[5]
Support of dependents, grantor trusts, 9.08[6]
Survivor's death benefits, 7.06
  exclusion from income, 7.06
  vested interests, 7.06

T

Target benefit plans, 5.02[4]
Tax-exempt bonds
  borrowing to purchase, 2.04[4][a][ii]
  generally, 2.04[4][a]
Tax-free exchanges. *See* Like-kind exchanges
Tax on generation skipping. *See* Generation skipping tax

[References are to paragraphs (¶) and notes (n.).]

Tax shelters
See also Partnerships
  cost of, 8.07[3]
  deductions, 8.06
    construction period, 8.06[2]
    intangible drilling expenses, 8.06[3]
    organizational expense, 8.06[1]
    syndication fees, 8.06[1]
  definition, 8.01[1]
  estate planning for, 8.08
  evaluation of, 8.07
  generally, 8.01
  goals, 8.01[2]
    deferral of taxes, 8.01[2][a]
    leverage, 8.01[2][c]
    limited liability, 8.01[2][d]
    ordinary income, capital gain, 8.01[2][b]
  hobby losses, 8.04
  how to evaluate, 8.07
  profit from, 8.07[5]
  retroactive allocation losses, 8.05
  tax risks, 8.07[2]
Terminable interests. *See* Marital deduction
Trustee, irrevocable trusts
  beneficiary as, trustee, 12.08[4]
  grantor as, 12.08[1]
  removal powers, 12.08[2]
  third party as, 12.08[3]
Trust for minor, 11.10[1]
Trusts. *See* Foreign trusts; Grantor trusts; Irrevocable lifetime trusts; Life insurance trusts; Revocable trusts

U

Unified credit, 10.02[2]
  amount of, 10.01 n.3
  using by gifts, 11.08
Uniform Gifts to Minors Act, 11.10[2]

V

Valuation
  annuity promise, 16.02[2][c]
  life insurance gift, 13.03[2]
  private annuity, 16.02[2][c]

W

Wash sales
  See also Capital gain
  generally, 2.03[2]
Wills
  charitable bequests, 15.05[2]
  disclaimers, 15.05[1]
  drafting marital deduction, 15.04
  equalization clauses, 15.04[3]
  fractional share provisions, 15.04[1]
  income tax planning, 15.05[3]
  joint returns, 15.05[3][c]
  marital bequest, amount of, 15.02[1]
    drafting of, 15.04
  pecuniary bequests, 15.04[2]
  "pick-and-choose" clause, 15.04[2]
  purposes of, 15.01
Workmen's compensation, 7.04[2]
  exclusion from income, 7.04[2]